BEST BABY NAMES 2020

Vermilion
LONDON

This updated edition published in 2019
First published by Vermilion in 2012

1 3 5 7 9 10 8 6 4 2

Vermilion, an imprint of Ebury Publishing,
20 Vauxhall Bridge Road,
London SW1V 2SA

Vermilion is part of the Penguin Random House group of
companies whose addresses can be found at global.
penguinrandomhouse.com

Penguin
Random House
UK

www.penguin.co.uk

A CIP catalogue record for this book is available from the British Library

ISBN 9781785042997

Printed and bound in Great Britain by Clays Ltd, Elcograf S.p.A.

Penguin Random House is committed to a sustainable future
for our business, our readers and our planet. This book is made
from Forest Stewardship Council® certified paper.

MIX
Paper from
responsible sources
FSC® C018179

SIOBHAN THOMAS

BEST
BABY
NAMES
2020

This book is dedicated to your new baby

Contents

Acknowledgements

Enormous thanks to Rosanne Rivers, a freelance writer, novelist and leader of writing workshops for young people. Her work was invaluable in compiling and editing the thousands of names in this book. Rosanne's novel *After the Fear* is available now.

I would also like to thank James Macfarlane for giving me the opportunity to write this book and for his continuous encouragement and good humour from beginning to end.

Thanks, also, to James Brighton, Alan Jones and Annabel Freer for their assistance and input.

Finally I must thank Helen O'Shea and Dan Holt for their reviews of the manuscript and for their honest opinions and feedback. My mum, Pat, and my husband, Owen, also did their share of rereading – but more importantly I want to thank them, and Orla Goncalves, for all their help with the children, without which this book would never have been completed!

Introduction

Congratulations! A new baby is on the way!

It is an incredibly amazing, exciting and life-changing time whether it's your first child or another in your ever-extending family. Suddenly, you are doing loads of planning in preparation for your new arrival. You may be rearranging your home or deciding which of the numerous items to buy to welcome your baby. There is so much to do and somehow you have to think of a good name as well. At first, it can seem a rather daunting responsibility as you want to find the very best name for them, but remember it can also be great fun. The wonderful thing about name-choosing is that it is not limited, not by income or space or anything at all. You are completely free to choose as many options and combinations as you like from the seemingly infinite number of names out there.

To choose a name for a brand new person is a uniquely special part of your preparations and a lovely experience to look back upon. By just relaxing and setting a little time aside, you can give your baby a very special gift that will really become as much a part of them in the future as the way they smile!

Naturally, you'll be keen to get it right so how are you going to decide the perfect name for them? The answers are in this book – which will help you on your baby-naming journey! Perhaps you like Richard, Hassan, Zeke or Montague or maybe Natasha, Lily-May or Havana. There are so many to consider that it can be confusing to work out how to begin. In the following pages are ways to start thinking about names, consider your ideas, any possible drawbacks and how to tackle them. You will also discover how and where to find inspiration, how to focus your choices, narrow them down to a shortlist and make that very final decision, arriving at the perfect baby name.

We hope to give you the confidence to plunge in, not worry too much and enjoy yourself. This experience may well become part of your earliest happy memories with your new baby. There is definitely a name out there that you will love and that you will be very happy to say and hear in the coming years. Sit back and let your imagination run wild as you begin to browse through this book. After all, you are very likely to be holding your brilliant final choice in your hands at this very moment!

Using This Book

This book does not have to read from beginning to end. In fact, that probably isn't the best way at all. It is designed for you to dip in anywhere by browsing or using the contents page. There are pointers and inspiration for everyone; couples and single parents who often like to involve siblings, wider family and close friends in helping to choose the perfect name. Stick markers in, make notes in the margins, highlight your favourites and cross out any names you want to veto. You might also be surprised how different a name can sound when you say it aloud.

Part One is a complete how-to guide on choosing baby names. It helps kick off the journey with ideas and suggestions on how and where to start. It helps in recognising various drawbacks with some names, how to come to agreement with your partner and how to cope with other people's opinions.

Part Two is all about inspiration. It offers famous names from categories such as film, sport, high achievers, fiction and many others. It is also reassuring to see a wide range of names, complete with a surname, written down and established as completely acceptable by the wider world.

Many people like to dive straight into page 49 and find out what the latest Top 100 most popular names are for England and Wales. While there will always be traditional names, and famous name trends, 2019 looks set to be more diverse than ever as new parents seek wider areas of inspiration. Everything from classical and traditional, mythological, fictional, the natural world including plants and food culture to gender-neutral options, aspirational and even outer space and the universe.

Part Three is the name section, with an alphabetical list of over nine thousand names from all over the world. It is in two sections – boys' names and girls' names with gender-neutral names being identified in both sections. Each entry includes additional information on the origin, meaning, spelling and pronunciation of each name.

PART ONE

Finding the Right Name for Your Baby

Choosing the Perfect Name

What Makes a Good Name?

What makes a good name is hugely dependent on when and where. We can look back over the last century and recognise some of the baby names that were popular 100 years ago; however, many of our modern names would be completely alien to parents of that time. The same is true about all of us who have grown up in different countries and different cultures around the world. Apart from our generation and where we live, our own very individual life experiences will affect our attitudes towards certain names. The names of friends, family, film stars, heroes, bullies, private relationships or public personalities are all going to affect how we view any particular name.

Old-fashioned differences between our aspirations for girls and boys still influence our choice of names today. With girls' names, many parents still say that they are seeking something 'feminine', or 'pretty'. For boys, parents often say they are looking for a 'strong' name. Of course, that isn't to say that a girls' name can't be pretty and strong, or a boys' name can't be gentle without being weak. There are also plenty of names that are widely used for both genders, which may well support a recent trend for names that are gender neutral.

In some cultures, such as Greek Orthodox, the name of a new baby is often determined by the father's name; having a 'Junior' in the family has long been associated with Americans too, but it has become much less popular there in recent years as parents seek out more unique names. Elsewhere names are determined by a whole host of factors: a baby girl, born at the end of the week to Ghanaian parents, might be called 'Afia', which means 'born on a Friday'; many Native American names are drawn from nature (direct translations include Rainbow and Butterfly); and African cultures often draw on their aspirations for their children, using names such as 'Prosperity' or 'Beautiful'.

In the UK we have been experimenting with new ideas for some time. In 2011, there was a raging debate on the baby forums when the Beckhams named their daughter 'Harper Seven' and when Beyoncé and Jay-Z called their baby girl 'Blue Ivy Carter'. Some people loved these unique and audacious choices for names, while others disagreed, saying that they were too self-consciously unusual. However, five years later when Jamie and Jools Oliver named their baby son River Rocket it hardly created a murmur. Indeed some public speculation was supportive along the lines that the names probably had relevance as the River Cafe is where Jamie Oliver had his big break into TV. Rocket was fine as it is either aspirational or a salad, appropriately for a chef.

If you do not want anything too off the wall and want to be sure of a name that will be considered 'good' and already in circulation for your baby's generation, you can look at the Top 100 currently most popular baby names on pages 49 – 5. Of the nearly 340,000 baby girls in the latest register, 42% of them share the top 100 spot for girls. With boys, over half of the 350,000 baby boys share the top 100 spot at 51%. The top 10 most popular girls' names are shared by 10% of baby girls and the Top 10 most popular boys' names are shared by 13% of baby boys. Many parents have said how they thought they had made an unusual choice only to find out later that it appeared surprisingly high on the popularity lists.

In recent decades the UK has become more cosmopolitan and people today are no longer surprised by unfamiliar names. With names from many countries, cultures and languages with several spelling options, unusual and unique names themselves have become more acceptable and far less of a social risk than in Granny's time. The emergence of the

young royals into parenthood has created a renewed interest in the royal family and the names they choose for their
babies. The Duke and Duchess of Cambridge's choice of
Louis Arthur Charles for their new arrival may well become
popular as people of all backgrounds will become interest-
ed in names seen as 'far too posh or old-fashioned' one or
two generations ago. Celebrities in the entertainment world
are often pioneers in naming creativity and names such as
Hart, True, Stormi and Chicago may soon start to appear as
popular choices.

When to Choose a Name

For those who have had their children's names ready and
waiting before their babies were even conceived, the pressure is off – unless you change your mind, of course! In
theory, there is no rush – you have nine months to consider your baby's name. You'd think that this would be long
enough, but it isn't always! Lots of people find that their
baby is in their arms before they have made up their mind.
In fact, there are many parents who have their name options
finalised well ahead of baby's arrival, only to find that they
change their mind after meeting their newborn. There is no
need to panic if you aren't ready to name the baby straight
away. It is perfectly acceptable to give yourselves a little time
with your new arrival to consider what name you are going
to give them. Don't feel under pressure from your friends
and family who absolutely need to know what to write in the
new baby card, or the grandparents who just have to have
the name to tell their friends. This is your baby, and you'll do
it in your own good time! Cuddle them, talk to them, try out
your shortlist (and any others that come to mind) and you'll
soon find a name that feels right for your baby. However, do
keep in mind that in the UK parents are legally obliged to

register their child's name before they are six weeks old. But this should give you plenty of time to decide!

Registering Your Baby

Birth Registration Overview

All births in England, Wales and Northern Ireland must be registered within 42 days of the child being born. You should do this by making an appointment at the local register office in the area where the baby was born or at the hospital before the mother leaves. The hospital will tell you if you can register the birth there. If you can't register the birth in the area where the baby was born, you can go to another register office and they will send your details to the correct office.

The child's surname is usually that of either the mother or the father but, in cases where the parents are unmarried and the father does not attend the registration, it is possible to give the child an alternative surname. The government website (see link below) will provide full details. There are also directions to the appropriate registration districts for those outside the above geographical areas.

https://www.gov.uk/register-birth

How to Choose a Name

Start the process with an open mind. If you're raising the baby with a partner, you'll both need to give proper consideration to one another's suggestions. It is helpful saying names aloud to one another; a name you like might not work on paper for your partner, but when they hear it spoken it might sound more appealing – of course it may also sound less appealing, so be prepared for that too! Respect one another's opinions on names. Avoid setting your heart on just one name too early; try to be flexible and listen to your partner's suggestions and objections. A name that sounds perfect to you may have been the name of the bully at your partner's primary school, and these associations can be hard to let go of.

It's OK to be experimental. Don't feel silly suggesting or trying out names that are a bit more adventurous than people may expect. If David Bowie's alter ego Ziggy Stardust was your teenage idol and you fancy bringing the name back into your life, see what it sounds like! You never know – your partner may approve!

If you find that you have lots of name possibilities, then a list will help you to keep track of your ideas. It is particularly useful if you start considering names early on in your pregnancy. You may find that your attitude to some of them changes over time, and when you look back at the list a couple of months down the line you may be surprised at what you initially wrote down!

Another good way to make your mind up on a name is to imagine its use in different situations. Consider whether a name appeals to you when used on a toddler and when used on an adult. Can you imagine it being accepted in both the playground and the boardroom? Perhaps some names are more Mercury Prize than Nobel Prize, or more stuntman than clergyman. Of course, everyone's opinions on this will differ, but thinking about names in this way might make a difference to your preferences.

Naming Babies after Other People

Going Double-Barrelled

Girls' names are more commonly hyphenated than boys' names, but there are still lots of possibilities for both sexes. Rose and May are popular second names for girls

('Anna-Rose', 'Lily-May'); Lee and James are quite common in double-barrelled boys' names ('Tommy-Lee', 'Tyler-James'). Other combinations that work well include 'Emily-Grace', 'Mia-Louise', 'Thomas-Jay' and 'Alfie-Joe'.

It's a creative way of making a name more interesting or to modernise an older name that you want to use. Hyphenating a double-barrelled name isn't strictly necessary but without it people may confuse the second half of the name for a middle name. Experiment with combinations, but avoid hyphenating names with lots of syllables and stick to just two names!

Taking things on a step from name association, some babies are named directly after a family member. In some families it is tradition to name a baby after the father, or grandfather; in other cases, children may be named after a recently deceased member of the family. Sometimes people choose the name of an aunt, uncle or other person who they particularly looked up to or got on with, or who they feel was a significant influence on them while growing up. Of course, the delivery of a baby can be very special and emotional, so there have been babies who were named after the person who delivered them!

Other Ideas for Inspiration

Once you know you're having a baby, regardless of how important it is to you to find a name quickly, start paying more attention to the names that are spoken around you every day. It is a good way to pick up new ideas, to gauge the popularity of a name, to hear different pronunciations and nicknames, and sometimes it can help to dispel your existing feelings towards a name. For example, a name you always associated with a miserable elderly aunt might actually be the name of that pretty, cheerful and well-spoken newsreader you like – suddenly the name is more appealing. Likewise, a name you think is a little unusual may actually be coming back into fashion again.

Listen out for parents talking to (and sometimes shouting at!) their children out and about.

Here are some ideas for finding a completely random list of names to inspire you.

- Credits at the end of television programmes and films
- Names of the players in televised sports games
- Authors' names on book spines along a bookshelf – at home, the library or a bookshop
- Birth, death and marriage announcements in local or national newspapers
- Names of journalists and the people who feature in newspaper and magazine articles

If you are a keen reader, cast your eyes back over your bookshelf and remind yourself of the various character names that featured in them. Or see our list of suggested names from well-known literature in our Inspiration Lists (see pages 35–38).

You can also use the book in conjunction with the baby-names.co.uk website. Here you can set up an account and save names to a shortlist that you can come back to as and when you like. You can also find further information on the current popularity of names, as well as suggestions for inspiration, including a random names generator. There is a huge community of mums and mums-to-be there, and discussions take place night and day on the subject of baby names. You can have a go at anonymously bouncing ideas off other people who are in the same boat as you, especially if you have decided not to divulge your potential baby names to friends and family.

When you're done with taking this naming business seriously, you can always try the 'Are you feeling lucky?' approach with this book. Choose a page at random and get your partner to point to a name with their eyes covered. OK, this isn't an altogether serious suggestion but you never know, it might find you a winner!

Useful Factors to Consider

Personal Associations with Names

As already discussed, people's attitudes and opinions on different names vary hugely. Your favourite name might provoke quite unexpected reactions when suggested to your partner or family. The strong, on-trend choice that you have in mind for your son is old-fashioned and dull according to your best friend. People can catch you unawares with their disapproval, insinuating that your choice of baby name is trashy, tacky or has other unattractive connotations.

Opinions on names are formed by naming trends and personal associations, i.e., who you know (or know of) with that name. You may not even be able to recall where you have heard that name; it may have been in a film, a news article or a distant connection, such as a friend of a friend that you have heard about but never met. You may have formed an opinion on it as a result of this very vague association. Sometimes we form an opinion on a name based on its stereotypical image – perhaps you associate a certain name with the age-old 'blonde bimbo' persona, or maybe you think of another name as being 'posh' – appropriate only for the kind of character Hugh Grant plays in a romantic comedy film.

Often, however, our connections with a name are much stronger than this. If you grew up knowing a person, or there is someone frequently in the public eye – a celebrity or politician – then you may find that they are the first person to enter your mind when you hear it. Your impression of this person is likely to shape your attitude towards that name. Cameron is a unisex name that has been popular in the name charts for many years, and may previously have owed its popularity to celebrities such as Cameron Diaz. Since 2010, however, when David Cameron became Prime Minister of the United Kingdom, the name has had a more political connotation.

Another example is names of pets. For those who have never owned a pet or had much contact with one it might sound rather silly, but if you grew up with a spaniel called Tom or a moggy named Megan, the thought of the name on your newborn baby might seem like calling your child Spot or Patch!

Some of our personal associations with names can be more negative. When you put a name to your partner and they say 'no' because of a girl they didn't like at primary school, put yourself in their shoes before you get frustrated. Childhood relationships can leave emotions etched into our memories forever, and nearly all of us can recall the name of the school bully. Unless someone else with that name has become known to you later in life, your personal feelings towards it are likely to be negative and you probably won't want it for your baby. Other common associations with names that can put you off using them for your child can be names of ex-partners, or people you work with. Even if these are people you like and get on with, it can often just seem unsuitable to take their name and use it on your child.

Popularity of a name also influences our attitudes towards it. There are notable trend cycles with names, and some names are seen as old-fashioned because they were more popular among our grandparents' and great-grandparents' generations than they are now. There are some names that haven't been fashionable for several generations, such as Winifred or Walter. For many people, the more popular a name is, the more attractive it is – to a point. People can also be deterred by a very popular name. They may prefer to avoid their child having to be known by their first name together with their last initial to differentiate them from the other children in their class with the same name – for example, 'Oliver T' or 'Olivia T' (both very popular names in recent years). Teachers often have the added problem that they know so many children that they find it hard to find a name they like that they don't already associate with another child! See the popularity charts (pages 49–51) for more information on what is popular now and has been in recent years.

A Name that Works with the Child's Surname

Your baby's surname will affect the suitability of his or her first name. Some combinations just won't sound right to your ears. Try saying first names out loud with your last name – it is surprising how different a name sounds once it is paired with a surname. As with nearly every aspect of choosing your baby's name, it is pretty subjective as to what sounds 'good'.

Sometimes parents choose alliterative names such as Emma Edwards or Sebastian Summers. There are numerous celebrity examples of alliterative names: Janet Jackson, Lucy Liu and Lennox Lewis to name just a few. These are fine if you are naming your first child, but if you go on to have several more and want to continue the theme you could find the naming process becomes more and more challenging!

While it is a subjective matter, there are also some things you might want to avoid when pairing a name with a surname.

- **Rhyming:** Most people would choose to avoid a first name that rhymes with their second name – such as 'Carys Harris' or 'Mark Clark'. Such a name might be amusing, and even attractively quirky – particularly if you imagine them on a musician or artist – but what if you put these names on a troubled teenager who lacks confidence in their own self-image? Even in the wild world of celebrities you don't find many examples of rhyming names. Jack Black is an example but he was born Thomas Jacob Black. It might be better to let your child adopt a stage name when they start frequenting the red carpets and in the meantime maybe opt for something a little less rock n' roll, just in case they grow up to be an accountant.
- **Famous names:** In general, people tend to steer clear of giving their child the same first and second name as famous people. So if your surname is Brand, the names Jo or Russell are likely to be put into the 'No' list pretty quickly. This is especially the case if the person is famous for all the wrong reasons, such as Fred West or Myra Hindley.
- **Common pairings:** If you have a common surname, think carefully about the first name you choose. A name that is very popular combined with a common surname might mean that your son or daughter shares his or her name with a classmate or friend!
- **Very long names:** If your child is going to have a double-barrelled surname, then you might want to steer clear of double-barrelled or very long first names to keep the potential mockery in the future to a minimum – and to give the poor child a chance to learn to spell it!

Unless you have the time or inclination to think about the issue of pairing a first name with a surname, you needn't get too consumed with the subject. It can sometimes be easy to overthink these things. The important thing is that you choose a first name for your baby that *you* like. Provided it sounds like a pretty good fit with the second name, doesn't have any glaringly obvious rhymes or innuendos and the initials don't spell out an obscenity, then the combination of names will be perfectly acceptable.

Spelling Variations

The name you give your baby, how it is spelt and how it is pronounced is entirely down to you. If you want to call your baby 'James', but spell it 'Jaymes', that is your decision and nobody can stop you.

The subject of name spellings can provoke a hot debate. It is understandable that some people decide to alter a traditional spelling of a name in order to make it more unique or more interesting, but at the same time you should consider what issues this might present in the future. Is it likely to result in misspellings, mispronunciations and questioning over its origin for the rest of the child's life?

While new spellings can be ridiculed for their simplification of traditional names, old-fashioned spellings are criticised sometimes for being confusing (particularly Gaelic names from Irish or Scottish traditions). Names such as 'Ciaran' are familiar to many of us, but when written down, the spelling can surprise people. More extreme examples of tricky Gaelic names include 'Fionnghuala' or 'Aoife' – but many people enjoy having a less obvious name spelling. And perhaps it is more widely accepted when your unusual name has a cultural tradition that you can explain to other people, so that you cannot be accused of having a 'made-up' name.

If the difficult original spellings of popular names are an issue for you, then you may choose to use an anglicised or phonetic spelling; 'Neve', for example, is becoming an increasingly popular spelling of the classic Irish name 'Niamh'. Consider your reasons for simplifying a name, though. We live in an ever-more diverse society, where names from different cultures are being introduced all the time. The assumption that a name that is a little unusual or hard to spell will cause significant problems for that child growing up might be exaggerated. Perhaps we should assume a greater level of intelligence and acceptance on the part of others!

Pronunciation Variations

Pronunciation of names can vary, and some people have strong views as to the correct way to pronounce certain names. Differences may simply be the result of different accents and dialects, or even different nationalities – for example 'Tanya' where some people pronounce it '*Tarn*-yah' and others pronounce it '*Tan*-yah'. Even if the pronunciation of a name does seem obvious to you, it is worth double-checking, just to make sure you haven't misunderstood it. That might sound unlikely but it does happen. In her teens, writer Caitlin Moran changed her name from 'Catherine' to 'Caitlin' after seeing the name in a Jilly Cooper novel. She believed at the time that the correct pronunciation was '*Cat*-lin' and continues to pronounce it that way today – she says it has caused confusion for people all of her adult life!

If you are in any doubt whatsoever, do some quick checks on your name before making it final. Ensure you know what the popular or original spelling of that name is, and how it is commonly pronounced – regardless of whether or not you intend to follow suit.

Names that Work with Twins and Other Siblings

There are no rules when it comes to what you can and can't call children based on the names of their siblings. For some people it is important that their children's names complement one another, while other people don't give it much thought. When people talk about finding names that work they usually just mean that they *sound OK*.

However, as with pairing first names with surnames, there are some general dos and don'ts when it comes to drawing the line between endearing and eccentric, or amusing and absurd. Again, this is down to personal opinion.

- **Themes:** You may decide that a theme would work for your family. Perhaps flower names like Rose and Daisy or names that start with the same letter like Jack and James. Of course, the more children you have, the harder it becomes to continue with a theme, so consider what you will do if in the future you extend your family.
- **Rhyming:** Rhyming your children's names with each other may sound sweet to you at first, but could become cloying in the future so think carefully about choosing names that rhyme. If you are totally against rhyming names, make sure to consider how your children's names might be shortened. For example, if you have decided on naming your twins Matilda and William, they could well end up being Tilly and Willy or Tilly and Billy.
- **Suitability:** Many names are categorised by people as traditional or modern, simple or fussy, popular or unusual. If your first two children have names that clearly fall into such a category, it might be unfair to give the third child something totally different. Imagine the protest from your youngest child after being named 'Tallulah-Belle', when her sisters are named Jane and Clare.

- **Combinations:** Consider whether your choices of sibling names match any famous partnerships or celebrity couples such as 'Brad and Angelina', fashion labels such as 'Florence and Fred' at Tesco or fictional television duos such as 'Charlie and Lola'. This isn't to say that you should avoid these well-known associations, but it is better for you to have thought them through ahead of time rather than have them brought to your attention by other people after the baby (or babies) have been born and named.

Middle Names

There are no rules as to how many names you can give your child. The most common format in the UK is a first name, which is used for everyday purposes, and a second name (or middle name), which is used less frequently. Second or third names are most commonly used on official documents or registration forms and sometimes they are abbreviated to their first initial in signatures, for example 'Siobhan E. Thomas'. If your child falls out of love with their first name then they may choose to use their second name in its place and it is a common port of call for those who do change their first name.

Common Hurdles

Disagreeing with Other People

While opinions will always be divided to some extent, it is easy to predict whether certain names, or types of names, will be accepted as 'good' names by the majority of people. Names that have remained popular through generations, such as William or Elizabeth, will come in for little criticism.

Unusual names, such as 'Blade' or 'Cruz', are more controversial and often meet more resistance from friends, family and the wider public.

When it comes to pleasing other people, what you must bear in mind is that once the baby has been born, their previous opinions on the name will really matter very little to them. The subject of names is much more divisive before the baby's arrival. As soon as people get to know your child, most of them will forget their earlier associations; the name will become the baby's – not the name of a character in *EastEnders*, a famous footballer or the lady who works in the post office. While it may take friends and family some time to get used to, they'll soon associate the name with your baby and in no time at all it will stop feeling strange to them and start to feel treasured – it will become part of your child. Many a grandparent has been heard to say 'I wasn't sure about it at first but now I love it!'

Ultimately, the name of a baby is down to his or her parents. It can be fun talking through name ideas with your best friend or your mum, but if you want to be open about your baby's name ahead of their arrival, be prepared for other people's reactions. If you think that negative comments will knock the wind out of your sails, keep the names to yourself. Perhaps think twice before publicising your shortlist too widely.

Disagreeing with Your Partner

With a bit of luck, you and your partner may find that you agree on a name, or a list of names, quite easily. But what happens when you don't?

If you feel that your partner is repeatedly rejecting your suggestions of names then perhaps you need to think about changing your approach. Firstly, consider exactly how you make your suggestions. Launching into a list of names at eleven o'clock at night, pouncing on them as they walk in the door from work or informing them in no uncertain terms that Trixabelle is the perfect name for your daughter is more than likely going to get you a 'no'. Pick your moment – everyone has times when they are more open to discussing these things. You must also allow your partner time to consider a name. You may have been thinking about it all day and imagining it in wooden letters on the nursery room door, but they will need time to process and digest it too. So don't expect an immediate response; just ask them to consider it in their own time.

Also, try to find out what it is about certain names that your partner doesn't like. Are you repeatedly offering names with tricky Gaelic spellings that he thinks will make life hard for the child? Are you only coming up with long-winded, double-barrelled names that she thinks are too fussy? Understanding your partner's reasons for rejecting a name will help you to find one that you both like.

If there is a name that you really love, and your partner refuses to agree to it, don't push them too hard on the subject. You can't (or at least you shouldn't) force some-one into agreeing to a name for their baby. If you are both going to be bringing this child up then it is important that you do things in agreement as much as possible from Day 1, and your baby's name is the best place to start. It may be the case that you need to go back to the drawing board, but sometimes it can be possible to persuade your partner into thinking of the name more favourably. Avoid getting into an argument, but let them know that a name is a strong contender for you and that you would really like them to consider it seriously before writing it off alto-gether. If they have particular negative associations with that name then you could attempt to override these associations by pointing out other, more appealing people or characters that have this name. For example, if your partner dismisses the name Harry because of Harry Potter, point out that not all Harrys are associated with wizardry and wearing small round glasses – prior to Mr Potter the best-known Harry on screen was 'Dirty Harry', a different image altogether! So if you want to be more persuasive do a bit more research on the name you like and see whether you think the meaning, history or popularity of the name might help your partner to see it in a different light.

The powers of persuasion must be allowed to work both ways, of course! It is easy to become preoccupied with convincing your partner to accept a name that you are in love with. However, you need to be open-minded to their suggestions too. If there is a name that they would really like for your baby then don't rule it out immediately. Keep it on your shortlist and give it a chance to grow on you – you may be surprised at how your feelings change, given some time.

Quick Checks Before You Name Your Baby!

Once you have fallen in love with a name you can become blinkered to its downsides – if it has any. There are some key points that are worth checking in order to establish certain associations or drawbacks to the name. If you find any, it doesn't mean that you should discard it; it's just better to know these things ahead of time. If Angelina is the name you have settled on, wouldn't you rather you were already aware of the fictional world of Angelina Ballerina before your baby girl gets given three stuffed tutu-wearing mice as new baby presents?

Nicknames and Shortenings

As they grow up, the child's name might evolve if they, or others, decide to use it differently. These changes can be a result of shortenings, nicknames or simply differences in pronunciation. It is worth considering the obvious possibilities with a name from the outset, so if the familiar form 'Jimmy' from 'James' really bothers you then you can either choose to avoid the name altogether or make a point of explaining to other people that you would prefer his full name used as much as possible. Of course, this might work with close relations, but be realistic about how much influence you are going to have over playground and sporting friendships in the future.

Changes to names come about in different ways. Names are often shortened and there are some very obvious examples such as 'Dan' from 'Daniel' or 'Liz' from 'Elizabeth'. Many names have a familiar form such as 'Bill' from 'William' or 'Maggie' from 'Margaret'. Of course, you may actually prefer some of these diminutives to their longer originals, so you can bypass the lengthy alternative altogether. For many years 'Max' has been much more popular than 'Maxwell', and recently 'Thomas' remains the same at 9th place in the popularity charts while 'Tommy' has made a remarkable leap, shooting up more than 21 places to rank 57. Other names have less obvious, or less frequently used, shortened forms. It is quite common for names of more than one syllable to be shortened informally to just the one syllable, especially by close friends and family. You might hear 'Lucy' affectionately shortened to 'Luce', or 'Siobhan' to 'Shiv'. You can usually be sure that these nicknames weren't the driving factor for choosing that name in the first place. They wouldn't offend most parents but it is still worth giving a thought to how a name might be shortened in the future by other people.

Nicknames aren't always the result of shortening a name or using its familiar form, and consequently they can be hard to predict. We all know of people who live with a nickname that forever prompts the question 'Why?' and the answer is often long-winded, nonsensical or ridiculous. In some cases, nobody knows how the nickname came about. Sometimes a name may originate from a story about that person (John 'Two Jags' Prescott), or from an aspect of their personality, hobby or job (David 'Golden Balls' Beckham). In these incidences all you can do is hope that if your child gets such a nickname, it is tasteful and in good humour. Many people have nicknames that are short-lived, used for a period of their lives such as their time at college or university, or used only by their work colleagues or teammates in the sport that they play. You do come across people who have lived by their nickname for so long that few people actually know their real name any more, but in most cases people grow out of their nicknames in the long run – often to their relief!

Sometimes a nickname can result from the modification of a person's first name, surname or both, which is another reason to try out name ideas with the surname. Say the name over a few times and make sure you don't think that there are any glaringly obvious innuendos, spoonerisms or jokes to be had – such as the English football player Fitz Hall who is known by his nickname as 'One Size'. The use of someone's surname, or a variant of their surname, as their nickname is a phenomenon particularly associated with team sports such as football – Paul Gascoigne's nickname 'Gazza' being one of the most famous examples. This tends to be more common among boys.

Once you have considered the obvious potential for nicknames, don't get bogged down with the idea that there may be some horrific double meaning or pet form of the name; if you can't think of it now, the chances are most other people won't either. And if your child does end up with a nickname that you don't approve of, it will probably have been unavoidable – do you think Scarlett Johansson's parents could have seen 'Scar-Jo' coming?

Check out Common Associations

You will probably have already thought of any obvious celebrity namesakes – for example, there are few women of childbearing age in the UK who haven't heard of the Hollywood actress Angelina Jolie. But in the case of Angelina Ballerina, dancing mice aren't necessarily going to be at the forefront of your mind, unless you already have (or spend time with) young children. Arduous research into popular children's television culture won't be required; just ask a friend who has children whether they think the name is popular or has any associations for them. You might also want to run the name through a quick search on the Internet just to see who is attracting attention at the moment with that name – particularly with your surname. The latest D-list celebrity hitting the headlines for a drunken gaffe is unlikely to affect your decision to use a name (nobody will remember them this time next year) but you might like to know if there are any public figures out there (good or bad) with that name.

Of course, it's not just people (or mice) that you want to look out for when it comes to names. Popular names are used as brand names for all sorts of products and services, for example Jessica nail varnish and George clothing at Asda. If you work in a beauty salon and shop at Asda then these names might lose some appeal, or it might be what gave you the idea in the first place! Remember that associations don't just fall into 'good' and 'bad' categories; some of these associations (even strong ones) will have no impact on our personal preferences for a name.

Consider the Initials

Most children in the UK are given at least one middle name and the English language has over 1,000 three-letter words, so there are plenty of name combinations that will spell out a real word when the initials are written down. More often than not these are unremarkable – S.I.T., H.A.T. and so on. At best they can be amusing, but in some rare cases initials can spell out a swear word or a slang term for something inappropriate (you can use your own imagination for examples of these!).

Also consider the first initial(s) together with the surname, as mistakes can occasionally happen in this way too – for example, it might not take the school children long to notice that 'Caleb Oliver Ward' could be abbreviated to 'C.O.Ward' or 'Una Grace Lee' to 'U.G.Lee'!

It is quite common to give your child the same first initial as their siblings or parents but remember that this can lead to confusion when it comes to mail sent to your address. Even if the middle initial differs, a lot of mail is sent to 'S. Thomas' without the Mr/Mrs prefix or sometimes with an incorrect title. Generally this would be a minor thing to niggle about when the postman arrives but it could also lead to embarrassing situations or arguments when people open the wrong mail!

Coordinated Names

For those parents who are really coordinated, you might want to take into account the first names of everyone else in the family. But how a name works with both siblings' and parents' names should still be a consideration – you might not want to be signing off your Christmas cards next year 'from Pat, Rick & Baby Patrick' but until you consider the name alongside your names this kind of mistake can easily go unnoticed.

Is There a Joke to be Had?

When it comes to ensuring that your child's name is not going to make for an easy target, you have to accept that there is no such thing as a 'bully-proof' name. Bullies are innovative and if they are going to bully a person they will seek out something about that person to pick on. However, you can certainly do your child a favour by avoiding a name that has an obvious joke 'built in'. Look out for:

- **Double meanings:** Ben Dover, Harry Pits, Amanda Hugenkiss, Hugh Jass … if you're a lover of *The Simpsons* you will be familiar with all these gag names that Bart Simpson gets the bartender, Moe, to call out. It's an old joke but spare a second to check that when you say your child's names aloud there is no suggestion of an alternative word or expression in there.
- **Silly spoonerisms:** Some names can also fall into the trap of *spoonerism*, where a joke is made by swapping corresponding consonants or vowels of the first and last name around – 'Kelly Smith' would become 'Smelly Kith', 'Mary Hegg' would become 'Hairy Megg' and so on. These are easy to spot when you think about them and might make a name worth ruling out if you think the spoonerism is likely to be used offensively.
- **Awkward anagrams:** Let's face it, it really isn't the end of the world if your baby's name can be rearranged to spell 'This Moaner' (Erin Thomas), but it is quite interesting. There are a number of free anagram checkers online so it is easy to find out what anagrams could be made of their potential name(s) if you would like to know.
- **Rhyming slang:** The use of rhyming slang comes and goes and there are many people who are unfamiliar with this use of replacing words or phrases with other

(unrelated) rhyming words. A couple of popular terms use people's names and consequently you should definitely avoid naming your child 'Ruby Murray' (curry) or 'Pete Tong' (wrong).

Finally, it's best to avoid your child's name becoming the joke of the class by steering clear of the plain ridiculous. You know how much our society likes to make fun of one another. Celebrities may get away with naming their children 'Jermajesty' (Jermaine Jackson), 'Blue Angel' (The Edge, U2) or Pilot Inspektor (Jason Lee) – and there is possibly even an argument for having to differentiate the child so that they stand out from their parents' glittering star status – but in your average classroom 'Denim' and 'Diezel' (Toni Braxton's children) are going to stand out like a sore thumb. There is a lot to be said for being different, but draw a line between *unusual* and *absurd*.

PART TWO

Inspiration

Naming Trends for 2019/20

There is no accurate way to predict the name charts – popularity of certain names is often generated by recent events and media coverage of high-profile people. Award-winners, musicians, Netflix characters, reality stars, novelists, book characters, royal babies, sports medal winners – all can bring a name back into fashion, inspire new trends, or even stop it becoming popular!

While traditional names remain as popular as ever, we have also seen a rise in the quest for unique names, with unusual spelling variations. As the world becomes ever-more globally connected, parents are choosing names from around the world and country origin is no boundary. There is a rise in names also inspired by geographical place names such as Dakota and Florence as people travel more and more. Gender-neutral names such as Bobbie and Charlie have always been popular but now seem to be a more conscious choice, as are names inspired by nature such as Sky, Storm and Bay.

Gender-neutral names

Campbell	River
Robin	Bobbie
Avery	Ashley
Drew	Kelsey
Storm	Alex
Charlie	Ryan

Recent high achievers

The primary reason for choosing a name is that you like it, but finding out that it is associated with one or more successful people in the world is always going to be pleasing! Whether or not you think you might be about to raise the next prize-winning physicist, musician, actor or literary prize winner doesn't matter – a name that has positive associations is bound to make you feel good about your choice.

Boys
Denis Mukwege Mukengere (The Nobel Prize for Peace, 2018)
Rami Malek (Best Actor, Oscars, 2019)
Mahershala Ali (Best Supporting Actor, Oscars, 2019)
Kyle Soller (Best Actor, Olivier Awards, 2019)
George Ezra (Best British Male Artist, Brit Awards 2019)
Sam Fender (Critics' Choice, Brit Awards 2019)
Stuart Turton (Best First Novel, Costa Book Awards 2019)
Geraint Thomas (BBC Sports Personality of the Year, 2018)

Girls
Nadia Murad (The Nobel Prize for Peace, 2018)
Donna Strickland (The Nobel Prize for Physics, 2018)
Olivia Colman (Best Actress, Oscars, 2019)
Regina King (Best Supporting Actress, Oscars 2019)
Patsy Ferran (Best Actress, Olivier Awards 2019)
Jorja Smith (Best British Female Solo Artist, Brit Awards 2019)
Anna Burns (Booker Prize Winner 2018)
Charlotte Prodger (Turner Prize, 2018)

Popular culture

The names of actors, musicians, models, writers and television stars are part of our everyday conversations and this is often reflected in the most popular baby name charts. Harper is now in the top 10 for girls' names, and may be inspired by Harper Beckham or Harper Lee. Liam, currently in the top 5 for boys, could be inspired by Liam Payne or Liam Hemsworth.

The real change here has been in the rise in popularity of social media influencers, who many of us follow on a daily basis, whether via Instagram, Twitter, Youtube or reality television shows and vlogs. The Kardashian children's names ('Dashlets') include North, Dream, Chicago and

True, leading the way for non-traditional, although very recognisable names.

Young actors and celebrities might also inspire baby names. Milo and Millie are very popular and this might be influenced by Milo Parker and Millie Bobby Brown.

Hollywood actors

Boys
Bradley Cooper
Donald Glover
Zac Efron
Rami Malek
Ryan Gosling
Jamie Foxx
Daniel Kaluuya
Eddie Redmayne

Girls
Viola Davis
Alicia Vikander
Brie Larson
Felicity Jones
Halle Berry
Dakota Johnson
Octavia Spencer
Saoirse Una Ronan

Television actors

Boys
Ben Wishaw
Kit Harrington
Aziz Ansari
Benedict Cumberbatch
Richard Madden
Babou Ceesay
Idris Elba
Dominic West

Girls
Vanessa Kirby
Jodie Comer
Thandie Newton
Michelle Keegan
Olivia Colman
Sofia Vergara
Karen Gillan
Natalie Dormer

Stage actors

Boys
Rory Kinnear
Mark Rylance
Adrian Lester
Tom Hiddleston
Charlie Stemp
Ralph Fiennes
Joel Montague
Trevor Dion Nicholas

Girls
Anne-Marie Duff
Noma Dumezweni
Imelda Staunton
Denise Gough
Katherine McPhee
Carrie Hope Fletcher
Billie Piper
Sheridan Smith

Child actors

Boys
Milo Parker
Finn Wolfhard
Caleb McLaughlin
Joel Dawson
Angus Imrie
Louis Serkis
Bleu Landau
Noah Jupe

Girls
Millie Bobby Brown
Landry Bender
Mackenzie Foy
Pixie Davies
Skai Jackson
Ramona Marquez
Dafne Keen
Tisha Martin

Comedians

Boys
Jack Whitehall
Jay Pharoah
Dara O Briain
Noel Fielding
James Acaster
Josh Widdicombe
Romesh Ranganathan
Sacha Baron Cohen

Girls
Shappi Khorsandi
Amy Poehler
Phoebe Waller-Bridge
Tina Fey
Gina Yashere
Tiffany Haddish
Rachel Brosnahan
Tracey Ullman

Fashion

Boys
Tyson Beckford
Zac Posen
Presley Walker Gerber
Marc Jacobs
Erdem Moralioglu
David Gandy
Lucky Blue Smith
Toby Huntington-Whiteley

Girls
Kendall Jenner
Paloma Elsesser
Gigi Hadid
Stella McCartney
Kaia Gerber
Coco Chanel
Noah Carlos
Cara Delevingne

Reality television

Boys
Spencer Matthews
Karamo Brown
Antoni Porowski
Rylan Clark-Neal

Girls
Sam Faiers
Nadiya Hussain
Binky Felstead
Georgia Toffolo

Mark Wright	Millie Mackintosh
Ollie Locke	Davina McCall
Marvin Humes	Megan McKenna
Scott Disick	Khloe Kardashian

Social media

Boys	*Girls*
Kurtis Conner	Susie Bubble
Eugene Lee Yang	Alexa Chung
Alfie Deyes	Haley Pham
Brooklyn Beckham	Avery Ovard
Caspar Lee	Zoe Sugg
Nickelson Wooster	Iskra Lawrence
Louis Cole	Tanya Burr
Joe Wicks	Dina Torkia

Celebrity Babies

Boys
Miles Theodore Stephens (John Legend & Chrissy Teigen)
Romeo Alejandro David (Alec Baldwin & Hilaria Thomas)
River Rocket (Jamie & Jools Oliver)
Hart (Miranda Kerr & Evan Spiegel)
Ennis Howard (Kirsten Dunst & Jesse Plemons)
Luke Richard (Eddie and Hannah Redmayne)
Beckett (Michael Phelps & Nicole Johnson)
Francisco (Lin-Manuel Miranda & Vanessa Nadal)

Girls
Marvel Jane (Pete Wentz & Meagan Camper)
True (Khloe Kardashian & Tristan Thompson)
Dream (Rob Kardashian & Blac Chyna)
Stormi Webster (Kylie Jenner & Travis Scott)
James (Ryan Reynolds & Blake Lively)
Dusty Rose (Adam Levine & Behati Prinsloo)
Story (Aaron Paul & Lauren Parsekian)
Apple (Gywneth Paltrow & Chris Martin)

Visual artists

Boys	*Girls*
Damien Hirst	Chantal Joffe

Leonardo da Vinci	Georgia O'Keeffe
Jack Vettriano	Beryl Cook
Vincent van Gogh	Barbara Hepworth
Antony Gormley	Marlene Dumas
Grayson Perry	Tamara de Lempicka
Anish Kapoor	Francine van Hove
Chris Ofili	Rachel Whiteread

FICTIONAL NAMES

We continue to be inspired by characters from our favourite books and films. Disney films evoke happy memories from our own childhoods, and the more recent films have provided fresh names to consider. And whether you love Harry Potter or Game of Thrones (or both!) there are some wonderful, creative names to choose from these books and films. Luna has now made it into the top 20 list for girls. Classic and contemporary children's books are also a rich source of name inspiration.

Disney film characters

Boys	*Girls*
Mickey	Belle
Donald	Ariel
Kristoff	Minnie
Flynn	Anna
Olaf	Elsa
Eric	Jasmine
Jack	Tiana
Georgie	Aurora
	Annabel

Star Wars characters

Boys	*Girls*
Han Solo	Leia Organa
Anakin Skywalker	Padmé Amidala
Luke Skywalker	Rey
Kylo Ren	Qi'ra

Lando Calrissian
Finn
Mace Windu
Tobias Beckett

Mara Jade
Maz Kanata
Shmi Skywalker
Jyn Erso

Marvel characters

Boys
Loki Laufeyson
Peter Quill
Clint Barton
Tony Stark
Thor Odinson
Bruce Banner
Scott Lang
Steven Rogers

Girls
Hope Pym
Peggy Carter
Wanda Maximoff
Natasha Romanoff
Virginia Potts
Maria Hill
Jane Foster
Carol Danvers

Game of Thrones

Boys
Robb Stark
Ned Stark
Brandon Stark
Jon Snow
Jaime Lannister
Theon Greyjoy
Stannis Baratheon
Joffrey Baratheon

Girls
Arya Stark
Catelyn Stark
Sansa Stark
Cersei Lannister
Lysa Arryn
Daenerys Targaryen
Brienne of Tarth
Margaery Tyrell

Hunger Games

Boys
Peeta Mellark
Gale Hawthorne
Haymitch Abernathy
Coriolanus Snow
Finnick
Cato

Girls
Katniss Everdeen
Primrose ("Prim") Everdeen
Effie Glimmer
Rue
Johanna
Delly

Harry Potter

Boys
Ron Weasley

Girls
Ginny Weasley

Albus Dumbledore
Sirius Black
Cedric Diggory
Fred Weasley
George Weasley
Arthur Weasley
Frank Longbottom

Luna Lovegood
Fleur Delacour
Cho Chang
Hermione Granger
Lavender Brown
Lily Potter

Contempory fiction characters

Boys
Charles Wallace
Max (*Where the Wild Things Are*)
Edmund Pevensie
Klaus Baudelaire
Greg Heffley
Alex Rider
Jack (*Grandpa's Great Escape*)
Atticus Finch

Girls
Alice Liddel
Violet Baudelaire
Arrietty Clock
Lyra Belacqua
Meg Wallace
Becky Thatcher
Petrova Fossil
Roberta (Bobbie) Waterbury

Shakespeare play characters

Boys
Benedick
Cassio
Romeo
Lysander
Edgar
Antonio
Orsino
Mark

Girls
Miranda
Ophelia
Olivia
Cordelia
Beatrice
Juliet
Desdemona
Hermia

Classic fiction characters

Boys
Arthur Huntingdon
Edward Rochester
Edgar Linton
Oliver Twist
Fitzwilliam Darcy
Charles Bingley
George Knightley
Edwin Drood

Girls
Elinor Dashwood
Lydia Bennet
Fanny Price
Harriet Smith
Adele Varens
Agnes Grey
Clara Peggotty
Rosa Bud

MUSICAL NAMES

Music is a rich source of name inspiration, from musical terms to classic and contemporary musicians. You could choose the name of your favourite artist (Bowie, Dolly), from a song title (Layla) or a musical term (Harmony), for example.

Musical terms

Boys	Girls
Largo	Aria
Forte	Harmony
Lieder	Allegra
Opus	Chanson
Fife	Calypso
Reed	Piper
Solo	Viola
Bene	Seraphine

Classical musicians

Boys	Girls
Johann Sebastian Bach	Renée Fleming
Wolfgang Amadeus Mozart	Clara Butt
Frederic Chopin	Nicola Benedetti
Benjamin Britten	Sarah Chang
Hans Zimmer	Vanessa-Mae Vanakorn Nicholson
Alfie Boe	Kathleen Ferrier
Andrea Bocelli	Jessye Norman
Sheku Kanneh-Mason	Laura Wright

Musical theatre characters

Boys	Girls
Alexander Hamilton	Cosette
Evan Hansen	Elle Woods
Emmett Forrest	Miss Adelaide
Oliver Twist	Carlotta Giudicelli
Fiyero Tiggular	Annie Warbucks
Joseph	Inez Stubbs

Danny Zuko   Velma Kelly
Simba   Nala

Pop music

Boys   *Girls*
George Ezra   Perrie Edwards
Olly Murs   Ellie Goulding
Justin Bieber   Selena Gomez
Zayn Malik   Ariana Grande
Jason Derulo   Jess Glynne
Adam Levine   Taylor Swift
Ed Sheeran   Fleur East
Matthew Healy   Rae Morris

Dance and RnB

Boys   *Girls*
Taio Cruz   Rita Ora
Kendrick Lamar   Missy Elliott
Pharrell Williams   Beyonce
Aloe Blacc   Iggy Izalea
Sean Combs   Alicia Keys
Frank Ocean   Maya Jane Coles
Calvin Harris   Lisa Lashes
Richie Hawtin   Jorja Smith

Rock and indie

Boys   *Girls*
Van McCann   Alecia Moore (Pink)
Robby Takac   Avril Lavigne
Chester Bennington   Beth Ditto
Gerard Way   Gwen Stefani
Ricky Wilson   Ellie Rowsell
Noel Gallagher   Nadina Shah
Chad Kroeger   Shirley Manson
Alex Turner   Phillipa (Pip) Brown

Soul

Boys   *Girls*
Bruno Mars   Emeli Sande

Marvin Gaye	Paloma Faith
Jason Mraz	Toni Braxton
Otis Redding	Jill Scott
Usher Raymond IV	Aretha Franklin
Levi Stubbs	Jennifer Hudson
George Michael	Etta James
Elton John	Joss Stone

Jazz

Boys	*Girls*
Jack Savoretti	Esperanza Spalding
Sonny Rollins	Ella Fitzgerald
Jools Holland	Eva Cassidy
Gregory Porter	Norah Jones
Jamie Cullum	Sade Adu
Louis Armstrong	Billie Holiday
Michael Bublé	Diana Krall
Chet Baker	Nina Simone

Sport and dance

We all have favourite sports that we watch or play. Whether you are into tennis, football, athletics, skiing or only watch once every four years when the Olympics occurs, the international world of sports is a rich inspiration for names.

Boys	*Girls*
Eden Hazard	Jeannie Longo
Dane Coles	Marta Vieira da Silva
Maro Itoje	Melanie Behringer
Mason Crane	Ada Hegerberg
Rafael Nadal	Nikita Parris
Max Whitlock	Rochelle Clark
Geraint Thomas	Simone Biles
Marcel Hirscher	Carly Patterson

Olympic greats

Boys	*Girls*
Usain Bolt	Jessica Ennis-Hill
Bradley Wiggins	Laura Trott
Steve Redgrave	Katherine Grainger
Paavo Nurmi	Jayne Torvill
Nikolai Andrianov	Birgit Fischer
Mark Spitz	Larisa Latynina
Sebastian Coe	Tanni Grey-Thompson
Daley Thompson	Kelly Holmes

Dance

Girls	*Boys*
Isadora Duncan	Gorka Marquez
Sofia Boutella	Kevin Clifton
Shriya Saran	Sergei Polunin
Otlile Mabuse	Carlos Acosta
Katya Jones	Matthew Morrison
Misty Copeland	Ashley Banjo
Tamara Rojo	Fred Astaire
Ginger Rogers	Joaquin Cortés

History-makers

Your baby will have a wonderful impact on your world, but there are some babies that go on to change the world for all of us. Here are some of the people who have inspired us all.

Boys	*Girls*
Barack Obama	Ada Lovelace
Martin Luther King	Virginia Woolf
Nelson Mandela	Mary Wollstonecraft
Simon Bolivar	Emmeline Pankhurst
Guy Fawkes	Indira Ghandi
Oskar Schindler	Harriet Tubman
Bill Gates	Rosa Parks
Thomas Jefferson	Margaret Thatcher

Mythological names

Greek and Roman names continue to inspire us; they are not common in the most popular names lists, but will be recognisable and your child might enjoy reading about their namesake one day!

Greek gods

Boys	*Girls*
Hermes	Artemis
Zeus	Hera
Chronos	Athena
Hades	Demeter
Ares	Nyx
Phanes	Eirene
Poseidon	Hestia
Dionysus	Hemera

Roman gods

Boys	*Girls*
Jupiter	Juno
Sol	Venus
Liber	Diana
Neptune	Vesta
Cupid	Ceres
Sancus	Luna
Saturn	Fortuna
Mars	Veritas

Names from the Bible

Boys	*Girls*
David	Eve
Zachariah	Esther
Luke	Tamar
Abraham	Judith
Ethan	Leah
Isaac	Naomi
Reuben	Zelda
Solomon	Delilah

Names from the Quran

Boys	*Girls*
Darim	Aisha
Bashir	Daneen
Kaamil	Jahida
Ghalib	Lafiza
Nahid	Omera
Taheem	Reyah
Madani	Tahira
Habib	Zahra

Natural world names

Boys	*Girls*
Robin	Willow
Bay	Flora
Flint	Hazel
Forrest	Anise
Rio	Saffron
Sky	Posie
Tiger	Ivy
Wolfie	Gaia

TRADITIONAL NAMES BY COUNTRY

You are not restricted to choosing a name from your own or your child's birth country. It could be that you lived in another country, or had a memorable holiday there. With many babies having parents from different countries, you could choose a name that works in both too. Names inspired by places, such as a city or state, have become more popular too, such as Savannah and Austin.

Place names

Boys	*Girls*
Brooklyn	Siena
Paris	Bristol

Phoenix	Chelsea
Austin	Savannah
Caspian	Dakota
Hamilton	Jordan
Indiana	Florence
Lincoln	Carmel

England

Boys	*Girls*
Harold	Mavis
Percy	Mabel
Horace	Ethel
Alfred	Doris
Cyril	Dolly
Herbert	Edie
Reginald	Winifred
Bernard	Geraldine

Nicknames

Boys	*Girls*
Spike	Blue
Sonny	Honey
Buster	Angel
Buddy	Bee
Jonty	Star
Ace	Bonnie
Skipper	Rosie
Rex	Betsy

UK royal names

The British monarchy has been riding a wave of international popularity and media interest for the past few years. The wedding of Meghan and Harry captured hearts around the world and with the arrival of their first baby, Archie is set to be the favourite name for many!

William and Catherine have three children: Prince George Alexander Louis, Princess Charlotte Elizabeth Diana, and the latest addition, Prince Louis Arthur Charles.

Boys	Girls
William	Meghan
Harry	Charlotte
Archie	Catherine
Charles	Elizabeth
George	Victoria
Louis	Beatrice
Alfred	Diana
Andrew	Eugenie

International Royal names

Boys	Girls
Daniel (Sweden)	Silvia (Sweden)
Harald (Norway)	Madeleine (Sweden)
Albert (Monaco)	Estelle (Sweden)
Philipp (Liechtenstein)	Ingrid (Norway)
Hans-Adam (Liechtenstein)	Caroline (Monaco)
Alois (Liechtenstein)	Stephanie (Monaco)
Frederik (Denmark)	Tatjana (Liechtenstein)
Hussein (Jordan)	Margrethe (Denmark)

Ireland

Boys	Girls
Seamus	Niamh
Connor	Orlagh
Ronan	Roisin
Patrick	Ciara
Oisin	Saoirse
Sean	Grace
Daniel	Aoife
Jack	Clodagh

Wales

Boys	Girls
Bryn	Anwen
Gethin	Ffion

Idris	Sian
Ceri	Tegan
Evan	Carys
Owen	Rhiannon
Tristan	Lowri
Rhodri	Angharad

Scotland

Boys	*Girls*
Cameron	Isla
Logan	Iona
Donald	Fiona
Douglas	Mackenzie
Gordon	Moire
Alisdair	Elspeth
Clyde	Flora
Alexander	Morven

United States of America

Boys	*Girls*
Tyler	Madison
Kyle	Emma
Jackson	Ensley
Lincoln	Madelyn
Caden	Harper
Logan	Avery
Ashton	Skylar
Carter	Ava

France

Boys	*Girls*
Etienne	Alice
Paul	Anais (double dot over the I)
Armand	Chloé
Yanis	Camille
Gabriel	Manon
Mathis	Jeanne
Louis	Louise
Enzo	Lea

Italy

Boys	*Girls*
Matteo	Anna
Alessandro	Maria
Luca	Rosa
Lorenzo	Giovanna
Luigi	Sofia
Antoni	Alessia
Marco	Chaira
Stefano	Antonia

Spain

Boys	*Girls*
Javier	Lucia
Mario	Martina
Carlos	Maria
Matias	Sofia
Alejandro	Paula
Sebastian	Ana
Hugo	Carla
Pablo	Gabriela

The Netherlands

Boys	*Girls*
Levi	Saar
Luuk	Mila
Stijn	Sanne
Daan	Anouk
Sem	Eva
Bram	Lotte
Lars	Isa
Markus	Lieke

Greece

Boys	*Girls*
Christos	Eleni
Nikolaos	Katerina
Ioannis	Dimitra

Panagiotis	Sophia
Vasileios	Angeliki
Adonis	Cassia
Homer	Anastasia
Quinn	Athena

Russia

Boys	*Girls*
Maxim	Anastasia
Ivan	Daria
Alexandr	Polina
Dmitry	Zoya
Mikhail	Viktoria
Nikolas	Alissa
Daniil	Tatiana
Vladimir	Mischa

Sweden

Boys	*Girls*
William	Ella
Oscar	Ebba
Liam	Lilly
Elias	Astrid
Isak	Saga
Axel	Alicia
Ludvig	Freja
Nils	Maja

Germany

Boys	*Girls*
Leon	Leonie
Lucas	Lena
Finn	Hannah
Jonas	Mila
Maximilian	Mia
Elias	Johanna
Moritz	Mathilda
Emil	Greta

Top 100 Boys Girls

Rank	Boys Name	Change in Rank	Rank	Girls Name	Change in Rank
1	OLIVER	–	1	OLIVIA	–
2	HARRY	–	2	AMELIA	–
3	GEORGE	↘	3	ISLA	↗
4	NOAH	↗	4	AVA	↗
5	JACK	↘	5	EMILY	↘
6	JACOB	↘	6	ISABELLA	↗
7	MUHAMMAD	↗	7	MIA	↗
8	LEO	↗	8	POPPY	↗
9	OSCAR	↗	9	ELLA	–
10	CHARLIE	↘	10	CHARLOTTE	↗
11	WILLIAM	–	11	LILY	↘
12	HENRY	↗	12	SOPHIA	↘
13	ALFIE	↗	13	GRACE	↗
14	THOMAS	↘	14	EVIE	↗
15	JOSHUA	↗	15	JESSICA	↘
16	FREDDIE	↗	16	SOPHIE	↘
17	JAMES	↘	17	ALICE	–
18	ARTHUR	↗	18	FLORENCE	↗
19	ARCHIE	↘	19	DAISY	↗
20	LOGAN	↗	20	FREYA	–
21	ALEXANDER	–	21	PHOEBE	↗
22	EDWARD	↗	22	SIENNA	↗
23	THEO	↗	23	EVELYN	↗
24	ISAAC	↘	24	ISABELLE	↘
25	LUCAS	↗	25	IVY	↗
26	ETHAN	↘	26	MATILDA	↘
27	MAX	↘	27	WILLOW	↗
28	JOSEPH	↘	28	ELSIE	↗
29	SAMUEL	↘	29	CHLOE	↘
30	MOHAMMED	↘	30	SCARLETT	↘
31	DANIEL	↘	31	SOFIA	↘
32	BENJAMIN	↗	32	RUBY	↘
33	FINLEY	↗	33	EVA	↘
34	SEBASTIAN	↗	34	HARPER	↗
35	HARRISON	↘	35	EMILIA	↗
36	ADAM	↗	36	ROSIE	↗

37	THEODORE	↗	37	MILLIE	↘
38	MASON	↘	38	LAYLA	↗
39	TEDDY	↗	39	MAYA	↘
40	DYLAN	↘	40	IMOGEN	↘
41	ELIJAH	↗	41	ELIZA	↗
42	ARLO	↗	42	ESME	↘
43	DAVID	–	43	ELIZABETH	↘
44	RILEY	↘	44	LOLA	↘
45	ZACHARY	↘	45	MAISIE	↗
46	LOUIE	–	46	ERIN	↗
47	HUGO	↗	47	LUNA	↗
48	JUDE	↗	48	LUCY	↘
49	TOBY	↘	49	EMMA	↗
50	REUBEN	↘	50	HARRIET	↘
51	REGGIE	↗	51	ARIA	↗
52	HARLEY	↗	52	ELEANOR	↘
53	JAXON	↘	53	ELLIE	↘
54	RORY	↗	54	PENELOPE	↗
55	LUCA	↘	55	THEA	↘
56	ALBIE	↗	56	HANNAH	–
57	JAKE	↘	57	HOLLY	↘
58	ALBERT	↗	58	MOLLY	↘
59	JENSON	↗	59	BELLA	↗
60	FRANKIE	↗	60	ROSE	↗
61	TOMMY	↘	61	VIOLET	↗
62	RONNIE	↗	62	AMBER	↘
63	CARTER	↗	63	GEORGIA	↘
64	GABRIEL	↗	64	JASMINE	↘
65	BOBBY	↗	65	LILLY	↘
66	MATTHEW	↘	66	ANNABELLE	↘
67	HARVEY	↘	67	NANCY	↗
68	MICHAEL	↘	68	DARCIE	↗
69	STANLEY	↘	69	ZARA	↘
70	ELLIOT	↘	70	MARIA	↘
71	FREDERICK	↗	71	LOTTIE	↗
72	CHARLES	↘	72	AMELIE	↘
73	JAYDEN	↘	73	ABIGAIL	↘
74	LUKE	↘	74	MILA	↗
75	JACKSON	↗	75	ANNA	↘
76	MOHAMMAD	↘	76	MARTHA	–
77	ROMAN	↗	77	MARYAM	–

78	ELLIOTT	↘	78	GRACIE	–
79	HUNTER	↗	79	ROBYN	↗
80	LOUIS	↘	80	IRIS	↗
81	CALEB	↗	81	SARA	↗
82	RYAN	↘	82	HEIDI	↘
83	EZRA	↗	83	ARABELLA	↗
84	NATHAN	↘	84	AURORA	↗
85	LEWIS	↘	85	BEATRICE	↘
86	DEXTER	↘	86	ORLA	↗
87	BLAKE	↘	87	SUMMER	↘
88	ELLIS	↗	88	CLARA	↘
89	JESSE	↗	89	FRANCESCA	↘
90	LIAM	↗	90	AISHA	↘
91	OLLIE	↘	91	JULIA	↗
92	ALEX	↘	92	VICTORIA	↘
93	IBRAHIM	↗	93	EDITH	↗
94	KAI	↘	94	LYLA	↗
95	RALPH	↗	95	DARCEY	↘
96	FELIX	↗	96	BONNIE	↗
97	TYLER	↘	97	DARCY	↗
98	LEON	↘	98	SARAH	↘
99	FINN	↗	99	LEAH	↘
100	AUSTIN	↘	100	FELICITY	↘

PART THREE

Baby Names

Names for Baby Boys A–Z

Names For Baby Boys A–Z

A

Aadyha

Meaning: Security
Origin: Arabic
Pronunciation: AH maan
Description: Amaan is an alternative spelling of the name Aman. It is a popular name in both English- and Arabic-speaking countries, and is a name that appears in the Quran.
Alternative spellings: Aman

Aahil

Meaning: Prince
Origin: Arabic
Pronunciation: AH hill
Description: Aahil is an Arabic word meaning 'prince.' Although it translates to prince, it generally refers to a king or ruler who presides over multiple nations and countries.
Alternative spellings: Ahil, Ahel, Aahel

Aaran

Meaning: Strong mountain
Origin: Hebrew
Pronunciation: AH ran
Description: Aaran is a Hebrew name derived from the Egyptian name Aharan and was the name given to the older brother of Moses.
Alternative spellings: Aarin, Aaryn, Arran

Aarav

Meaning: Peaceful
Origin: Sanskrit
Pronunciation: AH raav
Description: This name originates from the Indian word '*rav*', which means 'calm' or 'peaceful.' More specifically, it means 'rustling sound' or 'melodious music,' to describe a person who is at peace with himself.
Alternative spellings: Arav, Araav

Aariz

Meaning: Respectable
Origin: Arabic
Pronunciation: AH riz
Description: Aariz is of Arabic origin and has many meanings. It is most commonly understood to mean 'respectable' and 'intelligent man'.
Alternative spellings: Ariz, Arris

Aaron

Meaning: Strong mountain
Origin: Hebrew
Pronunciation: AIR ron
Description: As well as being a biblical name borne by the brother of Moses, the origin of Aaron could be linked to Egypt. Widely popular since the 1990s, it is the name of well-known figures Aaron Carter (singer) and Aaron Lennon (footballer).

Alternative spellings: Aaran, Aron, Arran, Arron, Arun

Aarush
Meaning: First ray of sun
Origin: Sanskrit
Pronunciation: ah ROOSH
Description: Aarush is Sanskrit in origin. It is derived from a Hindi word that means 'first ray of the sun'.
Alternative spellings: Aaroosh, Arush

Aaryan
Meaning: From Hadria
Origin: Latin
Pronunciation: ar REE an
Description: This name comes from the Latin name Hadrianus, hence the meaning 'from Hadria'. The name Hadrianus has belonged to six popes and also several early Christian saints and martyrs.
Alternative spellings: Aarian, Aryan

Aayan
Meaning: Era
Origin: Arabic
Pronunciation: UH yan
Description: Aayan is an alternative spelling of the name Ayan. Consequently it also means 'era' or its various synonyms. It is a name that is frequently mentioned in the Quran and thus is extremely popular in Muslim communities.
Alternative spellings: Ayan

Abbas
Meaning: Austere; lion
Origin: Hebrew
Pronunciation: AH bas
Description: A male name of Arabic origin, which means 'lion' or 'austere' and is favoured by Muslim parents. Abbas was the name of the prophet Muhammad's uncle and ancestor of the Abbasid caliphs who formerly ruled the Islamic world.
Alternative spellings: Abas

Abdirahman
Meaning: Servant to the merciful
Origin: Arabic
Pronunciation: AB DEE rah man
Description: Abdirahman is thought to be a variant of the Arabic name Abdulrahman, meaning 'servant to the merciful.' It is built from the Arabic words 'abd,' 'al' and 'rahman.' It is also sometimes found as a surname.
Alternative spellings: Abdulrahman, Abdur-Rahman, Abdurahman, Abdurrahman

Abdul
Meaning: Servant of Allah
Origin: Arabic
Pronunciation: AB dul
Description: Abdul is of Arabic origin and is the shortened form of Abdullah. Abdul means 'servant' and is commonly used together with its longer form, Abdullah. Also used as a surname.
Alternative spellings: Abdal, Abdel

Abdullah
Meaning: Servant of Allah
Origin: Arabic
Pronunciation: ab DUL ah

Description: This name, popular with Muslim parents, means 'God's servant'. One of the most popular names in the Islamic world, it is believed to be the name of the father of the prophet Muhammad.
Alternative spellings: Abd-Allah, Abdallah

Abdullahi
Meaning: Allah's servant
Origin: Arabic
Pronunciation: AB dul ah hee
Description: Abdullahi is an Arabic boys' name, and means 'Allah's servant.' It is a variant of the more commonly used name Abdullah.

Abdur
Meaning: Servant
Origin: Arabic
Pronunciation: AB dur
Description: Abdur is a variant of the Arabic name Abdul, which is short for Abdullah, meaning 'servant.' It is commonly followed by a second Muslim theophoric (God-invoking) name, such as Rahman or Razzaq, to make Abdul Rahman or Abdul Razzaq.

Abe
Meaning: Father
Origin: Hebrew
Pronunciation: AIB
Description: Abe is a Jewish name thought of as a shortened form of Abraham. It could also be from the Aramaic word *'abba'*, meaning 'father'.
Alternative spellings: Aabe, Aybe

Abel

Meaning: Breath; vapour
Origin: Hebrew
Pronunciation: AY bull
Description: In the Bible, Abel is the youngest son of Adam and Eve. As the story goes, he was murdered by his jealous brother Cain. This name is especially popular in Spain.
Alternative spellings: Abal, Aybel

Abid
Meaning: God's follower
Origin: Arabic
Pronunciation: AH bid
Description: Abid is the masculine version of the feminine name Abida, meaning God's follower.
Alternative spellings: Abbid

Abida
Meaning: God's follower
Origin: Hebrew
Pronunciation: AB ee dah
Description: This name comes from two separate origins depending on the gender of the bearer. The masculine version of the name is of Hebrew origin while the feminine version is Arabic and said to mean 'God's follower'.
Alternative spellings: Abbida, Abeeda

Abir
Meaning: Fragrance
Origin: Arabic
Pronunciation: A BIR
Description: Abir is an Arabic name found on both boys and girls. Abir is also the name of a dye found in India.
Alternative spellings: Abeer

Abner

Meaning: Father of light
Origin: Hebrew
Pronunciation: AB ner
Description: Abner is a biblical name meaning 'father of light'. The name was borne by the leader of King Saul's army and relative to the king himself. Abner is now fairly uncommon.
Alternative spellings: Abna, Abnur

Abraham

Meaning: Father of many nations
Origin: Hebrew
Pronunciation: AY bruh ham
Description: Abraham is a biblical name, borne by a man of great faith who was given a child aged 100. It is also heavily linked to Abraham Lincoln, the 16th president of America.
Alternative spellings: Abrahim, Ibrahim

Abram

Meaning: Father of many nations
Origin: Hebrew
Pronunciation: AY bram
Description: Abram is another variant of the name Abraham, meaning 'father of many nations'. It is often shortened to Bram and is also used as a surname.
Alternative spellings: Abbram, Abriam

Absalom

Meaning: Father of peace
Origin: Hebrew
Pronunciation: AB sa lom
Description: Absalom is a biblical name that means 'father of peace'. It is believed to be the name of the third son of King David but isn't very commonly used due to its relationship with grief within the Bible.
Alternative spellings: Abshalom, Absolom, Absolon

Abu

Meaning: Father
Origin: Arabic
Pronunciation: AH boo
Description: Abu is a name that has both African and Arabic roots. The name was brought into the limelight in Western culture by the Disney film *Aladdin*, in which it is the name of Aladdin's monkey.
Alternative spellings: Abbu, Aboo

Abubakar

Meaning: Father of the Camel
Origin: Arabic
Pronunciation: ABU baak err
Description: Abubakar is a popular name in the Muslim world as it was the name of one of the sahabas of the Holy Prophet. The name is composed of two words, 'abu' meaning 'father' and 'bakr' meaning 'young camel'. Abu Bakr as-Siddiq was the closest companion of the prophet Muhammad. In naming their children Abubakar, Muslims show their respect to the Holy Prophet. It is also the name of Pahang's royal mosque in Malaysia.
Alternative spellings: Abu-Bakr, Abubakr

Acacus

Meaning: Mountain
Origin: Greek
Pronunciation: AH ka cus
Description: Acacus is an uncommon name of Greek origin. In Greek mythology, Acacus was a king of Acacesium in Arcadia. It is said that he raised Hermes, an Olympian god and the son of Zeus.
Alternative spellings: Acakus, Akacus, Akakus

Ace

Meaning: Number one
Origin: Latin
Pronunciation: AYS
Description: Ace is a word commonly used to describe an expert, coming from the notion of being 'number one'. An ace is also one of the most powerful cards to hold in many card games. It has now become a popular name.
Alternative spellings: Ase, Ayce

Acheron

Meaning: River of woe
Origin: Greek
Pronunciation: AYK er on
Description: In Greek mythology, Acheron was the name of a river bordering Hades, the Greek Underworld. Originally Acheron was the son of Demeter and was punished for helping the Titans by being cast into the Underworld, where he turned into the river.
Alternative spellings: Akeron, Akheron

Achilles

Meaning: Unknown
Origin: Greek

A

Pronunciation: a KIL ees
Description: In Greek mythology the warrior Achilles was made invincible by being dipped into the River Styx by his goddess mother. However, his mother held on to his heel so this part of his body was able to be harmed, hence the phrase to have an 'Achilles heel'.
Alternative spellings: Achiles, Akilles

Actaeon

Meaning: Herdsman
Origin: Greek
Pronunciation: AK tay on
Description: In Greek mythology, Actaeon was a huntsman who saw the goddess Artemis naked and as a result was turned into a stag and torn to pieces by his own dogs.
Alternative spellings: Aktaeon, Aktaion

Adair

Meaning: Rich owner of spears
Origin: English
Pronunciation: ad DARE
Description: Derived from the English name Edgar meaning 'rich owner of spears'. It can also be used as a girls' name but is more usually used for boys.
Alternative spellings: Adare

Adam

Meaning: Red earth
Origin: Hebrew
Pronunciation: AD dum
Description: A very popular modern name with biblical roots. According to the Bible, Adam is the name of the first man on Earth. The name derives from the word

'*adama*', which means earth in Hebrew.
Alternative spellings: Aadam, Adem

Addison

Meaning: Son of Adam
Origin: English
Pronunciation: AD iss on
Description: The name Addison would have originally been given as a surname, meaning 'son of Adam'. Although the name is technically masculine, it has evolved into a unisex given name.
Alternative spellings: Addisonne, Adison

Aden

Meaning: Full of fire
Origin: Gaelic
Pronunciation: Ay den
Description: A respelling of Aiden, which itself is a modern variant of Aodh. Aden is a unisex name as well as the place name of a city in South Yemen.
Alternative spellings: Aedan, Aidan, Aiden, Aodh, Ayden

Adil

Meaning: Just; righteous; fair
Origin: Arabic
Pronunciation: AH deel
Description: Adil, meaning just, righteous or fair, is fairly uncommon in Britain, but may be more popular in the Middle East due to its Arabic origins.
Alternative spellings: Adeel, Adill

Adina

See entry in 'Names for Baby Girls A–Z'

Aditya

Meaning: Belonging to Aditi
Origin: Sanskrit
Pronunciation: a DEET ya
Description: In Hindu legend the name Aditya belonged to one of Aditi's 33 children. The word Aditya also refers to the sun. It is most commonly used in English- and Hindi-speaking countries.
Alternative spellings: Adeetya, Adityah

Adlai

Meaning: God is just
Origin: Hebrew
Pronunciation: AD lye
Description: Adlai is a concentrated version of the Hebrew name Adaliah and carries the meaning 'God is just'. It is borne by a minor figure in the Bible.
Alternative spellings: Addlai, Adlye

Adnan

Meaning: Settler
Origin: Arabic
Pronunciation: AD nan
Description: The name Adnan gets its meaning from the story of Adnan, a descendant of Ishmael who settled in the Arabian Peninsula.
Alternative spellings: Addnan

Adrian

Meaning: From Hadria
Origin: Latin
Pronunciation: AY dri uhn
Description: Adrian means 'from Hadria'. Hadria is a town in northern Italy, which also gave its name to the Adriatic Sea.

Alternative spellings: Adrean, Adrien

Adriel
Meaning: Of God's flock
Origin: Hebrew
Pronunciation: AY dree el
Description: Adriel is a name of biblical origin meaning 'of God's flock' or a follower of God. It has been more recently associated with angels and in particular the Angel of Death.
Alternative spellings: Adriell

Advik
Meaning: Unique
Origin: Sanskrit
Pronunciation: AAD viik
Description: Advik is a Indian boys' Sanskrit name meaning 'unique'.
Alternative spellings: Aadvik

Adyan
Meaning: Son of Ad
Origin: Muslim
Pronunciation: AD yan
Description: Adyan is a rare Muslim name derived from one of the prophets of Islam.
Alternative spellings: Adian, Adyann

Ahad
Meaning: Servant of the only one
Origin: Arabic
Pronunciation: AH had
Description: Al-Ahad is one of the names of God in the Quran and is a common name in the Arabic world. Ahad is often used

following Abdul, which means 'servant of Allah'.
Alternative spellings: Ahed

Ahmad
Meaning: Highly commendable
Origin: Arabic
Pronunciation: AH med
Description: Ahmad is a short-ened version of the popular baby name Muhammad. It is of Arabic origin and is said to mean 'highly commendable'. Ahmed is an alternative of this name and is also extremely popular.

Ahmed
Meaning: Worthy of praise
Origin: Arabic
Pronunciation: AH med
Description: Ahmed is one of the names given to the prophet Muhammad. It is popular with Muslim parents as a variant of Muhammad, one of the most com-monly found boys' names in the world.
Alternative spellings: Achmad, Achmat, Achmed, Achmet, Ahmad, Ahmat, Ahmeed, Ahmet

Ahyan
Meaning: Era
Origin: Arabic
Pronunciation: AYE an
Description: Ahyan is a variant spelling of the name Ayan, which is an Arabic name. The name covers a variety of words that all have similar meanings i.e. time, era, epoch. As it features heav-ily in the Quran it is extremely popular among Muslim families.

Ai
See entry in 'Names for Baby Girls A–Z'

Aiden
Meaning: Full of Fire
Origin: Gaelic
Pronunciation: AY den
Description: This name can be traced to both Gaelic and Celtic origin. The translation of both origins relates to fire, to be full of fire or bright with fire.
Alternative spellings: Aidan, Ayden

Ailsa
See entry in 'Names for Baby Girls A–Z'

AJ
Meaning: No meaning
Origin: English
Pronunciation: AYE jay
Description: AJ is a modern English invention composed of two letters and as such, has no real meaning. It is pronounced like the two letters as well. Although AJ is usually initials for two separate names, it is sometimes used as a given name as well.
Alternative spellings: Ajay

Ajax
Meaning: Name of Greek hero
Origin: Greek
Pronunciation: AY jaks
Description: Ajax is the name of two Greek heroes, Ajax the Great, who was the cousin of Achilles, and Ajax the Lesser, who was a leader during the Trojan War.

Alternative spellings: Ajaks

Ajay
Meaning: Invincible
Origin: Sanskrit
Pronunciation: AY jay
Description: Ajay is a popular Indian name for boys. It originates from the Sanskrit word for 'invincible' and can also be considered a phonetically spelt variation of the initials 'A' and 'J'.
Alternative spellings: A.J.

Akash
Meaning: Open air
Origin: Sanskrit
Pronunciation: a KASH
Description: Akash is a boys' given name derived from the Hindi term 'Akasha', meaning 'open air'. In Hindu philosophy there are five basic elements that make up the human body – Akash is one of these.
Alternative spellings: Akaash, Akkash

Akito
Meaning: Bright person
Origin: Japanese
Pronunciation: ah KEE to
Description: Akito is a Japanese boys' name composed of the elements of '*aki*' meaning 'bright' and '*to*' meaning 'person'.

Akram
Meaning: Noblest
Origin: Arabic
Pronunciation: AK ram
Description: Akram is a common Muslim name and surname. Like many Islamic names, it owes its history to the prophet

A

Muhammad, and it is said to mean 'noblest'. The name's popularity has risen due to international Pakistan cricketer Wasim Akram.

Akshara
Meaning: Unchangeable
Origin: Sanskrit
Pronunciation: ak SHA rah
Description: A unisex name said to mean 'unchangeable'. Popular in India, this versatile name is a favourite among Indian parents.
Alternative spellings: Akhshara, Aksara

Akshay
Meaning: Eternal
Origin: Sanskrit
Pronunciation: AHK shay
Description: Akshay is a boys' given name of Sanskrit origin, meaning 'eternal'. It is a rare variant of the Hindi name 'Akash'.
Alternative spellings: Akshaay, Akshai

Alaa
Meaning: Servant of Allah
Origin: Arabic
Pronunciation: ah LAH
Description: This name can be used for both girls and boys. It is often used as a shortened version of Aladdin and is said to mean 'servant of Allah'. Alaa is often given as a name by Muslim parents.
Alternative spellings: Ala, Allaa

Alan
Meaning: Rock
Origin: Gaelic
Pronunciation: A lun
Description: Alan is of Celtic origin, with the uncertain derivation probably being from a word meaning 'rock'. It is also a river running through Wales. It was introduced to England by followers of William the Conqueror.
Alternative spellings: Allan, Allen

Aland
Meaning: Precious
Origin: Gaelic
Pronunciation: AH land
Description: Aland is a variant of the name Alan. This name is uncommon in England but can be found more often in Wales. It is also the name given to a series of islands in the Baltic Sea.
Alternative spellings: Alland, Allund, Alund

Alastair
Meaning: Defender of man
Origin: Gaelic
Pronunciation: AL is ter
Description: Alastair is the Gaelic equivalent of the masculine name Alexander, and both are said to mean 'defender of man'. This is a more popular variant of the Scottish name Alasdair.
Alternative spellings: Alasdair, Alaster, Alisdair, Alistair, Alister

Albert
Meaning: Noble; bright; famous
Origin: German
Pronunciation: AL burt
Description: A popular name among European royal families. It became popular in Britain in the late 19th century, thanks to

Queen Victoria's husband Prince Albert.
Alternative spellings: Alburt, Allbert

Alberto

Meaning: Noble
Origin: Italian
Pronunciation: al BEHR tow
Description: Alberto is the Italian, Portuguese and Spanish form of Albert. It is particularly popular in Italy and is the name of Alberto Aquilani, an Italian footballer.
Alternative spellings: Albert, Albertio

Alby

Meaning: From Alba
Origin: Latin
Pronunciation: AL bee
Description: Alby is a variant of the Latin boys' name Alban. Alby is regarded as a unisex name given to both boys and girls.
Alternative spellings: Albie, Albye

Aldrin

Meaning: Old and wise ruler
Origin: English
Pronunciation: AL drin
Description: Aldrin is an English name meaning 'old and wise ruler'. It is also the last name of famous astronaut, Buzz Aldrin, who was one of the first people to land on the moon.

Alec

Meaning: Defender of man
Origin: Greek
Pronunciation: A lik

Description: Alec is a shortened form of Alexander, originating from the UK. 'A smart Alec' is also a derogatory term for someone attempting to be clever.
Alternative spellings: Alek, Alic, Alick, Alik

Aled

Meaning: Defender of man; child
Origin: Welsh
Pronunciation: A led
Description: This name is thought to derive from the more common name Alexander. It is believed that people named Aled are very affectionate and take huge pride in their appearance. As well as 'defender of man', Aled could also mean 'child'.
Alternative spellings: Aledd

Alejandro

Meaning: Defender of man
Origin: Greek/Spanish
Pronunciation: al ay HAHN droh
Description: Alejandro is a Mediterranean variant of the Greek name Alexander predominantly found in Greece and Spain. It has been a popular name for many years.
Alternative spellings: Alehandro, Aleyandro

Alessandro

Meaning: Defender of man
Origin: Italian
Pronunciation: al les SAHN dro
Description: Another variant of the Greek name Alexander, Alessandro is particularly popular in Italy.
Alternative spellings: Aleksandro, Alexandro, Alexandru, Alexsandro,

Aliksandro, Alisandro, Alissandro, Alixandro, Alyxandro

Alessio
Meaning: Defender of man
Origin: Italian
Pronunciation: a LESS see oh
Description: Alessio is a popular Italian boys' name and a variant of the Greek name Alexander.
Alternative spellings: Alecio, Allecio, Elessio

Alexander
Meaning: Defender of man
Origin: Greek
Pronunciations: AL eks ahn duh; al eks AHN duh
Description: From the Latin form of the Greek name Alexandros, which means 'to defend' and 'man warrior'. Alexander became very popular in the post-classical period and means 'defender of man'. Usage is largely derived from the fame of Alexander the Great, King of Macedon.
Alternative spellings: Aleksander, Alessander, Alexsander, Aliksander, Alisander, Alissander, Alixander, Alyxander

Alexandre
Meaning: Defender of man
Origin: French
Pronunciation: Alex ON druh
Description: This unisex name is the French form of the Greek name Alexander. However, more emphasis is put on the middle 'a', which is pronounced 'o'. Commonly used in countries across the world, this name has been extremely popular for many years.

Alternative spellings: Aleksandre, Alessandre, Alexsandre, Aliksandre, Alisandre, Alissandre, Alixandre, Alyxandre

Alexandros
Meaning: Defender of man
Origin: Greek
Pronunciation: al ex HAHN dros
Description: Alexandros is another variant of the Greek name Alexander. It is popular in the Mediterranean as an exotic twist on the traditional Greek boys' name.
Alternative spellings: Alexendros, Alyxandros

Alexandru
Meaning: Defender of man
Origin: Greek/Spanish
Pronunciation: al ex HAHN dru
Description: Alexandru is a Greek and Spanish boys' name that is another Mediterranean variant of the Greek name Alexander and the Greek/Spanish name Alejandro. It is more commonly seen as a surname.
Alternative spellings: Aleksandro, Alessandro, Alexandro, Alexsandro, Aliksandro, Alisandro, Alissandro, Alixandro, Alyxandro

Alexis
See entry in 'Names for Baby Girls A–Z'

Alexus
Meaning: Defender of man; helper
Origin: Greek
Pronunciation: ah LEX us
Description: A modern variant of the name Alexis. Lexus is a pet form of this name as well as being a name in its own right.

Alternative spellings: Aleksus, Alexis, Alexsus

Alf
Meaning: Elf
Origin: Norse
Pronunciation: ALF
Description: Alf is derived from the Old Norse word '*álf*', meaning 'elf'. It is often the short form of names such as Alfie or Alfred, but can stand as a first name on its own as well.

Alfie
Meaning: Elf counsel
Origin: English
Pronunciation: AL fee
Description: Pet form of Alfred, proving to be a popular name in recent years. This might be to do with the remake of cult film *Alfie*, starring Jude Law.
Alternative spellings: Alfi, Allfie

Alfonso
Meaning: Noble; brave
Origin: German
Pronunciation: AL phon SO
Description: Alfonso is a variation of the name Alphons, and is composed of the elements of '*apal*' meaning '*noble*' and '*funs*' meaning 'brave'.
Alternative spellings: Alphonso

Alfred
Meaning: Elf counsel
Origin: English
Pronunciation: AL fred
Description: A relatively common name before the Norman Conquest of Britain, Alfred was borne by Alfred the Great. It is an example of an Old English name that

spread impressively over Europe. Nowadays, its pet form, Alfie, is more popular.
Alternative spellings: Alfrid, Allfred, Alvred

Alger
Meaning: Elf spear
Origin: English
Pronunciation: AL ga
Description: Alger is a transferred surname of Old English origin that means 'elf spear'. Also a shortened version of the name Algernon.
Alternative spellings: Alga, Algar, Algare

Algernon
Meaning: With a moustache; elf spear
Origin: French
Pronunciation: AL ger non
Description: Algernon was originally a Norman nickname given to those with a moustache as the Normans were generally clean-shaven. Alger also means 'elf spear' in Old English so the meaning of Algernon could be similar. It is quite a rare name nowadays.
Alternative spellings: Alganon, Algarnon

Ali
Meaning: Sublime
Origin: Arabic
Pronunciation: AH lee
Description: According to Islamic belief, Ali was the name of Muhammad's cousin who married his daughter Fatima. Ali is also a shortened form of female names like Alice and Alison.

Alternative spellings: Ahlee, Aly

Alison
See entry in 'Names for Baby Girls A–Z'

Alix
See entry in 'Names for Baby Girls A–Z'

Alpha
Meaning: Strongest
Origin: Greek
Pronunciation: AL fuh
Description: An unusual name given to boys, Alpha is also the first letter of the Greek alphabet. It is sometimes used as a word to describe the strongest male in a pack of animals.
Alternative spellings: Alfa

Alvin
Meaning: Elf friend
Origin: English
Pronunciation: AL vin
Description: As this name derives from an Old English origin meaning 'elf' or 'magical being', it has many magical connotations.
Alternative spellings: Alfin, Alven, Alvyn, Elvin

Alyaan
Meaning: Supreme
Origin: Sanskrit
Pronunciation: AL yaan
Description: Alyaan is a Sanskrit Indian boys' name meaning 'supreme' or 'exalted'. It is also often spelt Alyan.
Alternative spellings: Alyan

Amal
Meaning: Hard-working
Origin: Hebrew
Pronunciation: ah MAHL
Description: This name has Hebrew origins and therefore has many meanings. Most famous from the protagonist of Gian Carlo Menotti's opera, *Amahl and the Night Visitors*.
Alternative spellings: Ahmal, Amel

Aman
Meaning: Security
Origin: Arabic
Pronunciation: AH maan
Description: This name is mostly used in Arabic- and English-speaking countries. In East Malaysia there is a town called Sri Aman, which is the trade centre for timber, rubber and pepper.
Alternative spellings: Arman, Eman

Amani
Meaning: Desires
Origin: Arabic
Pronunciation: ah MAH ne
Description: In Arabic-speaking countries Amani is used as a male name, but in Swahili-speaking countries it has also been taken up as a feminine name.
Alternative spellings: Ahmani

Amar
Meaning: Immortal
Origin: Sanskrit
Pronunciation: AH mar
Description: Amar is an Indian name and comes from the Sanskrit word for 'immortal'. Similar names include Amare, Amari and Ammar.
Alternative spellings: Ammar

A

Amarachi
See entry in 'Names for Baby Girls A–Z'

Amarah
Meaning: God's grace
Origin: African
Pronunciation: ah MAR ah
Description: A spelling variant of the shortened form of Amarachi, Amara. It could also derive from an Arabic word meaning 'eternal' or 'unfading'. It is most commonly used by Muslim parents and is a unisex name.
Alternative spellings: Amara, Ammara

Amari
Meaning: Prince
Origin: Arabic
Pronunciation: ah MARH ee
Description: Used as both a girls' and a boys' name, the name Amari could have been inspired by the feminine Arabic name Amira, which means 'princess'. The name is mostly found in America and is favoured by African-American parents.
Alternative spellings: Amarie

Ambrose
Meaning: Immortal
Origin: Greek
Pronunciation: AM broze
Description: Ambrose is a name borne by a 4th-century bishop of Milan. It derives from the Greek word *'ambrose'*, meaning 'immortal'. It is more common in Ireland than England or the USA.
Alternative spellings: Ambroze

Ameen
Meaning: Truthful
Origin: Arabic
Pronunciation: ah MEEN
Description: A variant of the Arabic name Amin. A popular name in Muslim communities.
Alternative spellings: Amin

Ameer
Meaning: Prince
Origin: Arabic
Pronunciation: ah MAR
Description: Ameer is a variant of the popular boys' name Amir. The origins of the name can be found in both the Muslim and Jewish religions, and it can mean 'prince' or 'treetop'.
Alternative spellings: Ameir, Amer, Amir, Emeer, Emir

Amos
Meaning: Born of God
Origin: Hebrew
Pronunciation: AI muhs
Description: Amos is a name of Hebrew origin, meaning 'to carry, born of God'. It has biblical references in the 'book of Amos'. The name was once very popular in America but is now rarely used.
Alternative spellings: Amoss, Emos

Amrit
Meaning: Nectar of immortals
Origin: Sanskrit
Pronunciation: AM rit
Description: Amrit is a unisex name often used by Hindu parents. It is of Sanskrit origin and is found in the Vedic epics to refer to a physical object that gives immortality.
Alternative spellings: Amreet

Anakin

Meaning: No meaning
Origin: English
Pronunciation: ANA kin
Description: Anakin is a modern invented name, most famously the name of Anakin Skywalker, the antagonist in the Star Wars franchise.

Anas

See entry in 'Names for Baby Girls A–Z'

Anders

Meaning: Different
Origin: Scandinavian
Pronunciation: AN ders
Description: Anders is the Scandinavian variant of Andrew.

Andre

Meaning: Manliness
Origin: Greek
Pronunciation: AN drey
Description: A French form of the Greek name Andrew.
Alternative spellings: Andrei

Andreas

Meaning: Manliness
Origin: Greek
Pronunciation: an DREY as
Description: Andreas is the New Testament Greek form of Andrew. Like its feminine equivalent, it comes from the word *'andreia'*, meaning 'manliness' or 'virility'.
Alternative spellings: Andreass, Andreyas

Andrei

Meaning: Warrior
Origin: Greek
Pronunciation: AN drey

Description: Andrei is the Bulgarian, Moldovan, Russian or Romanian form of Andrew.
Alternative spellings: Andrej, Andres, Andrey

Andrew

Meaning: Manliness
Origin: Greek
Pronunciation: AN droo
Description: The name Andrew has long been popular in the English-speaking world, especially in Scotland.
Alternative spellings: Andru

Andy

Meaning: Manliness
Origin: Greek
Pronunciation: AN dee
Description: Originally a pet form of Andrew, Andy is now a name in its own right. It is used as both a boys' and a girls' name, although its spelling variant Andi is specifically feminine.
Alternative spellings: Andi, Andie

Anees

Meaning: Friendly
Origin: Arabic
Pronunciation: a NEES
Description: Anees is a name of Arabic origin, meaning 'friendly'.
Alternative spellings: Aanees, Ahnees

Aneurin

Meaning: Pure
Origin: Welsh
Pronunciation: AN yur in
Description: Aneurin is a mistranscription of the name Aneirin; a scribal mistake in the 17th century has made this variant the far

more common version of the name today.
Alternative spellings: Aneirin

Angel
Meaning: Messenger of God
Origin: Greek
Pronunciation: AYN gel
Description: A common Spanish name from the Greek *'angelos'*, meaning 'messenger'. New Testament Greek suggests a more specific definition of 'messenger of God'.
Alternative spellings: Aingel, Ayngel

Angelo
Meaning: Messenger of God
Origin: Italian
Pronunciation: AN jeh lo
Description: Angelo is Italian in origin and is a variation of Angel, which means 'messenger of God'. It is more common in America and may be used as a tribute to Michelangelo, the famous artist.
Alternative spellings: Angello, Angeloh

Angus
Meaning: One; choice
Origin: Gaelic
Pronunciation: ANG gus
Description: Anglicised form of the Scottish name Aonghas, meaning 'one' or 'choice'.
Alternative spellings: Aonghas, Aonghus

Anis
Meaning: Friendly; pure
Origin: Arabic/Greek
Pronunciation: Ah nees

Description: Anis is an Arabic boys' name popular in Tunisia, meaning 'friendly'. It is also popular in Greece as a girls' name, meaning 'pure' or 'holy'.
Alternative spellings: Anais, Anees, Annis

Anish
Meaning: Supreme
Origin: Sanskrit
Pronunciation: a NEESH
Description: Anish is derived from Sanskrit. Meaning 'supreme' in Hindi, the name is sometimes applied to both Krishna and Vishnu. It is also the name of a river in Russia.
Alternative spellings: Aneesh, Annish

Ansh
Meaning: Portion
Origin: Indian
Pronunciation: AAN sh
Description: Ansh is an Indian boys' name meaning 'portion'. Other variations include Aansh, Aanshi and Aanush, although they all have different meanings.
Alternative spellings: Aansh

Anton
Meaning: Priceless
Origin: Latin
Pronunciation: an TON
Description: Anton is a shortened form of Anthony. The name is of Old Roman origins and shares the same meaning. Anton is also popular in Scandinavian countries and Russia.

Anthony
Meaning: Protector
Origin: Latin

Pronunciation: AN ton ee; AN thon ee
Description: An Old Roman name of uncertain origin. It could derive from Antonius, a popular Latin name that itself is thought to have spawned from Adonis, an ancient Greek. A common shortening of this name is Tony.
Alternative spellings: Anthoni, Antoni, Antony

Antoine
Meaning: Beyond praise
Origin: French
Pronunciation: AHN twahn
Description: Antoine is a boys' name meaning 'beyond praise'. It is the French form of Anthony and was very popular in France in the early 1990s.
Alternative spellings: Anthony, Antwone

Antonio
Meaning: Protector
Origin: Spanish
Pronunciation: an TONE ee oh
Description: Antonio is a variation of the Roman family name Antonius. Often this name is shortened to Tony and is used mainly in English- and Spanish-speaking countries, especially America.
Alternative spellings: Anthonio

Anusha
See entry in 'Names for Baby Girls A–Z'

Anwar
Meaning: Bright
Origin: Arabic
Pronunciation: AN war

Description: Anwar is an uncommon name of Arabic origin, meaning 'bright' or 'clear'.
Alternative spellings: Aanwar, Anwaar

Apollo
Meaning: Destroy
Origin: Greek
Pronunciation: a POL oh
Description: In Greek mythology, Apollo was the god of medicine, the sun, dancing, music and poetry. He was the sun of Zeus and Leto and his twin sister was Artemis. He is recognised as one of the most important and complex Olympian deities.
Alternative spellings: Apolo, Appollo, Appolo

Aqeel
Meaning: Wise
Origin: Arabic
Pronunciation: AH keel
Description: Aqeel is an uncommon name of Arabic origin, meaning 'wise'. Aqeel ibn Abi Talib was a cousin of the prophet Muhammad.
Alternative spellings: Akeel, Aqel

Aqib
Meaning: Successor
Origin: Arabic
Pronunciation: AH kib
Description: Aqib is an uncommon name of Arabic origin, meaning 'successor'.
Alternative spellings: Akib, Aqeeb

Aran
Meaning: Mountain of strength

Origin: Hebrew
Pronunciation: AH ran
Description: Aran has Hebrew roots and means 'mountain of strength'. It is variation of the biblical name Aaron, and therefore has a similar meaning to it.
Alternative spellings: Arann, Araan

Aras

Meaning: Eagle
Origin: Lithuanian
Pronunciation: AH ras
Description: Aras is a Lithuanian name meaning 'eagle'. It is most likely influenced by the Old German word '*arn*' and the Old Norse word '*örn*', both of which mean 'eagle'. A related name is Arnold, which has a similar meaning of 'eagle power'.
Alternative spellings: Araas

Archer

Meaning: Bowman
Origin: English
Pronunciation: AR cher
Description: Archer is a common surname in England, though it can be used as a given name. It is derived from the Middle English word '*archere*' and was given as an occupational name for skilled bowmen in the 14th century.
Alternative spellings: Archere, Archier

Archibald

Meaning: Courageous
Origin: German
Pronunciation: ARCH i bold

Description: Archibald is of Old German origin, but has made its way to Britain and is extremely popular in Scotland. Its shortened version, Archie, is even more popular.
Alternative spellings: Archibold

Archie

Meaning: Courageous
Origin: German
Pronunciation: AR chee
Description: Short for Archibald but now given as a name in its own right. Currently a very popular name in Britain.
Alternative spellings: Archi, Archy

Arda

Meaning: Bronze
Origin: Hebrew
Pronunciation: AR dah
Description: Arda is a unisex name that comes from the Hebrew word for 'bronze'. It could also be a variant of the unisex name Arden, said to mean 'great forest'.
Alternative spellings: Ardah, Arder

Areeb

Meaning: Helpful; skilful
Origin: Arabic
Pronunciation: a REEB
Description: Areeb is an Arabic boys' name meaning 'helpful' or 'skilful'.
Alternative spellings: Ahreeb

Arham

Meaning: Compassion
Origin: Arabic
Pronunciation: ARR haam
Description: Arham is an Arabic male name meaning 'mercy' or

'compassion'. Variations of the name include Erhem, Arhem, Arhamme and Arhamm.
Alternative spellings: Erhem, Arhem, Arhamme, Arhamm

Ari

Meaning: Lion; eagle
Origin: Hebrew
Pronunciation: AH ree
Description: Ari is a Hebrew boys' name meaning 'lion' or 'eagle'. It is the shortened version of the ancient Greek name Aristides and the more common Greek name Ariel.
Alternative spellings: Aree, Arri

Aria

Meaning: Lion
Origin: Hebrew
Pronunciation: AHR ee ah
Description: Aria has various origins and meanings. It could come from the Italian word for 'air' although in Hebrew its meaning is said to be 'lion'. It is unisex, but is more common in the Middle East as a masculine name.
Alternative spellings: Ariha

Arian

Meaning: Silver
Origin: Welsh
Pronunciation: AIR ee an
Description: Most predominantly found in Wales, Arian is a Welsh name derived from the Greek name Arion. The meaning of the name Arian is said to be associated with the element silver.
Alternative spellings: Arion, Aryan

A

Ariel

Meaning: God's lion
Origin: Hebrew
Pronunciation: AR ee el; AIR ee al
Description: This unisex name widely increased in popularity after Shakespeare's play *The Tempest* was performed.
Alternative spellings: Arial

Arif

Meaning: Knowledgeable
Origin: Arabic
Pronunciation: a REEF
Description: Arif is a common boys' name in the Arabic world. It means 'smart, widely knowledgeable and wise'.
Alternative spellings: Aarif, Aref

Aris

Meaning: War
Origin: Greek
Pronunciation: AIR ees
Description: Aris is an alternative spelling of the Greek name Ares, who was the god of war.
Alternative spellings: Ares

Ariyan

Meaning: Noble
Origin: Indian
Pronunciation: AREE yan
Description: Ariyan is most likely a different spelling of the Indo-Iranian name Aryan, which means 'noble'. In fact, the word is actually used as a designation and ethnic label for the Indic people of the Vedic period.
Alternative spellings: Arian

Arjan

Meaning: From Hadrian
Origin: Dutch

Pronunciation: AR jaan
Description: Arjan is a Dutch version of the name Adrian, meaning 'from Hadria'. Arjan is also an Indian name, but the Punjabi version is pronounced differently.
Alternative spellings: Arjun

Arley

Meaning: Heap of stones; hare wood
Origin: English
Pronunciation: ARR lee
Description: Arley is a variation of the name Harley, which is an English name meaning 'heap of stones' or 'hare wood'. It is most likely a modern invention, although it does have roots in a traditional name.
Alternative spellings: Arlie

Arlo

Meaning: Fortified hill
Origin: English
Pronunciation: AHR loh
Description: Arlo is a variation on the Old English '*harlow*', which means 'fortified hill'. It has been modified into the modern form Arlo over the years. In Spain Arlo means 'bayberry'.

Armaan

Meaning: Goal; longing
Origin: Persian
Pronunciation: AR mon
Description: Armaan is a Hindi/Urdu name of Persian origin. Its original meaning is thought to be 'goal'; however it was confused in translation and it now means 'longing' or 'wishing' in Hindi. It is used frequently in the Punjabi region of India for both Hindu and Sikh males.

Alternative spellings: Arman, Armon

Arman

Meaning: Soldier
Origin: Israeli
Pronunciation: ARR maan
Description: Arman is the Israeli version of the German name Armand, which means 'soldier'. Both names are actually related to Herman, which means 'army man'.
Alternative spellings: Armaan

Armand

Meaning: Soldier
Origin: German
Pronunciation: ARR maand
Description: Armand is a German name meaning 'soldier'. It is also related to Herman, which has the similar meaning of 'army man'.

Armani

Meaning: Free
Origin: Italian
Pronunciation: ah MAR nee
Description: Armani is an Italian surname that is said to mean 'free'. The success of the Italian designer Giorgio Armani has led to the use of Armani as a first name, given to both boys and girls.
Alternative spellings: Armaani, Armanie

Arnav

Meaning: Ocean water
Origin: Sanskrit
Pronunciation: Arh NAHV
Description: Arnav is a variation of the name Arnava and

shares its meaning of 'ocean water'. Arnav is a popular name in Arabic-speaking countries and it is one of the most commonly found Muslim boys' names in America.
Alternative spellings: Ahnav, Arhnav

Arnie
Meaning: Ruler; strong as an eagle
Origin: German
Pronunciation: ARN ee
Description: Arnie is the diminutive of the German name Arnold, meaning 'ruler' or 'strong as an eagle'. It is derived from the elements of '*arn*' meaning 'eagle' and '*wald*' meaning 'power'. It died out as an English name after the Middle Ages but was revived in the 19th century.
Alternative spellings: Arnee

Arnold
Meaning: Powerful eagle
Origin: German
Pronunciation: AR nold
Description: Arnold is a Frankish name derived from the words for 'eagle' and 'ruler'.
Alternative spellings: Arnald

Aronas
Meaning: Unknown
Origin: English
Pronunciation: eh ROW nah
Description: Aronas is most likely a contemporary invention, and as such has no real meaning. The closest name to Aronas is the girls' name Arona, which is a Maori name meaning 'colourful'.

Arooj
Meaning: Unknown
Origin: Persian
Pronunciation: ah ROOGE
Description: Arooj is a very unusual name and there is not much documentation on it. It is found used as a unisex name, but the variant Urooj is usually masculine. It originates from the Middle East and is possibly a Persian name.
Alternative spellings: Urooj

Arran
Meaning: Strong mountain
Origin: Hebrew
Pronunciation: AH run
Description: Arran could be seen as a variation of Aaron, meaning 'strong mountain'. However, Arran could also originate from the Scottish Isle of Arran.
Alternative spellings: Aaran, Aaron, Aron, Arron, Arun

Arthur
Meaning: Bear; stone
Origin: Gaelic
Pronunciation: AR thur
Description: The origin of this name is unclear, but it may come from the Celtic word '*artos*', which means 'bear' or the Irish word '*art*' for stone. The name is strongly associated with King Arthur.
Alternative spellings: Arther, Arthor, Arthur

Arun
Meaning: Dawn sky
Origin: Sanskrit
Pronunciation: AH roon
Description: Arun originates from a Sanskrit word referring to

a reddish-brown colour, which is associated with the sky at dawn.
Alternative spellings: Ahrun, Aroon

Arvin
Meaning: People's friend
Origin: English
Pronunciation: AR vin
Description: Arvin is an uncommon boys' name of English and Old German origin. It means 'people's friend', and is also a city in California and a type of plant.
Alternative spellings: Aarvin, Arvyn

Arya
See entry in 'Names for Baby Girls A–Z'

Aryaan
Meaning: Illustrious
Origin: Sanskrit
Pronunciation: air ee AHN
Description: Aryaan is derived from the Indian word for 'illustrious' and the Sanskrit word for 'gentleman'. It is an uncommon name in England.
Alternative spellings: Aaryan, Arryan

Asa
Meaning: Faithful
Origin: Hebrew
Pronunciation: AY sah
Description: Asa can be found in the Bible as the name of a king of Judah. He was renowned for his faithfulness and the meanings associated with the name stem from this.
Alternative spellings: Esa, Isa

Asad
Meaning: Lion
Origin: Arabic
Pronunciation: a SAAD
Description: Asad is one of many Arabic boys' names meaning 'lion'. Assad is the more common spelling in English, though Asad is the more accurate transliteration.
Alternative spellings: Assad

Asaph
Meaning: Collector
Origin: Hebrew
Pronunciation: AY saff
Description: Asaph is a name that features in the Bible and for that reason is sometimes considered a religious name.
Alternative spellings: Aisaph, Asaff, Aysaph

Ash
Meaning: Ash tree clearing
Origin: English
Pronunciation: AH sh
Description: Ash is a short form of the common unisex name Ashley, meaning 'ash tree clearing'. Although it is often used as a nickname, it can also be a name on its own.

Asha
See entry in 'Names for Baby Girls A–Z'

Ashby
Meaning: From the ash tree
Origin: English
Pronunciation: ash BEE
Description: Ashby was originally an Anglo-Saxon last name and is connected to the tribe of the

same name. It was given to a group of people who once lived in a dwelling near an ash tree, hence the meaning of the name. This follows the contemporary trend of using last names as first names.

Ashden
Meaning: Belonging to Ashton
Origin: English
Pronunciation: ash DEN
Description: Ashden was originally a surname referring to people who came from Ashton, a place in England.
Alternative spellings: Ashdon

Asher
Meaning: Fortunate
Origin: Hebrew
Pronunciation: ASH er
Description: A biblical name borne by one of the sons of Jacob who was promised a life of abundance and blessing. Often shortened to Ash.
Alternative spellings: Asha, Ashah

Ashley
Meaning: Field of ash
Origin: English
Pronunciation: ASH lee
Description: Ashley was originally a male name but is now unisex, most commonly used for girls. It comes from an English surname referring to a 'field of ash'. However, 'ash' is a type of tree and the 'ley' suffix suggests 'wood', so it could also mean 'ash wood/tree'.
Alternative spellings: Ashlee, Ashleigh

Ashton
Meaning: Ash tree settlement
Origin: English
Pronunciation: ASH tun
Description: Originally a surname, Ashton was used as the name of ash tree settlements. Now Ashton is a popular boys' name, possibly due to the fame of model and actor Ashton Kutcher.
Alternative spellings: Ashtan, Ashtun

Ashwin
Meaning: Calendar month
Origin: Sanskrit
Pronunciation: ASH win
Description: Ashwin is said to derive from Ashvin, the name of the seventh month on the Hindu calendar. It is most predominantly found in Hindi-speaking countries.
Alternative spellings: Ashvin

Asim
Meaning: Protector
Origin: Arabic
Pronunciation: a SEEM
Description: Asim is a popular Arabic boys' name meaning 'protector, guardian and defender'.
Alternative spellings: Aseem, Azim

Aspen
Meaning: Aspen tree
Origin: English
Pronunciation: ASS pen
Description: Aspen is a unisex name that has derived from the aspen tree, known by its delicate leaves and white bark. As

a given name, Aspen is found predominantly in America.
Alternative spellings: Aspun

Aston

Meaning: Ash tree settlement
Origin: English
Pronunciation: ASS tun
Description: The unisex name Aston comes from an Old English place name meaning 'east town settlement with an ash tree'. It may owe its increase of use as a first name to the popularity of the English sports car, the Aston Martin.
Alternative spellings: Astan, Asten, Astun

Astor

Meaning: Thunder god
Origin: Scandinavian
Pronunciation: AS ter
Description: Astor is a Scandinavian derived from the elements of '*as*' meaning 'God' and '*tor*' meaning 'thunder'.
Alternative spellings: Aster

Atif

Meaning: Compassionate
Origin: Arabic
Pronunciation: a TEEF
Description: Atif is a boys' given name of Arabic origin, meaning 'compassionate' or 'sympathetic'.
Alternative spellings: Ateef, Atiff

Atlas

Meaning: Not enduring
Origin: Greek
Pronunciation: AT lass
Description: In Greek mythology, Atlas was one of the primordial Titans. He was a giant forced to hold up the heavens on his shoulders as punishment from Zeus.
Alternative spellings: Atlass, Atlus

Atticus

Meaning: Man of Attica
Origin: Latin
Pronunciation: AT a kuss
Description: Atticus is a name from ancient Greece, meaning 'man of Attica or 'a man from Athens'. The name's popularity has risen considerably in recent years, possibly due to the enduring appeal of Harper Lee's novel, *To Kill a Mockingbird*.
Alternative spellings: Aticus, Attikas

Aubrey

Meaning: Elfin
Origin: German
Pronunciation: AW bree
Description: Aubrey comes from the Germanic name Alberic, which means 'elfin king'. It is now popular as a girls' name due to its similarity to the popular name Audrey.
Alternative spellings: Aubree, Aubrie, Awbrey

Audley

Meaning: From the old meadow
Origin: English
Pronunciation: ODD lee
Description: Audley is a surname originally derived from the placename Audley, in Staffordshire. This follows the contemporary trend of using last names as first names.

August

Meaning: Eighth month of the year
Origin: English
Pronunciation: AUH gust
Description: August is a boys' name that comes from the English word of the same spelling and refers to the eighth month of the year. Like June and May, these are popular contemporary name choices for parents who want to name their child something a bit more modern.

Auguste

Meaning: Great; magnificent
Origin: Latin
Pronunciation: ohg USTE
Description: Derived from the name Augustus, the name comes from the Latin word '*augere*' meaning 'great' or 'magnificent' and was a title given to Roman emperors.
Alternative spellings: August

Augustus

Meaning: To increase
Origin: Latin
Pronunciation: or GUSS tuss
Description: Augustus is a Latin name taken from the word '*augere*', meaning 'to increase'. It was borne by the Emperor Augustus in 27 BC. It is after him that the calendar month of August was named.
Alternative spellings: Augustuss, Orgustus

Aurelio

Meaning: Golden
Origin: Italian
Pronunciation: or EL ee OH
Description: Aurelio is the Italian version of the name Aurelius, derived from the Latin word '*aureus*' meaning 'golden' or 'gilded'.

Austen

Meaning: Great
Origin: Latin
Pronunciation: AU sten
Description: Austen is a variant of the Latin names Augustine and Augustus – meaning 'great' or 'magnificent'. Despite sounding similar, it is not to be confused with the American unisex name of similar spelling, Austin, which has risen in popularity since the Austin Powers movies.
Alternative spellings: Austin, Austyn

Austin

Meaning: Great; magnificent
Origin: Latin
Pronunciation: OSS tin
Description: Austin is a unisex name particularly popular in America.
Alternative spellings: Orstin, Ostin

Avery

Meaning: Elf counsel
Origin: English
Pronunciation: AYE ver ee
Description: Avery is an English name meaning 'elf counsel'. The name is a variation of Alfred, which is composed of 'alf' meaning 'elf' and 'fred' meaning 'counsel'. It used to be a surname, but is now widely used as a given name for both boys and girls.

A

Avi

Meaning: Father of many nations
Origin: Hebrew
Pronunciation: AH vee
Description: Avi is a boys' name very common in the Jewish state of Israel. It is a shortened variant of the well-known biblical name Abraham.
Alternative spellings: Ave, Avy

Awais

Meaning: Gifted
Origin: Arabic
Pronunciation: AH ways
Description: Awais is a masculine Arabic name said to mean 'gifted'. It is extremely unusual in Britain and its use in other parts of the world is scarce too.
Alternative spellings: Ahwais, Aways

Axel

Meaning: Father of peace
Origin: Hebrew
Pronunciation: AK suhl
Description: Axel, which is Hebrew in origin, is a common name in Scandinavia, central Europe and America. Axel Witsel is a Belgian international footballer and Axl Rose (a slight variant of Axel) is the lead singer of rock band Guns N' Roses.
Alternative spellings: Aksel, Axell, Axil, Axill, Axl

Ayaan

Meaning: Good luck
Origin: African
Pronunciation: ie YAHN
Description: Ayaan is a word used in the Quran said to refer to good luck and destiny. Someone who is experiencing particularly good luck may be referred to in Somalia as an 'ayaan'. Now it is used as a unisex name.
Alternative spellings: Ayahn, Iyaan

Ayaz

Meaning: Respected
Origin: Arabic
Pronunciation: AY yaz
Description: Ayaz is an uncommon Arabic boys' name that is more commonly seen as a surname. The name is derived from the city of Ayask in Iran.
Alternative spellings: Ayaaz

Ayden

Meaning: Full of fire
Origin: Gaelic
Pronunciation: AY den
Description: This variant of the name Aiden has become popular since 2001 in line with other misspellings of old names. Unlike Aiden, Ayden can be used as a girls' name.
Alternative spellings: Aden, Aedan, Aidan, Aiden, Aodh, Aydan

Ayman

Meaning: Lucky
Origin: Arabic
Pronunciation: EYE mun
Description: Derived from the Arabic for 'right', this name

literally means 'he who is on the right-hand side', meaning a moral or lucky person. Another variation of the name is Aymeen; however both versions are uncommon names today.
Alternative spellings: Aiman, Aymaan

Ayomide
See entry in 'Names for Baby Girls A–Z'

Ayub
Meaning: Prophet of God
Origin: Hebrew
Pronunciation: AY yoob
Description: The origin and meaning of this name are hard to trace; however Ayub is thought to be a Muslim variant of the Hebrew name 'Job', the name of a character in the Bible.
Alternative spellings: Ayoob, Ayuub

Ayush
Meaning: Long life
Origin: Sanskrit
Pronunciation: AH yush
Description: Because of its meaning, Ayush is used as a given name in the hope that it will bring prosperity.
Alternative spellings: Aiyush

Azaan
Meaning: Power
Origin: Hebrew
Pronunciation: ah ZAHN
Description: Azaan is a spelling variation of Azan, which is Hebrew

in origin and can be found in the Old Testament.
Alternative spellings: Azan, Azahn

Azariah
Meaning: Yaweh has helped
Origin: Hebrew
Pronunciation: az AIR ee ah
Description: Azariah is a Hebrew name meaning 'Yaweh Has Helped'. It was the name of many an Old Testament character in the Bible.

Azlan
Meaning: Lion
Origin: English
Pronunciation: AZ laan
Description: Azlan is most likely a variation of the name Aslan, which is a Turkish name meaning 'lion'. That is why the author C. S. Lewis used it to name the lion protagonist of the Chronicles of Narnia.
Alternative spellings: Azlaan

Azriel
Meaning: Helper of God
Origin: Hebrew
Pronunciation: az ree ELL
Description: Azriel is a variant of the Hebrew name Azreal, who is an archangel in many religions. Although it is predominatnly found as a boys' name it is also sometimes used as a girls' name.
Alternative spellings: Asriel, Azreel, Azryel

B

Bacchus
Meaning: Grapevine
Origin: Latin
Pronunciation: BAK uss
Description: The uncommon name Bacchus is the Latin name for the Greek god Dionysus who was the god of the grape harvest, winemaking, wine and of ritual madness.
Alternative spellings: Bachus, Bakhus

Baha
Meaning: Splendour
Origin: Arabic
Pronunciation: BA ha
Description: Baha is predominantly found as a boys' name, but is also used for girls. This could be to do with its associations of splendour and beauty. Baha could also be seen as a variant of the Spanish girls' name Baja, meaning 'lower'.
Alternative spellings: Bahah

Baker
Meaning: Person who bakes
Origin: English
Pronunciation: BAKE er
Description: Baker, like Taylor and Hunter, is an occupational name given to people who baked for a living. It derives from the English vocabulary word of the same spelling and meaning.

Bailey
Meaning: Bailiff
Origin: English
Pronunciation: BAY lee
Description: Originally a surname given to those who lived near a bailey, Bailey is now predominantly used as a unisex first name. The name prevails among girls in America and boys in the UK.
Alternative spellings: Bailee, Baileigh, Bailie, Baylee, Bayleigh, Bayley, Baylie

Balius
Meaning: Dappled
Origin: Greek
Pronunciation: BAH li uss
Description: In Greek mythology, Balius was one of two immortal horses (the other being Xanthus) sired by Zeus.
Alternative spellings: Balios, Ballius

Barack
Meaning: Blessed
Origin: Hebrew
Pronunciation: bah RAHK
Description: Barack is a boys' given name of Hebrew origin, meaning 'blessed'. It is an anglicisation of the Hebrew 'Baruch' and is borne by former US president Barack Hussein Obama.
Alternative spellings: Barach, Baruch

Baran
Meaning: Noble warrior; ram; rain
Origin: Various
Pronunciation: bah RAHN
Description: Baran has various origins and meanings. In Russian, the name means 'ram,' the Gaelic meaning is 'noble warrior' and the Turkish meaning is 'rain'. It is also closely related to the name Baron.

Bardo

Meaning: Water; bright wolf
Origin: Tibetan; German
Pronunciation: BAR doh
Description: Bardo is found in both Tibetan and German cultures although it means different things in each. In Tibet, the name means 'water', while in German, Bardo is most likely a short form of the name Bardolph, meaning 'bright wolf'.

Barkley

Meaning: No meaning
Origin: English
Pronunciation: BARK lee
Description: Barkley is most likely a modern invention, and as such does not have a meaning. It may be connected to the names Berkeley and Barclay. Barkley is also an English surname, borne by many famous sportspeople.
Alternative spellings: Barklee

Barnabas

Meaning: Son of consolation
Origin: Aramaic
Pronunciation: BAR nah bus
Description: The name Barnabas is quite popular in Britain and is often shortened to Barney. St Barnabas was a Jewish Cypriot and early Christian missionary who gave all his property to the Church.
Alternative spellings: Barnabus, Barnubus

Barnaby

Meaning: Son of consolation
Origin: Aramaic
Pronunciation: BAR na bee

Description: Barnaby shares its meaning of 'son of consolation' with Barnabas. It is an alternative to the popular name.
Alternative spellings: Barnabi

B

Barney

Meaning: Son of consolation
Origin: Aramaic
Pronunciation: BAR nee
Description: Originally the pet form of Barnabas or Barnaby, Barney is now a name in its own right.
Alternative spellings: Barni, Barny

Baron

Meaning: Title of nobility
Origin: English
Pronunciation: BARE on
Description: Baron is taken from the English vocabulary name of the same spelling and meaning, and it is a title often given to members of nobility.

Barry

Meaning: Fair-haired
Origin: Gaelic
Pronunciation: BA ree
Description: Barry is an anglicised form of the Irish name Barra, which comes from 'Fionnbarr'.
Alternative spellings: Barri, Barrie

Bart

Meaning: Farmer's son
Origin: Aramaic
Pronunciation: BART
Description: Bart is short for both Barton and Bartholomew. It was made famous by the success of American cartoon show *The Simpsons,* where Bart is one of the Simpson children.
Alternative spellings: Barte

Bartholomew

Meaning: Son of Talmai
Origin: Hebrew
Pronunciation: bar THOL o mew
Description: Bartholomew is a name of Hebrew origin. There are several saints named Bartholomew, although the apostle is the most famous. The name is often shortened to Bart.
Alternative spellings: Bartholomew, Bartolowmew

Bartlomiej

Meaning: Farmer's son
Origin: Hebrew
Pronunciation: bart lo MEY
Description: Bartlomiej is a Polish variation of the masculine name Bartholomew.
Alternative spellings: Bartholomew

Bartosz

Meaning: Son of Talmai
Origin: Polish
Pronunciation: BART ozz
Description: Bartosz is the Polish form of the name Bartholomew. Bartholomew is a boys' name of Greek origin. There are several saints named Bartholomew, although the apostle is the most famous. The name is often shortened to Bart, popularised by Bart Simpson of the TV cartoon *The Simpsons*.

Basil

Meaning: Royal; kingly
Origin: Greek
Pronunciation: BA zil
Description: Basil, despite it being the name of a herb, is actually derived from the Greek name Vassilios, meaning 'royal' or 'kingly'. Basil Rathbone was a famous British actor with this name.

Baxter

Meaning: Baker
Origin: English
Pronunciation: BAKS ter
Description: Baxter is a name derived from the Old English word for 'baker'. It was popular throughout the late 19th century and early 20th century, but the name has a certain modern ring to it that makes it a popular choice for contemporary babies.

See entry in 'Names for Baby Girls A–Z'

Bear

Meaning: Animal
Origin: English
Pronunciation: BEH ar
Description: The name bear most likely comes from the animal of the same name, and is usually used as a nickname. Edward Michael Grylls is better known as 'Bear Grylls,' and is a famous British adventurer and television presenter.

Beau

Meaning: Beautiful
Origin: French
Pronunciation: BOH
Description: Beau has had a surge in popularity recently. It originates from France and like Belle, its feminine counterpart, means 'beautiful'. It can sometimes be used as a girls' name too.
Alternative spellings: Bo, Bow

Beck

Meaning: Dweller near the brook
Origin: English
Pronunciation: BECK
Description: Beck is an uncommon boys' given name of English origin, meaning 'dweller near the brook'. It is a common surname in Scandinavian countries.
Alternative spellings: Bec, Bekk

Beckett

Meaning: Bee Cottage
Origin: English
Pronunciation: BECK ett
Description: Beckett is a variation of the name Becket, an English; Irish name meaning 'bee cottage'. It is a name that has been popular in recent years and is the name of many celebrity babies.
Alternative spellings: Becket

Bellerophon

Meaning: Great hero
Origin: Greek
Pronunciation: behl LEH ro fon
Description: In Greek mythology, Bellerophon was a great hero of monster slaying.
Alternative spellings: Bellerofon, Bellerophos

Ben

Meaning: Son of my sorrow
Origin: Hebrew
Pronunciation: BEN
Description: Ben can be short for Benjamin, Benedict or Bennett as well as being a first name in its own right.
Alternative spellings: Benn

Benas

Meaning: Son of my sorrow
Origin: Hebrew
Pronunciation: BEN ass
Description: Benas is an uncommon, exotic variant of the old Hebrew name Benjamin. It is more common in Hispanic regions.
Alternative spellings: Benass, Bennas

Benedict

Meaning: Blessed
Origin: Latin
Pronunciation: BEN ee dikt
Description: The name Benedict is mainly used in English-speaking countries. This name is very common among popes and was also the name of the saint who inspired the Catholic monastic order, the Order of St Benedict.
Alternative spellings: Benedikt, Benedyct

Benicio

Meaning: Blessed
Origin: Spanish
Pronunciation: ben EE see oh
Description: Benicio is a Spanish boys' name meaning 'blessed'. It is the Spanish version of the name Benedict, and as such shares the same meaning. Benicio del Toro is a famous Puerto Rican actor.

Benjamin

Meaning: Son of my sorrow
Origin: Hebrew
Pronunciation: BEN jah min
Description: A biblical name borne by the youngest of the

B

12 sons of Jacob. In the Bible, Benjamin's mother Rachel died giving birth to him. In her last moments she named him Benoni, meaning 'son of my sorrow'. His father did not wish him to bear such an ill-omened name, and renamed him Benyamin.
Alternative spellings: Benjaman, Benyamin

Bennett
Meaning: Blessed
Origin: Latin
Pronunciation: BEN et
Description: Bennett is derived from the Latin word '*benedict*'. Today it is more commonly found as a surname.
Alternative spellings: Bennet

Benny
Meaning: Son of my right hand
Origin: Hebrew
Pronunciation: BEN ee
Description: Benny is a name of Hebrew origin, meaning 'son of my right hand'. It is a common nickname for children named Benjamin, and a variant of the nickname Ben.
Alternative spellings: Benni, Bennie

Benson
Meaning: Son of Ben
Origin: English
Pronunciation: ben SON
Description: Benson was originally an English surname meaning 'son of Ben'. In recent years, it has also become a popular first name.
Alternative spellings: Bensen

Bentley
Meaning: Bent grass meadow
Origin: English
Pronunciation: BENT lee
Description: The name Bentley has passed down the generations from Old England. It is a place name in many counties across England, appearing in Suffolk, Essex, Derbyshire, Warwickshire and Hampshire. It is most commonly known due to the famous English car company of the same name.

Benton
Meaning: Town in the bent grass
Origin: English
Pronunciation: ben TUN
Description: Benton was originally an English surname referring to people who lived in a 'town in the bent grass'. This follows the contemporary trend of using last names as first names.

Berat
Meaning: Letters patent
Origin: Turkish
Pronunciation: beer AAT
Description: It is not entirely known what this Turkish name means, but it most likely means 'letters patent', which is an open document issued by a monarch or government granting an office, right, monopoly, title or status to a person.

Berlin
Meaning: Boardline
Origin: German
Pronunciation: ber LIN
Description: Berlin is an edgy baby name coming from the

capital city of Germany. Berlin is the largest city in Germany and, like Camden and Brooklyn, is part of the trend of using place names as baby names.

Bernard
Meaning: Brave bear
Origin: German
Pronunciation: BER nard
Description: Bernard is an old-fashioned name of German origin. Meaning 'strong, brave bear', the name was one of the most popular in the English-speaking world in the early 20th century; however, it is far less common in recent years.
Alternative spellings: Barnard, Bearnard, Bernd, Burnard

Bertie
Meaning: Noble; famous; bright
Origin: German
Pronunciation: BUR tee
Description: Bertie is commonly a nickname for those given the birth name Albert or Bertram, but it has recently found its way into popularity as a name in its own right. Bertie Ahern was the taoiseach of Ireland for 10 years.
Alternative spellings: Bertee

Bertrand
Meaning: Bright raven; bright shield
Origin: German
Pronunciation: BURT rand
Description: Bertrand is a German name derived from the elements of '*berht*' meaning 'bright' and '*hramn*' meaning 'raven' or '*rand*' meaning 'shield.' Bertrand Russell was a famous British philosopher.

Bilal
Meaning: Refreshing
Origin: Arabic
Pronunciation: BIH lal
Description: The name Bilal is the Arabic form of Billy. It is thought that the first convert of the prophet Muhammad was a slave who went by the name of Bilal. He then went on to become the very first high priest and treasurer of the muslim Empire.
Alternative spellings: Billal

Bill
Meaning: Seeking protection
Origin: German
Pronunciation: BILL
Description: Bill is a shortened form of the popular name William, but is also a name in its own right.
Alternative spellings: Bil

Billie
Meaning: Seeking protection
Origin: German
Pronunciation: BIL ee
Description: Billie also originates as a pet form of the name William. Although the name is unisex, this particular spelling is favoured for girls.
Alternative spellings: Billi, Billy

Billy
Meaning: Seeking protection
Origin: German
Pronunciation: BILL ee
Description: The most masculine spelling of the shortened form of William.
Alternative spellings: Billi, Billie

B

Bishop
Meaning: Priest
Origin: English
Pronunciation: BISH up
Description: Bishop is originally an English occupational name given to religious priests. While it is usually used as a last name, it has also become a first name in recent years.

Bjorn
Meaning: Bear
Origin: Swedish
Pronunciation: BY urn
Description: Bjorn is a Swedish boys' name that means 'bear'. Note that the 'j' is not pronounced. It is also one of the more common Swedish names.

Blake
Meaning: Black; white
Origin: English
Pronunciation: BLAYK
Description: Interestingly, Blake has two meanings that are opposite to one another. The Old English words for black and white are both linked to this name and it was often given as a nickname for someone with very bright or very dark hair.
Alternative spellings: Blaike, Blayke

Blakely
Meaning: Dark wood
Origin: English
Pronunciation: BLAKE lee
Description: Blakely was originally an English last name referring to people who lived next to a dark wood or clearing.

This follows the contemporary trend of using last names as first names.

Blythe
See entry in 'Names for Baby Girls A–Z'.

Bob
Meaning: Bright fame
Origin: German
Pronunciation: BOB
Description: Bob is an altered short form of Robert, meaning 'bright fame'.

Bobbie
Meaning: Bright fame
Origin: English
Pronunciation: BOB ee
Description: Bobbie can be used as both a boys' and girls' name. It is a more modern variant of the English shortened name Bob, which derives from Robert.
Alternative spellings: Bobbee, Bobbey, Bobby

Bodhi
Meaning: Wise
Origin: Sanskrit
Pronunciation: BOHD ee
Description: Bodhi is an uncommon name of Sanskrit origin, meaning 'wise', 'enlightening' or 'knowledge'. In Buddhism, it is the word given to the understanding possessed by a Buddha.
Alternative spellings: Bodhee, Bodhie

Bogdan
Meaning: Gift from God
Origin: Russian
Pronunciation: BOG daan

Description: Bogdan is of Russian and Ukrainian origins, meaning 'gift from God'.
Alternative spellings: Bogdon

Boreades

Meaning: Son of Boreas
Origin: Greek
Pronunciation: bo READ ess
Description: In Greek mythology, the Boreades were three giant sons of Boreas (the north wind) and Khione (goddess of snow).
Alternative spellings: Boreads, Boredes

Boris

Meaning: Glorious in battle
Origin: Russian
Pronunciation: BOH riss
Description: Originally thought to come from the Russian '*bogoris*' meaning 'small', the name Boris is now considered a short form of the Russian name Borislav, meaning 'glorious in battle'.
Alternative spellings: Borris, Boriss, Borys

Bosco

Meaning: Forest
Origin: Italian
Pronunciation: BOSS koh
Description: Bosco is an Italian boys' name meaning 'forest' or 'from the woods'. It is taken from the Latin word '*boscus*' meaning 'shrub' or 'undergrowth'.

Bowden

Meaning: Curved hill
Origin: English
Pronunciation: BOW den

Description: Bowden is an English surname made from the Old English words '*boga*' meaning 'bow' and '*dùn*' meaning 'hill' – together they mean a hill that is curved. This follows the contemporary trend of using last names as first names.
Alternative spellings: Bowdon

Bowie

Meaning: Blond
Origin: Scottish
Pronunciation: BOW ee
Description: Bowie is a Scottish boys' name meaning 'blond'. It was made popular in recent years due to the glam rock star, David Bowie.
Alternative spellings: Bowee

Bracken

Meaning: Descendant of Breacain
Origin: Gaelic
Pronunciation: BRAH ken
Description: Bracken is a unisex name derived from the Gaelic surname Breacain. The surname was originally given to the descendants of the clan that Saint Breacain belonged to. Bracken is also the name for a fern.
Alternative spellings: Bracain, Braken

Brad

Meaning: Broad wood clearing
Origin: English
Pronunciation: BRAD
Description: The name Brad came about as a shortened form of the name Bradley, but is now a first name in its own right.
Alternative spellings: Bradd

Braden

Meaning: Salmon
Origin: Gaelic
Pronunciation: BRAY den
Description: Braden is a popular boys' name in America and Canada in recent years. It derives from the Irish surname O'Bradan, which is the Gaelic word for 'salmon'. There are over 20 variants of the name, all of which are increasingly popular.
Alternative spellings: Bradin, Bradyn, Braedan, Braiden, Brayden

Bradley

Meaning: Broad wood clearing
Origin: English
Pronunciation: BRAD lee
Description: Bradley was originally used as a place name that meant 'broad wood clearing'. It then became a surname before being transferred to a forename.
Alternative spellings: Bradlee, Bradly

Brady

Meaning: Descendant of Brádach
Origin: Irish
Pronunciation: BRAY dee
Description: Brady is originally an Irish surname meaning 'descendant of Bradach'. However, in contemporary usage, it is not uncommon to see it used as a given name as well.
Alternative spellings: Bradee

Brandon

Meaning: Gorse hill
Origin: English
Pronunciation: BRAN den
Description: Brandon was originally used as a surname that combined the Old English words for a broom or gorse *(brom)* and a hill *(dun)*. It may also be considered a variant of Brendan.
Alternative spellings: Brandan, Branden, Brandun, Brandyn

Braxton

Meaning: Bracca's town
Origin: English
Pronunciation: BRAKS ten
Description: Braxton was originally an English surname from the Old English, referring to a place name 'Bracca's town'. The 'tun' part of the name refers to 'town' while the first part of the name is the name of the town itself.

Breckin

Meaning: Freckled
Origin: Irish
Pronunciation: breck IN
Description: Breckin is a variant spelling of the Irish name Breckin, meaning 'freckled'. Breckin Meyer is a famous American actor with this name.
Alternative spellings: Breccan

Brendan

Meaning: Prince
Origin: Gaelic
Pronunciation: BREN dan
Description: Brendan derives from the Old Irish name Breannain. It is widely used in Ireland in homage to St Brendan, known as 'the voyager'.
Alternative spellings: Brenden, Brendon

Brennan

Meaning: Teardrop

Origin: Gaelic
Pronunciation: BREN ann
Description: Brennan is a name for boys and girls that rose to popularity in the 1990s. It is of Irish and Gaelic origin and means 'teardrop'.
Alternative spellings: Brenan, Brennen, Brennon, Brenyn

Brent

Meaning: From a high place
Origin: English
Pronunciation: brent
Description: Brent is an English last name referring to someone who came from a high place or a steep hill. It also indicates people who lived in a place called Brent. This follows the contemporary trend of using last names as first names.

Brett

Meaning: Inhabitant of Britain
Origin: English
Pronunciation: BRET
Description: Brett is a very popular boys' name in America and Canada. It is common as both a surname and a given name.
Alternative spellings: Bret, Brette, Brit

Brian

Meaning: Strength
Origin: Gaelic
Pronunciation: BRY un
Description: Brian is a Gaelic name popular in Britain and Ireland. It is often spelt Bryan.
Alternative spellings: Brien, Brion, Bryan

Brody

Meaning: Muddy place
Origin: Gaelic

Pronunciation: BROH dee
Description: The meaning for this name originates from the Celtic word *'brothaigh'*. It was used as a surname for those who lived by muddy places and over time it has transferred into a forename.
Alternative spellings: Brodi, Brodie

Brogan

Meaning: Shoe
Origin: Gaelic
Pronunciation: BRO gun
Description: Brogan is a unisex name that was originally an Irish surname. Brogan is Gaelic in origin and is said to be derived from the word *'brog'*, which means 'shoe'.
Alternative spellings: Brogun

Brook

See entry in 'Names for Baby Girls A–Z'

Brooks

Meaning: Of the brook
Origin: English
Pronunciation: BRUK ss
Description: Brooks is an English boys' name meaning 'of the brook,' referring to a small stream.

Brooklyn

Meaning: Stream
Origin: English
Pronunciation: BRUK lin
Description: Brooklyn derives from the name of a borough in New York. It is very popular due to its combination of two well-loved names: Brooke and Lynn. The name is very popular in the USA and Canada.

Alternative spellings: Brooklin, Brooklynn

Bruce
Meaning: Unknown
Origin: Gaelic
Pronunciation: BROOS
Description: The name Bruce was originally a Scottish surname, notably belonging to Robert Bruce, a Scottish king in the 14th century.
Alternative spellings: Brooce, Bruse

Bruno
Meaning: Brown
Origin: German
Pronunciation: BRU no
Description: Bruno started life as a name given to upper-class families in the Middle Ages in Germany. It has been long established in America and may have been introduced to Britain from there.
Alternative spellings: Broono, Brunoh

Bryan
Meaning: High; noble
Origin: Gaelic
Pronunciation: BRY un
Description: Bryan is an alternative spelling of the popular Gaelic name Brian. It has long been the name associated with Brian Boru the Irish warrior king.
Alternative spellings: Brian

Bryce
Meaning: Of Britain
Origin: Scottish
Pronunciation: BRI-se
Description: Bryce is a popular boys' name of Scottish origin, meaning 'of Britain'. It is common as both a surname and a given name. Bryce Canyon, America is one of the most breathtaking natural geological sites in the world.
Alternative spellings: Brice, Bryse

Bryn
Meaning: Hill
Origin: Greek
Pronunciation: BREN, BRIN
Description: Bryn was originally a Welsh place name describing a dwelling next to a hill. It was then adopted into a unisex first name.
Alternative spellings: Bren, Brenne, Brin

Bryson
Meaning: Son of Brice
Origin: English
Pronunciation: BRY son
Description: Bryson is an English boys' name meaning 'son of Brice,' where Brice is a Scottish surname.
Alternative spellings: Brysen

Buddy
Meaning: Brother
Origin: English
Pronunciation: BUD dee
Description: Buddy is an uncommon boys' name, often shortened to Bud. Buddy is often used as a word signifying friendship or for a loved pet.
Alternative spellings: Buddey, Buddie

Burhan
Meaning: Proof
Origin: Arabic
Pronunciation: BUR hahn

Description: Burhan is an un-common Arabic name meaning 'proof'. It is an epithet of the prophet Muhammad. The name is somewhat popular in Turkey.
Alternative spellings: Buran, Burhaan

Burt

Meaning: Bright; glorious
Origin: English
Pronunciation: burt
Description: Burt is a name de-rived from the Old English '*beorht*' meaning 'bright' or 'glorious'. Burt Reynolds and Burt Lancaster were two famous actors with this name.
Alternative spellings: Bert

Buster

Meaning: A person who breaks things

Origin: English
Pronunciation: BUS tar
Description: The name Buster was originally a nickname meaning 'a person who broke things', from the word 'bust'. Buster Keaton was an American actor and director from the silent film era who made the name popular.

Byron

Meaning: Cattle shed
Origin: English
Pronunciation: BY ron
Description: This name originates from the surname of those who lived near cattle sheds or those who worked there, but was slowly adopted as a first name.
Alternative spellings: Biron, Byrun

C

Cade

Meaning: Barrel maker
Origin: English
Pronunciation: KADE
Description: Cade is an Old English surname said to refer to a barrel maker. It has now been adopted as a unisex name.
Alternative spellings: Caid, Cayde, Kade, Kayd

Caden

Meaning: Son; spirit of battle
Origin: Gaelic
Pronunciation: KAY den

Description: This name is mainly used in English-speaking countries, where it is thought to mean 'son'. It also has Welsh origins, where it is said to mean 'spirit of battle'. For this reason it is common among Welsh families.
Alternative spellings: Cadon, Caiden, Caidon, Cayden, Caydon, Kaden, Kadon, Kaiden, Kaidon, Kayden, Kaydon

Cadmus

Meaning: Alphabet
Origin: Greek

Pronunciation: CAD mus
Description: In Greek mythology, Cadmus was the son of Agenor and the brother of Europa. He went on to found the city of Thebes. He was credited with the introduction of the Phoenician alphabet.
Alternative spellings: Cadmos, Kadmos, Kadmus

Caelan
Meaning: Slender
Origin: Gaelic
Pronunciation: Kay laahn
Description: Caelan is a name of Gaelic origin. Its meaning is debated but some agree that it means 'slender'. It is an uncommon name in England but is more widely used in Ireland. Although it is most commonly found as a name for boys, it is in fact unisex.
Alternative spellings: Caolan, Caylan, Kaelan, Kaolan, Kaylan

Cai
Meaning: Rejoice
Origin: English
Pronunciation: KY
Description: Cai is an alternative spelling of the Scandinavian name Kai, which means 'rejoice'. It has become common in recent years for parents to slightly change the spelling of a name to suit their own choice.
Alternative spellings: Kai

Cain
Meaning: Spear
Origin: Hebrew
Pronunciation: KAYN
Description: Cain can be traced to several origins. In the Bible it was the name of the first son of Adam and Eve, who killed his own brother, and it means 'a spear'. However, in Wales Cain is a girls' name that means 'full of beauty'.
Alternative spellings: Caine, Kain, Kane, Kayne

Caio
Meaning: Happy
Origin: Latin
Pronunciation: CAY o
Description: Caio is an exotic boys' name meaning happy. It is a variant of the Welsh name Caeo and the Latin name Caius. It is more commonly seen as a surname.
Alternative spellings: Cayo, Kaio

Cairo
Meaning: Victorious
Origin: Arabic
Pronunciation: KY ro
Description: Cairo is the place name of Egypt's capital city and it means 'victorious'. It is therefore a fitting name for a child conceived or born in Egypt.
Alternative spellings: Kairo, Kyro

Cairon
Meaning: Victorious
Origin: Arabic
Pronunciation: KY ron
Description: This name derives from the city of Cairo. Cairo was originally given as a name to those who resided in the city; however, over time the name has developed into Cairon. The name could also be seen as a variant of the name Kieran.

Alternative spellings: Kairon, Kyron

Calchas
Meaning: Bronze man
Origin: Greek
Pronunciation: KAHL kas
Description: In Greek mythology, Calchas was a seer with a gift of interpreting the flight of birds and the entrails of the enemy during the tide of battle.
Alternative spellings: Calchus, Calkas

Caleb
Meaning: Dog; loyal
Origin: Hebrew
Pronunciation: KAY leb
Description: Caleb is a biblical name meaning 'dog'. It is also considered to mean 'loyal' or 'whole-hearted', depending on how the Hebrew is translated. Caleb was the name of one of Moses' followers on the journey to the Promised Land.
Alternative spellings: Kaleb, Kayleb

Callan
Meaning: Rock
Origin: Gaelic
Pronunciation: KAL an
Description: Callan is an uncommon boys' name of Gaelic origin. A British TV series by the name of *Callan* caused the name's popularity to rise in the 1970s.
Alternative spellings: Caelan, Calan, Caolan, Callen

Calum
Meaning: Peace
Origin: Latin
Pronunciation: KAL lum
Description: This name is very popular among followers of the Christian faith due to the symbolism of a dove, peace and the Holy Spirit. It also became popular due to St Columba, who was an influential Irish missionary in the 16th century.
Alternative spellings: Callum, Kallum, Kalum

Calvin
Meaning: Bald
Origin: French
Pronunciation: CAL vin
Description: Originally a French surname, Calvin meant 'little bald one' from the diminutive *'calve'*. The name's popularity in modern times is largely due to the success of designer fashion label Calvin Klein.
Alternative spellings: Kalvin

Camden
Meaning: Enclosed valley
Origin: English
Pronunciation: KAM den
Description: Camden is most likely an Old English surname meaning 'enclosed valley'. It is also a borough in north-west London, and as such is part of the trend where place names also double as given names.

Cameron
Meaning: Crooked nose
Origin: Gaelic
Pronunciation: KAM er uhn
Description: Cameron is a name of Scottish origin. It is a quite common surname, but has become

increasingly popular as a first name for both boys and girls.

Alternative spellings: Camron, Kameron, Kamran, Kamron

Camille

See entry in 'Names for Baby Girls A–Z'

Campbell

Meaning: Crooked mouth
Origin: Gaelic
Pronunciation: CAM bell
Description: Campbell is a common Scottish, English and American surname. Recently the name has become a popular given name in America for both boys and girls.
Alternative spellings: Campbel, Kampbell

Carey

Meaning: Dark
Origin: Irish
Pronunciation: care EE
Description: Carey was originally an Irish surname taken from the Old Irish adjective 'ciar' meaning 'dark' or 'black'. This follows the contemporary trend of using last names as first names.

Carl

Meaning: Free man
Origin: English
Pronunciation: KARL
Description: Carl derives from the Old English word *'ceorl'* meaning 'free man'. It is also the German form of Charles.
Alternative spellings: Karl

Carlo

Meaning: Free man

Origin: Spanish
Pronunciation: CAR lo
Description: Carlo is a shortened version of Carlos, a popular Spanish boys' name. Originating from the German name Charles, its Italian form, Carlo, has remained popular in the last century.
Alternative spellings: Carloh, Carlow

Carlos

Meaning: Free man
Origin: Spanish
Pronunciation: KARH lohs
Description: Carlos is the Spanish equivalent of the English name Charles.
Alternative spellings: Karlos

Carlton

Meaning: Free peasant settlement
Origin: English
Pronunciation: KARL ton
Description: Carlton is an American and English boys' name that was popular in the early 20th century.
Alternative spellings: Karlton

Carmel

See entry in 'Names for Baby Girls A–Z'

Carson

Meaning: Carr's son
Origin: English
Pronunciation: CAR sun
Description: Carson would originally have been a surname given to someone who hailed from a marshy area, or whose father had lived there. It has

developed into a first name throughout history, but is rare in the UK today.

Alternative spellings: Karson

Carter

Meaning: Cart transporter
Origin: English
Pronunciation: CAR ter
Description: Carter was originally used as a surname for those who transported goods in a cart. It is now used as both a first name and a surname.
Alternative spellings: Carta, Karter

Carwyn

Meaning: Love; fair; blessed
Origin: Welsh
Pronunciation: CAR win
Description: Carwyn is a Welsh boys' name meaning 'love, fair and blessed'. It is the masculine form of Carwen.
Alternative spellings: Caerwyn, Carwin, Corwyn

Casey

Meaning: Alert
Origin: English
Pronunciation: CAY see
Description: The name Casey derives from the Gaelic name Cathasaigh. It also comes from the folk hero 'Casey' Jones, who died while saving the lives of passengers on board the *Cannonball Express*. His name comes from his birth town, Cayce, Kentucky.
Alternative spellings: Casie, Cayce, Caycie, Caysie, Kacey, Kaci, Kacie, Kacy, Kasey, Kasie, Kaycee, Kaycie, Kaysie

Cash

Meaning: Cash
Origin: English
Pronunciation: CASH
Description: Cash is an uncommon English name meaning 'cash' or 'profit'. It is more recognised as a surname, borne by famous singer Johnny Cash.
Alternative spellings: Cassh, Kash

Caspar

Meaning: Treasurer
Origin: Persian
Pronunciation: CAS par
Description: Caspar is a Dutch form of the name Jaspar. In Christian belief it was borne by one of the three wise men who visited Christ.
Alternative spellings: Casper, Kacper, Kaspar, Kasper

Caspian

Meaning: Sea
Origin: English
Pronunciation: KAS pee an
Description: The Caspian Sea is a landlocked sea in north-west Asia, which was named after the ancient Caspians who used to live on its shore.
Alternative spellings: Caspean, Kasspian

Cassidy

Meaning: Curly
Origin: Gaelic
Pronunciation: CASS id ee
Description: Cassidy comes from the Gaelic surname O'Caiside. It can be seen as both a boys' and a girls' name.
Alternative spellings: Cassidey, Cassidi, Cassidie

Cassius

Meaning: Hollow
Origin: Latin
Pronunciation: cass EE us
Description: Cassius is a name that is likely to be of Latin origin, and may have been a Roman clan. There is also the suggestion that the name may have come from the Shakespeare character Caius Cassius. Cassius Clay was the birth name of heavyweight boxing champion of the world Muhammad Ali.
Alternative spellings: Kassius

Castiel

Meaning: Speed of God; God is my anger
Origin: Hebrew
Pronunciation: cast EE el
Description: Castiel is most likely a variation of the name Cassiel, who is an angel found in the Bible. Cassiel is one of the Seven Archangels, and the name means 'speed of God' or 'God is my anger'.
Alternative spellings: Kastiel

Cavan

Meaning: Handsome
Origin: Gaelic
Pronunciation: CA van
Description: Cavan is an uncommon boys' name of Irish and Gaelic origin, meaning 'handsome'. Cavan is also the name of a town in Ireland.
Alternative spellings: Cavann, Cavyn

Cayson

Meaning: No meaning
Origin: American
Pronunciation: CAY sun
Description: Cayson is most likely a modern, American invented name and as such has no meaning. It can be a combination of the names Casey and Jason, or a variation of Cason.
Alternative spellings: Cason, Kason

Cecil

Meaning: Blind
Origin: Latin
Pronunciation: see SIL
Description: Cecil comes from the name Cecilius, which is derivted from the Latin word 'caecus' meaning 'blind'.

Cedric

Meaning: Bounty
Origin: Celtic
Pronunciation: SED rick
Description: Cedric is a Celtic name that was created by Scottish writer Sir Walter Scott for his novel, *Ivanhoe*. It is a Celtic name meaning 'bounty'. It was also made popular by J.K. Rowling, who named one of her more memorable characters Cedric Diggory.
Alternative spellings: Cedrick

Celyn

See entry in 'Names for Baby Girls A–Z'

Chace

Meaning: Huntsman
Origin: English
Pronunciation: chAYce
Description: Chace is an Old English surname given as an occupational name for huntsman. As a given name it was uncommon

but in recent years it has become popular in America.
Alternative spellings: Chas, Chayce, Chayse

Chad

Meaning: Unknown
Origin: English
Pronunciation: CHAD
Description: The name Chad is a respelling of the Old English name Ceadda. Its meaning is unknown; however, it is the name of an African country so could be good for someone with African roots.
Alternative spellings: Chadd

Chaim

Meaning: Life
Origin: Hebrew
Pronunciation: CHAIM
Description: Chaim is a common name for Jewish boys. It is a variant of the Hebrew name Chayyim, which is derived from the Hebrew word for 'life'. It was believed that giving a baby this name would help the baby to remain healthy.
Alternative spellings: Chayim, Chayyim

Chance

Meaning: Chance; opportunity
Origin: English
Pronunciation: CHANSE
Description: Chance derives from the English vocabulary word 'chance' meaning 'opportunity' or 'luck'. It is also a derivation of Chauncey, a French name that means 'chancellor'. It can be used for girls or boys.
Alternative spellings: Chanse

Chandler

Meaning: Candle seller
Origin: French
Pronunciation: CHAND ler
Description: Chandler originated as a surname for those who made or sold candles and derives from the Old French word 'chandele'. The name is associated with one of the characters in the hit TV sitcom *Friends*.
Alternative spellings: Chandla, Chandlar

Channing

Meaning: People of Cana; wolf cub
Origin: English
Pronunciation: CHANN ing
Description: Channing is an English name meaning either 'people of Cana' or 'wolf cub'. It has become a popular modern name due to actor Channing Tatum.
See entry in 'Names for Baby Girls A–Z'

Charles

Meaning: Free man
Origin: German
Pronunciation: CHARLZ
Description: From the Germanic word 'karl', which means 'free man'. Charles was a popular name in the 17th century, thanks to its royal usage during that time.
Alternative spellings: Charls

Charlie

Meaning: Free man
Origin: German
Pronunciation: CHAR lee
Description: Pet form of Charles and Charlotte, now commonly

given as an independent name to both boys and girls.
Alternative spellings: Charlee, Charleigh, Charley, Charli, Charly

Charon

Meaning: Fierce brightness
Origin: Greek
Pronunciation: KARE on
Description: In Greek mythology, Charon was the boatman over the River Styx who carried the dead into the Underworld.
Alternative spellings: Charron, Karon

Chase

Meaning: Hunter
Origin: French
Pronunciation: CHAY ce
Description: While more popular as a boys name, it has also been given to girls. It would originally have been a given surname for a hunter in France or England. It is particularly popular in the US.

Che

Meaning: Argentine speech interjection
Origin: Spanish
Pronunciation: CHE
Description: Che was most likely made popular by Che Guevara (he was actually born Ernesto Guevara, and 'Che' was his nickname), the Argentine revolutionary. The word 'che' is actually an Argentine speech interjection, similar to 'bro' in English. Che Guevara often used the word, and that was how he got his famous nickname.

Chester

Meaning: Fort

Origin: Latin
Pronunciation: CHES ter
Description: Chester was originally an English surname, derived from the name of the city Chester. The city's name originates from the Latin word for 'fort', due to its connections with Hadrian's Wall.
Alternative spellings: Chesta, Chestar

Chevy

Meaning: Knight
Origin: French
Pronunciation: CHEV ee
Description: Chevy is a shortening of the French word 'chevalier' meaning 'knight'. Chevy Chase is an American comedian with this name.

Chris

Meaning: Follower of Christ
Origin: Greek
Pronunciation: KRIS
Description: Chris is a short form of Christopher, Christophe, Christine and other similar names, as well as being a male name in its own right.
Alternative spellings: Chriss, Kris

Christian

Meaning: Follower of Christ
Origin: Latin
Pronunciation: KRIS ti an
Description: Christian is a unisex name that literally means 'follower of Christ'. Incidentally, the name 'Christ' is a translation of the Hebrew term 'messiah', meaning 'anointed'.

Alternative spellings: Christian, Christien, Cristian, Kristian, Krystian

Christophe
Meaning: Follower of Christ
Origin: Greek
Pronunciation: KRIS toff
Description: Christophe is the French form of the Greek name Christopher, meaning 'bearer or follower of Christ'. Christophe is also seen as a surname.
Alternative spellings: Christoff, Kristophe

Christopher
Meaning: Follower of Christ
Origin: Greek
Pronunciation: KRIS toff ur
Description: Popular among early Christians who wanted to honour Christ with a personal link, Christopher is a name that largely rose in popularity in the 16th century.
Alternative spellings: Christofer, Christophar, Kristopher

Cian
Meaning: Ancient
Origin: Gaelic
Pronunciation: KEE ann
Description: In Irish mythology the name Cian was borne by a son-in-law of Brian Boru, and also by the ancient and influential clan who were known as the Cianachta. The name is still popular in Ireland and other parts of the world today.
Alternative spellings: Kean, Kian

Ciaran
Meaning: Dark-haired
Origin: Gaelic
Pronunciation: KEER rahn

Description: The name Ciaran derives from the Irish word *'ciar,'* which means 'black' or 'dark' and can be linked back to Ciar, son of Fergus, King of Ulster.
Alternative spellings: Keiran, Keiron, Kieran, Kieren, Kieron, Kiran

Cillian
Meaning: Fiesty
Origin: Gaelic
Pronunciation: KILL yan
Description: Cillian is a Gaelic boys' name, possibly a variation of Killian. Both names are said to have originated with meanings associated with war, but as a given name we would assume the meaning of Cillian to be 'feisty'.
Alternative spellings: Cillyan, Killian

Clark
Meaning: Clerk
Origin: English
Pronunciation: CLARK
Description: Clark is a name originally given to someone with the occupation of a clerk, which in the Middle Ages was a holy man with the ability to read and write.
Alternative spellings: Clarke

Clay
Meaning: Clay
Origin: English
Pronunciation: CLAY
Description: Clay may have originated as a surname used for those who lived in areas known to contain clay soils. It is also the shortened form of the name Clayton.
Alternative spellings: Cley, Klay

C

Clayton

Meaning: Clay settlement
Origin: English
Pronunciation: CLAY ton
Description: Like Clay, Clayton originated as a surname for those who lived near clay soils. It is still a very common surname but is also a very popular first name choice especially in the US.
Alternative spellings: Claiton, Cleyton, Klayton

Clement

Meaning: Merciful; gentle
Origin: English
Pronunciation: kle MENT
Description: Clement is the English form of the Latin name Clemens, which means 'merciful' and 'gentle'. It is also related to the English vocabulary word 'clemency,' also meaning 'merciful'. This was the name of 14 different popes.

Clint

Meaning: Town on a hilltop
Origin: English
Pronunciation: clint
Description: Clint is a shortened version of the name Clinton, meaning 'town on a hilltop'. Clint Eastwood is a famous American actor with this name.

Clive

Meaning: Lives near a cliff
Origin: English
Pronunciation: clive
Description: Clive is an English baby name that was originally given to people who lived near or on a cliff. Clive Owen is a famous British actor with this name.

Clyde

Meaning: From the banks of the River Clyde
Origin: Scottish
Pronunciation: cul LYDE
Description: Clyde was originally a Scottish surname to refer to people who lived near the banks of the River Clyde. The name of the river is taken from the Gaelic '*cluaidh*', although the meaning of this is unclear.

Coby

Meaning: Supplanter
Origin: English
Pronunciation: coh BEE
Description: Coby is a modern construction, and was probably originally a nickname for those named Jacob. This means that Coby has the same meaning as Jacob, which is 'supplanter'.
Alternative spellings: Cobie, Cobee, Kobe

Cody

Meaning: Obliging
Origin: Gaelic
Pronunciation: KOH dee
Description: The origin of the name Cody can be traced back to Gaelic surnames, specifically MacOda, which has become abbreviated and Americanised, and then translated from a surname to a first name. It is said to mean 'obliging' and can be used for both girls and boys.
Alternative spellings: Codey, Codie, Kody

Coen

Meaning: Brave
Origin: Dutch

C

Pronunciation: KOE en
Description: Coen is a Germanic variant of the name Conrad. It is most common in the Netherlands.
Alternative spellings: Coewn, Cohen, Kohen

Cohen

Meaning: Priest
Origin: Hebrew
Pronunciation: KOE en
Description: Cohen originates from the Hebrew name Kohen, borne by a priest and the brother of Moses in Jewish belief. It could also be the anglicised version of the Old Irish surname Cadhan.
Alternative spellings: Coen, Koen, Kohen

Colby

Meaning: Settlement
Origin: English
Pronunciation: KOHL bee
Description: Colby was originally a surname derived from an Old English place name. As a first name it has increased in popularity over the past 20 years.
Alternative spellings: Colbey, Colbi, Colbie, Kolby

Cole

Meaning: Dark
Origin: English
Pronunciation: COLE
Description: Cole is an English surname that has been transferred into a given name. It is taken from the Old English word *cola*, meaning 'dark complexion'. Other sources suggest the name to be a short form of the surname Coleman.

Alternative spellings: Cohl

Colin

Meaning: Young creature
Origin: Gaelic
Pronunciation: COLL in; CO lin
Description: Colin is a Gaelic name meaning 'young creature', but may also be considered a pet form of Nicholas.
Alternative spellings: Collin, Kolin

Colton

Meaning: From the coal or dark town
Origin: English
Pronunciation: COHL ton
Description: Colton is an English name meaning 'from the coal or dark town'. The 'coal' in the name is what most likely gave the name its meaning.
Alternative spellings: Kolton

Conall

Meaning: Strong wolf
Origin: Gaelic
Pronunciation: KON al
Description: Conall is a Scottish and Irish boys' name associated with the early chieftains and warriors of Ireland.
Alternative spellings: Conal, Connal, Connell

Conan

Meaning: Little wolf; little hound
Origin: Irish
Pronunciation: COH nan
Description: Conan is an Irish name that maeans 'little wolf' or 'little hound.' The name comes from the Gaelic element of *cù*, meaning 'wolf' or 'hound'. Conan

O'Brien is a famous American talk show host.

Connor
Meaning: Lover of hounds
Origin: Gaelic
Pronunciation: CON nor
Description: Taken from the Gaelic name Conchobhar, Connor has become increasingly popular outside of Ireland and has many variants. It is also derived from the Irish name Conaire, which can be found in Irish legends.
Alternative spellings: Conner, Conor, Konner, Konnor

Conrad
Meaning: Bold counsel
Origin: German
Pronunciation: KON rad
Description: Conrad is the usual English spelling of German name Konrad. It is often seen as a sur-name and means 'brave', 'counsel' or 'ruler'. It is often abbreviated to Kurt in Britain.
Alternative spellings: Konrad

Constantine
Meaning: Steadfast
Origin: Latin
Pronunciation: KON stan teen
Description: Constantine was originally a boys' name but is now a unisex name. It shares the same Latin roots as the word 'constant' and means 'steadfast'.
Alternative spellings: Constan-teen, Konstanteen, Konstantine

Cooper
Meaning: Barrel maker
Origin: English
Pronunciation: COO pur
Description: Before being adapted to a given name, Cooper was originally an occupational surname for one who made and sold barrels and tubs. It is still a common surname but is slowly becoming popular as a first name too.
Alternative spellings: Couper

Corban
Meaning: Gift to God
Origin: Hebrew
Pronunciation: KOR ban
Description: Corban is a variant of the Hebrew name Korban, meaning a 'blessing from God dedicated back to God'. The name can be found within Jewish communities but is rare elsewhere.
Alternative spellings: Corben, Corbin, Korbin

Corben
Meaning: Dark-haired
Origin: Gaelic
Pronunciation: CORE bin
Description: Corben derives from the Old French name Corbin, which means 'raven-coloured' or 'black-haired'.
Alternative spellings: Corbin, Corbyn, Korbin

Corey
Meaning: Spear
Origin: Gaelic
Pronunciation: COR ee
Description: The name Corey is of disputed origin. It could de-rive from the Gaelic word *'coire'*, meaning 'seething pool', 'cauldron' or 'hollow'. It may also be an anglicised version of

Corra, meaning 'spear'. It is a unisex name.
Alternative spellings: Coree, Corie, Cory, Koree, Korey, Kory

Corin
Meaning: Spear
Origin: Latin
Pronunciation: KOR in
Description: Corin is an uncommon Latin name meaning 'spear'. The story of Corin descends from the Sabine name Quirinus, a Roman god of war.
Alternative spellings: Coren, Corrin, Korin

Cormac
Meaning: Cart driver
Origin: Gaelic
Pronunciation: KOR mac
Description: Cormac is thought to have derived from a Gaelic word to describe a horseman or cart driver. It is a popular name in Ireland and America.
Alternative spellings: Cormack, Kormac, Kormack

Cosmo
Meaning: Harmony; order; beauty
Origin: Italian
Pronunciation: COS mo
Description: Cosmo is a boys' name of Italian and Greek origin, meaning 'order, harmony and beauty'. The name came to Britain with the arrival of the Duke of Gordon in the 17th century.
Alternative spellings: Cosimo, Cosme, Kosmo

Craig
Meaning: Rock
Origin: Gaelic
Pronunciation: krAYG
Description: Craig comes from the Gaelic word 'creag', meaning 'rock'.
Alternative spellings: Craeg, Kraig

C

Creon
Meaning: Heir to the throne
Origin: Greek
Pronunciation: KREE on
Description: In Greek mythology, Creon was the ruler of Thebes in the legend of Oedipus.
Alternative spellings: Creonn, Kreon

Cristiano
Meaning: Follower of Christ
Origin: Latin
Pronunciation: cris tee AH no
Description: Cristiano is a boys' given name of Latin origin, popular in Italian- and Portuguese-speaking countries. The meaning of the name is 'follower of Christ'.
Alternative spellings: Christian, Cristian, Kristiano

Cruz
Meaning: Cross
Origin: Spanish
Pronunciation: KROOZE
Description: Cruz is a unisex name that derives from the Spanish word for 'cross'. It has connotations of the cross of crucifixion and religion. It is better known as a boys' name.
Alternative spellings: Crooz, Cruise, Cruze, Kruise, Kruz, Kruze

Curtis
Meaning: Courteous
Origin: French

Pronunciation: CUR tiss
Description: Curtis derives from the word 'courteous' and was given as a nickname in the Middle Ages.
Alternative spellings: Kurtis

Cyprian
Meaning: Cypriot
Origin: Greek
Pronunciation: SEE pree ahn
Description: Cyprian is an uncommon name of Greek origin. It is from the Greek word *'kyprios'*, meaning 'the Cypriot'.

Alternative spellings: Ciprian, Siprian

Cyrus
Meaning: Throne
Origin: Persian
Pronunciation: SI russ
Description: Cyrus comes from the Persian word for 'throne'. Its meaning may come from the many Persian kings who took this name. It is popular in America.
Alternative spellings: Cyruss, Sirus

D

Daedalus
Meaning: Cunning worker
Origin: Greek
Pronunciation: DAY dah lus
Description: In Greek mythology, Daedalus was a skilled craftsman and artisan. He was the father of Icarus. In modern English the word Daedalus has been used extensively in the video-game industry.
Alternative spellings: Daedelus, Daydalus, Daydelus

Dafydd
Meaning: Beloved
Origin: Hebrew
Pronunciation: DAV ith
Description: Dafydd is the Welsh form of the Hebrew name David. The name Dafydd has religious tendencies as David features prominently in the Bible.
Alternative spellings: David

Dainton
Meaning: From Dainton
Origin: English
Pronunciation: DAIN ton
Description: Dainton is an unusual name in Britain, despite its origins as an English place name.
Alternative spellings: Daintan, Daynton

Dale
Meaning: Valley dweller
Origin: English
Pronunciation: DAIL
Description: Dale was originally a surname given to those local to a dale or valley. Now it is used as a given name.
Alternative spellings: Dail, Dayle

Dallas
Meaning: Skilled
Origin: Irish
Pronunciation: DAAL as

Description: Dallas is an Irish name meaning 'skilled,' and it is also the name of a city in Texas. This name is part of the growing trend of names taken from places.

Dalton
Meaning: From the valley
Origin: English
Pronunciation: DOLL ton
Description: Dalton is an Old English name meaning 'from the valley town'. There are many locations dotted across England with this name. In the last 20 years Dalton has become a popular name for boys in America.
Alternative spellings: Dallton, Dalten, Delton

Damian
Meaning: To tame
Origin: Greek
Pronunciation: DAY me en
Description: Damian derives from the Greek name Damianos. The name has religious connotations as St Damian is said to be the patron saint of physicians.
Alternative spellings: Damien, Damion, Daymian

Damon
Meaning: To tame
Origin: Greek
Pronunciation: DAY mon
Description: Damon is a derivative of *'daman'*, meaning 'to tame' or 'subdue'.
Alternative spellings: Daimon, Daymon

Dan
Meaning: God is my judge

Origin: Hebrew
Pronunciation: DAN
Description: Dan is the shortened version of Daniel, a common name in the English-speaking world. Daniel was mentioned often in the Bible and is of Hebrew origin.
Alternative spellings: Dann

Dana
Meaning: Fertility; from Denmark
Origin: Gaelic
Pronunciation: DAY na
Description: Although Dana is used for both boys and girls, the masculine and feminine forms have separate origins. Dana in the feminine form comes from Gaelic origin and in Irish mythology was the name of the goddess of fertility. As a boys' name it means 'from Denmark'.
Alternative spellings: Danah, Dayna

Dane
Meaning: From Denmark
Origin: English
Pronunciation: DAYN
Description: Dane is an English boys' name originally used to signify Danish ancestry. More recently the name has lost its Danish origins to become a name in itself.
Alternative spellings: Dain, Daine, Dayne

Daniel
Meaning: God is my judge
Origin: Hebrew
Pronunciation: DAN yule
Description: Daniel is a biblical name borne by the prophet, whose story is told in the Book

of Daniel. His story was a favourite tale in the Middle Ages and was often represented in miracle plays.
Alternative spellings: Danial, Daniyal, Danyaal, Danyal, Danyel, Danyl

Danielius
Meaning: God is my judge
Origin: Hebrew
Pronunciation: dan ee EL ee us
Description: Danielius is a Greek variant of Daniel, which is a very common name in the English-speaking world. Daniel was mentioned frequently in the Bible and is of Hebrew origin.
Alternative spellings: Danielios

Danny
Meaning: God is my judge
Origin: Hebrew
Pronunciation: DAN nee
Description: Originally a pet form of Daniel, Danny is now used as a first name in its own right.
Alternative spellings: Dannie

Dante
Meaning: Enduring
Origin: Spanish
Pronunciation: DAHN tay
Description: A historical name most associated with Dante Alighieri, the author of *The Divine Comedy*. He is considered one of the greatest poets of all time. Dante can be used as a shortened version of Durante. The name is mainly used in Italy today.
Alternative spellings: Dantay

Danyl
Meaning: God is my judge
Origin: Hebrew
Pronunciation: DAN il
Description: Danyl is a modern and shortened variant of the Hebrew name Daniel. Much like Danyaal, it took the phonetic spelling of the name.
Alternative spellings: Danil, Danyll

Dara
Meaning: Oak tree
Origin: Gaelic
Pronunciation: DAH ruh
Description: Dara is a boys' name originating in Ireland and recently has become popular in both America and Ireland.
Alternative spellings: Daire, Darragh

Darcy
Meaning: From Arcy
Origin: English
Pronunciation: DAR see
Description: Darcy is a unisex name created from the surname d'Arcy. The name Darcy became well established in England during the Middle Ages. Now, the name has links with Jane Austen's *Pride and Prejudice*, in which Mr Darcy is a main character.
Alternative spellings: Darcey, Darci, Darcie

Darin
Meaning: Dwelling by a hill
Origin: English
Pronunciation: DARE en
Description: Often thought of as a variation of the name Darren, Darin is also a name in its own right. Darin is an Old English surname that could mean 'dwelling by

a hill'. It is pronounced differently to Darren.
Alternative spellings: Darein

Darius
Meaning: Guardian
Origin: Persian
Pronunciation: DAH ree us
Description: Darius is a name of Persian origin and was borne by the king of the Persians in the 6th century BC.
Alternative spellings: Daryus

Darragh
Meaning: Dark oak
Origin: Gaelic
Pronunciation: DAH ruh
Description: Darragh is a boys' name from Ireland. In America it is more commonly seen as a surname rather than a given name.
Alternative spellings: Daire, Dara

Darrell
Meaning: From Airelle
Origin: French
Pronunciation: dare ELL
Description: Darrell is a French name taken from the Norman-French 'd'Airelle', referring to a person who came from the French town of Airelle.
Alternative spellings: Daryl, Darryl, Daryll, Darryll, Darrel

Darren
Meaning: Great
Origin: Gaelic
Pronunciation: DA ren
Description: The origins of Darren are somewhat blurred – it is thought to come from the Gaelic

surname meaning 'great', but it is also linked to a Welsh mountain named Moel Darren.
Alternative spellings: Darran, Darrin, Darryn

Darsh
Meaning: Lord Krishna; moonlight
Origin: Sanskrit
Pronunciation: DARSH
Description: Darsh is an Indian Gujarati boys' name that has the meanings 'Lord Krishna' and 'moonlight'.
Alternative spellings: Daarsh

Darwin
Meaning: Dear friend
Origin: English
Pronunciation: DAR win
Description: Darwin comes from the surname used in Old English, derived from the personal name 'Deorwine'. It is famously linked to Charles Darwin, who was responsible for the theory of evolution. The name is gathering popularity as a given name.
Alternative spellings: Darwinn

Dashiell
Meaning: Unknown
Origin: French
Pronunciation: Dash EEL
Description: It is thought that this name is the anglicised form of the French family name de Chiel, but there is no documented meaning of the name. Samuel Dashiell Hammett was a famous American novelist in the 1930s and 40s, and the name is found most often in America.
Alternative spellings: Dashiel

D

Dave

Meaning: Darling
Origin: Hebrew
Pronunciation: DAYV
Description: Dave is a shortened form of the biblical name David but is also a name in its own right.
Alternative spellings: Daive, Dayv

David

Meaning: Darling
Origin: Hebrew
Pronunciation: DAY vid
Description: A biblical name borne by King David of Israel, who killed the giant Goliath with a slingshot before his rise to power. David is a very popular name in English-speaking countries.
Alternative spellings: Daivid, Davide

Davis

Meaning: Son of David
Origin: Welsh
Pronunciation: day VIS
Description: Davis is more common as a surname but it is also a popular choice for first names. It is taken from the Welsh 'Dafydd', which when anglicised becomes David. Davis refers to people whose fathers were called David.

Dawood

Meaning: Beloved
Origin: Hebrew
Pronunciation: DA wood
Description: Dawood is an uncommon name of Hebrew origin, meaning 'beloved'.
Alternative spellings: Dawud, Duwood

Dawson

Meaning: Son of David
Origin: English
Pronunciation: DAW son
Description: Most commonly a surname, Dawson is an English boys' name that has risen in popularity as a first name over the last 10 years in America and England.
Alternative spellings: Dayson, Dowson

Dawud

Meaning: Darling
Origin: Hebrew
Pronunciation: dah WOOD
Description: Dawud is the Arabic variant of the Hebrew name David. It is rarely found in Britain but would make a nice alternative to the popular name David.
Alternative spellings: Dahwud, Dawood

Dax

Meaning: Town in France
Origin: French
Pronunciation: DAAX
Description: Dax is a French name taken from a town in south-western France from before the Roman occupation.

Dayton

Meaning: Day's settlement
Origin: English
Pronunciation: DAY ton
Description: Dayton is an uncommon English boys' name. Its popularity has increased in America in recent years. It is also the name of a city in Ohio, America.

Alternative spellings: Daytan, Dayten

Deacon
Meaning: Messenger
Origin: Greek
Pronunciation: DEE kan
Description: Thought to have derived directly from the name for a cleric in the Christian church who is not yet a priest or minister. It is a common surname in Britain and is now also used as a first name.
Alternative spellings: Deacon, Deecon

Dean
Meaning: Valley; church official
Origin: English
Pronunciation: DEEN
Description: Dean comes from the Old English word *'denu'*, which would have been given as a surname to those who lived near a valley. It is also an occupational name for a church, university or group supervisor. Now it is commonly used as a first name.
Alternative spellings: Deen, Deyn

Declan
Meaning: Endowed with goodness
Origin: English
Pronunciation: DEK lin
Description: Declan is the anglicised version of the Irish name Deaglan. It is thought that an Irish saint had this name.
Alternative spellings: Declin, Deklan

Demetrius
Meaning: Follower of Demeter

Origin: Greek
Pronunciation: de MEE tree uhs
Description: Demetrius is a Greek name meaning 'follower of Demeter'. Demeter is the goddess of the harvest. The name Demetrius appears in a number of William Shakespeare's plays, including *A Midsummer Night's Dream*.
Alternative spellings: Dametrius, Demetris, Dimetrius

Dennis
Meaning: Servant of Dionysus
Origin: Greek
Pronunciation: DEN niss
Description: Dennis comes from the name of the Greek god of revelry, Dionysus. As such, the name connotes a person who is amiable and very social. Denny and Den are short forms of this name.
Alternative spellings: Denis

Denny
Meaning: The Dane's village; servant of Dionysus
Origin: English
Pronunciation: DEN nee
Description: Denny is a variant of the Scandinavian name Denby and the English name Dennis. In most cases Denny is likely to be a shortened version of Dennis.
Alternative spellings: Denney

Denver
Meaning: Dane crossing
Origin: English
Pronunciation: DEN ver
Description: Denver was originally used as a surname for those located near Denver in Norfolk. It is also the capital of Colorado,

D

USA. Denver is now used as a given name as well as a surname.
Alternative spellings: Denvar

Denzel
Meaning: From Denzell
Origin: English
Pronunciation: DEN zell
Description: Denzell is a Cornish village that provides the root of the name Denzel.
Alternative spellings: Denzell, Denzil

Derek
Meaning: Ruler
Origin: German
Pronunciation: DER ick
Description: Derek derives from the Germanic name Theoderic, which means 'ruler of people'. The name arrived on British shores in the 1400s and gained traction in the 19th century.
Alternative spellings: Dereck, Derick, Derik, Derrek

Desmond
Meaning: From South Munster
Origin: Gaelic
Pronunciation: DEZ muhnd
Description: Desmond is a common Irish name, which is commonly shortened to Des.
Alternative spellings: Desmund, Dezmond

Dev
Meaning: God-like
Origin: Sanskrit
Pronunciation: DEHV
Description: The name Dev is commonly used as a shortened version of several longer names including Devlin, Devin and Devan. Dev is a name often favoured by Indian parents.
Alternative spellings: Dehv

Devon
Meaning: From Devon
Origin: English
Pronunciation: DEH vun
Description: Devon is a unisex name that derives from the place name of Devon in southwest England. Originally it was used for those born in Devon, but it is now becoming a popular name countrywide and in America.
Alternative spellings: Devone, Devun

Dewi
Meaning: Beloved
Origin: Welsh
Pronunciation: DOO ee
Description: Dewi is a modern variation of the name Dewey, which is thought to have been derived from the name David.
Alternative spellings: Dewey, Dewie

Dexter
Meaning: Right-handed; prosperous
Origin: Latin
Pronunciation: DEX ter
Description: As well as a name, Dexter is also a Latin word meaning 'right-handed'. As a given name it also means 'prosperous'.
Alternative spellings: Deckster

Dhruv
Meaning: North Star
Origin: Sanskrit

Pronunciation: DROOHV
Description: In Hindu belief Druhv was the name of an often-ignored second son of a king. He prayed to the god Vishnu, who turned him into the North Star so that he would never again be ignored.
Alternative spellings: Dhruve, Droov

Diego

Meaning: Supplanter
Origin: Spanish
Pronunciation: dee AY go
Description: Diego is a Spanish boys' name that is said to be a variant of the name James. It is a fairly unusual name in Britain but popular in Spain and America.
Alternative spellings: Diaygo

Digby

Meaning: Dyke; ditch; farm; town
Origin: English
Pronunciation: dig BEE
Description: Digby is both a given name and a surname. The name comes from the name of an English town, which comes from a combination of the Old English '*dic*' meaning 'dyke' or 'ditch' and the Old Norse '*byr*', meaning 'farm or 'town'.

Digory

Meaning: Lost one
Origin: French
Pronunciation: dig OR ee
Description: Digory is a variation of Diggory, a French name that means 'lost one'. Digory Kirke is a fictional character in C. S. Lewis' Chronicles of Narnia books.

Alternative spellings: Diggory

Dilan

Meaning: Sea
Origin: English
Pronunciation: dill EN
Description: Dilan is an alternative spelling of the name Dylan. In Welsh mythology, Dylan was the god of the sea, accidentally slain by his uncle Govannon.
Alternative spellings: Dhilan, Dylan, Dillon

Dillan

Meaning: Sea; loyal
Origin: Gaelic
Pronunciation: DIL un
Description: Dillan is an alternative spelling of the name Dylan. It could either come from the Gaelic god of the sea, Dylan, or from the Gaelic name Dillon, which is said to mean 'loyal'.
Alternative spellings: Dillon, Dylan

Dimitri

Meaning: Earth mother
Origin: Greek
Pronunciation: dee MEE tree
Description: Dimitri is a name of Greek origin, meaning 'earth mother'. It is the Slavic version of Demetrius and one of the most popular boys' names in Russia.
Alternative spellings: Dimitrie, Dimitry

Diomedes

Meaning: God-like cunning
Origin: Greek
Pronunciation: di o MEED ez

D

Description: In Greek mythology, Diomedes was a hero who fought in the Trojan War.
Alternative spellings: Diomeedes, Dyomedes

Dion
Meaning: Servant of Dionysus
Origin: Greek
Pronunciation: DYE on
Description: Dion is a unisex name derived from the name of the Greek god of revelry, Dionysus. Dione is a specifically feminine form of the name, while Deon is the spelling more often used for boys.
Alternative spellings: Deon, Dione, Dionne

Dionysus
Meaning: Grapevine
Origin: Greek
Pronunciation: dye on EYE suss
Description: In Greek mythology, Dionysus was the god of the grape harvest, winemaking, wine and of ritual madness. Its Latin form is Bacchus.
Alternative spellings: Dionisus, Dyonisus

Diya
See entry in 'Names for Baby Girls A–Z'

Dominic
Meaning: Lord
Origin: Latin
Pronunciation: DOM in ik
Description: Dominic comes from the Latin name Dominicus, derived from the word for 'lord'. Dominic is a popular Roman Catholic name

in honour of St Dominic and the name has grown in popularity since the 1970s.
Alternative spellings: Domenic, Dominik

Diyan
Meaning: Lamp
Origin: Indian
Pronunciation: DEE yaan
Description: Diyan is an Indian boys' name meaning 'lamp' or 'bright light'.
Alternative spellings: Diyaan

Domas
Meaning: Twin
Origin: Dutch
Pronunciation: doh MAS
Description: Domas is the Dutch version of the name Thomas, meaning 'twin'. In the New Testament, the name was borne by one of Christ's 12 Apostles, referred to as Thomas, called Didymus. Didymos is the Greek word for 'twin', and the name is the Greek form of an Aramaic byname meaning 'twin'.
Alternative spellings: Thomas

Dominykas
Meaning: Lord
Origin: Lithuanian
Pronunciation: dom IN ikas
Description: Dominykas is the Lithuanian version of the name Dominic. Dominic comes from the Late Latin name Dominicus, derived from the word for 'lord'. A popular Roman Catholic name in honour of St Dominic, the name has grown in popularity since the 1970s.
Alternative spellings: Dominic

Dominique
See entry in 'Names for Baby Girls A–Z'

Don
Meaning: World ruler
Origin: Gaelic
Pronunciation: DON
Description: The name Don came about as the shortened form of Donald; however it is a name in its own right.
Alternative spellings: Donn

Donald
Meaning: World ruler
Origin: Gaelic
Pronunciation: DON ald
Description: Donald is the anglicised form of the Scottish name Domhnall, which is formed from the words meaning 'world' and 'rule'. The 'd' at the end of the name Donald comes from an English misinterpretation fuelled by German names such as 'Ronald'.
Alternative spellings: Donalde, Donold

Donovan
Meaning: Brown-haired chieftain
Origin: Gaelic
Pronunciation: DON na vun
Description: Donovan is an Irish and Gaelic name that is popular for boys in America. The meaning of the name implies 'dark- or brown-haired chieftain'.
Alternative spellings: Donavan, Donavon, Donevon, Donoven

Dorian
Meaning: Member of the Greek tribe
Origin: Greek
Pronunciation: daw REE an
Description: Dorian was first used, and made popular, by Oscar Wilde's famous novel, *The Picture of Dorian Gray*. Wilde most likely took the name from an ancient Greek tribe called the Dorians.

D

Dougie
Meaning: Black river
Origin: Gaelic
Pronunciation: DUG less
Description: Dougie is a nickname that has become used as a first name in recent years. It is an abbreviated version of the name Douglas, which means 'black river' and was the name given to two powerful Scottish clans.

Douglas
Meaning: Black river
Origin: Gaelic
Pronunciation: DUG less
Description: Originally used both as a first and surname, the name Douglas was actually given to females in the 17th century, but it is used exclusively as a male name today. It is very popular in Scotland.
Alternative spellings: Douglass, Dougless

Drew
Meaning: Manliness
Origin: Greek
Pronunciation: DROO
Description: Drew is primarily a short form of the Greek name Andrew.
Alternative spellings: Dru

Drey
Meaning: No meaning
Origin: English

Pronunciation: drey
Description: Drey is a modern invented name and, because of this, has no meaning attached to it.
Alternative spellings: Dray

Duke

Meaning: Leader
Origin: English
Pronunciation: duke
Description: Duke is originally a title for the English nobility, derived from the Latin '*dux*' meaning 'leader'. It is now a common given name for boys. Duke Ellington was a famous American composer and originator of big-band jazz.

Duncan

Meaning: Brown chief
Origin: Gaelic
Pronunciation: DUN cun
Description: Duncan is an anglicised form of the Gaelic name Donnchadh. It was considered to be a royal name in early Scotland.
Alternative spellings: Duncun, Dunkan

Dustin

Meaning: Thor's stone
Origin: English
Pronunciation: DUST inn
Description: Dustin is an English surname that was originally taken from a Norman surname, Torsten. It is composed of the elements of '*thor*' and '*stone*'.

Dusty

Meaning: Full of dust
Origin: American

Pronunciation: dust EE
Description: Dusty is an American name taken from the English vocabulary word of the same spelling and meaning. It is a rather contemporary name and not often found outside of America.

Dwayne

Meaning: Dark
Origin: Gaelic
Pronunciation: DWAYN
Description: Dwayne is a name of Gaelic origin, meaning 'dark' or 'black'.
Alternative spellings: Duwayne, Dwayn

Dwight

Meaning: God of wine
Origin: English
Pronunciation: dwy ITE
Description: Dwight is an English name that comes from the medieval name Diot, which in turn is a diminutive of Dionysia, the feminine form of Dionysus. Therefore, it shares the same meaning as Dionysus, who was the Greek god of wine.

Dyfan

Meaning: To tame; subdue
Origin: Welsh
Pronunciation: DIE fan
Description: Dyfan is the Welsh form of the Greek name Damon. The name is a derivative of '*daman*', meaning 'to tame' or 'subdue'. Dyfan is also the name of a Welsh saint, although he is a highly obscure figure who is often mistaken with Sain Deruvian.

E

Eamon

Meaning: Wealthy protector
Origin: Irish
Pronunciation: AYE mon
Description: Eamon is a variant of the name Eamonn and the Irish version of the name Edmund. It is composed of two Old English words - '$\bar{e}ad$' ('prosperity, riches') and '$mund$' ('protector').
Alternative spellings: Eamonn

Earl

Meaning: Warrior; nobleman
Origin: English
Pronunciation: ERL
Description: The name Earl comes from the title of an earl. An earl is a British peer ranking below a marquess and above a viscount.
Alternative spellings: Earle, Erle, Urle

Easton

Meaning: Town in the east
Origin: English
Pronunciation: east TUN
Description: Easton was originally a surname but has now become a popular choice for a first name. It is composed of the Old English words '$east$' meaning the direction, and 'ton' meaning town, giving its meaning of 'town in the east'.

Eben

Meaning: Stone
Origin: Hebrew
Pronunciation: EE ben

Description: Eben is a shortened variant of the Jewish name Ebenezer.
Alternative spellings: Eauben, Ebenn, Eeben

Edan

Meaning: Little fire
Origin: Gaelic
Pronunciation: EE dan
Description: Edan is an uncommon name of Gaelic origin. The more common English variant is Aidan, but Edan has become popular in recent years.
Alternative spellings: Eden, Edun

Eddie

Meaning: Guardian of prosperity
Origin: English
Pronunciation: Eh DEE
Description: Eddie came about as a pet form of names beginning with Ed, such as Edward and Edwina. It is now used as a unisex name in its own right. It is a very common first name.
Alternative spellings: Eddi, Eddy

Eden

See entry in 'Names for Baby Girls A–Z'

Edgar

Meaning: Rich owner of spears
Origin: English
Pronunciation: ED gar
Description: The name Edgar is derived from the Old English

name Eadgar. The name was borne by an English king and St Edgar the Peaceful.
Alternative spellings: Edger

Edison
Meaning: Son of Edward
Origin: English
Pronunciation: ED ih sun
Description: Edison was the surname of famous American inventor Thomas Edison, and has since become a given name across the world. In English it literally means 'son of Edward'.
Alternative spellings: Adison, Eddison, Edisson

Edmund
Meaning: Guardian of prosperity
Origin: English
Pronunciation: ED mund
Description: The name Edmund derives from two elements of the Old English language: *'ead'*, meaning 'riches', and *'mund'*, which means 'protection'.
Alternative spellings: Edmond, Edmunde

Eduard
Meaning: Guardian of prosperity
Origin: English
Pronunciation: ED wood
Description: Eduard is an alternative spelling of the name Edward. Derived from Old English *'ead'* (meaning 'prosperity') and *'weard'* (meaning 'guard'), Edward is one of the most perennially popular of all Old English names. Edward was the name of three Anglo-Saxon kings and eight kings of England. Edward the Confessor, penultimate

Anglo-Saxon king of England, had a reign marked by peace and prosperity.
Alternative spellings: Edward, Eduardo

Edwin
Meaning: Lucky
Origin: English
Pronunciation: ED win
Description: The name Edwin is Old English in origin and is said to mean 'lucky'.
Alternative spellings: Edwen, Edwinn

Eesa
Meaning: Salvation
Origin: Hebrew
Pronunciation: EE sa
Description: Eesa is a name that is considered possibly the true name of Jesus Christ. It has become increasingly popular in the UK in recent years.
Alternative spellings: Eisa

Efan
Meaning: God is gracious
Origin: Welsh
Pronunciation: EF fan
Description: Efan is a variant of the Welsh name Evan, which in turn is the Welsh form of the English name John. Efan is uncommon as a given name in England. Efan was the nickname given to Efangwu 'Efan' Ekoku, an English-born Nigerian footballer.
Alternative spellings: Evan

Efe
Meaning: Older brother
Origin: Turkish
Pronunciation: EH fee

Description: Efe is an uncommon Turkish boys' name, which means 'older brother'. It is also a shortened variant of the Nigerian boys' name Efetobore.
Alternative spellings: Efee, Effe

Ehsan
Meaning: Perfection; excellence
Origin: Arabic
Pronunciation: ee SHAAN
Description: Ehsan is an Arabic boys' name meaning 'perfection' or 'excellence'. It is actually a religious term, referring to a Muslim's responsibility to obtain perfection in worship. It is one of the three dimensions of the Islamic religion.

Eisa
Meaning: Jesus
Origin: Arabic
Pronunciation: EYE sah
Description: Eisa is the Arabic form for Jesus. It is also a feminine name in Scandinavian countries, and the female version of Eisa means 'glowing embers' in Old Norse.
Alternative spellings: Eesa

Eli
Meaning: Jehovah is good
Origin: Hebrew
Pronunciation: EE ly
Description: Shortened form of Elijah, a Hebrew prophet who ascended into heaven in a blazing chariot.
Alternative spellings: Ely

Elia
Meaning: Jehovah is good

Origin: Hebrew
Pronunciation: EH le ah
Description: Elia is a unisex name that comes from the same root as the Hebrew name Elijah, which means 'Jehovah is good'.
Alternative spellings: Elea, Eliah

E

Elias
Meaning: The Lord is my God
Origin: Hebrew
Pronunciation: ee LYE us
Description: Elias is a Biblical name, and was originally used for followers of the Christian religion. While it has not been a traditionally popular name, it is now growing in popularity.
Alternative spellings: Elyas

Elijah
Meaning: Jehovah is good
Origin: Hebrew
Pronunciation: eh LY jah
Description: Elijah was a Hebrew prophet who ascended to heaven in a blazing chariot.
Alternative spellings: Elija, Elijeh

Elio
Meaning: Sun
Origin: Greek
Pronunciation: el EE oh
Description: Elio is a variation of the Greek name Helios. In Greek mythology, Helios was the god of the sun who rode his chariot across the sky each day.

Eliot
Meaning: My God is the Lord
Origin: Hebrew
Pronunciation: ell EE ott

Best Baby Names

Description: Eliot, a variation of the more common Elliot, is a unisex given name as well as a surname. It comes from the same Hebrew roots as Elias or Elijah.
Alternative spellings: Elliot, Elliott

Elisha
See entry in 'Names for Baby Girls A–Z'

Ellis
Meaning: Jehovah is good
Origin: Hebrew
Pronunciation: ELL iss
Description: Ellis derives from a medieval version of Elias. Often used as a transferred surname, Ellis has enjoyed good stints of popularity as a unisex name.
Alternative spellings: Eliss, Elliss

Ellison
Meaning: My God is the Lord
Origin: English
Pronunciation: ell ISS sun
Description: Ellison is the English variation of the name Ellis, and they share the same meaning, which is 'my God is the lord'. It is also both a surname and a unisex given name.
Alternative spellings: Elison

Elvis
Meaning: Unknown
Origin: English
Pronunciation: EL viss
Description: The name Elvis is famously borne by Elvis Presley, supposed founder of rock and roll. 2010 was the first year the name did not appear in the top 1,000 baby names in the US since 1954.
Alternative spellings: Ellvis, Elviss

Elwood
Meaning: Elder tree forest
Origin: English
Pronunciation: ed WUWD
Description: Elwood is an English name and surname that means 'elder tree forest' in Old English and comes from a place name.

Eman
Meaning: Faith
Origin: Arabic
Pronunciation: EE man
Description: Eman is a unisex name of separate origins. It can be a variant of the unisex name Iman, which is of Arabic origin and is said to mean 'faith'. Alternatively, the name could be a short form of the male name Emmanuel.
Alternative spellings: Eeman, Emaan, Iman

Emanuel
Meaning: God is with us
Origin: Hebrew
Pronunciation: ih MAN you uhl
Description: Emanuel is a popular boys' name meaning 'God is with us'. It is a variant of the Hebrew name Emmanuel.
Alternative spellings: Emanual, Emanuele, Imanuel

Emerson
Meaning: Son of Emery
Origin: English
Pronunciation: EM er sun

Description: Emerson is an Old English boys' name literally meaning 'Emery's son'. While quite uncommon as a given name, Emerson is more common as a surname in England and America.
Alternative spellings: Emersson, Emmerson

Emil
Meaning: Enthusiastic
Origin: Latin
Pronunciation: AY mul
Description: Emil is said to be of Latin origin and is derived from the Roman surname Aemilius. It is said to mean 'enthusiastic'.
Alternative spellings: Amil, Emile

Emile
Meaning: Eager
Origin: Latin
Pronunciation: em EEL
Description: Emile is an uncommon boys' name originating from the Latin name Emil. Emile is considered to be the French version of the name.
Alternative spellings: Emil

Emilio
Meaning: Imitating
Origin: Latin
Pronunciation: eh MEE li O
Description: This name is most commonly found in Italian-, Portuguese- and Spanish-speaking countries. It comes from the Latin element *'aemulus'*, which means 'imitating'.
Alternative spellings: Emelio, Emileo

Emilis
Meaning: Enthusiastic

Origin: Lithuanian
Pronunciation: ey MIL us
Description: Emilis is the Lithuanian form of the name Emil, meaning 'enthusiastic'. Emil (and Emilis) is said to be of Latin origin and is derived from the Roman surname Aemilius.

E

Emir
Meaning: Ruler
Origin: Arabic
Pronunciation: eh MEER
Description: Emir is a variation of the name Amir, meaning 'ruler'. It was a name that would originally have been given to rulers of Arabic caliphates, which are areas containing an Islamic steward who is a leader of a Muslim community.
Alternative spellings: Amir

Emmanuel
Meaning: God is with us
Origin: Hebrew
Pronunciation: ih MAN you uhl
Description: Also spelt Emanuel, in Hebrew this name means 'God is with us'. It is sometimes shortened to the Spanish version Manuel or Manny. In Christianity Emmanuel is sometimes used as a name for Jesus.
Alternative spellings: Emanuel

Emmett
Meaning: Universal
Origin: English
Pronunciation: EHM eht
Description: Emmett is the English masculine version of Emma, which is a German name meaning 'universal'. The element of *'ermen'* means 'whole' or

'universal' in German. It also has Hebrew roots and also means 'truth'.

Alternative spellings: Emet, Emmet, Emett

Emory

Meaning: House strength; industrious leader

Origin: German

Pronunciation: em ORR ee

Description: Emory has Old German origins and means 'house strength' and 'industrious leader'. Historically it was a last name, but has become a first name in the modern age.

Alternative spellings: Emre, Emery

Emre

Meaning: Friend

Origin: Turkish

Pronunciation: EM ree

Description: Emre is a Turkish boys' name meaning 'friend'. Related names include Emra, Emrah and Emreh.

Alternative spellings: Emory, Emery

Emrys

Meaning: Immortal

Origin: Welsh

Pronunciation: EHM rees

Description: Emrys is the Welsh form of the Greek name Ambrose. Ambrose, meaning 'immortal,' is a name borne by a 4th-century bishop of Milan. The name is generally more common in Ireland than England or the USA.

Enes

Meaning: Human being

Origin: Turkish

Pronunciation: EH nes

Description: Enes is an uncommon name of Turkish origin, meaning 'human being'.

Alternative spellings: Ehnes, Enees

Enoch

Meaning: Dedicated

Origin: Hebrew

Pronunciation: EE nuk

Description: Enoch means 'trained and vowed', 'dedicated and profound'. The name was popular in the early 20th century but has been less common since.

Alternative spellings: Enock

Enrico

Meaning: Home ruler

Origin: Italian

Pronunciation: ehn REE ko

Description: Enrico is a name of German and Italian origin, meaning 'home ruler'. It is regarded as the Italian form of Henry.

Alternative spellings: Enriko, Enrique

Enrique

Meaning: Home ruler

Origin: Spanish

Pronunciation: en REE kay

Description: Enrique is a popular boys' name meaning 'home ruler'. It is the Spanish variant of the name Henry.

Alternative spellings: Enricay, Enrikay

Enzo

Meaning: Ruler of the home

Origin: Italian

Pronunciation: EN zo

Description: Enzo could be considered the shortened form of many Italian names ending with

'enzo', such as Lorenzo. The name could also be the Italian variant of the name Henry, in which case it means 'ruler of the home'.
Alternative spellings: Enso, Enzoh

Eoghan
Meaning: Born of yew; youth
Origin: Gaelic
Pronunciation: YEW en
Description: Eoghan is an old Irish name meaning 'born of yew; youth'. Anglicised variants of the name include Owen.
Alternative spellings: Euan, Ewan, Owen

Eoin
Meaning: God is gracious
Origin: Hebrew
Pronunciation: OH en
Description: Eoin is a Gaelic variant of John, meaning 'God is gracious'. Eoin is derived specifically from the Latin Johan, where the 'j' was pronounced 'y'.
Alternative spellings: Eohin

Ephraim
Meaning: Fruitful
Origin: Hebrew
Pronunciation: EF ram
Description: Ephraim is a popular name for Jewish boys but remains uncommon in the wider UK population. It is of Hebrew origin and is said to mean 'fruitful'.
Alternative spellings: Efraim, Efrayim, Efrem

Eren
Meaning: Saint; holy person
Origin: Turkish
Pronunciation: eh REN

Description: Eren is a Turkish name meaning 'saint' or 'holy person'. It is also likely to be related to the girls' name Erin, which means Eren can be used for both boys and girls as a name choice.

E

Eric
Meaning: Eternal ruler
Origin: Norse
Pronunciation: EH rik
Description: The name Eric is of Old Norse origin. It consists of the words *'ei'* and *'rikr'* and its meaning is 'eternal ruler'. As a given name, Eric arrived on British shores over 1,000 years ago before the Norman Conquest of Britain.
Alternative spellings: Erick, Erik, Eryk

Ernest
Meaning: Sincere
Origin: German
Pronunciation: ER nest
Description: The name Ernest derives from the Old German word *'eornost'* meaning 'serious battle'. The name first spread to England from mainland Europe in the 18th century. The spelling 'Earnest' comes from the modern English adjective of the same spelling, meaning 'sincere'.
Alternative spellings: Earnest

Ernie
Meaning: Serious
Origin: German
Pronunciation: ER nee
Description: Ernie is a variant of the German name Ernest. It was

quite popular as a given name in the early 20th century but is now uncommon.

Alternative spellings: Erne, Erno

Errol
Meaning: Warrior; nobleman
Origin: Scottish
Pronunciation: ERE rol
Description: Errol is the Scottish version of the name Earl, meaning 'warrior' or 'nobleman'. Errol Flynn was a famous Australian-born actor who had this name.

Erwin
Meaning: Army friend
Origin: German
Pronunciation: err WIN
Description: Erwin is a German name derived from the Old German elements of '*heri*' meaning 'army' and '*wini*' meaning 'friend'.
Alternative spellings: Irwin

Esa
Meaning: Faithful
Origin: Hebrew
Pronunciation: ESS ah
Description: This unisex name has several spelling variations. The name appears in the Bible several times but is mostly known as the name of the third king of Judah, who ruled for 40 years.
Alternative spellings: Asa, Isa

Eshaan
Meaning: Worthy
Origin: Arabic
Pronunciation: esh AAN
Description: Eshaan is an uncommon Arabic boys' name meaning 'one who is worthy' or 'one who is in Allah's grace'.
Alternative spellings: Eshaann, Eshan

Eshan
Meaning: Another name for Lord Shiva
Origin: Indian
Pronunciation: EE shan
Description: Eshan is one of the many names of the Hindu god, Lord Shiva. He is one of three major deities in the Hindu religion and is known as 'the Destroyer,' although he is both benevolent and fearsome at the same time.
Alternative spellings: Eeshan, Eshaan

Esme
See entry in 'Names for Baby Girls A–Z'

Essa
See entry in 'Names for Baby Girls A–Z'

Eteocles
Meaning: Truly glorious
Origin: Greek
Pronunciation: e TEE o kleez
Description: In Greek mythology, Eteocles was the son of Oedipus, who became a king of Thebes.
Alternative spellings: Eteokles, Eteucles

Ethan
Meaning: Firm; long-lived
Origin: Hebrew
Pronunciation: EE than
Description: The name Ethan is seen in the Bible. It was popular

in the US in the 18th century following the fame of Ethan Allen, leader of a Vermont patriot group in the American Revolution.
Alternative spellings: Ethen, Ethun

Etienne
Meaning: Crown
Origin: French
Pronunciation: ETT ee en
Description: Etienne is the French variant of Stephen, meaning 'crown'.
Alternative spellings: Eitan, Etien, Ettenne

Euan
Meaning: Born from the yew
Origin: Greek
Pronunciation: YUH wen
Description: Scottish form of the name Eugene. Euan is Celtic for 'born from the yew'.
Alternative spellings: Eoghan, Ewan, Ewen

Eugene
Meaning: Wellborn; noble
Origin: Greek
Pronunciation: YUH jeen
Description: Greek in origin; the common shortened form of Eugene is Gene.
Alternative spellings: Eugen

Eurus
Meaning: The east wind
Origin: Greek
Pronunciation: YOO ros
Description: Eurus (sometimes spelt Euros) is a Greek name that means 'the east wind'. In Greek myth, Eurus is one of the Anemoi, who were the wind gods; each was responsible for a different direction in which the

wind blew. Eurus was associated with autumn, and was found near the palace of the sun god, Helios.
Alternative spellings: Euros

Evan
Meaning: God is gracious
Origin: Hebrew
Pronunciation: EH van
Description: Evan may be considered an anglicised form of the Welsh Iefan, which itself came from Ieuan. These are forms of John and mean 'God is gracious'.
Alternative spellings: Evun

Everly
See entry in 'Names for Baby Girls A–Z'

Everson
Meaning: Son of Everard
Origin: English
Pronunciation: ever SUN
Description: Everson was originally an English name referring to people who were the 'son of Everard'. This follows the contemporary trend of using last names as first names.

Ewan
Meaning: Born from the yew
Origin: Gaelic
Pronunciation: YOO an
Description: Ewan is the anglicised form of Eoghan, or Eugene.
Alternative spellings: Euan, Ewan

Eyad
Meaning: Support; might; strength
Origin: Arabic

E

Pronunciation: EE yad
Description: Eyad is an Arabic boys' name that means 'support,' 'might' and 'strength'.
Alternative spellings: Eyaad

Ezekiel

Meaning: God will provide strength
Origin: Hebrew
Pronunciation: ee ZEE kyul
Description: Ezekiel was the name of a prophet in the Old Testament.

It is Hebrew in origin and is said to mean 'God will provide strength'.
Alternative spellings: Ezekial

Ezra

Meaning: Helpful
Origin: Hebrew
Pronunciation: AIRZ ra
Description: The name Ezra comes from the Hebrew for 'helpful'. It was popular in the 17th century but is now uncommon.
Alternative spellings: Esra, Ezrah

F

Fabian

Meaning: Bean grower
Origin: Latin
Pronunciation: FAY bee en
Description: The name Fabian comes from the Latin surname Fabianus, which is generally held to refer to a family of bean growers. Several Roman emperors have been called this, as well as a total of 16 saints. This is a very popular name over the whole of Europe.
Alternative spellings: Fabien, Fabiun

Fabio

Meaning: Bean grower
Origin: Latin
Pronunciation: FAB ee oh
Description: Fabio is the Spanish equivalent of the name Fabian.
Alternative spellings: Fabeo, Fabyo

Fabrice

Meaning: Craftsman

Origin: French
Pronunciation: fab REECE
Description: Fabrice is a French name derived from the Roman Fabricius, meaning 'craftsman' or someone who worked with their hands.

Fahad

Meaning: Panther
Origin: Arabic
Pronunciation: fah HAHD
Description: Fahad is said to mean 'panther', the connotations of which are of stealth, courage and grace. It is most commonly found in Islamic communities.
Alternative spellings: Fahd

Faheem

Meaning: Mastermind
Origin: Arabic
Pronunciation: fah HEEM

Description: Faheem is an Arabic boys' name, which literally means 'to mastermind'. Faheem hence means 'one who understands with ease and is greatly blessed with wisdom'.
Alternative spellings: Fahim

Faisal

Meaning: Resolute
Origin: Arabic
Pronunciation: FAY saal
Description: Faisal is an Arabic name that means 'resolute'. King Faisal of Saudi Arabia ruled for over 10 years.
Alternative spellings: Faysal, Feisal

Faiz

Meaning: Successful
Origin: Arabic
Pronunciation: FAH eez
Description: Faiz is an uncommon name of Arabic origin, meaning 'successful' or 'victorious'.
Alternative spellings: Faez, Fahiz

Faizaan

Meaning: Generosity; abundance; benefit
Origin: Arabic
Pronunciation: FAY zaan
Description: Faizaan is an uncommon Arabic boys' name meaning 'generosity', 'abundance' or 'benefit'.
Alternative spellings: Fayzaan

Falak

Meaning: Star
Origin: Arabic
Pronunciation: FAL AK
Description: Falak is a unisex name of Arabic origins, meaning 'star'. It

is favoured by Muslim parents and often given as a baby name because of its bright meaning.
Alternative spellings: Falach, Falack

Farhaan

Meaning: Happiness; euphoria
Origin: Arabic
Pronunciation: FAR haan
Description: Farhaan is an Arabic boys' name. The name is said to mean 'happiness' and 'euphoria'.
Alternative spellings: Farhan, Farhann

Farhad

Meaning: Happiness
Origin: Persian
Pronunciation: FAR haad
Description: Farhad was the protagonist of an ancient series of Persian poems depicting his failed attempt to woo Armenian Princess Shirin away from Khosrau II. Its meaning makes it the perfect name for a very happy baby boy.
Alternative spellings: Fahad

Faris

Meaning: Stone
Origin: Greek
Pronunciation: fair IS
Description: As well as being a variant of the name Farris, this name is also the Middle English version of the more traditional name Peter.
Alternative spellings: Fariss, Farris

Faruq

Meaning: One who can distinguish the truth

F

Origin: Arabic
Pronunciation: fah RUK
Description: Faruq is an alternative spelling to the Arabic name Farouk. It means 'one who can distinguish right from wrong; truth from a lie'.
Alternative spellings: Farouk, Farouq

Fateh
Meaning: Conqueror
Origin: Arabic
Pronunciation: FAH tey
Description: Fateh is an Arabic name meaning 'conqueror'.
Alternative spellings: Fatih

Faunus
Meaning: Horned god
Origin: Latin
Pronunciation: fa UH nus
Description: According to ancient Roman myth, Faunus was the horned god of the forest, plains and field.
Alternative spellings: Fanus, Faunas

Federico
Meaning: Peaceful ruler
Origin: Spanish
Pronunciation: fed er EE co
Description: Federico is a Mediterranean boys' name meaning 'peaceful ruler'. It is the Spanish and Italian variant of the German name Frederick.
Alternative spellings: Frederico

Felipe
Meaning: Friend of horses
Origin: Spanish
Pronunciation: FEL eep
Description: Felipe is the Spanish version of the name Philip, which means 'friend of horses'. Felipe is a name that is popular in Brazil.
Alternative spellings: Philip

Felix
Meaning: Happy; fortunate
Origin: Latin
Pronunciation: FEE liks
Description: Felix is a Latin name meaning 'happy and fortunate'. It managed to penetrate Western culture largely thanks to its positive undertones.
Alternative spellings: Felicks, Felics

Fenton
Meaning: Settlement on the marsh
Origin: English
Pronunciation: FEN ton
Description: Fenton is an English surname meaning 'settlement on the marsh'. Though uncommon, it is sometimes used as a boys' given name.
Alternative spellings: Fennton, Fentonn, Fentton

Fergus
Meaning: Man of force
Origin: Gaelic
Pronunciation: FUR gus
Description: Fergus is a name of Gaelic origin, and has been popular in both Ireland and Scotland for many years. It is said to mean 'man of force,' and was the name given to an Irish prince who crossed the sea to settle in Argyll, Scotland. It is once again proving popular across the UK.

Fernando

Meaning: Intelligent
Origin: Spanish
Pronunciation: fehr NAN doh
Description: Fernando is a boys' given name of Spanish origin, meaning 'intelligent' and 'brave'. It is a popular name in Spain.
Alternative spellings: Fernandho, Fernandoh

Fernley

Meaning: Fern field
Origin: English
Pronunciation: fern LEE
Description: Fernley is an Old English name meaning 'fern field' or 'fern meadow'. This is a name that follows the historical trend of using place names as first names.

Filip

Meaning: Lover of horses
Origin: Greek
Pronunciation: FIL ip
Description: Filip is a Polish variation of the Greek name Phillip. The use of the version spelt Filip is unusual in Britain with Phillip being the more prominent version.
Alternative spellings: Philip, Phillip

Finbar

Meaning: Fair-haired
Origin: Irish
Pronunciation: fin BAR
Description: Finbar is derived from the Old Irish word 'fionn-bharr' meaning 'fair-haired'. The shortened, anglicised version of the name is Barry.
Alternative spellings: Finbarr, Finbarre, Finnbar

Finch

Meaning: Bird
Origin: English
Pronunciation: finch
Description: Finch comes from the bird of the same name. In the Middle Ages, these birds were often caught and sold as songbirds or to cook them, so the name may be an occupational name referring to the people who captured the birds.

Findlay

Meaning: Fair-haired courageous one
Origin: Gaelic
Pronunciation: FIND lay
Description: Findlay is a variant of the Gaelic name Finlay, which is an Irish surname meaning 'fair-haired courageous one'. Though uncommon, it is sometimes used as a boys' given name.
Alternative spellings: Findley, Finlay, Fyndlay, Fynley

Finn

Meaning: Fair-haired
Origin: Gaelic
Pronunciation: FIN
Description: Finn, an Irish boys' name, is derived from the Gaelic word 'fionn' meaning 'fair'.
Alternative spellings: Fin, Phin

Finnian

Meaning: Fair
Origin: Gaelic
Pronunciation: FINN i an
Description: Finnian is an uncommon boys' name of Irish and Gaelic origin meaning 'fair'. It is a variant of the more popular spelling, Finian.

Alternative spellings: Finian,
Finyan, Phinnian

Fintan
Meaning: Little fair one
Origin: Gaelic
Pronunciation: FIN tan
Description: Fintan is an uncommon Irish boys' name of Gaelic origin. It means 'little fair one'.
Alternative spellings: Finton,
Fintun

Fionn
Meaning: Fair
Origin: Gaelic
Pronunciation: FYE on
Description: Fionn is a variant of the Gaelic boys' name Finbar. The name is understood to mean 'white or fair hair; fair'.
Alternative spellings: Ffion, Fion,
Fyon

Fisher
Meaning: One who fishes
Origin: English
Pronunciation: fish ER
Description: Fisher was an English occupational surname given to those who fished for a living. Like Taylor and Hunter, these occupational names are very popular modern baby name choices.

Fletcher
Meaning: Arrow maker
Origin: English
Pronunciation: FLETCH er
Description: The name Fletcher first came into use as a surname in England in the Middle Ages, used to describe a maker of arrows. This is because the

Old French word *'fletch'* means 'arrow'.
Alternative spellings: Fletcha

Florian
Meaning: Blooming; flowering
Origin: Latin
Pronunciation: floor EE an
Description: Florian is a Latin name that comes from the Roman name Florianus. The prefix 'flōs' suggests the blooming or flowering of plants.
Alternative spellings: Florien

Flynn
Meaning: Red-haired
Origin: Gaelic
Pronunciation: FLIN
Description: Flynn is a unisex name and also a common surname, first recorded in 1255. It is popular in Ireland.
Alternative spellings: Flinn,
Flinne, Flyn

Ford
Meaning: Someone who lives near a ford
Origin: English
Pronunciation: ford
Description: Ford is an old English surname that refers to someone who lived near a ford. It is now better known as a famous American car manufacturer.

Forrest
Meaning: Forest
Origin: English
Pronunciation: FAWR est
Description: Forrest is from an English surname meaning 'forest,' which belonged to someone who

lived near a forest. The world's most famous Forrest is perhaps Forrest Gump, played by Tom Hanks in the 1994 movie of the same name.

Alternative spellings: Forest

Foster

Meaning: Forester
Origin: English
Pronunciation: fos TUR
Description: Foster is an old English occupational name that refers to someone who keeps the forest. Like Taylor or Hunter, Foster can now be used as a first name choice.

Fox

Meaning: Animal of the same name
Origin: English
Pronunciation: fahks
Description: Fox is most likely from the English word of the same meaning, referring to the animal. It can also be used as a nickname or a surname, such as George Fox, the founder of the Quakers.

Fran

See entry in 'Names for Baby Girls A–Z'

Francesco

Meaning: Free man
Origin: Italian
Pronunciation: fran CHESS co
Description: Francesco is the most common boys' name in Italy. It has seen a rise in popularity in England in recent years. It is the Italian variant of the French name Francis. The name means 'free man'.

Alternative spellings: Franchesco, Franchesko

Francis

Meaning: From France
Origin: Latin
Pronunciation: FRAN sis
Description: The name Francis derives from an Italian nickname for someone from France. History suggests that St Francis of Assisi is the original bearer of this name. He was originally baptised Giovanni but was renamed by his father when he returned from France.

Alternative spellings: Franciss, Fransis

Francisco

Meaning: Free man
Origin: Latin
Pronunciation: fran CEES co
Description: Francisco is a name of Latin origin. It has seen a rise in popularity in England in recent years. It is the Spanish variant of the French name Francis. The name means 'free man'.

Alternative spellings: Francesco, Franchesco, Franchesko

Franciszek

Meaning: From France
Origin: Latin
Pronunciation: FRAN cee shek
Description: This Polish variation of the name Francis is rare in Britain but popular in Poland.

Alternative spellings: Franciszeck

Franco

Meaning: Name of German tribe
Origin: Italian
Pronunciation: FRANC oh

Description: Franco is a common Italian surname and given name. It is closely related to the name Frank, which refers to the old Germanic tribe called the Franks, who invaded modern-day France.
Alternative spellings: Franko

Frank

Meaning: Spear; sincere
Origin: German
Pronunciation: FRANK
Description: Frank is an English form of the French name 'Francois', from the German tribe the Franks. The name was first derived from the German for 'spear' or 'javelin'. As an English vocabulary word, Frank also has the meaning of 'sincere'.
Alternative spellings: Franke

Frankie

See entry in 'Names for Baby Girls A–Z'

Franklin

Meaning: Liberated
Origin: English
Pronunciation: FRAN klen
Description: The name Franklin comes from an Old English word meaning 'liberated'. In medieval England a franklin was a man who owned his own portion of land but was not a man of gentility. Franklin owes its use as a first name to American Benjamin Franklin, as people named their children in honour of him.
Alternative spellings: Franklen, Franklyn

Franky

Meaning: He who is free

Origin: French
Pronunciation: FRAN kee
Description: Frankie as a name in itself is perhaps most widely used as a girls' name, whereas Franky is most usually the pet form of one of the masculine French names, either Frank or Francis – both of which share the meaning 'He who is free'. Frankie may be popularised by the fame of The Saturdays' singer Frankie Bridge.
Alternative spellings: Frankie

Fraser

Meaning: Unknown
Origin: English
Pronunciation: FRAY zer
Description: Fraser is a Scottish surname transferred into a given name. It is ultimately derived from the Norman place name and is of uncertain meaning.
Alternative spellings: Frasier, Frazer

Frazer

Meaning: Of the forest men
Origin: French
Pronunciation: fr aa SHER
Description: Frazer is a variant of the male name Fraser. There is also a possible Old English meaning belonging to the name and it is that of 'curly hair'. Although the name is close to the French word *fraise* meaning strawberry, it is not believed to have any association.
Alternative spellings: Fraiser

Fred

Meaning: Peaceful ruler
Origin: English

Pronunciation: FRED
Description: A short form of Alfred and Frederick, now given as a first name in its own right.
Alternative spellings: Fread

Freddie
Meaning: Peaceful ruler
Origin: German
Pronunciation: FRED dee
Description: A pet form of Frederick, Fred and occasionally Frederica, the name Freddie is now seen as a unisex given name.

Alternative spellings: Freddi, Freddy

Frederick
Meaning: Peaceful ruler
Origin: German
Pronunciation: FRED ur rik
Description: Frederic is of Old German origin and is comprised of the words for 'peace' and 'ruler'. The name failed following its Norman introduction, but was resurrected in the 18th century.
Alternative spellings: Frederic, Frederik, Fredric, Fredrick, Fredrik

G

Gabriel
Meaning: Strength from God
Origin: Hebrew
Pronunciation: GAY bree uhl
Description: A biblical name borne by archangel Gabriel, who according to the Old Testament appeared to Daniel after he was thrown into the lion's den. In the New Testament, Gabriel announced Christ's immaculate conception to Mary.
Alternative spellings: Gabrial

Gael
Meaning: Irishman
Origin: Gaelic
Pronunciation: GUY el
Description: Gael is a Gaelic name that refers to a group of people from a Celtric tribe and, as such, means 'Irishman'.

Gage
Meaning: Oath
Origin: French
Pronunciation: GAY ge
Description: Gage is a French name created in the 14th century that means 'oath' or 'pledge'. It was a surname originally but has become a first name in modern times.

Gale
Meaning: Father of exaltation
Origin: Hebrew
Pronunciation: GAYL
Description: Gale, the male form of the girls' name Gail, is a character in the hugely popular *Hunger Games*, book and film, and because of that may be a popular choice for boys.
Alternative spellings: Gael

Gareth
Meaning: Gentle
Origin: Welsh
Pronunciation: GA reth
Description: Gareth was first seen in the 15th century in Malory's Morte d'Arthur tales and is said to mean 'gentle'.
Alternative spellings: Garreth

Garrett
Meaning: Spear strength
Origin: German
Pronunciation: GARE ett
Description: Garrett is a name that is derived from the German elements of 'gēr' meaning 'spear' and 'hard' or 'strong'. While it is usually found as a surname in the UK, it is a popular given name choice in the US.
Alternative spellings: Garret

Gary
Meaning: Spear
Origin: German
Pronunciation: GA ree
Description: Gary was originally a surname that derived from the Old English word 'gar' meaning 'spear'.
Alternative spellings: Garey, Garry

Gavin
Meaning: White hawk
Origin: Welsh
Pronunciation: GAV en
Description: Gavin is a popular British boys' name derived from the Welsh name Gawain, meaning 'white hawk'.
Alternative spellings: Gavan, Gaven, Gavyn

Gene
Meaning: Noble
Origin: Greek

Pronunciation: JEEN
Description: Gene is a unisex name derived from the masculine name Eugene.
Alternative spellings: Gine, Jean

George
Meaning: Farmer
Origin: Greek
Pronunciation: JORJ
Description: St George is the patron saint of England, and is well known from the legend of St George and the dragon. Popularity was bolstered in the 18th century when George I became king of England.
Alternative spellings: Jeorge, Jorge

Georgie
Meaning: Farmer
Origin: Greek
Pronunciation: JORGE ee
Description: Georgie is used as a pet name for the names George, Georgina and Georgiana. The names are commonly associated with knighthood and chivalry due to heavy use of the name in legends associated with dragons.
Alternative spellings: Georgi, Georgy, Jorgie, Jorgy

Gerard
Meaning: Strength of the spear
Origin: German
Pronunciation: JEH rard
Description: Gerard is a boys' given name of German origin, popular in English-speaking countries. The name means 'strength of the spear'.
Alternative spellings: Geraud, Gerrard, Jerard

Gethin

Meaning: Dark
Origin: Welsh
Pronunciation: GETH in
Description: A Welsh name that would have originally been given as a surname, but eventually developed into a first name. Welsh names went out of popularity until the 19th century, and Gethin has been popular since.

Gian

Meaning: God is gracious
Origin: Hebrew
Pronunciation: Jee ahn
Description: Gian is a unisex name of Hebrew and Italian origin. It is commonly used as the shortened form of Giovanni or other names starting with Gian-.
Alternative spellings: Giann, Jian

Gianluca

Meaning: John Luke
Origin: Italian
Pronunciation: jee an LEW ka
Description: Gianluca is an Italian boys' name that translates into English as 'John Luke'. It is the shortened version of Giovanni Luca.
Alternative spellings: Gianluka

Gianni

Meaning: God is gracious
Origin: Hebrew
Pronunciation: jee AN nee
Description: Gianni is a name of Hebrew and Italian origin. It is a variant of the name Giovanni, which means 'God is gracious'.
Alternative spellings: Giani, Jianni

Gibson

Meaning: Son of Gib
Origin: Scottish
Pronunciation: GIB sun
Description: Gibson is a Scottish name and refers to someone who was the son of Gib (or Gilbert).

Gideon

Meaning: Mighty warrior
Origin: Greek
Pronunciation: Gid EE On
Description: This name derives from the transcription of Gidon in Hebrew, which means 'mighty warrior'. The name is also in the Old Testament and belongs to an Israelite judge. For this reason it is seen as a very biblical name.
Alternative spellings: Gidion

Gilbert

Meaning: Bright promise
Origin: French
Pronunciation: GILL bert
Description: Gilbert is the English variant of the French name of the same spelling. The French pronunciation has a soft 'g' making it sound like 'Jilber'. It was popular at the beginning of the 20th century but is far less common in recent years.
Alternative spellings: Gilburt, Guilbert

Giles

Meaning: Small goat
Origin: Greek
Pronunciation: JYE ulls
Description: Giles is a common surname in England, and was once a relatively popular given name. It refers to goatskin

G

from which ancient shields were made.
Alternative spellings: Gilles, Gyles, Jiles, Jyles

Giorgio
Meaning: Farmer
Origin: Greek
Pronunciation: JIYOR jiyo
Description: Giorgio is a boys' given name of Greek and Italian origin. It is a variant of the Greek name George, meaning 'farmer'.
Alternative spellings: Georgio, Giorgi

Giovanni
Meaning: God is gracious
Origin: Italian
Pronunciation: GEE oh VAR nee
Description: Giovanni is the Italian form of the name John, which means 'God is gracious'.
Alternative spellings: Giovani, Giovannie

Glen
Meaning: Valley
Origin: Gaelic
Pronunciation: GLEN
Description: Glen is a boys' name coined from the Scottish word 'glen', meaning 'valley'.
Alternative spellings: Glenn

Glyn
Meaning: Valley
Origin: Welsh
Pronunciation: GLIN
Description: Taken from the Welsh word 'glyn', meaning 'valley', this boys' name is mostly found in Wales.
Alternative spellings: Glin, Glynn

Gordon
Meaning: Place name; hill
Origin: Scottish, English
Pronunciation: GORE dun
Description: Thought to be derived from one of a number of place names, including Gordon in Berwickshire.
Alternative spellings: Gordan, Gorden

Gracie
See entry in 'Names for Baby Girls A–Z'

Gracjan
Meaning: Grace
Origin: Polish
Pronunciation: GRAY shan
Description: Gracjan is an uncommon Polish boys' name meaning 'grace'.
Alternative spellings: Gracian, Graczan

Grady
Meaning: Noble
Origin: Irish
Pronunciation: GRAY dee
Description: Grady is a name of Irish origin and comes from the Irish word 'gráda' meaning 'noble'. This name is a popular given name choice in the US.

Graham
Meaning: Gravel homestead
Origin: English
Pronunciation: GRAY am
Description: The name Graham is of Scottish origin, and was originally a surname. It is thought to have been related to Grantham, Lincolnshire.
Alternative spellings: Grayham, Greham

Grayson

Meaning: Son of grey-haired man
Origin: English
Pronunciation: GRAY sun
Description: Grayson is an increasingly popular boys' name of Old English origin. The name, and similar variants such as Carson, have seen a surge of popularity in America over the last 20 years.
Alternative spellings: Graysen, Greyson

Greg

Meaning: Watchful
Origin: Greek
Pronunciation: greg
Description: Greg is a short form of the name Gregory, a Greek name that means 'watchful' or 'alert'. Both names come from the Latin name Grēgorios.
Alternative spellings: Gregg

Gregor

Meaning: Vigilant
Origin: Greek
Pronunciation: GREY gor
Description: Gregor is a variant of the popular Greek name Gregory. Gregor is widely used as a surname but is less common as a given name in recent years.
Alternative spellings: Greger, Grigor, Grygor

Gregory

Meaning: Sentry
Origin: Greek
Pronunciation: GREG ger ree
Description: Gregory comes from a Greek word meaning 'sentry'. It was introduced to England by St Gregory the Great and has been a popular boys' name since the Norman Conquest.
Alternative spellings: Gregorey, Gregorie

Greyson

Meaning: Son of a grey-haired man
Origin: English
Pronunciation: GRAY sun
Description: Greyson is a variation of the name Grayson. The name has Old English roots, and as the name itself suggests, the meaning refers to a man who is the 'son of a grey-haired man'.
Alternative spellings: Grayson

Griff

Meaning: Lord; prince
Origin: English
Pronunciation: Griff
Description: Griff is a variation, and the English form of the Welsh name Gruffudd, meaning 'lord' or 'prince'. It can also be a nickname for the names Griffin and Griffith.

Griffith

Meaning: Lord; strong fighter
Origin: Welsh
Pronunciation: GRIH fith
Description: Griffith is a name of Welsh origin meaning lord, strong fighter or strong leader.
Alternative spellings: Griffeth, Gruffudd, Gruffydd

Gruffydd

Meaning: Lord
Origin: Welsh
Pronunciation: gruf FITH
Description: Gruffydd is the old Welsh form of the name Griffith. Both are considered to be equally

G

141

standard forms of the same name. Unlike Griffith, Gruffydd is very uncommon in recent years.
Alternative spellings: Griffith

Guillermo
Meaning: Protection
Origin: Spanish
Pronunciation: GEE eyre mo
Description: Guillermo is the Spanish version of the name William, and as such shares the same meaning of 'protection'. Guillermo del Toro is a famous Mexican film director.

Gunnar
Meaning: Fighter; soldier; warrior
Origin: Nordic
Pronunciation: GOON ar
Description: Gunnar is a popular Nordic first name composed of the elements of 'gunnr' meaning 'war' and 'arr' meaning 'warrior'.
Alternative spellings: Gunar

Gus
Meaning: Strong choice
Origin: Gaelic
Pronunciation: GUS
Description: Gus is often a diminutive for names such as Angus, August, Augustine or Augustus. However, it can also be a standalone name that is derived from the Old Irish word 'gusmhar' or

'gusair' meaning 'strength' or 'force' and 'gusto' meaning 'choice'.

Guto
Meaning: Lord; prince
Origin: Welsh
Pronunciation: gi TAW
Description: Guto is the diminutive of the Welsh name Gruffudd. The name is derived from two Welsh elements – the first part is of uncertain meaning, but 'udd' means 'lord' or 'prince'. It was a common name among medieval Welsh royalty.

Guy
Meaning: Guide
Origin: French
Pronunciation: GAI
Description: The name Guy derives from the French word for 'guide', 'guider'. It is also British slang for a man.

Gwion
Meaning: Anger
Origin: Welsh
Pronunciation: GWUY on
Description: Gwion is an uncommon Welsh name derived from the Welsh boys' name Gavin.
Alternative spellings: Gawion, Gwain

H

Haaris
Meaning: Vigilant guard
Origin: Arabic
Pronunciation: haah REES

Description: Haaris, not to be mistaken for the English Harris, is a masculine name of Arabic origin. It is a variant form of the name

Haris and both are said to mean 'vigilant guard'.
Alternative spellings: Haahris

Habib
Meaning: Beloved one
Origin: Arabic
Pronunciation: ha BEEB
Description: Habib is the masculine version of the Arabic name Habiba. Habib can also be considered a shortened form of the name Habibullah.
Alternative spellings: Habeeb

Hadi
Meaning: True direction
Origin: Arabic
Pronunciation: HAH dee
Description: Hadi is a masculine name of Arabic origin and it is said to mean 'true direction'.
Alternative spellings: Hadie, Haydi

Hadley
Meaning: Heather meadow
Origin: English
Pronunciation: HAD ley
Description: Hadley is an uncommon given name but a popular surname. It is of Old English origin meaning 'heather meadow'.
Alternative spellings: Hadlee, Hadleigh, Hadli, Hadlie, Hadly

Haidar
Meaning: Lion
Origin: Arabic
Pronunciation: HAY dar
Description: Haidar is an uncommon Arabic boys' name meaning 'lion'.
Alternative spellings: Haider, Haydar, Hyder

Haider
Meaning: Lion
Origin: Arabic
Pronunciation: HAY dar
Description: Haidar is an uncommon Arabic boys' name meaning 'lion'.
Alternative spellings: Hayder

Hakeem
Meaning: Wise
Origin: Arabic
Pronunciation: hah KEEM
Description: Hakeem is a common Arabic boys' name meaning 'wise' or 'intelligent'.
Alternative spellings: Hakim

Hammand
Meaning: Praiseworthy
Origin: Arabic
Pronunciation: HAH mad
Description: Hammad is an uncommon Arabic boys' name that is a variant of the Arabic name Mohammed, after the prophet Muhammad.
Alternative spellings: Hamad

Hamid
Meaning: Praiseworthy
Origin: Arabic
Pronunciation: HAH meed
Description: Hamid is a common Arabic surname and is sometimes used as a given name for baby boys. When spelt with an additional 'a' (Haamid), the name takes on a new meaning as 'praiser (of God)'.
Alternative spellings: Haamid, Hammad, Hameed, Hammid

Hamish
Meaning: Supplanter
Origin: Gaelic

H

Pronunciation: HAY mish
Description: Hamish is a name deriving from the Gaelic name Seamus and is the Scottish equivalent of the English name James. Hamish can be seen as a surname or a given name.
Alternative spellings: Hamishe, Hammish

Hamza

Meaning: Steadfast
Origin: Arabic
Pronunciation: HAM zuh
Description: It is possible that this name derives from the Arabic word *'hamuza'*, which means 'strong'. This name was used by one of Muhammad's uncles and is favoured by Muslim parents. Hamza is also a letter in the Arabic alphabet.
Alternative spellings: Hamzah

Hank

Meaning: Home ruler
Origin: English
Pronunciation: HANK
Description: Hank is a diminutive form of the name Henry, but has been a rather uncommon name in the UK and is more commonly found in the United States.

Hansel

Meaning: God is gracious
Origin: German
Pronunciation: han SELL
Description: Hansel is a variation of the German name Hans, meaning 'God is gracious'. It is also found in the popular Brothers Grimm children's story, 'Hansel and Gretel', about a pair of siblings captured by an evil witch who wants to eat them.

Hansen

Meaning: Son of Hans
Origin: Scandinavian
Pronunciation: han SON
Description: Hansen is a popular surname in Scandinavian countries, particularly Denmark, and means 'son of Hans'. This follows the contemporary trend of using last names as first names.
Alternative spellings: Hanson

Hao

Meaning: The good
Origin: Chinese
Pronunciation: HOW
Description: Hao is an uncommon boys' given name of Chinese origin, meaning 'the good'. The name can be spelt in a variety of ways but all are uncommon in English-speaking countries.
Alternative spellings: Hao, Hau, Hauo

Hari

Meaning: Colour
Origin: Sanskrit
Pronunciation: Hah ree
Description: Hari is considered a unisex name and has the bright meaning of 'colour'. The name is sometimes used as an alternative to Vishnu and Krishna. Hari could also be considered a respelling of the popular boys' name Harry, meaning 'ruler of the home'.
Alternative spellings: Harie, Harri, Harrie, Harry

Haris

Meaning: Son of Harry
Origin: English
Pronunciation: HA ris

Description: Haris would have been a name originally given to someone whose father was called Harry. It is an alternative spelling to Harris, and would have been a surname before it became a first name.
Alternative spellings: Harris

Harlan
Meaning: From the hare's land
Origin: English
Pronunciation: HAAR lahn
Description: Harlan is an English name meaning 'from the hare's land'.
Alternative spellings: Harlen

Harley
Meaning: Clearing of stones
Origin: English
Pronunciation: HAR lee
Description: Harley was originally a surname but was transferred to a boys' first name. Harley has recently become a popular name for girls, too.
Alternative spellings: Harlee, Harli, Harlie, Harly

Harlow
Meaning: Rocky hill
Origin: English
Pronunciation: HAR low
Description: Harlow was originally given as a surname to those who lived near a rocky hill. Due to the trend for surnames as first names, Harlow is now found as a unisex given name.
Alternative spellings: Hahlow, Harlo

Harman
Meaning: Grey man
Origin: English

Pronunciation: HAR man
Description: Harman is a known surname in America and England but a less popular given name. It is of Old English origin meaning 'grey man', where it is believed to have derived from Hardman.
Alternative spellings: Harmann, Harmen, Harmon, Harmonn

Harold
Meaning: Army leader
Origin: Norse
Pronunciation: HA rold
Description: Harold is an Old English name ultimately of Scandinavian origin, from the Old Norse name 'Haraldr'. Harold is often shortened to the popular boys' name Harry.
Alternative spellings: Harald, Harrold

Haroon
Meaning: Strong mountain
Origin: Hebrew
Pronunciation: HAH roon
Description: Haroon is a phonetic variation of the name Haroun. It is thought that both of these names mean 'strong mountain'.
Alternative spellings: Haroone, Haroun

Harper
See entry in 'Names for Baby Girls A–Z'

Harri
Meaning: Home ruler
Origin: German
Pronunciation: hah REE
Description: Modern spelling of the name Harry. Harry started as a nickname for Henry but became

H

a name in it own right. A popular name in modern times, its usage has increased from 2001 potentially due to the popularity of J.K. Rowling's fictional wizard Harry Potter.
Alternative spellings: Harry

Harrison
Meaning: Son of Harry
Origin: English
Pronunciation: HAH risson
Description: Harrison originated as a surname, meaning 'son of Harry'.
Alternative spellings: Harrison, Harrysson

Harris
Meaning: Son of Harry
Origin: English
Pronunciation: HA ris
Description: Harris is an English name that would have been given to someone whose father was called Harry. It was previously interchangeable with Harrison, but both have now become names in their own right. It is more commonly seen as a surname.
Alternative spellings: Haris

Harry
Meaning: Ruler of the home
Origin: German
Pronunciation: HAH ree
Description: Harry originated as a pet form of Henry, but has long since been a name in its own right. Since the publication of J.K. Rowling's first Harry Potter book in 1997, the name has grown in popularity.
Alternative spellings: Hari, Harie, Harri, Harrie

Harun
Meaning: Strong mountain
Origin: Arabic
Pronunciation: hah ROON
Description: The name Harun is Arabic in origin and thought to be linked with the Hebrew name Aaron. It may have the meaning 'strong mountain'.
Alternative spellings: Haaron, Haarun, Haron

Harvey
Meaning: Battleworthy
Origin: English
Pronunciation: HAR vee
Description: Originally a surname, Harvey is gaining popularity as a first name.
Alternative spellings: Harvay, Harvi, Harvie, Harvy

Hasan
Meaning: Good; beautiful
Origin: Arabic
Pronunciation: ha SAN
Description: Hasan is an Arabic name meaning 'good' or 'beautiful'. There are, in fact, two different spellings of Hasan although both have similar meanings – Hasan is the more common name, while Hassaan is the variation.
Alternative spellings: Hassan, Hassaan

Haseeb
Meaning: Respected
Origin: Arabic
Pronunciation: hah SEEB
Description: Haseeb is generally taken to mean 'respected' and is a popular name in Pakistan.
Alternative spellings: Hasibe, Hazeeb

Hashim

Meaning: Force for good
Origin: Arabic
Pronunciation: ha SHEEM
Description: Hashim is a commonly found family name in the Middle East, but is also used as a given name. Hashim was the title given to the great-grandfather of the prophet Muhammad.
Alternative spellings: Hasheem, Hashime

Hashir

Meaning: Collector
Origin: Arabic
Pronunciation: hah SHEER
Description: Hashir is a common Arabic surname. The name Hashir is another name for the prophet Muhammad or 'one who collects or gathers'.
Alternative spellings: Hasheer, Hashiir

Hasnain

Meaning: Handsome
Origin: Arabic
Pronunciation: HAS na IYN
Description: Hasnain was developed as a mixture of the Arabic names Hussain and Hassan. Generally the name Hasnain means 'handsome one'.
Alternative spellings: Hasnane

Hassan

Meaning: Handsome
Origin: Arabic
Pronunciation: HAH san
Description: Hassan is a popular boys' name in Arabic culture and is said to mean 'handsome'. Hasani is a Swahili variant of this name.
Alternative spellings: Hasan, Hasani

Hayden

Meaning: Hedged valley
Origin: English
Pronunciation: HAY den
Description: A unisex name that means 'hedged valley'. In German, the meaning of the name is 'pagan'.
Alternative spellings: Haiden, Haydn, Heydan, Haydon, Heydon

Haytham

Meaning: Young eagle
Origin: Arabic
Pronunciation: HAY tham
Description: Haytham is an uncommon boys' given name of Arabic origin, meaning 'young eagle' or 'lion'.
Alternative spellings: Haaytham, Haythaam

Hazem

Meaning: Firm; resolute
Origin: Arabic
Pronunciation: HAZ um
Description: Hazem is an Arabic boys' name meaning 'firm' or 'resolute'. It is both a surname and a given name in Arabic countries.
Alternative spellings: Hazm, Hazim

Heath

Meaning: Heath; place
Origin: English
Pronunciation: Hee th
Description: Originally used as a surname for those who lived near a heath, the word has now become a well-loved first name for both boys and girls.

H

Alternative spellings: Heathe, Hethe

Heathcliff
Meaning: From the heath cliff
Origin: English
Pronunciation: heeth CLIFF
Description: Heathcliff is an English place name referring to someone who is 'from the heath cliff'. Of course, Heathcliff is also a character in Emily Brontë's novel, *Wuthering Heights*.

Hector
Meaning: Anchor
Origin: Greek
Pronunciation: HEK tor
Description: Latinised form of the Greek Hektor, this name is popular as both a first name and surname. In Greek legend Hector was a Trojan champion killed by Achilles during the Trojan War.
Alternative spellings: Hecktor, Hektor

Helios
Meaning: Sun
Origin: Greek
Pronunciation: HEE lee os
Description: Helios is a name of Greek origin. In Greek mythology, Helios was the god of the sun who rode his chariot across the sky each day.
Alternative spellings: Helius, Hellios

Hemi
Meaning: God is gracious
Origin: Maori
Pronunciation: hemmy
Description: Hemi is of Maori origins and means 'God is gracious'. It is the Maori version of James, and therefore shares the same meaning.
Alternative spellings: Hemy, Hemmy

Henderson
Meaning: Son of Henry
Origin: Scottish
Pronunciation: hen DER sun
Description: Henderson was originally a Scottish last name meaning 'son of Henry'. This is a very common last name in Scotland. This follows the contemporary trend of using last names as first names.

Hendrix
Meaning: Home ruler
Origin: Dutch
Pronunciation: hen DRICKS
Description: Hendrix is the Dutch version of the name Henry, meaning 'home ruler'. Comprised of 'haim' (home) and 'ric' (power; ruler), Henry is a German name adopted by Normans who introduced it to Britain. The name was borne by numerous British kings including Henry VIII in the Tudor period.
Alternative spellings: Hendricks, Henryk

Henley
Meaning: High wood
Origin: English
Pronunciation: HEN lee
Description: The name Henley originated as a place name and then a surname. It is made up of the Old English words *'heah'* meaning 'high' and *'lea'* meaning 'clearing'. It is part of the growing

trend to use surnames as unisex first names.
Alternative spellings: Henlay, Henlee, Henleigh

Henry
Meaning: Ruler of the home
Origin: German
Pronunciation: HEN ree
Description: Henry is a German name adopted by Normans who introduced it to Britain. It quickly became a favoured royal name and was most notoriously borne by King Henry VIII.
Alternative spellings: Henrey, Henri, Henrie

Henryk
Meaning: Home ruler
Origin: Polish
Pronunciation: hen RICK
Description: Henryk is the Polish form of the name Henry, which is originally a German name meaning 'home ruler'. Comprised of haim (home) and ric (power; ruler), Henry is a German name adopted by Normans who introduced it to Britain. A more common spelling variation of this name is Henrick.
Alternative spellings: Hendrix, Hendricks

Hephaestus
Meaning: He who shines by day
Origin: Greek
Pronunciation: heh FYE stuss
Description: In Greek mythology, Hephaestus was the god of technology, blacksmiths, craftsmen and fire.
Alternative spellings: Hephaestos, Hephastus, Hephestus

Heracles
Meaning: Glory of Hera
Origin: Greek
Pronunciation: HER ah kleez
Description: In Greek mythology, Heracles was a divine hero and the son of Zeus.
Alternative spellings: Heraclus, Herakles, Hercules

Herb
Meaning: Bright warrior
Origin: German
Pronunciation: herb
Description: Herb is a German name and a shortened form of Herbert, so the name shares the same meaning of 'bright warrior'. It can also refer to the English vocabulary word of the same name.

Herbert
Meaning: Famous soldier
Origin: German
Pronunciation: HER bert
Description: The name Herbert is derived from the Germanic words *'hari'* and *'berht'* meaning 'soldier'.
Alternative spellings: Herburt

Herbie
Meaning: Famous soldier
Origin: German
Pronunciation: HER bee
Description: Herbie is the pet form of the masculine name Herbert. It became popular in the 19th century when it became fashionable to adopt aristocratic surnames as given names.
Alternative spellings: Herbi, Herby

Hercules
Meaning: Glory of Hera
Origin: Latin

H

Pronunciation: HERK yoo lees
Description: Hercules is the Roman name for the Greek demi-god Heracles.
Alternative spellings: Heracles, Heraclus, Herakles

Hermes
Meaning: Travel
Origin: Greek
Pronunciation: HER meez
Description: In Greek mythology, Hermes was the god of travellers, shepherds, literature and commerce.
Alternative spellings: Hermees, Hermeez

Heston
Meaning: From Heston
Origin: English
Pronunciation: HES ton
Description: Heston is an English surname and occasional given name. It literally means 'from Heston', which is a borough of London.
Alternative spellings: Hesston, Hestan, Hestonn

Hippolytus
Meaning: Loosener of horses
Origin: Greek
Pronunciation: hee POL ee tus
Description: In Greek mythology, Hippolytus was cursed by his own father, Theseus, and subsequently was dragged under the ocean's waves by horses.
Alternative spellings: Hippolitus

Hira
Meaning: Diamond
Origin: Sanskrit
Pronunciation: HIH rar; HIH rah

Description: The name Hira can be used for both boys and girls and comes from an old Sanskrit word said to mean 'diamond'. The masculine form is pronounced 'hih-rar' whereas the feminine form is pronounced 'hih-ra'.
Alternative spellings: Hirah, Hirra

Hirohi
Meaning: Abundant benevolence
Origin: Japanese
Pronunciation: hee RO hee
Description: This Japanese name can be written using the character 'hiro', which means 'abundant', and 'hito', meaning 'benevolence'. We can therefore take the name to mean 'abundant benevolence'.
Alternative spellings: Hirohie

Hiroki
Meaning: Wide trees
Origin: Japanese
Pronunciation: hee RO key
Description: Hiroki can be written using the Japanese character 'hiro' when it means 'large and wide' with 'ki', meaning 'woods' – to mean 'large woods'. It is also possible to write it 'hiro' for 'abundance' and 'ki' for 'radiance' – to mean 'abundant radiance'.
Alternative spellings: Hirokie

Hiromi
Meaning: Abundant beauty
Origin: Japanese
Pronunciation: hi row mee
Description: Hiromi is a unisex name often found in Japan. It consists of the characters 'hiro', meaning 'abundance', and 'mi', meaning 'beauty'.

Alternative spellings: Hiromie, Hiromy

Hiromitsu
Meaning: Large light
Origin: Japanese
Pronunciation: hee ROW mee tsoo
Description: The name Hiromitsu is made up of the Japanese characters *'hiro'* and *'mitsu'*. *'Hiro'* can either mean 'wide and large' or 'abundance', while *'mitsu'* could mean 'ray of light' or 'support'.
Alternative spellings: Hiromittsu

Hisham
Meaning: Generous
Origin: Arabic
Pronunciation: HE sham
Description: Hisham is an Arabic boys' name and a variant of Hicham. It is uncommon in English-speaking countries but is quite popular in Morocco.
Alternative spellings: Hicham, Hishaam

Honor
See entry in 'Names for Baby Girls A–Z'

Horatius
Meaning: Hour
Origin: Latin
Pronunciation: hoh RAY tee us
Description: Horatius is an uncommon name of Latin origin.
Alternative spellings: Horatios, Horaytius

Howard
Meaning: Garden worker
Origin: French
Pronunciation: HOW ard
Description: Howard originated as an aristocratic surname and became popular as a first name in the 19th century. It is thought to derive from the French for 'worker with a hoe'.
Alternative spellings: Haward, Howerd

Hubert
Meaning: Clever
Origin: German
Pronunciation: HUGH burt
Description: Although Hubert was a common name in the Middle Ages, it has since diminished in popularity. It is of Old German origin from a word that means 'clever'.
Alternative spellings: Huebert, Hughbert

Hudson
Meaning: Son of Hugh
Origin: English
Pronunciation: HUD sun
Description: Hudson was originally an Old English surname meaning 'son of Hugh'. It has since been adapted as a first name for boys.
Alternative spellings: Hudsonne, Hudsun

Huey
Meaning: Mind; spirit; heart
Origin: German
Pronunciation: HEW ee
Description: Huey is an uncommon boys' given name of German origin, meaning 'mind', 'heart' or 'spirit'. It is a variant of Hugh.
Alternative spellings: Hew, Hughey

H

Hugh

Meaning: Mind; spirit; heart
Origin: German
Pronunciation: HEW
Description: The name Hugh derives from the Old French name Hugues. It has been widely used since the Middle Ages and is the name of various saints.
Alternative spellings: Hue, Huw

Hugo

Meaning: Mind; spirit; heart
Origin: German
Pronunciation: HEW go
Description: Hugo is a Latin diminutive form of the name Hugh. It first emerged as a given name in the 19th century.
Alternative spellings: Hugoe

Humphrey

Meaning: Peaceful warrior
Origin: German
Pronunciation: HUM free
Description: Humphrey is a common surname and an uncommon given name of Old German origin.
Alternative spellings: Humfrey, Humfry, Humphry

Humza

Meaning: Steadfast
Origin: Arabic
Pronunciation: HUM za
Description: Humza is a variant of the popular Arabic boys' name Hamza. Hamza ibn Abd al-Muttalib was one of the prophet Muhammad's uncles, known for his strength and bravery in battle.
Alternative spellings: Hamza, Humzaa

Hunter

Meaning: Hunter
Origin: English
Pronunciation: HUN tur
Description: Hunter comes literally from the English noun. It was originally a surname, given to a family who hunted as a profession, but like a lot of surnames it has been taken up as a boys' name. In its original usage as a first name it was specifically a masculine name, but it has now become popular as a name for both girls and boys.

Huntley

Meaning: From the hunter's meadow
Origin: English
Pronunciation: hunt LEE
Description: Huntley was originally an English surname composed of the Old English elements of '*hunt*' and '*leah*' meaning 'wood' or 'clearing'. This follows the contemporary trend of using last names as first names.

Husnain

Meaning: Good
Origin: Arabic
Pronunciation: hus NAYN
Description: Husnain is a Persian alternative spelling and variant of the popular Arabic boys' name Hussein. It is a diminutive of Hassan, meaning 'good', 'handsome' or 'beautiful'.
Alternative spellings: Husnein, Hussnain, Hussnein

Hussein

Meaning: Handsome
Origin: Arabic
Pronunciation: hu SAYN

Description: Hussein is one of the many variations of the name Hassan. All are of the same Arabic origin, and share meanings of 'worthy' and 'handsome'.
Alternative spellings: Husain, Husayn, Husein, Huseyin, Hussain

Huxley
Meaning: Hugh's meadow
Origin: English
Pronunciation: hux LEE
Description: Huxley is an English male name meaning 'Hugh's meadow'.
Alternative spellings: Huxlee

Huzaifah
Meaning: Small sheep

Origin: Arabic
Pronunciation: huz EYE fah
Description: Huzaifah is an uncommon Arabic boys' name and a modern variant of Huthaifah, meaning 'small sheep'. Huzaifah Ibn Al-Yaman was a companion of the prophet Muhammad.
Alternative spellings: Hudhayfah, Huthaifah, Huzaifa

Hylas
Meaning: Companion
Origin: Greek
Pronunciation: HI lass
Description: In Greek mythology, Hylas served as a companion of Heracles.
Alternative spellings: Hilas, Hylass

H
I

I

Ian
Meaning: God is gracious
Origin: Gaelic
Pronunciation: EE en
Description: Ian originated as the Scottish form of John and is sometimes found spelt Iain, especially in Scotland.
Alternative spellings: Ean, Iain

Ianis
Meaning: God is gracious
Origin: Greek
Pronunciation: YAN iss
Description: Ianis is a variant spelling of the name Yannis, meaning 'God is gracious'. Both are variants of the popular boys name John.
Alternative spellings: Yannis

Iasus
Meaning: Fire bringer
Origin: Greek
Pronunciation: EYE ah suss
Description: In Greek mythology, Iasus was a king of Argos.
Alternative spellings: Iaisos, Iasos

Ibraheem
Meaning: Father of nations
Origin: Arabic
Pronunciation: ib ra HEEM
Description: Ibraheem, a variant of Ibrahim, is the Arabic form of the Hebrew name Abraham.
Alternative spellings: Abraham, Ibrahim, Ibrahime

Icarus
Meaning: He follows

Origin: Greek
Pronunciation: IK ah rus
Description: In Greek mythology, Icarus attempted to escape from King Minos by flying to safety with wings made by his father. Icarus flew too close to the sun, melting the wax that held the wings together, and he fell into the ocean.
Alternative spellings: Icaros, Ikarus

Idris
Meaning: Fiery leader
Origin: Welsh
Pronunciation: ID riss
Description: Idris was the name given to a giant in Welsh legend who was said to have an observatory on Cader Idris. The giant had a feisty nature and so the name carries these connotations.
Alternative spellings: Idrees, Idreez, Idriss, Idriz

Iestyn
Meaning: Righteous
Origin: Latin
Pronunciation: YES tin
Description: Iestyn is a popular name in Wales derived from the Latin word for 'righteous'. The name could also be considered a Welsh variation on the name Justin, which means 'just'.
Alternative spellings: Iestin

Ieuan
Meaning: God is gracious
Origin: Welsh
Pronunciation: YUGH yan
Description: Ieuan is the Welsh version of the popular boys' name John. It is a very uncommon name, even in Wales. It is a unique alternative to Ewan and Ian.

Ifan
Meaning: God is gracious
Origin: Welsh
Pronunciation: EEF an
Description: Ifan is the Welsh variant of the name John, more widely found in its anglicised form Evan. Ifan can also be found as a surname.
Alternative spellings: Ifanne

Iggy
Meaning: Fire
Origin: Latin
Pronunciation: igg EE
Description: Iggy is a name derived from the Latin word '*ignis*' meaning 'fire'. It is sometimes a shortened form of Ignatius.
Alternative spellings: Iggie

Igor
Meaning: Warrior
Origin: Scandinavian
Pronunciation: EYE gore
Description: The name Igor derives from the English name George and is very common in Polish-, German- and Russian-speaking countries. It can also be considered a variation of the Irish, Welsh and Scottish name Ivor.
Alternative spellings: Egor

Ihsan
Meaning: Perfection
Origin: Arabic
Pronunciation: ih SAHN
Description: In Islamic belief the concept of ihsan is to take your inner faith and project it into the world by performing deeds and

duties. The word Ihsan is also found in Hindu belief where it can refer to the third eye of the deity Shiva. As a baby name it means 'perfection'.
Alternative spellings: Isaan, Isan

Ike
Meaning: Laughter
Origin: English
Pronunciation: IYKE
Description: Ike is the shortened version of the name Isaac, and as such, shares the same meaning of 'laughter'.

Ikram
Meaning: Honour
Origin: Arabic
Pronunciation: ih KRAM
Description: Although the name Ikram is unisex, the masculine version is usually spelt Ikraam. The name comes from an Arabic word meaning 'honour' and is mainly found used by Muslim parents.
Alternative spellings: Ickram, Ikraam

Ilias
Meaning: The Lord is my God
Origin: Hebrew
Pronunciation: IH lee as
Description: Ilias is an uncommon name of Hebrew and Arabic origin. It is a variant of Ilyas and Elijah. The name is somewhat popular in Greece.
Alternative spellings: Elijah, Ilyas

Illyrius
Meaning: Cyclops
Origin: Greek
Pronunciation: ill LYE ree us

Description: In Greek mythology, Illyrius was the son of the cyclops Polyphemus.
Alternative spellings: Illirius, Illiryus

Imad
Meaning: Pillar
Origin: Arabic
Pronunciation: EE mahd; IH mad
Description: Imad is an uncommon boys' given name of Arabic origin. The name generally refers to Allah being a pillar or source of great strength.
Alternative spellings: Ihmad, Imaad

Imam
Meaning: Leader
Origin: Arabic
Pronunciation: EE mam
Description: The word imam refers to a leader within the Islamic faith. It could refer to someone claiming to be descended from Muhammad or to a leader of a Muslim community.
Alternative spellings: Emam, Imaam

Iman
Meaning: Faith
Origin: Arabic
Pronunciation: EE man
Description: The name Iman came about as a shortened form of the name Immanuel, itself a variant of the name Emmanuel. The names carry separate meanings although they are both related to faith. Iman originated as a boys' name but is now often found on girls.
Alternative spellings: Eman, Imaan

I

Imran

Meaning: Glorious nation
Origin: Arabic
Pronunciation: EEM ran
Description: This name is a spelling variation from the Hebrew name Amran. The name also derives from the Quran, where the grandfather of Jesus is noted to be called Imran.
Alternative spellings: Amran, Imaran

Indiana

Meaning: India
Origin: English
Pronunciation: in dee AHR nah; in dee ANN ah
Description: Indiana is an elaboration on the feminine name India. However, Indiana is the name of the male character from the Indiana Jones franchise.
Alternative spellings: Indianah, Indyana

Inigo

Meaning: Unknowing
Origin: Spanish
Pronunciation: EE ne go
Description: Inigo is a boys' name popular in Spain. The name is derived from Ignatius, which is thought to come from the Roman name Egnatius, meaning 'unknowing' in Latin.
Alternative spellings: Eneko, Inego, Ingo

Ioan

Meaning: Gift from God
Origin: Welsh
Pronunciation: yo AN
Description: Ioan is the Welsh version of the popular baby name John. It has been popular in Wales for many years, although has only recently become popular in other countries.

Iolo

Meaning: Handsome lord
Origin: Welsh
Pronunciation: eye OH lo
Description: Iolo is the diminutive of Iorwerth, a Welsh boys' name meaning 'handsome lord'. This name is sometimes used as a Welsh form of Edward.
Alternative spellings: Iolyn, Iorwerth

Iona

See entry in 'Names for Baby Girls A–Z'

Iosif

Meaning: God shall add another son
Origin: Romanian
Pronunciation: yo SEEF
Description: Iosif is the Russian, Romanian and Greek form of the biblical name Joseph. The name itself means 'God shall add another son'. It was an important biblical name, although it was uncommon in Britain until the mid-17th century.
Alternative spellings: Yosif, Yousif

Irfan

Meaning: Wisdom
Origin: Arabic
Pronunciation: EER fahn
Description: Irfan is an uncommon boys' given name of Arabic origin, meaning 'wisdom' or 'wise one'.
Alternative spellings: Irfahn, Irrfan

Isaac

Meaning: To laugh
Origin: Hebrew
Pronunciation: EYE zak
Description: Isaac is a biblical name borne by the son of Abraham, who was close to being sacrificed by his father. Instead, a ram was sacrificed, as Abraham had proven his devotion to God.
Alternative spellings: Isaak, Isack, Issac, Izaak

Isha

Meaning: The Lord
Origin: Sanskrit
Pronunciation: Ee Shaa
Description: Isha can be used as a girls' or boys' name and is often found in India. As a feminine name it means 'woman' and is the name of the goddess Durga, whereas in the male form it means 'the Lord'.
Alternative spellings: Esha, Ishah

Ishaan

Meaning: Guardian of the sun
Origin: Sanskrit
Pronunciation: ee sh AAAN
Description: This male name is predominantly used in Indian speaking countries. It is also a variation of the name Ishan, which can also be spelt Isan. Within the Hindu tradition Ishan is the guardian of the North East and is often associated with Lord Shiva. The Indian meaning of this name is 'guardian of the sun'.
Alternative spellings: Ishan

Ishaaq

Meaning: To laugh

Origin: Muslim
Pronunciation: ee SHAACK
Description: Ishaaq is the Muslim version of the biblical name Isaac, meaning 'to laugh'. Isaac is a biblical name borne by the son of Abraham, who was close to being sacrificed by his father until God changed his mind. Instead, a ram was sacrificed, as Abraham had proven his devotion.
Alternative spellings: Isaac, Issac

Ishan

Meaning: The Lord Vishnu; sun guardian
Origin: Sanskrit
Pronunciation: ee SHAN
Description: Ishan is an increasingly popular Hindi boys' name of Sanskrit origin and the male form of the name Ishana.
Alternative spellings: Eshaan, Ishaan

Ishaq

Meaning: To laugh
Origin: Hebrew
Pronunciation: EES hak
Description: Ishaq is the Arabic variant of the Hebrew name Isaac, which is said to mean 'to laugh'.
Alternative spellings: Ishak

Isaiah

Meaning: Salvation of the Lord
Origin: Aramaic
Pronunciation: eye ZYE ah
Description: Isaiah is a biblical name, and was the name given to one of the sons of Amos. It has slowly been growing in popularity in recent years.
Alternative spellings: Issaiah, Isaia

I

Ismaeel

Meaning: God will hear
Origin: Hebrew
Pronunciation: ees ma EHL
Description: Ismaeel is a variant of the Arabic name Ishmael, which is of Hebrew origin and means 'God will hear'. It is often seen as religious as Ishmael is said to have built the temple of Kaaba in Mecca.
Alternative spellings: Ishmaeel, Ishmael, Ishmail, Ismael, Ismail

Israel

Meaning: God will conquer
Origin: Hebrew
Pronunciation: IZ rale
Description: Israel is used in the Bible as the name of the land of Israel, and is now the name of a state in the Middle East tracing its roots back to this biblical land. It is now used as a unisex given name.
Alternative spellings: Israelle, Israil

Issa

Meaning: Salvation
Origin: African
Pronunciation: Ess ah
Description: Issa is a variant of the African name Essa, meaning 'salvation' or 'protection'. It is a unisex name.
Alternative spellings: Essa, Essah

Ivan

Meaning: God is gracious
Origin: Hebrew
Pronunciation: EYE van
Description: Ivan is the Slavic version of the English name John. Widely used in Russia, it was the name of many rulers, including the infamous 'Ivan the Terrible'.
Alternative spellings: Eivan

Ivo

Meaning: Yew
Origin: French
Pronunciation: EE voh
Description: Ivo is an uncommon name of French and German origin. It is a form of the French name Yves.
Alternative spellings: Ivoh, Yvo

Ivor

Meaning: Bow warrior; archer
Origin: Norse
Pronunciation: EYE vor
Description: Ivor is an Old Norse name that is made up of the elements 'yr' meaning 'bow' and 'arr' meaning 'warrior'. Together, it creates the name's meaning of 'bow warrior'. It was brought to Britain by Scandinavian settlers in the Middle Ages.
Alternative spellings: Ivorr

Iwan

Meaning: God is gracious
Origin: Welsh
Pronunciation: EE wan
Description: Iwan is the Welsh variation of Ivan, which itself comes from the Hebrew name John. Iwan is quite an unusual name as its variants Evan or Ivan are more popular.
Alternative spellings: Ewan, Iwun

Izaan

Meaning: Obedience
Origin: Arabic
Pronunciation: IZ aan
Description: Izaan is an uncommon Arabic name for boys meaning 'obedience' and 'disciplined'.
Alternative spellings: Izan, Izzan

J

Jac

Meaning: God is gracious
Origin: Hebrew
Pronunciation: jak
Description: Jac is an alternative spelling of the popular baby name Jack, which itself was a pet form of John. Whilst Jac is not a common version of the spelling, it has grown in popularity in the UK.
Alternative spellings: Jack

Jace

Meaning: Healer
Origin: Greek
Pronunciation: JAYSS
Description: Jace is a name of Greek origin. The name is increasingly popular as a modern variant form of Jason, which has been in vogue in recent years, along with its counterpart, Jase.
Alternative spellings: Jase, Jayce

Jack

Meaning: God is gracious
Origin: Hebrew
Pronunciation: JAK
Description: Jack was originally a pet form of John, but is now a well-established given name in its own right. It is also sometimes used as an informal pet form of James, perhaps influenced by the French form Jacques. It has been an extremely popular boys' name in England and Wales since 1995.
Alternative spellings: Jak, Jac

Jackson

Meaning: Son of Jack
Origin: English
Pronunciation: JAX sun
Description: Jackson originated as a surname, which meant 'son of Jack', but is now used as a first name in its own right.
Alternative spellings: Jakson, Jaxon

Jacob

Meaning: Supplanter
Origin: Hebrew
Pronunciation: JAY cobb
Description: From the Hebrew name Yaakov. Jacob is a biblical name borne by the cunning son of Isaac and Rebecca. The name has experienced a recent popularity boost due to the character Jacob in the successful Twilight franchise.
Alternative spellings: Jacub, Jakob, Jakub

Jacobi

Meaning: Supplanter
Origin: Hebrew
Pronunciation: jah COH bee
Description: Jacobi is the Ashkenazic Jewish version of the name Jacob and as such, shares the same meaning of 'supplanter'.
Alternative spellings: Jacoby

Jacques

Meaning: He who supplants
Origin: French
Pronunciation: ZHA hk
Description: Jacques is a popular French name and the French variant of James. It is derived from the Latin name Iacobus, which is now commonly referred to as Jacob.

Alternative spellings: Jacque, Jaq, Jaques

Jad
Meaning: Benevolent
Origin: Arabic
Pronunciation: jad
Description: Jad is an Arabic boys' name meaning 'benevolent'. It is also the short form of the name Jadallah.
Alternative spellings: Jaad

Jadon
Meaning: Thankful
Origin: Hebrew
Pronunciation: JAY don
Description: Jadon is a common boys' name that has become increasingly popular in America. The name has many variant forms, all originally more common as surnames, which in recent years have been used as given names.
Alternative spellings: Jaden, Jaeden, Jaedon, Jaidin, Jaidon, Jaydan, Jayden, Jaydon

Jago
Meaning: Supplanter
Origin: Cornish
Pronunciation: jay GOH
Description: Jago is the Cornish version of the name Jacob. From the Hebrew Yaakov, Jacob was borne by the biblical father of twelve sons, who gave their names to the 12 tribes of Israel. Son of Isaac and Rebecca and twin brother of Esae, Jacob was the cunning younger twin who tricked his brother into trading his inheritance for a bowl of soup. He later

tricked his blind, dying father into blessing him instead of Esau.
Alternative spellings: Jaygo

Jaheim
Meaning: Raised up
Origin: Hebrew
Pronunciation: yah HEEM
Description: Jaheim is a name of Hebrew origin, meaning 'raised up'. The name is somewhat popular in America.
Alternative spellings: Jahaim, Jaheem

Jai
Meaning: Champion
Origin: Sanskrit
Pronunciation: JAY
Description: Jai could be the short form of names such as Jaimal, but it is also a name in its own right. Although its meaning is 'champion' when used as a given name, it changes into 'chatty' when used as a pet name.
Alternative spellings: Jay

Jaiden
Meaning: Champion
Origin: Greek
Pronunciation: JAY den
Description: The name Jaiden is thought to be a fairly modern creation, perhaps a combination of the names Hayden and Jai, meaning 'champion'. Although there is a similar Hebrew name, Jadon, there is not thought to be any relation between this and the modern name Jaiden, which only became popular in about the late 1990s.
Alternative spellings: Jadan, Jaden, Jadon, Jaidan, Jaidon, Jaydan, Jayden, Jaydon

Jak

Meaning: Gracious is the Lord
Origin: Hebrew
Pronunciation: jak
Description: Jak is a spelling variant of the name Jack, which is derived as a pet form of the name John. John is Hebrew in origin and means 'gracious is the Lord'. Jak is the more unusual spelling of the name, and the version Jack has been one of the most popular names in Britain for quite some time.
Alternative spellings: Jac, Jack

Jake

Meaning: God is gracious
Origin: Hebrew
Pronunciation: JAYK
Description: Jake is a variant of the name Jack but also a name in its own right. The name re-turned to fashion in the 1990s and may be used as a short form for Jacob.
Alternative spellings: Jaike, Jayk

Jakob

Meaning: He who grasps the heel
Origin: Hebrew
Pronunciation: yah KUB
Description: Jakob, also seen spelt Jakub, can be seen as a Czech, Polish or Slovakian take on the Hebrew name Jacob. The Hebrew translation of the name Jacob is 'he who grasps the heel'. In the Bible, Jacob was an ancestor of the tribes of Israel.
Alternative spellings: Jacob, Jakub

Jalen

Meaning: No meaning
Origin: American
Pronunciation: JAY len
Description: Jalen is a modern American invention and, for this reason, has no meaning attached to it.
Alternative spellings: Jalan, Jalon, Jaylen, Jaylan, Jaylon

Jamal

Meaning: Handsome
Origin: Arabic
Pronunciation: ja MAHL
Description: Jamal is often found as a surname as well as a given name. It has associations with male beauty.
Alternative spellings: Jamaal, Jamall, Jameel, Jamel, Jamil

James

Meaning: Supplanter
Origin: English
Pronunciation: JAY mes
Description: The English form of the name borne in the New Testa-ment by two of Christ's disciples, James son of Zebedee and James son of Alphaeus. James is a royal name in Britain associated with James I of Scotland.
Alternative spellings: Jaimes, Jaymes

Jamie

Meaning: Supplanter
Origin: Hebrew
Pronunciation: JAY mee
Description: Originally a pet form of James; Jamie is now a common given name for both boys and girls.
Alternative spellings: Jaime, Jaimey, Jaimi, Jaimie, Jaimy, Jamey, Jaymey, Jaymi, Jaymie

J

Jan

Meaning: Gift from God
Origin: Scandinavian
Pronunciation: jan; yan
Description: Jan has been a popular name across Scandinavia for many years, and is said to mean 'Gift from God' it could possibly originally derive from a Hebrew name. It is also a common nickname for women with the name Janet for example. Jan Molby is a former footballer.
Alternative spellings: Jann

Jared

Meaning: He descends
Origin: Hebrew
Pronunciation: JAH red
Description: Jared is a biblical name, taken from the Old Testament. He was a descendant of Adam, and lived for many years.

Jarvis

Meaning: Spear man
Origin: English
Pronunciation: JAAR vis
Description: Jarvis is the English form of the German last name Gervais, which in turn comes from the uncommon name Gervasius. The meaning of the names is derived from the Germanic element of '*ger*,' meaning 'spear'.

Javier

Meaning: The new house
Origin: Spanish
Pronunciation: HAV yer
Description: Javier is the Spanish form of the name Xavier. Both names come from the Catholic saint, Francis de Xavier, where Xavier is his birthplace. The place name comes from the word '*etxaberri*,' which in Basque means 'new house'.
Alternative spellings: Xavier

Jason

Meaning: Healer
Origin: Greek
Pronunciation: JAY sun
Description: Jason comes from the Greek name Iason, borne by the mythological hero and leader of the Argonauts. The name comes from the Greek word '*iasthai*', meaning 'to heal'.
Alternative spellings: Jaison, Jayson

Jasper

Meaning: Treasurer
Origin: Persian
Pronunciation: JASS per
Description: Jasper is the modern English form of Casper, the name of one of the three wise men (or Magi) who brought gifts to Jesus Christ at his birth.
Alternative spellings: Jaspar

Jawad

Meaning: Generous
Origin: Arabic
Pronunciation: jah WAHD
Description: Jawad is an Arabic word meaning 'open-handed' or 'generous'. It can also be used as a name, though it is uncommon. Jawad is said to be one of the names used to describe Muhammad. It is also the name of a town in India.
Alternative spellings: Jahwad, Jawaad, Jawahd

Jax

Meaning: Son of Jack
Origin: English
Pronunciation: JACKS
Description: Jax is a modern shortened form of the English name Jackson, which literally means 'son of Jack'. It is often given as a nickname to boys named Jack.
Alternative spellings: Jacks, Jaxx

Jaxon

Meaning: Son of Jack
Origin: English
Pronunciation: JAX sun
Description: The name Jaxon can be seen as a variant of the name Jason or a variant spelling of the name Jackson.
Alternative spellings: Jackson, Jakson, Jaxson, Jaxxson

Jay

Meaning: Victory
Origin: Sanskrit
Pronunciation: JAY
Description: Jay is an Indian name meaning 'victory' in Sanskrit. It can also be seen as a shortened form of names beginning with J, like Jason. Although it is most commonly found as a boys' name, it is unisex.
Alternative spellings: Jai

Jaya

Meaning: Victory
Origin: Sanskrit
Pronunciation: JAY ah
Description: Jaya is a unisex name originating from a Sanskrit word meaning 'victorious'. In Hindu belief Jaya is one of the gatekeepers of the domain of the god Vishnu.
Alternative spellings: Jaia

Jayce

Meaning: Healer
Origin: Greek
Pronunciation: jays
Description: Jayce is a different spelling of the name Jace, which in turn is a shortened form of the Greek name Jason. The name comes from the Greek name Iason, borne by the mythological hero and leader of the Argonauts, who sailed to Colchis to discover the golden fleece. Jason fell in love with sorceress Medea during this adventure, but was later killed by a timber beam falling from his ship the *Argo*. The name comes from the Greek word '*iasthai*,' meaning 'to heal'.
Alternative spellings: Jaice, Jays

Jaydan

Meaning: Thankful
Origin: Hebrew
Pronunciation: JAY den
Description: Jaydan is a very popular boys' name in America and originates from the Hebrew name Jadon. The spelling variant Jayden can sometimes be used as a unisex name.
Alternative spellings: Jadan, Jaden, Jadon, Jaidan, Jaiden, Jaidon, Jayden, Jaydon

Jaylan

Meaning: Calm
Origin: Hebrew
Pronunciation: JAY lan
Description: Jaylan is a unisex name that has seen increased popularity in America in recent years. It is a modern variant of

J

Jaylen, which descends from Jalon who was a descendant of Judah.
Alternative spellings: Jaelan, Jaelon, Jailan, Jalan, Jaylen, Jaylon

Jean
See entry in 'Names for Baby Girls A–Z'

Jed
Meaning: Loved by God
Origin: Hebrew
Pronunciation: JED
Description: The name Jed was originally used as a pet form of the name Jedidiah. This name is first seen in the Bible and derives from the element of *'yahew'*, which means 'beloved'.
Alternative spellings: Jedd

Jedidiah
Meaning: Beloved of Yahweh
Origin: Hebrew
Pronunciation: jed I DIE ya
Description: Jedidiah is a Hebrew name, derived from the name Yedidyah, meaning 'beloved of Yahweh'. In the Old Testament, this was a name given by God to Solomon, who is King David's second son.

Jeevan
Meaning: Life; bringer of life
Origin: Indian
Pronunciation: jee VAAN
Description: Jeevan is a male Indian given name meaning 'life' or 'bringer of life'. It comes from the Sanskrit language but is most often a Punjabi name.
Alternative spellings: Jevan

Jeffrey
Meaning: God's peace
Origin: English
Pronunciation: JEFF rey
Description: Jeffrey is a common English boys' name. The name Geoffrey is the precursor to Jeffrey, from the German word *Gottfried* meaning 'God's peace'.
Alternative spellings: Geoffrey, Jeffery, Jeffory, Jefrey, Jeffry

Jem
Meaning: He who supplants
Origin: English
Pronunciation: JEM
Description: Jem is an uncommon boys' name, often used as a nickname for James or Jeremy. It is a variant of the Hebrew name James, meaning 'he who supplants'.
Alternative spellings: Gem, Jemm

Jensen
Meaning: Son of Johannes
Origin: Scandinavian
Pronunciation: JEN son
Description: The name Jensen has Scandinavian roots and is said to mean 'son of Jens'. It could also be the Scandinavian version of the surname Johnson. Jensen is part of a group of surnames growing popular as first names.
Alternative spellings: Jenson, Jensun

Jenson
Meaning: Son of Jan
Origin: Scandinavian
Pronunciation: jen SUN
Description: Jenson is an unusual name, it that is hard to find much history of its usage. It can

be traced back to Scandinavia, and is thought to be a variation on the name Janson, which literally means 'son of Jan'. It is rare as a first name, but does occur as a boys' name, although more commonly it is a surname.
Alternative spellings: Jensen

Jeremiah
Meaning: Appointed by God
Origin: Hebrew
Pronunciation: jer eh MY yah
Description: Jeremiah has biblical associations as the name of the prophet Jeremiah. He wrote the Book of Jeremiah and it is also believed that he wrote the Book of Lamentations.
Alternative spellings: Jeremia, Jerimiah

Jeremy
Meaning: Appointed by God
Origin: Hebrew
Pronunciation: JEH ruh me
Description: Jeremy is an anglicised form of the biblical name Jeremiah. The name Jeremy may be seen in the Authorised Version of the New Testament.
Alternative spellings: Jeremey, Jeremie

Jermaine
See entry in 'Names for Baby Girls A–Z'

Jerome
Meaning: Sacred name
Origin: Greek
Pronunciation: jeh ROME
Description: The name Jerome comes from the biblical word *'hieros'*, which means 'holy' or 'sacred', and also the word *'onoma'*, which means 'name'.
Alternative spellings: Gerome, Jerrome

Jerry
Meaning: Spear ruler
Origin: English
Pronunciation: JEH ree
Description: Jerry is a unisex given name of Old English origin. It is the modern diminutive form of Gerald.
Alternative spellings: Gerri, Gerrie, Gerry, Jerri, Jerrie

Jess
See entry in 'Names for Baby Girls A–Z'

Jesse
Meaning: Gift
Origin: Hebrew
Pronunciation: JESS ee
Description: Jesse is a unisex name originally borne by the father of King David, meaning 'gift' in Hebrew. The more common spelling of 'Jesse' is used for boys; however Jessic is sometimes seen.
Alternative spellings: Jessie

Jethro
Meaning: Pre-eminence
Origin: Hebrew
Pronunciation: JETH ro
Description: Jethro is an uncommon name of Hebrew origin, meaning 'pre-eminence'.
Alternative spellings: Jethroe, Jethrow

Jett
Meaning: Black gemstone
Origin: English
Pronunciation: JET

J

Description: Jett is a common surname in America and has recently become a more popular given name in English-speaking countries.
Alternative spellings: Jet

Jibril
Meaning: Angel
Origin: Arabic
Pronunciation: jib RIL
Description: Jibril is an uncommon Arabic boys' given name. In Abrahamic religions, Gabriel (transliterated in Arabic as Jibril) is an angel who typically serves as a messenger to humans from God.
Alternative spellings: Gibral, Jibra'il

Jim
Meaning: Supplanter
Origin: Hebrew
Pronunciation: JIM
Description: Jim is a shortened form of James and is now seen as a name in its own right.
Alternative spellings: Jym

Jimmy
Meaning: Supplanter
Origin: Hebrew
Pronunciation: JIM ee
Description: Jimmy is a pet form of either James or Jim.
Alternative spellings: Jimmi, Jimmie

Joachim
Meaning: Established by God
Origin: Hebrew
Pronunciation: wa KEEM
Description: Comes from the Hebrew name Johoiachin. Joaquin is a common modern spelling variant of this name. It was believed that Joachim was the name of the Virgin Mary's father in medieval Catholic tradition.
Alternative spellings: Jachim, Joaquin

Joan
See entry in 'Names for Baby Girls A–Z'

Joao
Meaning: God has given
Origin: Portuguese
Pronunciation: zh WOW
Description: Joao is the Portuguese form of the common boys' name John, which means 'God has given'. The name is a prominent one in the Bible and is of great importance to early Christianity, since it was borne by many saints. It is also the name of 23 popes.

Jobey
Meaning: Persecuted
Origin: Hebrew
Pronunciation: joe BEE
Description: Jobey is a Hebrew name meaning 'persecuted' and is also a variation of the name Joby. This name can also be used for girls.
Alternative spellings: Joby

Jocelyn
See entry in 'Names for Baby Girls A–Z'

Jody
Meaning: From Judea
Origin: English
Pronunciation: JO dee

Description: Jody is a unisex name evolving from numerous other names such as George, Jude and Joseph. It is thought to mean 'from Judea' as it is similar to the name Jude.
Alternative spellings: Jodi, Jodie

Joe
Meaning: The Lord gave more
Origin: Hebrew
Pronunciation: JO
Description: Joe is the shortened form of the Hebrew name Joseph, but is now a given name in its own right.

Joel
Meaning: One true God
Origin: Hebrew
Pronunciation: JOLE
Description: Joel is a biblical name borne by one of King David's 'mighty men', and a prophet in the 8th century BC. Largely popular as a Jewish name, Joel has enjoyed success across the English-speaking world.
Alternative spellings: Jole

Joey
Meaning: The Lord gave more
Origin: Hebrew
Pronunciation: JO ee
Description: Joey is a pet form of Joe or Joseph, as well as an independent given name. It is also the name of a baby kangaroo.
Alternative spellings: Joeiy

Johann
Meaning: God is gracious
Origin: Hebrew
Pronunciation: YO hahn

Description: Johann is a name of Hebrew origin, meaning 'God is gracious'. It is the German form of Johan, which is derived from John.
Alternative spellings: Johan, Johanne

John
Meaning: God is gracious
Origin: Hebrew
Pronunciation: JON
Description: The name John was of great importance in early Christianity. It was borne by John the Baptist and John the Apostle. The name was also borne by many saints and by 23 popes. In its various forms in different languages, it has been the most perennially popular of all Christian names.
Alternative spellings: Jon, Jonne

Johnathan
Meaning: Gift of God
Origin: Hebrew
Pronunciation: JON er thun
Description: Johnathan is a variant of the popular boys' name Jonathan. Both are of Hebrew origin and have strong links with the Bible. Jonathan was the son of King Saul and was noted for his manliness, generosity and unselfishness.
Alternative spellings: Jonathan, Jonathon, Jonothon

Johnny
Meaning: God is gracious
Origin: Hebrew
Pronunciation: JON nee
Description: Johnny originally came about as a pet form of the

J

name John; however it is now found as a given name in its own right.
Alternative spellings: Johnni, Johnnie, Jonni, Jonnie, Jonny

Jokubas
Meaning: Supplanter
Origin: Lithuanian
Pronunciation: jok OO bas
Description: Jokubas is the Lithuanian version of the name Jacob. The name means 'supplanter' and is from the Hebrew, Yaakov. Jacob was borne by the biblical father of 12 sons, who gave their names to the 12 tribes of Israel. Son of Isaac and Rebecca and twin brother of Esae, Jacob was the cunning younger twin who tricked his brother into trading his inheritance for a bowl of soup. He later tricked his blind, dying father into blessing him instead of Esau.

Jolyon
Meaning: Youthful; soft-haired
Origin: Latin
Pronunciation: jolee ON
Description: Jolyon is a variation of the names Julian and Julien, and as such shares the same meaning of 'youthful' and 'soft-haired'.

Jon
Meaning: Gracious Lord
Origin: Hebrew
Pronunciation: jon
Description: Jon was the shortened form of the Latin Johannes, before it became John. John is a Hebrew name meaning 'Gracious Lord'. Although the version spelt John is more popular in modern times, both of the spellings can

be found in Britain and the name in general is and has been one of the most popular boys' names for many years.
Alternative spellings: John

Jonah
Meaning: Peace
Origin: Hebrew
Pronunciation: JOE nah
Description: The name Jonah features in the Bible in the legendary tale of Jonah and the whale. Yonah is the original form of this name and influences how it is pronounced in some languages.
Alternative spellings: Jona, Yonah

Jonas
Meaning: Peace
Origin: Hebrew
Pronunciation: YOH nas
Description: Jonas is the Greek variation of the Hebrew name Jonah, seen in the Old Testament. It can also be found as a surname.
Alternative spellings: Jonass, Jonasse

Jonty
Meaning: Gift of God
Origin: Hebrew
Pronunciation: JON tay
Description: Jonty is an American variant of Jonte, which is derived from the Hebrew name Jonathan. It is often given as a nickname to boys named Jonathan but has recently become a stand-alone name.
Alternative spellings: Johntay, Jonte, Jontey

Jordan
Meaning: Flowing down
Origin: Hebrew

Pronunciation: JOR den
Description: The unisex name Jordan was originally given to children baptised using the holy water from the River Jordan. It is also the name of a country.
Alternative spellings: Jorden, Jordon, Jordun, Jordyn

Jorge

Meaning: Farmer
Origin: Greek
Pronunciation: JORJ
Description: Jorge is a phonetically spelt variation of the popular name George, meaning 'farmer'. The variant Jorge is more widely found in Europe but is gaining popularity in the UK.
Alternative spellings: George, Jeorge

Jose

Meaning: The Lord gave more
Origin: Hebrew
Pronunciation: ho ZAY
Description: Jose is the Spanish form of the Hebrew name Joseph, which means 'the Lord gave more'.
Alternative spellings: Josay

Joseph

Meaning: The Lord gave more
Origin: Hebrew
Pronunciation: JO zeff
Description: English form of the biblical Hebrew name Yosef, meaning 'the Lord gave more', often in reference to having another son. This was borne by the favourite son of Jacob in the Bible. The name is still very popular today.
Alternative spellings: Josef, Joseff, Josif, Joszef, Jozef

Josh

Meaning: God is salvation
Origin: Hebrew
Pronunciation: JOSH
Description: Josh originally came about as a pet name of Joshua but is now found as a given name in its own right.
Alternative spellings: Joshe

Joshua

Meaning: God is salvation
Origin: Hebrew
Pronunciation: JOH shoo ah
Description: Borne in the Bible by the Israelite leader who took command of the Children of Israel after the death of Moses. The name enjoyed a great surge of popularity in the 1990s.
Alternative spellings: Jeshua

Jovan

Meaning: The supreme God
Origin: Latin
Pronunciation: JO vahn
Description: Jovan is a boys' name of Latin origin that originated from the Roman supreme deity, Jupiter. It is popular in Serbia as the equivalent to the English name John.
Alternative spellings: Jovon, Jovun

Jowan

Meaning: God has given
Origin: Cornish
Pronunciation: joh WAAN
Description: Jowan is the Cornish version of the common boys' name John. It is a prominent biblical name meaning 'God has given,' and is used many times in the Bible. It is also the name of many saints and 23 popes.

J

Juan

Meaning: God is gracious
Origin: Spanish
Pronunciation: WAHN
Description: Juan is the Spanish variant of the Hebrew name John. It is a very popular name in Spain and in Spanish-speaking communities worldwide.
Alternative spellings: Huon, Juwan

Judah

Meaning: Praised
Origin: Hebrew
Pronunciation: joo DAH
Description: In the Bible, Judah was the fourth of Jacob's 12 sons. The name is rising in popularity in recent years. The Greek form of the name is Judas and is very rarely used due to the infamy of the betrayer Judas Iscariot.
Alternative spellings: Juda, Yudah

Jude

Meaning: Praise
Origin: Greek
Pronunciation: JOODE
Description: Jude is a short form of Judas, and is used in the Bible to distinguish between the Judas who betrayed Christ and other men of that name.
Alternative spellings: Jeude,Jood

Jules

See entry in 'Names for Baby Girls A–Z'

Julian

Meaning: Bearded youth
Origin: Latin
Pronunciation: JOO lee un

Description: Julian is derived from the Latin name 'Julius'.
Alternative spellings: Juliun, Julyan

Julio

Meaning: Bearded youth
Origin: Greek
Pronunciation: HOO lee oh; JOO lee oh
Description: Julio is a Spanish form of Julius, introduced to the English-speaking world by Hispanic settlers in the US.
Alternative spellings: Julioh

Julius

Meaning: Bearded youth
Origin: Latin
Pronunciation: JOO lee us
Description: Julius is a Roman family name notably borne by Julius Caesar.
Alternative spellings: Julyus, Yulius

Junaid

Meaning: Warrior; soldier; shield
Origin: Arabic
Pronunciation: yun AID
Description: This name derives from the Urdu word meaning 'warrior' or 'fighter'; however, it is also believed that the name comes from the Arabic word 'jund'meaning 'solider' or 'shield'.Either way, the name hasconnotations of strength and fighting.
Alternative spellings: Junade, Junaide

Junior

Meaning: Son
Origin: English
Pronunciation: JOO ni uh

Description: Junior is a nickname used to distinguish a son from his father. It is of recent coinage as a given name and exists mostly in the United States.
Alternative spellings: Gunior, Juniur

Jupiter
Meaning: Father god
Origin: Latin
Pronunciation: JOOP it er
Description: In Roman mythology, Jupiter was the king of the gods – the Latinised version of the original Greek god Zeus. It is also the name of the fifth planet from the sun and the largest planet within the solar system.
Alternative spellings: Joopiter, Jupyter

Justin
Meaning: Fair, righteous
Origin: Latin
Pronunciation: JUS tin
Description: Justin is an English form of the Latin name Justinus, from 'Justus'. It was a name borne by several early saints.
Alternative spellings: Justen, Justinn

K

Kabir
Meaning: The Great
Origin: Arabic
Pronunciation: kah BEER
Description: Kabir is a common boy's name originating from the Arabic Al-Kabir, which means 'The Great' – the 37th name of God in Islam. Kabir was a mystic poet and saint of India whose writings have greatly influenced the Bhakti movement.
Alternative spellings: Kaabir, Kabeer

Kade
Meaning: Round
Origin: English
Pronunciation: Kayd
Description: Kade is a different spelling of the name Cade, which comes from an Old English surname meaning 'round'.
Alternative spellings: Cade

Kaden
Meaning: Son; spirit of battle
Origin: Gaelic
Pronunciation: KAY den
Description: Kaden is the popular anglicised form of Kaiden. Kaiden is Celtic in origin and is said to mean 'warrior'.
Alternative spellings: Caden, Cadon, Caiden, Caidon, Cayden, Caydon, Kadan, Kaden, Kaedan, Kaeden, Kaidan, Kaydan Kayden

Kaede
See entry in 'Names for Baby Girls A–Z'

Kaelan
Meaning: Slender
Origin: Gaelic
Pronunciation: KAY lan
Description: Kaelan is a unisex name of Gaelic origin. Its meaning is debated but some agree that it

means 'slender'. It is most commonly used for boys.
Alternative spellings: Caelan, Caolan, Caylan, Kaolan, Kaylan

Kai
Meaning: The sea
Origin: Hawaiian
Pronunciation: KY
Description: Kai is a Hawaiian word meaning 'the sea'. The Welsh version of this name means 'keeper of the keys'. It has recently become more popular as a baby name in Britain.
Alternative spellings: Ky, Kye

Kain
Meaning: Acquire
Origin: Hebrew
Pronunciation: KAYN
Description: Kain is an uncommon given name but a popular surname. It is a variant of Kenan, which is a Hebrew name meaning 'acquire'. It could also be considered a variant of the Gaelic name Kane.
Alternative spellings: Caine, Cane, Kaine, Kane, Kayne

Kaine
Meaning: Spear
Origin: Gaelic
Pronunciation: KAYN
Description: Kaine is a variant form of the masculine Gaelic name Kane. It could also be considered a variant of the Hebrew name Cain.
Alternative spellings: Caine, Cane, Kaine, Kane, Kayne

Kairo
Meaning: Victorious
Origin: Arabic
Pronunciation: KYE ro

Description: Kairo is an uncommon Arabic boys' name and is a variant of Cairo, which is also the capital of Egypt and the oldest city in the Arabic world. It is derived from 'al Qahir', which is the Arabic name of the planet Mars.
Alternative spellings: Cairo, Kyro

Kairon
Meaning: Dark-haired
Origin: Gaelic
Pronunciation: KYE ron
Description: Kairon is a less popular variant of the Irish name Kieran, although the two are pronounced differently. It is also an uncommon Indian name, named after a small Indian village.
Alternative spellings: Kyron

Kaiser
Meaning: Emperor
Origin: German
Pronunciation: KAI sur
Description: Kaiser is the German word for 'emperor' and refers to the title that the ruler holds. This is an unusual boys' name choice and could be a good option for more adventurous parents.

Kaison
Meaning: No meaning
Origin: American
Pronunciation: KAI sun
Description: Kaison is an invented, modern name and as such has no meaning. It can also be spelt in a variety of different ways.
Alternative spellings: Kayson, Kason, Cayson, Cason

Kajus

Meaning: Rejoice
Origin: Latin
Pronunciation: KAH ee us
Description: Kajus is a variant of the Roman surname Caius, related to the Latin term *'guadere'*, meaning 'Aelto rejoices'. The name also features in the Bible, belonging to a saint.
Alternative spellings: Caius, Cajus, Kaius

Kaleb

Meaning: Dog
Origin: Hebrew
Pronunciation: KAY leb
Description: Kaleb is an alternative spelling of Caleb. It is a biblical name that means 'dog'. Caleb was one of Moses' followers, and the change to add a K at the start of the name would have been a modern construction.
Alternative spellings: Caleb

Kaleem

Meaning: Lecturer
Origin: Arabic
Pronunciation: kah LEEM
Description: Kaleem is an uncommon name of Arabic origin, meaning 'lecturer'.
Alternative spellings: Caleem, Kahleem

Kalen

Meaning: Slender
Origin: Gaelic
Pronunciation: KAY len
Description: Kalen is an uncommon name of Gaelic origin, meaning 'slender' or 'uncertain'.
Alternative spellings: Caelan, Kaelen

Kamar

Meaning: The moon
Origin: Arabic
Pronunciation: KAH maar
Description: Kamar is an Arabic boys' name meaning 'the moon'. This name is not to be confused with Kumar, which has a different meaning.
Alternative spellings: Qamar

Kamil

Meaning: Sacrifice
Origin: Arabic
Pronunciation: kah MEAL
Description: The name Kamil derives from the name Camillus, which means 'altar server'. It is most popular in Arabic-, Polish- and Czech-speaking countries.
Alternative spellings: Camil, Kamill

Kamile

Meaning: Sacrifice
Origin: Italian
Pronunciation: kah MEEL
Description: Kamile is the Polish variant of the French Camille, a name used for both boys and girls that originates from Roman mythology.
Alternative spellings: Camile, Camille, Kamille

Kamran

Meaning: Crooked nose
Origin: Gaelic
Pronunciation: CAM ren
Description: Kamran is one of the many spelling variations for the name Cameron. This spelling also has a Persian meaning, which is 'prosperous'.

K

Alternative spellings: Cameron, Camron, Kameron, Kamron

Kane
Meaning: Battle; a spear
Origin: Hebrew
Pronunciation: KAYN
Description: The name Kane is a variation of Cain. In the Bible, Cain killed his brother, Abel. In English the name Cane derived from the medieval word for 'cane' or 'reed'.
Alternative spellings: Caine, Cane, Kaine

Kaoru
Meaning: Fragrant
Origin: Japanese
Pronunciation: Kah o roo
Description: This name can most commonly be found in Japan and is written using only one Japanese character meaning 'fragrant'. It can be adopted as both a girls' and a boys' name.
Alternative spellings: Kaoruh, Kayoru

Karam
Meaning: Generous
Origin: Arabic
Pronunciation: KAH raam
Description: This Arabic name is most commonly used for boys, but can be found as a girls' name. The name is thought to have derived from the name Karim, which can also be spelt Kareem.
Alternative spellings: Karaam, Kharam

Karan
Meaning: Ear
Origin: Sanskrit
Pronunciation: kar AHN

Description: Karan is an old Indian name that has been transliterated from Sanskrit as meaning 'ear'. It is also the name of a town in Mali.
Alternative spellings: Kaaran, Karaan

Karim
Meaning: Generous
Origin: Arabic
Pronunciation: kah REEM
Description: Karim is a popular name among Muslim families, thought to mean 'generous'.
Alternative spellings: Kareem, Kareme

Karl
Meaning: Free man
Origin: German
Pronunciation: KARL
Description: Karl is a German variant of the English name Charles. It is also a variant spelling of the name Carl.
Alternative spellings: Carl

Karol
Meaning: Free man
Origin: Latin
Pronunciation: KA rawl
Description: The name Karol comes from Carolus, the Latin form of Charles. The form Karol is rarely found in Britain.
Alternative spellings: Carol

Karson
Meaning: Carr's son
Origin: English
Pronunciation: karr SUN
Description: Karson is a variation of the English name Carson. It was originally a surname given to someone who hailed

from a marshy area, or whose father had lived there. It has developed into a first name throughout history, but is rare in the UK today.
Alternative spellings: Carson

Karter
Meaning: Cart transporter
Origin: English
Pronunciation: kar TUR
Description: Kartor is a modern, variant spelling of the English name Carter. Carter is taken from the surname originally given to those who transported goods in a cart. The use of the letter K breathes fresh life into the traditional name.
Alternative spellings: Carter

Kasey
Meaning: Vigilant guard
Origin: Gaelic
Pronunciation: KAY see
Description: Kasey is a spelling variant of the names Casey and Kaci. It derives from the Gaelic name Cathasaigh and is popular in America and Ireland.
Alternative spellings: Casey, Casie, Cayce, Caycie, Caysie, Kacey, Kaci, Kacie, Kacy, Kasie, Kaycee, Kaycie, Kaysie

Kasim
Meaning: Divided
Origin: Arabic
Pronunciation: kah SEEM
Description: Kasim is an alternative spelling of the Arabic boys' name Kassim. It is more common as a surname but has increased in popularity as a given name in recent years.
Alternative spellings: Kaseem, Kassim

Kason
Meaning: No meaning
Origin: American
Pronunciation: kay SUN
Description: Kason is a different version of the name Kayson. Both names are modern American inventions and as such have no real meaning.
Alternative spellings: Kayson, Cason, Cayson

Kasper
Meaning: Treasurer
Origin: Persian
Pronunciation: KASS per
Description: Kasper is a popular Danish name of Persian origin, meaning 'treasurer'.
Alternative spellings: Caspar, Casper, Kacper, Kaspar

Kay
See entry in 'Names for Baby Girls A–Z'

Kaya
See entry in 'Names for Baby Girls A–Z'

Kayan
Meaning: High status
Origin: Persian
Pronunciation: kai YAAN
Description: Kayan is a Persian name meaning 'high status,' referring to someone who is important. It also has Indian connections, and in Hindi the name means 'name of a dynasty of King Kaikobad'.
Alternative spellings: Cayan

K

...el maker
...

Pronunciation: KAYD
Description: Kayd is a modern variant of the name Cade, said to refer to a barrel maker. It is now used as a unisex name. Kayd may also be found used as an abbreviation of the masculine name Kaden, which is Celtic in origin and means 'warrior'.
Alternative spellings: Cade, Caid, Cayde, Kayd

Kaylan

Meaning: Slender
Origin: Gaelic
Pronunciation: KAY lan
Description: Kaylan is a modernised and American version of the Gaelic name Caelan. Though previously uncommon, the name has increased in popularity in recent years as a given name for both boys and girls.
Alternative spellings: Caelan, Caolan, Caylan, Kaelan, Kaolan

Kaylum

Meaning: Peace
Origin: Latin
Pronunciation: KAY lum
Description: Kaylum could be a variation of the name Calum, which comes from the Latin word 'columba', meaning 'dove'. It is a very popular name in Britain, especially in Scotland.
Alternative spellings: Caylum

Kayson

Meaning: Healer
Origin: Greek
Pronunciation: KAY sun

Description: Kayson is a name of Greek origin. It is a modern coinage thought to be based on the name Jason, which has become popular in recent years.
Alternative spellings: Cayson, Kasen, Kason

Kazumi

Meaning: Beautiful harmony
Origin: Japanese
Pronunciation: Ka zoo mee
Description: This Japanese name is written using the characters of 'kazu', meaning 'peace and harmony', along with 'mi', which means 'beautiful'. It is most commonly found in Japan and can be used for both boys and girls.
Alternative spellings: Kazumie

Kazuo

Meaning: First born
Origin: Japanese
Pronunciation: ka ZOO oh
Description: This Japanese name means 'first born', so is most commonly given to sons who are born first in the family.
Alternative spellings: Kazuoh, Kazzuo

Keagan

Meaning: Fiery
Origin: Irish
Pronunciation: KEE gan
Description: Keagan is an Irish baby name that has connotations of fire and therefore means 'fiery'. This name would be ideal for a little redheaded baby.
Alternative spellings: Keegan

Keane

Meaning: Ancient

Origin: Gaelic
Pronunciation: KEEN
Description: Keane is the pet form of the name Keenan, but is also used in its own right. Both are Gaelic in origin and are said to mean 'ancient'.
Alternative spellings: Kean, Keene

Keanu

Meaning: Cool breeze from the mountains
Origin: Hawaiian
Pronunciation: ki AH nu
Description: Keanu is a Hawaiian name meaning 'cool breeze blowing down from the mountains'.
Alternative spellings: Kearnu

Keaton

Meaning: Kite town
Origin: English
Pronunciation: KEE ton
Description: Keaton is of Old English origin, meaning 'shed' or 'kite town'. It is more commonly found as a surname.
Alternative spellings: Keeton, Keyton

Keegan

Meaning: Fiery
Origin: Irish
Pronunciation: KEE gan
Description: Keegan is a variant spelling of the Irish name Keagan, and shares the same meaning of 'fiery'.
Alternative spellings: Keagan

Keelan

Meaning: Graceful
Origin: Gaelic
Pronunciation: Key lan

Description: Keelan is the unisex version of the Gaelic name Keeley. Depending on which origin is taken, Keelan could mean 'graceful' or 'slender'.
Alternative spellings: Ceelan, Keylan

Keenan

Meaning: Ancient
Origin: Gaelic
Pronunciation: KEE nan
Description: Keenan, a name that means 'ancient' or 'distant', is a more anglicised version of the Irish name Cian. Keenan is more commonly found as a surname.
Alternative spellings: Keenen, Keenon, Kenan

Kei

Meaning: Joyful
Origin: Japanese
Pronunciation: KAY i
Description: Kei is a unisex name more commonly found on boys. This name was originally a pet form of the name Keiko; however, over time it has transferred into a forename in its own right.
Alternative spellings: Kehi

Keir

Meaning: Dark-haired
Origin: Gaelic
Pronunciation: KEE er
Description: Keir is an uncommon boys' name of Gaelic origin. The meanings vary and include 'dusky', 'dark-haired', 'dark-skinned' and 'swarthy'.
Alternative spellings: Keer, Keirr

Keith

Meaning: Woodland

K

Origin: Gaelic
Pronunciation: KEETH
Description: Keith is a commonly found surname, especially in Scotland, where it is considered to be aristocratic. It is also a popular given name for boys.
Alternative spellings: Keeth, Keyth

Kelly
See entry in 'Names for Baby Girls A–Z'

Kelsey
Meaning: Victorious ship
Origin: English
Pronunciation: KEL see
Description: The name Kelsey comes from the Old English word *'ceolsige',* which means 'victorious ship'. It was originally used as a surname but is now a unisex given name.
Alternative spellings: Kelsea, Kelsi, Kelsie, Kelsy

Kelvin
Meaning: Narrow water
Origin: Gaelic
Pronunciation: KEHL vin
Description: Kelvin is a Gaelic boys' name meaning 'narrow water'. It is also a scientific unit for temperature, named after Scottish physicist William Thomson, Lord Kelvin, who created the measurement.
Alternative spellings: Calvin

Kendrick
Meaning: Keen power; summit; son of Henry
Origin: English
Pronunciation: KEN drik

Description: Kendrick is an English surname that means 'keen power'. It is also an Old Welsh and Scottish given name where it means 'summit' and 'son of Henry' respectively.
Alternative spellings: Kendric, Kendrik

Kennedy
Meaning: Leader
Origin: Gaelic
Pronunciation: KEH na dee
Description: Kennedy derives from the Gaelic element of *'ceann',* meaning 'head'. It was most likely first used as a nickname for a clan leader, before transferring to a surname. It is now a given name for both boys and girls.
Alternative spellings: Kenedy, Kennedey, Kennedi, Kennedie

Kenneth
Meaning: Fire born; handsome
Origin: Gaelic
Pronunciation: KEN neth
Description: Kenneth is a popular boys' name of Gaelic origin. Kenneth derives from the Gaelic *'coinneach',* which means 'handsome', and it also means 'fire born'. Often shortened to Ken or Kenny, the name was at its highest popularity in the early 20th century and is less common since.
Alternative spellings: Keneth, Kennith

Kenny
Meaning: Handsome
Origin: Gaelic
Pronunciation: KEH nee

Description: Kenny is the abbreviated form of the name Kenneth. Kenny is often found as a surname as well as a boys' first name.
Alternative spellings: Kennie

Kent
Meaning: Border
Origin: English
Pronunciation: KENT
Description: Originally a surname, Kent is also a county in England. It has recently gained popularity as a boys' given name.
Alternative spellings: Kente

Kenzie
Meaning: The fairest
Origin: Gaelic
Pronunciation: KEN zee
Description: Kenzie is a unisex name and is a shortened form of Mackenzie, which derives from the Gaelic surname McKenzie, originally MacCoinneach. The meaning of the name varies. For a girl it is said to mean 'the fairest' yet for a boy it means 'handsome one'.
Alternative spellings: Kenzee, Kenzi, Kenzy

Kenzo
Meaning: Wise
Origin: Japanese
Pronunciation: KEN zo
Description: The name Kenzou is built from the Japanese characters for 'intelligent; wise' (*ken*) and 'three' (*zou*). The name is usually transcribed in English as Kenzo.
Alternative spellings: Kenzou

Keon
Meaning: God is gracious

Origin: Gaelic
Pronunciation: KEE on
Description: Keon is a boys' name of Gaelic and Hebrew origins. It is a variant of Ewan, from John, meaning 'God is gracious'. It has risen in popularity in recent years.
Alternative spellings: Kion, Kyon

Kerem
Meaning: Vineyard
Origin: Hebrew
Pronunciation: KER ehm
Description: Kerem is a unisex name of Hebrew origin, meaning 'vineyard'. It is thought to be derived from Jeremy.
Alternative spellings: Karim, Kereem, Kerim

Kerry
See entry in 'Names for Baby Girls A–Z'

Keston
Meaning: Area in London
Origin: English
Pronunciation: kes TUN
Description: Keston is a place name, specifically a town in the London Borough of Bromley and on the border of Greater London and Kent.
Alternative spellings: Kestin, Kesten

Kevin
Meaning: Beloved
Origin: Gaelic
Pronunciation: KEH vin
Description: Kevin is an anglicised version of the Gaelic name Caoimhin. It is a popular name worldwide, but has fallen from the top 100 boys' names in the UK.

K

Alternative spellings: Keven, Kevyn

Keyaan
Meaning: Kingly
Origin: Arabic
Pronunciation: keh YAHN
Description: Keyaan seems to be a masculine name of Arabic origin. Its meaning is believed to be 'kingly'.
Alternative spellings: Keyahn, Keyarn

Keyan
Meaning: God is gracious
Origin: Gaelic
Pronunciation: kee YAN
Description: Keyan is a variation of the Gaelic name Kiyan, meaning 'God is gracious'. The names are in turn a variant of Ewan, from John, which means they all share the same meaning.
Alternative spellings: Kiyan

Khalid
Meaning: Immortal; eternal
Origin: Arabic
Pronunciation: KAH leed
Description: Khalid is a popular name among the Arabic community and is said to mean 'immortal' or 'undying'. It has grown in popularity in the UK in recent years.

Khalil
Meaning: Friend
Origin: Arabic
Pronunciation: kah LEEL
Description: Khalil is an Arabic name meaning 'friend'. It is rare in the UK.
Alternative spellings: Kalil, Khaleel

Kian
Meaning: Ancient
Origin: Gaelic
Pronunciation: KI an
Description: Kian is the anglicised version of Cian.
Alternative spellings: Cian, Kean

Killian
Meaning: Feisty
Origin: Gaelic
Pronunciation: KILL yan
Description: Killian is an alternate spelling of the Gaelic name Cillian. Both names are said to have originated with meanings associated with war, but as a given name we would assume the meaning of Cillian to be 'feisty'
Alternative spellings: Cillian

Kim
See entry in 'Names for Baby Girls A–Z'

Kimberley
See entry in 'Names for Baby Girls A–Z'

King
Meaning: Leader
Origin: English
Pronunciation: king
Description: King can be both a given name and a surname, and is derived from the English word of the same spelling and means 'head' or 'leader'. The word itself comes from the Old English word *cyning* meaning 'tribal leader'.

Kingsley
Meaning: King's meadow
Origin: English

Pronunciation: KINGS lee
Description: Kingsley was originally given as a surname to those who cared for the king's land. It has evolved into a first name and is very popular in the US.
Alternative spellings: Kingslee, Kingsleigh

Kingston
Meaning: King's town
Origin: English
Pronunciation: KINGS tun
Description: Kingston is an uncommon name of English origin, meaning 'King's town' after the Jamaican city.
Alternative spellings: Kingstun

Kip
Meaning: Bearer of Christ
Origin: English
Pronunciation: kip
Description: Kip, like Kit, is a shortened version of Christopher and as such, shares the same meaning of 'bearer of Christ'.

Kiran
Meaning: Beam of light
Origin: Sanskrit
Pronunciation: KEE ran
Description: Kiran is a unisex name of Sanksrit origin, said to mean 'beam of light'. It could also be considered a spelling variant of the Gaelic name Kieran.
Alternative spellings: Ciaran, Keiran, Keiron, Kieran, Kieron

Kieron
Meaning: Dark one
Origin: Gaelic
Pronunciation: KIER ron

Description: This name is mainly used in English-speaking countries such as America, Canada, England and Australia. This spelling is a variant of the English and Irish name Kieran. There is also a Hindi variation of this name, which is spelt Kiran. In Hindi it means 'beam of light'.
Alternative spellings: Kieran

Kishan
Meaning: Krishna
Origin: Sanskrit
Pronunciation: kee SHAAN
Description: Kishan is an uncommon boys' name of Sanskrit origin. It is a modern form of Krishna, the name of a Hindu deity believed to be an incarnation of the god Vishnu.
Alternative spellings: Keeshan, Kishaan

K

Kit
Meaning: Follower of Christ
Origin: Greek
Pronunciation: KIT
Description: Kit is an abbreviation of the name Christopher, meaning 'follower or bearer of Christ'. It is especially popular in America.
Alternative spellings: Kitt

Kiva
See entry in 'Names for Baby Girls A–Z'

Kiyan
Meaning: God is gracious
Origin: Gaelic
Pronunciation: KEE yan
Description: Kiyan is a boys' name of Gaelic and Hebrew origins. It is a variant of Ewan, from John,

| is gracious'. It has
| arity in recent years.
| **pellings:** Kean,
Keon, Kian, Kion

Klay
Meaning: Clay
Origin: English
Pronunciation: CAH lay
Description: Klay is a different spelling of the name Clay. Clay is a name that either exists as a shortened form of Clayton, a transferred surname or a name given to somebody who lived on clay soils.
Alternative spellings: Clay

Knox
Meaning: Round hill
Origin: English
Pronunciation: NOX
Description: Knox is an unusual boys' name of Old English origin, where it originally meant 'hill with a rounded peak'.
Alternative spellings: Nox

Kobe
Meaning: Supplanter
Origin: Hebrew
Pronunciation: koh BEE
Description: Kobe is a rather uncommon baby name and is likely to be a diminutive form of the name Jacob. A famous bearer of the name is Kobe Bryant, LA Lakers basketball player – although his parents chose Kobe due to the Japanese beef.
Alternative spellings: Kobi, Kobie, Koby, Cobe, Coby

Kodi
Meaning: Helpful
Origin: Gaelic
Pronunciation: KOH dee
Description: Kodi is a modern variant of the common Gaelic name Cody, meaning 'helpful'. It can be used for girls and boys.
Alternative spellings: Codey, Codie, Cody, Kody

Kofi
Meaning: Born on Friday
Origin: Ghanaian
Pronunciation: KOH fi
Description: Kofi is a Ghanaian boys' name signifying birth on a Friday.
Alternative spellings: Kofey, Kofii, Kofy

Kohen
Meaning: Priest
Origin: Hebrew
Pronunciation: koe EN
Description: Kohen is an alternative spelling of the name Cohen, which is borne by a priest and the brother of Moses in Jewish belief. It could also be the anglicised version of the Old Irish surname Cadhan.
Alternative spellings: Cohen

Kole
Meaning: Dark
Origin: English
Pronunciation: kole
Description: Kole is a variation of the common boys' name Cole, which is an English surname that was transferred into a given name. It is taken from the Old English word '*cola*,' meaning 'dark complexion'. Other sources suggest the name to be a short form of the name Coleman.
Alternative spellings: Cole

Konrad

Meaning: Bold counsel
Origin: German
Pronunciation: KON rad
Description: Konrad is a German name meaning 'brave', 'counsel' or 'ruler', often seen just as 'bold counsel'.
Alternative spellings: Conrad

Korenl

Meaning: Horn
Origin: English
Pronunciation: corn EL
Description: Kornel is most likely a modern respelling of the traditional name Cornel, which is a diminutive of Cornelius. The name means 'horn', because it comes from the Latin element of 'cornu'. The respelling injects an element of fresh modernity into the name.
Alternative spellings: Cornel

Korey

Meaning: Spear
Origin: Norse
Pronunciation: KOR ree
Description: The name Korey is a variant of Cory, a given name common for both boys and girls in America. It comes from a surname that was possibly either derived from the Gaelic 'corra', meaning 'spear', Old Norse given name Kori (meaning 'the chosen one') or from 'ravine' in Gaelic, 'hollow' in Irish, 'seething pool' in Scots, or 'horn' in French.
Alternative spellings: Coree, Corey, Corie, Cory, Koree, Kory

Kostas

Meaning: Constant; steadfast

Origin: Greek
Pronunciation: kos TAS
Description: Kostas is a short form of the Greek name Konstantinos. The name is the Greek version of the name Constantine and means 'constant' or 'steadfast'.
Alternative spellings: Costas

Krishan

Meaning: Black
Origin: Sanskrit
Pronunciation: KRISH an
Description: Krishan is a variant of the name Krishna. The spelling of the Hindu god Krishna varies from region to region. The name is said to derive from a Sanskrit word meaning 'black'.
Alternative spellings: Krishaan, Krishann

Krishna

Meaning: Deity
Origin: Sanskrit
Pronunciation: KRISH naa
Description: Krishna is the name of a Hindu deity believed to be an incarnation of the god Vishnu.
Alternative spellings: Krishnah

Kristian

Meaning: Follower of Christ
Origin: Latin
Pronunciation: KRIS ti en
Description: Kristian is the Scandinavian version of the name Christian. It is unisex and means 'follower of Christ'.
Alternative spellings: Christian, Christien, Cristian, Krystian

Krzysztof

Meaning: Bearer of Christ

K

Origin: Polish
Pronunciation: kriss TOFF
Description: Krzysztof is the Polish version of the name Christoph, meaning 'bearer of Christ'. The roots of the name come from the Greek words *'christo'* referring to Christ, and 'phero' meaning to bear or carry. Early Christians used this as a metaphorical name to express how they always carry Christ in their hearts.
Alternative spellings: Kristophe, Christophe

Ksawery

Meaning: The new house
Origin: Polish
Pronunciation: ksa VE ri
Description: Ksawery is the Polish version of the name Xavier, which in turn is a Hispanicised version of the Basque place name *'etcheberria,'* meaning 'the new house'.

Kuba

Meaning: Supplanter
Origin: Polish
Pronunciation: kuw BAH
Description: Kuba may sound like Cuba (as in the Caribbean island), but it is actually a Polish diminutive of the Hebrew name Jacob, and as such shares the same meaning with it.
Alternative spellings: Cuba

Kunal

Meaning: Lotus
Origin: Sanskrit
Pronunciation: koo NAL
Description: Kunal has several meanings in Sanskrit including

'lotus', 'bird with beautiful eyes' and 'one with beautiful eyes'.
Alternative spellings: Kunall

Kurt

Meaning: Courageous
Origin: German
Pronunciation: KURT
Description: Kurt is a boys' name popular in America. It is a variant of Conrad, which is of Old German origin.
Alternative spellings: Curt, Kert

Kurtis

Meaning: Considerate
Origin: French
Pronunciation: KER tiss
Description: Kurtis is a spelling variation of the name Curtis. Both names come from the word 'courteous'.
Alternative spellings: Curtis

Kush

Meaning: Son of Lord Rama
Origin: Sanskrit
Pronunciation: KUSH
Description: Kush is a variant of Kusha, who was one of the twin sons of Lord Rama in Hindu mythology. It is an uncommon name in English-speaking countries as Kush is the name given to a strain of cannabis.
Alternative spellings: Koosh, Kuush

Kyan

Meaning: Little king
Origin: English
Pronunciation: KYE un
Description: Kyan is a modern variation of the name Ryan and is especially popular in America.

Alternative spellings: Kyanne

Kye
Meaning: Key keeper
Origin: Welsh
Pronunciation: KY
Description: Kye is the phonetically anglicised version of the Welsh name Kai, meaning 'keeper of the keys'. The name Kai also originates from Hawaii, where it means 'ocean'.
Alternative spellings: Kai, Ky

Kylan
Meaning: Narrow water
Origin: Gaelic
Pronunciation: KI lan
Description: Kylan derives from an Irish place name, referring to a place where water becomes very narrow. It is also a variant of the name Kyle.
Alternative spellings: Kylanne, Kylon

Kyle
Meaning: Narrow water
Origin: Gaelic
Pronunciation: KY all
Description: Kyle is derived from a term that means a narrow channel between two land masses.
Alternative spellings: Kyill

Kylo
Meaning: No meaning
Origin: English
Pronunciation: KY loh
Description: Kylo is an invented name and as such, there is no meaning. It has grown in popularity in recent times due to the Star Wars character, Kylo Ren, played by actor Adam Driver in the film *Star Wars: The Force Awakens*.

Kymani
Meaning: Adventurous traveller
Origin: Jamaican
Pronunciation: ki MAN ee
Description: Kymani, often written Ky-Mani, is a Jamaican boys' name. It literally means an 'adventurous traveller'.
Alternative spellings: Kymanee, Kymanie, Kymany

Kyran
Meaning: Black
Origin: Gaelic
Pronunciation: keer AN
Description: Kyran is a Gaelic name that has been popular for many years, although you may recognise the alternative spelling of Keiran.
Alternative spellings: Keiran

Kyron
Meaning: Master
Origin: Greek
Pronunciation: KYE ron
Description: The name Kyron derives from the Greek legend of Chiron the centaur. It is thought that the name inspired the modern name Tyrone, used widely in the UK and US. Kyron is mainly found in Europe and Russia. It could also be considered a variant spelling of the Gaelic name Kairon.
Alternative spellings: Kairon

K

L

Lacey
See entry in 'Names for Baby Girls
A–Z'

Lachlan
Meaning: Viking settler
Origin: Gaelic
Pronunciation: LAHK lin
Description: Lachlan is a Gaelic
name originally used in Scotland
as a name for the settling Vikings.
It then spread to Canada and
Australia, where it is particularly
popular.
Alternative spellings: Laclan,
Laklan, Lochlan

Laertes
Meaning: Avenger
Origin: Greek
Pronunciation: Lye ER teez
Description: In Greek myth-
ology, Laertes was the king of
the Cephallenians and father
of Odysseus. In Shakespeare's
Hamlet, Laertes is the brother of
Ophelia.
Alternative spellings: Laertees,
Layertees

Laith
Meaning: Lion
Origin: Arabic
Pronunciation: LAYTH
Description: Laith is an uncom-
mon Arabic boys' name that means
'lion', 'strong' or 'brave'. It is more
commonly seen as a surname in
the Arabic world.
Alternative spellings: Laithe,
Lathe, Layth

Lance
Meaning: Land
Origin: French
Pronunciation: LANCE
Description: Lance is a popular
boys' name of French origin, de-
rived from the Old German name
Lanzo, meaning 'land'.
Alternative spellings: Lanse,
Lantz

Lando
Meaning: Famous throughout the
land
Origin: Italian
Pronunciation: lan DOH
Description: Lando is an Italian variation of the name Roland,
meaning 'famous throughout the
land'. Lando Calrissian is a character in the Star Wars franchise.

Landon
Meaning: Long hill
Origin: English
Pronunciation: LAN don
Description: Landon is a boys'
name of English origin that
means 'long hill'. It is a variant of
Langdon.
Alternative spellings: Landan,
Landen

Laney
See entry in 'Names for Baby Girls
A–Z'

Landry
Meaning: Land ruler
Origin: English
Pronunciation: LAN dree

Description: Landry is a name with English and French origins and means 'ruler'. It was imported into Britain by the Normans.
Alternative spellings: Landrey

Larry
Meaning: Man from Laurentum
Origin: Latin
Pronunciation: LAIR ee
Description: Larry is a shortened version of the name Laurence, meaning 'man from Laurentum'. Both names come from the name Laurentius.

Larson
Meaning: Son of Lars
Origin: Scandinavian
Pronunciation: LAAR sun
Description: Larson is a Scandinavian surname meaning 'son of Lars'. Lars comes from the Roman name Laurentius. This follows the contemporary trend of using last names as first names.

Laurel
Meaning: Laurel
Origin: English
Pronunciation: LOH rul
Description: Originally Laurel was a feminine name, deriving from the Old English laurel tree. Recently the name has picked up popularity as a boys' name, possibly due to the fame of the comedy duo Laurel and Hardy.
Alternative spellings: Loral

Laurence
Meaning: From Laurentum
Origin: Latin
Pronunciation: LOR rents

Description: Laurence originates from the Roman name Laurentius. It can be found as a male English name and a French feminine name.
Alternative spellings: Laurince, Laurynce, Lawrence, Lorence

Laurie
Meaning: Victory
Origin: Latin
Pronunciation: LAW ree
Description: The name Laurie can be used as a unisex name, as it was originally a shortened version of the names Laura and Laurence. It is now used as a name in its own right and is seen to mean 'victory'.
Alternative spellings: Lauri, Laury, Lawrie, Lowry

Lawrence
Meaning: Crowned with a laurel
Origin: French
Pronunciation: LOR rents
Description: The anglicised form of Laurence, brought to Britain during the Norman Conquest.
Alternative spellings: Laurence, Laurince, Laurynce, Lorence

Lawson
Meaning: Son of Lawrence
Origin: English
Pronunciation: LAW sun
Description: Lawson is part of a group of surnames that have been adapted as a boys' given name.
Alternative spellings: Lawsonne, Lorson

Layson
Meaning: Crowned with a laurel
Origin: English
Pronunciation: LAAY sun

L

Description: Layson most likely came from the name Law, as in Lawrence and as such shares the meaning of 'crowned with a laurel'. It is found as a surname but it can also be used as a given name.

Layton

Meaning: Leek settlement
Origin: English
Pronunciation: LAY tun
Description: Layton is a modern adaption of the Old English surname Leighton, which refers to 'a settlement with leeks growing'.
Alternative spellings: Laiton, Leighton, Leyton, Lleyton

Lazarus

Meaning: God has helped
Origin: Hebrew
Pronunciation: laaz AH rus
Description: Lazarus is a Hebrew surname and given name meaning 'God has helped'. He was also a figure in the Bible who was brought back from the dead by Jesus.

Leandro

Meaning: Lion man
Origin: Spanish
Pronunciation: lee ANN droh
Description: Leander is the Spanish version of the Greek name Leander, which comes from the Greek elements of *'leon'* meaning 'lion' and *'aner'* meaning 'man'. In Greek mythology, Leander fell in love with Hero, a priestess of Aphrodite who lived in a tower in Sestos. Every night Leander would swim across the Hellespont to be with her.
Alternative spellings: Leander

Ledley

Meaning: Living near a field or stream
Origin: English
Pronunciation: led LEE
Description: Ledley is a place name that referred to people who lived near a physical feature such as a field or stream. Although more common as a surname, it can be used as a given name as well.

Lee

Meaning: Wood; clearing
Origin: English
Pronunciation: LEE
Description: The name Lee comes from the Old English word *'lea'* meaning 'clearing' or 'meadow'. It is a unisex name.
Alternative spellings: Lei, Leigh

Leland

Meaning: Land lying fallow
Origin: English
Pronunciation: Lee lund
Description: Leland is an Old English surname, sometimes given as a unisex given name. It has risen in popularity as a given name in the last five years.
Alternative spellings: Leeland, Leelund

Lennie

Meaning: Brave lion
Origin: English
Pronunciation: LEN nee
Description: Lennie is a variant of the Old German name Leonard, meaning 'brave lion'.
Alternative spellings: Lenney, Lenni, Lenny

Lennon

Meaning: Dearest
Origin: English
Pronunciation: LEN on
Description: Lennon is a commonly found surname that has been adopted as a given name for boys. Popularity of this name is highly likely to be linked with the fame of the Beatles star John Lennon.
Alternative spellings: Lenon

Lennox

Meaning: Field on River Leven
Origin: Gaelic
Pronunciation: Len KNOCKS
Description: Lennox is a name made from the Scottish *'ach'*, meaning 'field', and *'llyfn'*, meaning 'smooth' or 'docile'. It was originally given as a surname for those living by the River Leven.
Alternative spellings: Lennux, Lenox, Lenux

Lenny

Meaning: Brave Lion
Origin: German
Pronunciation: len NEE
Description: Lenny is an abbreviated version of the German name Leonard. St. Leonard is the patron saint of peasants and horses.

Leo

Meaning: Lion
Origin: Latin
Pronunciation: LEE oh
Description: From the Latin for 'lion'. It is borne by numerous Christian saints and is most commonly found as the pet name for Leonardo.
Alternative spellings: Leoh, Lio

Leon

Meaning: Lion
Origin: Latin
Pronunciation: LEE on
Description: Leon is a derivative of Leo, the Latin personal name meaning 'lion'.
Alternative spellings: Leeon

Leonard

Meaning: Brave lion
Origin: German
Pronunciation: LEN ard
Description: Leonard is an Old French name, comprised of German elements to mean 'brave lion'. A French saint named Leonard lived in the 5th century and was the patron of peasants and horses.
Alternative spellings: Lenard, Leonerd

Leonardo

Meaning: Brave lion
Origin: German
Pronunciation: lee on ARDdough
Description: Leonardo is an elongation of the German name Leonard, despite the two names having different pronunciations of the *'leo'* element.
Alternative spellings: Lionardo

Leonidas

Meaning: Strong
Origin: Greek
Pronunciation: lee on EYE dass
Description: Leonidas was borne by the legendary King of Sparta who is said to have held off the entire Persian army with only 300 of his guard. To this day the name carries connotations of bravery and strength.
Alternative spellings: Leonydas, Lionidas

L

Leopold

Meaning: Bold people
Origin: German
Pronunciation: lee UH pold
Description: Leopold is a name of German origin. The name comes from the German words *'liut'* meaning 'people' and *'bold'* meaning 'brave'. Then *'liut'* was altered to the Latin *'leo'*.
Alternative spellings: Leopolde, Leupold

Leroy

Meaning: The king
Origin: French
Pronunciation: LEE roy
Description: Leroy is a French name that was popular in English-speaking countries in the early 20th century, though its popularity has decreased in recent years. The meaning of Leroy is 'the king', from the French phrase *'Le roi'*.
Alternative spellings: Leeroy, Leroi

Leslie

Meaning: Holly garden
Origin: Gaelic
Pronunciation: LEZ lee
Description: Leslie derives from the Scottish surname, meaning 'garden of holly'. It is also used as a unisex given name.
Alternative spellings: Leslee, Lesley, Lesli, Lesly

Levi

Meaning: Allied
Origin: Hebrew
Pronunciation: LEE vye
Description: Levi could be a shortened version of the name Levon. Levi is also a brand of jeans and so the forename may be derived from this. It is unisex but more commonly found on boys.
Alternative spellings: Leevi

Levin

Meaning: Dear friend
Origin: German
Pronunciation: LEH vin
Description: Levin is a modern German version of the Old German name Leobwin or Liebwin, meaning 'dear friend'. An English variation of this name is Lewin.

Levison

Meaning: Son of Levy
Origin: Hebrew
Pronunciation: leh VEE sun
Description: Levison is traditionally a Jewish last name meaning 'son of Levy'. It is rarely used as a first name but could be an adventurous choice for parents looking for something more unusual.

Levy

Meaning: Joining
Origin: Hebrew
Pronunciation: lev EE
Description: Levy is a Hebrew surname meaning 'joining'. It is also a surname found in Scotland and is a shortened form of Donlevy, meaning 'brown mountain'.
Alternative spellings: Levi

Lewis

Meaning: Famous warrior
Origin: French
Pronunciation: LOO iss
Description: Lewis first appeared as an English form of the French

name Louis. It could have also derived from the surname Lewis.
Alternative spellings: Lewys, Loui, Louie, Louis, Luis

Lewys
Meaning: Famed warrior
Origin: Welsh
Pronunciation: LOO is
Description: Lewys is the Welsh variant of the English name Lewis, which is the anglicisation of the French name Louis, meaning 'renowned fighter'. It is a popular name in Wales but the spelling is uncommon elsewhere.
Alternative spellings: Lewis, Loui, Louie, Louis, Luis

Leyton
Meaning: Meadow settlement
Origin: English
Pronunciation: lay TON
Description: The name Leyton is a variant of the Old English name Leighton, which has been used as a first name since the early 1800s. Can also be spelt Lleyton or Layton. It is found as both first name and surname, but currently isn't found very often as either.
Alternative spellings: Layton

Lex
Meaning: Defender of man
Origin: Greek
Pronunciation: LEX
Description: Lex is a shortened form of the Greek name Alexander, meaning 'defender of man'. It is a common boys' name in the Netherlands. Lex Luthor is the fictional nemesis of Superman.
Alternative spellings: Lecks, Lexx

Lexus
Meaning: Law
Origin: Latin
Pronunciation: LEX us
Description: Lexus derives from the Latin word for 'law' and is now used as a unisex forename.
Alternative spellings: Lexsus, Lexuss

Liam
Meaning: Protection
Origin: German
Pronunciation: LEE uhm
Description: Liam was originally a shortened version of the name William, but is now a name in its own right.
Alternative spellings: Lyam

Liev
Meaning: Lion
Origin: Russian
Pronunciation: lee EHV
Description: Liev is the Russian form of Leo, and means 'lion'. Liev Schreiber is a famous American actor with this name.

Lincoln
Meaning: Lake settlement
Origin: English
Pronunciation: LINK on
Description: This name is derived from the city of Lincoln in England, and has now become a very popular forename. It is also found as a surname.
Alternative spellings: Lincon

Linden
Meaning: Lime tree hill
Origin: German
Pronunciation: LIN den

L

Description: Linden is a name of German origin. Linden can also be a variant of the name Lyndon. The linden tree is a deciduous tree known as a 'lime' tree in British English, though not related to the citrus tree of the same name.
Alternative spellings: Lindan, Lindon, Lyndan, Lyndon

Linus
Meaning: Flax
Origin: Greek
Pronunciation: LYE nus
Description: In Greek mythology Linus is the musician son of Apollo. This is an uncommon boys' name.
Alternative spellings: Linas, Linnus

Lleyton
Meaning: Leek settlement
Origin: English
Pronunciation: LEY ton
Description: Lleyton is a modern variant of the Old English name Leighton, which literally means 'leek or meadow settlement'.
Alternative spellings: Laiton, Layton, Leighton, Leyton

Lloyd
Meaning: Grey
Origin: Welsh
Pronunciation: LOYD
Description: Lloyd is the transferred use of a Welsh surname that originates from a nickname meaning 'grey-haired'.
Alternative spellings: Loyd, Loyde

Lochlan
Meaning: Viking settler
Origin: Gaelic
Pronunciation: LOK lahn

Description: Lochlan comes from the Gaelic name Lochlann, a term used in the Highlands for 'Viking settlers'.
Alternative spellings: Lochlann, Lockan Locklan

Lockie
Meaning: From the land of the lakes
Origin: Scottish
Pronunciation: lock EE
Description: Lockie is a Scottish name meaning 'from the land of the lakes,' thought to have been used originally for Norse immigrants.
Alternative spellings: Locky

Logan
Meaning: Hollow
Origin: Gaelic
Pronunciation: LO gun
Description: Logan is a Scottish surname that has now transferred into a forename for both girls and boys. It is popular in Canada and New Zealand.
Alternative spellings: Logun

Loki
Meaning: Mischievous
Origin: Norse
Pronunciation: LOCK ee
Description: Loki is an uncommon boys' name of Old Norse origin. In the Old Norse mythology, Loki was the mischievous troublemaker in the Norse pantheon of gods.
Alternative spellings: Lokee, Lokey Lokie

Lorcan
Meaning: Little fierce one
Origin: Gaelic
Pronunciation: LOR ken

Description: Lorcan is an uncommon name of Irish and Gaelic origin, meaning 'little fierce one'. It is sometimes equated with Laurence, though Lorcan is a name in its own right. The name is growing in popularity in Ireland in recent years.
Alternative spellings: Lorcen, Lorkan, Lorken

Lorenzo
Meaning: Crowned with a laurel
Origin: Latin
Pronunciation: lor EN zoh
Description: Lorenzo is an Italian version of the English name Lawrence. It was originally a name given to a person from the Roman city Laurentum. It is a fairly uncommon name in the UK, but more popular in the US.

Louie
Meaning: Famed warrior
Origin: French
Pronunciation: LOO ee
Description: Louie is the English variation of the French name Louis, meaning 'renowned or famed warrior'.
Alternative spellings: Lewis, Lewys, Loui, Louis, Luis

Louis
Meaning: Famed warrior
Origin: French
Pronunciation: LOO ee; LOO is
Description: Louis was a very common name among French royals and noblemen. The name was borne by 16 French kings up to the French Revolution.
Alternative spellings: Lewis, Lewys, Loui, Louie, Luis

Lowell
Meaning: Wolf cub
Origin: French
Pronunciation: loh UHL
Description: The name Lowell is an Old French name meaning 'wolf cub'. It is also the name of a city in the American state of Massachusetts.

Lowen
Meaning: Joyful
Origin: Cornish
Pronunciation: loh WEN
Description: Lowen is a Cornish name that comes from a modern Cornish vocabulary word meaning 'joyful'. It is quite a rare name, even in the Cornish language.

Luc
Meaning: From Lucanus
Origin: Greek
Pronunciation: LUKE
Description: Luc is a variant of the Greek boys' name Luke, meaning 'from Lucanus'. The spelling Luc is common in French- and Dutch-speaking regions and is rarely seen in English-speaking regions.
Alternative spellings: Louke, Luke

Luca
Meaning: From Lucanus
Origin: Greek
Pronunciation: LOO cuh
Description: Luca is the Italian equivalent of the Greek name Luke and is extremely popular as a boys' name in Italy. It can also be spelt with a 'k', in which case its origin becomes Russian.
Alternative spellings: Louka, Lucca, Luka

L

Lucas

Meaning: From Lucanus
Origin: Greek
Pronunciation: LOO cuhs
Description: Lucas derives from the Greek name Loukas, meaning 'from Lucanus'. Lucas is an extremely popular name in Australia, America, Brazil, Canada, France and Germany.
Alternative spellings: Loukas, Lucas, Lucus, Lukas, Lukus

Lucien

Meaning: Light
Origin: Latin
Pronunciation: LOO shen; LOO see en
Description: Lucien is the French variant of the Latin boys' name Lucian, meaning 'light'. The name has recently had an upsurge in popularity.
Alternative spellings: Lucian, Lucjan

Lucius

Meaning: Light
Origin: Latin
Pronunciation: LOO shuss
Description: Lucius is a Greek name of Latin origin. It is derived from the Latin word *'lux'* meaning 'light'. Lucio is the Italian, Spanish and Portuguese translation of the name.
Alternative spellings: Lucio, Lucios

Luis

Meaning: Famed warrior
Origin: Spanish
Pronunciation: LOO ees
Description: Luis is the Spanish variation of the French name Louis. The spelling is rarely found in Britain.
Alternative spellings: Lewis, Lewys, Loui, Louie, Louis

Luka

Meaning: From Lucanus
Origin: Russian
Pronunciation: loo KA
Description: Luka could be considered a spelling variant of the Italian name Luca but is also a Russian name in its own right.
Alternative spellings: Louka, Luca, Lucca

Lukasz

Meaning: From Lucanus
Origin: Greek
Pronunciation: LOO kash
Description: Lukasz is a Polish variant of the Greek boys' name Luke.
Alternative spellings: Lukaj, Lukash

Luke

Meaning: From Lucanus
Origin: Greek
Pronunciation: LUKE
Description: Luke is the Middle English form of the Greek name Loukas. The third gospel in the New Testament has been ascribed to Luke, which may have helped its popularity.
Alternative spellings: Louke, Luc

Luqman

Meaning: Wise
Origin: Arabic
Pronunciation: LUK mahn
Description: The name Luqman is found in early Arabic and Turkish literature and also features in the

194

Quran. It carries the meaning of 'wise one'.
Alternative spellings: Lukman, Lukmahn, Luqmahn

Lyle
Meaning: Island
Origin: English
Pronunciation: lie YAL
Description: Lyle is an English surname derived from the French word *l'isle*, meaning 'island'.

Lyndon
Meaning: Lime tree hill
Origin: English
Pronunciation: LIN don
Description: Lyndon is the name of an area of Leicestershire. It most likely started as a family name for those from Lyndon, then became a boys' first name.
Alternative spellings: Lindan, Linden, Lindon, Lyndan

M

Mac
Meaning: Son of
Origin: Gaelic
Pronunciation: MAK
Description: Mac is a common first element in Scottish and Irish surnames. It is also often used as a nickname for given names such as MacKenzie.
Alternative spellings: Mack, Mak

Macaulay
Meaning: Son of righteousness
Origin: Scottish
Pronunciation: mac ALL lay
Description: Macaulay, sometimes written as MacAulay, is a Scottish boys' name meaning 'son of righteousness'. It is a surname as well as a first name.
Alternative spellings: MacAulay, McAulay

Maciej
Meaning: Gift from God
Origin: Hebrew
Pronunciation: MAH chey

Description: Maciej is the Polish variant of Matthew or Matthias, both of which mean 'gift from God'.
Alternative spellings: Maciaj

Mackenzie
Meaning: The fairest
Origin: Gaelic
Pronunciation: ma KEN zee
Description: Mackenzie derives from the Gaelic surname McKenzie, originally MacCoinneach. The meaning of the name varies. For a girl it is said to mean 'the fairest' yet as a boys' name it means 'handsome one'.
Alternative spellings: Mackenzi, Mackenzy, Makenzie, Mckenzi, Mckenzie, Mckenzy

Maddox
Meaning: Generous
Origin: Welsh
Pronunciation: MAH docks
Description: It is thought that the boys' name Maddox came from the Welsh surname Maddocks, which

L
M

means 'descendant of Maddock'. Now the name carries the meaning of 'generous'.
Alternative spellings: Maddocks, Madox

Madison
Meaning: Matthew's son
Origin: English
Pronunciation: MADD isson
Description: The name Madison started life as a surname, meaning 'son of Mad'. Mad was used as a pet form of Matthew in the Middle Ages. Although it has masculine roots, it is now a unisex name.
Alternative spellings: Maddison, Madisyn, Madyson

Mads
Meaning: Gift from God
Origin: Scandinavian
Pronunciation: mads
Description: Mads is the Scandinavian version of the name Matthew, and shares the same meaning of 'gift from God'. Mads Mikkelsen is a famous Danish actor with this name.

Magnus
Meaning: Great
Origin: Latin
Pronunciation: MAG nus
Description: Magnus is considered a royal name in Norway and Denmark and is often found in Germany and Scotland.
Alternative spellings: Magnes, Magnuss

Magor
Meaning: Council spear

Origin: German
Pronunciation: MAH goor
Description: Magor comes from the Old German name Malger, meaning 'council spear'. The name arrived in England in 1066, after the Norman Conquest.

Mahad
Meaning: The one who is great
Origin: Arabic
Pronunciation: mah HAD
Description: Mahad is an Arabic name meaning 'the one who is great'.
Alternative spellings: Maahad, Mahaad, Mahhad

Mahdi
Meaning: Guided by Allah
Origin: Arabic
Pronunciation: MAH dee
Description: Mahdi is an Arabic name, often favoured by Muslim parents due to its meaning of 'guided by Allah'.
Alternative spellings: Madi

Mahir
Meaning: Talented
Origin: Arabic
Pronunciation: ma HEER
Description: Mahir is an Arabic name popular in Turkey.
Alternative spellings: Maheer

Mahmoud
Meaning: Praiseworthy
Origin: Arabic
Pronunciation: mah MOOD
Description: Mahmoud is an Arabic name meaning 'praiseworthy'.
Alternative spellings: Mahmud

Maison

Meaning: One who works with stone
Origin: English
Pronunciation: may SUN
Description: The name Maison is a modern spelling variant of the name Mason. It can be a boys' or girls' name and be used as a first name or surname. The original spelling has been around since the Middle Ages, but this variant is very modern and fairly uncommon.
Alternative spellings: Mason, Mayson

Maiwand

Meaning: Name of a village in Afghanistan
Origin: Afghan
Pronunciation: mai WAND
Description: Maiwand is actually a place name, referring to a village in Afghanistan. It is notable for the 1880 Battle of Maiwand.

Major

Meaning: Greater; military rank
Origin: Latin
Pronunciation: may JOOR
Description: Major is a Latin name meaning 'greater'. It is also a military rank, given to officers in higher positions.

Maksim

Meaning: The greatest
Origin: Russian
Pronunciation: MACK sim
Description: Maksim is the Russian form of the name Maxim, meaning 'the greatest'. Both names come from the name Maximus, which had Roman origins. However, this form of the name is most commonly used in Slavic countries.
Alternative spellings: Maxim

Maksymillian

Meaning: The greatest
Origin: Latin
Pronunciation: mac CEE mil ee an
Description: Maksymilian is an alternative spelling of the Latin name Maximilian, which means 'greatest'. It is likely to be a name that hails from Eastern Europe. The name Maximilian was created when Fredrick the Third, the German Emperor, combined the names Scipio Aemilianus and Quintus Fabius Maximus to name his son; they were both Roman generals.
Alternative spellings: Maximilian

Malachy

Meaning: My messenger
Origin: English
Pronunciation: MAL a kye
Description: From the Hebrew name Malachi, who was a prophet and the writer of the final book in the Old Testament. The name has risen greatly in popularity in recent years.
Alternative spellings: Malachey, Malachi, Malakai, Malaki

Malak

Meaning: Angel
Origin: Arabic
Pronunciation: MAH lak
Description: Malak is the name of an archangel in Islamic belief and the name still carries that meaning.

M

It is a unisex name more often found on boys.
Alternative spellings: Malach

Malcolm
Meaning: Devotee of St Columba
Origin: Gaelic
Pronunciation: MAL kum
Description: Malcolm derives from the Gaelic name 'Mael Coluim', meaning 'devotee of St Columba'. St Columba was a popular 6th-century Irish monk.
Alternative spellings: Malcom

Malik
Meaning: King
Origin: Arabic
Pronunciation: MAL ik
Description: Malik comes from the Arabic word for 'king'. It has risen in popularity since its use by African-American activist Malcolm X, who took the Islamic name El-Hajj Malik El-Shabazz.
Alternative spellings: Malic, Malick

Manal
See entry in 'Names for Baby Girls A–Z'

Manraj
Meaning: The heart's king
Origin: Punjabi
Pronunciation: man RAJ
Description: The name Manraj has its origins in the Punjabi language. It is used largely in English and Indian as both a given name and a surname. The meaning of Manraj is 'heart's king'.
Alternative spellings: Maanraj, Manraaj

Manson
Meaning: Son of Magnus
Origin: Scottish
Pronunciation: man SUN
Description: Manson is a Scottish surname meaning 'son of Magnus' and is most often found in the far north-east of the country. This is a very common last name in Scotland. This follows the contemporary trend of using last names as first names.

Manu
Meaning: Wisdom
Origin: Sanskrit
Pronunciation: man OO
Description: Manu, when translated from Sanskrit, means 'wisdom'. It is also the name of the progenitor of mankind in the Hindu religion.

Manuel
Meaning: God is with us
Origin: Hebrew
Pronunciation: mah noo EL
Description: Manuel is a name of Hebrew origin, meaning 'God is with us'. It is the Spanish and Portuguese form of Immanuel.
Alternative spellings: Manwell

Manveer
Meaning: Brave-minded
Origin: Punjabi
Pronunciation: man VEER
Description: Manveer is a common boys' name meaning 'brave-minded'. It has its origins in the Punjabi language. Manveer is a variant form of the Indian name Manvir.
Alternative spellings: Maanveer, Manvir

Marc

Meaning: From the god Mars
Origin: Latin
Pronunciation: MARK
Description: Marc is the French form of the name Mark, and this spelling is becoming increasingly popular around the globe. It is most likely derived from the name of the Roman god of war, Mars.
Alternative spellings: Mark

Marcel

Meaning: From the god Mars
Origin: Latin
Pronunciation: MAR sell
Description: The name Marcel derives from the Latin name Marcellus, itself derived from the name of the Roman god of war, Mars. This name was also borne by many popes and saints. Forms of this name include the Spanish variant Marcelo and the French version Marceau.
Alternative spellings: Marcell, Marrcel

Marco

Meaning: From the god Mars
Origin: Latin
Pronunciation: MAR koh
Description: Marco is the Italian, Spanish and Portuguese form of the name Mark. This name was commonly used among the Romans and given to boys who were born in March, as this is the month of the god Mars.
Alternative spellings: Marcoh, Marko

Marcus

Meaning: From the god Mars
Origin: Latin
Pronunciation: MAR kus
Description: The name Marcus, like Marcel and Marco, is derived from the name of the Roman god of war, Mars. It may have typically been given to boys born in March.
Alternative spellings: Markus

Marek

Meaning: Dedicated to Mars
Origin: Latin
Pronunciation: MAR ik
Description: Marek is a popular Czech, Polish and Slovak name, the equivalent of Mark in English. Marek is of Latin origin and means 'dedicated to Mars'.
Alternative spellings: Marec, Mareck, Marik

Mario

Meaning: God of war; male
Origin: Italian
Pronunciation: MAH ryo
Description: Mario is the Italian form of the name Marius, which either comes from Mars, the name of the Roman God of war, or the Latin root *maris*, meaning 'male'. A popular Mario is the hero of the Nintendo video game, Super Mario Bros.

Mark

Meaning: From the god Mars
Origin: Latin
Pronunciation: MARK
Description: The name Mark derived from the Roman god of war, Mars. According to Arthurian legend, King Mark was the aged ruler of Cornwall, whose name may be derived from the Celtic word *'march'*, meaning 'horse'.
Alternative spellings: Marc

M

Marley

Meaning: Forest of joy
Origin: English
Pronunciation: MAHr ley
Description: Marley is an Old English surname, which has now been transferred to a unisex given name.
Alternative spellings: Marlee, Marli, Marlie, Marly

Marlon

Meaning: Little hawk
Origin: English
Pronunciation: MAR lon
Description: Marlon is a unisex name of English origin, meaning 'little hawk'. The name gained popularity in the 1900s, perhaps due to the fame of actor Marlon Brando.
Alternative spellings: Marlan, Marlen, Marlonn

Marlow

Meaning: Driftwood
Origin: English
Pronunciation: mar LOW
Description: Marlow is an Old English name meaning 'driftwood'. It was also a place name in England and was given as a surname to people who lived in the area.
Alternative spellings: Marlowe

Marsh

Meaning: Marsh
Origin: English
Pronunciation: MARSH
Description: The name Marsh was originally a surname adopted by those who lived on marshy ground. The name may also be thought of as a short form of the German name Marshall, meaning 'horse worker'.
Alternative spellings: Marshe

Marshall

Meaning: Horse worker
Origin: German
Pronunciation: MAR shawl
Description: Marshall is a transferred surname, ultimately derived from the German for 'horse servant'. It is now a popular first name.
Alternative spellings: Marshal, Marshell

Martin

Meaning: From the god Mars
Origin: Latin
Pronunciation: MAR tin
Description: The name Martin is derived from the Latin name Martinus, originally attributed to the Roman god of war, Mars.
Alternative spellings: Martinn

Marty

Meaning: God of War
Origin: Latin
Pronunciation: MAR tee
Description: Marty is a short form of the name Martin. Both names are derived from the Latin name Martinus, originally attributed to the Roman god of war, Mars.

Marvin

Meaning: Sea friend
Origin: Welsh
Pronunciation: MAR vin
Description: Marvin is a popular boys' name of Welsh origin and is a variant of Mervin. It is common as both a given name and as a surname. Its popularity has fallen since the middle of the 20th century.
Alternative spellings: Marven, Marvin, Marvyn

Marwan

Meaning: Solid stone
Origin: Arabic
Pronunciation: MAR wan
Description: Marwan is a name of Arabic origin, meaning 'solid stone'. It is common in some Arabic states such as Egypt, Lebanon and Tunisia.
Alternative spellings: Marwen

Mason

Meaning: Stoneworker
Origin: French
Pronunciation: MAY son
Description: This name has been around since the Middle Ages. It used to be given as a surname to those who worked with stone but has now transferred into a unisex given name.
Alternative spellings: Maison, Mayson

Massimo

Meaning: The greatest
Origin: Latin
Pronunciation: MA see mo
Description: Massimo is a name of Latin origin, meaning 'the greatest'. It is the Italian form of Maximus.
Alternative spellings: Masimo, Massimoh

Matas

Meaning: Gift from God
Origin: Hebrew
Pronunciation: MA tas
Description: Matas appears to be a variant of the name Matthew, coming from northern Europe. It is very popular in Britain, whereas Matas is usually found on the continent.
Alternative spellings: Mathas, Mattas

Matei

Meaning: Gift of God
Origin: Bulgarian
Pronunciation: MAH tei
Description: Matei is the Bulgarian form of the name Matthew, meaning 'gift of God'. Mattew was the author of the first gospel in the New Testament and was a Christian evangelist.

Mateo

Meaning: Gift of God
Origin: Spanish
Pronunciation: mah TEE oh
Description: Mateo is the Spanish form of the name Matthew, which in turn is the English form of the name of the Christian evangelist and author of the first gospel in the New Testament. The name is a form of the Hebrew name Mattathia, which means 'a gift from God'.
Alternative spellings: Matteo

Mateusz

Meaning: Gift from God
Origin: Hebrew
Pronunciation: MA tee oosh
Description: Mateusz is derived from the biblical name Matthew and is used commonly in the Polish language.
Alternative spellings: Mateuzs

Mathis

Meaning: Gift of God
Origin: French
Pronunciation: math US
Description: Mathis is the French version of the name Matthew, and as such shares the same meaning of 'gift of God'.

M

Matthew

Meaning: Gift from God
Origin: Hebrew
Pronunciation: MATH yoo
Description: Matthew is the English form of the name of the Christian evangelist, author of the first gospel in the New Testament. It derives from the Hebrew name Mattathia, meaning 'gift from God'.
Alternative spellings: Mathew

Matthias

Meaning: Gift of God
Origin: Greek
Pronunciation: ma THYE us
Description: Matthias is a name of German, Greek and Hebrew origin. The name is used across Europe in a variety of variant forms as both a given name and a surname. In the Christian Bible, Matthias was the disciple selected to replace Judas as an apostle.
Alternative spellings: Mathias, Mathyas

Maurice

Meaning: One From Mauritania
Origin: Latin
Pronunciation: MORE us
Description: Maurice is a Latin name, derived from the words 'mauritius' or 'mauricius' and refers to a person who is from Mauritania, which corresponds to modern-day Morocco.

Maverick

Meaning: Independent
Origin: English
Pronunciation: mav ER rik
Description: Maverick is a name whose meaning is derived from the English word of the same spelling, meaning 'independent'. It was first used in the 1950s Western TV series of the same name.
Alternative spellings: Maverik

Max

Meaning: The greatest
Origin: Latin
Pronunciation: MAKS
Description: Max is a short form of Maximillian and to a lesser extent Maxwell, but it is now often found as a name in its own right.
Alternative spellings: Maks

Maxim

Meaning: The greatest
Origin: Latin
Pronunciation: MACK sim
Description: This Russian name derives from Maksim, a variation of the name Maximus. This name had Roman origins and is most commonly used in Slavic-speaking countries.
Alternative spellings: Maksim, Maxsim

Maxime

Meaning: The greatest
Origin: Latin
Pronunciation: mahk SEEM
Description: Maxime is a name of Latin origin, meaning 'the greatest'. It is the French form of Maximus.
Alternative spellings: Macsime, Maksime, Maxeem

Maximilian

Meaning: The greatest
Origin: Latin
Pronunciation: MAC cee MIL ee an
Description: Derived from the Latin word *'maximus'*, meaning 'greatest'. The name was invented

by German emperor Frederick the Third, by combining the surnames of Roman generals Scipio Aemilianus and Quintus Fabius Maximus to name his son. The name is popular in German-speaking countries.
Alternative spellings: Maximillian, Maxymilian

Maximus
Meaning: The greatest
Origin: Latin
Pronunciation: MAX i muus
Description: Maximus is a variant of the name Maxim. The name was borne by a variety of saints and was very popular among early Christians.
Alternative spellings: Maksimus, Maxymus

Maxwell
Meaning: Mac's well
Origin: English
Pronunciation: MAKS wel
Description: Maxwell comes from a Scottish surname meaning 'well belonging to Mac'.
Alternative spellings: Macswell, Makswell, Maxwel

McKenzie
Meaning: Fair One
Origin: Gaelic
Pronunciation: ma KEN zee
Description: This can also be spelt as Mackenzie. This name can be applied to both boys and girls, with the meaning varying between 'the fairest' for a girl, or 'son of the fair one' for a boy. It originated from the Gaelic surname 'Mac Coinnich'.
Alternative spellings: Mackenzie

McKinley
Meaning: Son of fair hero
Origin: Scottish
Pronunciation: mac KIN lee
Description: McKinley is a Scottish surname meaning 'son of fair hero'. This follows the contemporary trend of using last names as first names.
Alternative spellings: MacKinley

Md
Meaning: Praiseworthy
Origin: Arabic
Pronunciation: EM dee
Description: Md is an uncommon Arabic boys' name that is a much shortened variant of the Arabic name Muhammad, named after the prophet.

Mehdi
Meaning: Rightly guided
Origin: Arabic
Pronunciation: MEHH dee
Description: A variant of the Arabic name Madhi, meaning 'rightly guided'.
Alternative spellings: Mehdie, Mehdy

Mehmet
Meaning: Praiseworthy
Origin: Arabic
Pronunciation: meh MET
Description: Mehmet is an Arabic boys' name and a variant of the old Turkish name Mehmed, which is derived from the prophet Muhammad. Mehmed II was Sultan of the Ottoman Empire and a national hero in Turkey. He conquered Constantinople and brought an end to the Byzantine Empire. His name and its variants

M

are among the most popular boys' names in Turkey.

Alternative spellings: Mehmed, Mehmett, Mehmud

Mekhi

Meaning: Who is like God?
Origin: Hawaiian
Pronunciation: MEH kay
Description: Mekhi is an increasingly popular name of Hawaiian and Hebrew origin. It is a modern variant of the popular Hebrew name Michael. The name transliterates as the question 'who is like God?'
Alternative spellings: Mechi, Mekhai

Meleager

Meaning: Burning fire
Origin: Greek
Pronunciation: mel EE ah gar
Description: In Greek mythology, Meleager was a fierce warrior, second only to Heracles in his abilities.
Alternative spellings: Meleaeger, Meleger

Melvin

Meaning: Bad town
Origin: English
Pronunciation: MEL vin
Description: Melvin is a boys' given name of English and French origin. It is probably derived from the surname Melville, from the French for 'bad town'.
Alternative spellings: Melven

Memphis

Meaning: Place in United States
Origin: English
Pronunciation: MEM fiss

Description: Memphis is a place name, more specifically a city in the American state of Tennessee. Like Brooklyn and Paris, this is a trendy place name that would be a good choice for adventurous parents.

Menelaus

Meaning: Hero
Origin: Greek
Pronunciation: men uh LAOW us
Description: In Greek mythology, Menelaus was a legendary king of Mycenaean Sparta and the husband of Helen of Troy. He was a hero of the Trojan war.
Alternative spellings: Menelaos, Menelyos

Mercury

Meaning: Merchandise
Origin: Latin
Pronunciation: MEHR cure ree
Description: In Roman mythology, Mercury was a messenger who wore winged sandals. He was the god of trade, thieves and travel. It is also the name of the closest planet to the sun in the solar system.
Alternative spellings: Mercuri, Murcury

Merrick

Meaning: Dark-skinned; Moorish
Origin: Latin
Pronunciation: MEH rick
Description: More commonly found as a surname and often associated with Joseph Merrick (the Elephant Man), Merrick as a first name is thought to have come from the name Maurice, which has Latin roots.
Alternative spellings: Merrick

Micah

Meaning: Who is like God?
Origin: Hebrew
Pronunciation: MY kah
Description: The name Micah is a variation of the name Michael and therefore carries biblical associations. Micah wrote the book prophesising the breakdown of Jerusalem. The original spelling of the name Micah is actually Micaiah.
Alternative spellings: Mica

Michael

Meaning: Who is like God?
Origin: Hebrew
Pronunciation: MY cal
Description: Michael is a biblical name borne by an archangel protector of the Hebrews, regarded as a Catholic saint. The name was also borne by a Persian prince mentioned in the Book of Daniel. Michael has been a relentlessly popular name since the early 20th century.
Alternative spellings: Micael, Micel, Michel, Michul, Mikal, Mikael, Mikail, Mikhail

Mick

Meaning: Who is like god?
Origin: English
Pronunciation: mick
Description: Mick is a shortened version of Michael and as such, shares the same meaning of 'who is like God?'. Mick Jagger is the lead singer of the Rolling Stones.

Miguel

Meaning: Who is like God?
Origin: Hebrew
Pronunciation: mee GHEL
Description: Miguel is the Spanish form of the name Michael.

Alternative spellings: Migel

Mike

Meaning: Who is like God?
Origin: Hebrew
Pronunciation: MYK
Description: A common short form of the Hebrew name Michael, now given as a first name in its own right.
Alternative spellings: Myke

Mikel

Meaning: Who is like God?
Origin: Hebrew
Pronunciation: MEE kel
Description: Mikel is an uncommon name of Hebrew origin. It is a modern American-English variant of Michael, meaning 'who is like God?'
Alternative spellings: Mikil

Mikey

Meaning: Who is like God?
Origin: Hebrew
Pronunciation: MY kee
Description: The name Mikey is a variant of Micah and also Michael. It is often used as a pet form for Michael or Mick.
Alternative spellings: Mikie, Mykey, Myki, Mykie

Mikolaj

Meaning: Victory of the people
Origin: Greek
Pronunciation: Mee CO low
Description: Although this name derives from Old Greek it is mainly used in Polish- and Russian-speaking countries. It is a form of the English and French name Nicholas.
Alternative spellings: Mickolaj

M

Milan

Meaning: Loving
Origin: Slavic
Pronunciation: mih LAN
Description: Milan was originally a name of Slavic origin, meaning 'loving'. However it is also the name of a major Italian city, and is given to both boys and girls after the city of Milan.
Alternative spellings: Milanne, Millan

Miles

Meaning: Mild and merciful
Origin: Latin
Pronunciation: MY ulls
Description: Miles is thought to have come from the Latin name Milo, meaning 'mild and merciful'. It could also have come into usage as a shortened form of Michael.
Alternative spellings: Myels, Myles

Miller

Meaning: Grain mill worker
Origin: English
Pronunciation: MIH ler
Description: Miller is an English surname given to a person working in a grain mill. It had been adapted as a first name by the 19th century, although it has never been particularly common.
Alternative spellings: Miler

Milo

Meaning: Mild and merciful
Origin: Latin
Pronunciation: MY lo
Description: Milo is a Roman name, meaning 'mild and merciful'. It could also be a shortened form of Miles.
Alternative spellings: Miloh, Mylo, Myloh

Milosz

Meaning: Lover of glory
Origin: Czech
Pronunciation: MEE los
Description: Milosz, the pet form of Miloslav, is the Polish variant of the Czech name Milos. It is common as both a given name for boys and as a surname.
Alternative spellings: Meelos, Milos

Minako

See entry in 'Names for Baby Girls A–Z'

Miran

Meaning: Peace; World
Origin: Slavic
Pronunciation: MEER an
Description: Miran is a Slavic name derived from the element of '*miru*,' meaning 'peace' or 'world'. This is quite an unusual name, but would be a good choice for parents looking for somthing more unusual.

Mischa

See entry in 'Names for Baby Girls A–Z'

Mitch

Meaning: Who is like God?
Origin: English
Pronunciation: mitch
Description: Mitch is derived from Mitchell, which in turn is a variant of Michael and as such, shares the same meaning of 'Who is like God?'.

Mitchell

Meaning: Who is like God?
Origin: Hebrew
Pronunciation: MITCH ell
Description: The forename Mitchell has been transferred from a common surname that derived from Michel (a medieval alternative of Michael).
Alternative spellings: Mitchel, Mitchull

Mohammed

Meaning: Worthy of glory and praise
Origin: Arabic
Pronunciation: moh HAM mad; moh HAM med
Description: Mohammed and its spelling variants are some of the most frequently used boys' names in the world. It is popular with Muslim parents as it is the name of the prophet Muhammad.
Alternative spellings: Mohamad, Mohamed, Mohammad, Mohammod, Muhammad, Muhamed Muhammed, Muhamad

Mohsin

Meaning: Charitable
Origin: Arabic
Pronunciation: moh SEEN
Description: Mohsin is an Arabic name said to mean 'charitable' or 'beneficial'.
Alternative spellings: Muhsin

Moise

Meaning: Delivered from the water
Origin: Romanian
Pronunciation: MOO ise
Description: Moise is the Romanian spelling of the name Moses and as such, shares the same name meaning. Moses is the name of the Biblical character in the Old Testament, who leads the Israelites out of Egypt.

Mona

See entry in 'Names for Baby Girls A–Z'

Montague

Meaning: Pointed hill
Origin: French
Pronunciation: MON tay gu
Description: Montague is a name of French origin, meaning 'pointed hill'. It was common as a given name in the 19th century. It is also the name of a number of cities in America and Canada.
Alternative spellings: Montagew, Montagu

Montgomery

Meaning: Gomeric's hill
Origin: French
Pronunciation: mont GOM err ree
Description: Montgomery was originally a surname that gradually transformed into a first name over time. Mainly used in English-speaking countries, this name has fallen out of popular use.
Alternative spellings: Montgomerey

Monty

Meaning: Pointed hill
Origin: French
Pronunciation: mont EE
Description: Monty is a short form of the name Montague, a name of French origin, meaning 'pointed hill'. It was common as a given name in the 19th century.

M

Morgan

Meaning: Great circle
Origin: Welsh
Pronunciation: MOR gun
Description: The name Morgan derives from the Old Welsh masculine name Morcant, which can mean 'bright or great sea' or 'great circle'.
Alternative spellings: Morgann, Morganne

Morris

Meaning: Dark-skinned
Origin: English
Pronunciation: MORE us
Description: Morris is derived from the Latin Mauritius, meaning Moorish and referring to the Moors, a group of Arabic people who had dark colouring.
Alternative spellings: Morriss, Moris

Morrison

Meaning: Son of Morris
Origin: English
Pronunciation: moriss SUN
Description: Morrison is an English surname meaning 'son of Morris'. This follows the contemporary trend of using last names as first names.

Moses

Meaning: Delivered from the water
Origin: Hebrew
Pronunciation: MOZ es
Description: Moses is a biblical name associated with the famous story in the Old Testament, where he was abandoned as a baby but grows up to lead the Israelites out of Egypt and to the Promised Land, as well as receiving the Ten Commandments from God.

Moshe

Meaning: Taken from the water
Origin: Hebrew
Pronunciation: mo SHEH
Description: Moshe is the original Hebrew name for Moses. Due to their biblical use the names are often said to mean 'taken from the water' because of the story of Moses.
Alternative spellings: Mosh

Murray

Meaning: Lord and master
Origin: Gaelic
Pronunciation: MUH ree
Description: Murray is a boys' name of Gaelic origin, meaning 'lord and master'. It is one of the most common surnames in the world, and was once common as a given name.
Alternative spellings: Murrey, Murry

Muriel

Meaning: Sea; bright
Origin: Celtic
Pronunciation: MUR ee AL
Description: Muriel is a Celtic name that was originally spelt Muirgheal. The name is composed of 'muir' meaning 'sea,' and 'gheal' meaning 'bright'.

Murphy

Meaning: Sea warrior
Origin: Irish
Pronunciation: MUR fee
Description: Murphy is an Irish surname that was originally spelt Murchadh. Composed of the elements 'muir' meaning 'sea' and 'cath' meaning 'battle'. Although it was originally a surname it is now a popular choice for a first name.
Alternative spellings: Murphee

Musa

Meaning: Taken from the water
Origin: Hebrew
Pronunciation: MOO sa
Description: The name Musa is the Arabic version of the biblical name Moses. It is mainly used in Turkish-, Arabic- and Hebrew-speaking countries. Although the name is technically masculine, it can also be found used for girls.
Alternative spellings: Musah

Musab

Meaning: Undefeatable
Origin: Arabic
Pronunciation: mu SAAB
Description: Musab is an uncommon name, said to mean 'undefeatable'. In Islamic belief, Musab was the name of a sahabah, a companion of the prophet Muhammad.
Alternative spellings: Musabe, Mussab

Mustafa

Meaning: Lordly
Origin: Arabic
Pronunciation: MOO staf fa
Description: The name Mustafa derives from the same word in Arabic to mean 'chosen'. The name is popular within Muslim families as Mustafa was often used as one of the names for the prophet Muhammad.
Alternative spellings: Mustafah

Myles

Meaning: Fighter
Origin: German
Pronunciation: my ULZZ
Description: Myles is a variation of the name Milon, which is Germanic in origin. It is also a variation of Miles, which was brought over to England via the means of the Norman Conquest. However, there is also a Latin version in which it may have derived, Milo, which means soldier.
Alternative spellings: Miles

Myron

Meaning: Sweet oil; perfume
Origin: Greek
Pronunciation: my RON
Description: Myron was used originally to honour the Greek sculptor of the same name and means 'sweet oil' or 'perfume' in Ancient Greek. This name is more popular in the United States but has declined in popularity since the 1960s.
Alternative spellings: Miron

M
N

N

Nabeel

Meaning: Noble
Origin: Arabic
Pronunciation: nah BEEL
Description: Nabeel is a masculine name of Arabic origin and it is said to mean 'noble'.

Alternative spellings: Nabeal, Nabel, Nabil

Nadeem

Meaning: Life of the party
Origin: Arabic
Pronunciation: nah DEEM

Description: Nadeem is an Arabic name meaning 'life of the party', referring to a friend or companion that you would like to wine and dine with.

Nana
See entry in 'Names for Baby Girls A–Z'

Napoleon
Meaning: Lion of Naples
Origin: Italian
Pronunciation: nap OH lee ON
Description: Napoleon is an Italian name meaning 'lion of Naples'. It is derived from the elements of '*Napoli*' meaning 'Naples' and '*leone*' meaning 'lion'.

Narcissus
Meaning: Sleep
Origin: Greek
Pronunciation: nar SISS suss
Description: Narcissus is an uncommon name of Greek origin. In Greek mythology, Narcissus fell in love with his own reflection in a pool, and there he remained, mesmerised, until he turned into a flower – the narcissus, commonly known in English as a daffodil.
Alternative spellings: Narkissos, Narssisus

Nat
See entry in 'Names for Baby Girls A–Z'

Natan
Meaning: God has given
Origin: Hebrew
Pronunciation: NEE tan
Description: Natan is a variant of the name Nathan and is very popular in Russian- and Spanish-speaking countries. It is seen in the Bible as belonging to a prophet who overthrew King David.
Alternative spellings: Naytan

Nate
Meaning: God has given
Origin: Hebrew
Pronunciation: NAYT
Description: Nate is a short form of Nathan or Nathaniel, but it is now given as a first name in its own right.
Alternative spellings: Nayte

Nathan
Meaning: God has given
Origin: Hebrew
Pronunciation: NAYTH ann
Description: Nathan is considered a biblical name as it is the name of a prophet who overthrew King David. It can also be a shortened form of Nathaniel or Jonathan.
Alternative spellings: Nathen

Nathanial
Meaning: God has given
Origin: Hebrew
Pronunciation: Na THAN yel
Description: Nathanial is derived from Nathan, both of which are Hebrew in origin and are said to mean 'God has given'. Nathanial was the first name of an apostle, but he was referred to as his surname Bartholomew. Nathaniel is less commonly found than Nathan but is becoming increasingly popular.
Alternative spellings: Nathaneal, Nathaniel, Nathanyal

Ned
Meaning: Wealthy guardian
Origin: English

Pronunciation: NED
Description: Ned is a pet form of Edward, but also a name in its own right.

Nehemiah
Meaning: Comforter
Origin: Hebrew
Pronunciation: nee ah MYE ah
Description: Nehemiah is a name of Hebrew origin. In the Hebrew Bible he is the central figure of the Book of Nehemiah. The name has risen in popularity in America in recent years.
Alternative spellings: Nahumiah, Nehemia, Nehumiah

Neil
Meaning: Champion
Origin: Gaelic
Pronunciation: NEEL
Description: The name Neil comes from the Irish name Niall, the origin of which is disputed. Possible meanings are 'cloud', 'passionate' and 'champion'.
Alternative spellings: Neal, Neel, Neill

Nelson
Meaning: Son of Neil
Origin: English
Pronunciation: NEL sun
Description: Nelson has been a common name for boys for many centuries. It is also one of the most common surnames in the English-speaking world.
Alternative spellings: Nellson, Nelsen, Nelsun

Neo
Meaning: Gift; new
Origin: African, English

Pronunciation: NEE oh
Description: The name Neo can be found in several countries. It could originate from the English word 'new' or the African word meaning 'gift'.
Alternative spellings: Neoh, Neyo

Neptune
Meaning: God of the sea
Origin: Latin
Pronunciation: NEP tune
Description: In Roman mythology, Neptune was the Roman god of water, the sea and religion. Neptune is also the name of a planet in the solar system.
Alternative spellings: Neptoone

Nessus
Meaning: Centaur
Origin: Greek
Pronunciation: NESS us
Description: In Greek mythology, Nessus was a famous centaur who was killed by Heracles, and whose tainted blood in turn killed Heracles.
Alternative spellings: Nessos, Nessuss

Nestor
Meaning: Return
Origin: Greek
Pronunciation: NES tor
Description: Nestor appeared in Homer's epic poem *The Odyssey*, where, despite his old age, he is noted for his bravery and oratorical ability.
Alternative spellings: Nesstor, Nestur

Neville
Meaning: New village
Origin: French

N

Pronunciation: neh VILLE
Description: Neville is a French name meaning 'new village'. Originally a surname, it has been used as a first name since the 19th century.

Niall

Meaning: Champion; cloud; passionate
Origin: Gaelic
Pronunciation: NY al
Description: Niall is the Irish root of the English name Neil. Niall's origin is somewhat disputed; as well as 'champion', it could mean 'cloud' or 'passionate'.
Alternative spellings: Nial, Nihal, Nyle

Niam

Meaning: Happiness; comfort
Origin: Arabic
Pronunciation: nah EEM
Description: Niam is a variation of the boys' name, Naeem, meaning 'happiness' or 'comfort' in Arabic. However, it is also a Hebrew name and in that language, the name means 'pleasant'.
Alternative spellings: Naeem

Nicholas

Meaning: Victory of the people
Origin: Greek
Pronunciation: NI cuh lus
Description: Nicholas comes from the Greek name Nikolaos, derived from the words for 'victory' and 'people'. Nicholas was a 4th-century bishop who brought gifts to children around Christmas time and earned the name of St Nicholas.
Alternative spellings: Nicolas, Nikolas

Nick

Meaning: Victory of the people
Origin: Greek
Pronunciation: NIK
Description: Nick is a shortened form of Nicholas, but it is now given as a name in its own right.
Alternative spellings: Nic, Nik

Nicky

Meaning: Victory of the people
Origin: Greek, English
Pronunciation: NIK ee
Description: Nicky is a unisex name of Greek and English origin. It is a shortened variant of the Greek name Nicholas, meaning 'victory of the people'.
Alternative spellings: Nickee, Nicki, Nickie

Nico

Meaning: Victory of the people
Origin: Greek
Pronunciation: NICK oh
Description: Nico can be considered a shortened form of the name Nicholas and is often seen in Europe as a given name in its own right.
Alternative spellings: Nicoh, Niko

Nicol

Meaning: Victory of the people
Origin: Greek
Pronunciation: nih KOL
Description: Nicol is a rare unisex variant of the masculine name Nicholas.
Alternative spellings: Nicoll

Nihal

Meaning: Joyous
Origin: Arabic
Pronunciation: nih HAHL

Description: Nihal is a unisex Arabic name. It could also be considered a spelling variant of the Irish name Niall.
Alternative spellings: Niall, Nihall

Nikhil
Meaning: Whole
Origin: Sanskrit
Pronunciation: nih KEEL
Description: Nikhil is a boys' name, meaning 'whole'. It is often found in India.
Alternative spellings: Nichil, Nikhill

Nikita
Meaning: Undefeated
Origin: Russian
Pronunciation: nee KEE ath
Description: In its original Russian form Nikita is a masculine name said to mean 'undefeated'. It has since been found in many languages used as a unisex or a feminine name.
Alternative spellings: Nichita, Nicita, Nikitah

Nikko
Meaning: Victory
Origin: English
Pronunciation: nee KOH
Description: Nikko is a version of the Greek name Nike meaning 'victory'. It is also the basis of the common name Nicholas.
Alternative spellings: Niko

Niko
Meaning: Victory of the people
Origin: Greek
Pronunciation: nee KOH
Description: Niko is a variation of the name Nico, which itself is a variation of Nicholas. It can be presumed to share the same meaning as Nicholas, which is 'victory of the people'.
Alternative spellings: Nikko

Nikolai
Meaning: Victory of the people
Origin: Greek
Pronunciation: NIK oh lye
Description: Nikolai is a Slavic variant of the boys' name Nicholas, of Greek origin, meaning 'victory of the people'.
Alternative spellings: Nicholai, Nicholi, Nikolay, Nikoli

Nikodem
Meaning: Conquerer of the people
Origin: Slavik
Pronunciation: ni KO dem
Description: Nikodem is a name that has been popular in Poland for many years, and has now begun to rise in popularity in the UK. It is likely to be an alternative spelling of the name Nikodemus. It means 'conqueror of the people' or 'people's conqueror'.

Nile
Meaning: Champion; cloud; passionate
Origin: English
Pronunciation: nay AL
Description: Nile is a variation of the name Niall, which is the Irish root of the English name Neil. The origin of Niall is somewhat disputed - as well as 'champion', it could mean 'cloud' or 'passionate'. It can also refer to the Nile River in Egypt.
Alternative spellings: Niall

N

Noah

Meaning: Rest
Origin: Hebrew
Pronunciation: NO uh
Description: Noah is the biblical character who built an ark to save two animals of every species from God's flood. It is currently experiencing a burst of popularity.
Alternative spellings: Noa

Noel

Meaning: Birthday of Christ
Origin: French
Pronunciation: NO ell
Description: Noel is a unisex name that comes from a French word meaning 'birthday'. The word now has associations with Christ's birthday, Christmas Day. The spelling Noelle is favoured for girls.
Alternative spellings: Nowell

Nojus

Meaning: Rest
Origin: Hebrew
Pronunciation: NO jus
Description: There is not much known about the origin of this name; however it is thought to derive from the biblical name Noah.
Alternative spellings: Nojius

Noran

See entry in 'Names for Baby Girls A–Z'

Norbert

Meaning: Bright north
Origin: German
Pronunciation: NOR bert
Description: Norbert is an old-fashioned name of German origin, meaning 'bright north' or 'famous north'.
Alternative spellings: Norburt

Norman

Meaning: North man
Origin: English
Pronunciation: nor MAN
Description: Common among the English before the Norman invasion in 1066, it gained in popularity afterwards. Although originally a surname, it is also a popular choice as a given name.

Norton

Meaning: North settlement
Origin: English
Pronunciation: NOR tun
Description: Norton is most commonly found as a surname. It was originally given to those who lived in places dubbed 'Norton', meaning 'north town'. It is not frequently seen as a given name.
Alternative spellings: Norten

O

Oakley

Meaning: Oak wood
Origin: English
Pronunciation: OKE lee

Description: Oakley came about as a surname, given to those who lived in places near to a wood full of oak trees. The name is part of

a growing trend to give children surnames as first names.
Alternative spellings: Oaklee, Oakleigh

Ocean
Meaning: The ocean
Origin: English
Pronunciation: OH shun
Description: Ocean is a name that comes from the noun in the English language to refer to a very large expanse of sea. It is a modern name and can be found on both boys and girls.
Alternative spellings: Oshun

Octavius
Meaning: Eighth
Origin: Latin
Pronunciation: oc TAY vee us
Description: From the Latin word *'octavus'*, meaning 'eighth'. It was the family name of the Roman Emperor Augustus before he changed his name.
Alternative spellings: Octayvius

Odysseus
Meaning: Full of wrath
Origin: Greek
Pronunciation: oh DIH see us
Description: Odysseus is the protagonist in Homer's epic poem *The Odyssey.*
Alternative spellings: Odisseus, Odyseus

Odin
Meaning: Inspiration; rage; frenzy
Origin: Norse
Pronunciation: oh DIN
Description: Odin is an Old Norse name derived from the Norse word *'óðr'* meaning 'inpiration,' 'rage' or

'frenzy'. In Norse mythology, Odin was the highest of the gods and resided in Valhalla, where warriors went after death.

Oisin
Meaning: Tiny deer
Origin: Gaelic
Pronunciation: OH sheen
Description: Oisin is a respelling of the name Ossain, which in Irish legend is the son of Finn and means 'tiny deer'.
Alternative spellings: Osain, Ossain

Ola
See entry in 'Names for Baby Girls A–Z'

Olaf
Meaning: Descendant of an ancestor
Origin: Norse
Pronunciation: OH laugh
Description: The name Olaf originates from the Old Norse word *'anleifr'*, meaning 'descendant of an ancestor'.
Alternative spellings: Ollaf

Olan
Meaning: Name of a saint
Origin: Irish
Pronunciation: oh LAHN
Description: Olan is the name of an Irish saint who is the patron saint of the parish of Aghabullogue, a village in Cork.

Ole
Meaning: Ancestor
Origin: Norse
Pronunciation: OH lee
Description: Ole is of Norse origin, meaning 'ancestor'. It is

O

215

popular in Danish- and Norwegian-speaking countries.
Alternative spellings: Olee, Olley, Ollie

Oliver

Meaning: Olive
Origin: Latin
Pronunciation: OH lih ver
Description: The name Oliver has many origins. It is the masculine form of Olive, derived from the fruit that grows on olive trees. Alternately it could be connected with the Old Norse '*oleifr*', meaning 'ancestral relic'.
Alternative spellings: Olifer

Olivier

Meaning: Olive tree
Origin: Latin
Pronunciation: oh lih VE ay
Description: Olivier is a name that was given to medieval ruler Charlemagne's closest companions. It is said that Olivier was thoughtful and cautious, and the name derives from the Latin for 'olive tree'. A common name in France, it is rarer in the UK.
Alternative spellings: Oliwier

Ollie

Meaning: Olive
Origin: Greek
Pronunciation: OLL lee
Description: A shortened form of Oliver or Olive; Ollie is often seen as a name in its own right. It is technically a unisex name, but more often used for boys.
Alternative spellings: Oli, Olie, Olli, Olly, Oly

Omar

Meaning: Long life
Origin: Arabic, Hebrew
Pronunciation: OH mar
Description: Omar is of both Arabic and Hebrew origin. It can be found in the Bible as the name of the son of Esau.
Alternative spellings: Omah, Omarr, Omer

Omari

Meaning: Long life
Origin: Arabic
Pronunciation: oh MAR ee
Description: Omari is a unisex variation on the masculine name Omar, meaning 'long life'.
Alternative spellings: Omarie, Omary

Ophion

Meaning: Ruler
Origin: Greek
Pronunciation: OH fi on
Description: In Greek mythology, Ophion ruled the world with Eurynome before the two of them were cast down by the Titans.
Alternative spellings: Ofion, Opheon

Oren

Meaning: Pine; ash
Origin: Hebrew
Pronunciation: oh REN
Description: Oren is a Hebrew boys' name meaning 'pine' or 'ash'. He was a character in the Book of Characters, one of the last books of the Bible. He was one of six sons of Jerahmeel.

Orestes

Meaning: Mountain
Origin: Greek
Pronunciation: Oh REH stehs

Description: An uncommon name of Greek origin, Orestes is derived from the Greek word *'oros'*, meaning 'mountain'.
Alternative spellings: Orestis, Orestus, Orestys

Orin
Meaning: Pale
Origin: Gaelic, Hebrew
Pronunciation: OH rin
Description: Orin is an uncommon boys' name of Gaelic and Hebrew origins. It is a variant of *oran* (Gaelic, meaning pale) and *oren* (Hebrew, meaning pine tree).
Alternative spellings: Oran, Oren

Orion
Meaning: Hunter
Origin: Greek
Pronunciation: oh RYE on
Description: Orion is an uncommon given name for boys. Orion was a mighty hunter, the son of Poseidon, who was turned into a constellation.
Alternative spellings: Oryon

Orlando
Meaning: Famous land
Origin: German
Pronunciation: or LAN doe
Description: The name Orlando is the Italian version of the Old German name Roland, meaning 'famous land'.
Alternative spellings: Orhlando, Orlandoh

Orpheus
Meaning: Darkness
Origin: Greek
Pronunciation: OR fee us

Description: In Greek mythology, Orpheus was a legendary poet and musician.
Alternative spellings: Orfeus, Orpheos

Orson
Meaning: Bear
Origin: French
Pronunciation: OR sun
Description: Orson comes from the French nickname for 'bear'.
Alternative spellings: Orsonne

Oscar
Meaning: Divine spear
Origin: English
Pronunciation: OSS car
Description: The name Oscar was originally used in James Macpherson's poems, which inspired Napoleon to name his godson Oskar. This is how the former king of Sweden came to have an English name.
Alternative spellings: Oscah, Oska, Oskar

Osian
Meaning: Poet
Origin: Welsh
Pronunciation: OSH an
Description: Osian is a Welsh name that would have derived from the legendary poet Oisin.

Oskar
Meaning: Lover of deer
Origin: Greek
Pronunciation: os KAHR
Description: Oskar is the Scandinavian version of Oscar. Its history can be traced back to usage in poems about the past of Scotland, written in the 1700s. Napoleon named his godson after the

O

character, who went on to become the king of Sweden. In 1895 Oscar Wilde was tried for homosexuality and as a result the popularity of the name Oscar dwindled, but it is now a very popular name, especially in America.
Alternative spellings: Oscar

Oslo
Meaning: Capital of Norway
Origin: English
Pronunciation: os LOW
Description: Oslo is taken directly from the name of the capital of Norway. Like London and Paris, this name follows the trend of using place names for baby names.

Osman
Meaning: Servant of God
Origin: Arabic
Pronunciation: OZ man
Description: Osman is a version of the male Arabic given name Uthman. The name was first used in Persia and was then adopted by Turkish, Bosnian, Indian and Pakistani communities, among others.
Alternative spellings: Osmann, Usman

Otis
Meaning: Prosperity and fortune
Origin: German
Pronunciation: OH tiss
Description: Otis comes from the German male name Oda, meaning 'prosperity and fortune'.
Alternative spellings: Oatis, Otiss

Otto
Meaning: Wealthy
Origin: German
Pronunciation: OTT oh; AW to

Description: The German name Otto is traditionally pronounced 'aw-to' but has been anglicised to 'otto'.
Alternative spellings: Autto, Otoh

Owain
Meaning: Born of the yew tree
Origin: Gaelic
Pronunciation: OH wen
Description: The name Owain is thought to be a variation of the Greek name Eugene. However, it may derive from the name Eoghan, meaning 'lamb'.
Alternative spellings: Owaine, Owayn

Owais
Meaning: Little wolf
Origin: Arabic
Pronunciation: oh-WAI
Description: Owais is an ancient Arabic name meaning 'little wolf'. It is formed from the Arabic word '*aws*', meaning wolf.
Alternative spellings: Uwais, Ouways, Ouweis.

Owen
Meaning: Well born
Origin: Gaelic
Pronunciation: OH win
Description: The name Owen could be a transferred use of the surname or an anglicised version of the Gaelic name Owain.
Alternative spellings: Owin

Ozzy
Meaning: No meaning
Origin: English
Pronunciation: ozz EE
Description: Ozzy is a short form of names such as Osvaldo

and Osborne. A famous English Ozzy is Ozzy Osbourne, who was the lead singer for the heavy metal band, Black Sabbath.
Alternative spellings: Ozzie

P

Pablo
Meaning: Humble
Origin: Spanish
Pronunciation: PAHB low
Description: The name Pablo has most certainly been popularised by the fame of the artist Pablo Picasso, to whom it owes its introduction to Britain and America. It is especially popular in Spain.
Alternative spellings: Pabloh

Paddy
Meaning: Patrician
Origin: Gaelic
Pronunciation: PAH dee
Description: The name Paddy first came about as a shortened version of the name Patrick, but is now a name in its own right. It arose in Ulster in the 17th century.
Alternative spellings: Paddi, Paddie

Paolo
Meaning: Small
Origin: Latin
Pronunciation: POW low
Description: Paolo is a name of Italian and Latin origin, meaning 'small' or 'humble'. It is a popular name in Italy.
Alternative spellings: Powlo

Paris
See entry in 'Names for Baby Girls A–Z'

Parker
Meaning: Gamekeeper
Origin: English
Pronunciation: PAR ka
Description: Parker was originally a surname given to gamekeepers in the Middle Ages. It is now being used as a first name and is predominantly American.
Alternative spellings: Parcer

Pascal
Meaning: Associated with Passover/Easter
Origin: Latin
Pronunciation: pass CAL
Description: Pascal is a name that is taken from the Latin word *'paschalis'* or *'pashalis'*, meaning 'associated with Passover or Easter'. This name is often given to baby boys born on Easter Day.
Alternative spellings: Pascale, Pasqual

Patrick
Meaning: Noble
Origin: Gaelic
Pronunciation: PAT rik
Description: Although the name Patrick derives from the Latin *'patricius'*, a title given to distinguish a nobleman, it is considered a Gaelic name. Patrick is the name of the patron saint of Ireland.
Alternative spellings: Patrik, Patryck

O
P

Paul

Meaning: Modest
Origin: Latin
Pronunciation: PAWL
Description: Paul comes from the Latin name Paulus, originally a Roman nickname meaning 'small' or 'modest'.
Alternative spellings: Paull, Pawel

Pavel

Meaning: Small; little
Origin: Slavic
Pronunciation: pah VEL
Description: Pavel is a common name found in Slavic countries and it means 'small' or 'little'.
Alternative spellings: Pavell

Pavish

Meaning: Bright
Origin: Hindi
Pronunciation: PAH vish
Description: Although there is some argument about the meaning of this name, Pavish is an Indian/Hindu name most likely meaning -'bright'.

Payton

Meaning: Town of peacocks
Origin: Old English
Pronunciation: PAY tun
Description: Payton is a unisex name of separate origins. Some believe it derives from the name Patrick, meaning 'noble'. It is also said to be made up of the two Old English elements of *'pawa'*, meaning 'peacock', and *'tun'*, meaning 'town'. This would make the meaning of the name 'town of peacocks'.
Alternative spellings: Peyton

Pedro

Meaning: Rock
Origin: Spanish
Pronunciation: PED roh
Description: Pedro is the Spanish variant of the name Peter.
Alternative spellings: Pedroh

Peleus

Meaning: Man of Pelion
Origin: Greek
Pronunciation: PEL ee us
Description: In Greek mythology, Peleus was the father of Achilles and a brave warrior who fought alongside Heracles.
Alternative spellings: Peleos

Percy

Meaning: Pierce valley
Origin: French
Pronunciation: PUR see
Description: Percy is a name of French origin, meaning 'pierce valley'. In medieval times, Percy was used as a nickname for Piers or Percival.
Alternative spellings: Percee, Perci, Percie

Perry

Meaning: Proximity to a pear tree
Origin: English
Pronunciation: PEH ree
Description: The name Perry derives from an Old English surname originally given to those who lived near a pear tree. Originally a masculine name, it is now unisex.
Alternative spellings: Perri, Perrie

Pete

Meaning: Rock
Origin: Greek

Pronunciation: PEET
Description: Although rarely seen as a given name in its own right, Pete is a popular pet name for those named Peter.
Alternative spellings: Peet, Peit

Peter

Meaning: Rock
Origin: Greek
Pronunciation: PEE tuh
Description: Peter is the English form of the most well known of Christ's apostles. The name means 'rock' and has been in constant use since the Middle Ages.
Alternative spellings: Peeta, Peita, Peta

Pharrell

Meaning: Descendant of the valorous man
Origin: American
Pronunciation: FAH rel
Description: Pharell is a modern American name for boys.
Alternative spellings: Farrell, Farryll, Pharryl

Phil

Meaning: Lover of horses
Origin: Greek
Pronunciation: FILL
Description: Phil is a unisex name that first came about as a shortened form for the names Philip, Philippa or Phyliss. It is usually a pet name, but is sometimes a name in its own right.
Alternative spellings: Phill

Philip

Meaning: Lover of horses
Origin: Greek
Pronunciation: FIL lip

Description: Philip comes from the Greek name Philippos, comprised of words meaning 'to love' and 'horse'. It has been popular since the classical period.
Alternative spellings: Philipe, Phillip, Phillipe

Phoebus

Meaning: Bright
Origin: Greek
Pronunciation: FEE bus
Description: In Greek mythology, Phoebus was one of the names given to Apollo, the son of Zeus.
Alternative spellings: Foebus, Phoebos

Phoenix

Meaning: Mythological bird
Origin: Greek
Pronunciation: FEE niks
Description: Phoenix as a given name comes from the mythological bird, said to die by fire, then rise from its own ashes. It is often found as a surname.
Alternative spellings: Fenix, Foenix, Phenix, Pheonix

Pierce

Meaning: Rock
Origin: Greek, English
Pronunciation: PEERS
Description: Pierce is an uncommon name of Greek and English origin.
Alternative spellings: Pearce, Peirs, Piers

Pierre

Meaning: Rock
Origin: French
Pronunciation: pee AIR

P

Description: The French variant of Peter.
Alternative spellings: Piere, Pierr

Piotr
Meaning: Rock
Origin: Greek
Pronunciation: PEA otr
Description: Piotr is a variation on Peter and is most commonly found in Slavic- and Polish-speaking countries.
Alternative spellings: Piotra, Piotre, Pietro

Pietro
Meaning: Stone; rock
Origin: Italy
Pronunciation: PEE et roh
Description: Piertro is the Italian version of the popular name Peter, and shares the same meaning of 'stone' or 'rock'.
Alternative spellings: Peter

Piper
Meaning: Pipe player
Origin: English
Pronunciation: PIPE er
Description: Piper was originally a surname given to those whose father played the pipe. It is now a unisex first name.
Alternative spellings: Pypa, Pyper

Poseidon
Meaning: God of the sea
Origin: Greek
Pronunciation: Poss EYE don
Description: In Greek mythology, Poseidon was the god of the sea.
Alternative spellings: Poseydon

Pranav
Meaning: Praise
Origin: Sanskrit
Pronunciation: PRA nav
Description: Pranav comes from the Sanskrit word for 'symbol'. It is a common name for Indian boys.
Alternative spellings: Praanav, Pranaav, Prannav

Prateek
Meaning: Image or symbol of God
Origin: Sanskrit
Pronunciation: prah TEEK
Description: Prateek is a Sanskrit name meaning 'image of symbol of God'.
Alternative spellings: Pratik

Presley
Meaning: Priest's meadow
Origin: English
Pronunciation: PRES ley
Description: Presley is a name of Old English origin, meaning 'priest's meadow'. Originally a surname, it has become a somewhat common given name.
Alternative spellings: Preslee, Presleigh, Presli, Preslie, Presly

Preston
Meaning: Priest's town
Origin: English
Pronunciation: PRES tun
Description: Preston is the name of a town in Lancashire and would have been given as a surname to those who lived there. The word originates from the Old English *'preost'*, meaning 'priest', and *'tun'*, meaning 'town'. It is now found as a given name.

Alternative spellings: Prestan, Presten, Prestun

Prince
Meaning: Prince
Origin: Latin
Pronunciation: PRINSE
Description: As well as being a royal title, Prince would have been given as a surname to those who worked in the prince's household. The name has had a surge in popularity as a first name since the fame of 80s singer Prince.
Alternative spellings: Prynce

Prisha
See entry in 'Names for Baby Girls A–Z'

Q

Qasim
Meaning: Generous; selfless
Origin: Arabic
Pronunciation: KAH sim
Description: Qasim derives from the Arabic word *'qasama'*, meaning 'to share' or 'portion'. It now carries the meaning of 'selfless' or 'generous'.
Alternative spellings: Quasim

Quentin
Meaning: Fifth born
Origin: Latin
Pronunciation: KWEN tin
Description: Quentin derives from the Latin name Quintinus, meaning 'fifth'.
Alternative spellings: Quenton, Quintin, Quinton

Quest
Meaning: Voyage of discovery
Origin: English
Pronunciation: KWEST
Description: Quest is a fairly modern name, often given as a baby name for a boy. It comes from the English word for a 'voyage of discovery'.
Alternative spellings: Qwest

Quincy
Meaning: Fifth born
Origin: Latin
Pronunciation: KWIN see
Description: Quincy derives from the Latin name Quintinus and means 'fifth'. It can also be a shortened form of the name Quentin.
Alternative spellings: Quency, Quincey, Quinci, Quincie

Quinn
Meaning: Descendant of Cuinn
Origin: Gaelic
Pronunciation: KWIN
Description: Traditionally, Quinn was used as a surname for the son of Cuinn. It transferred into a male given name and is now used for both boys and girls.
Alternative spellings: Quin, Quinne, Qwin

P
Q

R

Raees

Meaning: Chief
Origin: Arabic
Pronunciation: RACE
Description: Raees is an uncommon variant of the Arabic name Rais, meaning 'chief' or 'leader'. It is a title used by the rulers of Muslim states in the Middle East and South Asia.
Alternative spellings: Race, Raees, Rais

Rafael

Meaning: God has healed
Origin: Hebrew
Pronunciation: RAH fy elle
Description: Rafael is a variant of the biblical name Raphael. The name is made up of the elements of *'rapha'*, meaning 'to heal', and *'el'*, which means 'God'.
Alternative spellings: Rafaell, Rafaelle, Raffael, Raphael, Raphaell

Rafal

Meaning: God has healed
Origin: Hebrew
Pronunciation: RAF al
Description: Rafal is the Polish variant of the Hebrew name Raphael, meaning 'God has healed'.
Alternative spellings: Rafel, Raffal, Raphal

Rafe

Meaning: Wolf
Origin: Norse
Pronunciation: RAYF
Description: Rafe is a variant of the name Ralph, which comes from the Norse word for 'wolf'. It was popular in the 17th century but Ralph is now the preferred form. Rafe could also be seen as a shortened form of the name Rafael.
Alternative spellings: Raife, Rayfe

Rafferty

Meaning: One who will prosper
Origin: Gaelic
Pronunciation: RAF er tee
Description: The name Rafferty originally came about as an Irish surname, meaning 'prosperous'. It was then transferred into a boys' given name.
Alternative spellings: Rafertey, Raferti, Rafertie, Raferty, Raffertey, Rafferti, Raffertie

Rafi

Meaning: Holding high; servant of the exalted one
Origin: Arabic
Pronunciation: RA fi
Description: Rafi is a name used by Muslims, Jews and Christians of Armenian origin. The word Rafi is of Arabic origin, and its meaning is 'holding high' or 'servant of the exalted one'.
Alternative spellings: Rafee, Raffi, Raffy

Raheem

Meaning: Kind-hearted
Origin: Arabic
Pronunciation: rah HEEM
Description: Raheem is a phonetic spelling variant of the Arabic name Rahim, meaning 'kind-hearted'. It is also the shortened form of

Abdurrahim, meaning 'servant of the merciful'.
Alternative spellings: Rahim, Rahime

Rahim
Meaning: Compassionate
Origin: Arabic
Pronunciation: ra HEEM
Description: Rahim is an Arabic name meaning 'compassionate'. It is one of the most popular names in Afghanistan. In Islam, Rahim is one of the 99 attribute names of Allah.
Alternative spellings: Raheem, Rahiem

Rahman
Meaning: The compassionate; the most gracious
Origin: Arabic
Pronunciation: RAH mahn
Description: This name usually forms part of a compound, such as Abdur Rahman, 'servant of God'.

Raihan
Meaning: Sweet basil
Origin: Arabic
Pronunciation: ray HAN
Description: Raihan is considered to mean 'sweet basil'. It is not commonly found in Britain.
Alternative spellings: Rayhan

Raja
Meaning: Optimism
Origin: Arabic
Pronunciation: rah-JUH
Description: This Arabic name is considered unisex, but the feminine and masculine forms are often pronounced differently. For girls it is pronounced

'rah-jah', whereas for boys it is 'rah-juh'.
Alternative spellings: Raija, Raijah, Rajah

Rajan
Meaning: The radiant king
Origin: Sanskrit
Pronunciation: RA jan
Description: Rajan is a name of Hindi and Sanskrit origin, meaning 'the radiant king'. It can also be of Arabic origin, meaning 'anticipation'.
Alternative spellings: Raajan, Rajaan

Rajveer
Meaning: The hero of the land; kingdom's warrior
Origin: Punjabi
Pronunciation: RAJ veer
Description: Rajveer is a somewhat common Punjabi name. It means 'the hero of the land; kingdom's warrior'.
Alternative spellings: Rajvir

Ralf
Meaning: Wolf counsel
Origin: English
Pronunciation: RALF
Description: Ralf is a variant of the Old English name Ralph, meaning 'wolf counsel'. It was very common in the early 20th century but is now less popular.
Alternative spellings: Ralfe, Ralph, Ralphe

R

Ralphie
Meaning: Wolf counsel
Origin: English
Pronunciation: RALF ee

Description: Ralphie is a variant of the Old English name Ralph, meaning 'wolf counsel'. It was very common in the early 20th century but its usage has declined.
Alternative spellings: Ralphee, Ralphi, Ralphy

Ramla
See entry in 'Names for Baby Girls A–Z'

Rana
See entry in 'Names for Baby Girls A–Z'

Randall
Meaning: Wolf shield
Origin: Norse
Pronunciation: RAN dul
Description: Randall is a mainly US vernacular form of the Norse name Randolf.
Alternative spellings: Randalle, Randell

Randolf
Meaning: Wolf shield
Origin: Norse
Pronunciation: RAN dulf
Description: Randolf is a Norman name derived from the Old Norse name Rannulfr. This name is comprised of elements meaning 'wolf' and 'shield'. It is also seen as a surname.
Alternative spellings: Randolph

Randy
Meaning: Wolf shield
Origin: Norse
Pronunciation: RAN dee
Description: Most common in the US and Australia, Randy is a pet form of Randolf, Randall or Andrew, and it is also a name used for girls. It is also seen as a given name in its own right.
Alternative spellings: Randey, Randi, Randie

Ranveer
Meaning: Hero of the battle
Origin: Indian
Pronunciation: ran VEE er
Description: Ranveer is an Indian male name meaning 'hero of the battle'. The popular Bollywood actor, Ranveer Singh, has contributed to the popularity of this name. See entry in 'Names for Baby Girls A–Z'

Rashid
Meaning: Rightly guided
Origin: Arabic
Pronunciation: rash EED
Description: Rashid is a common Arabic boys' name meaning 'rightly guided'. It can be spelt in many different ways and is one of 99 names of Allah.
Alternative spellings: Raashid, Rachid, Rashed, Rachid, Rasheed

Rastus
Meaning: To love
Origin: German
Pronunciation: RAS tus
Description: Rastus is a name found in the New Testament. It is also a short form of the Greek name Erastus, derived from the word *'eran',* meaning 'to love'.
Alternative spellings: Rastuss

Raul
Meaning: Wolf counsel
Origin: Norse

Pronunciation: rah OOL
Description: Raul is the Spanish version of the masculine name Ralph.
Alternative spellings: Raoul, Raull

Ravi
Meaning: Sun
Origin: Sanskrit
Pronunciation: RA vi
Description: In ancient Hindu mythology, Ravi is the Hindu god of the sun.
Alternative spellings: Ravee, Ravvi

Ray
Meaning: Decision protector
Origin: German
Pronunciation: RAY
Description: Ray is a shortened form of Raymond, but is also given as a name in its own right. Although Ray is a specifically masculine name, many of its spelling variants are favoured for girls.
Alternative spellings: Rae, Rai, Raye

Rayan
Meaning: Gates to heaven
Origin: Sanskrit
Pronunciation: RY han
Description: Rayan is a unisex name that is said to refer to the gates of heaven in Islamic belief. Rayan is also a title used in India to distinguish those in power. As well as having Arabic roots, Rayan has origins in the Persian language where it is said to derive from the name Rayhan.
Alternative spellings: Raiyan, Rayann, Rayanne

Rayhan
Meaning: Fragranced herb

Origin: Persian
Pronunciation: RY hahn
Description: Rayhan is a Persian name that features in the Quran. It could also be considered a spelling variant of the Sanskrit name Rayan.
Alternative spellings: Raihan, Rayhaan, Rehan, Rihan

Raylan
Meaning: No meaning
Origin: American
Pronunciation: RAY laan
Description: Raylan is a modern baby name that was invented in America. As such, it has no meaning but it would be a great choice for parents looking for something interesting and unique.

Rayyan
Meaning: Gate of paradise; splendour
Origin: Arabic
Pronunciation: ray YAN
Description: Rayyan is an Arabic boys' name and is said to be one of the gates of paradise, especially for those who have fasted throughout their lives.
Alternative spellings: Rayan
See entry in 'Names for Baby Girls A–Z'

Raymond
Meaning: Decision protector
Origin: French
Pronunciation: RAY mund
Description: Raymond comes from the Old French name Raimund and was introduced to Britain by the Normans.
Alternative spellings: Raimond, Raymund

R

Razzaq

Meaning: The provider
Origin: Muslim
Pronunciation: ra ZAK
Description: Razzaq is a name that usually forms a compound, such as Abdur Razzaq, meaning 'servant of the all-provider'.

Reece

Meaning: Enthusiasm
Origin: Welsh
Pronunciation: reese
Description: An anglicised spelling of Rhys, the name Reece is now widespread outside Wales, among girls as well as boys. The name means 'enthusiasm'.
Alternative spellings: Rhys

Reed

Meaning: Red-haired
Origin: Scottish
Pronunciation: reed
Description: Reed is an Old English surname meaning 'red' and is usually given to people with red hair.
Alternative spellings: Reid
See entry in 'Names for Baby Girls A–Z'

Reese

See entry in 'Names for Baby Girls A–Z'

Regan

See entry in 'Names for Baby Girls A–Z'

Reggie

Meaning: Queen
Origin: Latin
Pronunciation: RED jee
Description: Reggie derives from the traditional boys' name Reginald. Reginald could be derived from the German name Reginwald, or from the Latin word *'regina'*, meaning 'queen'.
Alternative spellings: Reggi, Reggy

Reginald

Meaning: Queen
Origin: Latin
Pronunciation: REG in old
Description: Reginald could derive from the German name Reginwald, or from the Latin word *'regina'*, meaning 'queen'. It was very popular in the early 20th century but has recently fallen from favour.
Alternative spellings: Regienald, Reginold

Rehaan

Meaning: Sweet-scented
Origin: Arabic
Pronunciation: RAY han
Description: Rehaan is a variant of the popular Arabic name Rehan. Rehan features in the Quran and is said to mean 'sweet-scented'.
Alternative spellings: Reehan, Rehan

Reign

Meaning: To rule
Origin: English
Pronunciation: rayn
Description: Reign come from the English vocabulary word meaning 'to rule' or to 'hold royal office,' and is a unique name choice.

Reilly

Meaning: Unknown
Origin: Irish

Pronunciation: rye LEE
Description: Reilly is most likely a respelling of the Irish surname, Reilley, from an Irish personal name Raghallach. It is unknown what this name means, however. It can also be related to the more common name, Riley, which is a unisex English name meaning 'rye wood'.
Alternative spellings: Reilley, Riley, Ryleigh

Reiss
Meaning: Twig
Origin: German
Pronunciation: REESE; RICE
Description: Reiss is a German surname of Old German origin, sometimes used as a given name. It is most commonly used by Ashkenazic Jewish people as an occupational name for a rice dealer or as an ornamental name from the Old German word *'Reis'*, meaning 'twig' or 'branch'.
Alternative spellings: Reis, Ryce

Remi
Meaning: From Rheims
Origin: French
Pronunciation: reh ME
Description: The name Remi derives from the French town Rheims and would have originally been given to those who lived in the town. There was also a French saint who bore the name Remi.
Alternative spellings: Remy

Rene
See Renee in 'Names for Baby Girls A–Z'

Reon
Meaning: King

Origin: Gaelic
Pronunciation: RE on
Description: Reon is a rare variant of the boys' name Ryan, which is of Gaelic origin and means 'king'.
Alternative spellings: Rion, Ryon

Reuben
Meaning: Behold; a son
Origin: Hebrew
Pronunciation: ROO ben
Description: Reuben is a biblical name borne by one of Jacob's 12 sons, and hence a name of one of the 12 tribes of Israel.
Alternative spellings: Reuban, Ruben

Rex
Meaning: King
Origin: Latin
Pronunciation: REKS
Description: Rex is the Latin word for 'king' and it first came to exist as a given name in the 19th century.
Alternative spellings: Reks

Reyan
Meaning: Door of heaven
Origin: Indian
Pronunciation: REE yan
Description: Reyan is a variant spelling of the name Riyan, an Indian boys' name meaning 'door of heaven'.
Alternative spellings: Riaan, Riyan

R

Reyansh
Meaning: Ray of light
Origin: Hindi
Pronunciation: rey AANSH
Description: Reyansh is a Hindi boys' name meaning 'ray of light'.

It is also used as an alternative name for the Hindu god, Lord Vishnu.

Rhett

Meaning: Advice; counsel
Origin: Dutch
Pronunciation: reh ETT
Description: Rhett was a Dutch surname and anglicised form of de Raedt, where the Middle Dutch word '*raet*' means 'advice' or 'counsel'. It was brought to the United States by Dutch settlers in the 1600s, particularly the South Carolina region. One of the main characters in *Gone with the Wind* is Rhett Butler.

Rian

Meaning: Little king
Origin: Gaelic
Pronunciation: RIY an
Description: Rian is the anglicised spelling of the Irish name Ryan.
Alternative spellings: Ryan

Ricardo

Meaning: Powerful
Origin: German
Pronunciation: ree KAR doh
Description: Ricardo is a variation of the German name Richard, meaning 'powerful'. It is often found in Italy.
Alternative spellings: Ricardoh, Rikardo

Rich

Meaning: Powerful
Origin: German
Pronunciation: RITCH
Description: Rich is a shortened version of the German name Richard. It is now a given name in its own right. Rich also means 'wealthy' in English.
Alternative spellings: Ritch

Richard

Meaning: Powerful
Origin: German
Pronunciation: RICH urd
Description: Proving to be an enduringly popular given name, Richard is of Frankish origin and was introduced to the UK by the Normans. The name is particularly associated with Richard I, who earned the nickname 'lionheart'.
Alternative spellings: Richarde, Ritchard

Richie

Meaning: Powerful
Origin: German
Pronunciation: RITCH ee
Description: Richie is a shortened variant of the popular Old German name, Richard, meaning 'strong power'.
Alternative spellings: Richee, Richi, Richy, Ritchee, Ritchi, Ritchie, Ritchy

Rick

Meaning: Powerful
Origin: German
Pronunciation: RIK
Description: Rick is a shortened form of Richard and sometimes Frederick. It is now seen as a name in its own right.
Alternative spellings: Rik

Ricky

Meaning: Powerful
Origin: German

Pronunciation: RIK ee
Description: Ricky is a pet form of Richard and sometimes Frederick. It is now seen as a name in its own right and is regarded as a unisex name.
Alternative spellings: Ricki, Rickie, Riki, Rikie, Riky

Rico

Meaning: Ruler of the home; powerful
Origin: Italian
Pronunciation: REE ko
Description: Rico originated as a pet name for Enrico and Ricardo. Enrico means 'ruler of the home' while Ricardo is a form of Richard, meaning 'powerful'.
Alternative spellings: Reeco, Ricoh

Ridwan

Meaning: Merciful
Origin: Arabic
Pronunciation: rihd WAN
Description: Ridwan derives from the name of the keeper of the gates of heaven in Islamic belief. Connotations of the name are those of goodwill and mercifulness.
Alternative spellings: Riddwan

Ringo

Meaning: No meaning
Origin: English
Pronunciation: ring GOH
Description: Ringo is actually an invented nickname specifically for Ringo Starr, one of the members of The Beatles. Originally called Richard Starkey, Ringo was given this moniker for all the rings he wore.

Rio

Meaning: River
Origin: Spanish
Pronunciation: REE o
Description: Rio is a fairly modern unisex name derived from the Spanish word for 'river'. It is also linked to major Brazilian city Rio de Janeiro, which directly translates to 'river of January'.
Alternative spellings: Reo, Rioh

Rishi

Meaning: Wise
Origin: Sanskrit
Pronunciation: RIH shee
Description: The name Rishi derives from the seer said to reveal Vedic hymns when in a state of higher consciousness, called 'The Rishi'. The meaning of the name is therefore 'wise'.
Alternative spellings: Rhishi, Rishie

River

Meaning: River
Origin: English
Pronunciation: RIH vuh
Description: River is a fairly modern name, borne out of the so-called 'flower power' era in the 1960s. It is considered unisex.
Alternative spellings: Riva, Ryver

Riyad

Meaning: Meadows; gardens
Origin: Arabic
Pronunciation: ree AD
Description: Riyad is an Arabic boys' name meaning 'meadows' or 'garden'.
Alternative spellings: Riad

R

Roan

Meaning: Red-haired
Origin: Gaelic
Pronunciation: ro UN
Description: Roan is a modern variation on the masculine Gaelic name Rowan. Its Gaelic meaning is 'red-haired,' and although it used to be specifically a boys' name it can now be found used for girls. However, its most common feminine form is spelt Rowanne.
Alternative spellings: Rohan, Rowan

Robbie

Meaning: Bright Fame
Origin: German
Pronunciation: rob BIE
Description: Robbie is a nickname usually given to someone with the name Robert, although it has become popular as a given name in recent years. The name Robert was introduced into the UK by the Normans and has remained popular ever since.

Robert

Meaning: Bright fame
Origin: German
Pronunciation: ROB ert
Description: Introduced to Britain by the Normans, Robert has since remained in the spotlight as a popular first name. It is often shortened to Bob.
Alternative spellings: Roburt

Roberto

Meaning: Bright fame
Origin: German
Pronunciation: rob ER tow
Description: Roberto is a variant of Robert, a name of Old German origin meaning 'bright fame'. It is a common name in Italian-, Portuguese- and Spanish-speaking countries.
Alternative spellings: Roburto

Robin

Meaning: Bright fame
Origin: German
Pronunciation: ROB in
Description: Robin used to exist as a pet form of Robert, but has since gained credence as a given name for both boys and girls. It is also the English vocabulary name for the red-chested songbird seen around Christmas time.
Alternative spellings: Robinn, Robyn

Robson

Meaning: Son of Robert
Origin: English
Pronunciation: ROB son
Description: Robson is an English name derived from the German name Robert. Though commonly a surname, it is occasionally used as a given name.
Alternative spellings: Robsen, Robsun

Rocco

Meaning: Battle cry
Origin: German
Pronunciation: ROCK o
Description: Rocco is predominantly used within the Italian language and derives from the German name Rochbert, which is no longer in use.
Alternative spellings: Roccoh, Rocko

Rocket
Meaning: Spacecraft; herb
Origin: English
Pronunciation: rock ETT
Description: Taken from the English word of the same meanings, Rocket can either refer to the spacecraft or the herb used in cooking. Jamie Oliver and Pharrell Williams both chose this name for their sons.
Alternative spellings: Rockett

Rocky
Meaning: Rest
Origin: Italian
Pronunciation: ROH kee
Description: Rocky is derived from the name Rock, which itself is the anglicised form of the name Roch. Roch carries the meaning of 'rest'. Rocky is also an English word meaning 'rough' or 'many rocks'.
Alternative spellings: Rocki, Rockie

Roderick
Meaning: Famous ruler
Origin: German
Pronunciation: rod ERR rick
Description: Roderick is a German name composed of 'hrōþ', meaning 'glory' and 'rīks', meaning 'ruler'. A common shortened version of this name is Roddy.
Alternative spellings: Roderik

Rodin
Meaning: Unknown
Origin: French
Pronunciation: ro DAN
Description: Rodin is actually a French surname most attributed to the great French sculptor, August Rodin, who created *The Thinker*.

In terms of meaning, however, it is unknown.

Rodney
Meaning: Hroda's Island
Origin: English
Pronunciation: RAWD nee
Description: Rodney was originally a surname derived from a place name, Hroda's Island. It is now a popular first name choice for baby boys.

Rodrigo
Meaning: Ruled with fame
Origin: German
Pronunciation: roh DREE goh
Description: Rodrigo is the Spanish version of the German name Roderick, meaning 'ruled with fame'.
Alternative spellings: Roderigo, Rodrigoh

Rogan
Meaning: Red-haired
Origin: Irish
Pronunciation: ROH gan
Description: Rogan is an Irish baby name meaning 'red-haired'. Like the other Irish; Gaelic baby names starting with 'ro,' this name would be idea for a red-headed baby boy.

Roger
Meaning: Famous spear
Origin: German
Pronunciation: ROD jer
Description: Roger was one of the most popular boys' names during the medieval period.
Alternative spellings: Rodger

Rohin
Meaning: Rising

R

Origin: Indian
Pronunciation: row HIN
Description: Rohin is a common Hindu/Indian name meaning 'rising'.

Roland

Meaning: Famous country
Origin: German
Pronunciation: ROH lund
Description: Roland is a name of French and German origin, meaning 'famous country'.
Alternative spellings: Rolland, Rowland

Roma

See entry in 'Names for Baby Girls A–Z'

Roman

Meaning: Citizen of Rome
Origin: Latin
Pronunciation: ROH mun
Description: The name Roman derives from the Latin word referring to the citizens of Rome. The Romans are associated with power, pride and strength and the given name shares these connotations.
Alternative spellings: Romann

Romario

Meaning: Pilgrim to Rome
Origin: Italian
Pronunciation: ro MAR io
Description: Romario is a variant of the Italian name Romeo. It is often used as a nickname in Portuguese- and Spanish-speaking countries.
Alternative spellings: Romarioh, Romarrio

Rome

Meaning: Capital city of Italy
Origin: English
Pronunciation: rome
Description: Rome is most famously the capital city of Italy, and is derived from the Latin word 'roma'. It follows the trend where certain place names are used as baby names, such as India or Paris.

Romeo

Meaning: Pilgrim to Rome
Origin: Italian
Pronunciation: RO me oh; ro MAY oh
Description: Romeo is most famous for being the name of the hero in Shakespeare's play *Romeo and Juliet*. Because of this it has connotations of love. It derives from the Italian city of Rome.
Alternative spellings: Romio, Romyo

Ronald

Meaning: Open-minded
Origin: Norse
Pronunciation: RON uld
Description: Ronald is predominantly found in Scotland, especially in the form Ranald. The name is of Norse origin and was brought over by raiding Vikings.
Alternative spellings: Ronold, Ronuld

Ronan

Meaning: Little seal
Origin: Gaelic
Pronunciation: ROW nan
Description: Ronan was first made popular by the ancient king of Leinster, who was tricked into killing his own son. The meaning of this name comes from the Irish name Ron, meaning 'seal'.

Alternative spellings: Rohnan, Rownan

Ronnie
Meaning: Open-minded
Origin: Norse
Pronunciation: RON ee
Description: This unisex name is a spelling variant of the feminine name Ronni or the masculine name Ronny.
Alternative spellings: Ronni, Ronny

Ronny
Meaning: Open-minded
Origin: Norse
Pronunciation: RON knee
Description: Ronny is considered unisex although this spelling is often reserved for boys. Originally a shortened form of Ronald, it is now used as a given name in its own right.
Alternative spellings: Ronney, Ronni, Ronnie

Rory
Meaning: Red-haired king
Origin: Gaelic
Pronunciation: RAW ree
Description: Rory derives from the Gaelic words meaning 'red' and 'king'. Although it is technically masculine it is becoming popular as a girls' name.
Alternative spellings: Roari, Roary, Rori, Rorie

Roscoe
Meaning: Doe wood
Origin: Norse
Pronunciation: ross COE
Description: Roscoe has Norse origins, and is derived from a place name that meant 'doe wood'

in Old Norse. It was especially popular in the 1880s but has steadily declined in use over the years.
Alternative spellings: Rosco

Roshan
See entry in 'Names for Baby Girls A–Z'

Ross
Meaning: Headland
Origin: Gaelic
Pronunciation: ROSS
Description: Ross may be thought of as a transferred surname, but the word itself comes from the Gaelic term 'ros' meaning 'headland'.
Alternative spellings: Rosse

Roy
Meaning: Red
Origin: Gaelic
Pronunciation: ROY
Description: Roy originates from Scotland, where it means 'red'. It has since been reinterpreted in some places to mean 'king', from Old French.
Alternative spellings: Roi, Roye

R

Ruairi
Meaning: Red-haired king
Origin: Gaelic
Pronunciation: ROO ry
Description: Ruairi is a name of Goidelic (Irish and Scottish Gaelic) origin. It translates as 'red-haired king'. Historically, it has also been anglicised as Roderick. Its equivalent in the Welsh language is Rhodri, also meaning 'red'-haired king.
Alternative spellings: Rhodri, Ruairidh, Ruari, Ruaridh

Ruan

Meaning: Little red one
Origin: Gaelic
Pronunciation: ROO an
Description: Ruan comes from the Gaelic word for 'red', *'ruadh'*. The other form, from the tree, comes from a Norse word for the European plant. This word refers to the red leaves and berries of the rowan tree.
Alternative spellings: Rooan, Ruwan

Rudi

Meaning: Famous wolf
Origin: German
Pronunciation: roo DEE
Description: Although this name is predominantly used in its female form it is actually unisex and comes from the name Rudolph. The name is mostly used in German-, Hungarian- and Spanish-speaking countries although it is occasionally seen in Britain too. There are several spelling variations of this name including Rudie and Rudy.
Alternative spellings: Rudie, Rudy

Rudra

Meaning: The roarer
Origin: Hindi
Pronunciation: roo DRAH
Description: Rudra is a Hindu/Indian name that, directly translated, means 'the roarer'. It is also a deity in the Hindu religion who is associated with wind or storm and the hunt.
Alternative spellings: Rudrah

Rufus

Meaning: Red-haired

Origin: Latin
Pronunciation: ROO fuhs
Description: Rufus comes from the Latin nickname meaning 'red-haired'.
Alternative spellings: Ruffus

Rupert

Meaning: Bright fame
Origin: German
Pronunciation: ROO pert
Description: Rupert is a German form of Robert, and means 'bright fame'.
Alternative spellings: Rupurt

Russ

Meaning: Little red one
Origin: French
Pronunciation: RUSS
Description: Russ is a short form of Russell, and may be taken to merely mean 'red' or 'little red one' from the Old French word *'rous'*.
Alternative spellings: Rus

Russell

Meaning: Little red one
Origin: French
Pronunciation: RUSS el
Description: Russell, like Roan, means 'red-haired', yet is derived from an Old French nickname.
Alternative spellings: Rusel, Russel

Ryder

Meaning: One who rides
Origin: English
Pronunciation: RI der
Description: Ryder is a name of Old English origin. The name was given as an occupational name for horseback riders in

medieval times. It is more common as a surname but has recently become popular as a given name.
Alternative spellings: Rider, Rydar

Ryker
Meaning: Rich
Origin: Dutch

Pronunciation: RYE ker
Description: Ryker (and its related name, Riker) is the Dutch form of the name Richard, or Rich. The meaning of the name is also 'rich,' as in wealthy. There is a prison called Riker's Island in New York City, so parents may want to be careful with this name.
Alternative spellings: Riker

S

Saad
Meaning: Happy;
Origin: Arabic
Pronunciation: saa HD
Description: Saad is mainly used in Arabic- and Hebrew-speaking countries. It is also a variant of the name Sayid, which carries many meanings including 'happy'.
Alternative spellings: Saahd

Sacha
Meaning: Defender of man
Origin: Greek
Pronunciation: SA sha
Description: Sacha is a name of Russian and Greek origin. It is a diminutive of Alexander, meaning 'defender of man'.
Alternative spellings: Sascha, Sasha

Sachin
Meaning: Essence; existence
Origin: Sanskrit
Pronunciation: SA chin
Description: Sachin is a name of Sanskrit origin, meaning 'essence' or 'existence'. The name is an alternative name for the god Shiva.
Alternative spellings: Sachen, Sashin

Saeed
Meaning: Happy; mister
Origin: Arabic
Pronunciation: say EED
Description: Saeed is a name of Arabic origin, meaning 'happy'. It is a variant of Said.
Alternative spellings: Saaed, Said, Sayed, Syed

Safwan
Meaning: Purity
Origin: Arabic
Pronunciation: sahf WAHN
Description: Safwan is a masculine name of Arabic origin, the meaning of the name is said to be 'purity'.
Alternative spellings: Safwann, Sahfwan, Saphwan

Sahar
Meaning: Vigilant; moon
Origin: Arabic

R
S

Pronunciation: SAH hahr
Description: Sahar is a unisex name, which in Arabic means 'vigilant', or in Hebrew can mean 'moon'.
Alternative spellings: Sarhar

Sahib

Meaning: Master
Origin: Arabic
Pronunciation: SAH ib
Description: Sahib was used in India as a mark of respect. It is said to mean 'master'.
Alternative spellings: Sahibb

Sahil

Meaning: Sea shore
Origin: Hindi
Pronunciation: sah HIl
Description: Sahil is a male Hindu name derived from the Indian word for 'sea shore,' which in turn is borrowed from the Arabic.

Sai

Meaning: Paint
Origin: Japanese
Pronunciation: sai
Description: Sai is a Japanese boys' name meaning 'paint'. It is also an Indian name, although in Hindi it has a different meaning.

Saif

Meaning: Sword
Origin: Arabic
Pronunciation: say EEF
Description: Saif comes from the Arabic word meaning 'curved sword'. This sword is an important Arabic symbol.
Alternative spellings: Sayf

Sailor

Meaning: A crew member of a ship or boat
Origin: English
Pronunciation: SAY lor
Description: Traditionally an occupational surname for someone who worked aboard a boat. Slowly it is becoming popular as a given name for boys.
Alternative spellings: Saylor

Salahuddin

Meaning: Righteous of religion
Origin: Arabic
Pronunciation: salah HOO din
Description: Salahuddin is a variation of the name Salah Al-Din, an Arabic name meaning 'righteous of religion'. It is comprised of two Arabic words, '*salah*', meaning 'righteousness' and '*din*,' meaning 'religion'.

Salman

Meaning: Uppermost point
Origin: Arabic
Pronunciation: sal MAAN
Description: The name Salman, which derives from the name Solomon, is commonly used in Arabic- and Turkish-speaking countries. Other meanings of this name include 'healthy' and 'safe'.
Alternative spellings: Salmaan, Zalman

Sam

Meaning: God has listened
Origin: Hebrew
Pronunciation: SAM
Description: Short form of Samuel, and less frequently Samson. Sam is also short for the girls'

name Samantha, and for Arabic
names Samir and Samira.

Sameer

Meaning: Lively in conversation
Origin: Arabic
Pronunciation: SAH meer
Description: Sameer is a mascu-
line name of Arabic origin and is
said to refer to 'the one with lively
conversation'.
Alternative spellings: Samir

Sami

Meaning: Elevated status
Origin: Arabic
Pronunciation: SAH mee
Description: Sami is a unisex
name that comes from the Arabic
element of 'sami'.
Alternative spellings: Samie,
Sammey, Sammi, Sammie, Sammy,
Samy

Sammy

Meaning: God has listened
Origin: Hebrew
Pronunciation: SA me
Description: Sammy is the pet
form of both the masculine Samuel
and the feminine Samantha. It may
be used as a name in its own right
as well.
Alternative spellings: Sami, Samie,
Sammey, Sammi, Sammie, Samy

Samson

Meaning: Sun
Origin: Hebrew
Pronunciation: SAM sun
Description: Samson is Hebrew in
origin and comes from the biblical
story of Samson and Delilah.
Alternative spellings: Samsen,
Samsun

Samuel

Meaning: God has listened
Origin: Hebrew
Pronunciation: SAM yule
Description: Samuel is a bib-
lical name meaning 'he (God) has
hearkened'.
Alternative spellings: Samual,
Samuell

Sanchit

Meaning: Collection
Origin: Indian
Pronunciation: san CHIT
Description: Sanchit is an Indian
boys' name meaning 'collection' or
'accumulated', as in to have a large
number of things.

Sandeep

Meaning: Lighted lamp
Origin: Indian
Pronunciation: san DEEP
Description: Sandeep is a very
common Indian boys' name
meaning 'lighted lamp'. It is most
likely taken from the Sanskrit
'saṃdīpa'.
Alternative spellings:
Sundeep

Sandro

Meaning: Defender of man
Origin: Italian
Pronunciation: saan DROH
Description: Sandro is a short-
ened version of the name
Alexander or Alessandro, and as
such shares the same meaning of
'defender of man'.

Sandy

Meaning: Defender of man
Origin: Greek
Pronunciation: SAN dee

S

Description: Sandy is a unisex name and pet form of either 'Alexander' or 'Alexandra'.
Alternative spellings: Sandie

Sanjay
Meaning: Triumphant; victor
Origin: Sanskrit
Pronunciation: saan JAY
Description: Sanjay is a common Indian boys' name meaning 'triumphant' or 'victor'.

Santana
Meaning: Saintlike; Saint Ana
Origin: Spanish
Pronunciation: saan TAN UH
Description: Santana is a unisex name and is the condensed form of Saint Ana. Carlos Santana is a famous Mexian rock musician.

Santiago
Meaning: St James
Origin: Spanish
Pronunciation: san tee AH go
Description: Santiago comes from a combination of 'saint' and 'Diego'. St Diego is the patron saint of Spain. It is rare in Britain but popular in Europe.

Santino
Meaning: The saints
Origin: Spanish
Pronunciation: san TEE no
Description: Santino is a variant of the Spanish boys' name Santos, meaning 'the saints'.
Alternative spellings: Santeeno, Santinoh

Sanvir
Meaning: Strong; brave
Origin: Indian
Pronunciation: saan VEER
Description: Sanvir is an Indian boys' name meaning 'strong' and 'brave'.
Alternative spellings: Sanveer

Sasha
Meaning: Defender of man
Origin: Greek
Pronunciation: SASH a
Description: An English respelling of Greek names Alexander and Alexandra. It can be used for both boys and girls.
Alternative spellings: Sacha

Saul
Meaning: The child we asked for
Origin: Hebrew
Pronunciation: SAHL
Description: Saul originates from the Hebrew meaning 'the child we asked for'. It can be found in the Bible as the name of the first king of Israel and came into popular usage in the 17th century.
Alternative spellings: Saaul

Sawyer
Meaning: Sawer of wood
Origin: English
Pronunciation: SAW yar
Description: Sawyer was originally an occupational surname meaning 'sawer of wood' or 'woodcutter'. It was the name of the main character in Mark Twain's *The Adventures of Tom Sawyer*.

Saxon
Meaning: Swordsman
Origin: English
Pronunciation: sax ON
Description: Saxon was a surname taken from the Saxons,

who were a Germanic tribe. The name comes from the Germanic word '*sahs*' meaning 'knife'.

Scott
Meaning: Painted warrior
Origin: English
Pronunciation: SCOT
Description: Scott is a popular name, which historically was a surname and is still a common last name today. It means 'painted warrior'.
Alternative spellings: Scot

Seamus
Meaning: Supplanter
Origin: Gaelic
Pronunciation: SHAY mus
Description: Seamus is an Irish name and a variant of the Hebrew name James, meaning 'he who supplants'. Seamus is a common name for Irish families living in America.
Alternative spellings: Shamus, Sheamus, Seumas

Sean
Meaning: God is gracious
Origin: Gaelic
Pronunciation: SHAWN
Description: Sean is the anglicised spelling of the name Eoin, which is the Irish equivalent of John. The name means 'God is gracious'.
Alternative spellings: Sêan, Shaun, Shawn, Sion

Seb
Meaning: Revered
Origin: Greek
Pronunciation: SEB

Description: Seb is a diminutive of the Greek boys' given name Sebastian.
Alternative spellings: Sebb

Sebastian
Meaning: Revered
Origin: Latin
Pronunciation: seb ASS ti an
Description: Sebastian is an ever-popular name that means 'revered'. It comes from the Latin name Sebastos, which was the Greek translation of the title Augustus used for Roman emperors.
Alternative spellings: Sebastien

Seeley
Meaning: Blessed; silly
Origin: French
Pronunciation: see LEE
Description: Seeley is an Old French name meaning 'blessed'. It is also connected to the German word '*selig*', which forms the basis of the English word for 'silly'.
Alternative spellings: Sealey, Seely, Seelyee

Selby
Meaning: Willow farm
Origin: English
Pronunciation: sell BEE
Description: Derived from an English surname meaning 'willow farm' in Old Norse, Selby is now also a prominent given name choice.
Alternative spellings:

Selwyn
Meaning: Prosperous friend
Origin: English
Pronunciation: SEL win

S

Description: Selwyn is an Anglo-Saxon name meaning 'prosperous friend'. It is uncommon and can also be a surname.
Alternative spellings: Selwin

Sergio
Meaning: Servant
Origin: Latin
Pronunciation: SEHR gee o
Description: Sergio is a name of Latin origin, meaning 'servant'.
Alternative spellings: Sergeo

Seth
Meaning: Appointed
Origin: Hebrew
Pronunciation: SETH
Description: Seth is Hebrew in origin, and means 'appointed'.

Seymour
Meaning: St-Maur
Origin: French
Pronunciation: SEE moor
Description: Seymour comes from the name Saint-Maur, which is a settlement in Normandy, France. It is considered a British name.
Alternative spellings: Seamor, Seamore, Seamour, Seymore

Shaan
See entry in 'Names for Baby Girls A–Z'

Shae
Meaning: Full of majesty
Origin: Gaelic
Pronunciation: shey
Description: Shae is a variant of the name Shea, which is Irish in origin and means 'full of majesty'. It can be given to baby girls or boys. There are lots of variations in the spelling of this name: Shae is an anglicised version and is often a shortened version of Seamus.
Alternative spellings: Shea, Shay

Shah
Meaning: King
Origin: Persian
Pronunciation: SHAH
Description: Shah is the title of the ruler of certain Asian countries and derives from the Persian word meaning 'king'. It is a common name in Iran.
Alternative spellings: Sha, Shaah

Shane
Meaning: God is gracious
Origin: Hebrew
Pronunciation: SHE yn
Description: Shane is a masculine name derived from the Irish name Sean, which itself is derived from the Hebrew name John.
Alternative spellings: Shaine, Shayne

Shannon
See entry in 'Names for Baby Girls A–Z'

Shayaan
Meaning: Intelligent
Origin: Muslim
Pronunciation: shy AAN
Description: Shayaan is a Muslim boys' name meaning 'intelligent'. A similar girls' name is Shayan, although that is a variation of the Native American name Cheyeene.
Alternative spellings: Shayan

Shayan

Meaning: Deserving; worthy
Origin: Arabic
Pronunciation: shah YAN
Description: Shayan is an Arabic male name meaning 'deserving' and 'worthy'.
Alternative spellings: Shayaan

Shaye

See entry in 'Names for Baby Girls A–Z'

Shayne

See entry in 'Names for Baby Girls A–Z'

Shea

See entry in 'Names for Baby Girls A–Z'

Sheikh

Meaning: Scholar
Origin: Arabic
Pronunciation: SHEEK
Description: Sheik is an Arabic honorary term referring to a scholar or teacher. It has traditionally been given to the leader of a tribe or wise man. It is rare as a first name.
Alternative spellings: Sheek

Sheldon

Meaning: Steep valley
Origin: English
Pronunciation: SHEL den
Description: Sheldon is an English boys' name meaning 'steep valley' or 'flat-topped hill'. It was formerly popular, but its usage has decreased in recent years.
Alternative spellings: Shelden, Sheldin

Shepherd

Meaning: Sheep herder
Origin: English
Pronunciation: shep ERD
Description: Shepherd is an old English occupational name and given to those who were sheep herders. Like Taylor and Hunter, these occupational names are taken straight from the English vocabulary word.

Shiloh

Meaning: Sanctuary
Origin: Hebrew
Pronunciation: SHY lo
Description: In the Bible, Shiloh was a sanctuary near Jericho. It is mainly a boys' name, but can also be used for girls.
Alternative spellings: Shilo, Shylo, Shyloh

Shiro

Meaning: White
Origin: Japanese
Pronunciation: shee ROH
Description: Shiro is a Japanese character that means 'white'. In some contexts, Shiro can also mean 'castle'.

Shiv

Meaning: Pure
Origin: Sanskrit
Pronunciation: shiv
Description: Shiv is a boys' name and a variant of Shiva, a popular name of Hindi and Sanskrit origin. Shiva is the name of a Hindu god. The cult of Shiva is widespread throughout India and is given prominence in many legends.

S

Shivam

Meaning: Pure
Origin: Sanskrit
Pronunciation: SHIV ah
Description: Shivam is a variant of Shiva, the name of a Hindu god and a popular name of Hindi and Sanskrit origin.
Alternative spellings: Shivaam

Sholto

Meaning: Fruitfulness; sower of seeds
Origin: Scottish
Pronunciation: shol TOH
Description: Sholto is a Scottish name that has associations with harvesting, as it means 'fruitfulness' or 'sower of seeds'.

Shyanne

See entry in 'Names for Baby Girls A–Z'

Sia

Meaning: One who brings joy
Origin: Persian
Pronunciation: SEE ah
Description: Sia is an unusual name of uncertain origin. The name was originally masculine but can now be found for girls as well and means 'one who brings joy'.
Alternative spellings: Siia

Sid

Meaning: Wide meadow
Origin: English
Pronunciation: SID
Description: Sid is a shortened version of the Old English name Sidney, meaning 'wide meadow'. It was popular in the 19th century but is rarer in recent years.
Alternative spellings: Cid, Syd

Siddharth

Meaning: Achieved all wishes
Origin: Sanskrit
Pronunciation: sid HARTH
Description: Siddharth is a variant of the Indian boys' name, Siddhartha, meaning 'one who has achieved all wishes'.
Alternative spellings: Siddharthe, Sidharth, Sidharthe

Sidney

Meaning: Wide meadow
Origin: English
Pronunciation: SID nee
Description: Sidney is an old English name meaning 'wide meadow'. It was originally a surname and is now also a unisex given name.
Alternative spellings: Cydnee, Cydney, Sidnee, Sydnee, Sydney

Silas

Meaning: Forest dweller
Origin: Hebrew
Pronunciation: SY lus
Description: Silas is a masculine name of Hebrew origin. The name is taken to mean 'forest dweller'.
Alternative spellings: Silus, Sylas, Sylus

Simba

Meaning: Lion
Origin: Swahili
Pronunciation: sim BAH
Description: Simba is the Swahili word for 'lion', which is appropriate as it was the main character's name in Disney's *The Lion King*.

Simon

Meaning: Listen
Origin: Hebrew

Pronunciation: SYE mon
Description: Simon is a biblical name meaning 'hearkening' (listening).
Alternative spellings: Simeon, Symon

Siya
Meaning: Unknown
Origin: Arabic
Pronunciation: SEE ah
Description: Siya is a name that can be found used for both boys and girls. It appears to be of Arabic origin and is favoured by Muslim parents.
Alternative spellings: Siyah

Skyler
Meaning: Scholar
Origin: Dutch
Pronunciation: sky LER
Description: Skyler is a unisex name that comes from the Dutch surname Schuler, meaning 'scholar'. The name is not used in the Netherlands, however. It is uncertain why, but the name became popular as a first name in America in the 1980s.

Sohail
Meaning: Handsome
Origin: Arabic
Pronunciation: SU hel
Description: Sohail is an Arabic term meaning 'handsome', 'brilliant', 'noble', 'glorious', 'easy-going' and 'peaceful'.
Alternative spellings: Sohayle, Suhail

Sol
Meaning: Sun

Origin: Spanish
Pronunciation: SOL
Description: Sol is a name that can be used for both boys and girls. It is of Spanish origin as 'sol' is the Spanish word for the sun.

Solomon
Meaning: Peace
Origin: Hebrew
Pronunciation: SOL oh mon
Description: King Solomon, son of David and Bathsheba, was known for his wisdom. Solomon is mainly a Jewish name, and is derived from the word *'shalom'* for 'peace'.
Alternative spellings: Soloman

Sommer
Meaning: Summer
Origin: Scandinavian
Pronunciation: SOH mer
Description: Sommer is a Scandinavian form of the name Summer. It is unisex.
Alternative spellings: Summer

Sonny
Meaning: Son
Origin: English
Pronunciation: SUN ee
Description: The name Sonny can trace its origin back to use as a pet name. The name is taken to mean 'son of ours', although the name is actually unisex.
Alternative spellings: Sonnie, Sunny

Soren
Meaning: Apart
Origin: Danish
Pronunciation: SOR en

S

Description: Soren is a name of Danish origin, meaning 'apart'. The name may derive from an old Roman family name, Severinus, or also possibly from the Norse god of thunder, Thor.
Alternative spellings: Sorenn, Sorun

Spencer
Meaning: Dispenser
Origin: French
Pronunciation: SPEN sur
Description: Spencer comes from the French word for a dispenser of supplies in a manor house. The name is also a common surname.
Alternative spellings: Spencur, Spenser

Spike
Meaning: Pointed
Origin: English
Pronunciation: SPIKE
Description: Spike is an uncommon name of English origin. Spike literally means a 'pointed end'.
Alternative spellings: Spyke

Stanley
Meaning: Stone clearing
Origin: English
Pronunciation: STAN lee
Description: Stanley, originally a place name to describe a stony field, was adopted as a surname and then as a masculine first name. The name therefore means 'stone clearing'. It was very popular around the turn of the 20th century.
Alternative spellings: Stanlee

Stanislaw
Meaning: Someone who achieves glory
Origin: Polish
Pronunciation: stan ISS law
Description: Stanislaw is the Polish version of the name Stanislav, and means 'someone who achieves glory'. The name is formed of the Slavic elements of '*stani*', meaning 'to become' and '*slava*', meaning 'glory'.
Alternative spellings: Stanislav

Stefan
Meaning: Crown
Origin: Scandinavian
Pronunciation: STEFF ahn
Description: The name Stefan derives from the common name Stephen. There are biblical links to this name and Stefan is a popular name in German- and Polish-speaking countries.
Alternative spellings: Steffan, Stephan

Stephen
Meaning: Garland; crown
Origin: Greek
Pronunciation: STEE vun
Description: Stephen comes from the Greek word '*stephanos*', meaning 'garland; crown'. Stephen is also the name of the first Christian martyr, whose feast is celebrated on December 26th.
Alternative spellings: Steven

Steve
Meaning: Garland; crown
Origin: Greek
Pronunciation: STEEV
Description: Steve is a short form of Steven and is a popular name.
Alternative spellings: Steev

Stevie

Meaning: Honourable
Origin: Greek
Pronunciation: STE vee
Description: Stevie is a modern pet form of the name Stephen. It can be used for girls or boys.
Alternative spellings: Stevee

Stiles

Meaning: To climb
Origin: English
Pronunciation: styles
Description: Stiles is an Old English name taken from the word '*stigan*', which means 'to climb'.

Storm

Meaning: Storm
Origin: English
Pronunciation: STORM
Description: Storm is a rare unisex name that comes from the English word 'storm'.

Stuart

Meaning: Steward
Origin: English
Pronunciation: STEW ert; STOO ert
Description: Stuart comes from the French version of the surname 'Stewart', originally used for someone with the occupation of a steward, or someone who served in a royal manor.
Alternative spellings: Stewart

Subhaan

Meaning: Glory
Origin: Arabic
Pronunciation: soob HAAN
Description: Subhaan is an Arabic boys' name and is said to mean 'glory'.
Alternative spellings: Subhan

Sufyan

Meaning: Fast walker
Origin: Arabic
Pronunciation: soof YAN
Description: Sufyan is popular in Arabic-speaking countries and in the English-Arabic community.
Alternative spellings: Sufian, Sufyaan

Sufyyan

Meaning: Bearing a sword
Origin: Persian
Pronunciation: soof YAN
Description: Sufyaan, also spelt Sufyan or Sufjan, is a masculine name of Persian origin and its meaning is debated but it is generally held to mean 'bearing a sword'.
Alternative spellings: Sufjan, Sufyan

Sulaiman

Meaning: Peace
Origin: Arabic
Pronunciation: su LAY man
Description: Sulaiman is a spelling variation of the boys' name Sulayman. Both are Arabic in origin and are said to mean 'peace'. It is found in many similar forms in different countries such as the Turkish Suleiman or English Solomon.
Alternative spellings: Sulayman, Suleiman

Suleman

Meaning: Peace
Origin: Turkish
Pronunciation: SUL ee man
Description: Suleman is the Turkish form of Solomon, meaning 'peace'. Suleman the Magnificent

S

247

was a sultan of the Ottoman Empire in the 16th century.
Alternative spellings: Suleiman, Suleyman

Sullivan
Meaning: Dark eyes
Origin: Gaelic
Pronunciation: SULL li van
Description: Sullivan is one of the most common surnames in the English-speaking world. It is not very popular as a given name for boys. The name is of Gaelic origin and the meaning is 'dark eyes'.
Alternative spellings: Sullavan, Sullevan

Sully
Meaning: To stain
Origin: French
Pronunciation: sul LEE
Description: Sully is a name taken from the French word '*souiller*' meaning 'to stain' or to make something dirty.

Sultan
Meaning: Ruler
Origin: Arabic
Pronunciation: SUL tan
Description: Sultan is a common title to signify power and leadership, and is often used as a name in Arabic cultures. The word

transliterates as 'ruler', 'emperor' and 'king'.
Alternative spellings: Sulten, Sulton, Sultun

Sutton
Meaning: Town in the south
Origin: English
Pronunciation: SUT ton
Description: Sutton is an Old English place name referring to a 'town in the south', composed of the elements of '*suth*' meaning 'south' and 'tun' meaning 'town'. Sutton is also the name of many 'towns' in Britain.

Sven
Meaning: Lad
Origin: Norse
Pronunciation: SVEN
Description: From the Old Norse byname 'Sveinn'.
Alternative spellings: Svenn, Svven

Szymon
Meaning: Listen
Origin: Hebrew
Pronunciation: SHEE mon
Description: The name Szymon is a variation of the traditional English name Simon. The Hebrew element of this name comes from the biblical character Simon.
Alternative spellings: Szimon

T

Tadhg
Meaning: Poet; philosopher
Origin: Gaelic

Pronunciation: TAYg
Description: Tadhg is an Irish and Scottish name referring

to 'poet' or 'philosopher'.
It was the name of many Irish
kings in the 10th and 16th
centuries.

Taha

Meaning: Unknown
Origin: Arabic
Pronunciation: tah HA
Description: Taha is an Arabic
name that is used in reference to
prayers. The name is more com-
mon as a surname.
Alternative spellings: Tahaa,
Tahha, Tahhaa

Tai

Meaning: Great
Origin: Chinese
Pronunciation: TIE
Description: Tai is a Chinese
name meaning 'great' or
'extreme'. It might also mean
'from Thai', denoting someone
from Thailand.
Alternative spellings: Taio, Thai,
Ti

Talha

Meaning: Big tree
Origin: Arabic
Pronunciation: tahl HAH
Description: Talhah is an Arabic
masculine name meaning 'big tree'.
It was the name of one of the
prophet Muhammad's most well-
known companions (Talha ibn
Obaidullah).

Talon

Meaning: Bird claw
Origin: English
Pronunciation: TAL on
Description: This unusual name is
taken from the English vocabulary

word of the same name, referring
to a 'bird's claw'.

Tamika

See entry in 'Names for Baby Girls
A–Z'

Tanner

Meaning: Leather-maker
Origin: English
Pronunciation: tan NER
Description: Tanner is an English occupational name meaning
'leather-maker'. Like Taylor and
Hunter, these types of names
were given to people who held
these jobs but have now become
popular names in their own
right.

Taran

Meaning: Thunder
Origin: Gaelic
Pronunciation: TAH ran
Description: Taran is a unisex
name, and was probably intro-
duced by American writer Lloyd
Alexander in his novel *The Chron-
icles of Prydain*.
Alternative spellings: Tarann

Tariq

Meaning: Evening caller
Origin: Arabic
Pronunciation: TAH rik
Description: An Arabic name
meaning 'evening caller' and
'nocturnal visitor'.
Alternative spellings: Tarek,
Tareq, Tarick, Tarik

Tate

Meaning: Colourful
Origin: Norse
Pronunciation: TAY te

T

249

Description: Tate is a masculine name that originally began life as a surname.
Alternative spellings: Tait, Tayt, Tayte

Taylan
Meaning: Tailor
Origin: English
Pronunciation: tay LAAN
Description: This name is Turkish in origin, meaning 'elegant' or 'long and thin person'. It could also derive from Taylor.
Alternative spellings: Taylon, Teylan

Taylor
Meaning: Tailor
Origin: English
Pronunciation: TAY lor
Description: Taylor was originally a surname given to those with the occupation of tailor. It is a popular unisex name.
Alternative spellings: Tailor, Tayla, Taylah, Tayler, Teyla, Teylah, Teylor

Ted
Meaning: God's gift
Origin: Greek
Pronunciation: ted
Description: Ted is an abbreviated version of Theodore, but can also be shortened from Edward. Theodore means 'God's gift,' but is more commonly shortened to Theo in the UK.

Teddy
Meaning: Gift of god
Origin: Greek
Pronunciation: TED ee

Description: Teddy is a name in its own right, but could be a nickname for someone named Theodore or Edward.
Alternative spellings: Teddi, Tedi, Tedy

Teejay
Meaning: Crown
Origin: Sanskrit
Pronunciation: TEE jay
Description: Teejay is a name of Sanskrit and Punjabi origin. It is commonly used as a nickname for boys named Tajinder, which means 'crown'.
Alternative spellings: Tijay

Teo
Meaning: Gift of God
Origin: Greek
Pronunciation: TAY oh
Description: Teo is a name of Greek origin, meaning 'gift of God'. It is a shortened version of Teodor, a variant of Theodore. Teo is common in Italy and Spain, where the name is pronounced with an 'ay' sound instead of 'e'.
Alternative spellings: Tayo, Teodor, Teyo

Terence
Meaning: Instigator
Origin: Gaelic
Pronunciation: TEH rense
Description: Terence is derived from the Roman name Terentius, but it is also the anglicised form of the Gaelic word *'turlough'*.
Alternative spellings: Terance, Terrence

Terry
Meaning: Power of the people

Origin: German
Pronunciation: TEH ree
Description: Terry is commonly found as a masculine name, but it can be considered unisex if changed to the alternate spelling, Terri. It is also considered a shortened version of Terence.
Alternative spellings: Terrey, Terri, Terrie

Thatcher

Meaning: Person who thatches roofs
Origin: English
Pronunciation: thatch ER
Description: Thatcher is an old occupational name given to those who used to fix or thatch roofs for a living. Like Taylor and Hunter, these occupational names are taken straight from the English vocabulary word.

Theo

Meaning: Gift of God
Origin: French
Pronunciation: THEE oh
Description: Theo is a shortened version of the masculine name Theodore and has become very popular in its own right.
Alternative spellings: Theeo

Theodore

Meaning: Gift of God
Origin: Greek
Pronunciation: THEE a daw
Description: Theodore can be abbreviated to Ted or Teddy, but is commonly shortened to Theo in the UK.
Alternative spellings: Theodaw

Theon

Meaning: Godly
Origin: Greek
Pronunciation: thee ON
Description: Theon is a Greek boys' name meaning 'Godly'. It was also the name of a famous Greek mathematician.

Thiago

Meaning: Supplanter
Origin: Portuguese
Pronunciation: chee AH go
Description: Thiago is a different spelling of the name Tiago, which in itself is a dimiutive of Santiago. To make things more complicated, Santiago is the Spanish version of the name James. That is why all these names share the same meaning as James, which is 'supplanter'.
Alternative spellings: Tiago

Thierry

Meaning: People's ruler
Origin: French
Pronunciation: tee AIR ee
Description: Thierry is a name of French and Old German origin, meaning 'people's ruler'. It is also a variant of the Greek Theodoric, but is commonly used as the French form of the German name Terry.
Alternative spellings: Thierri, Thierrie

Thomas

Meaning: Twin
Origin: Aramaic
Pronunciation: TOM us
Description: Thomas is a biblical name, and is the name of one of Christ's 12 apostles. The name is

T

popular throughout the Christian world.
Alternative spellings: Tomas

Tiago
Meaning: St James
Origin: Spanish
Pronunciation: tee AY go
Description: Tiago is the abbreviated form of the Spanish name Santiago. This name comes from a combination of 'saint' and 'Diego', and the shortened version has become popular in the Iberian peninsula.
Alternative spellings: Tiaygo

Tim
Meaning: Honour God
Origin: Greek
Pronunciation: TIM
Description: Tim is an abbreviation of the name 'Timothy'. This shortened version has recently grown in popularity.

Timothy
Meaning: Honour God
Origin: Greek
Pronunciation: TIM uh thee
Description: This name has derived from the Greek name Timotheos. He was a companion of St Paul in the Bible. The name was not used in England before the Reformation, but has risen in popularity ever since.
Alternative spellings: Timothee

Timur
Meaning: Iron
Origin: Turkish
Pronunciation: tim OOR

Description: Timur is a Turkish name that means 'iron'. A famous historical figure with this name was Timur, also called Tamerlane, who was a Central Asian ruler in the 14th century.
Alternative spellings: Timor

Titus
Meaning: Unknown
Origin: Latin
Pronunciation: TIE tus
Description: Titus is a Latin name of unknown meaning, although it was the name of a Roman military commander who later became emperor. It was also the name of the main character of Shakespeare's play, *Titus Andronicus*.

Tobey
Meaning: God is good
Origin: Hebrew
Pronunciation: TOW bee
Description: Tobey is a variant of the Hebrew name Tobias and a different spelling of the English name Toby. It can be used for both boys and girls.
Alternative spellings: Tobee, Tobi, Tobie, Toby

Tobias
Meaning: God is good
Origin: Hebrew
Pronunciation: toe BY us
Description: Tobias is derived from the Hebrew 'Tobiah', meaning 'God is good'. It is a fairly common name in the Bible, and was popular in the Middle Ages.
Alternative spellings: Tobyas

Todd
Meaning: Fox

Origin: English
Pronunciation: TOD
Description: Todd would originally have been a surname, taken from the English dialect word meaning 'fox'. It is more common in the US than the UK.
Alternative spellings: Tod

Tom

Meaning: Twin
Origin: Aramaic
Pronunciation: TOM
Description: Tom is a pet form of Thomas, but has become popular as a name in its own right.
Alternative spellings: Thom

Tommy

Meaning: Twin
Origin: Aramaic
Pronunciation: TOM ee
Description: Tommy is an abbreviation of the name Thomas, but has become a popular name in its own right.
Alternative spellings: Tommey, Tommi, Tommie

Tommaso

Meaning: Twin
Origin: Italian
Pronunciation: tom MAS oh
Description: Tommaso is the Italian version of the traditional boys' name, Thomas. It is classic boys' name and has been popular for years and years. The name was originally borne in the Bible by the Apostle Thomas, who himself was a twin, which is where the meaning comes from. This name was given to Christians in the medieval period as a sign of honour.

Tony

Meaning: Protector
Origin: Latin
Pronunciation: TOE nee
Description: Originally a shortening of Anthony, Tony has now become a name in its own right. Its spelling variants Toni and Tonie are specifically feminine.
Alternative spellings: Toney, Toni, Tonie

Torin

Meaning: Chief
Origin: Gaelic
Pronunciation: TOR en
Description: Torin is a name often thought to be an anglicised form of the Gaelic name Torfhinn, meaning 'chief', or Toirneach, meaning 'thunder' (and thus linked to Thor, Norse god of thunder).
Alternative spellings: Toren, Torrin

Travis

Meaning: Traverser
Origin: French
Pronunciation: TRAV iss
Description: Travis would originally have been a name given to people who were traversers. The name has grown in popularity in recent years.
Alternative spellings: Traviss, Travys

Trent

Meaning: Floodwater
Origin: English
Pronunciation: TRENT
Description: The name Trent is taken from the English river of the same name. The river name actually means 'trespasser',

T

253

referring to its frequent flooding.
Alternative spellings: Trente

Trevor
Meaning: Large settlement
Origin: Welsh
Pronunciation: TREV va
Description: Trevor was originally a surname given to people from Welsh villages called 'Trefor'. It has risen in popularity across the English-speaking world.
Alternative spellings: Trever, Trevur

Trey
Meaning: Three
Origin: English
Pronunciation: trey
Description: Trey is an English name meaning 'three', and was originally a nickname for a son who was the third generation in a family. It is now being used as a given name, however.

Tristan
Meaning: Noise
Origin: Gaelic
Pronunciation: TRISS tan
Description: Tristan is a name of Welsh origin. In Arthurian legend this name belonged to one of the knights of King Arthur's round table, who gave his name to the tragic tale of Tristan and Isolde.
Alternative spellings: Tristin, Trystan, Trystin

Triumph
Meaning: To succeed
Origin:
Pronunciation: try UMPH

Description: Triumph is taken from the English vocabulary word of the same spelling and means 'to succeed'.

Troy
Meaning: Descendant of footsoldier
Origin: Gaelic
Pronunciation: TROI
Description: While Troy is a name of Gaelic origin, it is probably more well known for its Greek influence. Troy was a city in Greek legend that was besieged by the Greeks.
Alternative spellings: Troi

Truman
Meaning: Trusty man
Origin: English
Pronunciation: TROO man
Description: Truman is an Old English name that is very rare nowadays.
Alternative spellings: Trooman, Trueman

Tucker
Meaning: To torment
Origin: German
Pronunciation: tuck ER
Description: Tucker was originally a surname found in many parts of England and Ireland. The name comes from various German verbs meaning 'to torment'. In modern times, Tucker is much more commonly found in the USA than in Britain.

Tudor
Meaning: Ruler of the people
Origin: Welsh
Pronunciation: too DOOR

Description: Tudor is a Welsh name that means 'ruler of the people'. It is the Welsh equivalent of the German name Theodoric, which has the same meaning. The name is from the Germanic elements of *'peudo'* meaning 'people' and *'riks'* meaning 'ruler'.

Ty

Meaning: Unknown
Origin: English
Pronunciation: TIE
Description: While Ty is mainly used to shorten names such as Tyler, Tyson and Tyrone, it has become popular in its own right.
Alternative spellings: Tie

Tyga

Meaning: No meaning
Origin: American
Pronunciation: ty GAH
Description: Tyga is a modern invented name and as such, it has no meaning. It owes its popularity to rapper Tyga, who explained that his stage name means 'Thank you God always'.

Tyler

Meaning: Tile-maker
Origin: English
Pronunciation: TY ler
Description: Once a surname, Tyler has morphed into a first name. It can be unisex, but has risen in popularity among boys.
Alternative spellings: Tyla, Tylah, Tylar, Tylor

Tymon

Meaning: God's honour
Origin: Greek
Pronunciation: TY mon; ty MON
Description: Tymon is an uncommon name and a variant of Timothy, a Greek name meaning 'God's honour'.
Alternative spellings: Timon, Tymonn

Tymoteusz

Meaning: Honour God
Origin: Polish
Pronunciation: tim OOT ee usz
Description: Tymoteusz is the Polish form of the name Timothy, meaning 'Honour God'. The names come from the biblical name Timotheos, with 'time' meaning 'honour' and 'theeos' meaning 'God'.

Tyrell

Meaning: Puller
Origin: French
Pronunciation: TI rell
Description: It is thought that Tyrell derives from the Scandinavian god of battle Tyr.
Alternative spellings: Terrell, Tirell, Tyrel, Tyrrell

Tyrese

Meaning: No meaning
Origin: American
Pronunciation: TIE rees
Description: Tyrese is a modern, American invented name that is associated with names such as Terence, Tyree and Tyrone. As such, it has no real meaning.

Tyrone

Meaning: Irish county
Origin: Gaelic
Pronunciation: TYE rone

T

Description: Tyrone is derived from the name of a district in Ireland and has been adopted as a first name.
Alternative spellings: Tierone, Tyroan

Tyson
Meaning: High-spirited

Origin: French
Pronunciation: TY sun
Description: Tyson is a name of French origin, meaning 'high-spirited'. It has recently become popular in America.
Alternative spellings: Tycen, Tyeson, Tysen

U

Ulric
Meaning: Wolf power
Origin: English
Pronunciation: UL rik
Description: Ulric was originally coined in the Middle Ages where it meant 'wolf power'. It has become associated with the German name 'Ulrich' in recent times.
Alternative spellings: Ulrik

Ulysses
Meaning: Wrathful
Origin: Latin
Pronunciation: OO ly SEES
Description: Ulysses is the Latin form of the Greek name Odysseus. It was made famous by United States president Ulysses S. Grant and James Joyce's novel, *Ulysses*.

Umair
Meaning: Intelligent one
Origin: Arabic
Pronunciation: OO mare
Description: Umair is a popular name across Islamic communities.
Alternative spellings: Omair, Umaire

Umar
Meaning: Thriving
Origin: Arabic
Pronunciation: OO mar
Description: Umar is a favourite name across the Arabic world, although it is common in Sunni Muslim, rather than Shia Muslim communities.
Alternative spellings: Umer, Umur

Uri
Meaning: Light
Origin: Hebrew
Pronunciation: your EE
Description: Uri comes from the Hebrew word meaning 'light'. It is linked to 'Uriah' but not 'Yuri', as that name has a completely different meaning.

Uriah
Meaning: God is light
Origin: Hebrew
Pronunciation: yuh RY ah
Description: Uriah is a biblical name. It can be shortened to Uri.
Alternative spellings: Youriah

Usman

Meaning: Bustard
Origin: Arabic
Pronunciation: uss MAHN
Description: Usman is an Arabic boys' name meaning 'bustard,' which is a large, heavily-built, swift-running bird breed.

Uzair

Meaning: Helpful
Origin: Muslim
Pronunciation: oo ZAIR
Description: Uzair is the Muslim version of the Hebrew name, Ezra. It comes from the Hebrew word for 'helpful' and Ezra was the author of one of Old Testament books.

V

Valentin

Meaning: Strong; healthy
Origin: Latin
Pronunciation: val EN tin
Description: Valentin comes from the Latin name Valentinus, meaning 'strong' and 'healthy'. This name in common in Russia, Ukraine, Scandinavia and France.
Alternative spellings: Valentine, Valentino

Valentino

Meaning: Strong
Origin: Latin
Pronunciation: val en TEE no
Description: Valentino is a variant of the Latin boys' name Valentine, meaning 'strong' or 'healthy'. It is a common name in Italy and among Italian-Americans.
Alternative spellings: Valenteno, Valentyno

Vance

Meaning: One who lives near marshland
Origin: English
Pronunciation: vance
Description: Vance is an English surname that was given to people who lived near a marshland or a bog. However, the letter 'V' makes this a modern-sounding and edgy baby name.

Varin

Meaning: Rich in gifts
Origin: Indian
Pronunciation: VAAR in
Description: Varin is an Indian boys' name meaning 'rich in gifts'. It can also be found in France as a last name, particularly the members of aristocracy in the Burgundy region.

Vasco

Meaning: Crow
Origin: Spanish
Pronunciation: vaas COH
Description: Vasco is a Spanish name most likely taken from the surname Velázquez, which in turn became Velasco, which means 'crow' in Basque.

Vaughn

Meaning: Small

U
V

Origin: Welsh
Pronunciation: von
Description: Vaughn is derived from the Welsh word '*bychan*', meaning 'small'. Although more popular as a surname, it can also be used as a given name.

Viaan

Meaning: Lively
Origin: Indian
Pronunciation: vee AAHN
Description: Viaan is an Indian male name meaning 'lively' or 'full of life and energy'. An alternative spelling of the name is Vian, and has the same meaning as well.
Alternative spellings: Vian

Vicente

Meaning: Conquerer
Origin: Italian
Pronunciation: vee CENT eh
Description: Vicente is the Italian, Spanish and Portuguese version of the name Vincent, and as such shares the same meaning of 'conquerer'.

Veer

Meaning: Brave
Origin: Sanskrit
Pronunciation: VEER
Description: Veer seems to have come from the Sanskrit word meaning 'brave'. It is popular among Indian communities.
Alternative spellings: Vier

Victor

Meaning: Conqueror
Origin: Latin
Pronunciation: VIK tor
Description: Victor is a Latin name that would have been given to winners in a battle. While the name is uncommon today, it has previously been extremely popular.
Alternative spellings: Vicktor, Viktor, Wiktor

Vihaan

Meaning: Dawn; morning
Origin: Indian
Pronunciation: vee HAAN
Description: Vihaan is a male Indian name that comes from the Sanskrit word for 'dawn' or 'morning,' hence the meaning of the name. The female form of this name is Vihana, and that name also has the same meaning.
Alternative spellings: Vihan

Vincent

Meaning: Conquering
Origin: Latin
Pronunciation: VIN sent
Description: Vincent is derived from Latin, and has been a popular name across Europe for many years.
Alternative spellings: Vinsent

Vinny

Meaning: Friend
Origin: English
Pronunciation: VIN knee
Description: The name Vinny derives from the Old English names Alvina and Elvina. It could also be a shortened version of Vincent.
Alternative spellings: Vinni, Vinnie

Vivaan

Meaning: First rays of the sun
Origin: Sanskrit

Pronunciation: viv AAHN
Description: The name Vivaan comes from a Sanskrit word that means 'first rays of the sun'. Vivaan is also one of the names of the Hindu god, Lord Krishna.
Alternative spellings: Vivan

Vlad
Meaning: Rule
Origin: Russian

Pronunciation: vlahd
Description: Vlad is a Slavic name that comes from the element of '*vladeti*', meaning 'rule'. Vlad III, known as Vlad the Impaler, was the prince of Wallachia in the 15th century. He was the son of Vlad Dracul and was known as a cruel leader. He famously inspired Bram Stoker's 1897 vampire novel, *Dracula*.

W

Wade
Meaning: Able to go
Origin: English
Pronunciation: WAYDE
Description: Wade is a popular name of Old English and Scandinavian origin, meaning 'able to go'.
Alternative spellings: Waide, Wayde

Waldo
Meaning: Ruler
Origin: German
Pronunciation: wall DOH
Description: Waldo is a German name meaning 'ruler'. It was made famous by the children's books series Where's Waldo? (or as it is known in the UK, Where's Wally?)

Waleed
Meaning: Newborn
Origin: Arabic
Pronunciation: wah LEED
Description: Waleed is an Arabic name meaning 'newborn'. The name is also often spelt Walid. The name comes from the Arabic word '*walada*' meaning 'to give birth'.
Alternative spellings: Walid

Wali
Meaning: Custodian; protector; helper; friend
Origin: Arabic
Pronunciation: wall EE
Description: Wali is an Arabic word that has many meanings, including 'custodian,' 'protector,' 'helper' and 'friend'. This would be an ideal choice for parents looking for something with a variety of wonderful meanings.

Walter
Meaning: Army ruler
Origin: German
Pronunciation: WAL ter
Description: While the constituents of Walter are German, the name is actually Old French. It has recently become rare.
Alternative spellings: Wolter
Alternative spellings: Wally, Wallie

V

W

Waris

Meaning: Belong to the last one
Origin: Arabic
Pronunciation: WARE is
Description: Waris comes from an Urdu vocabulary word meaning 'belong to the last one', as in being a successor or heir to someone.

Warren

Meaning: Protector
Origin: French
Pronunciation: WAR run
Description: Warren would have been a common name for someone hailing from the French village of La Varrenne. It also has roots in the German language.
Alternative spellings: Warran, Warron

Waverly

Meaning: Meadow of quivering aspen
Origin: English
Pronunciation: wave ERR lee
Description: Waverly is a unisex name meaning 'meadow of quivering aspen'. The word 'waver' means to tremble or flicker.

Waylon

Meaning: Land beside the road
Origin: English
Pronunciation: WAY lon
Description: Waylon was originally an English surname meaning 'land beside the road'. The name comes from the Old English *wieland*.

Wayne

Meaning: Cartwright
Origin: English
Pronunciation: WAIN
Description: Wayne is a first name derived from a surname that would have been given to a carter or cartwright.
Alternative spellings: Wain, Wayn

Wesley

Meaning: West meadow
Origin: English
Pronunciation: WEZ lee
Description: Wesley was originally a surname meaning 'west meadow' but was adopted as a first name in tribute to founders of the Methodist Church Charles and John Wesley.
Alternative spellings: Weslee, Wesli, Weslie, Wesly, Wezlee, Wezli, Wezlie, Wezley

Weston

Meaning: Town in the west
Origin: English
Pronunciation: west TUN
Description: Like Easton, it was originally a surname but is now used regularly as a first name. In Old English, it is composed of 'west' meaning the direction and 'ton' meaning town, givingits meaning of 'town in the west'.
Alternative spellings: Victor

Wilberforce

Meaning: From Wilberfoss
Origin: English
Pronunciation: WIL ber forse
Description: Wilberforce comes from Old English and was given as the name to someone from Wilberfoss.
Alternative spellings: Wilbeforce, Wilburforce

Wilbur

Meaning: Wild boar; resolute; brilliant
Origin: English
Pronunciation: will BOOR
Description: Wilbur is from an English surname meaning 'wild boar'. However, it also has German roots and can mean 'resolute' or 'brilliant'.

Wilder

Meaning: To be wild
Origin: English
Pronunciation: wild ER
Description: Wilder comes from the English vocabulary word of the same spelling, meaning 'to be (even more) wild'. This is part of the trend of taking English words and turning them into names, such as Prince or Maverick.

Wilf

Meaning: Desires peace
Origin: English
Pronunciation: wilf
Description: Wilf is a short form of the name Wilfred, meaning 'desires peace'. Wilfred is a name that first appeared in Old English, and was the name of a saint in the 7th century.

Wilfred

Meaning: Will
Origin: English
Pronunciation: WIL fred
Description: Wilfred is an old-fashioned name of English origin, meaning 'will', 'desire' and 'peace'. It is often shortened to Wilf.
Alternative spellings: Wilfrid

Will

Meaning: Protection
Origin: German
Pronunciation: WILL
Description: Will is a shortened form of the name William.
Alternative spellings: Wil

Willem

Meaning: Protection
Origin: German
Pronunciation: WIL lem
Description: Willem is a Dutch variant of the popular German name William.
Alternative spellings: Wilem, Willum

William

Meaning: Protection
Origin: German
Pronunciation: WILL yum
Description: This name was introduced to England by the Normans, and was in fact the name of the conqueror himself. In the first century after the conquest it was the most common name in all of Britain. It has risen in popularity following the marriage of Prince William and Kate Middleton.
Alternative spellings: Wiliam, Willyam

Willie

Meaning: Will, desire; helmet, protection
Origin: German
Pronunciation: WILL ee
Description: Willie is a shortened version of the traditional boys' name, William. It has multiple meanings meaning 'will' and 'desire' and also 'helmet' and 'protection'.
Alternative spellings: Willy

Wilson

Meaning: Son of Will

W

Origin: English
Pronunciation: WIL son
Description: Wilson is a common surname derived from Old English. It has been a first name for many years, but is fairly uncommon.
Alternative spellings: Willson, Wilsun

Winston

Meaning: Joy stone
Origin: English
Pronunciation: WIN ston
Description: The name Winston is taken from the place in Gloucestershire. It has become rare in recent times.
Alternative spellings: Whinston, Whynston, Wynston

Wojciech

Meaning: Joy of war; smiling warrior
Origin: Polish
Pronunciation: voi CHEKH
Description: Wojciech is a Polish name formed from two components of archaic Polish: '*woj*' means 'war' or 'warrior' and '*ciech*' means 'joy,' hence the combined meaning of 'joy of war' or 'smiling warrior'.

Woodrow

Meaning: Row of houses by a wood
Origin: English
Pronunciation: wuhd ROW
Description: Woodrow is an English surname that means 'row of houses by a wood'. It was made popular by US president Woodrow Wilson.

Woody

Meaning: Row of houses by a wood
Origin: English
Pronunciation: WUH dee
Description: Woody came about as an abbreviation of such names as Woodrow. It probably came into fashion due to such film stars as Woody Allen.
Alternative spellings: Woodie, Woodee

Wyatt

Meaning: Brave
Origin: Greek
Pronunciation: WY att
Description: Wyatt, sometimes a pet form of William, was a medieval surname but has adapted to become a first name. It is popular in America.
Alternative spellings: Wyett

X

Xander

Meaning: Defender of man
Origin: Greek
Pronunciation: ZAN duh
Description: Xander is a shortened form of Alexander but has become a popular name in its own right.

Alternative spellings: Sander, Zander

Xavier

Meaning: The new house
Origin: Spanish
Pronunciation: ZAV ee air

Description: Xavier is a Hispanic version of the Basque place name Etcheberria.

Alternative spellings: Javier, Savier, Zavier

Y

Yaaqub
Meaning: Supplanter
Origin: Arabic
Pronunciation: yack UB
Description: Yaaqub is the Arabic version of the Hebrew name Jacob and as such, shares the same meaning of 'supplanter'.
Alternative spellings: Yaqub

Yaasir
Meaning: To be rich
Origin: Arabic
Pronunciation: yaas IR
Description: Yaasir is a variation of the more common Yasir, and the name means 'to be rich'. It comes from the Arabic word 'yasira' meaning 'one who makes things easier'.
Alternative spellings: Yasir

Yagiz
Meaning: Unknown
Origin: Turkish
Pronunciation: yaa GEEZ
Description: Yagiz is a Turkish boys' name. Because it is quite rare, not much is known about it.

Yahir
Meaning: He shines; he enlightens
Origin: Arabic
Pronunciation: YAH heer
Description: The entymology of Yahir is conflicted but it is most likely an Arabic name derived from the Hebrew name Yair, meaning 'he shines'.

Yahya
Meaning: He lives
Origin: Arabic
Pronunciation: YUH ya
Description: Yahya is a prophet in the Quran, and it is believed that the name means 'he lives' – which means his legacy will continue forever.

Yair
Meaning: He will enlighten
Origin: Hebrew
Pronunciation: yaah AIR
Description: Yair is a Hebrew verb that means 'He will enlighten'. It is found in ancient Jewish texts and is also a name often found in contemporary Israel.
Alternative spellings: Jair, Ya'ir

Yani
Meaning: Peace
Origin: Aboriginal
Pronunciation: yanny
Description: Yani is an Australian Aboriginal name meaning 'peace'. It is a unisex name that can be used for both boys and girls.
Alternative spellings: Yanny, Yanni

X
Y

Yanis

Meaning: God is gracious
Origin: Greek
Pronunciation: YAAN iss
Description: Yanis is a Greek variation of the common boys' name, John, and as such shares the same meaning with it. Other forms of the name include: Yannis, Yiannis and Giannis, all of them having Greek roots.
Alternative spellings: Yannis

Yaqub

Meaning: Held by the heel
Origin: Hebrew
Pronunciation: YA coob
Description: Yaqub is the Hebrew version of the name Jacob, and is mainly found in Muslim and Arabic areas.
Alternative spellings: Yacob, Yacoob

Yaseen

Meaning: Refers to a passage in the Quran
Origin: Arabic
Pronunciation: YAAS iyn
Description: Yaseen is a phonetically spelt variant of the Arabic name Yasin. Yasin is formed by combining two Arabic letters from a prolific extract in the Quran, 'Ya' and 'Seen,' and is also used in Egyptian folk-tales. The name is popular in Turkey.
Alternative spellings: Yasin

Yash

Meaning: Successful
Origin: Sanskrit
Pronunciation: YASH
Description: Yash is uncommon in the UK but it is common among Indian communities. It is said to mean 'success'.
Alternative spellings: Yashe

Yasir

Meaning: Rich
Origin: Arabic
Pronunciation: yah SEER; YAH sir
Description: Yasir is Arabic in origin and is popular throughout the Middle East. It is said to mean 'rich' and is a common name among Muslim families.
Alternative spellings: Yahsir, Yaseer

Yehuda

Meaning: Praise
Origin: Hebrew
Pronunciation: ye hu DA
Description: Yehuda is a biblical name that means 'praise', 'gratitude' and 'thanks'.
Alternative spellings: Yehudah

Yoshinobu

Meaning: Splendid faith
Origin: Japanese
Pronunciation: yosh in OO bu
Description: Yoshinobu is a common name in Japan and Japanese-speaking communities, but is found across Asia.
Alternative spellings: Yosinobu

Youssef

Meaning: The Lord gave more
Origin: Hebrew
Pronunciation: YOU sef
Description: Youssef is a boys' given name of Hebrew origin common in the Arabic world. It is a variant of Joseph.
Alternative spellings: Yousef, Youssef, Yousaf, Yousif, Yosef, Yosif, Yusef

Yu

Meaning: Unknown
Origin: Chinese
Pronunciation: YOO
Description: Yu is a unisex name, and has various different meanings due to the 13 different Chinese characters that represent the name.
Alternative spellings: Yoo

Yunus

Meaning: Dove
Origin: Hebrew
Pronunciation: YOU nus
Description: Yunus is the Arabic version of the English Jonas.
Alternative spellings: Yonus, Younus

Yuri

Meaning: Farmer; earth worker
Origin: Russian
Pronunciation: YOUR ee

Description: Yuri is the Russian translation of George.
Alternative spellings: Yury

Yuvraj

Meaning: Crown prince
Origin: Sanskrit
Pronunciation: yuv RAJH
Description: Yuvraj is a name that is popular among Indian communities, and was originally given to the son of one of the ruling maharajahs or chiefs of the various kingdoms in India. It has grown in popularity in the UK in recent years.

Yves

Meaning: Yew
Origin: French
Pronunciation: EEV
Description: Yves is a very rare name in the UK and is French in origin.

Z

Zac

Meaning: The Lord recalled
Origin: Hebrew
Pronunciation: ZAK
Description: Zac derives from Zachary, and has become a name in its own right. It has become extremely popular in recent years due to film star Zac Efron.
Alternative spellings: Zach, Zack, Zak, Zakk

Zachariah

Meaning: The Lord recalled
Origin: Hebrew

Pronunciation: zak ah RYE ah
Description: Zachariah is a biblical name and features 31 times in the Bible. It is popular in the UK.
Alternative spellings: Zacarias, Zaccaria, Zakaria

Zacharias

Meaning: The Lord recalled
Origin: Hebrew
Pronunciation: zak a RYE ass
Description: Zacharias is the Greek or northern African spelling of the Hebrew name Zachariah, meaning 'the Lord recalled'.

Y
Z

Alternative spellings: Zaccarias, Zacharius

Zachary
Meaning: The Lord recalled
Origin: Hebrew
Pronunciation: ZAK ah ree
Description: This name is a derivative of Zachariah and as such is a Hebrew name.
Alternative spellings: Zachari, Zachery, Zackary, Zakary

Zahir
Meaning: Helper; supporter
Origin: Arabic
Pronunciation: ZAH heer
Description: Zahir is an Arabic boys' name meaning 'helper' or supporter'. In the Quran and Islamic religion, al-Zahir is one of the 99 names of Allah.

Zaid
Meaning: He who progresses
Origin: Arabic
Pronunciation: ZADE
Description: Zaid is the anglicised variation of the name Zayd, which itself is Arabic.
Alternative spellings: Zade, Zayd

Zaiden
Meaning: No meaning
Origin: American
Pronunciation: ZAY den
Description: Zaiden is a variation of the name Zaden, which is a modern invention and has no meaning as such. This would be a great choice for parents looking for something very cool-sounding and unique.
Alternative spellings: Zaden, Zayden

Zain
Meaning: Handsome
Origin: Arabic
Pronunciation: zane
Description: Zain is an Islamic name that means 'beauty' or 'handsome'. The name is popular in Muslim communities and there is a Muslim singer and songwriter who shares this name, Zain Bhikha.
Alternative spellings: Zayn, Zane, Zayne

Zak
Meaning: Purity
Origin: Hebrew
Pronunciation: zak
Description: Zak spelt in this way can be taken as a name in itself. Its Hebrew meaning is 'purity'. It can however also be the shortened form of Zakaria or Zakarias, both of which have numerous spelling variations originating from both Hebrew and Arabic. The meaning of Zak when considered a shortened version of Zakaria is 'God has remembered'.
Alternative spellings: Zach, Zack

Zaki
Meaning: The Lord recalled
Origin: Greek
Pronunciation: ZAK ee
Description: Zaki and similar names have become extremely popular since the fame of film star Zac Efron. It is thought to be of Greek origin.
Alternative spellings: Zakki

Zakir
Meaning: The Lord recalled
Origin: Arabic
Pronunciation: za KEER

Description: This name means 'the one who remembers'. It is unusual in Britain but popular across the Arabic world.
Alternative spellings: Zahkir, Zakeer

Zana

Meaning: Wise; knowing
Origin: Kurdish
Pronunciation: zaan AH
Description: Zana is a Kurdish boys' name meaning 'wise' or 'knowing' and has connotations of knowledge and learning.
Alternative spellings: Zanna, Zanah, Zannah

Zander

Meaning: Defender of man
Origin: Greek
Pronunciation: ZAN der
Description: Zander is a Dutch and Slavic variant of the boys' name Xander, which is a variant of the Greek name Alexander, meaning 'defender of man'. Xander and Zander have both risen greatly in popularity in recent years.
Alternative spellings: Sander, Xander

Zayaan

Meaning: Graceful
Origin: Arabic
Pronunciation: ZAY aan
Description: Zayaan is a name and a variant of the Arabic name Zayan. It is common as both a given name and as a surname in the Arabic world.
Alternative spellings: Zayain, Zayan

Zaydan

Meaning: Grow; increase

Origin: Arabic
Pronunciation: zaay DAAN
Description: Zaydan is an Arabic boys' name that means 'growth' or 'increase'. It is similar to the name Zayd, which shares the similar meaning of 'abundance' or 'plentiful'. It is both a given name and a surname in Arabic countries.
Alternative spellings: Zayden

Zayer

Meaning: Tourist who visits holy places
Origin: Arabic
Pronunciation: zaay ER
Description: Zayer is an Arabic boys' name meaning 'tourist who visits holy places'. It is more commonly found in Muslim/Islamic communities.
Alternative spellings: Zayir

Zebediah

Meaning: Gift from God
Origin: Hebrew
Pronunciation: zeb EH DIE ah
Description: Zebediah is a Hebrew name meaning 'gift from God'. It is the name of several characters in the Old Testament.
Alternative spellings: Zebedia

Zeeshan

Meaning: Noble
Origin: Arabic
Pronunciation: ZEE sharn
Description: Zeeshan is said to mean 'possessor of high status' and is of Arabic origin. It is commonly used to signify nobility, and is also regularly abbreviated to Shan.
Alternative spellings: Zeesharn, Zeshan

Z

Zeke

Meaning: God will provide strength
Origin: Hebrew
Pronunciation: zee-kee
Description: Zeke is a shortened form or nickname of the Hebrew name Ezekiel. Ezekiel was the name of a prophet in the Old Testament. It is said to mean 'God will provide strength'.

Zenith

Meaning: Peak; most successful
Origin: English
Pronunciation: zen ITH
Description: Zenith is taken from the English vocabulary word of the same spelling, and it means 'peak' or 'most successful', as in the point at which something reaches its highest.

Zephaniah

Meaning: Yahweh is hidden
Origin: Hebrew
Pronunciation: zef ahn EYE ah
Description: Zephaniah is a biblical name meaning 'Yahweh is hidden'. He is the author of the Book of Zephaniah and one of 12 minor prophets of the Old Testament.
Alternative spellings: Zephinia

Zhi

Meaning: Nature
Origin: Chinese
Pronunciation: JHEE
Description: Zhi is a unisex name of Chinese origin, common as both a given name and a surname. It roughly transliterates as 'nature', 'character' or 'quality'.
Alternative spellings: Zhee, Zi

Zia

See entry in 'Names for Baby Girls A–Z'

Zidane

Meaning: Growth; progress; increase
Origin: Arabic
Pronunciation: zee dan
Description: Zidane is an Arabic boys' name, and because it has a 'zyd' root, the name means 'progress,' 'growth' or 'to increase'. It is the name of the famous French footballer and manager, Zinedine Zidane.
Alternative spellings: Zidan

Ziggy

Meaning: Victory; peace
Origin: English
Pronunciation: zig EE
Description: Ziggy is a variation of the name Siegfried, a German name that is composed of the elements of '*sig*' meaning 'victory' and '*frithu*' meaning 'peace'. The late David Bowie made the name popular because Ziggy Stardust was his alter ego.

Zion

Meaning: Highest point
Origin: Hebrew
Pronunciation: ZI on
Description: Zion is a masculine name of Hebrew origin. It is an extremely rare name, unlike many other Hebrew names in Britain. It is said to mean the 'highest point' or 'pinnacle'.
Alternative spellings: Zyon

Ziya

Meaning: Splendour; light; glow

Origin: Arabic
Pronunciation: ZEE yah
Description: Ziya is a name taken from the Arabic word '*diya*', which means 'splendour', 'light' and 'glow'.
Alternative spellings: Zia

Zohaib

Meaning: Leader
Origin: Arabic
Pronunciation: zo HAYB
Description: The name Zohaib comes from an Arabic word that means 'leader', 'king', 'gold' or 'ocean of knowledge'. It is common as both a given name and a surname.
Alternative spellings: Zohayb

Zorawar

Meaning: Strong; powerful
Origin: Indian
Pronunciation: zorah WAR

Description: Zorawar is an Indian boys' name meaning 'strong' or 'powerful'.

Zubair

Meaning: Proper name
Origin: Arabic
Pronunciation: zu BAYR
Description: The boys' name Zubair comes from the Arabic word that means 'proper name' or 'superior'. It is sometimes written as Zubayr, which is a city in Iraq. Zubair is also the name of a group of islands in the Red Sea.
Alternative spellings: Zubaair, Zubayr

Zylan

Meaning: No meaning
Origin: American
Pronunciation: zye LAAN
Description: Zylan is a modern invented name and as such, has no real meaning.

Z

Names for Baby Girls A–Z

A

Aamna

Meaning: Security
Origin: Arabic
Pronunciation: AHM na
Description: Aamna derives from an Arabic word meaning 'security'.
Alternative spellings: Amna

Aarna

Meaning: Strong mountain
Origin: Hebrew
Pronunciation: AHR nah
Description: Aarna originates from the longer Hebrew name Arnina, and is the feminine version of the name Aaron.
Alternative spellings: Aarrna, Arna

Aasiyah

Meaning: Caring one
Origin: Arabic
Pronunciation: ah SEE yah
Description: As Aasiyah is found in Islamic scriptures the name was initially favoured by Muslim parents, however its use has now spread to Africa.
Alternative spellings: Aasiya, Asiya, Asiyah

Aadya

Meaning: First power or the beginning
Origin: Hindi
Pronunciation: Ah DEE yah
Description: Aadya is a Hindu name of Indian origin. The translation is similar in many Eastern languages, meaning 'first power', 'goddess' and 'unequalled'. It is a popular name throughout the Hindu community and variations of the spelling have seen a rise in popularity in mainstream culture.
Alternative spellings: Aadyha, Adya

Aairah

Meaning: Noble; honourable; respectful
Origin: Urdu
Pronunciation: AY rah
Description: Aairah is a pretty, feminine name of Urdu origin, that means 'noble' or 'respectful'. Variations of the name include Aaira and Ayra.
Alternative spellings: Aaira, Ayra, Ayrah

Aaliya

Meaning: Exalted; ascending
Origin: Hebrew
Pronunciation: Ah LEE ah
Description: Aaliya is a feminine form of the Arabic name, Ali, that translates as 'exulted' or 'ascending'. The name had a huge surge in popularity in the late 90s thanks to Grammy and Academy Award nominated singer and actress, Aaliyah, who tragically died in a plane crash in 2001.
Alternative spellings: Aliya, Aaliyah, Aliyah, Alia

Aamina

Meaning: Dependable
Origin: Arabic
Pronunciation: Ah MEE nah
Description: Aamina is a spelling variation of Amina and translates as 'dependable'. It is a widely-used name in the Muslim community as it is understood that 'Āminah bint Wahb (who died in 577AD) was mother of the prophet Muhammad.
Alternative spellings: Amina, Ahmina, Aminah, Aaminah

Aanya

Meaning: Limitless
Origin: Hindi
Pronunciation: AHN yah
Description: Aanya is a Hindu name that means 'limitless' or 'resurrection'. The name is also a variation of Anya, a Russian form of Hannah that means 'with grace'.
Alternative spellings: Anya

Aariya

Meaning: Lioness
Origin: Hebrew
Pronunciation: Ah REE ah
Description: Aariya is a spelling variation of Arya, an Iranian name of Indian origin. The name received a surge in popularity in Western society thanks to the female character, Arya Stark in popular TV series *Game of Thrones*.
Alternative spellings: Aria, Arya, Aarya

Aasiya

Meaning: Healer; one who tends to the sick
Origin: Arabic
Pronunciation: ah SEE yah

Description: Aasiya, a spelling variation of Asiya, is a revered name within the Muslim community. In history, Asiya bint Muzahim was the wife of the Pharoah, who reigned during the time of Moses. She is regarded as one of the four greatest women of all time in Muslim faith, the other three being Mary (mother of Jesus), Khadija (wife of Muhammad) and Fatimah (daughter of Muhammad).
Alternative spellings: Asiya, Asija

Aayat

Meaning: Miracles of the Quran
Origin: Arabic
Pronunciation: AH yat
Description: The Islamic translation of Aayat is 'verse of the Quran' or 'miracles of the Quran'. It refers to 'signs' or proof of the validity of the verses of the Quran.
Alternative spellings: Ayat

Abbie

Meaning: Father's joy
Origin: Hebrew
Pronunciation: AB ee
Description: The most popular spelling variant of the pet form for Abigail. This name is a name in its own right.
Alternative spellings: Abbey, Abbi, Abby, Abi

Abida

Meaning: God's follower
Origin: Hebrew
Pronunciation: AB ee dah

Description: A feminine version of the masculine name Abid, meaning 'God's follower'.
Alternative spellings: Abbida, Abeeda

Abigail
Meaning: Father's joy
Origin: Hebrew
Pronunciation: AB ih gayl
Description: Abigail is a biblical Hebrew name meaning 'father in exaltation'.
Alternative spellings: Abbigail, Abygail

Abiha
Meaning: Father
Origin: Arabic
Pronunciation: ah BEE ah
Description: Abiha is a name of Arabic origins and it could share a root with the Hebrew name Abigail. In Islamic belief it was a title of one of the daughters of the prophet Muhammad.
Alternative spellings: Abbiha, Abeeha

Abilene
Meaning: Grass
Origin: Hebrew
Pronunciation: AB ih leen
Description: Abilene is both the name of a small town in Texas and the translation of a Hebrew word meaning 'grass'. According to the New Testament, Abilene is a region of the Holy Land.
Alternative spellings: Abelene, Abileen

Abir
See entry in 'Names for Baby Boys A–Z'

Abishag

A

Meaning: Wise; educated
Origin: Hebrew
Pronunciation: AB ih shag
Description: Abishag is a biblical name, borne by a beautiful virgin brought to King David on his death bed in an attempt to restore his vigour and lust for life. It is very rarely seen these days.
Alternative spellings: Abbishag, Abyshag

Abital
Meaning: Dewy
Origin: Hebrew
Pronunciation: AB ih tal
Description: Abital is a biblical name meaning 'dewy', so this name has connotations with dawn and nature.
Alternative spellings: Abbital, Abitel

Abla
Meaning: Woman with a full figure; wild rose
Origin: Arabic
Pronunciation: AB la
Description: The name Abla is thought to have Arabic roots and refers to 'a woman with a full figure'. It could also be Swahili in origin, in which case it could mean 'a wild rose'.
Alternative spellings: Ablah

Acacia
Meaning: Point; thorn
Origin: Greek
Pronunciation: ah KAY shuh; ah KAY see uh
Description: This unusual girls' name is also the name of a flower, the acacia, which is the national symbol of Australia. It is suggested

that the flower has the power to ward off evil.
Alternative spellings: Akacia, Akaysha, Akeisha

Ada
Meaning: Noble
Origin: German
Pronunciation: AY da
Description: Ada is sometimes used as a pet form of Adele, but is also a name in its own right.
Alternative spellings: Adah, Aida

Adah
Meaning: Adornment
Origin: Hebrew
Pronunciation: AY da
Description: Adah is a biblical name meaning 'adornment', or 'enhancement'. Particularly popular in Sweden.
Alternative spellings: Ada, Aida

Adaline
Meaning: Noble
Origin: Teutonic
Pronunciation: AD e lin
Description: An unusual spelling variation of Adeline that has risen in popularity in recent years. The name is of German origin, the diminutive of Adèle.
Alternative spellings: Adeline, Adelyn, Adaleine, Adalyn

Adamina
Meaning: Red earth
Origin: Hebrew
Pronunciation: AD ah ME na
Description: This name is the feminine form of Adam and shares the same meaning, 'earth'.
Alternative spellings: Adamena, Addamina

Addison
See entry in 'Names for Baby Boys A–Z'

Adela
Meaning: Noble
Origin: Teutonic
Pronunciation: a DEL a
Description: Adela is a further diminutive of the German name Adèle or the masculine form Adel, meaning 'noble'. In history, Saint Adela was a 7th-century Frankish princess who founded a monastery in France. It was also the name of one of William the Conqueror's daughters.
Alternative spellings: Adèle, Adele

Adelaide
Meaning: Noble; kind
Origin: German
Pronunciation: AD ee lade
Description: This name of Old German origin means 'full of kindness'.
Alternative spellings: Adelade, Adelayde

Adele
Meaning: Noble; kind
Origin: German
Pronunciation: a DELL
Description: Adele is a variant of the Old German name Adeline or Adelaide.
Alternative spellings: Adel, Adelle

Adelina
Meaning: Noble; kind; small-winged one
Origin: French
Pronunciation: A del EE na
Description: A popular girls' name that derives from the Old

German names Adelaide and Adeline. It is a name rich with associations and means 'noble', 'kind' and 'small-winged one'.
Alternative spellings: Adeleina, Adelena

Adina
Meaning: Slender
Origin: Hebrew
Pronunciation: a DEE na
Description: Adina was formerly a male name and was borne by a soldier in King David's army. Now it is more common with females due to its feminine sound.
Alternative spellings: Adeena, Adena

Aditi
Meaning: No boundaries
Origin: Sanskrit
Pronunciation: ah DEE tah
Description: Aditi is a name said to mean 'no boundaries'. It is the name of a Hindu goddess so is popular with Hindu parents.
Alternative spellings: Adeeti, Aditie, Adity

Admete
Meaning: Untamed
Origin: Greek
Pronunciation: ad MEE tee
Description: In Greek mythology, Admete's father asked Heracles to acquire for his daughter the belt of the queen of the Amazons.
Alternative spellings: Admeete, Admette

Adrianna
Meaning: From Hadria
Origin: Latin
Pronunciation: ah dre AH nah

Description: Adrianna is the feminine form of the masculine Adrian. This refers to a man from Hadria, so Adriana means 'girl from Hadria'.
Alternative spellings: Adreana, Adriana, Adrihanna

Adrianne
Meaning: From Hadria
Origin: Latin
Pronunciation: AY dri ann
Description: Another feminine variant of the popular boys' name Adrian.
Alternative spellings: Adreanne, Adrienne

Aeryn
Meaning: Ireland
Origin: Gaelic
Pronunciation: EH rin
Description: Aeryn is the American respelling of the Gaelic name Erin. In the 19th century many Irish poets used the name Erin to refer to Ireland or as a feminine personification of the land.
Alternative spellings: Aerin, Airin, Eirinn, Erin, Eryn

Afaf
Meaning: Chastity
Origin: Arabic
Pronunciation: AY faf
Description: Afaf is a popular name and has associations with virtue.
Alternative spellings: Avaf, Avaff

Afia
Meaning: Born on a Friday
Origin: African
Pronunciation: ah FEE ah
Description: Afia is a feminine form of the name Afua. Both of

A

the names are derived from the Ewe language spoken in Benin, Togo and Ghana in Africa.
Alternative spellings: Aafia, Aphia, Afiyah

Africa
Meaning: Africa
Origin: English
Pronunciation: AF ri ka
Description: Africa is a girls' name that first arose in the 18th century. It derives from the continent of the same name and is usually found as a baby name in English-speaking countries.
Alternative spellings: Africah, Afrika

Agatha
Meaning: Good
Origin: Greek
Pronunciation: AG a tha
Description: Derived from the Greek word for 'good', *agathos*, the name was also introduced to Britain in the 11th century by the Normans.
Alternative spellings: Agetha, Agata

Agnes
Meaning: Purity; lamb
Origin: Greek
Pronunciation: AG nes
Description: Agnes is said to come from the Greek word for 'purity'. It also originates from the Latin word '*agnus*', which means 'lamb'.
Alternative spellings: Agness, Agyness

Ahlam
Meaning: A pleasant dreamer
Origin: Arabic
Pronunciation: AH lam
Description: Ahlam is a popular

girls' name that means 'a pleasant dreamer' or 'imaginative dreams'.
Alternative spellings: Ahlaam, Arlam

Ai
Meaning: Love
Origin: Japanese
Pronunciation: AH ee
Description: This name is most commonly found within Japanese-speaking communities and is very popular. Although mainly used in a feminine capacity, Ai is actually unisex.

Aida
Meaning: Returning
Origin: Arabic
Pronunciation: AI ee dah
Description: The name is derived from the Arabic name Āyidah, meaning 'returning'. The name entered pop culture in the late 19th century with the release of Guiseppe Verde's opera of the same name.
Alternative spellings: Aeeda, Aide, Ayeeda, Ayida

Aiko
Meaning: Child of love
Origin: Japanese
Pronunciation: AYE koh
Description: Aiko is a Japanese name that is comprised of the elements of '*ai*' meaning 'love' and '*ko*' meaning 'child'.
Alternative spellings: Ayko

Aila
Meaning: Bird
Origin: Gaelic
Pronunciation: EYE luh
Description: Aila is a name that

can be found in several languages. In Scotland it is the shortened form of Aileen. The ultimate root of the name is thought to be the Latin word *'avis'*, which means 'bird.'

Alternative spellings: Ayla, Eila

Ailsa

Meaning: Elizabeth's rock
Origin: Gaelic
Pronunciation: AYL sah
Description: Ailsa comes from the island Ailsa Craig in Scotland, which originally meant Elizabeth's Rock. Although the root name is specifically feminine, many boys were also named Ailsa, after the island.
Alternative spellings: Eilsa, Elsa, Else

Aima

Meaning: Leader or ruler
Origin: Arabic
Pronunciation: aim ah
Description: Aima is an unconventional name that translates from Arabic as 'leader' or 'ruler'. It may also be adopted as an exotic form of the French name, Amy, meaning 'beloved'.
Alternative spellings: Ayma

Aimee

Meaning: Beloved
Origin: French
Pronunciation: AIM me
Description: A French name from the French verb *'aimer'*, meaning 'to love'.
Alternative spellings: Ami, Amie, Amiee, Amy

Aine

Meaning: Brightness
Origin: Gaelic

Pronunciation: ON ya
Description: Aine is the traditional Irish name of the fairy queen in Celtic mythology. It is also considered an Irish equivalent of Anne. Note the interesting pronunciation of this name.
Alternative spellings: Aina, Anya, Onya

Ainsley

Meaning: Meadow
Origin: Gaelic
Pronunciation: AINS lee
Description: Ainsley is a unisex Gaelic name that comes from a Scottish place of the same name. The name is derived from an Old English word for 'meadow'.

Aisha

Meaning: Prosperous
Origin: Arabic
Pronunciation: ah EE sha
Description: Aisha is a name of Arabic origin, most often found in Muslim communities. The prophet Muhammad's third wife was named Aisha.
Alternative spellings: Aiesha, Aishah, Ayesha, Ayisha, Aysha

Aisling

Meaning: Spirit of Ireland
Origin: Gaelic
Pronunciation: ASH ling
Description: Aisling, a name of Old Gaelic origin, is a mythical maiden who represents the spirit of Ireland. This is a very patriotic Irish name.
Alternative spellings: Aishling, Aisleyne, Aislin, Aisling, Aislinn, Aislynn, Ashleen, Ashlyn, Ashlynne, Eislinn and Isleen

Aiva

Meaning: Bird
Origin: Latin
Pronunciation: AY vuh
Description: Aiva is a variant form of the name Ava, which is short for Avalon. The name is derived from the Latin word *'avis'*, which means 'bird'. Very popular in English-speaking countries.
Alternative spellings: Aive, Ava, Ayva, Eva

Aiyana

Meaning: Flowering
Origin: Native American
Pronunciation: ay AHN na
Description: In Native American Aiyana means 'flowering'. It is also a variant of the name Ayanna, which originates from an African language.
Alternative spellings: Ayana, Ayanha, Ayanna

Aizah

Meaning: Prosperous
Origin: Arabic
Pronunciation: AY zah
Description: A favourite with Muslim parents, Aizah comes from the name Asia, after the continent, and means 'prosperous'. Unsurprisingly, it is most widely found in countries within Asia.
Alternative spellings: Aiza, Asia, Asiah, Asya

Akira

Meaning: Bright; intelligent; clear
Origin: Japan
Pronunciation: AK i rah
Description: Akira is predominantly a common Japanese male name but it has also begun to garner popularity as a female name. In Scotland, the name is a female version of the name Acair, meaning 'anchor'. It is also an Indian female name derived from the Sanskrit, meaning 'graceful strength'.
Alternative spellings: Akeera

Akshara

Meaning: Unchangeable
Origin: Sanskrit
Pronunciation: ak SHA rah
Description: A unisex name said to mean 'unchangeable'. This versatile name is popular with Indian parents.
Alternative spellings: Akhshara, Aksara

Alaa

Meaning: Servant of Allah
Origin: Arabic
Pronunciation: ah LAH
Description: This name can be used for both girls and boys. It is often used as a shortened version of Aladdin and is said to mean 'servant of Allah'. Alaa is often given as a name by Muslim parents.
Alternative spellings: Ala, Allaa

Alaia

Meaning: Joyful; happy
Origin: Basque
Pronunciation: ah LYE ah
Description: Alaia is of Arabic, Hebrew and Basque origin and means 'exulted', 'happy' and 'joyful'. This spelling variation has been rising in popularity in recent years as an alternative to similar-sounding names like Aaliyah, Ahalya and Alaya.
Alternative spellings: Allayah, Alaya, Alayah

Alaina

Meaning: Rock
Origin: Gaelic
Pronunciation: ah LANE ah
Description: Alaina, a name found mainly in Wales, is a variation of Alana and pronounced slightly differently. Its meaning is the same as Alana.
Alternative spellings: Alayna, Alena, Aleyna

Alana

Meaning: Rock
Origin: Gaelic
Pronunciation: a LAH nuh
Description: This is the feminine form of popular masculine name Alan, the name of a river that runs through Wales. The name has Celtic origins.
Alternative spellings: Alanah, Alannah, Allana, Allanah, Allannah

Alanis

Meaning: Rock
Origin: Gaelic
Pronunciation: ah LAN iss
Description: This is a Gaelic name meaning 'rock' and is the female version of Alan. Alanis Morissette is a famous Canadian singer with this name. She was named after her father, whose name is Alan.
Alternative spellings: Alannis

Alara

Meaning: One who brings brightness and happiness to the soul
Origin: Persian
Pronunciation: a LAR ah
Description: Alara is a popular name in Turkey and means 'the one who brings brightness and happiness to the heart and soul'.

Alara is also the name of a water fairy in Turkish mythology who must remain beside the water to maintain her youth and beauty.
Alternative spellings: Allara, Alarah, Elara

Alarna

Meaning: Rock
Origin: Gaelic
Pronunciation: ah LAR nah
Description: Alarna is another variation of the feminine form of Alan. It has a slightly different pronunciation than Alana and is mainly found in Wales thanks to its Celtic origin.
Alternative spellings: Alahna, Alarnah

Alaw

Meaning: Melodious river
Origin: Welsh
Pronunciation: AH low
Description: Alaw comes from a Welsh name of a river in Anglesey. The river's name means 'melodious'. The name is not common outside of Wales. It is pronounced like the word 'allow'.
Alternative spellings: Allaw, Alow

Alayna

Meaning: Light; torch; bright
Origin: Greek
Pronunciation: a LAY nah
Description: A variation of the name Elaine, a French cognate of the Greek Helenē, meaning light, torch or bright. Alternatively, Alayna can be used as a Scottish feminine form of Alan, meaning 'little rock'.
Alternative spellings: Alaina, Alana

Alba

Meaning: White; clear; bright
Origin: Latin
Pronunciation: al ber
Description: Alba is female name from the masculine, Albus or Albinus. Alba is also a prevalent place name (being the Gaelic name for Scotland as well as a poetic name for England). It is also a common surname in Spain.
Alternative spellings: Allba

Albany

Meaning: City in New York state
Origin: English
Pronunciation: al BAAN nee
Description: Albany is one of the major cities in the state of New York. Like London and Paris, this name follows the trend of using place names for baby names.

Alberta

Meaning: Noble; bright; famous
Origin: German
Pronunciation: al BER ta
Description: Alberta is the feminine form of Albert and the name of one of Queen Victoria's daughters, and the Canadian province of Alberta was named after her.
Alternative spellings: Alburta, Allberta

Aleah

Meaning: Noble
Origin: Hebrew
Pronunciation: AH lee yah
Description: A rare girls' name, Aleah is another variant of the name Aliyah. While Aliyah is popular among Muslim parents,

Aleah is a popular baby name with Jewish parents.
Alternative spellings: Aaleyah, Aalia, AAliyah, Aaliyah, Aleya, Alia, Aliya, Aliyah, Aliyyah

Aleena

Meaning: Noble
Origin: Arabic
Pronunciation: ah LEE nah
Description: This modern spelling of Alina is found mostly in America.
Alternative spellings: Aleenah, Alina

Aleeza

Meaning: Joyful
Origin: Hebrew
Pronunciation: Ah LEE zah
Description: Aleeza is a female Hebrew name that translates as 'joyful' or 'cheerful'. Aleeza can also be a diminutive for the Persian name, Aleezadeh, which means 'offspring of Ali' or 'high-born'.
Alternative spellings: Aliza

Aleisha

Meaning: Noble
Origin: German
Pronunciation: ah LEE sha
Description: Aleisha is a variant of the popular name Alisha.
Alternative spellings: Aleesha, Alesha, Alicia, Alicja, Aliesha, Alisha, Alysha, Elisha

Alena

Meaning: Light; torch; bright
Origin: Greek
Pronunciation: a LAY nah
Description: A variation of the name Elaine, a French cognate of the Greek Helenē, meaning light,

torch or bright. Alternatively, Alayna can be used as a Scottish feminine form of Alan, meaning 'little rock'.
Alternative spellings: Alaina, Alana

Alessia
Meaning: Defender of man
Origin: Greek
Pronunciation: ah LAY see ah
Description: This popular Italian name is a nice variation of Alicia.
Alternative spellings: Alecia, Alicia, Alicja, Alisia, Alissia, Alycia, Alysia, Alyssia, Elicia, Elissia

Alex
Meaning: Defender of man
Origin: Greek
Pronunciation: AL ix
Description: Alex is a shortened form of Alexander, Alexandra and Alexis. It is also a unisex name in its own right.
Alternative spellings: Alix

Alexa
Meaning: Defender of man
Origin: Greek
Pronunciation: ah LEX uh
Description: The feminine version of Alex, Alexa derives from the Greek name Alexander.
Alternative spellings: Aleksa, Alexah, Alixa

Alexandra
Meaning: Defender of man
Origin: Greek
Pronunciation: AL eks AHN druh
Description: Alexandra is the feminine form of Alexander and became popular in the UK after Alexandra of Denmark's marriage to Edward VII.
Alternative spellings: Aleksandra, Alessandra, Alexsandra, Aliksandra, Alisandra, Alissandra, Alixandra, Alyxandra

Alexandre
See entry in 'Names for Baby Boys A–Z'

Alexandria
Meaning: Defender of man
Origin: Greek
Pronunciation: ah leks AHN dree ah
Description: A variation of the name Alexandra, this is also the name of a major Egyptian city.
Alternative spellings: Aleksandria, Alessandria, Alexandrea, Alexsandria, Aliksandria, Alisandria, Alissandria, Alixandria, Alyxandria

Alexi
Meaning: Defender of man
Origin: Greek
Pronunciation: ah LEX ee
Description: Alexi is a shortened form of Alexis but can also be used as a name in its own right. As it derives from the Greek name Alexander it also shares the meaning of 'defender of man'.
Alternative spellings: Aleksi, Alexie, Alexsee, Alexy

Alexia
Meaning: Defender of man; helper
Origin: Greek
Pronunciation: ah LEX ee ah
Description: Alexia is a feminine alternative to the unisex name Alexis that derives from Alexander, meaning 'defender of man', or it could come from a Greek word meaning 'helper'.
Alternative spellings: Aleksia, Alexiya

Alexis

Meaning: Defender of man; helper
Origin: Greek
Pronunciation: a LEX iss
Description: Derived from Alexander, Alexis was originally a boy's name, but is now more common among girls.
Alternative spellings: Aleksis, Alexiss, Alexsis, Alexus

Ali

See entry in 'Names for Baby Boys A–Z'

Alice

Meaning: Noble
Origin: French
Pronunciation: AL iss
Description: A distinct name in medieval England, Alice enjoyed a surge of popularity in the 19th century and periods of favour ever since.
Alternative spellings: Alise, Aliss, Alys

Alicia

Meaning: Noble
Origin: French
Pronunciation: a LEE sha; a LEE si a
Description: A modern form of Alice, with two different pronunciations.
Alternative spellings: Alecia, Alessia, Alicja, Alisia, Alissia, Alycia, Alysia, Alyssia, Elicia, Elissia; Aleesha, Aleisha, Alesha, Aliesha, Alisha, Alysha

Alina

Meaning: Noble
Origin: French
Pronunciation: a LEE nah

Description: Commonly found in English-, Italian-, Polish-, Russian- and Spanish-speaking countries, this name is also considered the shortened form of the French name Adelaide.
Alternative spellings: Aleena, Alinah

Alishba

Meaning: Favoured by God
Origin: Hebrew
Pronunciation: ah LISH bah
Description: This Hebrew form of the English name Elizabeth is found in the the Old Testament. Alishba was the wife of Aaron, Moses' older brother. The name also has Islamic roots.
Alternative spellings: Allishba, Alyshba

Alison

Meaning: Noble; exalted
Origin: German
Pronunciation: AL iss on
Description: Alison is an Old German name that was originally derived from the name Alice. It is commonly shortened to Ali, or Ally.
Alternative spellings: Alicen, Alisson, Allison, Allyson, Alycen Alyson, Alysson

Alissa

Meaning: From the flower; alyssum
Origin: Greek
Pronunciation: ah liss ah
Description: A popular feminine name used across the world with origins in Greek, Arabic and Filipino. In Western countries the name is usually derived from the name of the flower, alyssum.

Alternative spellings: Alica

Alivia
Meaning: Olive
Origin: Latin
Pronunciation: ah LI vee ah
Description: Alivia is a modern American variation of Olivia, which originates from the Latin for an olive.
Alternative spellings: Alivya

Allegra
Meaning: Happy
Origin: Italian
Pronunciation: a LEG ra
Description: Allegra is a name taken from the Italian adjective meaning 'happy', and in music '*allegro*' is a tempo meaning 'cheerful' or 'brisk'.
Alternative spellings: Allegrah, Allegre

Alma
Meaning: Lift the Spirit
Origin: Latin
Pronunciation: AHL mah
Description: The origin of the name Alma is disputed but was most likely derived from the Latin word, '*almus*', which means 'kind' or 'nourishing'. It is a feminine form of Almo.
Alternative spellings: Elma

Aloha
Meaning: Love
Origin: Polynesian
Pronunciation: a LO ha
Description: Aloha is a modern name from the Polynesian word meaning 'love', which is often used as a greeting. Its popularity has rapidly increased.
Alternative spellings: Alloha

Alpha
See entry in 'Names for Baby Boys A–Z'

Althea
Meaning: Unknown; derived from Greek mythology
Origin: Greek
Pronunciation: al THEE uh
Description: Derived from the Greek name Althaea, the mother of the hero Meleager in Greek mythology. The name became better known in the late 70s when the Jamaican reggae duo Althea & Donna released their number 1 hit 'Uptown Top Ranking'.
Alternative spellings: Althaea, Althaia

Alya
Meaning: Sky; to ascend
Origin: Arabic
Pronunciation: AH lya
Description: Alya is a name used in many countries that originates from Ancient Greek, Hebrew and Arabic. The most common translation of the name refers to sky, heaven or ascent.
Alternative spellings: Aalya, Alia

Alyssa
Meaning: Noble
Origin: German
Pronunciation: ah LIS sah
Description: This name is another variation of Alice.
Alternative spellings: Alisa, Alissa, Alysa, Elisa, Elissa, Elyssa

Amaia
Meaning: Mother city
Origin: Spanish

A

Pronunciation: am EYE ya
Description: A given and surname of Spanish origins derived from the village of Amaya in Spain. The name is composed of the elements of '*am(ma)*', meaning 'mother' and the suffix '*ia*' that is used to form action names, suggesting the meaning of Amaia is 'mother city'.
Alternative spellings: Amayah, Ammaya, Amya

Amanah

Meaning: To uphold trust
Origin: Arabic
Pronunciation: AM an ah
Description: Amanah is the closest English translation of the word '*Al-Amanah*', 'The Trust', which refers to the moral responsibility of fulfilling one's obligations due to Allah.
Alternative spellings: Amana

Amal

See entry in 'Names for Baby Boys A–Z'

Amalia

Meaning: Hard-working
Origin: German
Pronunciation: ah MAHL ee ah
Description: Amalia is a variation of Amelia. Despite sharing its meaning with Amelia, Amalia is pronounced differently and is popular in Germany.
Alternative spellings: Amelia, Amilia, Emelia, Emilia, Emilija

Amalie

Meaning: Hard-working
Origin: German
Pronunciation: ah ma LEE

Description: Another name derived from the Old German name Amelia. This name is most widely used in France as a variant spelling of Amelie. This name is rising in popularity in the UK.
Alternative spellings: Amelie

Amana

Meaning: Security
Origin: Arabic
Pronunciation: ah MAN na
Description: Amana is an unusual name that can be found in several languages and its meaning is uncertain. As it is similar to the Arabic name Aman, it could share its meaning of 'security'.
Alternative spellings: Ahmana, Amanah

Amanda

Meaning: Loveable
Origin: Latin
Pronunciation: a MAN duh
Description: The name Amanda derives from the Latin '*amabilis*', meaning 'loveable'. When originating from Sanskrit, Amanda is also (rarely) seen as a boys' name.
Alternative spellings: Amander

Amani

Meaning: Desires
Origin: Arabic
Pronunciation: ah MAH ne
Description: In Arabic-speaking countries Amani is used as a male name; however in Swahili-speaking countries it is also used for females.
Alternative spellings: Ahmani

Amara

Meaning: Unfading
Origin: Greek

Pronunciation: a MAH ra
Description: This name may come from the Greek word *'amarantos'*, which means 'unfading'; however some believe that it derives from the Latin word *'amarus'*, which means bitter.
Alternative spellings: Amarah, Ammara

Amarachi

Meaning: God's grace
Origin: African
Pronunciation: ah MAR ah chi
Description: Amarachi comes from the language of the Igbo people who take it to mean 'God's grace'. Amara is the short form.
Alternative spellings: Amerachi

Amari

Meaning: Possessor of great strength
Origin: Africa
Pronunciation: am AR ee
Description: Amari is an attractive name of African origin. It translates as 'strength' or 'possessor of great strength'. It is also a feminine forn of the masculine Arabic name, Amar, which translates as 'moon'.
Alternative spellings: Amare

Amaris

Meaning: You are loved
Origin: Latin
Pronunciation: a MER iss
Description: Amaris is a Latin word that translates as 'you are loved'. It is popular in Latin America and Spain. It could also be a short form of the name Amarysia, a name that derives from Greek mythology.

Amaya

Meaning: High place
Origin: Spanish
Pronunciation: a MAY ah
Description: Amaya was the name of a heroine in the traditional Basque stories of the knight Teodosio de Goni.
Alternative spellings: Amaha, Amaia, Ammaya

Amba

Meaning: Amber; mother
Origin: English
Pronunciation: AM buh
Description: A variant of Amber, this name could also come from the Sanskrit word meaning 'mother'. In this case it is used mainly by Hindu parents.
Alternative spellings: Ambah, Amber

Amber

Meaning: Amber
Origin: English
Pronunciation: AM buh
Description: Amber is the word for a fossilised resin, derived from the Arabic word *'ambar'*.
Alternative spellings: Amba, Ambah

Ameena

Meaning: Honest; trustworthy
Origin: Arabic
Pronunciation: ah MEE nah
Description: A beautiful female given name originating from the Arabic for 'honest' or 'trustworthy'. It is popular within Muslim communities throughout the world as there are many important Islamic figures who share the name within the Islamic faith.
Alternative spellings: Amina, Amna, Aminah

Ameerah

Meaning: Princess
Origin: Arabic
Pronunciation: ah MEER ah
Description: Another spelling variant of the name Amira, found in both Arabic and Swahili-speaking countries.
Alternative spellings: Ameera, Amera, Amira, Amirah

Amelia

Meaning: Hard-working
Origin: German
Pronunciation: ah MEE lee uh
Description: One of the most popular girls' names in Britain, Amelia is comprised of the Latin name Emilia and the Germanic name Amalia.
Alternative spellings: Amilia, Emelia, Emilia, Emilija

Amelie

Meaning: Hard-working
Origin: French
Pronunciation: AH meh lee
Description: The French equivalent of Amelia, Amelie is used widely across the English-speaking world.
Alternative spellings: Amalie

Amiee

Meaning: Beloved
Origin: French
Pronunciation: AY mee
Description: Amiee is a name of French origin and it means 'beloved'. It is the original form of Amy, which is the more common version in Britain.
Alternative spellings: Aimee, Ami, Amie, Amy

Amika

Meaning: Loved friend
Origin: Latin
Pronunciation: AH mik ah
Description: Amika is a Latin name meaning 'loved friend'. It can also be related to the English vocabulary word 'amicable'.
Alternative spellings: Ammika

Aminata

Meaning: Serenity
Origin: Arabic
Pronunciation: ah min AH ta
Description: Aminata is of Arabic origin; however its use has spread into Swahili. The name can be found across Africa and the Middle East.
Alternative spellings: Aminahta

Amiyah

Meaning: Unknown
Origin: Arabic
Pronunciation: ah MEE yah
Description: Amiyah, an unusual name of uncertain origin and meaning, may come from the Arabic language.
Alternative spellings: Amiya

Amiya

Meaning: Beloved
Origin: Old French
Pronunciation: a MEE ah
Description: Amiya is a variant of the Old French and Latin name, Amy, meaning 'beloved' or 'to love'. A modern, neater alternative spelling of the name is Amia.
Alternative spellings: Amia

Amrit

Meaning: Nectar of immortals
Origin: Sanskrit
Pronunciation: AM rit
Description: Amrit, a unisex name, is of Sanskrit origin and is found in the Hindu Vedic epics to

refer to a physical object that gives immortality.

Alternative spellings: Amreet

Amrita

Meaning: Nectar of immortals
Origin: Sanskrit
Pronunciation: am REE tah
Description: Amrita is the feminine version of Amrit and is often favoured by Hindu parents.
Alternative spellings: Amreeta

Ana

Meaning: Favoured by God
Origin: Hebrew
Pronunciation: AH nah
Description: A variant of the popular girls' name Anna. This spelling is common in Eastern Europe.
Alternative spellings: Anna, Annah

Anaïs

Meaning: Love
Origin: Persian
Pronunciation: ah NAY ISS
Description: Commonly found in French-speaking countries, this name has its origins in Persian and Hebrew and is associated with the Persian goddess of love, Anaitis.
Alternative spellings: Anais, Annais

Anabia

Meaning: Turn towards Allah
Origin: Arabic
Pronunciation: anah BI ya
Description: Anabia is a feminine Arabic name meaning 'turn towards Allah.' A variation of this name is Anaba, a Quaranic word meaning 'he/she made repentance and returned to Allah'.

Anaiya

Meaning: God Answers
Origin: Hebrew
Pronunciation: A nay ah
Description: A derivative of the masculine Hebrew name, Anaiah, which means 'Yahweh (God) answers'.
Alternative spellings: Anaya, Anaiah, Anayah

Anam

Meaning: A blessing
Origin: Arabic
Pronunciation: AH nam
Description: Anam is an Arabic name used mainly by Muslim parents who feel their child is a blessing from Allah.
Alternative spellings: Ahnam

Ananya

Meaning: With no match
Origin: Sanskrit
Pronunciation: ah NAHN yah
Description: Ananya is mainly used in India and is popular with Hindu parents. Sometimes shortened to Anu.
Alternative spellings: Ananyah

Anas

Meaning: Friendly
Origin: Arabic
Pronunciation: Ah Nas
Description: A unisex name of Arabic origin. Anas is also a shortened form of names such as Anastasia.
Alternative spellings: Annas

Anastasia

Meaning: Resurrection
Origin: Russian
Pronunciation: a na STAY ZEE ah; a na STAY zhah

Description: Anastasia is a Russian name that has enjoyed solid popularity in Eastern Europe. The famous 'lost' Russian princess named Anastasia boosted the name's popularity.
Alternative spellings: Anastacia, Anastasja, Anastazia, Anastazja

Andrea
Meaning: Virility
Origin: Greek
Pronunciation: AN dree ah; an DREY ah
Description: This feminine form of the name Andreas or Andrew is derived from 'andreia', meaning 'virility'.
Alternative spellings: Andria

Andy
See entry in 'Names for Baby Boys A–Z'

Aneira
Meaning: Gold
Origin: Welsh
Pronunciation: a NEER ah
Description: The origin of this name is not definite but it is believed to come fron the Welsh word 'eur' meaning gold.
Alternative spellings: Aneera, Anira

Angel
See entry in 'Names for Baby Boys A–Z'

Angie
Meaning: Messenger of God
Origin: Latin
Pronunciation: an GEE
Description: Angie is the short form of the name Angelina and as such, shares the same meaning of 'messenger of God'. Starting out as a nickname, Angie is now a name in its own right.

Angela
Meaning: Messenger of God
Origin: Greek
Pronunciation: AN gel uh; an GEL uh
Description: This feminine form of Angelus is an elaboration of 'angel'.
Alternative spellings: Angella

Angelica
Meaning: Messenger of God
Origin: Latin
Pronunciation: an GEL ih ka
Description: Angelica is taken from the Latin word meaning 'angelic'.
Alternative spellings: Angellica, Anjelica

Angelina
Meaning: Messenger of God
Origin: Latin
Pronunciation: AN ja LEE na
Description: This variation of Angela is popular, especially in Italy.
Alternative spellings: Angeleena, Angelena

Angharad
Meaning: Beloved
Origin: Welsh
Pronunciation: ang HAH rad
Description: Angharad, a popular name in Celtic folklore, is a traditional Welsh name. It is becoming fashionable in other parts of Britain.
Alternative spellings: Angherad

Aniela

Meaning: Hard-working
Origin: German
Pronunciation: ah NEE lee ah
Description: Aniela is found mainly in Eastern European countries and is especially popular in Poland. It is thought to be a variant of Amelia.
Alternative spellings: Anelia

Anika

Meaning: Grace
Origin: Sanskrit
Pronunciation: AN i KAH
Description: This attractive name is of Sanskrit, Dutch, Hebrew and Japanese origin. In all but Japanese it has a similar meaning, roughly translating as 'grace'. In Japanese the name translates as 'apricot from Nara'.
Alternative spellings:

Anis

Meaning: Friendly; pure
Origin: Arabic; Greek
Pronunciation: Ah nees
Description: A popular girls' name in Greece, this is also a boys' name in Tunisia. In Arabic Anis means 'friendly' and in Greek, 'pure' or 'holy'.
Alternative spellings: Anais, Anees, Annis

Anisa

Meaning: Good companion
Origin: Arabic
Pronunciation: a NEE sa
Description: With roots in Hebrew and Arabic, this name is fairly popular in Arabic-speaking countries.
Alternative spellings: Aneesa, Anisah

Anisah

Meaning: One with no master
Origin: Sanskrit
Pronunciation: ah NEE sah
Description: A variant of Anise, Anisah also has Sanskrit origins.
Alternative spellings: Anisa, Aneesa, Anisha

Anise

Meaning: Anise seed
Origin: English
Pronunciation: uh NIECE
Description: Anise comes from the anise seed, a herb that is known for its licorice-like flavor. Like Basil and Rosemary, Anise is part of the trend of using herbs for given names.

Anita

Meaning: Favoured by God
Origin: Hebrew
Pronunciation: ah NEE tah
Description: Anita is one of many variations of Anne, which itself comes from the Hebrew name Hannah.
Alternative spellings: Aneeta, Anitah

Aniya

Meaning: Favoured by God; caring
Origin: Hebrew
Pronunciation: ah NEE yah
Description: Aniya is a variant of Ania, a name of Hebrew origin, and is found all over Europe and parts of Asia.
Alternative spellings: Aneeya, Aniyah, Anniya, Anniyah

Anjali

Meaning: Gift
Origin: Sanskrit
Pronunciation: AHN ja lee
Description: Anjali is an

uncommon name in English-speaking countries and is favoured more by Indian parents.
Alternative spellings: Anjaly, Anjuly

Annabel
Meaning: Loveable
Origin: Latin
Pronunciation: AN a bell
Description: Thought to derive from the Latin *'amabilis'* meaning 'loveable', this name is also a combination of Anne and the French word *'belle'* meaning 'beautiful'. As such, the name could also mean 'beautiful favoured one'.
Alternative spellings: Anabel, Anabelle, Annabell, Annabelle

Annabella
Meaning: Loveable
Origin: Latin
Pronunciation: AH na bel ah
Description: Annabella, like Annabel, is derived from the Latin *'amabilis'.*
Alternative spellings: Anabela, Anabella, Annabela

Annalese
Meaning: Noble and promised of God; graceful
Origin: German
Pronunciation: ah nah LEES
Description: Annalese is a compound name made up of Anna and Lisa. Its combined meaning is 'noble birth' and 'promised of God', as well as 'graceful'.
Alternative spellings: Annaliese, Annalise

Anne
Meaning: Favoured by God
Origin: Greek
Pronunciation: AN

Description: Anne is the English form of the Hebrew name Hannah. It is the name of many English queens, including Anne Boleyn and Anne of Cleves.
Alternative spellings: Ann

Annella
Meaning: Grace
Origin: Hebrew
Pronunciation: ANN ell a
Description: Annella is a contemporary variant of the Latin name, Anne, which evolved fom the Hebrew name, Hannah, which means 'favour' or 'grace'.
Alternative spellings: Anella, Anela

Annette
Meaning: Favoured by God
Origin: French
Pronunciation: ann ETTE
Description: Annette is a French diminutive of Ann, and as such shares the same meaning of 'favoured by God'.

Annie
Meaning: Favoured by God
Origin: Greek
Pronunciation: AN nee
Description: A pet form of Anne.
Alternative spellings: Anney, Anni, Anny

Annika
Meaning: Grace
Origin: Hebrew
Pronunciation: Ann ee kah
Description: A further modernised name from the traditional Latin name, Anne, developed from the Hebrew name, Hannah. The meaning of the name translates as 'grace' or 'grace of God'.

Alternative spellings: Anika

Anniyah
Meaning: Caring
Origin: Arabic
Pronunciation: ah NEE yah
Description: This Arabic name is popular with Muslim parents.
Alternative spellings: Aneeya, Aniya, Aniyah, Anniya

Annya
Meaning: Inexhaustible
Origin: Hebrew, Greek
Pronunciation: AHN yah
Description: This name, of both Hebrew and Old Greek origin, is pronounced in a similar way to the Russian Anya.
Alternative spellings: Annyah

Anouk
Meaning: Favoured by God
Origin: Hebrew
Pronunciation: AH nook
Description: Anouk is a variant of the name Anna and is more popular in French- and Dutch-speaking countries. It is also used in Arabic.
Alternative spellings: Anook

Anoushka
Meaning: Grace
Origin: Hebrew; Russian
Pronunciation: AN oosh kah
Description: A Russian diminutive of Anne that translates as 'little Anna'. The traditional name, Anne, means 'grace' or 'grace of God'.
Alternative spellings: Annoushka, Anoushkah, Annushka

Antigone
Meaning: The opposite of her forebears

Origin: Greek
Pronunciation: an TIG oh nee
Description: In Greek mythology, Antigone was the daughter of Oedipus and Jocasta.
Alternative spellings: Antigon, Antigonos

Antonia
Meaning: Protector
Origin: Latin
Pronunciation: an TO nee uh
Description: A Latin feminine form of Anthony and a common Roman family name in classical times.
Alternative spellings: Antoniah, Antonya

Antonina
Meaning: Protector
Origin: Latin
Pronunciation: ahn toh NEE nah
Description: This fairly unusual variant of Antonia is most commonly found in Eastern Europe and is often shortened to Nina.
Alternative spellings: Antoneena, Antonena

Anum
Meaning: Grace; God favours
Origin: Arabic
Pronunciation: AN oom
Description: Anum may be used as a variant of the classic Latin name, Anne. The name is also featured in the Quran and is a popular Muslim name. The Arabic translation is 'blessings of God'.
Alternative spellings: Annum

Anusha
Meaning: Beautiful sky
Origin: Sanskrit
Pronunciation: ah NOO sha

Description: Anusha is a unisex name thought to mean 'beautiful sky' or 'beautiful morning'. It is a popular baby name with Indian parents.
Alternative spellings: Anoosha

Anwen
Meaning: Very beautiful
Origin: Welsh
Pronunciation: AN wen
Description: Anwen is an attractive female name with a classic Welsh sound pattern. The name translates as 'very beautiful'.
Alternative spellings: Arnwen

Aoife
Meaning: Beaming radiance
Origin: Gaelic
Pronunciation: EE fa
Description: Aoife is a name of Gaelic origin, and means 'beaming radiance'. It is especially popular in Ireland.
Alternative spellings: Eefa, Efa, Efah

Aphrodite
Meaning: Risen from the foam
Origin: Greek
Pronunciation: AF ro DYE tee
Description: In Greek myth, Aphrodite was the goddess of love and beauty.
Alternative spellings: Afrodite, Afrodyte, Aphrodyte

April
Meaning: Blooming flowers
Origin: Latin
Pronunciation: AY pril
Description: The word April, from the Latin *'aprilis'*, meaning 'to open', is associated with spring.
Alternative spellings: Aprill

Aqsa
Meaning: Temple
Origin: Arabic
Pronunciation: AC sah
Description: The name Aqsa originates from Al-Aqsa in Jerusalem, the second-oldest mosque in Islam.
Alternative spellings: Acksa, Aksa

Arabella
Meaning: Loveable
Origin: Latin
Pronunciation: AH ra BELL ah
Description: With its Latin origins it is thought that the name Arabella either derives from Annabel or Annabella. It is likely that this name first occurred because of a misspelling in the 1600s.
Alternative spellings: Arabela, Arrabella

Araya
Meaning: Inspired by the town Araia, Spain
Origin: Basque
Pronunciation: uh RAY yuh
Description: Araia is originally a Basque surname, from the town Araia in Aspárrena, province of Alava, Basque Country. Although rare, it is used in Western countries as a female given name.
Alternative spellings: Araia, Arayah

Arda
See entry in 'Names for Baby Boys A–Z'

Areeba
Meaning: Witty; intelligent
Origin: Arabic
Pronunciation: ah REE bah
Description: Areeba is a name of

Arabic origin and means 'witty' or 'intelligent'. It is mainly used in the Middle East and other Muslim countries.
Alternative spellings: Areebah, Ariba

Areesha
Meaning: Under an umbrella; peace
Origin: Arabic
Pronunciation: AR eesh ah
Description: Areesha is an obscure name but may be of Arabic origin. Possible translations of the name include 'under an umbrella', 'peace' and 'living'.
Alternative spellings: Arisha, Arreesha, Aeresha

Aren
Meaning: Eagle ruler
Origin: German
Pronunciation: AIR ren
Description: Aren is an Old German name meaning 'eagle ruler'. It is also an African name that also means 'eagle'.

Aretha
Meaning: Excellence
Origin: Greek
Pronunciation: a RI thuh
Description: Aretha is intended as a derivative of the Greek word *'arete'* meaning 'excellence'.
Alternative spellings: Areetha, Aritha

Aria
See entry in 'Names for Baby Boys A–Z'

Ariadne
Meaning: Chaste; Most Holy
Origin: Greek

Pronunciation: a ree AD nee
Description: Ariadne is a popular Greek name composed of the elements of αρι (ari), 'most' and αδνος (adnos). 'holy'. In Greek mythology, Ariadne was the daughter of King Minos.
Alternative spellings: Arriadne

Ariana
Meaning: Silver
Origin: Welsh
Pronunciation: ah ree AH nah
Description: This name is chiefly used in Dutch-, German-, French- and Italian-speaking countries.
Alternative spellings: Arriana, Arianna, Aryana

Arianne
Meaning: Silver
Origin: Welsh
Pronunciation: ah ree AN
Description: A variant of Ariana and also the feminine form of Arian. This name can be shortened to Ari or Anne.
Alternative spellings: Arienne

Ariel
Meaning: God's lion
Origin: Hebrew
Pronunciation: AR ee el; AIR ee al
Description: This unisex name widely increased in popularity after Shakespeare's play *The Tempest*.
Alternative spellings: Arial

Ariella
Meaning: God's lion
Origin: Hebrew
Pronunciation: AR ee el ah
Description: Ariella derives from

the unisex name Ariel; however, this form is specifically feminine thanks to its use of 'a' at the end of the name.

Alternative spellings: Arialla, Ariela

Arielle

Meaning: Lion of God
Origin: Hebrew
Pronunciation: a REE ell
Description: Arielle is the femine form of the Hebrew *ariel*, which means 'lion of God'. Ariel is also an accepted girls' name, epitomised in the Hans Cristian Andersen story, 'The Little Mermaid', and its Disney adaptation.

Alternative spellings: Ariel

Arina

Meaning: Peaceful
Origin: Greek
Pronunciation: ah REE na
Description: Arina is an unusual name. It is a variant of Irina, the Russian equivalent of the name Irene. It is most predominantly found in Russia.

Alternative spellings: Irina

Arissa

Meaning: The best
Origin: Greek
Pronunciation: ah RIS ah
Description: The Greek word *'arista'*, meaning 'the best', was used to refer to a healthy ear of corn at harvest. A very popular name in continental Europe.

Alternative spellings: Arisa, Arisah, Arissah

Arla

Meaning: Eagle's hill; manly
Origin: English

Pronunciation: AR lah
Description: This is a comtemporary name that may have derived from the masculine name, Arlo or a shortening of the female name, Charlene.

Alternative spellings: Ala

Armani

Meaning: Free
Origin: Italian
Pronunciation: ah MAR nee
Description: Armani is an Italian surname that is said to mean 'free'.

Alternative spellings: Armaani, Armanie

Aroush

Meaning: Angel from paradise
Origin: Arabic
Pronunciation: ah ROOSH
Description: Aroush, an Arabic name, is used mainly by Muslim parents and means 'angel come from paradise'.

Alternative spellings: Aroosh

Artemis

Meaning: Strong-limbed
Origin: Greek
Pronunciation: AH teh mis
Description: In Greek mythology, Artemis was the goddess of the hunt and the twin sister of Apollo.

Alternative spellings: Artemus, Artimis, Artimus

Arwa

Meaning: Gracefulness; beauty
Origin: Arabic
Pronunciation: AR wah
Description: Arwa is a lyrical Muslim name that interprets as 'beauty', 'lightness', 'softness'. Arwa was also the name of one of the aunts of the prophet Muhammad,

which possibly contributes to the name's popularity.
Alternative spellings: Arwaa

Arwen
Meaning: Fair skin
Origin: Welsh
Pronunciation: AR wen
Description: Arwen is a name of Welsh origin and it means 'fair skin'. In Tolkien's *Lord Of The Rings* Arwen is the name of a main Elf character.
Alternative spellings: Ahwen

Aryana
Meaning: Chaste; most holy
Origin: Greek
Pronunciation: a ree ARN ah
Description: Arianna is a variant of the classical Greek name Ariadne. The name interprets as 'chaste' or 'most holy'. Ariadne was also a figure in Greek mythology, the daughter of King Minos.
Alternative spellings: Ariana, Arianna

Aseel
Meaning: Pure; genuine
Origin: Arabic
Pronunciation: AS il
Description: Aseel is an Arabic name more commonly chosen as a male given name but gaining popularity as a female name. The meaning of the name is 'authentic', 'pure' or 'genuine'. It is also an adjective used to describe people with good moral conduct.
Alternative spellings: Asil

Asha
Meaning: Full of aspiration
Origin: Greek

Pronunciation: AH shah
Description: Asha is a fairly uncommon name in Britain but is sometimes used as a variant of Aisha.
Alternative spellings: Ashah, Asher

Ashanti
Meaning: Ghanaian
Origin: African
Pronunciation: a SHAN tee; ah SHARN tee
Description: Ashanti is the name of a major ethnic group in Ghana and is also used as a surname by the Akan people of Ghana.
Alternative spellings: Ashantie, Ashanty

Ashlee
Meaning: Field of ash
Origin: English
Pronunciation: ASH lee
Description: A specifically feminine variant of the popular name Ashley. The name comes from an English surname that refers to a 'field of ash'.
Alternative spellings: Ashleigh, Ashley

Asma
Meaning: Important
Origin: Arabic
Pronunciation: AHS mah
Description: Asma, a popular girls' name among Muslim parents, is the daughter of the brother of Muhammad Abu-Bakr in Islamic belief.
Alternative spellings: Asmaa, Asmah

Aspen
Meaning: Aspen tree
Origin: English

Pronunciation: ASS pen
Description: Aspen is a unisex name derived from the aspen tree, known by its delicate leaves and white bark. As a given name, it is common in America.
Alternative spellings: Aspun

Aston
See entry in 'Names for Baby Boys A–Z'

Astra
Meaning: Star
Origin: Greek
Pronunciation: ASS tra
Description: This girls' name meaning 'star' is based on the Greek word *'aster'* or the Latin word *'astrum'*.
Alternative spellings: Astrah, Astre

Astrid
Meaning: Beautiful goddess
Origin: Norse
Pronunciation: ASS trid
Description: Astrid is of Old Norse origin and has strong associations with beauty. In Old Norse myth it was the name of a valkyrie.
Alternative spellings: Astryd

Asya
Meaning: Resurrection
Origin: Greek
Pronunciation: AHS ya
Description: Asya was originally a pet form of the name Anastasia, but has since become a name in its own right.
Alternative spellings: Aiza, Aizah, Asia, Asiah

Atarah
Meaning: Crown
Origin: Hebrew
Pronunciation: a TAH rah
Description: Atarah is a biblical name meaning 'crown'. According to the Bible, it was borne by one of the wives of Jerahmeel. Often shortened to Tara.
Alternative spellings: Atara, Attara

Athena
Meaning: Goddess of wisdom and war
Origin: Greek
Pronunciation: ah THEE nah
Description: Athena is the Latin form of the Greek name Athene, who was the goddess of wisdom and war in Greek mythology. Athena and Athene are popular girls' names in Greece.
Alternative spellings: Athina

Aubree
Meaning: Unknown
Origin: Latin
Pronunciation: OR bree
Description: A venacular form of the Latin name, Albereda. The etymology of this name is unclear but is different to the male derivation, which translates as 'Leader of the Elves'.
Alternative spellings: Aubrey, Aubrée, Aubrie

Aubrey
See entry in 'Names for Baby Boys A–Z'

Audra
Meaning: Noble strength
Origin: English
Pronunciation: OR dra
Description: Sometimes used as a pet form of Audrey, Audra is also a name in its own right.
Alternative spellings: Audre

Audrey

Meaning: Noble strength
Origin: English
Pronunciation: OR dree
Description: This Old English name, borne by actress Audrey Hepburn, also has associations with lace.
Alternative spellings: Audree, Audrie, Awdrey

Augusta

Meaning: Great; magnificent
Origin: Latin
Pronunciation: oog GUS tah
Description: Augusta is the female version of the Latin name Augustus. It is also used as a title given to empresses of the Roman and Byzantine Empires.

Aurelia

Meaning: Golden
Origin: Latin
Pronunciation: aw REE lee uh
Description: Aurelia has similar Latin roots to the name Aurora, which refers to the dawn. Both names have connotations of light and beauty.
Alternative spellings: Aureliah, Aureliya

Aurora

Meaning: Dawn
Origin: Latin
Pronunciation: aw RO rah
Description: Aurora, the Roman goddess of dawn, is also a meteorological term for light displays in the sky.
Alternative spellings: Arora, Aurara, Aurorah

Austeja

Meaning: Bee goddess
Origin: Lithuania

Pronunciation: ow STAY ah
Description: Austeja is a popular, contemporary name in Lithuania. It is derived from the name of an ancient Lithuanian bee goddess.
Alternative spellings: Austėja, Austeya

Austin

See entry in 'Names for Baby Boys A–Z'

Autumn

Meaning: Autumn
Origin: English
Pronunciation: AW tum
Description: Like Summer, this is a seasonal name.
Alternative spellings: Autum, Ortumn

Avani

Meaning: Earthly
Origin: Sanskrit
Pronunciation: ah VAH nee
Description: Avani is a name used predominantly, although not exclusively, by Hindu families. It comes from a Sanskrit word meaning 'earthly'.
Alternative spellings: Ahvani, Avahni, Avanee, Avany

Avaya

Meaning: Gift of God
Origin: Sanskrit
Pronunciation: avv AY ah
Description: An unusual Hindu name that means 'gift of God' or 'first ray of sun'.
Alternative spellings: Avayah, Avaia

Aveline

Meaning: Bird; struggle
Origin: French

Pronunciation: AV er leen
Description: The meaning of Aveline, a French name derived from Avis, may stem from the German for 'struggle' or the Latin *'avis'* meaning 'bird'.
Alternative spellings: Aveleen, Aveleene, Avelene

Avery
Meaning: Elf ruler
Origin: Old French
Pronunciation: AY var ee
Description: Originally an English surname derived from the Old English words *'aelf'*, meaning 'elf', and *'raed'*, meaning 'counsel'. In recent years the name has increased in popularity as a female given name, possibly as an extension of the name Ava.
Alternative spellings: Avary

Aviana
Meaning: Like a bird
Origin: Latin
Pronunciation: ah vee AH na
Description: Aviana translates from Latin as 'like a bird' or 'delicate one'.
Alternative spellings: Avianna

Avleen
Meaning: Blessed by God
Origin: Hindi
Pronunciation: AV leen
Description: Avleen is a unisex name of Indian origin. It translates as 'blessed by God' or 'different'.
Alternative spellings: Avline

Avneet
Meaning: God is light
Origin: Hebrew

Pronunciation: AHV neet
Description: In Hebrew, Avneet means 'God is light.'
Alternative spellings: Avneat

Avni
Meaning: Earth
Origin: Hindi
Pronunciation: AV nee
Description: An attractive girls' name of Indian origin that can be interpreted as 'earth' or 'princess of God'.
Alternative spellings: Avnee

Avril
Meaning: April
Origin: French
Pronunciation: AV ril
Description: Avril is the French word for the month of April. It may also be linked to the words 'boar' and 'battle' because of its Old English roots.
Alternative spellings: Avrill, Avrille

Aya
Meaning: Design; bird of prey
Origin: Japanese, Hebrew
Pronunciation: AH yah
Description: In Japan Aya is a girls' name and refers to paintings and objects of visual beauty. In Hebrew it is a boys' name, meaning a 'bird of prey'.
Alternative spellings: Ayah, Iya

Ayaan
See entry in 'Names for Baby Boys A–Z'

Ayah
Meaning: Miracle
Origin: Arabic
Pronunciation: AY yah
Description: This variant of Aya

has roots in Arabic. It comes from the word for 'miracle' and was first used in the Middle East.

Alternative spellings: Aya, Iyah

Ayana

Meaning: Flower of beauty
Origin: African
Pronunciation: AY an ah
Description: Ayana is a popular name with African parents and is also found in Arab countries.
Alternative spellings: Ayanna

Ayda

Meaning: Adornment; nobility
Origin: Hebrew
Pronunciation: AY dah
Description: Ayda is a biblical name that means 'adornment' or 'enhancement'. It also traces back to the Germanic element of 'adel', meaning 'nobility'.
Alternative spellings: Ada, Aida, Adah

Aydan

See Ayden in 'Names for Baby Boys A–Z'

Ayeza

Meaning: Noble
Origin: Arabic
Pronunciation: ay EE zah
Description: Ayeza is an Arabic feminine name. The meaning is difficult to determine exactly, but many think that it means 'noble'. It is most likely associated with the name Aiza, which has the same meaning.

Ayla

Meaning: Moonlight
Origin: Persian

Pronunciation: AY lah
Description: Ayla is of Turkish and Old Persian origin. In Turkish the name means 'halo of light around the moon' and in Old Persian it translates as 'moonlight'.
Alternative spellings: Isla, Eilah, Aila

Aylin

Meaning: Moon
Origin: Persian
Pronunciation: AY linn
Description: Aylin is a popular Turkish name that derives from the word 'ay', meaning 'moon'. It is a variant of Ayla.
Alternative spellings: Ayleen, Ayleene, Aylinn

Ayomide

Meaning: My joy has arrived
Origin: African
Pronunciation: Ey Aa Mayde
Description: Although Ayomide is a unisex name it is more common for girls. Owing to its meaning, the name is often given to children who suffered a traumatic or troublesome birth.
Alternative spellings: Ayomaid, Ayomayd

Aysha

Meaning: She who lives or womanly.
Origin: Arabic
Pronunciation: I eesh a
Description: Aysha is a variant spelling of the Arabic name Aisha. Aisha was the name of the last and youngest wife of the Islamic prophet, Muhammad.
Alternative spellings: Aisha, Ayeesha

Ayuka

Meaning: Sweetfish
Origin: Japanese
Pronunciation: a YU ka
Description: This name can most commonly be found in Japanese-speaking countries.
Alternative spellings: Aiuka, Ayooka

Ayva

Meaning: Bird
Origin: German
Pronunciation: AY vuh
Description: Ayva is a variant spelling of Ava, a popular name of German, Hebrew and Latin origin. It is most likely a derivative of the Latin '*avis*' meaning 'bird'.
Alternative spellings: Ava, Avah

Azalea

Meaning: Flower name
Origin: English
Pronunciation: azz AYE lee ah
Description: Azalea comes from the pink and red flower of the same name that is found all over the world. Like Rose and Tulip, Azalea is part of the trend of using flowers as given names.

Azra

Meaning: Helper; young maid
Origin: Hebrew
Pronunciation: AZ ra
Description: Azra may come from the Hebrew, Azara, meaning 'helper', or from Arabic, meaning 'young maid'.
Alternative spellings: Asra, Azrah

B

Baha

See entry in 'Names for Baby Boys A–Z'

Bahija

Meaning: Joyous
Origin: Arabic
Pronunciation: ba HE ja
Description: Bahija is a name primarily associated with good cheer and happiness. It would be a good name for a very smiley baby girl.
Alternative spellings: Bahijah

Bailey

See entry in 'Names for Baby Boys A–Z'

Barbara

Meaning: Foreign woman
Origin: Greek
Pronunciation: BAH bah ruh
Description: According to Roman Catholic custom, St Barbara is a protector against fire and lightning, as well as the patron saint of architects, stonemasons and fortifications.
Alternative spellings: Barbarah, Barbarer

Baylor

Meaning: Horse trainer
Origin: English
Pronunciation: BAY lor

Description: Baylor is an English girls' name meaning 'horse trainer'. It is an unusual name that is not very popular, but it is very unique.
Alternative spellings: Bayler

Bea
Meaning: Happy
Origin: Latin
Pronunciation: BEE
Description: Bea originally came about as a pet form of the name Beatrice but is now found as an independent name. Despite its spelling it is pronounced 'bee'.
Alternative spellings: Bee

Beatrice
Meaning: Happy
Origin: Latin
Pronunciation: BE-ah triss
Description: Derived from the Latin word *'beatus'*, Beatrice means 'happy'.
Alternative spellings: Beatriss, Beatrix, Beatriz

Becca
Meaning: Binding
Origin: Hebrew
Pronunciation: BEK cuh
Description: This modern form of Rebecca, sometimes used as a name in its own right, can be shortened to Bex.
Alternative spellings: Beca, Becka

Becky
Meaning: Binding
Origin: Hebrew
Pronunciation: BEK kee
Description: Originally a shortened form of Rebecca and now a name in its own right, Becky was

especially popular during the 18th and 19th centuries.
Alternative spellings: Beccy, Beci, Becki, Beckie, Beki

Belinda
Meaning: Beautiful
Origin: Italian
Pronunciation: buh LIN dah
Description: Belinda is a name taken from the Italian word *'bella'*, meaning 'beautiful'. Alternatively, it can also be from the Old German word *'betlinde'*, meaning 'bright serpent' or 'bright linden tree'.

Bella
Meaning: Beautiful
Origin: Hebrew
Pronunciation: BEL luh
Description: Bella is linked to both the French and Italian words for 'beautiful' and is also a shortened form of Isabella.
Alternative spellings: Bela

Belle
Meaning: Beautiful
Origin: Latin
Pronunciation: BELL
Description: Belle is the French word for 'beauty' and can be a pet form of Isabelle or Annabelle.
Alternative spellings: Bell

Bellona
Meaning: War
Origin: Latin
Pronunciation: bel LOH nah
Description: In Roman mythology, Bellona was a Roman goddess of war.
Alternative spellings: Bellonna, Belona

B

Bernice

Meaning: Bringer of victory
Origin: Greek
Pronunciation: BER niss
Description: This Hebrew name is said to derive from the Macedonian name Berenice.
Alternative spellings: Berneice, Bernisse

Beryl

Meaning: Pale green stone
Origin: Greek
Pronunciation: BEH rill
Description: This name of a semi-precious pale green stone peaked in popularity in the UK during the 1930s.
Alternative spellings: Beril, Berill, Beryll

Bessie

Meaning: Promised by God
Origin: Hebrew
Pronunciation: BESS ee
Description: Bessie came about as a pet form of the popular name Elizabeth, but is now a name in its own right.
Alternative spellings: Bessi, Bessy

Beth

Meaning: Promised by God
Origin: Hebrew
Pronunciation: BETH
Description: The name Beth is of Hebrew origin meaning 'house'. It is also a shortened form of Elizabeth.
Alternative spellings: Bethe

Bethan

Meaning: Promised by God
Origin: Hebrew
Pronunciation: BEH than
Description: As well as being a shortened form of Bethany and Elizabeth, the name Bethan can also be seen as a name in its own right.
Alternative spellings: Bethane, Bethann

Bethany

Meaning: Village
Origin: Hebrew
Pronunciation: BETH anny
Description: This name first appeared in the New Testament as the name of a village where Jesus stayed before his crucifixion. It could also derive from the name Elizabeth, meaning 'promised by God'.
Alternative spellings: Bethani, Bethanie

Bethel

Meaning: House of God
Origin: Hebrew
Pronunciation: beth ELL
Description: Bethel is a Hebrew name that, when translated, means 'house of God'. Although they sound similar, Bethel is not Bethlehem.
Alternative spellings: Bethell

Betsy

Meaning: Promised by God
Origin: Hebrew
Pronunciation: BET see
Description: Like Bessie, Betsy came about as a pet form for the name Elizabeth.
Alternative spellings: Betsi, Betsie

Betty

Meaning: Promised by God
Origin: Hebrew
Pronunciation: BET ee
Description: Another pet form of the name Elizabeth, Betty rose to popularity in the 1930s.

Alternative spellings: Betti, Bettie

Beverley
Meaning: Beaver stream
Origin: English
Pronunciation: BEV er lee
Description: Transferred use of the surname used by those from an East Yorkshire settlement.
Alternative spellings: Beverlie, Beverly

Bianca
Meaning: White
Origin: Latin
Pronunciation: bi AN cuh
Description: This name was used by Shakespeare in both *The Taming of the Shrew* and *Othello*. It derives from the French name Blanche.
Alternative spellings: Biancah, Bianka

Bibi
Meaning: Lady of the house
Origin: Persian
Pronunciation: BEE bee
Description: This nickname in several languages is also a given name.
Alternative spellings: Bebe, Beebi

Billie
Meaning: Seeking protection
Origin: German
Pronunciation: BIL ee
Description: Although the name is unisex, this particular spelling is favoured among girls.
Alternative spellings: Billi, Billy

Binky
Meaning: No
Origin: English
Pronunciation: BINK ee
Description: Binky is a modern invention and as such, has no real meaning. It was made popular by Made in Chelsea star Binky Felstead, whose real name is Alexandra.

Birdy
Meaning: Bird
Origin: English
Pronunciation: bird EE
Description: Birdy is a cuter version of the English word 'bird' and is both a nickname and a given name.
Alternative spellings: Birdie, Byrdie

Bisma
Meaning: Unknown
Origin: Arabic
Pronunciation: BIS ma
Description: This unusual name is found across Asia and seems to be favoured by Muslim parents.
Alternative spellings: Bismah, Bismer

Blake
Meaning: Dark; pale
Origin: Old English
Pronunciation: bl aike
Description: Blake is a contemporary name with two conflicting etymologies. Both from Old English, the first 'a derivative of '*blæc*', meaning 'black' and the second, '*blæac*', meaning 'pale'.
Alternative spellings: Blaike

Blanka
Meaning: White
Origin: French
Pronunciation: BLON kah
Description: Blanka, like Bianca, is a pet form of Blanche and is popular in Polish-speaking countries.
Alternative spellings: Blanca, Blankah

Blessing
Meaning: God-given treasure; fortunate event
Origin: English
Pronunciation: BLES ing
Description: With its positive meaning, this name is more common in America than in Britain.
Alternative spellings: Blesing

Bliss
Meaning: Happiness
Origin: English
Pronunciation: blyss
Description: Bliss is a feminine name that comes from the English vocabulary. The word used today can be traced back to the Old English word '*bliss*' meaning 'happiness'. The name has been used in England since the Middle Ages.

Blossom
Meaning: Flower blossom
Origin: English
Pronunciation: BLOH sum
Description: The name comes from the English word for 'flower' and was originally a term of affection.
Alternative spellings: Blosom, Blossum

Bluebell
Meaning: Grateful
Origin: English
Pronunciation: BLOO bell
Description: Bluebell, a wild flower, symbolises gratitude.
Alternative spellings: Bloobell, Bluebelle

Blythe
Meaning: Joyful
Origin: English
Pronunciation: BLYTH
Description: A more common variant of the unisex name Blithe. The word appears in Shelley's poem 'To a Skylark'.
Alternative spellings: Blithe, Blyth

Bo
See entry in 'Names for Baby Boys A–Z'

Bobbi
Meaning: Bright fame
Origin: German
Pronunciation: BOH bee
Description: A specifically feminine spelling of the unisex name Bobby and a diminutive of the name Roberta.
Alternative spellings: Bobbie, Bobby

Bobbie
See entry in 'Names for Baby Boys A–Z'

Bonnie
Meaning: Pretty; attractive; good
Origin: Scottish
Pronunciation: BON ee
Description: Bonnie is a direct translation of the Scottish adjective, meaning 'pretty', which traces back to the Latin word '*bonus*', meaning 'good'. The name is also a pet form of Bonita.
Alternative spellings: Bonny

Bow
Meaning: Handsome; pretty
Origin: French
Pronunciation: B oh
Description: Bow may be a spelling variant of the French, '*beau*', meaning 'pretty' or 'handsome'. It could

also be from the Old English, '*boga*', meaning 'to bend, bow or arch'.
Alternative spellings: Bo, Beau

Bracken
See entry in 'Names for Baby Boys A–Z'

Brandy
Meaning: Gorse hill
Origin: English
Pronunciation: BRAN dee
Description: The name refers to a type of alcohol but is more likely to be a feminine form of Brandon.
Alternative spellings: Brandee, Brandi, Brandie

Breanna
Meaning: The strength of grace
Origin: English
Pronunciation: bree ANN ah
Description: Breanna is a modern American name that combines Bree and Anna.
Alternative spellings: Brianna, Bryanna

Bree
Meaning: The exalted one
Origin: Gaelic
Pronunciation: BREE
Description: Bree is an anglicised form of the Irish name Brighe, linked to the Gaelic name Bridget.
Alternative spellings: Bri, Brie

Brenda
Meaning: Sword; torch
Origin: Nordic
Pronunciation: bren DAH
Description: Brenda is an Old Norse name. Its roots are found

in the Norse word '*brandr*' meaning 'sword' or 'torch'. It is also considered the female version of Brendan in many countries.

Brennan
See entry in 'Names for Baby Boys A–Z'

Bridget
Meaning: The exalted one
Origin: Gaelic
Pronunciation: BRID jet
Description: Bridget comes from the Gaelic name Brighid, which was borne by a Celtic goddess.
Alternative spellings: Bridjit

Bridie
Meaning: The exalted one
Origin: Gaelic
Pronunciation: BRI dee
Description: This pet form of the Gaelic Brighid is popular in Ireland.
Alternative spellings: Bridi, Bridy

Briella
Meaning: Strength from God
Origin: Hebrew
Pronunciation: BREE el lah
Description: Briella is a shortened form of the name Gabriella and as such, shares the same meaning of 'strength from God'.

Brises
Meaning: Mythical queen
Origin: Greek
Pronunciation: Briss ESS
Description: A variant of Briseis, the name of a Trojan widow taken by Achilles in Greek myth.
Alternative spellings: Briseis, Brisses, Brissess

Bristol
Meaning: City in England
Origin: English
Pronunciation: brist OL
Description: Bristol is a city in south-west England and, like Camden or Brooklyn, is part of the trend of using place names as baby names.

Britney
Meaning: Brittany
Origin: English
Pronunciation: BRIT nee
Description: A respelling of Brittany made famous by singer Britney Spears.
Alternative spellings: Brittany

Brittany
Meaning: Brittany
Origin: English
Pronunciation: BRIT a nee
Description: The name of the region of north-west France. Britannia was a 2nd-century Roman goddess. The name is especially popular in America.
Alternative spellings: Britney

Brogan
See entry in 'Names for Baby Boys A–Z'

Brontë
Meaning: Literary scribe
Origin: Gaelic
Pronunciation: BRON tay
Description: This first name has been adopted from the surname of the English writers Emily, Charlotte and Anne.
Alternative spellings: Brontay, Brontie

Bronwyn
Meaning: White breast
Origin: Welsh
Pronunciation: BRON win
Description: Bronwyn is a very popular girls' name in Wales. It is also found in many Welsh legends.
Alternative spellings: Bronwen, Bronwin

Brook
Meaning: Stream
Origin: English
Pronunciation: BRUCK
Description: The name comes from the English word for a little stream and was originally a surname. It can also be found as a boys' name.
Alternative spellings: Brooke

Brooklyn
Meaning: Stream
Origin: English
Pronunciation: BRUCK lin
Description: An extension of the English name, Brook, meaning 'little stream', with the common suffix -lyn. It has also been used as a name in honour of Brooklyn, the New York City borough.
Alternative spellings: Brooklin

Bryce
Meaning: Speckled
Origin: English
Pronunciation: brice
Description: Bryce is most likely a variant of the name Brice, which in term came from the Latin name Bricius, meaning 'speckled'. Bryce Dallas Howard is a famous American actress with this name.
Alternative spellings: Brice

Bryn
See entry in 'Names for Baby Boys A–Z'

Bryony
Meaning: Vine
Origin: Greek
Pronunciation: BRY o nee
Description: This name of a Greek climbing plant has connotations of nature and life.
Alternative spellings: Brioni, Brionie, Briony, Bryoni, Bryonie

Bunny
Meaning: Rabbit
Origin: English
Pronunciation: BUN nee
Description: Bunny i ... derived from names s ... bara and Bernice, but is also used as a first name.
Alternative spellings: Bunni, Bunnie

Bushra
Meaning: Good omen
Origin: Arabic
Pronunciation: BUSH ra
Description: The name is probably Arabic in origin and supposedly brings good luck to the bearer of the name and to the bearer's family.
Alternative spellings: Bushrah

C

Cade
See entry in 'Names for Baby Boys A–Z'

Cadence
Meaning: Flowing rhythm
Origin: English
Pronunciation: KAY dense
Description: Cadence is a musical term and its definition is 'the rhythm and movement of tone in sound'.
Alternative spellings: Caydence, Kaydence

Cadi
Meaning: Rhythm; flow
Origin: English
Pronunciation: CAY dee
Description: A diminutive of the name Cadence, from an English word meaning 'rhythym, flow'.
Alternative spellings: Cady

Caelan
See entry in 'Names for Baby Boys A–Z'

Cain
See entry in 'Names for Baby Boys A–Z'

Caitlyn
Meaning: Pure
Origin: Greek
Pronunciation: KATE lin
Description: Caitlyn is an alternative spelling of Caitlin, itself the Irish form of Katharine. Caitlyn is a well-loved name in English-speaking countries and is

especially popular in America.
Alternative spellings: Caitlin, Catelin, Catelyn, Kaitlin, Kaitlyn, Katelin, Katelyn, Katelynn

Callie

Meaning: Beautiful
Origin: Greek
Pronunciation: KAH lee
Description: Originally the pet form of the name Caroline, it is now used as a name in its own right. 'Cal' comes from the Greek word for 'beauty'.
Alternative spellings: Cali, Calleigh, Callie, Cally

Calliope

Meaning: Beautiful voice
Origin: Greek
Pronunciation: kuh LIE o pee
Description: Calliope is an uncommon name of Greek origin and an alternative spelling of Kalliope. In Greek mythology, Kalliope was the eldest of the seven muses and represented epic poetry.
Alternative spellings: Calleope, Calliopee, Kalliope

Callisto

Meaning: Most beautiful
Origin: Greek
Pronunciation: kah LISS toe
Description: Callisto is an uncommon name of Greek origin. In Greek mythology, Callisto was a nymph of Artemis. It is also the name of a moon, the third-largest in the solar system, of the planet Jupiter.
Alternative spellings: Calisto, Kallisto

Cameron

See entry in 'Names for Baby Boys A–Z'

Camilla

Meaning: Sacrifice
Origin: Italian
Pronunciation: cah MIL ah
Description: Camilla originates from Roman mythology in which Camilla was the queen of the Volsci.
Alternative spellings: Camila, Kamila, Kamilla

Camille

Meaning: Sacrifice
Origin: Italian
Pronunciation: kah MEEL
Description: The French version of the name Camilla. Whereas Camilla is specifically feminine, Camille is used as a name for both boys and girls.
Alternative spellings: Camill, Kamile, Kamille

Campbell

See entry in 'Names for Baby Boys A–Z'

Candace

Meaning: Queen; mother; clarity
Origin: Latin
Pronunciation: can DEESE
Description: Candace was the hereditary title of a succession of Ethiopian queens. It is now a first name but still carries the meaning of 'queen' or 'mother'. It could also have come from the Late Latin word *candita*, meaning 'clarity'.
Alternative spellings: Candice

Caoimhe

Meaning: Beautiful
Origin: Gaelic
Pronunciation: KEEV ah
Description: Caoimhe is a name of Gaelic origin that is usually

C

found in England anglicised as Keeva. It comes from the Gaelic word *'caomh'*, which means 'beautiful'.
Alternative spellings: Keeva

Caprice
Meaning: Fanciful
Origin: Italian
Pronunciation: CUH price
Description: Caprice is an Italian name that means 'fanciful'. It is the same spelling and meaning as the English word.

Cara
Meaning: Dearest
Origin: Italian
Pronunciation: KAR ah
Description: Cara is a variant spelling of the Italian name Kara.
Alternative spellings: Carah, Kara

Carla
Meaning: Free man
Origin: English
Pronunciation: CAR la
Description: Carla is a feminine version of the English name Carl. As such, it means 'free man'. It first came into general use in the 1940s.
Alternative spellings: Karla

Carley
Meaning: Free man
Origin: German
Pronunciation: CAR lee
Description: Carley is a spelling variant of the name Carlie. Carlie and Carley originally came about as pet forms of Carlene.
Alternative spellings: Carli, Carlie, Carly

Carmel
Meaning: Garden
Origin: Hebrew
Pronunciation: car MEL
Description: Carmel is a unisex name used mainly by Roman Catholics. In the 12th century a monastery was founded in Mount Carmel and the Carmelite order came about from that.
Alternative spellings: Karmel

Carmen
Meaning: Garden
Origin: Hebrew
Pronunciation: CAR mun; CAR men
Description: Carmen is the Spanish version of the name Carmel and can most commonly be found in English- and Spanish-speaking countries.
Alternative spellings: Carman, Karmen

Carlotta
Meaning: Free Man
Origin: Italian
Pronunciation: car LOT ah
Description: Carlotta is the Italian version of the name Charlotte, which in turn is the feminine version of the name Charles, meaning 'free man'.

Carolina
Meaning: Free man
Origin: German
Pronunciation: KARE oh lie nah
Description: Carolina is the feminine version of Carlo, which is itself the Spanish form of Charles. The names Carlo and Carolina are popular in Latin America. It may be given as a name to girls born in Carolina in America.

Alternative spellings: Carolena, Carolyna, Karolena, Karolina, Karolyna

Caroline
Meaning: Free man
Origin: German
Pronunciation: CA ruh line
Description: Caroline comes from the Latin name Carolina. It is thought to have been first borne by Lady Caroline Lamb, the mistress of Lord Byron.
Alternative spellings: Carolyne, Karoline

Carrie
Meaning: Free man
Origin: German
Pronunciation: KA ree
Description: A short form of Caroline.
Alternative spellings: Cari, Carri

Carys
Meaning: Love
Origin: Welsh
Pronunciation: CA riss
Description: Carys means 'love', deriving from the Welsh word *'caru'*, and is sometimes shortened to Cass.
Alternative spellings: Carice, Caris, Karice, Karis, Kariss, Karys

Casey
See entry in 'Names for Baby Boys A–Z'

Cassandra
Meaning: Entangler of men
Origin: Greek
Pronunciation: kah SAN dra
Description: Cassandra is a name associated with tragedy in Greek myth and legend. In Homer's epic poem *The Iliad*, Cassandra was a Trojan princess who foretold the fall of Troy, but no one believed her. She was considered both blessed and cursed.
Alternative spellings: Cassandre, Kassandra

Cassia
Meaning: Spice
Origin: Latin
Pronunciation: CAS see ah; CASH ah
Description: Cassia is a name that can be traced to two separate origins. It can be seen as the feminine form of the name Cassius, which is said to come from a Roman family name. Alternatively, Cassius could be of Greek origin, from the word *'kasia'*, which is the name of a spice.
Alternative spellings: Cashia, Cassiah, Cassier

Cassidy
Meaning: Curly
Origin: Gaelic
Pronunciation: CASS id ee
Description: Cassidy comes from the Gaelic surname O'Caiside. It can be seen as both a boys' and a girls' name.
Alternative spellings: Cassidey, Cassidi, Cassidie

Cassie
Meaning: Entangler of men
Origin: Greek
Pronunciation: KASS ee
Description: Originally a pet form of Cassandra, Cassie is now a first name in its own right. The name is most commonly used in English-speaking countries.

Alternative spellings: Cassi, Cassy, Kassey, Kassie

Cataleya

Meaning: Genus of orchids
Origin: English
Pronunciation: cat a lay ah
Description: A contemporary name that may be connected to the Cattleya orchids of Argentina. The flowers were named after English botanist, Wiliam Cattley.
Alternative spellings: Katalaya, Cattleya

Catalina

Meaning: Pure
Origin: Greek
Pronunciation: cat a lee nah
Description: Catalina is a Spanish form of Katherine, derived from the Greek name, Katerina, which translates as 'pure'.
Alternative spellings: Katalina

Catherine

Meaning: Pure
Origin: Greek
Pronunciation: CATH er in
Description: Catherine is an English name that can be traced back to the Greek name Aikaterina. It is linked to the word *'katharos'* meaning 'pure'. The name was introduced to England in the medieval period.
Alternative spellings: Catharin, Catharine, Catharyn, Catherin, Catheryn, Cathryn, Katharin, Katharine, Katherin, Katherine, Katheryn, Kathryn

Catrin

Meaning: Pure
Origin: Greek
Pronunciation: KAT reen
Description: Catrin derives from the same roots as Katherine or Catherine. Catrin may have come about as a pet form of Katrina.
Alternative spellings: Catrine, Katreen, Katrin

Catriona

Meaning: Pure
Origin: Greek
Pronunciation: kah tree OH nah
Description: Catriona is the Gaelic version of the Greek name Catherine. The name is mostly found in Scotland and Ireland; however Catriona has also spread to other countries.
Alternative spellings: Catrionah, Katriona

Cece

Meaning: Blind
Origin: Latin
Pronunciation: see see
Description: Cece is most likely a short form or nickname for the name Cecelia, meaning 'blind'. The name became popular because it was the name of Jim and Pam's baby in the US version of *The Office*.

Cecilia

Meaning: Blind
Origin: Latin
Pronunciation: seh SEE lee ah
Description: Cecilia is derived from the Latin *'caecus'*, which means 'blind'. It was introduced to the UK in the medieval period and is also a feminine equivalent of the name Cecil.
Alternative spellings: Cecelia, Cecillia

Cecily

Meaning: Blind
Origin: Latin

C

Pronunciation: SES ih lee
Description: Cecily is a variant of the name Cecilia, which is the feminine version of Cecil. Cecil is of Latin origin and it means 'blind'. When first used, Cecil was a name given to girls.
Alternative spellings: Ceciley, Cecili, Cecilie, Cicily

Celia

Meaning: Heavenly
Origin: Latin
Pronunciation: see lee ah
Description: Celia is a variant of the Roman family name, Caelius, meaning 'heaven'. It is also a pet form of Cecilia and Celeste.
Alternative spellings: Cilia

Celeste

Meaning: Heavenly
Origin: French
Pronunciation: sell EST
Description: Celeste is a French name now seen across the English-speaking world. It comes from the Latin *'caelestis'*, meaning 'heavenly'. In Greek mythology Celesta is the sister of Hades.
Alternative spellings: Celesta, Seleste

Celine

Meaning: Heavenly; follower of Mars
Origin: Latin
Pronunciation: su LEEN
Description: Celine may come from the same root as Celeste, Celina and Celia and mean 'heavenly'. It could also derive from the Roman Marceline, meaning 'follower of Mars'.
Alternative spellings: Celeen, Celline, Seline

Celyn

Meaning: Holly
Origin: Welsh
Pronunciation: KEH lin
Description: Celyn, a unisex name from the Celtic for 'holly', is a good name for a child born around Christmas time. It is more common in Wales.
Alternative spellings: Kelyn

Ceri

Meaning: Fair, blessed poetry
Origin: Welsh
Pronunciation: KER ee
Description: Ceri is a Welsh name meaning 'fair, blessed poetry'. It is the short form of Ceridwen and Cerise. Note that the name is pronounced different from how it is spelt.

Cerys

Meaning: Love
Origin: Welsh
Pronunciation: CARE iss
Description: Cerys is a variant of the Welsh name Carys. It should be noted that the two names have slightly different pronunciations.
Alternative spellings: Carys, Ceriss

Chana

Meaning: Favoured by God
Origin: Hebrew
Pronunciation: KAH na
Description: Chana is a spelling variant of the name Channah, which is itself a variant of the popular Hebrew name Hannah. Chana is a popular name in Israel with Jewish parents.
Alternative spellings: Channah

Chance
See entry in 'Names for Baby Boys A–Z'

Chanel
Meaning: Wine
Origin: French
Pronunciation: SHA nel
Description: Chanel was originally a surname, notably that of French fashion designer Gabrielle Coco Chanel. It was adopted as a first name due to Coco Chanel's success and has since developed connotations of couture and high society.
Alternative spellings: Chanelle

Chantelle
Meaning: Stone; song
Origin: French
Pronunciation: shon TELL; sharn TELL
Description: Chantelle was originally a French surname but has been adopted as a first name in France and many Dutch- and English-speaking countries. Derived from the word *'cantal'*, meaning 'stone', it is more commonly associated with the French for 'song'.
Alternative spellings: Chantal, Chantel

Chardonnay
Meaning: Chardonnay wine
Origin: French
Pronunciation: SHAR don ay
Description: Chardonnay, a variety of grape, is also a village in the Maconnais region of France. This name was made popular in the UK by the character in the TV show *Footballers' Wives*.

Alternative spellings: Chardonay, Shardonnay

Charis
Meaning: Graceful
Origin: Greek
Pronunciation: KA riss
Description: In Greek myth, Charis was a goddess said to have the best qualities of all women. The name came to England around the 17th century.
Alternative spellings: Cariss, Carys, Cerys

Charlee
Meaning: Free man
Origin: French
Pronunciation: CHAR lee; char LEE
Description: This is a modern spelling variation of the popular unisex name Charlie, which is short for Charlotte.
Alternative spellings: Charleigh, Charley, Charli, Charlie, Charly

Charlize
Meaning: Free Man
Origin: English
Pronunciation: char LEE ze
Description: Charlize is the feminine version of the name Charles, and as such shares the same meaning of 'free man'. The name was made popular by actress Charlize Theron.

Charlotte
Meaning: Free man
Origin: French
Pronunciation: SHAR lot
Description: French feminine diminutive of Charles, used in

England since the 17th century. It owed its popularity in the 18th and 19th centuries to Queen Charlotte and Charlotte Brontë.
Alternative spellings: Charlette, Charlott

Chaya

Meaning: Free man
Origin: German
Pronunciation: CHYE yah
Description: Chaya was originally a surname, and the forename version could have derived from that. It may also be a feminine form of Chay, which is itself a pet form of Charles.
Alternative spellings: Chayah, Cheya

Chelsea

Meaning: From Chelsea
Origin: English
Pronunciation: CHEL see
Description: Chelsea, introduced as a name from the south-west London district of Chelsea, could have also been influenced by the name Kelsey.
Alternative spellings: Chelci, Chelcie, Chelsey, Chelsie, Chelsy

Cherry

Meaning: Charity; fruit
Origin: Latin
Pronunciation: CHE ree
Description: Cherry, a short form of Charity, is now a name in its own right.
Alternative spellings: Cheri, Cherri, Cherrie

Cheryl

Meaning: Charity; fruit
Origin: Latin

Pronunciation: CHEH ral
Description: Cheryl is a relatively modern name and was coined in around the 1940s. It is thought to be a variation of the name Cherry, the short form of the name Charity.
Alternative spellings: Cheril, Cherrylle

Chiara

Meaning: Bright
Origin: Italian
Pronunciation: kee AR uh
Description: Chiara is a variant of the names Clare and Clara and means 'bright' or 'famous'. It is popular with Italian parents.
Alternative spellings: Chiarah, Ciara, Kiara

Chitose

Meaning: Strength of a thousand
Origin: Japanese
Pronunciation: ch it O see
Description: This name can be written by using different Japanese characters, as well as the traditional Japanese alphabet Hiragana. The different characters mean 'thousand', 'to climb or ascend' and 'strength and force'.
Alternative spellings: Chetose, Chetosi

Chloe

Meaning: A green shoot
Origin: Greek
Pronunciation: KLO ee
Description: From the Greek name Khloe, this was originally used in the classical period as an epithet of the fertility goddess Demeter.
Alternative spellings: Chloë, Chlöe, Chloé, Chloey, Cloe, Cloey, Khloe, Khloë, Kloé, Kloë, Kloey

Chris
See entry in 'Names for Baby Boys A–Z'

Christa
Meaning: Anointed; chosen one
Origin: Greek
Pronunciation: kris TAH
Description: Possibly a derivation of the Greek word '*Cristos*', meaning 'anointed' or 'chosen one'. It could also be a pet form of Christine, which translates as 'follower of Christ'.
Alternative spellings: Krista, Crista

Christabel
Meaning: Beautiful Christian
Origin: Latin
Pronunciation: KRIST ah bel
Description: This name of Latin and French origin combines Christian, a 'follower of Christianity' and *belle*, 'beauty'. We can take Christabel to mean 'beautiful Christian'.
Alternative spellings: Christa-belle, Kristabel

Christian
See entry in 'Names for Baby Boys A–Z'

Christiana
Meaning: Follower of Christ
Origin: English
Pronunciation: kris tee AH nah
Description: Christiana is a variant of the name Christine, which is the feminine version of Christian.

Christina
Meaning: Follower of Christ
Origin: Latin
Pronunciation: kris TEE nuh
Description: A simplified form of the Latin feminine form of Christian.
Alternative spellings: Christena, Cristina, Kristina

Christine
Meaning: Follower of Christ
Origin: French
Pronunciation: kris TEEN
Description: Christine is the feminine version of the name Christian, which means 'follower of Christ'. The name is often subject to variation and adaptation – Chris, Chrissy, Kirsty, Kristen and Kristine all bear links to the name Christine.
Alternative spellings: Christeen, Christene, Kristine

Ciara
Meaning: Dark-haired; bright
Origin: Gaelic
Pronunciation: see AIR ah; KEER ah; kee AR ah
Description: This feminine form of the Irish name Ciaran means 'dark' or 'black'. Ciara could also be a variant of the Italian Chiara, meaning 'bright'. The 'c' can be soft or hard.
Alternative spellings: Chiara, Chiarah, Kiara

Cienna
Meaning: From Siena
Origin: Italian
Pronunciation: see EN ah
Description: Cienna is an alternative spelling for Sienna, derived from the Italian city Siena. It is a fitting name given to baby girls conceived there. The variant form Cienna may have come about as

a way of distinguishing the given name from the name of the city.
Alternative spellings: Sienna

Cindy
Meaning: From Mount Cynthus
Origin: Greek
Pronunciation: SIN dee
Description: Cindy originally came about as a pet form of names such as Cynthia or Lucinda, but it is now used as a given name. It experienced a popularity boost in the 1960s with the launch of the popular Sindy doll.
Alternative spellings: Cindee, Cindi, Cindie, Sindy

Claire
Meaning: Bright
Origin: French
Pronunciation: KLARE
Description: Claire is the French form of the name Clara. It is a popular name in English-speaking countries and was introduced to Britain by the Normans.
Alternative spellings: Clare

Clancy
Meaning: Red-haired warrior
Origin: Irish
Pronunciation: clan SEE
Description: Clancy is an Irish name meaning 'red-haired warrior'. Translated directly from the Gaelic, it means 'son of Fhlannchadh', where 'flann' means 'reddish'.

Clara
Meaning: Bright
Origin: Latin
Pronunciation: CLAH ra
Description: Clara derives from the Latin word *'clarus'*,

meaning 'bright'. It is currently one of the top ten girls' names in France.

Clarice
Meaning: Bright
Origin: Latin
Pronunciation: CLA riss
Description: Clarice came about as an elaboration on the Latin name Clara.
Alternative spellings: Clarisse, Claryce

Clarissa
Meaning: Bright
Origin: Latin
Pronunciation: cla RISS a
Description: A Latinate form of Clarice. Sometimes shortened to Claire.
Alternative spellings: Clairissa, Clarica, Claryssa

Claudette
Meaning: Lame
Origin: French
Pronunciation: KLO dett
Description: Claudette is the French version of the Latin surname Claudius, which in turn is from *'claudus'*, meaning 'lame'. Alternatively it is also the female version of Claude.

Claudia
Meaning: Lame
Origin: Latin
Pronunciation: CLOR de uh
Description: This is a version of the Roman name Claudius. The French unisex form 'Claude' used to be very popular in France.
Alternative spellings: Claudier, Klaudia

Clemency
Meaning: Merciful
Origin: English
Pronunciation: clem EN see
Description: Clemency is from the English word of the same spelling and means 'merciful'. It comes from the Latin root 'clemens', which means the same thing.

Clementine
Meaning: Mild-mannered
Origin: Latin
Pronunciation: CLEH men tyne
Description: Clementine is the feminine equivalent of the name Clement. It is also associated with the fruit. A popular name in Germany.
Alternative spellings: Clementyne, Clemintine, Klementine

Cleo
Meaning: Father's glory
Origin: Greek
Pronunciation: KLEE oh
Description: Cleo is the short form of the name Cleopatra, which is Greek in origin. It was the name of a famous Egyptian queen, so carries connotations of allure and mystery.
Alternative spellings: Cleoh, Clio, Kleo

Cleopatra
Meaning: Glory father
Origin: Greek
Pronunciation: clee OH pat ra
Description: The name Cleopatra is famous for being borne by the ruler of Egypt, born 69 BC. She had children with both Caesar and Mark Anthony before dying aged 39 from a snakebite.

Clover
Meaning: Clover plant
Origin: English
Pronunciation: cloh VER
Description: Clover is a type of plant that is found almost all over the world. It is most often used as fodder, as in animal feed. Clovers usually have three leaves. Four-leaf clovers are very rare, and therefore considered to be tokens of luck.

Coco
Meaning: Chocolate
Origin: French
Pronunciation: KO ko
Description: Coco was the nickname of the pioneering French fashion designer, Chanel, and is associated with couture and high society.
Alternative spellings: Coko, Koco, Koko

Cody
See entry in 'Names for Baby Boys A–Z'

Colette
Meaning: Victory of the people
Origin: Greek
Pronunciation: coll ET
Description: Colette is a French feminine form of Colle, the medieval short form of Nicholas. Colette is also a shortened form of the name Nicolette.
Alternative spellings: Collette, Kolette

Connie
Meaning: Steadfast
Origin: Latin
Pronunciation: KOH nee

Description: Distinct from the masculine Conny, which is short for Connor, Connie is a pet form of Constance, but has become a name in its own right.
Alternative spellings: Conie, Conni, Conny

Constance
Meaning: Steadfast
Origin: Latin
Pronunciation: KON stanse
Description: The name derives from the Latin word for 'constant' or 'steadfast' and was popular in Norman times. It is often short-ened to Connie.
Alternative spellings: Constanse, Konstance

Constantine
See entry in 'Names for Baby Boys A–Z'

Cora
Meaning: Maiden
Origin: Greek
Pronunciation: KORE ah
Description: Cora derives from the Greek '*kore*' meaning 'the maiden'. Kore was another name for Persephone, a daughter of Zeus in Greek mythology.
Alternative spellings: Corah, Kora

Coral
Meaning: Coral
Origin: English
Pronunciation: KOH ral
Description: Coral, the skeleton of marine animals, became a name once the substance was considered rare and valuable. It has an exotic feel.
Alternative spellings: Corelle, Koral

Coraline
Meaning: Coral
Origin: Greek
Pronunciation: core UH ine
Description: It is a variation of the name Coral, referring to the hard, stone-like substance found in the sea.

Cordelia
Meaning: Heart
Origin: Latin
Pronunciation: kor DEE lee ah
Description: Cordelia is a variant of Cordellia. The name is thought to be derived from the Latin word '*cor*', which means 'heart'.
Alternative spellings: Cordellia, Kordelia

Corey
See entry in 'Names for Baby Boys A–Z'

Corinne
Meaning: Beautiful maiden
Origin: English
Pronunciation: COR inn
Description: Corinne is a vari-ation of the name Corina, and as such shares the meaning of 'beautiful maiden'. It has roots in the Greek word '*kore*' meaning 'maiden'.

Cornelia
Meaning: Horn
Origin: Latin
Pronunciation: kor NEE lee ah
Description: Cornelia is the feminine equivalent of Cornelius, a Roman family name thought to have come from the Latin word '*cornu*', meaning 'horn'.
Alternative spellings: Kornelia

Cosima

Meaning: Order; decency
Origin: Greek
Pronunciation: ko SEE ma
Description: The girls' name Cosima is derived from the Greek name Kosmas. In the 4th century St Cosmas was martyred along with his brother.
Alternative spellings: Cosimah, Kosima

Courtney

Meaning: Domain of Curtius
Origin: French
Pronunciation: KORT nee
Description: Once thought to mean 'short nose', this was a surname for those who lived in places called Courtenay, meaning 'Domain of Curtius'.
Alternative spellings: Cortney, Courteney, Kortney, Kourteney, Kourtney

Cressida

Meaning: Golden
Origin: Greek
Pronunciation: cress EE dah
Description: Cressida was created by Shakespeare for his play, *Troilus and Cressida*. He took it from the Greek name Chryseis, meaning 'daughter of Chryses'. All of these have a common Greek root, '*chrysos*' meaning 'golden'.

Cruz

See entry in 'Names for Baby Boys A–Z'

Crystal

Meaning: Crystal
Origin: English
Pronunciation: KRIS tall
Description: Crystal is derived from the Greek word '*krystallos*' meaning 'ice'. Crystal is suggestive of gemstones.
Alternative spellings: Chrystal, Kristel, Krystal

Cydney

Meaning: Wide meadow
Origin: English
Pronunciation: SID nee
Description: Cydney is a specifically feminine variant of the unisex name Sydney.
Alternative spellings: Cydnee, Sidnee, Sidney, Sydnee, Sydney

Cynthia

Meaning: From Mount Cynthus
Origin: Greek
Pronunciation: SIN thee ah
Description: Derived from the Greek mountain, this would have originally been the surname of those who lived by or on the mountain. It was also the name of a Greek goddess born there.
Alternative spellings: Cinthia, Cynthea, Synthia

D

Dahlia

Meaning: Dahlia flower; valley
Origin: English

Pronunciation: DAHL yuh
Description: The dahlia is a bushy flower native to Mexico, where it is

C
D

considered the national flower. It also means 'valley' in Swedish.
Alternative spellings: Dahlya, Dalia, Darlia

Daisy

Meaning: Day's eye
Origin: English
Pronunciation: DAY zee
Description: The yellow centre of the flower of the same name is covered by petals come dusk and was named 'day's eye'. This then became 'daisy' over time.
Alternative spellings: Daisi, Daisie, Daysie

Dalia

Meaning: Dahlia flower; grapevine
Origin: Arabic
Pronunciation: DAHL yuh
Description: Dalia is a common name in Arabic and Hebrew and stems from the word 'grapevine'. It is also a spelling variant of Dahlia, derived from the name of the flower.
Alternative spellings: Dahlya, Dahlia, Darlia

Dallas

Meaning: City in Texas
Origin: English
Pronunciation: DALL as
Description: Dallas is a city in the American state of Texas. Like London and Paris, this name follows the trend of using place names for baby names.

Dana

Meaning: Fertility; from Denmark
Origin: Gaelic
Pronunciation: DAY na
Description: In Irish myth, Dana was the name of the goddess of fertility.
Alternative spellings: Danah, Dayna

Danae

Meaning: Founder of Ardea
Origin: Greek
Pronunciation: dah NAY
Description: In Greek mythology, Danae was a daughter of King Acrisius of Argos and Queen Eurydice.
Alternative spellings: Danaea, Danay

Dania

Meaning: God is my judge
Origin: Hebrew
Pronunciation: DAN yah
Description: Dania is a variation of Danielle, the feminine form of Daniel.
Alternative spellings: Daniah, Daniya

Danica

Meaning: From Denmark
Origin: Slavic
Pronunciation: dah NEE kah
Description: Danica, thought to come from the word 'Dane', would have been given as a first name to Danish girls.
Alternative spellings: Danicah, Danika

Daniella

Meaning: God is my judge
Origin: Hebrew
Pronunciation: dan YELL ah
Description: The feminine form of the name Daniel. This spelling is mainly used in English-speaking countries.
Alternative spellings: Daniela, Daniyella, Danniella

Danielle

Meaning: God is my judge
Origin: Hebrew
Pronunciation: dan ee ELL; dan YELL
Description: A French feminine form of the Hebrew name Daniel and is a popular name in Britain.
Alternative spellings: Daniele, Daniyelle, Dannielle

Danni

Meaning: God is my judge
Origin: Hebrew
Pronunciation: DAH nee
Description: Danni came about as a pet form of the name Danielle, but is now used as a name in its own right.
Alternative spellings: Dani, Dannie

Daphne

Meaning: Laurel tree
Origin: Greek
Pronunciation: DAF nee
Description: In Greek mythology Daphne was a nymph who was pursued by Apollo. When she asked the gods to help they turned her into a laurel tree.
Alternative spellings: Daphnee, Daphney

Darcey

Meaning: From Arcy
Origin: French
Pronunciation: DAR see
Description: Darcey is the specifically feminine spelling of the unisex name Darcy. Darcy is a French surname, which means 'person from Arcy'. It is also found as a surname in Ireland.
Alternative spellings: Darci, Darcie, Darcy

D...

Me...
Orig...
Pronu...
Descript...
version of ...
Darius, whic...
and means 'gu...
Alternative sp...
Darya

Darla

Meaning: Darling
Origin: English
Pronunciation: daar LAH
Description: Darla is derive... the Old English 'dearling', or a... more commonly known in mod... English, 'darling'.

Davina

Meaning: Darling
Origin: Hebrew
Pronunciation: da VEE nuh
Description: Davina, or Davinia, is a Latinate feminine form of David, said to have originated in Scotland.
Alternative spellings: Davena, Davinah, Davinia

Dawn

Meaning: Daybreak
Origin: English
Pronunciation: DORN
Description: The name Dawn originates from the English word for the beginning of the day.
Alternative spellings: Dawne

Daya

Meaning: Man Destroyer

Darcy

See entry in 'Names for Baby Boys A–Z'.

...aria
...ning: Guardian
...: Persian
...ciation: DAR ee ah
...ion: Daria is the feminine
...he masculine name
... is of Persian origin
...ardian'.
...llings: Dariah,

...ten the pet
...Deborah
...used as
...begin-

...d from
...s it is
...ern

...Deana,

D

...ee ah
...na is of Greek
...generally translates as
...n from the island of Delos'.
...t is also a pet form of names such
as Cordelia and Odelia.
Alternative spellings: Deliah

...ning: Bee
Origin: Hebrew
Pronunciation: DEB bee
Description: Debbie came about
as a pet form of the name Deborah,
but is now a name in its own right.
Alternative spellings: Debbee,
Debbi, Debby

Deborah

Meaning: Bee
Origin: Hebrew
Pronunciation: DEB or ah
Description: This biblical name,
which was very popular in the
1960s, can often be shortened to
Debbie or Bee.
Alternative spellings: Debbora,
Debborah, Debora

Delilah

Meaning: Flirtatious
Origin: Hebrew
Pronunciation: de LYE lah
Description: Delilah is the
biblical name of the woman
who gave Samson up to the
Philistines.
Alternative spellings: Delila,
Delylah

Delphine

Meaning: Of Delphi
Origin: French
Pronunciation: DEHL feen
Description: Delphine is the
French form of the name Del-
phina, which is from the Latin
meaning 'of Delphi', which
refers to the city in Ancient
Greece that was the site of the
oracle Apollo.

Delta

Meaning: Fourth born
Origin: Greek
Pronunciation: del TAH
Description: Delta is actually the fourth letter of the Greek alphabet and refers to children who are the fourth born in a family.

Delyth

Meaning: Pretty
Origin: Welsh
Pronunciation: del ITH
Description: Delyth is a Welsh name and is derived from the Welsh word for 'pretty'.

Demelza

Meaning: Place in Cornwall
Origin: Cornish
Pronunciation: deh MEL zah
Description: Demelza is a Cornish place name, specifically a hamlet in St. Wenn, Corwall. It is the name of the heroine in Winston Graham's Poldark series.

Demeter

Meaning: Earth mother
Origin: Greek
Pronunciation: deh MEE ter
Description: In Greek mythology, Demeter was the goddess associated with the fertility of the earth and also protected the sanctity of marriage.
Alternative spellings: Demeta, Demetre

Demi

Meaning: Half
Origin: French
Pronunciation: DEH me
Description: Demi is a name coined in modern times. It may also be a pet form of Demetria or Demetrius, making its meaning 'earth'.
Alternative spellings: Demie, Demy

Denisa

Meaning: Servant of Dionysus
Origin: Greek
Pronunciation: deh NEES ah
Description: Denisa is a variant of the French name Denise.
Alternative spellings: Deneesa, Denisah

Denise

Meaning: Servant of Dionysus
Origin: Greek
Pronunciation: deh NEECE
Description: Like Denisa, Denise is the feminine form of Denis, derived from the name of the Greek god, Dionysus.
Alternative spellings: Deneese, Dineese

Desiree

Meaning: Desired
Origin: French
Pronunciation: DES er RAY
Description: An anglicisation of the French name Désirée meaning 'desired'.
Alternative spellings: Desirée

Destiny

Meaning: Fate
Origin: Latin
Pronunciation: DES tih nee
Description: Destiny, from the word meaning 'the power of fate', derives from the Latin *'destinare'*. It is very popular in the US.
Alternative spellings: Destini, Destinie

Devin
Meaning: Fawn
Origin: Irish
Pronunciation: deh VIN
Description: Devin is the anglicised version of the Irish name, Ó Damháin, which is a reference to the given name 'Damán Allaid', meaning 'fawn'.

Devon
Meaning: From Devon
Origin: English
Pronunciation: DEH vun
Description: Devon is a unisex name that derives from the county in south-west England.
Alternative spellings: Devone, Devun

Devora
Meaning: Bee
Origin: Hebrew
Pronunciation: dev OR ah
Description: Devora is a Hebrew name meaning 'bee'. In the Torah, Devorah was a prophetess who taught the Jewish nation for forty years.

Diamond
Meaning: Diamond
Origin: English
Pronunciation: DIE mund
Description: The name of one of the most precious stones, Diamond is still fairly rare but is used for girls who are considered very precious.
Alternative spellings: Dyamond

Diana
Meaning: Pure
Origin: Latin
Pronunciation: dy AH nah
Description: Diana was the Roman goddess of the moon and virginity. The name increased in popularity after the death of Diana, Princess of Wales.
Alternative spellings: Dianah, Dyana

Didi
Meaning: A Pet Name
Origin: English
Pronunciation: dee dee
Description: Didi is a pet name given to people with names such as Diana. However, it can also be a given name on its own as well.

Dilara
Meaning: Heart's desire
Origin: Persian
Pronunciation: dee LAH rah
Description: Dilara is a name of both Persian and Turkish origins. It comes from the Persian word *'dil'*, which means 'heart', and shares a root with *'dilek'*, which means 'desire' in Turkish.
Alternative spellings: Delara, Dilarah

Dima
Meaning: Torrential rain
Origin: Arabic
Pronunciation: DI ma
Description: Dima is said to refer to rain; however it could come from the Arabic word meaning 'life'. It could also be a shortened version of the Russian name Dmitri, which means 'of Demeter'.
Alternative spellings: Dema, Dimah

Dina
Meaning: Judgement; daytime; valley

Origin: Hebrew
Pronunciation: DEE nah
Description: Dina is a name that can be traced back to three separate origins. It could come from a Sanskrit word meaning 'daytime'. Equally, it could derive from a Hebrew word meaning 'judgement' or the name could come from an Old English word meaning 'valley'.
Alternative spellings: Deena, Dena, Denah, Dinah

Dion

Meaning: Servant of Dionysus
Origin: Greek
Pronunciation: DYE on
Description: Dion is a unisex name that is derived from the name of the Greek god of revelry, Dionysus. Dione is a specifically feminine form of the name, while Deon is the spelling more often used for boys.
Alternative spellings: Deon, Dione, Dionne

Disha

Meaning: Direction
Origin: Indian
Pronunciation: dee SHAH
Description: Disha is an Indian girls' name meaning 'direction'.

Divine

Meaning: Heavenly
Origin: Latin
Pronunciation: dih VINE
Description: Divine is a girls' name that is a variant of Divina. Divine has religious implications and the name means 'heavenly' or 'of heaven'.
Alternative spellings: Davine, Devine, Divina, Divinia, Divyne

Divya

Meaning: Divine
Origin: Sanskrit
Pronunciation: div YAAH
Description: Divya comes directly from the Sanskrit word of the same spelling and means 'divine'.

Dixie

Meaning: Southerner
Origin: English
Pronunciation: DICK see
Description: The name Dixie comes from the term used to describe those who lived south of the line drawn up to settle disputes between British colonies in America in the 1700s.
Alternative spellings: Dixi, Dixy

Diya

Meaning: Bright
Origin: Arabic
Pronunciation: DI ya
Description: Although Diya was originally a masculine name it is becoming popular as a girls' name.
Alternative spellings: Deya, Dia, Diyah

Dolcie

Meaning: Sweet
Origin: Italian
Pronunciation: Dolt je; Doll see
Description: *Dolce*, the Italian word for 'sweet', may refer to: Dolcè, an Italian municipality located in the province of Verona. The name may also be used in honour of luxury fashion house, Dolce & Gabbana.
Alternative spellings: Dolce, Dolcè, Dulcie

Dolly

Meaning: Gift of God

Origin: Greek
Pronunciation: DOR oth ee
Description: A diminutive of
Dorothy, from the Greek, Dorothea,
meaning 'God's gift'. The shortening
became popular in the 16th century.
Alternative spellings: Dollie,
Dolley

Dominica
Meaning: Lord
Origin: Latin
Pronunciation: do me NEE kah
Description: Dominica is the less
common feminine equivalent of
Dominic and is from the Latin
'dominicus' meaning 'from the
Lord' or just 'Lord'.
Alternative spellings: Dominika,
Dominikah

Dominique
Meaning: Lord
Origin: Latin
Pronunciation: dom in EEK
Description: Dominique is the
more usual feminine version of
Dominic, although in France and
America it is used as a unisex name.
Alternative spellings: Domineke

Donna
Meaning: Lady
Origin: Italian
Pronunciation: DON na
Description: The name Donna
comes from the Italian word for
'lady' and was first taken up by
English speakers in the early 20th
century.
Alternative spellings: Dona,
Donnah

Dora
Meaning: Gift of God

Origin: Greek
Pronunciation: DOR ah
Description: A further diminutive
of the Greek, Dorothea, Dora is
now a popular name on its own. It
is also a shortening of the female
name, Theodora.
Alternative spellings: Dorah

Doris
Meaning: From Dorian; gift
Origin: Greek
Pronunciation: DOR riss
Description: Doris was originally a
name given to women of the Greek
Dorian tribe. *'Doron'* means 'gift'.
Alternative spellings: Doriss,
Dorris

Dorothy
Meaning: God's gift
Origin: Greek
Pronunciation: DOR oth ee
Description: Dorothy, from the
Greek Dorothea, is a combina-
tion of the words *'doron'* and
'theos', meaning 'gift' and 'God'
respectively.
Alternative spellings: Dorothi,
Dorothie

Dottie
Meaning: Gift of God
Origin: Greek
Pronunciation: DOT ee
Description: Dottie is a further
shortening of the English name,
Dorothy, which in turn derives
from the Greek, Dorothea.
Alternative spellings: Dotty

Dream
Meaning: To Dream
Origin: English
Pronunciation: dreem

Description: Dream is taken from the English vocabulary word of the same meaning. Like Faith or Grace, this is part of the trend to use English words as baby names.

Drew

See entry in 'Names for Baby Boys A–Z'

Dua

Meaning: Prayer
Origin: Arabic
Pronunciation: doo AH
Description: Dua derives from the Arabic word that means 'prayer'. It is an unusual name in Britain but is popular in the Middle East.
Alternative spellings: Dewa

Dusty

See entry in 'Names for Baby Boys A–Z'

E

Eadie

Meaning: Riches; blessed
Origin: English
Pronunciation: ee dee
Description: A sweet variation of the traditional English name, Edith, meaning 'riches' or 'blessed'. Further variations include Ditte and Edyth.
Alternative spellings: Edie

Easha

Meaning: She who lives or womanly
Origin: Arabic
Pronunciation: eesh ah
Description: A variant of the popular Islamic name, Aisha. Aisha was the name of the last and youngest wife of the prophet Muhammad.
Alternative spellings: Isha

Ebony

Meaning: Dark wood
Origin: Latin
Pronunciation: EH ben ee
Description: This name of an extremely dark wood is popular with African-Americans. It has Latin, Greek and Egyptian origins.
Alternative spellings: Eboni, Ebonie

Echo

Meaning: Echo
Origin: Greek
Pronunciation: EK oh
Description: In Greek myth, Echo was a nymph used by the adulterous Zeus to distract his wife Hera.
Alternative spellings: Ecko, Ekho

Eden

Meaning: Paradise
Origin: Hebrew
Pronunciation: E den
Description: Eden may be considered a short form of Edith, but is more likely to be used in relation to the 'garden of Eden' where, according to the Bible, Adam and Eve lived in paradise.
Alternative spellings: Edan, Edon

Eddie
See entry in 'Names for Baby Boys A–Z'

Edith
Meaning: Ambitious
Origin: English
Pronunciation: EE dith
Description: Edith is an Old English name that is made up of the elements of *'ead'*, which means 'riches', and *'gyth'* meaning 'strife'.
Alternative spellings: Edithe

Efa
Meaning: Beaming radiance
Origin: Hebrew
Pronunciation: EE fah
Description: Efa is a variant of the name Eva, and is usually found in Wales. It is very similar in pronunciation to the Irish name Aoife.
Alternative spellings: Aoife, Eefa, Efah

Effie
Meaning: Beautiful silence
Origin: Greek
Pronunciation: EH fee
Description: Effie, a pet form of Euphemia, is now used as a name in its own right and is especially popular in Scotland.
Alternative spellings: Effi, Effy

Eiko
Meaning: Prosperous child
Origin: Japanese
Pronunciation: ee EE koh
Description: Although this name has its roots in Japanese, it is commonly found in many other Asian countries. The character *'ei'* means 'flourish and prosperity' while *'ko'* means 'child'.
Alternative spellings: Eheko, Eyko

Eileen
Meaning: Pleasant
Origin: Gaelic
Pronunciation: eye LEEN
Description: This anglicised form of Eibhlin is linked to Helen and Evelyn.
Alternative spellings: Aileen, Eyleen

Eilidh
Meaning: Pleasant; bright
Origin: Gaelic
Pronunciation: AY lee
Description: Eilidh is thought to be a Gaelic variant of either Eileen, which means 'pleasant' or Ellie, which means 'bright'.
Alternative spellings: Ailidh, Eiledh

Eira
Meaning: Snow
Origin: Welsh
Pronunciation: AIR ah; AY rah
Description: Eira is a name of Welsh origin, and comes from the Welsh word for 'snow'.
Alternative spellings: Aira, Eyra

Ela
Meaning: Beautiful; fairy maiden
Origin: Greek
Pronunciation: ELL ah
Description: A modern contraction of Ella, which has many derivations. It is often used as a shortening for names beginning with 'El', including Elizabeth and Eleanor. It is also a pet name for names such as Annabella or Danniella.
Alternative spellings: Ella

Elaina

Meaning: Bright
Origin: French
Pronunciation: eh LAY nah
Description: Elaina is a variant of the Greek name Elaine.
Alternative spellings: Elana, Elayna, Eliana

Elaine

Meaning: Bright
Origin: Greek
Pronunciation: eh LANE
Description: Elaine is the French form of the Greek name Helen. In English legend, Elaine is the name of a woman who falls in love with Sir Lancelot.
Alternative spellings: Elane, Elayne

Elana

Meaning: Bright
Origin: Greek
Pronunciation: eh LAH nah
Description: As well as being a variant of Elaina, Elana is also considered a phonetically spelt variant of Eleanor. It is also found as a Hebrew name in its own right and in this form means 'tree'.
Alternative spellings: Elaina, Elanor, Eleana, Eleanor, Elena

Elara

Meaning: One who brings brightness and happiness to the soul
Origin: Persian
Pronunciation: ell AR ah
Description: Elara is a variant spelling of Alara, a popular name in Turkey that means 'the one who brings brightness and happiness to the heart and soul'. Alara is also the name of a water fairy in Turkish mythology who must remain beside the water to maintain her youth and beauty.
Alternative spellings: Alara

Eleanor

Meaning: Bright
Origin: French
Pronunciation: ELL a nor
Description: An Old French respelling of the Old Provencal name Aliénor. Introduced to England in the 12th century by Eleanor of Aquitaine, who came from France to wed King Henry II.
Alternative spellings: Elana, Elanor, Eleana, Elena, Ellena, Elina

Eleonora

Meaning: Bright
Origin: French
Pronunciation: ELL ee oh nor
Description: A variant spelling of Eleanor, itself a contraction of the traditional French name Aliénor.
Alternative spellings: Eleanor, Elanor, Eleanora

Electra

Meaning: Shining
Origin: Greek
Pronunciation: el LEHK tra
Description: Electra is of Greek origin and an alternative spelling to Elektra. It is the name given to one of the nine brightest stars in the Pleiades star cluster, in the constellation of Taurus.
Alternative spellings: Elektra

Elen

Meaning: Mischievous
Origin: Gaelic
Pronunciation: EH len
Description: Elen is a Gaelic

name associated with a nymph and carries with it connotations of mischievousness.
Alternative spellings: Elin, Elinn, Ellen

Eleni

Meaning: Bright
Origin: Greek
Pronunciation: eh LEH ne
Description: Like Elaine, Eleni comes from the Greek name Helen and shares its meaning of 'bright'.
Alternative spellings: Elene, Elleni

Eleri

Meaning: River
Origin: Welsh
Pronunciation: EH lee ree
Description: This unusual, predominantly Welsh name is likely to have associations with the Welsh river Eleri.
Alternative spellings: Elerie, Elery, Elleri

Elia

Meaning: Jehovah is good
Origin: Hebrew
Pronunciation: EH le ah
Description: Elia, a unisex name, comes from the same root as Elijah, which means 'Jehovah is good'.
Alternative spellings: Elea, Eliah

Elif

Meaning: Symbol
Origin: Arabic
Pronunciation: ELL eef
Description: The name occurs in the Old Testament, the female form of Aleph. Although not

attributed a meaning, the name is also the name for many powerful symbols in Arabic and Hebrew.
Alternative spellings: Alif, Aleph, Eliph

Elija

Meaning: My God is Yaweh
Origin: Hebrew
Pronunciation: ELL aye ja
Description: A variant of Elijah, who was a prophet in Israel in the 9th century BC mentioned in many holy texts. It has been predominantly used as a male name but is now considered unisex.
Alternative spellings: Elijah, Elias

Elin

Meaning: Beautiful nymph
Origin: Welsh
Pronunciation: ELL in
Description: Welsh form of Helen, which translates as 'beautiful nymph', or 'intelligent, beautiful'.
Alternative spellings: Elyn, Ellin

Elisa

Meaning: Promised by God
Origin: Hebrew
Pronunciation: eh LEE sah
Description: Elisa is a modern variant of the name Eliza, itself a pet form of Elizabeth.
Alternative spellings: Alisa, Alissa, Alysa, Alyssa, Elissa, Elyssa

Elise

Meaning: Promised by God
Origin: Hebrew
Pronunciation: ell EEZ
Description: Elise is a pet form of

the Hebrew name Elizabeth, and hence means 'promised by God'. It is the title of Beethoven's piano piece 'Für Elise'.

Alternative spellings: Eleese, Elize, Ellisa, Elyse

Elisha

Meaning: Powerful
Origin: Hebrew
Pronunciation: ell EE sha; ell ISH a
Description: This name is thought to derive from the biblical name 'El', which means 'powerful', and 'Sha' which means 'to help and deliver'. It can also be considered a variant of the name Alisha, meaning 'noble'.
Alternative spellings: Aleesha, Aleisha, Alesha, Alicia, Alicja, Aliesha, Alisha, Alysha, Eleisha, Elisher

Elissia

Meaning: Noble
Origin: German
Pronunciation: eh LIS ee ah
Description: Elissia is a German variant of the popular name Alicia.
Alternative spellings: Alecia, Alessia, Alicia, Alicja, Alisia, Alissia, Alycia, Alysia, Alyssia, Elicia

Eliza

Meaning: Promised by God
Origin: Hebrew
Pronunciation: ey LYE zah
Description: Eliza was originally a pet form of the name Elizabeth.
Alternative spellings: Aliza, Alyza, Elyza

Elizabeth

Meaning: Promised by God

Origin: Hebrew
Pronunciation: eh LIZ a buth
Description: From Elisabet, the Greek form of the Hebrew name Elisheva. The name was made popular by Queen Elizabeth I in the 16th century and is still favoured by royals.
Alternative spellings: Elisabeth

Ella

Meaning: All bright
Origin: German
Pronunciation: ELL lug
Description: The name Ella was introduced to Britain by the Normans. It derives from a word meaning 'all' or 'inclusive' but is also a form of Helen, which means 'bright'.
Alternative spellings: Ellah

Elle

Meaning: Bright woman
Origin: French
Pronunciation: ELL
Description: Elle is a modern name from the French word for 'she'. It could also be considered a variant of the Greek name Helen, meaning 'bright'.
Alternative spellings: Ell

Ellen

Meaning: Bright
Origin: Greek
Pronunciation: ELL en
Description: Ellen is a variant form of the Greek name Helen. It originally came into use in the 16th century.

Ellia

Meaning: Promised by God; bright
Origin: Hebrew
Pronunciation: ELL ee ah

Description: A modern contraction of Ella, which has many deriviations. It is often used as a shortening for names beginning with 'El', including Elizabeth and Eleanor.
Alternative spellings: Ellie, Elia

Elliana
Meaning: God has answered; bright
Origin: Hebrew
Pronunciation: ELL ee arn ah
Description: Composed of the Hebrew elements of '*El*', meaning God and '*ana*', meaning '*answered*'. It could also be considered as a variation of the Greek, Helene, meaning 'bright'.
Alternative spellings: Eliana, Eleana

Ellie
Meaning: Bright woman
Origin: French
Pronunciation: ELL lee
Description: Ellie is generally a pet name for a variety of names beginning 'El', in particular the name Eleanor.
Alternative spellings: Elli, Elly

Elliot
See entry in 'Names for Baby Boys A–Z'

Ellis
Meaning: Jehovah is good
Origin: Hebrew
Pronunciation: ELL iss
Description: Ellis derives from a medieval version of Elias. Often used as a transferred surname, Ellis has enjoyed popularity as a unisex name.
Alternative spellings: Eliss, Elliss

Ellise
Meaning: Promised by God
Origin: Hebrew
Pronunciation: eh LEECE
Description: As well as being a spelling variant of the name Elise, Ellise could also have developed in France as a feminine version of the name Elisee. It shares its meaning of 'promised by God' with Elizabeth.
Alternative spellings: Eleese, Elise, Elize, Elyse

Elodie
Meaning: Wealthy
Origin: German
Pronunciation: ell LOAD ee
Description: This name is extremely popular in German- and French-speaking countries and is a variation of the German name Elodia. The element of '*od*' means 'wealth and riches'.
Alternative spellings: Elodi, Elody

Eloisa
Meaning: Famed warrior
Origin: French
Pronunciation: eh loh EE sa
Description: Eloisa comes from the same roots as the name Louise, which is popular in Britain. It could also derive from the French Heloise.
Alternative spellings: Elloisa, Eloisah, Elouisa

Eloise
Meaning: Sun
Origin: French
Pronunciation: EH lo eez
Description: Eloise is the anglicised form of Heloise. It is seen as

a more unique alternative to the name Louise.
Alternative spellings: Elloise, Elouise

Elora
Meaning: Bright
Origin: Greek
Pronunciation: EH lor ah
Description: Elora originally came about as a variation of Eleanor, the French version of the Greek name Helen. It may also be a variation of the name of a group of caves in India.
Alternative spellings: Elaura, Ellora, Elorah

Elowen
Meaning: Elm Tree
Origin: Cornish
Pronunciation: ELL oh wen
Description: From the Cornish word, 'elowenn', meaning 'elm tree'.
Alternative spellings: Ellowen

Elsa
Meaning: Promised by God
Origin: English
Pronunciation: ELL sa
Description: Elsa is a girls' name predominantly seen in Sweden, Germany and England. It is derived from the classic name Elizabeth.
Alternative spellings: Ailsa, Eilsa, Else

Elsie
Meaning: Promised by God
Origin: Hebrew
Pronunciation: ELL see
Description: The name Elsie is a pet form of Elspeth, which

itself is a Scottish variation of the Hebrew name Elizabeth. Elsie is currently experiencing a surge in popularity.
Alternative spellings: Ellsi, Ellsie, Ellsy, Elsi, Elsy

Elspeth
Meaning: Promised by God
Origin: Hebrew
Pronunciation: ELL speth
Description: Elspeth is a Scottish variation of the name Elizabeth. It is gaining popularity and can be found in many places outside of Scotland.
Alternative spellings: Ellspeth, Elsbeth

Elvie
Meaning: Bright white
Origin: Gaelic
Pronunciation: ELL vee
Description: Elvie is a variant of the feminine Irish name Elva. It is thought that the original Gaelic name is Ailbhe, which means 'bright white'.
Alternative spellings: Elvi, Elvy

Elysia
Meaning: Blissful heaven
Origin: Latin
Pronunciation: eh LIZ ee ah
Description: Elysia is a name that comes from the Latin Elysium, the destination of the blessed after death and equivalent to Christianity's heaven.
Alternative spellings: Elisia, Elisya

Eman
See entry in 'Names for Baby Boys A–Z'

Emaan
Meaning: Belief; faith

Origin: Arabic
Pronunciation: ee MAHN
Description: A variation of the name Iman, which can be used as a name for boys and girls. It translates as 'faith' or 'faith in the metaphysical realities of Islam'.
Alternative spellings: Eman, Iman

Ember

Meaning: Spark burning low
Origin: English
Pronunciation: EM burgh
Description: Ember is an English noun that describes the smouldering remains of a fire that appear in the form of glowing ashes.
Alternative spellings: Unknown

Emelia

Meaning: One who excels; friendly
Origin: Latin
Pronunciation: em EE lee uh
Description: This name derives from the Latin name Emily, and in Greek the name means 'friendly'. It could also come from the Germanic Amelia.
Alternative spellings: Amalia, Amelia, Amilia, Emilia, Emilija

Emersyn

Meaning: Son of Emery
Origin: English
Pronunciation: emer SON
Description: Emersyn is a different spelling of the more common Emerson. It is a unisex name that used to be a surname given to those whose father was named Emery.
Alternative spellings: Emerson

Emi

Meaning: All-encompassing

Origin: German
Pronunciation: EH me
Description: Emi is a variant form of Emmi, which is a pet form of the popular name Emma. Emi is now found used as a name in its own right. Emi could also be considered a Japanese name, meaning 'blessed with beauty'.
Alternative spellings: Emmi, Emmie, Emmy, Emy

Emilie

Meaning: One who excels
Origin: French
Pronunciation: EH mill ee
Description: A modern respelling of the popular name Emily.
Alternative spellings: Emilee, Emily

Emilija

Meaning: One who excels
Origin: Latin
Pronunciation: eh MEE lee ah
Description: Emilija is a variant of Emilia, a variation of Emily. The name is Latin in origin, but this spelling is more common in the Baltics.
Alternative spellings: Amalia, Amelia, Amilia, Emelia, Emilia

Emma

Meaning: All-encompassing
Origin: German
Pronunciation: EM muh
Description: Originally a Frankish name, Emma was first used as a short form of names such as Ermintrude.
Alternative spellings: Ema

Emmanuella

Meaning: God is with us

Origin: Hebrew
Pronunciation: eh man yu EH lah
Description: Emmanuella is a variation on Emanuelle, the feminine version of Emanuel.
Alternative spellings: Emmanuela

Emmanuelle
Meaning: God is with us
Origin: Hebrew
Pronunciation: eh man yu EH lah
Description: Emmanuelle is the feminine version of Emanuel.

Emme
Meaning: All-encompassing
Origin: German
Pronunciation: EH me
Description: Emme is a pet form of Emma, a name of Old German origin and one of the most popular girls' names in Britain. Emme is becoming more widely used as a name in its own right.
Alternative spellings: Em, Emm

Emmeline
Meaning: One who excels
Origin: Latin
Pronunciation: EM uh leen
Description: This French version of Emily is part of a current British trend for French names.
Alternative spellings: Emeline, Emmalene, Emmaline, Emmelene

Emmylou
Meaning: All-encompassing
Origin: English
Pronunciation: emmi LOO
Description: Emmylou is a variant of the name Emma and Emmy, both of which mean 'all-encompassing'. Emmylou Harris is a famous country singer with this name.

Enid
Meaning: Purity or soul
Origin: Welsh
Pronunciation: EE nid
Description: From the Welsh, 'eneit', meaning 'purity' or 'soul'. The given name of popular British children's writer Enid Blyton.
Alternative spellings: Eanid, Énide

Eniola
Meaning: Wealthy
Origin: African
Pronunciation: eh ne OH lah
Description: Eniola is an African name, found predominantly in Nigeria. It is thought to come from the Yoruba language, and means 'wealthy one'.
Alternative spellings: Eneola, Eniolah

Enya
Meaning: Kernel
Origin: Gaelic
Pronunciation: EN yah
Description: Enya is a modern variation of the name Eithne, a name found in Irish history, legend and poetry.
Alternative spellings: Enyah

Enyo
Meaning: Warlike
Origin: Greek
Pronunciation: EN yo
Description: In Greek mythology, Enyo was an ancient goddess of war, acting as a companion to the war god Ares.
Alternative spellings: Ennyo, Enyoh

Eowyn
Meaning: Horse lover
Origin: Old English

E

Pronunciation: EOO win
Description: Eowyin is an Old English name meaning 'horse lover'. It was made famous by J. R. R Tolkein, who named one of his *Lord of the Rings* characters Eowyn.

Erica
Meaning: Eternal ruler; heather
Origin: Norse
Pronunciation: EH rih kah
Description: Erica is the feminine version of the Old Norse name Eric. In this sense it shares its meaning of 'eternal ruler'. However, the name Erica could also have roots in Latin, where it would mean 'heather'.
Alternative spellings: Ericka, Erika

Erin
Meaning: Ireland
Origin: Gaelic
Pronunciation: EH rin
Description: This anglicised version of the Irish name Eirinn was used as a poetic name for Ireland for centuries.
Alternative spellings: Aerin, Aeryn, Airin, Eirinn, Eryn

Esa
See entry in 'Names for Baby Boys A–Z'

Esha
Meaning: Desire
Origin: Arabic
Pronunciation: ISH ah
Description: Esha is of Arabic origin and means 'desire'. It is particularly popular with Hindu parents.
Alternative spellings: Eesha, Eshah

Eshal
Meaning: Heavenly flower

Origin: Arabic
Pronunciation: ESH ahl
Description: Eshal is a Quranic baby name that translates as 'heavenly flower'. It is derived from the SH-AIN-L root, similar to other Muslim names includung Ashal and Shaalah.
Alternative spellings: Eshaal

Esma
Meaning: To esteem
Origin: French
Pronunciation: EZ mah
Description: An unusual variant, most likely a deriviation of Esme, an English name from the French word *'esmer'*, meaning 'to esteem'.
Alternative spellings: Esme, Esmé, Esmée, Esmae, Esmai

Esme
Meaning: Respected
Origin: French
Pronunciation: EZ may
Description: Esme is a French name, originally unisex but now more commonly given to girls. It is sometimes thought of as a pet form of Esmerelda.
Alternative spellings: Esmae, Esmee, Esmie

Esmerelda
Meaning: Emerald
Origin: Spanish
Pronunciation: EZ mer EL da
Description: Deriving from the Spanish for emerald.
Alternative spellings: Esmeralda

Esperanza
Meaning: Hope; expectation
Origin: Spanish

Pronunciation: es per AN zah
Description: Esperanza comes from the Spanish vocabulary word for 'hope' or 'expectation'. It has been made popular by jazz singer, Esperanza Spalding.

Essa

Meaning: Salvation
Origin: African
Pronunciation: ESS ah
Description: Essa is a variant of the African unisex name Issa, meaning 'salvation' or 'protection'.
Alternative spellings: Essah, Issa

Estella

Meaning: Star
Origin: Latin
Pronunciation: ESY ell ah
Description: A French feminine name, a derivative of the Latin 'stella', meaning 'star'.
Alternative spellings: Stella, Estellar

Estelle

Meaning: Star
Origin: Latin
Pronunciation: eh STEL
Description: Estelle is from the French 'estella', which derives from the Latin word for 'star', 'stella'.
Alternative spellings: Estell

Estera

Meaning: Star
Origin: Persian
Pronunciation: ESS tair ah
Description: A variant of the Hebrew female name, Esther, based on the name of the Persian goddess, Ishtar, a translation of the word 'star'.

Alternative spellings: Esthera, Esther

Esther

Meaning: Star
Origin: Persian
Pronunciation: ESS ter
Description: Esther is the Hebrew variation of the name of the Persian goddess Ishtar, which means star.
Alternative spellings: Ester, Estha

Ethel

Meaning: Noble
Origin: English
Pronunciation: ETH ell
Description: Ethel, an Old English name meaning 'noble', was popular in the early 1900s.
Alternative spellings: Ethal, Ethelle

Etta

Meaning: Keeper of the hearth
Origin: Germanic
Pronunciation: ETT ah
Description: Etta is a short form of the English name Henrietta, derived from the French Henriette. The female version of Henri, meaning 'home ruler' or 'keeper of the hearth'.
Alternative spellings: Eta, Ette

Ettie

Meaning: Keeper of the hearth
Origin: Germanic
Pronunciation: ETT ee
Description: Ettie is a further variant of the English name Henrietta, derived from the French Henriette. It is originally from the Germanic name Heimiric, derive from the word elements, of 'heim' meaning 'home' and 'ric', meaning of 'power'.
Alternative spellings: Etty, Hetty

E

Eunice
Meaning: Good victory
Origin: Greek
Pronunciation: yoo NIS
Description: Eunice is the Latinised form of the Greek name Eunike, meaning 'good victory'. It is made up of the elements of *'eu'* meaning *'good'* and *'nike'*, which means 'victory'.

Europa
Meaning: Wide eyes
Origin: Greek
Pronunciation: yoo RO pah
Description: In Greek mythology, Europa was seduced by Zeus and became the first queen of Crete. It is also the name of the sixth moon of Jupiter.
Alternative spellings: Europe, Eurupa

Eurydice
Meaning: Broad justice
Origin: Greek
Pronunciation: yur ri DIH see
Description: In Greek mythology, Eurydice was the wife of Orpheus. The story of Eurydice and Orpheus became a popular theme in Renaissance art.
Alternative spellings: Euredice, Euridice

Eva
Meaning: Living
Origin: Hebrew
Pronunciation: EE vuh
Description: The name Eva comes from the Hebrew name Eve, which means 'living' and is the name of the first woman put on the earth in Christian belief.
Alternative spellings: Ewa

Evadne
Meaning: Well
Origin: Greek
Pronunciation: ee VAD nee
Description: In Greek mythology, Evadne was the wife of Capaneus of Argos, who committed suicide after the death of her husband.
Alternative spellings: Evadnee, Evedne

Evalyn
Meaning: Bird
Origin: Latin
Pronunciation: EH va lin
Description: Closely related to the name Evelyn, both names come from the Latin *'avis'*, which means 'bird'.
Alternative spellings: Evelyn

Evangeline
Meaning: Good news
Origin: Greek
Pronunciation: ee VAN geh lene
Description: This name is most often used in English- and French-speaking countries and derives from the word *'evange'*, which is a term for the gospels.
Alternative spellings: Evangelene, Evangilene, Evangiline

Evanna
Meaning: God is gracious
Origin: Welsh
Pronunciation: ee VAN uh
Description: Evanna is a Welsh name meaning 'God is gracious'. Evanna Lynch is a famous British actress who played Luna in the Harry Potter series.

Eve
Meaning: Life

Origin: Hebrew
Pronunciation: EVE
Description: In the Christian tradition, Eve, from the Hebrew *'havva'*, was the first woman. Eve also means 'animal'.
Alternative spellings: Eeve

Evelina

Meaning: Hazelnut
Origin: Norman French
Pronunciation: EV ah LEEN ah
Description: Evelina is a variation of Evelyn, which originated from the Norman French surname, Aveline. The modern French translation of aveline is 'hazelnut'.
Alternative spellings: Evelyna, Evelin, Evelyn

Eveline

Meaning: Hazelnut
Origin: Norman French
Pronunciation: EV eh lin
Description: Eveline is a variant spelling of the English given name, Evelyn. The name originated from the Norman French surname, Aveline, that translates as 'hazelnut'.

Alternative spellings: Evelyn, Aveline, Evelynn

Everly

Meaning: Grazing meadow
Origin: English
Pronunciation: EV er lee
Description: Everly is a unisex variation on the feminine name Evelyn.
Alternative spellings: Everli, Everlie

Evie

Meaning: Life
Origin: Hebrew
Pronunciation: EE vee
Description: Evie originated as a pet form of the names Eve, Eva or Evelyn and is currently extremely popular.
Alternative spellings: Evi, Evy

Evita

Meaning: Living one
Origin: Hebrew
Pronunciation: eh VEE tah
Description: Evita is a Hebrew name meaning 'living one'. It has connections to Eve, who was the first woman in the bible.

F

Fabienne

Meaning: Bean grower
Origin: French
Pronunciation: fa BEE en
Description: Fabienne is a French name meaning 'bean grower'. It is also the feminine version of the name Fabien.

Fahima

Meaning: Chaste
Origin: Arabic
Pronunciation: fah HEE mah
Description: Fahima is a variation of the name Fatima.
Alternative spellings: Faatimah, Fatema, Fathima, Fatima, Fatimah

Fahmida

Meaning: Full of knowledge
Origin: Arabic
Pronunciation: fah ME dah
Description: Fahmida is a name of Arabic origins said to mean 'full of knowledge'. It is predominantly used by parents of the Muslim faith.
Alternative spellings: Fameda, Famida

Faith

Meaning: Faith
Origin: English
Pronunciation: FAYTH
Description: The name Faith comes directly from the word meaning 'confident belief in the truth or a person or idea'.
Alternative spellings: Faithe, Fayth

Faiza

Meaning: Successful
Origin: Arabic
Pronunciation: FAH ee za
Description: Faiza is a name of Arabic origin that means 'successful'. Although uncommon in Britain, Faiza is a popular name in African and Arabic countries.
Alternative spellings: Faizah, Fayiza

Falak

See entry in 'Names for Baby Boys A–Z'

Fallon

Meaning: Chief
Origin: Gaelic
Pronunciation: FAH lin
Description: Fallon is an anglicised version of the Irish surname Fallamhain, which means 'chief'.
Alternative spellings: Fallan

Farah

Meaning: Cheerful
Origin: Arabic
Pronunciation: FAH rah
Description: Farah is a name of Arabic origin and means 'cheerful'.
Alternative spellings: Fara, Farrah

Faria

Meaning: Happiness; towering
Origin: Arabic
Pronunciation: FAH ree ah
Description: Faria could be of Arabic origin and mean 'towering'. It could also mean 'happiness'.
Alternative spellings: Fariah, Farya

Fariha

Meaning: Happiness
Origin: Arabic
Pronunciation: fah REE ha
Description: Fariha comes from an old Arabic word meaning 'happiness'.
Alternative spellings: Farihah, Faryha

Faryal

Meaning: Angel
Origin: Arabic
Pronunciation: far YAAL
Description: Faryal is an Arabic feminine name meaning 'angel'. Related names include Faryaal, Farryal and Farryaal.
Alternative spellings: Faryaal, Farrya, Farryaal

Fatma

Meaning: Chaste
Origin: Arabic
Pronunciation: FAT ma
Description: Fatma is a Turkish variation of the feminine Arabic

name Fatima. It is a popular name among Muslim parents.
Alternative spellings: Fatmah

Faustina
Meaning: Fortunate
Origin: Latin
Pronunciation: foss TEEN ah
Description: Faustina is a Latin name meaning 'fortunate'. It comes from the Latin word *'faustus'*, which gives the name its meaning.

Favour
See entry in 'Names for Baby Boys A–Z'

Fay
Meaning: Fairy
Origin: English
Pronunciation: FAY
Description: Fay is the traditional word for 'fairy'. It is commonly used as a pet form for Faith.
Alternative spellings: Faye

Felicia
Meaning: Happy times
Origin: Latin
Pronunciation: feh LEE shah; feh LISS eh ah
Description: Felicia derives from the Latin phrase *'tempora felicia'* meaning 'happy times'. It is thought to be the feminine equivalent of Felix.
Alternative spellings: Felicya, Felisia

Felicity
Meaning: Happy; fortunate
Origin: Latin
Pronunciation: feh LISS it ee
Description: Like Felicia, Felicity derives from the Latin *'felicia'*

meaning 'happy'. It is also the feminine form of Felix, which means good fortune.
Alternative spellings: Feliciti, Felicitie

Fern
Meaning: Fern plant
Origin: English
Pronunciation: fern
Description: Fern is a feminine name of English origin and comes from the English word for the fern plant. The variant form Fearne has developed to differentiate the name from the plant, and is becoming the more popular form, aided perhaps by the fame of the English radio and television presenter Fearne Cotton.
Alternative spellings: Fearne, Ferne

Ffion
Meaning: Foxglove
Origin: Welsh
Pronunciation: FEE on
Description: Ffion is a name of Welsh origin and is derived from the Welsh name for the foxglove flower.
Alternative spellings: Fion, Fionn, Fyon

Fifi
Meaning: The Lord gave more
Origin: French
Pronunciation: fee fee
Description: Fifi is a diminutive of the name Josephine and as such, shares the same meaning of 'the Lord gave more'.

Fiona
Meaning: Fair-haired

Origin: Gaelic
Pronunciation: fee OH na
Description: Fiona derives from the Gaelic word *'fionn'* meaning 'fair', and shares this derivation with the masculine names Finn and Finlay.
Alternative spellings: Fionah, Fyona

Fiza

Meaning: Breeze
Origin: Urdu
Pronunciation: FEE zah
Description: The name Fiza is most likely of Urdu origin and is popular with Muslim parents.
Alternative spellings: Fizah, Fyza

Fleur

Meaning: Flower
Origin: French
Pronunciation: FLURE
Description: Fleur comes from the French word for 'flower'.

Flick

Meaning: Happy; fortunate
Origin: Latin
Pronunciation: FLIK
Description: Flick is a colloquial pet name for a girl named Felicity. It is not often used as a name in its own right.
Alternative spellings: Flic, Flik

Fliss

Meaning: Happiness; luck; good fortune
Origin: Latin
Pronunciation: flyss
Description: Fliss is an English name that is related to Felicity and shares the same meaning, 'happiness'. Both names have roots in

the Latin word 'felicitas', meaning 'luck' or 'good fortune'.

Flo

Meaning: Flower
Origin: Latin
Pronunciation: FLO
Description: Flo is a short form for Florence or Flora, but is also becoming a name in its own right. Thanks to its meaning of 'flower' the name Flo has connotations of beauty and serenity.
Alternative spellings: Flow

Flora

Meaning: Flower
Origin: Latin
Pronunciation: FLOR ah
Description: The name Flora comes from the Latin word *'flos'*, meaning 'flower'. It is also the name of the Roman mythological goddess of flowers and the spring.
Alternative spellings: Flaura, Florah

Florence

Meaning: Blossoming
Origin: Latin
Pronunciation: FLOR ence
Description: Florence derives from the Latin male name Florentius.
Alternative spellings: Florense, Florenze

Florentina

Meaning: Blooming
Origin: Latin
Pronunciation: floor EN teen uh
Description: Florentina is a Latin name meaning 'blooming'. The Latin root 'flora' means that this name has a strong connotation with flowers and plants.

Florrie

Meaning: Blossoming
Origin: Latin
Pronunciation: FLOH ree
Description: Florrie came about as a pet form of the name Florence, but is now found used as a name in its own right.
Alternative spellings: Flori, Florri, Florry

Flynn

See entry in 'Names for Baby Boys A–Z'

Fran

Meaning: From France
Origin: English
Pronunciation: FRAN
Description: Fran is a short form of names such as Francesca, Francis or Frances. It is sometimes used as a name in its own right.
Alternative spellings: Franne

Frances

Meaning: From France
Origin: Italian
Pronunciation: FRAN sis
Description: The feminine equivalent of Francis, an Italian nickname for a man from France.
Alternative spellings: Francesse

Francesca

Meaning: From France
Origin: Italian
Pronunciation: fran CHESS cuh
Description: The Italian form of Frances, Francesca originally existed as a word for 'French' and still carries its meaning of 'from France'.
Alternative spellings: Franceska, Franchesca

Francine

Meaning: From France
Origin: French
Pronunciation: fran SEEN
Description: Francine is the feminine version of Francis and as such, shares the same meaning of 'from France'.

Frankie

Meaning: Liberated person from France
Origin: French
Pronunciation: FRAN kee
Description: Frankie is a unisex name that means 'he who is free' if taken from the French name Frank, or 'person from France' if taken from the Latin name Francis.
Alternative spellings: Franckie, Franki, Franky

Freida

Meaning: Peace
Origin: German
Pronunciation: FREE dah
Description: Freida is a name of German origin and is a shortened variant of Alfreda. It was common in the early 20th century but has since declined in popularity.
Alternative spellings: Freda, Frida

Frenchy

Meaning: Nickname
Origin: English
Pronunciation: fren CHEE
Description: Frenchy is a possible nickname for Francine or Francesca, but could stand as a given name on its own. Frenchy is a character from the popular movie, *Grease*.
Alternative spellings: Frenchie

F

Freya

Meaning: Goddess of love
Origin: Scandinavian
Pronunciation: FRAY yuh
Description: Freya was the goddess of love in Scandinavian mythology, whose name was derived from the Germanic word *'frouwa'*, meaning 'lady'.
Alternative spellings: Freja, Freyja

Fujiko

Meaning: Wisteria child
Origin: Japanese
Pronunciation: foo JEE ko
Description: This popular Japanese girls' name is made up of the element *'fuji'*, which means 'wisteria', and *'ko'*, which means 'child'.
Alternative spellings: Fujeko, Fujico

Fumiko

Meaning: Strong beautiful child
Origin: Japanese
Pronunciation: foo MEE ko
Description: This Japanese girls' name may mean 'child of treasured body' or 'child of abundant beauty'. Parents hope a child with this name will grow to be a strong successful woman.
Alternative spellings: Fumeko, Fumico

G

Gabriella

Meaning: Strength from God
Origin: Hebrew
Pronunciation: GAB ree EL la
Description: Gabriella is an elaboration upon the girls' name Gabrielle, derived from the archangel Gabriel in Christian belief.
Alternative spellings: Gabriela

Gabrielle

Meaning: Strength in God
Origin: Hebrew
Pronunciation: GAB ree ELL
Description: Gabrielle is the feminine equivalent of the biblical name Gabriel and means 'strength in God'.
Alternative spellings: Gabriele

Gaby

Meaning: Strength from God
Origin: French
Pronunciation: gah BEE
Description: Gaby is a French feminine version of the name Gabriel and as such, shares the same meaning of 'strength from God'.
Alternative spellings: Gabby

Gaia

Meaning: Earth mother
Origin: Greek
Pronunciation: GAY a; GUY a
Description: In Greek mythology, Gaia was the goddess of Earth and the great mother of all.
Alternative spellings: Gaiaa, Gaiya, Gaya

Gail

Meaning: Father of exaltation
Origin: Hebrew
Pronunciation: GAYL
Description: Gail is a girls' name of Hebrew origin and a shortened variant of Abigail.

Alternative spellings: Gael, Gale

Gemma
Meaning: Precious stone
Origin: Italian
Pronunciation: JEM ma
Description: The popular name Gemma comes from an Italian nickname for 'gem', a 'precious stone'.
Alternative spellings: Jemma

Gene
See entry in 'Names for Baby Boys A–Z'

Genesis
Meaning: Birth
Origin: Greek
Pronunciation: jeh EH sis
Description: Genesis is a Greek name meaning 'birth'. It is also one of the most famous books in the Old Testament in the Bible, which tells of the creation of the world and Adam and Eve. Because it is the name of the creation story, the meaning of 'birth' is very appropriate.

Genevieve
Meaning: Woman
Origin: German
Pronunciation: JEN eh veev
Description: Genevieve is a French name of Old German origin. It comes from the words *'geno'* meaning 'people', and *'wefa'* meaning 'woman'. Genevieve is the name of the patron saint of Paris.
Alternative spellings: Geneveve, Genevive

Georgette
Meaning: Farmer; earth worker

Origin: French
Pronunciation: jorge ETTE
Description: Georgette is the female version of the name George, and as such shares the same meaning of 'farmer' or 'earth worker'.

Georgia
Meaning: Farmer
Origin: Greek
Pronunciation: JAW yuh
Description: This feminine form of George was borne by a 5th-century saint. Georgia is a country on the east coast of the Black Sea and a US state.
Alternative spellings: Georgea, Jorgia, Jorja

Georgiana
Meaning: Farmer
Origin: Greek
Pronunciation: jor jee AHN ah
Description: Georgiana is a feminine version of the Greek name George. Georgiana was popular in the 18th century but now the preferred feminine version is Georgina.
Alternative spellings: Georgeana, Jorgiana

Georgie
See entry in 'Names for Baby Boys A–Z'

Georgina
Meaning: Farmer
Origin: Greek
Pronunciation: jor JEE na
Description: First rising to popularity in Scotland in the 18th century, the name Georgina is the feminine version of the Greek name George, meaning 'farmer'.
Alternative spellings: Georgena, Jorgina

G

Geraldine

Meaning: Spear ruler
Origin: French
Pronunciation: geral DEEN
Description: Geraldine is the French and feminine version of the name Gerald and as such, they share the same meaning of 'spear ruler'.

Gertrude

Meaning: Spear strength
Origin: German
Pronunciation: gert RUDE
Description: Gertrude is a German name composed of the elements of *'ger'* meaning 'spear' and *'thrud'* meaning 'strength'.
Alternative spellings:

Gia

Meaning: God is gracious
Origin: Italian
Pronunciation: GEE ah
Description: Gia is a pet form of the name Gianna, which itself is a shortened version of the Italian name Giovanna. Gia is now given as a first name in its own right.
Alternative spellings: Giah, Jia

Gigi

Meaning: Farmer; earth worker
Origin: French
Pronunciation: gee gee
Description: Gigi is most likely a French diminutive of Georgine, which in turn is the female version of George, meaning 'farmer' or 'earth worker'.

Gian

See entry in 'Names for Baby Boys A–Z'

Gianna

Meaning: God is gracious
Origin: Italian
Pronunciation: gee AR na
Description: Gianna is a short form of the Italian name Giovanna, the feminine version of Giovanni. The name is popular in Italy and America.
Alternative spellings: Geanna, Jianna

Gilly

Meaning: Gillyflower
Origin: English
Pronunciation: jil EE
Description: Gilly was invented for the *Game of Thrones* series, and is named after the gillyflower. She is one of the many daughters of Craster in the story.

Gina

Meaning: Queen; farmer
Origin: Italian
Pronunciation: JEE na
Description: Gina came about as a pet form of the names Regina and Georgina. Regina is an Italian name that means 'queen', while Georgina, like George, means 'farmer'.
Alternative spellings: Gena, Jeana

Ginny

Meaning: Of the virgin
Origin: Latin
Pronunciation: jin EE
Description: Ginny is a Latin name meaning 'of the virgin'. Ginny Weasley is a well known character in the Harry Potter series.
Alternative spellings: Jinny

Giovanna

Meaning: God is gracious

Origin: Italian
Pronunciation: GEE oh VAR na
Description: Giovanna is the feminine form of the Italian name Giovanni, itself derived from the name John. Giovanna, Giovanni, Gianna and Gio all share the same meaning as the name John, which is 'God is gracious'.
Alternative spellings: Giovana, Giovannah

Giselle

Meaning: Promised
Origin: German
Pronunciation: ji ZEL
Description: Giselle is of Old German origin, said to mean 'one who was promised'. The spelling Gisele is very popular in France.
Alternative spellings: Gisele, Gisell

Giulia

Meaning: Youth
Origin: Italian
Pronunciation: JOO le ah
Description: Guilia is an Italian girls' name. The anglicised version is Julia.
Alternative spellings: Jiulia, Julia

Giuliana

Meaning: Youthful; graceful
Origin: Italian
Pronunciation: giu LEE ana
Description: Giuliana is an Italian name derived from the Latin word '*iuliana*' meaning 'youthful' or 'graceful'. Many argue that it is a combination of Julia and Anna.

Gladys

Meaning: Country
Origin: Welsh
Pronunciation: GLAD iss

Description: Gladys is a Welsh girls' name of many possible origins. It could come from the Old Welsh name 'gwladus', which means 'country' or 'nation'. There are also suggestions that the name could stem from '*gwledig*' meaning 'ruler', or even that it might be a Welsh version of Claudia.
Alternative spellings: Gladis, Gladiss, Gladyss

Gloria

Meaning: Glory
Origin: Latin
Pronunciation: GLOR ee ah
Description: The name Gloria derives directly from the Latin word for 'glory'.
Alternative spellings: Gloriah, Gloriya

Glory

Meaning: High honour
Origin: English
Pronunciation: gloor EE
Description: Glory comes from the English vocabulary word of the same spelling and means 'high honour'.

Goda

Meaning: River Godavari
Origin: Sanskrit
Pronunciation: GOH da
Description: Goda is a very rare and unusual name of uncertain meaning. It seems to have Sanskrit origins and is thought to come from the name of the River Godavari in India.
Alternative spellings: Godah

Grace

Meaning: Elegance
Origin: Latin

Pronunciation: GRAYSE
Description: The name Grace, meaning 'elegance', came to prominence in the 1540s and was particularly popular in Scotland and northern England.
Alternative spellings: Grayce

Gracie

Meaning: Elegance
Origin: Latin
Pronunciation: GRAY see
Description: Gracie came about as a pet form of the name Grace. It is now a name in its own right and is sometimes given to boys.
Alternative spellings: Gracey, Graci

Greta

Meaning: Pearl; light's creation
Origin: Latin
Pronunciation: GREH ta
Description: Greta, an abbreviated form of Margaret, originates from Sweden and means 'light's creation'.
Alternative spellings: Gretah, Gretta

Gretel

Meaning: Pearl
Origin: German
Pronunciation: gret EL
Description: Gretel is a diminuitive of Grete, which in turn is the short form of Margaret, meaning 'pearl'. Gretel is one half of Hansel and Gretel, from the famous Brothers Grimm fairytale of a witch trying to eat the siblings.

Gurleen

Meaning: Absorbed in the guru's readings
Origin: Sanskrit

Pronunciation: GOOR leen
Description: Gurleen is a name of Punjabi origin, and it means 'absorbed in the guru's readings'. It is often found in India where it is used mostly by Hindu parents.
Alternative spellings: Gerleen, Gurline

Guadalupe

Meaning: From the Guadalupe River
Origin: Spanish
Pronunciation: GUA de loop eh
Description: Guadalupe is a Spanish place name referring to the town that was near the source of the Guadalupe River, which is a pilgrimage site due to the apparition of Our Lady of Guadelupe.

Gwen

Meaning: Fair-haired
Origin: Welsh
Pronunciation: GWEN
Description: Gwen is both an independent name and the shortened form of the names Gwendolen and Gwyneth.
Alternative spellings: Gwenn, Gwyn

Gwendolen

Meaning: Fair-haired; white ring
Origin: Welsh
Pronunciation: GWEN do len
Description: Gwendolen was the wife of the mythical Welsh king, Locrine. It is made up of *'gwen'*, meaning 'fair' and *'dolen'*, a word for 'eyebrows'.
Alternative spellings: Gwendolyn, Gwyndolen

Gwyneth

Meaning: Fair-haired
Origin: Welsh
Pronunciation: GWIN eth
Description: Gwyneth comes from the Welsh name Gwynned, which is derived from the place in North Wales.
Alternative spellings: Gweneth, Gwenyth

Gypsy

Meaning: Wanderer
Origin: English
Pronunciation: gyp SEE
Description: Gypsy is derived from the English vocabulary word of the same spelling and means 'wanderer'.

H

Haaniya

Meaning: Happy; delighted; content
Origin: Indian
Pronunciation: haa NEE ya
Description: Haaniya is an Indian girls' name meaning 'happy,' 'delighted' or 'content'.
Alternative spellings: Hanniyah, Haniya, Haniyah

Habiba

Meaning: Beloved one
Origin: Arabic
Pronunciation: hah BEE bah
Description: Habiba is a name of Arabic origin and means 'beloved one'. It is a popular name with parents of Pakistani descent and those following the Islamic religion.
Alternative spellings: Habbiba, Habibah

Hadassah

Meaning: Myrtle tree
Origin: Hebrew
Pronunciation: had AH saah
Description: Hadassah is a Hebrew name meaning 'myrtle tree'

and was the name of Queen Esther in the Old Testament. The myrtle tree is one of four types of tree that forms the *lulav*, a bouquet made up of palm fronds, willow, citron and myrtle tree branches for the Jewish holiday of Sukkot.
Alternative spellings: Hadassa

Hadia

Meaning: Religious guide
Origin: Urdu
Pronunciation: HAH de ah
Description: Hadia is a name of Urdu origin, most commonly found in Pakistan and in Muslim communities across the world. Its meaning refers to a 'guide on the path of righteousness'.
Alternative spellings: Hadiah, Hadya

Hadiya

Meaning: Religious guide
Origin: Arabic
Pronunciation: HAH dee yah
Description: Hadiya is the feminine version of the masculine name Hadi,

which is said to come from the Arabic for 'true direction of religion'.
Alternative spellings: Hadija, Hadiyah

Hadley
Meaning: Heather meadow
Origin: English
Pronunciation: HAD ley
Description: Hadley is an uncommon given name but a popular surname. It is of Old English origin meaning 'heather meadow'. It is also a unisex name.

Hafsa
Meaning: Lioness
Origin: Arabic
Pronunciation: HAHF sa
Description: Hafsa means 'lioness'. It is the name of one of the wives of the prophet Muhammad who looked after the Quran after Muhammad's death. Hafsa is a popular girls' name within Muslim communities.
Alternative spellings: Hafsah, Hafza

Hajar
Meaning: Emigrant
Origin: Arabic
Pronunciation: hhaa JHAA r
Description: Hajar is a feminine Arabic name meaning 'emigrant'. It also has Hebrew roots and can also mean 'flight'.

Hajra
Meaning: Promise of pilgrimage
Origin: Arabic
Pronunciation: HIJ rah
Description: Hajra is a name that comes from 'Hajj', the name of the annual pilgrimage to Mecca made by Muslims. The name signifies a promise of pilgrimage to the newborn.
Alternative spellings: Hajrah

Halia
Meaning: Island nymph
Origin: Greek
Pronunciation: HAY lee ah
Description: In Greek mythology, the nymph Halia lived alone on the island that would later be named Rhodes.
Alternative spellings: Haliah, Hallia

Halima
Meaning: Gentle-mannered
Origin: Arabic
Pronunciation: ha LEE mah
Description: This Arabic name has some of its roots in the Swahili language and means 'gentle' or 'mild mannered'. It is often shortened to pet forms such as Halma or Hallie.
Alternative spellings: Haleema, Haleemah, Halimah

Halle
Meaning: Ruler of the home
Origin: English
Pronunciation: HAL lee
Description: Halle is pronounced 'hallie' and could derive from the name Hallie or Hayley. The name Hallie has Norwegian and German roots, whereas Hayley is of Old English origin.
Alternative spellings: Halley, Halli, Hallie, Hally

Halo
Meaning: Circular aura of light
Origin: English
Pronunciation: Halo comes from

the English vocabulary word of the same spelling and refers to the circle of light often seen on depictions of angels.
Description: hay LOH

Hamna

Meaning: Dark-coloured berry
Origin: Arabic
Pronunciation: HAM na
Description: Hamna comes from an Arabic word for a 'dark-coloured berry'. In Islamic belief it was the name of the sister of one of the wives of the prophet Muhammad.
Alternative spellings: Hamnah

Hana

Meaning: Blissful
Origin: Arabic
Pronunciation: HA nah
Description: Hana is a name of Arabic origin and its meaning is said to be 'blissful'. It could also be considered a respelling of the popular name Hannah.
Alternative spellings: Hanna, Hannah

Hanan

Meaning: Tenderness
Origin: Arabic
Pronunciation: hah NAN
Description: Hanan is a feminine Arabic name with roots meaning 'tenderness'. Other variations of the name include Haneen, Hanin and even the Hebrew name, Hannah, which has a very similar meaning.

Hania

Meaning: Favoured by God; grace; blissful
Origin: Hebrew

Pronunciation: HAH nee ah
Description: Hania is a name that comes from the Middle East and can be found in Hebrew and Arabic languages. It could be from the same origin as the names Anna and Hannah.
Alternative spellings: Haniah, Haniya

Hanifa

Meaning: Upholder of Islam
Origin: Arabic
Pronunciation: hah NEE fah
Description: The name Hanifa is the feminine form of the masculine Hanif and is popular with Muslim parents.
Alternative spellings: Hanifah, Hanifer

Hannah

Meaning: Favoured by God
Origin: Hebrew
Pronunciation: HAN nuh
Description: A biblical name borne by the mother of the prophet Samuel, from the Hebrew name Hanna. Hannah enjoyed a huge revival in the 1990s.
Alternative spellings: Hana, Hanna

Hari

See entry in 'Names for Baby Boys A–Z'

Harleen

Meaning: Hare and eagle
Origin: English
Pronunciation: HAR leen
Description: Harleen is a feminine variation of the now unisex name Harley. Harleen also shares Harley's meaning of 'hare and eagle'.

Alternative spellings: Harlene, Harline

Harley
See entry in 'Names for Baby Boys A–Z'

Harlow
See entry in 'Names for Baby Boys A–Z'

Harmonia
Meaning: Harmony
Origin: Greek
Pronunciation: har MOAN ee a
Description: In Greek mythology, Harmonia was the immortal goddess of harmony and concord.
Alternative spellings: Harmoniai, Harmoniya

Harmony
Meaning: Pleasing musical sound
Origin: English
Pronunciation: HAR moh nee
Description: The name Harmony has been adapted from the English word. Like the name Melody, it is often used by parents who are fans of music.
Alternative spellings: Harmoney, Harmoni, Harmonie

Harper
Meaning: Harp-player
Origin: English
Pronunciation: HAR per
Description: Harper was originally a surname used by those who had a history of playing the harp. It is now used as a unisex given name and was made famous in 2011 when David and Victoria Beckham named their first daughter Harper Seven Beckham.

Alternative spellings: Harpah, Harpor

Harriet
Meaning: Ruler of the home
Origin: German
Pronunciation: HA ri et
Description: Harriet is an anglicised version of the French name Henriette, the feminine form of Henry. It first appeared in the 17th century then rose in popularity over the next 200 years.
Alternative spellings: Hariet, Harriett, Harriette

Hasna
Meaning: Beautiful one
Origin: Arabic
Pronunciation: HAS nah
Description: Hasna is a name of uncertain meaning but it is generally considered to mean 'beautiful one' or 'strong'.
Alternative spellings: Hasnah, Hazna

Hattie
Meaning: Ruler of the home
Origin: German
Pronunciation: HAT ee
Description: This pet form of Harriet is now a name in its own right.
Alternative spellings: Hatti, Hatty

Havana
Meaning: Capital of Cuba
Origin: Spanish
Pronunciation: hah VAH nah
Description: Havana is the capital city of Cuba, but is also a very popular modern name that is common in Spanish-speaking countries.
Alternative spellings: Havanah

Haven

Meaning: Place of safety; shelter
Origin: English
Pronunciation: HAY ven
Description: Haven is directly taken from the English vocabulary word meaning 'place of safety' or 'shelter'. While its literal meaning is a safe place for ships to dock, it has come to take on a general meaning of refuge.

Hawwa

Meaning: Full of life
Origin: Arabic
Pronunciation: HA wah
Description: Like Hawa, Hawwa is the Arabic equivalent to the name Eve, the first woman created by Allah and predominantly used by Muslim parents.
Alternative spellings: Hawa, Hawwah

Haya

Meaning: Full of life
Origin: Hebrew
Pronunciation: HAH yah
Description: Haya is a variation of the Hebrew name Chava, which means 'full of life'. The name has long been used in the Middle East but is now spreading into other parts of the world.
Alternative spellings: Hayah, Hayar

Hayden

See entry in 'Names for Baby Boys A–Z'

Hayley

Meaning: Clearing of hay
Origin: English
Pronunciation: HAY lee
Description: The name Hayley comes from the surname adopted by those from Hailey in Oxfordshire. It is also a more modern spelling of the Old English name Hayleigh, which comes from the elements of 'hay' and 'leigh', meaning 'a clearing of land'.
Alternative spellings: Hailey, Haylee, Hayleigh, Hayli, Haylie, Hailie

Hazel

Meaning: Hazel tree; light brown
Origin: English
Pronunciation: HAY zell
Description: Hazel, a nut-bearing tree, is also a colour commonly used to describe light-brown eyes.
Alternative spellings: Hazelle, Hazile

Heath

See entry in 'Names for Baby Boys A–Z'

Heather

Meaning: Heather
Origin: English
Pronunciation: HEH ther
Description: The name Heather comes from the moorland plant.
Alternative spellings: Heatha, Hether

Heba

Meaning: Gift
Origin: Arabic
Pronunciation: HE ba
Description: From an Arabic word meaning 'gift', Heba is mainly used by Muslim parents and is popular in Africa and the Middle East. It could also be a variation of the Greek name Hebe.

H

Alternative spellings: Heaba, Hebah

Hebe
Meaning: Youthful
Origin: Greek
Pronunciation: HEE bee
Description: In Greek myth, Hebe was the name of the goddess of youth. The name could also come from New Zealand, where Hebe is a native plant.
Alternative spellings: Heaby, Hebi, Hebie

Hecate
Meaning: Triple-formed
Origin: Greek
Pronunciation: HEK a tee
Description: In Greek mythology, Hecate was an ancient goddess of dark places, often associated with ghosts, witches and sorcery.
Alternative spellings: Hecatee, Hekate

Hecuba
Meaning: Worker
Origin: Greek
Pronunciation: HEK yoo bah
Description: In Greek mythology, Hecuba was married to King Priam of Troy, with whom she had 19 children.
Alternative spellings: Hecabe, Hecueba, Hekuba

Heidi
Meaning: Noble
Origin: German
Pronunciation: HI dee
Description: Heidi is a Swiss pet form of Adelheid, the German form of Adelaide.
Alternative spellings: Heidie, Heidy

Helen
Meaning: Bright
Origin: Greek
Pronunciation: HEL en
Description: The mythical Helen of Troy was known as 'the face which launched a thousand ships'. The name has associations of extreme beauty.
Alternative spellings: Hellen

Helena
Meaning: Bright
Origin: Greek
Pronunciation: HEL eh nuh; hel AY nah
Description: A Latinate form of Helen. Helena carries the same associations of beauty as the name Helen.
Alternative spellings: Helenah, Helene

Helice
Meaning: She-bear
Origin: Greek
Pronunciation: HEL ee see
Description: In Greek mythology, Helice was beloved by Zeus, but Hera, out of jealousy, metamorphosed her into a she-bear, whereupon Zeus placed her among the stars.
Alternative spellings: Helise, Helyce

Hemera
Meaning: Day
Origin: Greek
Pronunciation: he MEE ra
Description: In Greek mythology, Hemera was one of the earliest Greek deities and the personification and goddess of daytime.
Alternative spellings: Hemerah, Hemira

Henley
See entry in 'Names for Baby Boys A–Z'

Hennessy
Meaning: Choice
Origin: Irish
Pronunciation: hen ESS ee
Description: Hennessy is a surname meaning derived from the Irish word '*aonghus*' meaning 'choice.' This follows the contemporary trend of using last names as first names.

Henrietta
Meaning: Ruler of the home
Origin: German
Pronunciation: hen ree EH tah
Description: Henrietta, the feminine equivalent of Henry, was made popular in 17th-century England when Charles I married Henrietta Marie.
Alternative spellings: Henriette, Henryetta

Hera
Meaning: Lady
Origin: Greek
Pronunciation: HEH rah
Description: In Greek mythology, Hera was the queen of the ancient Greek pantheon. She was the wife of Zeus and the goddess of marriage, childbirth and the home.
Alternative spellings: Heera, Herah

Hermione
Meaning: Travel
Origin: Greek
Pronunciation: her MY o nee
Description: In Greek mythology, Hermione was the daughter of Helen of Troy and Menelaus, King of Sparta.
Alternative spellings: Hermioney, Hermioni

Hero
Meaning: Courage
Origin: Greek
Pronunciation: HERE row
Description: In Greek mythology, Hero was a priestess of Aphrodite. In modern English, a hero is a man admired for his courage or noble qualities. Heroine is the female equivalent.
Alternative spellings: Hiro

Hester
Meaning: Star
Origin: English
Pronunciation: hes TAR
Description: Hester is the Latin form of the biblical name, Esther. It is a name most commonly found in England but it was also popularised by Nathaniel Hawthorne's book, *The Scarlet Letter*, where the protagonist was called Hester Prynne.

Hestia
Meaning: Home
Origin: Greek
Pronunciation: HESS tee ah
Description: In Greek mythology, Hestia was the virgin goddess of the hearth, the family and the state.
Alternative spellings: Hestiaa, Hestya

Hetty
Meaning: Star
Origin: Greek
Pronunciation: HEH tee
Description: Hetty came about as a pet form of the name Hester, but

H

is now used as a name in its own right. Hester is Greek in origin and means 'star'.
Alternative spellings: Hetti, Hettie

Hiba
Meaning: Gift
Origin: Arabic
Pronunciation: HIB ah
Description: Hiba is a name of Arabic origin and comes from an Arabic word meaning 'to give' or 'gift'. It is very important in Islamic belief to give charitably and it is from this that the name Hiba has come about.
Alternative spellings: Hibah, Hibba

Hilary
Meaning: Cheerful
Origin: Latin
Pronunciation: HIL uh ree
Description: Hilary is from the Latin word *'hilaris'*, which shares the same root as 'hilarious'.
Alternative spellings: Hilari, Hilarie, Hillary

Hilda
Meaning: Battle
Origin: German
Pronunciation: HILL da
Description: Hilda is a German girls' name, from the element of *'hild'* meaning 'battle'.
Alternative spellings: Hildah

Himeko
Meaning: Princess child
Origin: Japanese
Pronunciation: HEE meh ko
Description: This baby name can be written using a variety of Japanese character combinations. Depending on the characters used it can either mean 'princess child'

or 'sun and rice child'.
Alternative spellings: Himekoh

Hippodamia
Meaning: Ladybird
Origin: Greek
Pronunciation: hee po DAY mee ah
Description: In Greek mythology, Hippodamia was the bride of King Pirithous of the Lapiths. It is also the scientific name given to the ladybird.
Alternative spellings: Hippodaymia, Hippodaymya

Hippolyta
Meaning: Loosener of horses
Origin: Greek
Pronunciation: he POL it ah
Description: In Greek mythology, Hippolyta was an Amazonian queen who possessed a magical girdle. The male version of the name is Hippolytus.
Alternative spellings: Hippolita

Hira
Meaning: Diamond
Origin: Sanskrit
Pronunciation: HIH rah
Description: The name Hira can be unisex, although using different pronunciations. The masculine form is pronounced 'hih-rar' whereas the feminine form is pronounced 'hih-ra'. The name comes from an old Sanskrit word said to mean 'diamond'.
Alternative spellings: Hirah, Hirra

Hiromi
See entry in 'Names for Baby Boys A–Z'

Holly

Meaning: Holly
Origin: English
Pronunciation: HOLL lee
Description: The name Holly comes from the word for the ever-green tree. It was traditionally given to girls born around Christmas.
Alternative spellings: Holley, Holli, Hollie

Honey

Meaning: Honey
Origin: English
Pronunciation: HUN ee
Description: The name Honey comes from the word for the sweet substance produced by bees. It is also a term of affection but a rare given name.
Alternative spellings: Hunnie, Hunny

Honor

Meaning: Honour
Origin: Latin
Pronunciation: Hon Or
Description: Honor derives from the Latin name Honoria, which also means 'honour'. The name could be considered a variant of the English word for 'personal integrity' or 'fame and glory'.
Alternative spellings: Honour

Hope

Meaning: Hope
Origin: English
Pronunciation: HOPE
Description: From the word meaning 'a feeling of desire or expectation for a certain thing to happen.' Hope is considered one of the 'quality names' like Charity and Faith and is often favoured by Christian parents.

Huda

Meaning: Guidance
Origin: Arabic
Pronunciation: HOO dah
Description: Huda, popular among Muslim parents, means 'guidance'.
Alternative spellings: Hudah, Hudda

Humaira

Meaning: Reddish colour
Origin: Arabic
Pronunciation: hugh MARE ah
Description: The name Humaira means 'reddish colour' in Arabic. In Islamic belief it was the nickname that the prophet Muhammad gave to his wife Aisha due to her rosy red cheeks.
Alternative spellings: Humairah, Humera

Husna

Meaning: Kindness
Origin: Arabic
Pronunciation: HOOS nah
Description: Husna means 'kindness' and is a popular name in Pakistan.
Alternative spellings: Husnah

Hyacinth

Meaning: Flower
Origin: English
Pronunciation: high AH synth
Description: Hyacinth refers to the flower of the same name and is found throughout the world. Like Rose and Tulip, Hyacinth is part of the trend of using Flowers for given names.

H

I

Ianthe
Meaning: Violet flower
Origin: Greek
Pronunciation: eye AN theh
Description: From the Greek words *'ion'* and *'anthos'*, meaning 'violet' and 'flower' respectively.
Alternative spellings: Ianthie

Ida
Meaning: Hard-working
Origin: German
Pronunciation: EYE dah
Description: The name Ida was brought to Britain by the Normans and was made popular in the 19th century by Lord Alfred Tennyson. It can mean both 'hard-working' and 'princess'.
Alternative spellings: Idah, Iyda

Iga
Meaning: Fight
Origin: German
Pronunciation: EE gah
Description: The name Iga originally came about as a pet form of the name Jadwiga, which is itself the Polish variant of the German name Hedwig. Hedwig means 'battle fight' and Iga also shares this meaning.
Alternative spellings: Igah, Iyga

Ikram
See entry in 'Names for Baby Boys A–Z'

Imaan
Meaning: Faith
Origin: Arabic
Pronunciation: im MAAN
Description: Imaan is the feminine version of the name Iman. It comes directly from the Arabic word *'iman'*, which means 'faith' and 'believer'.
Alternative spellings: Imarn

Iman
See entry in 'Names for Baby Boys A–Z'

Imani
Meaning: Faith; dependable
Origin: Arabic
Pronunciation: ee MAH nee
Description: Imani can be seen as the feminine version of the Arabic name Iman, meaning 'faith', or a diminutive form of the name Amina, meaning 'dependable'.
Alternative spellings: Imanie

Imogen
Meaning: Maiden
Origin: Shakespeare
Pronunciation: IHM oh jen
Description: This name derives from the Celtic name Innogen, meaning 'maiden'. Imogen features in Shakespeare's play *Cymbeline* where it is the name of a strong heroine.
Alternative spellings: Imojen

Inaaya
Meaning: Gift from God
Origin: Arabic
Pronunciation: ihn AH yah
Description: Inaaya is a name of Arabic origin, believed to mean 'gift from God' or 'one to behold'. Of the spelling variations, some

have separate meanings. The short form is Inny or Immy,
Alternative spellings: Inaiya, Inaya, Inayah, Inyaih

Inaya
Meaning: Empathy
Origin: Arabic
Pronunciation: in NY yah
Description: Inaya is another spelling variation of the Arabic name Inaaya; however its meaning of 'empathy' is different to Inaaya, which is 'gift from God'.
Alternative spellings: Inaaya, Inaiya, Inayah, Inyaih

India
Meaning: India
Origin: English
Pronunciation: IN dee uh
Description: India is a relatively modern name, taken from the name of the Asian country.
Alternative spellings: Indiya, Indya

Indiana
Meaning: India
Origin: English
Pronunciation: in dee AHR nah; in dee ANN ah
Description: Indiana is an elaboration on the feminine name India. However, Indiana Jones is the name of the fictional male character from the Indiana Jones franchise.
Alternative spellings: Indianah, Indyana

Indie
Meaning: India; blue; independent
Origin: English
Pronunciation: IN dee

Description: Indie seems to have come about as a pet form of the names India and Indigo and its meaning can therefore vary. The name can either mean 'blue' or 'from India'. The word 'indie' is often used in English as a shortened form of the word 'independent'.
Alternative spellings: Indi, Indy

Indigo
Meaning: Indian plant
Origin: English
Pronunciation: IN dih go
Description: Indigo, like India, became popular in the 1970s when Indian culture was fashionable and it is the name of an Indian plant. Recently, Indigo has surged in popularity along with other colour names such as Blue and Violet.
Alternative spellings: Indygo

Indira
Meaning: Beauty
Origin: Sanskrit
Pronunciation: In DEER ah
Description: A name of Hindu and Sanskrit origin, Indira means 'beauty' or 'splendid'. The name became well known in the 1970s and 80s when Indira Gandhi was India's first female Prime Minister.
Alternative spellings: Indeera

Ines
Meaning: Pure
Origin: Greek
Pronunciation: EE ness
Description: Ines is a variant of the name Agnes, which is Greek in origin and means 'pure'. The form Ines is the Spanish version of the name. It is popular in

I

Spanish-speaking countries, especially Mexico.
Alternative spellings: Inez

Ingrid
Meaning: Beauty
Origin: Norse
Pronunciation: IN grid
Description: The name Ingrid comes from the Norse element of *'ing'* meaning 'beauty'. Ing was also the name of a Norse god of fertility. The name is mostly popular in Scandinavia.
Alternative spellings: Engrid, Ingryd

Ino
Meaning: White goddess
Origin: Greek
Pronunciation: EYE no
Description: In Greek mythology, Ino was a mortal queen of Thebes who, after her death, was worshipped as a goddess.
Alternative spellings: Eyno, Iyno

Io
Meaning: Heifer
Origin: Greek
Pronunciation: EYE oh
Description: In Greek mythology, Io was a young maiden who was loved by Zeus. She was turned into a heifer – a young female cow – by Zeus to protect her from Hera.
Alternative spellings: Eyo

Ioana
Meaning: God is gracious
Origin: Greek
Pronunciation: ee OH ah nah
Description: Ioana is a variation of the name Ioanna, which in turn is a Greek variation of the name Joanna. The name ultimately means 'God is gracious,' as the name has its roots in the biblical name John. Related names include the Bulgarian Yoana, as well as the variant spellings of Joanna.

Iole
Meaning: Violet
Origin: Greek
Pronunciation: EYE oh lee
Description: Iole is an uncommon girls' name of Greek origin. The name is the transliteration of the classic Greek word for a violet.
Alternative spellings: Eyole

Iona
Meaning: Island
Origin: Norse
Pronunciation: Eye Own Ah
Description: The name Iona comes from the Scottish island Ioua, named as the 'dew-tree island'. It could also derive from the English name Ione, which means 'violet'.
Alternative spellings: Ionah

Iqra
Meaning: To read
Origin: Arabic
Pronunciation: ihk RAH
Description: The name Iqra comes from an Islamic word that refers to the process of reading, hence its meaning of 'to read'. It is a rare name in Britain, used mainly in Islamic communities.
Alternative spellings: Ikra, Iqrah

Irene
Meaning: Peace
Origin: Greek

Pronunciation: eye REEN
Description: Irene is a Greek name meaning 'peace'. Eirene was the Greek goddess of peace.

Irina

Meaning: Peace
Origin: Greek
Pronunciation: ee REE nah
Description: Irina is a popular girls' name of Greek origin. The name is one of the most common female names in Eastern Europe and Russia.
Alternative spellings: Arina, Irene, Iryna

Iris

Meaning: Rainbow
Origin: Greek
Pronunciation: EYE riss
Description: The name Iris derives from Greek mythology, where Iris was a messenger of the gods and the personification of the rainbow. It is now linked to the English flower name.
Alternative spellings: Iriss

Isabella

Meaning: Promised by God
Origin: Latin
Pronunciation: IS uh BELL luh
Description: The Latin form of Isabel and derived from the name Elizabeth. Along with its alternate spellings, the name has surged in popularity recently, possibly due to the success of the Twilight franchise, in which Isabella is the full name of the main character.
Alternative spellings: Isabela, Isobela, Isobella, Izabela, Izabella, Izzabella

Isabelle

Meaning: Promised by God
Origin: French
Pronunciation: IS uh BELL
Description: This French form of Isabel is derived from Elizabeth. Isabelle is the most popular spelling of this name.
Alternative spellings: Isabel, Isabell, Isobel, Isobelle, Izabel, Izabelle, Izzabelle

Isadora

Meaning: Gift from Isis
Origin: Greek
Pronunciation: eye sa DOR ah
Description: The name Isadora derives from the male name Isadore, meaning 'gift from Isis', the Egyptian god. It can also be considered a feminine version of the name Iadore, which was used in Greece before and during the Christianisation of the Roman Empire.
Alternative spellings: Isadorah, Isadorra

Isha

Meaning: Woman; goddess
Origin: Sanskrit
Pronunciation: EE shaa
Description: Isha is a unisex name and is often found in India. As a feminine name it means 'woman' and is the name of the goddess Durga, whereas in the male form it means 'the Lord'.
Alternative spellings: Esha, Ishah

Isla

Meaning: From Islay
Origin: English
Pronunciation: EYE luh
Description: First coined in the 20th century in Scotland, the name

I

Isla originates from the island of Islay in the Hebrides.
Alternative spellings: Eila

Isma

Meaning: Protection
Origin: Arabic
Pronunciation: IS ma
Description: Isma is an unusual name in the UK, though is more popular in the Middle East. It is of Arabic origin and means 'protection' or 'safeguarding of the prophets'.
Alternative spellings: Ismah

Ismene

Meaning: Knowledgeable
Origin: Greek
Pronunciation: is MEE nee
Description: Ismene is Greek in origin. In Greek mythology, Ismene was a daughter of Oedipus.
Alternative spellings: Ismeneh, Ismine

Isra

Meaning: Night journey
Origin: Arabic
Pronunciation: IS ra
Description: Isra is of Arabic origin and means 'night-time journey'. Its meaning refers to the prophet Muhammad's night journey to Jerusalem, where he met Jesus and Moses before returning to Mecca that night.
Alternative spellings: Israh

Israel

See entry in 'Names for Baby Boys A–Z'.

Issa

Meaning: Salvation
Origin: African
Pronunciation: ESS ah

Description: Issa is a variant of the African name Essa, meaning 'salvation' or 'protection'. It can be used for both baby boys and girls.
Alternative spellings: Essa, Essah

Ivana

Meaning: Gift from God
Origin: Russian
Pronunciation: EE van na
Description: Ivana is the feminine form of the name Ivan, which is the Slavic form of the name John, which is where the meaning 'gift from God' comes from. Related names include Ivanka, Iva and Ivka.
Alternative spellings: Ivanah

Ivie

Meaning: Faithfulness
Origin: English
Pronunciation: i VEE
Description: The name Ivy is taken straight from the creeping green plant often seen growing on the site of buildings or gardens. The name was popular at the beginning of the 20th century, though is far less common nowadays.
Alternative spellings: Ivy

Ivory

Meaning: White
Origin: English
Pronunciation: EYE voree
Description: Ivory comes from the English vocabulary word of the same name, referring to the white-ish colour. The name also refers to the tusks of animals, especially elephants, which are the same colour.

Iyla

Meaning: Moonlight
Origin: Sanskrit

Pronunciation: EYE la
Description: It is thought that Iyla originates from India and means 'moonlight'. It could also be considered a variant of the Persian name Lyla.
Alternative spellings: Eila, Ila

Iylah

Meaning: Scottish island
Origin: Scottish
Pronunciation: ie LAH
Description: Iylah is a variation of the Scottish name Isla and that in turn is a variation of the name Islay, referring to the island off the west coast of Scotland.

Alternative spellings: Iyla, I sla

Izzy

Meaning: Promised by God
Origin: Hebrew
Pronunciation: IH zee
Description: Izzy originally came about as a shortened form of the name Elizabeth or Isabelle. Izzy is a relatively modern name in its own right and is especially popular in Britain. Izzy can also be found as a boys' name; however it is rare and does not come from the name Elizabeth.
Alternative spellings: Izzi, Izzie

I
J

J

Jacinta

Meaning: Hyacinth
Origin: Spanish
Pronunciation: jah SIN tah
Description: Jacinta is the Spanish name for the flower, hyacinth. It ultimately comes from the Greek word '*hyakinthos*'.
Alternative spellings: Jacintah

Jacqueline

Meaning: Supplanter
Origin: Hebrew
Pronunciation: JAK eh lin; JAK eh leen
Description: Jacqueline is the feminine diminutive form of Jacques, the French version of James.
Alternative spellings: Jacquelean, Jacqueleen, Jacquelyn

Jada

Meaning: Green stone; precious
Origin: English
Pronunciation: JAY dah
Description: Jada is a relatively modern name and can be seen as a development of Jade.
Alternative spellings: Jaida, Jayda

Jade

Meaning: Green stone; precious
Origin: English
Pronunciation: JAYD
Description: Jade comes from the Spanish name for the precious stone. The word can be literally translated as 'stone of the bowels', and jade was believed to offer protection against intestinal disorders. The name also means 'precious'.
Alternative spellings: Jaide, Jayde

Jagoda

Meaning: Berry
Origin: German
Pronunciation: yah GOW dah
Description: Jagoda is an unusual name that comes from a Slavic word meaning 'berry'. It is often found in Croatia and Poland.
Alternative spellings: Jagodah

Jaime

Meaning: Supplanter; love
Origin: Hebrew
Pronunciation: JAY me
Description: A variation of the unisex name Jamie. The verb *'aimer'* means 'to love' in the French language, which gives this name a double meaning.
Alternative spellings: Jaimy, Jamie

Jamila

Meaning: Beautiful
Origin: African
Pronunciation: jah MEEL ah
Description: Jamila is the feminine version of Jamil or Jamal. The names mean 'handsome' so we can take the feminine meaning to be 'beautiful'.
Alternative spellings: Jameela, Jamela, Jamilah

Jana

Meaning: God is gracious
Origin: Hebrew
Pronunciation: JAH nah
Description: Jana is a variant of the name Jane, itself a version of the masculine name John.
Alternative spellings: Janah

Jane

Meaning: God is gracious
Origin: Hebrew
Pronunciation: JAYN
Description: Jane was originally a feminine form of John, but is now a given name in its own right.
Alternative spellings: Jaine, Jayne

Janelle

Meaning: God is gracious
Origin: English
Pronunciation: je NEL
Description: Janelle is a modern version of the name Jane and has only been used since the 20th century. It is ultimately derived from the name John, meaning 'God is gracious'.

Janet

Meaning: God is gracious
Origin: Hebrew
Pronunciation: JAN et
Description: The name Janet is a diminutive of the name Jane. It also derives from the French Jeanette.
Alternative spellings: Janett, Janette, Jannet

Jannah

Meaning: Garden of heaven
Origin: Arabic
Pronunciation: JAH nah
Description: The Arabic name Jannah refers to the Islamic paradise or 'garden of heaven' and is a popular name with Muslim parents.
Alternative spellings: Janah, Janna

Jannat

Meaning: Heaven
Origin: Persian
Pronunciation: ja NAT

Description: Jannat is a name of Persian origin, which has become popular in India too. It is said to mean 'heaven'. Jannat is also the name of a famous Bollywood film.
Alternative spellings: Janat

Jasleen

Meaning: Jasmine flower
Origin: Persian
Pronunciation: JAZ leen
Description: Jasleen is a modern variant form of the name Jasmine. Often shortened to Jas or Jaz.
Alternative spellings: Jaslene, Jasline

Jasmin

Meaning: Jasmine flower
Origin: Persian
Pronunciation: JAZ min; YAZ min
Description: The name Jasmin is of Persian origin and can also be found in its original form: Yasmin. The flower is used in Thailand as a symbol for 'mother'.
Alternative spellings: Jasmine, Jazmin, Jazmine, Yasmin

Javeria

Meaning: Bringer of happiness
Origin: Arabic
Pronunciation: jah VEER ah
Description: In Islamic belief, Javeria is the name of one of the wives of the prophet Muhammad.
Alternative spellings: Javeriah, Javeriya

Jay

See entry in 'Names for Baby Boys A–Z'

Jaya

See entry in 'Names for Baby Boys A–Z'

Jayda

Meaning: Precious
Origin: English
Pronunciation: jay DAH
Description: Jayda is likely to be a development of Jade, and is a relatively modern name. Jade is a feminine name that comes from the English noun referring to the precious stone, similar to the name Ruby. In this way its meaning is 'precious'.

Jayla

Meaning: Unknown
Origin: English
Pronunciation: JAY la
Description: Jayla is a relatively modern name created from the names Kayla and Jay. Jayla is part of a trend to form new names that have no specific meaning but are phonetically pleasing.
Alternative spellings: Jaila, Jaylah

Jaylan

See entry in 'Names for Baby Boys A–Z'

Jean

Meaning: God is gracious
Origin: Hebrew
Pronunciation: JEEN; ZHAHN
Description: Jean is a unisex name most often found on girls. As a male name it derives from the Hebrew name John, as a feminine name it comes from Jane.
Alternative spellings: Gene, Gine

Jeanette

Meaning: God is gracious

Origin: French
Pronunciation: jean ETT
Description: Jeanette is a French name meaning 'God is gracious' and is a variation of the name Jeanne. It is also related to Janet and Janette.

Jeanne

Meaning: God is gracious
Origin: French
Pronunciation: jee ANNE
Description: Jeanne is a French, feminine version of the name John and as such, shares the same meaning of 'God is gracious'.

Jemima

Meaning: Handsome
Origin: Hebrew
Pronunciation: je MYE ma
Description: In the Old Testament, Jemima was the eldest daughter of Job. Although its peak of popularity was in the 19th century, it is still used today.
Alternative spellings: Gemima, Jemimah

Jemma

Meaning: Precious stone
Origin: Italian
Pronunciation: JEM ah
Description: Jemma is a version of the Italian name Gemma.
Alternative spellings: Gemma

Jenna

Meaning: White-haired
Origin: Gaelic
Pronunciation: JEN na
Description: Originally a shortened form of Jennifer, but can now be found as a name in its own right.
Alternative spellings: Jena, Jenah

Jennifer

Meaning: White-haired
Origin: Gaelic
Pronunciation: JEN ih fur
Description: Jennifer, a very popular baby name in the UK, derives from the Welsh name Guinevere, which is the name of the legendary King Arthur's wife.
Alternative spellings: Jenifer

Jenny

Meaning: White-haired
Origin: Welsh
Pronunciation: JEH ne
Description: Jenny came about as a pet form of the name Jennifer, but can now be seen as a name in its own right.
Alternative spellings: Jeni, Jenney, Jenni, Jennie

Jermaine

Meaning: Of Germany
Origin: German
Pronunciation: JER mane
Description: Jermaine is an alternative spelling for the more usual Germaine, and is thought to mean 'from Germany'.
Alternative spellings: Germaine, Germane, Jermane

Jerry

See entry in 'Names for Baby Boys A–Z'

Jersey

Meaning: From Jersey
Origin: Norse
Pronunciation: JER zee
Description: Jersey, the name of the largest of the Channel Islands, is also an American state. The

name has Norse origins and means 'grassy island'.
Alternative spellings: Jersie, Jersy

Jess

Meaning: Gift
Origin: Hebrew
Pronunciation: JESS
Description: Jess originally came about as a shortened form of the girls' names Jessie or Jessica but is now found as a unisex name in its own right.
Alternative spellings: Jesse

Jessa

Meaning: Gift
Origin: Hebrew
Pronunciation: jess AH
Description: Jessa is a short form of the name Jessica, and shares the same meaning of 'gift'.

Jessica

Meaning: Gift
Origin: Hebrew
Pronunciation: JESS ikker
Description: This name is thought to have been created by Shakespeare in his play *The Merchant of Venice*. It could also be a name of Hebrew origin.
Alternative spellings: Jessicah, Jessicka, Jessika

Jessie

Meaning: Gift
Origin: Hebrew
Pronunciation: JESS ee
Description: Jessie is often used as a pet form of the names Jessica and Jess and is often seen as a unisex name in its own right.
Alternative spellings: Jesse, Jessi, Jessy

Jia

Meaning: Champion
Origin: Sanskrit
Pronunciation: jay
Description: Jai could be the short form of several names but it is also a name in its own right. It is also spelt Jay, is of Sanskrit origin and in this form is usually masculine but is found used for both boys and girls. It is said to mean 'champion'. When used as a short form of any name starting with a 'Jay' sound it was originally given as a nickname meaning 'chatty,' in reference to the jay bird.

Jiay

Meaning: Sweet heart
Origin: Sanskrit
Pronunciation: jee YA
Description: Jiya is a name popular among Hindus and other religious groups in India. It is said to mean 'sweet heart'. It is not very common in the UK but is slowly gaining in popularity.

Jo

Meaning: God is gracious
Origin: Hebrew
Pronunciation: JO
Description: Jo may be the shortened form of any girls' name beginning with 'Jo—', such as Joanna or Jolene.
Alternative spellings: Joe

Joan

Meaning: God is gracious
Origin: Hebrew
Pronunciation: JONE
Description: One of the more old-fashioned female variants of 'John'. Predominantly a female name, this

can occasionally be found as a male name.

Joanna

Meaning: God is gracious
Origin: Hebrew
Pronunciation: jo AN nuh
Description: Joanna is a variation of the name Joanne, itself a feminine version of the masculine name John.
Alternative spellings: Joana, Joannah

Joanne

Meaning: God is gracious
Origin: Hebrew
Pronunciation: jo AN
Description: Joanne is one of a few feminine versions of the Hebrew name John. In France the name started as Johan, before coming to Britain in the 12th century and developing into Joanna and Joanne.
Alternative spellings: Johanne

Jocelyn

Meaning: Lord
Origin: English
Pronunciation: JOSS sa lin
Description: It is thought that the name Jocelyn is a mixture of the feminine names Joyce and Lynn. While Joyce is of Latin origin and means 'Lord', Lynn comes from an Old English surname meaning 'water pool'.
Alternative spellings: Jocelin, Josslin, Josslyn

Jodie

Meaning: From Judea
Origin: English
Pronunciation: JO dee
Description: Jodie is a feminine spelling of the unisex name Jody.
Alternative spellings: Jodi, Jody

Jody

See entry in 'Names for Baby Boys A–Z'

Joelle

Meaning: One true God
Origin: French
Pronunciation: jo ELLE
Description: Joelle is the feminine version of the name Joel, and as such shares the same meaning of 'one true God'.

Joely

Meaning: Pretty
Origin: French
Pronunciation: jo LEE
Description: Joely has its roots in French and is most likely a variation of the word '*jolie*' meaning 'pretty'. Joely Richardson is a famous British actress with this name.

Johanna

Meaning: God is gracious
Origin: Hebrew
Pronunciation: yoh HAN nah
Description: Johanna is a continental variant of the name Joanna. Both of the names are ultimately of Hebrew origin and mean 'God has given'. Note the difference in pronunciation.
Alternative spellings: Johannah, Yohanna

Jojo

Meaning: Nickname
Origin: English
Pronunciation: jojo

Description: Jojo is a nickname for names such as Jolene and Josephine, but can also stand as a given name on its own. Jojo is a famous American singer with this name.

Jolene

Meaning: No meaning
Origin: English
Pronunciation: jo LEEN
Description: Jolene is a modern, invented name combining 'jo' with the suffix 'lene'. As such, it has no meaning.

Jolie

Meaning: Pretty
Origin: French
Pronunciation: jo LEE
Description: Jolie comes from the French word for 'pretty' and has recently been adopted into a girls' given name.
Alternative spellings: Joley, Joli

Joni

Meaning: God is gracious
Origin: Hebrew
Pronunciation: JONE ee
Description: A modern spelling variant of the name Joanie.
Alternative spellings: Joanie, Joany, Jonie

Jordan

Meaning: Flowing down
Origin: Hebrew
Pronunciation: JOR den
Description: The name Jordan was originally given to children baptised using the holy water from the River Jordan. It is also the name of a country.
Alternative spellings: Jorden, Jordon, Jordun, Jordyn

Jorgie

Meaning: Farmer
Origin: Greek
Pronunciation: jorge EE
Description: Jorgie is an alternative spelling of the name Georgie, which itself is a pet name of names such as Georgina. While Jorgie is a more modern construction, Georgina and similar names are heavily featured in legendary stories.
Alternative spellings: Georgie

Jorja

Meaning: Farmer
Origin: Latin
Pronunciation: JORJ aah
Description: Jorja is a fairly modern variation of the English name Georgia. The meaning derives from the Greek word *'georgos'*, which means 'farmer'.
Alternative spellings: Georga, Jorga

Josephina

Meaning: The Lord gave more
Origin: German
Pronunciation: JO zeh FEE nuh
Description: Josephina is a variant of the Hebrew name Josephine.
Alternative spellings: Josefina, Josephena

Josephine

Meaning: The Lord gave more
Origin: Hebrew
Pronunciation: JO zeh feen
Description: The name Josephine is one of the feminine versions of the biblical name Joseph and shares its meaning of 'God will give more'.
Alternative spellings: Josefine, Josephene

J

Josie

Meaning: The Lord gave more
Origin: Hebrew
Pronunciation: JO see
Description: Although Josie started as a pet name for the name Josephine, it is a first name in its own right.
Alternative spellings: Josey, Josi, Josy

Josslyn

Meaning: Member of German tribe
Origin: German
Pronunciation: JAWS lin
Description: Josslyn is a variation of the more common Joselyn and comes from the French name Gautzelin, which is a name for a member of an old German tribe called the Gauts.
Alternative spellings: Joselyn

Joy

Meaning: Joy
Origin: Latin
Pronunciation: JOY
Description: The name Joy comes from the word meaning 'extreme happiness'. It may also be considered a pet form of Joyce.

Joyce

Meaning: Lord; joy
Origin: Breton
Pronunciation: JOYS
Description: Joyce originally comes from the Breton name 'Iodoc', meaning 'Lord'. It was first adapted to Jodocus, then to the male name Josce. Joyce disappeared as a male name in the 14th century.
Alternative spellings: Joyse

Judith

Meaning: Of Judea
Origin: Hebrew
Pronunciation: JOO dith
Description: Judith is a biblical name borne by a Jewish heroine and beautiful widow who delivered her people from invading Assyrians. Judith can be taken to mean 'from Judea'.
Alternative spellings: Judithe, Judyth

Judy

Meaning: Of Judea
Origin: Hebrew
Pronunciation: JOO dee
Description: Judy is a Hebrew name that is closely related to Judith, meaning 'of Judea'. Judith is a biblical name borne by a Jewish herione.
Alternative spellings: Judi, Judie

Jules

Meaning: Bearded youth
Origin: Latin
Pronunciation: JOOLZ
Description: Jules is a unisex baby name of Latin origin, meaning 'down-bearded youth'. It is found in both English- and French-speaking countries. The name is the French form of Julius. In English, as a girls' name, it is often used as a pet form of Julia.
Alternative spellings: Jools

Julia

Meaning: Youth
Origin: Latin
Pronunciation: JOO lee ah
Description: Julia is a feminine form of the Roman family name

Julius, famously shared by Julius Caesar.
Alternative spellings: Guilia, Juliah

Julianna
Meaning: Youth
Origin: Latin
Pronunciation: JOO lee AN uh
Description: The name Julianna is a modern combination of Julia and Anna. It could also be considered as a spelling variant of the Latin name Juliana, which is the feminine form of Julian.
Alternative spellings: Juliana, Juliannah, Julyanna

Julianne
Meaning: Youth
Origin: Latin
Pronunciation: JOO lee AN
Description: The feminine form of the male name Julian. Or it is often considered to be a modern combination of the names Julia and Anne.
Alternative spellings: Juliane, Julyanne

Julie
Meaning: Youth
Origin: Greek
Pronunciation: JOO lee
Description: Julie is the French form of Julia, but is also used as a pet form of Juliana and Juliette. All of these names stem from the masculine name Julius, which is of Latin origin.
Alternative spellings: Juley, Juli

Juliet
Meaning: Youth
Origin: Latin

Pronunciation: JOO lee et
Description: Juliet is a form of the Latin name Julia, made famous by the lead female character in Shakespeare's play *Romeo and Juliet*. Juliette is the French version of this name.
Alternative spellings: Juliett, Juliette

June
Meaning: Month of June
Origin: English
Pronunciation: JOON
Description: June is a name coined from the English word for the summer month, and is popular with babies either born or conceived at this time of year. Interestingly, the month of June was named after the Roman goddess Juno.
Alternative spellings: Gune

Juniper
Meaning: Juniper tree
Origin: English
Pronunciation: JOON ip er
Description: The name Juniper comes from the type of tree of the same name, which has evergreen-like needles and a distinctive type of berry that is used in a variety of culinary dishes and is a primary flavouring in gin. Juniper is one of a long line of flower-and plant-related names.

Juno
Meaning: Queen of heaven
Origin: Latin
Pronunciation: JOO no
Description: Juno is a name of Latin origin. In Roman mythology it was the name of the queen of the

J

gods; the equivalent of the Greek goddess Hera.
Alternative spellings: Junoh

Justina
Meaning: Fair; just
Origin: Latin
Pronunciation: JUST een ah
Description: Justina is the anglicised version of Latin name Iustina and the female version of the name Justin. Both names are

related to the word 'justice' and as such, mean 'fair' or 'just'.

Justine
Meaning: Fair; just
Origin: Latin
Pronunciation: jus TEEN
Description: Justine is the feminine form of the name Justin, which is of Latin origins.
Alternative spellings: Justeen, Justene

K

Kacey
Meaning: From Cayce
Origin: English
Pronunciation: kay CEE
Description: Kacey is a modern alternative spelling of the name Casey. It is more commonly given as a female name but could be also given as a boys' name. Casey was a name given to Casey Jones as he hailed from a town called Cayce. This name could also be given to someone with the initials K.C.
Alternative spellings: Kaci, Kacie, Casey

Kadie
Meaning: Pure
Origin: Greek
Pronunciation: KAY dee
Description: Kadie is a modern name that has come about as an elongated version of the name Kay or a variation of the popular name Katie. Most of these names come from the Greek name Kathoros, which means 'pure'.

Alternative spellings: Kadi, Kady

Kaede
Meaning: Maple
Origin: Japanese
Pronunciation: kah eh DH
Description: This unisex Japanese name is written using only one character. It is an unusual character also used for the word 'maple'. The name could also be considered a spelling variation of the name Kayda.
Alternative spellings: Kaeida, Kaeide

Kaelan
See entry in 'Names for Baby Boys A–Z'

Kai
See entry in 'Names for Baby Boys A–Z'

Kaia
Meaning: Pure

Origin: Greek
Pronunciation: KAY ah
Description: The name Kaia is thought to be an elongated version of Kay, which is a pet form for many names starting with the letter K. It could also be a unisex name meaning 'restful place'.
Alternative spellings: Kaiya, Kaja, Kaya

Kaira
Meaning: Dark-haired
Origin: Gaelic
Pronunciation: KARE ah
Description: Kaira is a variant of the more commonly found Keera, or Keira. These names are all feminine versions of the masculine name Kieran, meaning 'dark one'.
Alternative spellings: Kaera, Kayra

Kaitlin
Meaning: Pure
Origin: Greek
Pronunciation: KATE lin
Description: It is believed that this name derives from the Old Greek name Catherine and is a spelling variant of the Irish name Caitlin. Like Katherine, it is often shortened to Kate.
Alternative spellings: Caitlin, Caitlyn, Catelin, Catelyn, Kaitlyn, Katelin, Katelyn, Katelynn

Kaja
Meaning: No meaning
Origin: English
Pronunciation: kye AH
Description: Kaja is a feminine name, thought to be an elongated version of the name Kay. Kay originated as a pet form for many

names starting with a K such as Katherine. It later became a name in its own right and since the variations Kaja and Kaya have formed.

Kali
Meaning: The dark one
Origin: Sanskrit
Pronunciation: KAH lee
Description: Kali is the name of the Hindu goddess of time. It derives from a Sanskrit word meaning 'the dark one'. Kali is thought of as the bringer of death, but depending on the beliefs of the individual she can also been seen as a benevolent god.
Alternative spellings: Cali, Kalli

Kamila
Meaning: Sacrifice
Origin: Latin
Pronunciation: cah MIL ah
Description: Kamila is a variant of Camilla, a name that originates from Roman mythology. It was the name for the queen of the Volsci, who was known for being a fast runner and a great warrior. This spelling is usually found in Poland.
Alternative spellings: Camila, Camilla, Kamilla

Kamile
See entry in 'Names for Baby Boys A–Z'

Kaori
Meaning: Fragrant fabric
Origin: Japanese
Pronunciation: kah O ree
Description: This Japanese name is considered one of the prettiest

K

for girls in Japan. This name is often spelt using the character of *'kao'* meaning 'incense' or 'perfume' together with the character *'ri'*, which stands for 'fabric' or 'to weave'.

Alternative spellings: Kaorhi, Kaorie

Kaoru

See entry in 'Names for Baby Boys A–Z'

Kara

Meaning: Dearest
Origin: Italian
Pronunciation: KAR ah
Description: Kara is a spelling variant of the name Cara, which is of Italian origin and means 'dearest'.
Alternative spellings: Cara, Carah

Karen

Meaning: Pure
Origin: Greek
Pronunciation: KA ren
Description: A Danish equivalent of Katherine introduced to America by Scandinavian settlers.
Alternative spellings: Caren, Karin, Karren

Karina

Meaning: Loved one
Origin: Italian
Pronunciation: ka REE nah
Description: Karina derives from an Italian word for 'dearest one'. A spelling variant can be found in the Italian phrase *'che carina'*, meaning 'how lovely'. It is a relatively modern name also often found in northern Europe.

Alternative spellings: Careena, Carina, Kareena

Karis

Meaning: Graceful
Origin: Greek
Pronunciation: KARE iss
Description: Karis is a Greek name that has spread throughout Europe.
Alternative spellings: Carice, Caris, Carys, Karice, Kariss, Karys

Karla

Meaning: Free man
Origin: German
Pronunciation: KAR lah
Description: Karla is the feminine version of the name Karl. This spelling is more common in continental Europe.
Alternative spellings: Carla

Karlie

Meaning: Free man
Origin: English
Pronunciation: KAR lee
Description: Karlie is a variation of the name Carly, which in turn is the feminised version of the name Carl, meaning 'free man'. Karlie Kloss is a famous supermodel.
Alternative spellings: Carlie, Carly

Karolina

Meaning: Free man
Origin: German
Pronunciation: ka ro LINE a
Description: The name Karolina ultimately derives from the masculine name Charles, which means 'free man'. It is a spelling variant of Carolina and can be most

commonly found in English- and Polish-speaking countries.
Alternative spellings: Carolina, Carolyna

Kasey
See entry in 'Names for Baby Boys A–Z'.

Katarina
Meaning: Pure
Origin: Greek
Pronunciation: kah tah REE nah
Description: Katarina is a variant of the popular name Katherine. Although ultimately Greek in origin, Katarina is most likely to be found in Eastern European countries.
Alternative spellings: Catarena, Catarina, Caterena, Caterina, Katarena, Katerena, Katerina

Katarzyna
Meaning: Pure
Origin: Greek
Pronunciation: kat ar ZEE nah
Description: Katarzyna is a variant of the Greek name Catherine and is one of the most popular names in Poland at this time. The name comes from the Greek word 'katharos', meaning 'pure'.
Alternative spellings: Katarzena, Katarzina

Kate
Meaning: Pure
Origin: Greek
Pronunciation: KAYT
Description: Kate is a short form of Katherine, and shares the meaning of 'pure'.
Alternative spellings: Cate, Kaite

Katherine
Meaning: Pure
Origin: Greek
Pronunciation: KATH er in
Description: Katherine is another form of the name Catherine. The name has many variants but all of them derive from the Greek word 'katharos', which means 'pure'.
Alternative spellings: Catharin, Catharine, Catharyn, Catherin, Catherine, Catheryn, Cathryn, Katharin, Katharine, Katherin, Katheryn, Kathryn

Kathleen
Meaning: Pure
Origin: Greek
Pronunciation: kath LEEN
Description: Kathleen is one of the many variants based on the name Katherine. Kathleen seems to have come from Ireland, where it is most popular.
Alternative spellings: Cathleen, Cathlene, Kathlene

Kathy
Meaning: Pure
Origin: English
Pronunciation: KATH ee
Description: Kathy is a shortened version of the name Katherine and both names mean 'pure'. Kathy is often a nickname of Katherine but can stand as a name in its own right as well.
Alternative spellings: Cathy

Katie
Meaning: Pure
Origin: Greek
Pronunciation: KAY tee
Description: The name Katie

K

started as a pet form of Katherine but is now a first name in its own right.

Alternative spellings: Kaity, Katey, Kati, Katy

Katrina

Meaning: Pure
Origin: Greek
Pronunciation: cah TREE nah
Description: Katrina is one of the many variants of the name Katherine and shares its meaning of 'pure'.

Alternative spellings: Catrina

Katya

Meaning: Promised by God
Origin: Russian
Pronunciation: kat YAH
Description: Katya is a shortened version of the Russian name Yekaterina and Ekaterina, meaning 'pure'. All of these names are the Russian version of the Hebrew name Elizabeth and share the meaning 'promised by God'.

Alternative spellings: Katja

Kay

Meaning: Pure
Origin: English
Pronunciation: KAY
Description: Kay is a pet form of any name beginning with the letter K, but also a name in its own right.

Alternative spellings: Kae

Kaya

Meaning: Pure
Origin: English
Pronunciation: KAY ah
Description: Kaya is thought to be an elongated version of the name Kay.

Alternative spellings: Kaia, Kaiya, Kaja

Kaya

Meaning: Restful place
Origin: Japanese
Pronunciation: KAY ah
Description: Kaya is an unusual unisex name. Its origins are Japanese, Zulu, Turkish, Hopi and Hindi, and other meanings are 'yew tree', 'forgiveness', 'home' and 'wise child'.

Alternative spellings: Kaia, Kaiya, Kaja

Kaycee

Meaning: Vigilant guard
Origin: Gaelic
Pronunciation: KAY see
Description: A phonetically spelt variant of the unisex Casey and Kasey.

Alternative spellings: Casey, Casie, Cayce, Caycie, Caysie, Kacey, Kaci, Kacie, Kacy, Kasey, Kasie, Kaycie, Kaysie

Kayd

See entry in 'Names for Baby Boys A–Z'

Kaydee

Meaning: Pure
Origin: Greek
Pronunciation: KAY dee
Description: Kaydee is a phonetic spelling of Kady, and both are likely to be a modern variant of Katie.

Alternative spellings: Kadi, Kadie, Kady, Kaydey, Kaydi, Kaydie

Kaydence

Meaning: Rhythm
Origin: English

Pronunciation: KAY dense
Description: Kaydence, derived from cadence, follows the trend for phonetically spelt names. It has risen in popularity in recent years.
Alternative spellings: Cadence, Kadence

Kayla

Meaning: Who is like God?
Origin: Hebrew
Pronunciation: KAY lah
Description: Probably a pet form of the name Michaela, this relatively modern name is popular in the US.
Alternative spellings: Kaela, Kaylah

Kaylee

Meaning: Slender
Origin: Gaelic
Pronunciation: KAY lee
Description: Although the origin of Kaylee is uncertain, some speculate that it is a variant of Kayla. Both names could come from the Gaelic name Caoilainn, meaning 'slender' or from the name Michaela meaning 'who is like God?'.
Alternative spellings: Kayleigh, Kayley

Kaysha

Meaning: Fruit tree
Origin: Hebrew
Pronunciation: KAY shuh
Description: Kaysha is a name of uncertain origin. It is possible it is a Hebrew name that means 'fruit tree'. However, it could also derive from the modern name Keisha.
Alternative spellings: Caysha, Kaesha, Kaisha

Kazumi

See entry in 'Names for Baby Boys A–Z'

Keavy

Meaning: Precious
Origin: Gaelic
Pronunciation: KEE vee
Description: The name Keavy is a variant of the anglicised form of the Gaelic name Caoimhe, which is pronounced 'keeva'. The names come from the Old Gaelic word *'caomh'* meaning 'precious'.
Alternative spellings: Keavi, Keavie, Keevy

Keeva

Meaning: Beautiful; gentle; kind
Origin: Gaelic
Pronunciation: kee VAH
Description: Keeva is the phonetic spelling of the Irish name, Caoimhe. In Gaelic, the name comes from the word 'caomh,' meaning 'beautiful,' 'gentle' and 'kind'. The male version of the name is Caomhin – or Kevin, in English.

Keelan

See entry in 'Names for Baby Boys A–Z'

Keeley

Meaning: White; slender
Origin: Gaelic
Pronunciation: KEE lee
Description: Keeley is most likely to be derived from the Irish name 'Caoilfhionn' and is possibly the Gaelic version of Kelly. It could also come from 'Caoilinn', meaning 'slender'.
Alternative spellings: Keeli, Keelie, Keely

K

Kei
See entry in 'Names for Baby Boys A–Z'

Keiko
Meaning: Blessed child
Origin: Japanese
Pronunciation: KAY koh
Description: This name has its roots in the Japanese language and is one of the most popular Japanese names ending in 'ko'. Depending on the characters used to spell this name the meaning can vary from 'joyful child' to 'respectful child'.
Alternative spellings: Kaiko

Keira
Meaning: Dark-haired
Origin: Gaelic
Pronunciation: KEER uh
Description: Keira is a variant of the Gaelic name Ciara. Like Kiera, it is also the feminine form of Kieran.
Alternative spellings: Keirah, Kiera, Kira, Kyra

Keisha
Meaning: Prosperous
Origin: Arabic
Pronunciation: KEE sha
Description: The name Keisha became popular in the 1980s. It is probably a variation of the Arabic Aisha.
Alternative spellings: Keesha, Keysha

Kelis
Meaning: Unknown
Origin: American
Pronunciation: keh LEES
Description: As Kelis is most likely a recently created name, its meaning is uncertain.
Alternative spellings: Keliss, Kellis

Kelly
Meaning: Bright-headed
Origin: Gaelic
Pronunciation: KEL lee
Description: Kelly is most commonly found as a girls' name despite originating from the Irish male name Ceallach.
Alternative spellings: Kelli, Kellie

Kelsea
Meaning: Victorious ship
Origin: English
Pronunciation: KEL see
Description: Kelsea is a variant of the unisex name Kelsey, most commonly used for girls. The names are thought to derive from the Old English word *'ceolsige'*, which means 'victorious ship'.
Alternative spellings: Kelsey, Kelsi, Kelsie, Kelsy

Kelsey
See entry in 'Names for Baby Boys A–Z'

Kendra
Meaning: Keen power
Origin: English
Pronunciation: KEN dra
Description: Kendra is the feminine version of the English surname Kendrick and it shares its meaning of 'keen power'.
Alternative spellings: Kendrah

Kennedy
See entry in 'Names for Baby Boys A–Z'

Kenza

Meaning: The fairest
Origin: Gaelic
Pronunciation: KEN zah
Description: Kenza is the feminine variant of the name Kenzie, which derives from the Gaelic surname McKenzie – itself part of a group of surnames now popular as first names. Both Kenzie and Kenza share the surname's meaning of 'the fairest'.
Alternative spellings: Kensa, Kenzah

Kenzie

Meaning: Fair one
Origin: Gaelic
Pronunciation: ken ZEE
Description: When anglicised, Kenzie becomes Kenneth. Kenzie is usually adopted in the USA as a shortened form of Mackenzie. The meaning of Mackenzie varies between 'fair one' for a girl, or 'son of the fair one' for a boy.

Kerem

See entry in 'Names for Baby Boys A–Z'

Keren

Meaning: Ray of power
Origin: Hebrew
Pronunciation: KARE en
Description: Keren is a name of biblical origins. It means 'ray of power'. In the Bible Keren was the name of one of the three daughters of Job. It could also be considered a variant of the name Karen.
Alternative spellings: Kerin, Kerren

Kerry

Meaning: Descendants of Ciar
Origin: Gaelic
Pronunciation: KEH ree
Description: Kerry was originally a surname, from the Irish county of the same name. Kerry means 'descendants of Ciar' and the original Gaelic spelling is Chiarrai. The name is unisex, but is more commonly given to girls.
Alternative spellings: Kerrey, Kerri, Kerrie

Keya

Meaning: Flower
Origin: Sanskrit
Pronunciation: KAY ah
Description: The name Keya comes from the Bengali word for 'flower'. In Hindu scripture the god Brahma uses the name of the flower in a story called 'The Cursed Flower'.
Alternative spellings: Keeya

Kezia

Meaning: Cassia spice
Origin: Hebrew
Pronunciation: key ZYE ah
Description: Kezia comes from the Hebrew name for 'cassia spice', which is a general term for spices such as cinnamon. In the Bible it was the name of the second daughter of Job.
Alternative spellings: Keziah, Kezzia, Kezziah

Khadija

Meaning: Early child
Origin: Arabic
Pronunciation: ka DEE ja
Description: Khadija is an Arabic name meaning 'early baby' and

K

is traditionally given to babies born earlier than expected. In the Quran it is the name of one of the wives of the prophet Muhammad. The spelling variants of this name are all popular names.

Alternative spellings: Khadeeja, Khadeejah, Khadijah

Khaleesi
Meaning: Queen
Origin: English
Pronunciation: KA lee see
Description: A name derived from George. R. R. Martin's popular series, Game of Thrones, Khaleesi means 'queen' in Dothraki, a language invented for the series.

Khloe
Meaning: Greenery
Origin: Greek
Pronunciation: klowh EE
Description: Khloe is a variant spelling of Chloe, and is a modern form of the name that has appeared along with many other 'C' names that have been replaced by 'K,' which is a very modern trend. Chloe is of Greek origin and is said to mean 'greenery'; it was another name given to the Greek goddess Demeter, who was the protector of fields of greenery.
Alternative spellings: Chloe

Khushi
Meaning: Happiness
Origin: Sanskrit
Pronunciation: KUSH ee
Description: Khushi may have come about as a short form of the masculine name Khushiram, however the form Khushi is only seen on girls. The name is often found in India and its meaning is thought to relate to happiness.

Alternative spellings: Kushee, Kushi, Khushy

Kia
Meaning: Go well
Origin: English
Pronunciation: KEE ah
Description: The name Kia is thought to originate from New Zealand, where the phrase *'kia ora'* is used as a greeting to wish someone well.
Alternative spellings: Kiah

Kiana
Meaning: Ancient
Origin: English
Pronunciation: kee AHN ah
Description: The name Kiana may derive from the Gaelic name Cian, which means 'ancient'.
Alternative spellings: Chiana, Ciana, Kianah, Kianna

Kiara
Meaning: Bright
Origin: Latin
Pronunciation: kee AH ra; KEER ah
Description: The name Kiara is mainly used in English-speaking countries, especially England and America. It is thought that this name derives from the Italian name Chiara, which was borne by Saint Chiara of Assisi.
Alternative spellings: Chiara, Chiarah, Ciara

Kiki
Meaning: No meaning
Origin: French
Pronunciation: kee kee

Description: Kiki is a French name was originally a nickname at the turn of the last century. As such, it has no meaning as it is a nickname that has slipped into the mainstream as a given name.

Kim

Meaning: Wood clearing
Origin: English
Pronunciation: KIM
Description: Kim is a short form of Kimberley, but also an independent given name for both boys and girls.
Alternative spellings: Kimm

Kimberley

Meaning: Wood clearing
Origin: English
Pronunciation: KIM ber lee
Description: Kimberley is the name of a South African town named after a Lord Kimberley, whose surname originates from England. The name is unisex but most often found on girls in the UK.
Alternative spellings: Kimberlee, Kimberleigh, Kimberly

Kimmy

Meaning: Wood clearing
Origin: English
Pronunciation: kim EE
Description: Kimmy is a diminutive of the name Kimberley and as such, means 'wood clearing'.
Alternative spellings: Kimmi, Kimmie

Kimora

Meaning: Unknown
Origin: English
Pronunciation: ki MOH rah
Description: Kimora is a modern name thought to have evolved

from the name Kimberley.
Alternative spellings: Kimmora, Kimorah

Kinga

Meaning: Brave in war
Origin: German
Pronunciation: KIN gah
Description: Kinga is the pet form of the Old German name Kunegunda, meaning 'brave in war'. The name is often found in Germany, Poland and Hungary; however, its use is unusual in the UK.
Alternative spellings: Kingah

Kinsley

Meaning: King's woods
Origin: English
Pronunciation: kins LEE
Description: Kinsley is an English surname derived from the elements of 'cyne' meaning 'kingly' and 'lëah' meaning 'wood'. As a given name, it was first used in America.

Kinza

Meaning: Hidden treasure
Origin: Arabic
Pronunciation: KIN za
Description: The name Kinza comes from the Arabic word 'kinz', meaning 'hidden treasure'. The name has extreme associations with wealth.
Alternative spellings: Kinsa, Kinzah

Kiran

See entry in 'Names for Baby Boys A–Z'

Kirika

Meaning: Natural beauty
Origin: Japanese
Pronunciation: ki ri KA

Description: Kirika is written using the Japanese characters of *'kiri'*, meaning 'plant' and *'ka'*, meaning 'summer flower'. Therefore the name has lots of associations with nature and plant life.
Alternative spellings: Kirikah, Kiryka

Kirsten
Meaning: Follower of Christ
Origin: Latin
Pronunciation: KUR sten
Description: Kirsten is the Scandinavian form of the Latin name Christine.
Alternative spellings: Kirstenne, Kirstin

Kirsty
Meaning: Follower of Christ
Origin: Gaelic
Pronunciation: KUR stee
Description: Kirsty is a diminutive of the name Christine or Kirsten, but now a popular name in its own right.
Alternative spellings: Kirstey, Kirsti, Kirstie

Kitty
Meaning: Pure
Origin: Greek
Pronunciation: KIT ee
Description: Originally a short form of Katherine but now used as a name in its own right.
Alternative spellings: Kitti, Kittie

Kiva
Meaning: Protected
Origin: Hebrew
Pronunciation: KEY va
Description: The name Kiva is closely related to the Hebrew name Akiva, meaning 'protector'.

Though typically considered a girls' name, it is in fact unisex.
Alternative spellings: Keeva, Kivah

Kiya
Meaning: Unknown
Origin: Arabic
Pronunciation: KYE ah
Description: The name Kiya can be traced back to Egyptian history as the name of the wife of the Pharaoh Akhenaten. It is generally considered to have roots in the Arabic language but has an uncertain meaning.
Alternative spellings: Kiyah

Kizzy
Meaning: Spice
Origin: African
Pronunciation: KEE zee
Description: Kizzy is a name of uncertain origin, but possibly a pet form of Kezia, which could carry the same meaning of 'spice' as Cassia.
Alternative spellings: Kizzi, Kizzie

Klara
Meaning: Clarity
Origin: Latin
Pronunciation: KLAH ra
Description: Klara is an alternate spelling of Clara, meaning 'clarity'. This spelling is often found in Eastern Europe.
Alternative spellings: Clara

Klaudia
Meaning: Lame
Origin: Italian
Pronunciation: claw de AH
Description: Klaudia is a spelling variation of the name Claudia. It is popular to modernise names by

replacing 'c' with 'k'. Claudia is a feminine name of Roman origin and like its masculine equivalent, Claud, it comes from the Roman name Claudius, which is said to mean 'lame'.
Alternative spellings: Claudia

Kodi
See entry in 'Names for Baby Boys A–Z'

Korey
See entry in 'Names for Baby Boys A–Z'

Kornelia
Meaning: Horn
Origin: Latin
Pronunciation: kor nee lee AH
Description: Kornelia, more usually spelt Cornelia, is the feminine equivalent of the masculine name Cornelius. Cornelius was a Roman family name thought to have come from the Latin word 'cornu' meaning 'horn'.
Alternative spellings: Cornelia

Kristen
Meaning: Follower of Christ
Origin: Latin
Pronunciation: KRIS ten
Description: Kristen is a variant of the name Christine, meaning 'follower of Christ'. Kristen is found more in Eastern Europe where 'K' often replaces 'C' at the beginning of names.
Alternative spellings: Christen, Cristen, Kristenne, Kristin

Kristian
See entry in 'Names for Baby Boys A–Z'

Kristina
Meaning: Christian
Origin: English
Pronunciation: kris TEE nah
Description: Kristina is a feminine name that is derived from the name Christine, the feminine equivalent of the masculine Christian and used for the same purpose. It comes from the English word 'Christian' and refers to a follower of Christianity.
Alternative spellings: Cristina, Christina

Krystal
Meaning: Christian; precious
Origin: German
Pronunciation: KIRS tul
Description: Krystal is a modern spelling variation of Crystal. Crystal is a feminine name that can come from two sources. It could be from the English noun referring to the precious stone, similar to the name Jade. In this way its meaning is seen as 'precious'. However, it is also found as a variation of the German name Christel, which is itself a variation of Christine. Christine is the feminine version of Christian, and means literally 'Christian'.
Alternative spellings: Crystal

Kya
Meaning: Unknown
Origin: English
Pronunciation: KYE ah
Description: The name Kya is especially popular with African-American parents. It is thought to be a variation of the names Kyla or Kai, given for its phonetically pleasing sound.
Alternative spellings: Kyah

Kyla

Meaning: Beautiful or narrow spit of land
Origin: Gaelic
Pronunciation: kye LAH
Description: Kyla is a Gaelic name, which may have two meanings. It could be a derivative of the name Cadhla, which means 'beautiful', or it may be the feminine version of the name Kyle, which means 'narrow spit of land'.
Alternative spellings: Kylah

Kylie

Meaning: Boomerang
Origin: Australian
Pronunciation: KY lee
Description: An Australian name said to mean 'boomerang'. Kylie could also be of Irish origin and mean 'graceful'.
Alternative spellings: Kiley, Kyley, Kyli

Kyoko

Meaning: Respectful child
Origin: Japanese
Pronunciation: kyo KOH
Description: This name derives from the Japanese name Kyouko, which is pronounced with a longer 'o' sound.
Alternative spellings: Kioko, Kyokoh

L

Laaibah

Meaning: Most beautiful from heaven
Origin: Arabic
Pronunciation: LAY bah
Description: Laaibah is a popular Arabic girls' name. It means 'most beautiful from heaven' and has connotations with beauty and religion.
Alternative spellings: Laaiba, Laiba, Laibah, Layba, Laybah

Lacey

Meaning: Laced
Origin: English
Pronunciation: LAY see
Description: Lacey is a unisex name, taken from the surname Lassy. It could also derive from the fabric lace.
Alternative spellings: Laci, Lacie, Lacy, Laicee, Laicey, Laycie

Laila

Meaning: Dark-haired
Origin: Persian
Pronunciation: LAY la
Description: Laila is a variant of the Persian name Leila, meaning 'dark-haired'.
Alternative spellings: Lailah, Layla, Laylah, Leila, Leilah, Leyla

Lainey

Meaning: Bright
Origin: Greek
Pronunciation: LAYN ee
Description: Lainey is the pet form of the name Elaine, a French variant of the name Helen. The name carries

connotations of beauty and brightness.

Alternative spellings: Lainey, Laini, Lainie, Lainy, Laney, Lanie, Lany, Laynee, Laynie, Leni

Lana

Meaning: Little rock
Origin: Gaelic
Pronunciation: lahn AH
Description: Lana is likely to be a Gaelic name meaning 'little rock,' although it could also be a short-ened version of the German name Alana.

Laney

Meaning: Bright
Origin: French
Pronunciation: LAY nee
Description: As well as being a spelling variant of Lainey, mean-ing 'bright', the name Laney also derives from the French surname Delaney. A unisex name most com-monly found on girls.
Alternative spellings: Lainey, Laini, Lainie, Lainy, Lanie, Lany, Laynee, Laynie, Leni

Lara

Meaning: From Larissa; cheerful
Origin: Russian
Pronunciation: LA ra
Description: Lara is a shortened Russian form of the name Larissa, and it first ventured into the English-speaking world in the early 20th century. It is considered a name in its own right.
Alternative spellings: Larah, Larrah

Laraib

Meaning: Undoubting

Origin: Urdu
Pronunciation: lah RAYB
Description: Laraib is a name of Urdu origin, from a word meaning 'undoubting'. It is often favoured by parents following the Islamic faith.
Alternative spellings: Laraaib, Larayb

Larissa

Meaning: From Larissa; cheerful
Origin: Greek
Pronunciation: lah RISS ah
Description: Larissa originates from Greece where it is the name of a city. It may have originally been used for girls born there, but could also come from the Latin *'hilaris'*, meaning 'cheerful'.
Alternative spellings: Larisa, Larissah

Larna

Meaning: River; rock
Origin: Welsh
Pronunciation: LAHR na
Description: Larna is a variant of the Celtic name Lana. Both names derive from Alana, the feminine form of Alan.
Alternative spellings: Lahna, Lana

Latifah

Meaning: Gentle
Origin: African
Pronunciation: lah TEE fah
Description: The name Latifah comes from a Swahili word mean-ing 'gentle'. The name is found mainly in Africa.
Alternative spellings: Latefah, Latifa

Latisha

Meaning: Happy

L

Origin: Latin
Pronunciation: lah TEE sha
Description: Latisha is a variant of the Latin Laetitia, the Roman goddess associated with joy.
Alternative spellings: Laetitia, Latishah, Leticia

Latoya
Meaning: Victorious One
Origin: Latin
Pronunciation: la TOY ah
Description: Latoya is a Latin name meaning 'victorious one'. It originates from the Spanish Toya, which is a nickname for Victoria.

Laura
Meaning: Laurel
Origin: Latin
Pronunciation: LAW ruh
Description: Laura is the feminine form of the Latin name Laurus, meaning 'laurel'. The name was popularised in part by Italian poet Petrarch, who wrote love poems to a woman named Laura.
Alternative spellings: Laurah, Lora

Laurel
Meaning: Laurel
Origin: English
Pronunciation: LOH rul
Description: Originally Laurel was a feminine name, deriving from the Old English laurel tree.
Alternative spellings: Loral

Lauren
Meaning: From Laurentum
Origin: Latin
Pronunciation: LOR ren
Description: This feminine version of Laurence comes from the Roman name Laurentia.

Alternative spellings: Laurin, Lauryn, Lawren, Lorenne

Laurence
See entry in 'Names for Baby Boys A–Z'

Laurie
Meaning: Victory
Origin: Latin
Pronunciation: LAW ree
Description: Originally a shortened version of the names Laura and Laurence, this unisex name is now used in its own right and means 'victory'.
Alternative spellings: Lauri, Laury, Lawrie, Lowry

Lavender
Meaning: Flower name
Origin: English
Pronunciation: lav EN dur
Description: Lavender is derived from the name of the purple, strong-scented flower. Like Rose and Tulip, Lavender is part of the trend of using flowers as given names.

Lavinia
Meaning: Mother of Rome
Origin: Latin
Pronunciation: lah VEE ne ah
Description: The name of the mythical mother of Rome.
Alternative spellings: Laviniah, Lavinja, Lavinya

Layan
Meaning: Soft; gentle
Origin: Arabic
Pronunciation: lie YAAN
Description: Layan is a feminine Arabic name meaning 'soft'

and 'gentle'. It is a popular name given to newborn girls in the Arab world, and is related to names such as Lina, Leena and Lena, all of which have the same meaning.

Leah
Meaning: Spiritless
Origin: Hebrew
Pronunciation: LEE uh
Description: Leah, a biblical name, has grown in popularity since the 1990s and is now a favourite in Britain.
Alternative spellings: Lea, Leia, Leigha, Lia

Leanna
Meaning: Bright
Origin: Greek
Pronunciation: lee AHN ah
Description: A modern name, created by combining the names Lee and Anna, Leanna could also derive from Helen, meaning 'bright'.
Alternative spellings: Leana, Lianna

Leanne
Meaning: Bright
Origin: Greek
Pronunciation: lee AN
Description: Leanne is a variant of Leanna and a combination of the names Lee and Anne. It could also derive from the Greek name Helen.
Alternative spellings: LeAnn, Leann, Lianne

Lee
Meaning: Wood; clearing
Origin: English
Pronunciation: LEE
Description: From the Old

English word *'lea'* meaning 'clearing' or 'meadow', this is a unisex name.
Alternative spellings: Lei. Leigh

Leela
Meaning: Dark-haired
Origin: Persian
Pronunciation: LEE lah
Description: A phonetically spelt variation of the Persian name Leila, and most commonly pronounced 'lie-la', whereas Leela is pronounced 'lee-la'.
Alternative spellings: Leelah, Leila, Leilah, Lila

Leen
Meaning: Bright
Origin: Greek
Pronunciation: LEEN
Description: Leen is a Greek name, mainly found in Dutch-speaking countries. It derives as a pet name of the Dutch version of Helen, which is Helena, pronounced 'heh-leen-a'.
Alternative spellings: Lean, Lene

Leena
Meaning: Palm tree
Origin: Arabic
Pronunciation: LEE nah
Description: In origin, an elongation of the Greek name Leen or a variant of the name Lina.
Alternative spellings: Leenah, Lena, Lenah, Lina, Linah

Leja
Meaning: Weary
Origin: Lithuanian
Pronunciation: lee YA
Description: Leja is an alternative spelling of the Lithuanian name Leah.

L

The name ultimately comes from the Hebrew word 'le'ah', meaning 'weary'.
Alternative spellings: Leah

Leilani
Meaning: Heavenly lei
Origin: Hawaiian
Pronunciation: lay LAH nee
Description: This Hawaiian name is uncommon in Britain but gaining popularity in America. Lei is the Hawaiian name for flowers in a garland around the neck, which symbolise love, so Leilani may mean 'heavenly love'.
Alternative spellings: Lailani, Laylani, Leilanee

Leland
See entry in 'Names for Baby Boys A–Z'

Lena
Meaning: Bright
Origin: Greek
Pronunciation: LAY nah
Description: Lena is a shortened name of the Greek name Helena, or the Greek name Magdalena. It could also be a spelling variant of the name Lina.
Alternative spellings: Leena, Leenah, Lenah, Lina, Linah

Leni
Meaning: Bright
Origin: Greek
Pronunciation: LAY nee
Description: Leni is one of many pet forms of the name Helen and a variation on Laney, from the name Helena.
Alternative spellings: Lainey, Laini, Lainie, Lainy, Laney, Lanie, Lany, Laynee, Laynie

Leona
Meaning: Lion
Origin: Latin
Pronunciation: LEE oh na
Description: Leona is a Latinate feminine form of the masculine name Leo, meaning 'lion'.
Alternative spellings: Leonah, Liona

Leoni
Meaning: Courageous
Origin: Latin
Pronunciation: lee OH ne
Description: Leoni is a feminine version of the Latin name Leo, meaning 'lion' and was probably given as a virtuous name, meaning 'courageous'.
Alternative spellings: Leonie, Leony, Lioni, Lionie, Liony

Leonie
Meaning: Courageous
Origin: Latin
Pronunciation: LAY oh ne
Description: This name is a spelling variation of Leoni.
Alternative spellings: Leoni, Leony, Lioni, Lionie, Liony

Leslie
See entry in 'Names for Baby Boys A–Z'

Leticia
Meaning: Happy
Origin: Latin
Pronunciation: leh TEE shah
Description: Leticia is a variant of the Latin name Laetitia, the Roman goddess associated with joy.
Alternative spellings: Laetitia, Laticia, Latisha, Latishah

Lettie

Meaning: Joy; Happiness
Origin: English
Pronunciation: let EE
Description: Lettie is the English diminutive of Letitia, a Latin name meaning 'joy' and 'happiness'. Lettie can also be spelt Letty, and all three names have a traditional feel to them.
Alternative spellings: Letty

Levi

See entry in 'Names for Baby Boys A–Z'

Lexi

Meaning: Defender of man
Origin: Greek
Pronunciation: LEK see
Description: The name Lexi originated as a pet form of the names Alexandra, Alexa or Alexis, all feminine forms of the Greek name Alexander, meaning 'man's defender'.
Alternative spellings: Leksi, Leksy, Lexie, Lexy

Lexus

See entry in 'Names for Baby Boys A–Z'

Leya

Meaning: Always with God; law
Origin: Hebrew
Pronunciation: LEEY ah
Description: As well as being a variant of the Hebrew name Leeya, meaning 'always with God', Leya could also be considered a Spanish name, meaning 'law'.
Alternative spellings: Leeya, Liya

Liana

Meaning: Captivating
Origin: French
Pronunciation: lee AH nah
Description: Liana is a French given name as well as a name for a vine which is often found in the rainforest. These factors imply that the meaning of the given name is along the lines of 'ensnaring' or 'captivating'.
Alternative spellings: Leana, Lianah, Liyana

Libby

Meaning: Promised by God
Origin: Hebrew
Pronunciation: LIB ee
Description: Libby originally came about as the pet form of Elizabeth, meaning 'promised by God'. It is now a name in its own right, possibly based on a child's attempt to say 'Elizabeth'.
Alternative spellings: Libbi, Libbie

Liberty

Meaning: Freedom
Origin: Latin
Pronunciation: LIB er tee
Description: Liberty derives from the Latin word *'libertas'*, meaning 'free'. The name has strong links to America due to the Statue of Liberty.
Alternative spellings: Liberti, Libertie

Lila

Meaning: Dark-haired
Origin: Persian
Pronunciation: LEE lah; LYE la
Description: Lila is a phonetically spelt variation of the name Leila, which is of Persian origin and means 'dark-haired'.

L

Alternative spellings: Leela, Leelah, Leila, Leilah, Lilah, Lilla, Lillah

Lili
Meaning: Bright one; God is perfection
Origin: Welsh
Pronunciation: lil LEE
Description: This name has become very popular in English-speaking countries in recent years due to current trends. This name has roots in the Old Greek language, meaning 'bright one', and Old Hebrew, where it means 'God is perfection'. It was once that this name was a pet form of the name Elizabeth; however it is now considered a forename in its own right.
Alternative spellings: Lily, Lillie, Lilly

Lilia
Meaning: Lilies
Origin: Latin
Pronunciation: LIL ee ah
Description: The name Lilia comes from the Latin word *'lilia'*, meaning 'lilies'. Lily is a very popular name choice at the moment and Lilia could make a nice alternative.
Alternative spellings: Lilah, Lillia, Lilliah

Lilian
Meaning: Lily flower
Origin: Latin
Pronunciation: lil ee An
Description: Lilian is an elaboration upon the Latin name Lily, itself coming from the commonly white flower. As with the name Lily,

it can also be spelt with two Ls.
Alternative spellings: Lillian

Lilianna
Meaning: Peace and grace
Origin: Hebrew
Pronunciation: LIH lee AH nah
Description: Lilianna is thought to be a relatively new name, created by combining Lily and Anna. The lily is a Christian symbol of peace and Anna means 'grace', so Lilianna could mean 'graceful flower' or 'peace and grace'.
Alternative spellings: Liliana, Lilliana, Lillianna

Lilibeth
Meaning: Flower; promised by God
Origin: English
Pronunciation: lili BETH
Description: Lilibeth is a combination of Lily, the flower and Beth, from Elizabeth meaning 'promised by God'. As such, it has a combined meaning from both names.

Lilith
Meaning: Of the night
Origin: Assyrian
Pronunciation: lil ITH
Description: Lilith is the name of a demon in ancient Assyrian myths, and the name itself means 'of the night' in Akkadian. In Jewish tradition, she was Adam's first wife before she was cast out of Eden for not being submissive to him.

Lilla
Meaning: Peace
Origin: English
Pronunciation: LIH lee

Description: Lilla has come about as a variant of the extremely popular name Lily. Lily could be taken as a shortened form of Elizabeth or from the flower name.
Alternative spellings: Lila, Lilah, Lillah

Lillian

Meaning: Promised by God
Origin: Hebrew
Pronunciation: LIL ee an
Description: Lillian is an elaboration upon the Latin name Lily, which comes from the name of the white flower. It can be spelt so that there is an emphasis on the 'anne' element of the name.
Alternative spellings: Lilian, Lilianne, Lillianne

Lilo

Meaning: Generous one
Origin: Hawaiian
Pronunciation: lee LOH
Description: Lilo is a Hawaiian name meaning 'generous one'. It was made famous by the Disney animated film, *Lilo and Stitch*.

Lily

Meaning: White flower; purity
Origin: Latin
Pronunciation: LILL lee
Description: The name Lily comes from the English word for the flower. It is regarded in many cultures as a symbol of purity and in Christian belief it is a symbol of peace. The name has recently enjoyed a huge popularity boost and is very popular in the UK and US.
Alternative spellings: Lili, Lilli, Lillie, Lilly

Lina

Meaning: Palm tree
Origin: Arabic
Pronunciation: LEE nah
Description: Lina originally came about as a shortened form of Carolina and Avelina. It is now a given name in its own right and may originate from the Arabic for 'palm tree'.
Alternative spellings: Leena, Leenah, Lena, Lenah, Linah

Linda

Meaning: Pretty; neat; snake
Origin: English
Pronunciation: LIN da
Description: The popular name Linda may have originally developed as a shortened form of Belinda. The word *'linda'* also means 'pretty' in Spanish, 'neat' in Italian and 'snake' in German.
Alternative spellings: Lynda

Lindsay

Meaning: Lincoln island
Origin: English
Pronunciation: LIN zee
Description: Originally, Lindsay was a Scottish surname, but it is now a forename found worldwide. Sometimes seen as a boys' name in Scotland and Australia, it is usually a female name.
Alternative spellings: Lindsee, Lindsey, Lindsi, Lindsie, Linsay, Linsee, Linsey, Linsi, Linsie, Lyndsay, Lyndsey, Lynsay, Lynsey

Lisa

Meaning: Promised by God
Origin: Hebrew
Pronunciation: LEE suh
Description: Lisa is a variant of

L

the less popular name Liza, itself a shortened form of Elizabeth. It may also be considered a shortening of the spelling Elisabeth.
Alternative spellings: Leesa, Lissa

Lissa
Meaning: Honey bee
Origin: Greek
Pronunciation: LEE sah
Description: Lissa, once a short version of Melissa, is now a name in its own right. It can also be considered a variant of the name Lisa.
Alternative spellings: Leesa, Lisa

Livia
Meaning: Peace; olive
Origin: Latin
Pronunciation: LIV ee uh
Description: Livia is considered the shortened form of Olive, a tree that symbolises peace in Christian tradition. It is thought to have derived from the Roman family name Livius, meaning 'blue'. It is often shortened to Liv.
Alternative spellings: Liviah, Livja, Lyvia

Livvy
Meaning: Peace; olive
Origin: Latin
Pronunciation: LIV ee
Description: Livvy could be the pet form of the names Olivia, Olive or Livia. All of these names are of Latin origin and mean 'olive' or 'olive tree'.
Alternative spellings: Livi, Livie, Livvi, Livvi, Livvie, Livy

Liyana
Meaning: Captivating
Origin: French
Pronunciation: lee AH nah
Description: Liyana is probably a variant form of Liana, which is a feminine name of French origin and it is said to refer to twining around. It is the name of a tropical rainforest vine. These factors imply that the meaning of the name is along the lines of 'ensnaring' or 'captivating'.
Alternative spellings: Liyanah, Liana

Liz
Meaning: Promised by God
Origin: Hebrew
Pronunciation: LIZ
Description: Originally a short form of Elizabeth, Liz means 'promised from God' and is a name in its own right.
Alternative spellings: Lizz

Liza
Meaning: Promised by God
Origin: Hebrew
Pronunciation: LY zuh
Description: Liza is a shortened form of Eliza, which derives from the name Elizabeth. It is sometimes seen as an alternative to the name Lisa.
Alternative spellings: Lizah, Lyza

Lizzie
Meaning: Promised by God
Origin: Hebrew
Pronunciation: LIZ ee
Description: Lizzie is a pet form of the popular name Elizabeth, but it is also found as a name in its own right.
Alternative spellings: Lizzi, Lizzy

Logan

See entry in 'Names for Baby Boys A–Z'

Lois

Meaning: Unknown
Origin: Greek
Pronunciation: LOW is
Description: Lois is a biblical name of obscure origin and meaning. In the New Testament it is found as the name of the grandmother of Timothy. The family of Timothy all have names of Greek origin so it is presumed that Lois is also a Greek name.
Alternative spellings: Loiss, Lowis

Lola

Meaning: Sorrows
Origin: Spanish
Pronunciation: LO luh
Description: Lola was originally a pet form of the Spanish name Dolores, but is now an independent given name.
Alternative spellings: Lolah

Lorelai

Meaning: Rock in the River Rhine
Origin: German
Pronunciation: LOR eh lye
Description: Lorelai comes from an Old German myth about a woman who waited for her lover on a rock in the River Rhine. When he failed to arrive she jumped to her death. There is a rock in the river named after her.
Alternative spellings: Laurelai, Laureli, Lorelei, Loreli

Lorena

Meaning: From the province of Lorraine

Origin: Spanish
Pronunciation: lo RAYN ah
Description: Lorena is the Spanish form of the name Lorraine, a French name meaning 'from the province of Lorraine,' a region in north-eastern France. Lorena is a name often heard in Hispanic communities.

Lorie

Meaning: Laurel tree
Origin: English
Pronunciation: LAWR ee
Description: Lorie has a strong connotation with the English name Laurel, which refers to the laurel tree.
Alternative spellings: Laurie, Lory, Lori

Lorna

Meaning: From Lorn
Origin: Scottish
Pronunciation: lor NAH
Description: Lorna is a name that developed in Scotland, and would have referred to someone who hailed from the town of Lorn.

Lottie

Meaning: Womanly
Origin: French
Pronunciation: LOT ee
Description: Lottie is a pet form of the name Charlotte; however it carries a separate meaning of 'womanly'.
Alternative spellings: Lotti, Lotty

Louella

Meaning: Beautiful warrior
Origin: American
Pronunciation: loo ELL ah
Description: Louella is a fairly

L

modern name that combines the names Louise and Helen. Louise is of French origin and means 'famed warrior', while Ella derives from the Greek Helen meaning 'bright' and associated with beauty. We can therefore take the meaning to be 'beautiful warrior'.
Alternative spellings: Loella, Louela, Luella

Louisa
Meaning: Famed warrior
Origin: Latin
Pronunciation: loo EE zah
Description: Louisa is the feminine form of the French name Louis, originally derived from Latin.
Alternative spellings: Louesa, Louiza, Luisa

Louise
Meaning: Famed warrior
Origin: French
Pronunciation: LOO ease
Description: Louise is the primary feminine version of the French name Louis and is a popular name in Britain.
Alternative spellings: Louize, Luise

Lourdes
Meaning: Craggy slope
Origin: Basque
Pronunciation: lords
Description: Lourdes is a Basque name meaning 'craggy slope'. It was made popular because Madonna named her daughter Lourdes.
Alternative spellings: Lords, Lordes

Lowenna
Meaning: Joy

Origin: English
Pronunciation: lo EN na
Description: Lowenna is a rare English name, specifically deriving from the county of Cornwall. It is found as a place name in many parts of the world. It means 'joy' and can also be found spelt with a single 'n'.
Alternative spellings: Lowena, Lowenah

Lowri
Meaning: Crown of laurels
Origin: Latin
Pronunciation: LAUW ree
Description: Lowri is the Welsh equivalent of the name Laura, which is derived from the Latin word for 'laurel'. It is quite a well-known name in Wales.
Alternative spellings: Lauri, Laurie, Laury, Lawrie

Lua
Meaning: Moon
Origin: Latin
Pronunciation: LOO ah
Description: Lua is an uncommon girls' name of Latin origin and a variant of the name Luna, the Latin word for moon and the name of the Roman goddess of the moon.
Alternative spellings: Looa, Luah

Luana
Meaning: Favoured warrior
Origin: French
Pronunciation: loo AHN ah
Description: Luana is thought to be a combination of the names Louise and Anna. Louise is of French origin, meaning 'famous

warrior', while Anna is of Hebrew origin, meaning 'grace' and 'God favours'.
Alternative spellings: Louana, Louanna, Luanna

Lucia

Meaning: Light
Origin: Latin
Pronunciation: loo CHEE ah
Description: St Lucia, a popular saint in northern Europe, represents light and is celebrated on 13 December, when light is scarce.
Alternative spellings: Loucia, Lucya

Lucinda

Meaning: Light
Origin: Latin
Pronunciation: loo SIN dah
Description: Lucinda came about as an embellished version of the name Lucy, meaning 'light'. Traditionally the Romans used to give the name to baby girls born at dawn.
Alternative spellings: Loucinda, Lucindah, Lucynda

Lucy

Meaning: Light
Origin: French
Pronunciation: LOO see
Description: Lucy comes from the Old French name Lucie, derived from the Latin word *'lux'*, meaning 'light'. It was in fairly widespread use back in the Middle Ages, increasing greatly in popularity in the 1990s.
Alternative spellings: Luci, Lucie

Luella

Meaning: Famed warrior

Origin: French
Pronunciation: loo EH la
Description: Luella is a variant of Louella, a feminine name of relatively modern coinage. The name is a compound of the two favourite feminine names, Louise and Ella. Louise is of ultimately French origin and comes from the masculine Louis meaning 'famed warrior'. Ella is the pet form of the French Eleanor, which is itself the French variant of the Greek Helen. Although both the root names are French in origin, Luella is thought to have been invented in English-speaking countries.
Alternative spellings: Louella

Lula

Meaning: No meaning
Origin: English
Pronunciation: loo LAH
Description: Lula is a diminutive of Louise and another other name that starts with Lu. It is also a nickname that is similar to Lulu, Lula or Lou.

Lulu

Meaning: Light; famed warrior
Origin: German
Pronunciation: LOO loo
Description: Lulu came about as a pet form of the names Lucy and Louise, but is now often found as a name in its own right.
Alternative spellings: Loulou

Luna

Meaning: Moon
Origin: Latin
Pronunciation: LOO nah
Description: The name Luna

comes from the Latin word for the moon.
Alternative spellings: Loona, Louna, Lunah

Lydia
Meaning: Woman from Lydia
Origin: Greek
Pronunciation: LID ee uh
Description: Lydia was originally a place name for an area in Asia. In the New Testament, Lydia was converted by St Paul to Christianity.
Alternative spellings: Lidia, Lidiya, Lidya

Lyla
Meaning: Dark-haired
Origin: Persian
Pronunciation: LYE lah
Description: Lyla can be seen as a spelling variant of the names Leila and Lila. Unlike these names, there is only one common pronunciation of Lyla.

Alternative spellings: Leila, Leilah, Lila, Lilah, Lylah

Lynn
Meaning: Pretty
Origin: English
Pronunciation: LIN
Description: Lynn is a name of uncertain origin. It is thought to be a shortened form of Linda, in which case it would mean 'pretty'. It could also be a Gaelic surname related to water.
Alternative spellings: Lyn, Lynne

Lyra
Meaning: Lyre
Origin: Latin
Pronunciation: LY ra
Description: Lyra is a modern name derived from the Latin for 'lyre', a stringed instrument. Lyra is also the name of a star constellation and so has connotations of brightness.
Alternative spellings: Lyrah

M

Maame
Meaning: Mother; pearl
Origin: African
Pronunciation: MAYM
Description: The name Maame could derive from an African word meaning 'mother' or it could be a form of the pet name Mame, from Margaret. In this case it would mean 'pearl'.
Alternative spellings: Mayme

Mabel
Meaning: Loveable
Origin: Latin
Pronunciation: MAY bell
Description: Mabel is a short form of the Latin name Amabel, itself thought to be related to the name Annabel.
Alternative spellings: Mabelle, Maybel

Mabli
Meaning: Loveable

Origin: Welsh
Pronunciation: mahb LEE
Description: Mabli is the Welsh form of the name Mabel, meaning 'loveable'. It was made popular by C.M Yonge's novel *The Heir of Redclyffe* (1854), which featured a character called Mabel.

Macie

Meaning: Estate of Marcius
Origin: French
Pronunciation: may SEE
Description: Macie is a form of the feminine Macy, which comes from the French surname that means 'the Estate of Marcius'. The surname is thought of as masculine; however as a first name Macy is only used for girls. It is especially popular in America, famous because of Macy's department store.
Alternative spellings: Macy, Maci, Macey

Mackenzie

Meaning: The fairest
Origin: Gaelic
Pronunciation: ma KEN zee
Description: Mackenzie derives from the Gaelic surname McKenzie, originally MacCoinneach. The meaning of the name varies. For a girl it is said to mean 'the fairest' yet as a boy's name it means 'handsome one'.
Alternative spellings: Mackenzi, Mackenzy, Makenzie, Mckenzi, Mckenzie, Mckenzy

Maddie

Meaning: Relative of Maud
Origin: English
Pronunciation: mad DEE
Description: The female name Maddie is actually the shortened version of the name Madison, but has now become a forename in its own right. Beginning life as a unisex name, it quickly became more common to be used for females. This name is most commonly found in English-speaking countries.
Alternative spellings: Maddy

Maddison

Meaning: Matthew's son
Origin: English
Pronunciation: mad ISSON
Description: Maddison is a variation of the more common Madison, meaning 'Matthew's son'. Maddison can also be a boys' name.
Alternative spellings: Madison

Madeline

Meaning: From Magdala
Origin: Hebrew
Pronunciation: MAD uh line
Description: Madeline derives from the French form of Magdalene, which means 'from Magdala'. Magdala was the birthplace of Mary Magdalene, found in the Bible. The name was brought over from France in the 12th century.
Alternative spellings: Madeleine, Madelene, Madelyn

Madiha

Meaning: Praiseworthy
Origin: Arabic
Pronunciation: mah DEE hah
Description: Madiha is a popular name in the Middle East and Swahili-speaking countries.
Alternative spellings: Madeeha

M

Madina

Meaning: City of Islam
Origin: Arabic
Pronunciation: meh DEE nah
Description: Madina is a spelling variation of the name Medina, deriving from the city in the Middle East. Medina was the first city that the prophet Muhammad introduced Islam to, so it has great importance in that religion.
Alternative spellings: Madeena, Medeena, Medina

Madison

See entry in 'Names for Baby Boys A–Z'

Madonna

Meaning: My lady
Origin: Italian
Pronunciation: ma DON na
Description: Madonna comes from the Italian title of the Virgin Mary and means 'my lady'.
Alternative spellings: Madona, Madonnah

Mae

Meaning: Star of the sea
Origin: Hebrew
Pronunciation: may
Description: Unlike May, the name Mae does not possess a link to the calendar month. However, the two names do share meaning. Both are pet forms of Mary, hence meaning 'star of the sea'.
Alternative spellings: May

Maeve

Meaning: Intoxicating
Origin: Gaelic
Pronunciation: MAYV
Description: Maeve is a phonetically spelt variation of the Irish name Meadhbh. Maeve is the name of a powerful figure in Irish mythology.
Alternative spellings: Maieve, Mayeve

Mafalda

Meaning: Mighty in battle
Origin: Italian
Pronunciation: ma FAL dah
Description: Mafalda is the Italian version of the German name Matilda and as such, shares the same meaning of 'mighty in battle'.

Magdalena

Meaning: From Magdala
Origin: Hebrew
Pronunciation: mag dah LAY nah
Description: Magdalena derives from the name Magdalene, meaning 'from Magdala'.
Alternative spellings: Magdalina

Maggie

Meaning: Pearl; light's creation
Origin: Latin
Pronunciation: MA gee
Description: Maggie came about as a pet name of Margaret, meaning 'pearl'. It has now become a name in its own right.
Alternative spellings: Maggey, Maggi, Maggy

Magnolia

Meaning: Flower
Origin: English
Pronunciation: ma NO lee ah
Description: Magnolia comes from the white and pink flowers of the same name. Like Rose and Tulip, Magnolia is part of the

trend of using flowers as given names.

Maha
Meaning: Great
Origin: Sanskrit
Pronunciation: MAH ha
Description: Maha derives from the Sanskrit word meaning 'great'. It is used in many titles in Hinduism, such as *maharaj*, meaning 'great king' and *mahashi*, which means 'great saint'.
Alternative spellings: Mahar

Mahdiya
Meaning: Guided by Allah
Origin: Arabic
Pronunciation: MAH dee ah
Description: Mahdiya is the feminine version of the name Mahdi. Both are Arabic in origin and are favoured by Muslim parents due to their meaning.
Alternative spellings: Madiya, Madiyah, Mahdiyah

Maheen
Meaning: Moonlight
Origin: Arabic
Pronunciation: mah HEEN
Description: The name Maheen derives from an Arabic word referring to the moon. It is quite a rare name.
Alternative spellings: Mahene, Mahine

Mahi
Meaning: Goddess
Origin: Sanskrit
Pronunciation: muh HEE
Description: In Indian mythology Mahi is the name of an earth goddess. Mahi is also the name of

a village in India, and in several languages it means 'fish'.
Alternative spellings: Mahee

Mahima
Meaning: Great one
Origin: Sanskrit
Pronunciation: mah HEE mah
Description: Mahima derives from a Sanskrit word meaning 'great one' and is often favoured by Hindu parents.
Alternative spellings: Maheema, Mahema, Mahimah

Mahira
Meaning: Talented
Origin: Arabic
Pronunciation: meh HEER ah
Description: Mahira is the feminine version of the name Mahir and found mainly in the Middle East. Its origins are probably either Hebrew or Arabic.
Alternative spellings: Maheera, Mahirah

Mahnoor
Meaning: Moonlight
Origin: Arabic
Pronunciation: MAH noor
Description: Mahnoor is a phonetically soft name with the beautiful meaning of 'moonlight'.
Alternative spellings: Mahnor

Maia
Meaning: Mother; illusion
Origin: Greek
Pronunciation: MAY ah
Description: Maia is found in Greek and Roman mythology, where it is the name of the goddess of spring and the mother of the god Hermes. Maia is also a

M

variation of the name Maya, which means 'illusion' and is often found in Hindu philosophy.
Alternative spellings: Maiya, Maja, Maya, Mya, Myah

Maira
Meaning: Sea dew
Origin: Hebrew
Pronunciation: MAY rah
Description: Maira is the Irish equivalent of the name Mary. The Maira is also the name of an Italian river, and the name is used in Italy.
Alternative spellings: Mairah, Mayra

Maisha
Meaning: Prosperous
Origin: Arabic
Pronunciation: mah EE sha
Description: Maisha is a popular variant of the name Aisha. Aisha was the name of the third wife of the prophet Muhammad.
Alternative spellings: Maesha, Maishah

Maisy
Meaning: Pearl; light's creation
Origin: Latin
Pronunciation: MAY zee
Description: This very popular name may have come about as a pet name for Margaret or the Gaelic Mairead. Both names come from the Latin *'margarita'*, meaning 'pearl'.
Alternative spellings: Maisee, Maisey, Maisie, Maizie, Maysie, Mazie

Makayla
Meaning: Who is like God?
Origin: Hebrew
Pronunciation: mee KAY lah

Description: Makayla is a fairly modern name, created as a phonetically spelt version of Michaela. It is often shortened to Kayla.
Alternative spellings: Michaela

Malaika
Meaning: Angel
Origin: Arabic
Pronunciation: mah lah EE kah; mah LIE kah
Description: Malaika is the female form of the Arabic name Malak, meaning 'angel'. It is often shortened to Mal.
Alternative spellings: Malaikah, Malayka

Malak
See entry in 'Names for Baby Boys A–Z'.

Malala
Meaning: Grief-stricken
Origin: Afghan
Pronunciation: ma LA LA
Description: Malala is an Afghan name meaning 'grief-stricken'. Malala Yousafzai is a Pakistani activist and the world's youngest Nobel Prize laureate.

Maleeha
Meaning: Beautiful one
Origin: Sanskrit
Pronunciation: MAH lee ah
Description: Maleeha is a variant of Maliha, which is a feminine name that originates from a Sanskrit word meaning 'beautiful one'. It is quite a popular name with Muslim parents and is found used mostly in the Middle East and Africa.
Alternative spellings: Maliha

Mali

Meaning: Star of the sea
Origin: Welsh
Pronunciation: mal LEE
Description: Mali is a popular Welsh name, derived from the English name Molly, which is itself a pet form of Mary, meaning 'star of the sea'. It could also refer to the African country of the same name, or the Thai name Mali, which means 'flower'.

Malia

Meaning: Sea dew
Origin: Hebrew
Pronunciation: mah LEE ah
Description: Malia is a variant of the name Mary, and is popular in Hawaii.
Alternative spellings: Maliah, Maliya

Malika

Meaning: Nobility
Origin: Arabic
Pronunciation: MAH lee kah
Description: Malika is the feminine equivalent of Malik. It is sometimes used in Pakistan for the title of lady, which gives it the meaning of 'nobility'.
Alternative spellings: Maleeka, Malikah

Malina

Meaning: Raspberry
Origin: Russian
Pronunciation: ma LEE nah
Description: Malina, when directly translated from Russian, means 'raspberry'. It could also be a variation of the name Melina.

Maliyah

Meaning: Bitter
Origin: Hawaiian
Pronunciation: MAH lee yah
Description: Maliyah is the Hawaiian version of the name Mary, and shares the same meaning of 'bitter'.
Alternative spellings: Maliya

Malka

Meaning: Queen
Origin: Hebrew
Pronunciation: MAHL kah
Description: Malka derives from the Hebrew word meaning 'queen'.
Alternative spellings: Malca, Malcah, Malkah

Mallory

Meaning: Unfortunate
Origin: French
Pronunciation: mal OR ee
Description: Mallory is a name derived from the French word 'maloret,' which means 'unfortunate'. Despite the meaning, it would still make a lovely baby name for a girl.
Alternative spellings: Malory

Mamie

Meaning: Sea dew
Origin: English
Pronunciation: maim EE
Description: Mamie is a nickname for the name Mary, but can also be used as a given name on its own. As such, it shares the same meaning of 'sea dew'. Mamie Gummer is an American actress and daughter of Meryl Streep.

Mamrie

Meaning: No meaning
Origin: English

Pronunciation: maim REE
Description: Mamrie is a modern invented name and as such, has no real meaning. It is associated with YouTube personality, Mamrie Hart, whose great-grandmother's middle name was Mamrie.

Manahil
Meaning: Atmosphere of paradise
Origin: Urdu
Pronunciation: MAH na hil
Description: Manahil is a variant of the name Minahil, which is of Urdu origin. Some sources claim the name means 'atmosphere of paradise'.
Alternative spellings: Manahill

Manal
Meaning: One who attains
Origin: Arabic
Pronunciation: MAH nal
Description: Manal is a unisex name; however it is most often found used for girls. As well as having Arabic roots, it is also thought to derive from a Sanskrit word meaning 'bird'.
Alternative spellings: Manel, Mannal

Mandy
Meaning: Loveable
Origin: Latin
Pronunciation: MAN dee
Description: Mandy is a pet form of the Latin name Amanda, and therefore means 'loveable'. It is now a name in its own right.
Alternative spellings: Mandi, Mandie

Manha
Meaning: Gift from Allah; morning

Origin: Arabic
Pronunciation: man HA
Description: Manha is often favoured by those of the Muslim faith and is currently quite a popular name for girls. In Portuguese it means 'morning'.
Alternative spellings: Manhah

Mannat
Meaning: Special prayer
Origin: Sanskrit
Pronunciation: MAN nat
Description: Mannat is quite an unusual name in Britain but when found it is mainly favoured by Sikh parents. It is quite a popular name in India, and can often be found in the UK as a surname.
Alternative spellings: Manat, Mannatt

Manon
Meaning: Sea dew
Origin: French
Pronunciation: mah NON
Description: Manon came about as a French pet form of the Hebrew name Mary.
Alternative spellings: Mannon

Mara
Meaning: Sea dew
Origin: Hebrew
Pronunciation: MAHR ah
Description: Mara was once a pet name of Mary, but is now a name in its own right. It could also be considered the pet form of longer names such as Tamara or Samara, in which case it would carry their meaning.
Alternative spellings: Marah, Marar

Marcelina
Meaning: From the god Mars

Origin: Latin
Pronunciation: mar suh LEE nah
Description: Marcelina is a feminine version of the name Marcel, derived from the name of the Roman god of war, Mars.
Alternative spellings: Marceleena, Marcelena, Marcelinah

Marcella

Meaning: From the god Mars
Origin: Italian
Pronunciation: mar SELL uh
Description: Marcella is the Italian, feminine version of the name Mark and as such, shares the same meaning of 'from the god Mars'.

Marcheline

Meaning: From the god Mars
Origin: Latin
Pronunciation: MAR shuh LEEN
Description: Marcheline is a variation of the French name Marceline, ultimately derived from the name of the Roman god of war, Mars. It could also be seen as a name taken from the month of March.
Alternative spellings: Marchaline, Marchalyne, Marchelyne, Marsheline

Marcia

Meaning: From the god Mars
Origin: Latin
Pronunciation: MAR sha; MAR cee a
Description: Marcia comes from the same roots as Marcella and Marcelina. These are feminine versions of the Latin name Marcel, derived from the name of the Roman god of war, Mars.
Alternative spellings: Marciah, Marcya

Marcie

Meaning: From the god Mars
Origin: Italian
Pronunciation: MAR see
Description: Marcie was originally the pet form of Latin names such as Marcella and Marcia, but is also found used as a name in its own right.
Alternative spellings: Marci, Marcy

Margaret

Meaning: Pearl; light's creation
Origin: Greek
Pronunciation: MAR gah ret
Description: Margaret has been an enduringly popular name ever since the Middle Ages. It is derived from the Greek word *'margaron'* meaning 'pearl'.
Alternative spellings: Margeret, Margret

Margo

Meaning: Pearl
Origin: Latin
Pronunciation: mar GO
Description: Margo is a variation of the name Margot, meaning 'pearl'. It is also likely influenced by the wine-making French town. Both names are also connected to Margaret, which also has the same meaning.
Alternative spellings: Margaux, Margot

Marguerite

Meaning: Pearl
Origin: French
Pronunciation: marg ARR eet
Description: Marguerite is the French version of the name Margaret and shares the same meaning of 'pearl'.

M

Marhaw

Meaning: Plant
Origin: Arabic
Pronunciation: MAR wah
Description: Marhaw is thought to be of Arabic origin, although its meaning is debated. It is thought to come from the Arabic name of a plant.
Alternative spellings: Marhow

Maria

Meaning: Sea dew
Origin: Latin
Pronunciation: ma REE ah; ma RYE ah
Description: Maria is the Latin form of Mary. It is especially popular in Spain. The name has religious connotations in Christian belief as it is the name of the mother of Christ.
Alternative spellings: Maariya, Maariyah, Mariah, Mariya, Mariyah

Mariam

Meaning: Uncertain
Origin: Arabic
Pronunciation: MAR ee um
Description: Mariam is an Arabic girls' name and a variant of Miryam, the Arabic alternative form of Mary, the mother of Jesus. It is an uncommon name for girls, meaning 'uncertain'.
Alternative spellings: Marian, Marium, Mariyam, Maryam

Mariama

Meaning: Sea dew
Origin: Hebrew
Pronunciation: mah ree AH ma
Description: Mariama is a more modern variation of the name Miriam, which is the original form of Mary. Its first appearance is as the name of the sister of Moses. However, some argue that its origins lie further back in ancient Egypt and its meaning is debated.
Alternative spellings: Mariamah, Maryama

Mariana

Meaning: Sea dew
Origin: Hebrew
Pronunciation: mah ree AH nah
Description: Mariana is a variant of Marian, which comes from the same source as the name Mary. The variant Mariana is popular in Spanish-speaking countries.
Alternative spellings: Marianah, Marianna

Marianna

Meaning: No Meaning
Origin: English
Pronunciation: mer EE an ah
Description: Marianna is a combination of the names Maria and Anna. It should not be confused with the name Mariana, which is Roman in origin. Marianna is also sometimes the Latinised form of the name Marianne.

Marianne

Meaning: Sea dew
Origin: Hebrew
Pronunciation: MAH ree an
Description: Marianne is a variant of Marian, which comes from the same source as the name Mary.
Alternative spellings: Marian, Mariane

Marie

Meaning: Sea dew
Origin: Hebrew
Pronunciation: muh REE
Description: Marie, the French form of Maria, can also be considered a spelling variant of the biblical name Mary.
Alternative spellings: Mari, Mary

Mariella

Meaning: Sea dew
Origin: Hebrew
Pronunciation: mah re EH lah
Description: Mariella is an elaborated version of the popular name Mary.
Alternative spellings: Mariela, Mariellah, Maryella

Marigold

Meaning: Flower
Origin: English
Pronunciation: mary GOLD
Description: Marigold comes from the bright yellow-orange flower of the same name. Like Rose and Tulip, Marigold is part of the trend of using flowers as given names.

Marilyn

Meaning: No meaning
Origin: English
Pronunciation: mer LIN
Description: Marilyn is a combination of Mary and Lynn, and thus has no real meaning. Perhaps the most famous bearer of this name is Marilyn Monroe. Other names related to Marilyn are Maralyn, Marie, Mary, Marylyn and Merrilyn.

Marina

Meaning: Sea dew
Origin: Latin
Pronunciation: ma REE nah
Description: Marina derives from the Latin name Marino, meaning 'man of the sea'. Shakespeare introduced many to the name in his play *Pericles, Prince Of Tyre*.
Alternative spellings: Marinah, Maryna

Marion

Meaning: Sea dew
Origin: French
Pronunciation: mary ON
Description: Marion is the French version of the name Marie, which in turn comes from the Hebrew Miryam. All of these names mean 'sea dew'.

Marisa

Meaning: Sea dew
Origin: Hebrew
Pronunciation: mar EES ah
Description: Marisa is a spelling variant of the name Marissa and pronounced 'mar EES ah', whereas Marissa is usually pronounced 'ma RIS ah'.
Alternative spellings: Marisah, Marissa, Marissah

Marisol

Meaning: Mary of the solitude
Origin: Spanish
Pronunciation: mary SOL
Description: Marisol is the Spanish title given to the Virgin Mary. It is a shortened form of María de la Soledad, meaning 'Mary of the solitude'.

Marjorie

Meaning: Pearl
Origin: Latin

Pronunciation: mar JOOR ee
Description: Marjorie is a variation of the name Margaret, and both names come from the Latin word '*margarita*' meaning 'pearl'. It is also said that Marjorie is influenced by marjoram, a type of herb.

Marla
Meaning: No meaning
Origin: German
Pronunciation: MAAR lah
Description: Marla is the German version of Marlene. The name is a combination of Mary and Magdalen, and as such has no meaning.

Marley
See entry in 'Names for Baby Boys A–Z'

Marlie
Meaning: Forest of joy
Origin: English
Pronunciation:
Description: Marlie is a variation of Marley, which is from Old English words meaning 'forest' and 'pleasure'. The name Marley can be seen to mean 'forest of joy'. Adopted as a first name in fairly modern English, Marley can be both a masculine and feminine name.
Alternative spellings: Marley

Marlon
See entry in 'Names for Baby Boys A–Z'

Marlowe
Meaning: Driftwood
Origin: English
Pronunciation: mar LOW
Description: Marlowe is an English girls' name meaning

'driftwood'. It is attributed to the 16th-century poet and playwright, Christopher Marlowe.
Alternative spellings: Marlow

Marnie
Meaning: Sea dew
Origin: Latin
Pronunciation: MAR nee
Description: Marnie is a name that is derived from Marina, meaning 'from the sea'. Marnie has become a name in its own right and is especially popular in English-speaking countries.
Alternative spellings: Marney, Marni, Marny

Marta
Meaning: Lady
Origin: Hebrew
Pronunciation: MAR tah
Description: Marta is a name seen as a variation of Martha, meaning 'lady'. Marta is a popular name on the continent.
Alternative spellings: Martah

Martha
Meaning: Lady
Origin: Aramaic
Pronunciation: MAR tha
Description: In the New Testament, Martha was the sister of Lazarus. Due to this character's life, the name Martha is associated with hard domestic work.
Alternative spellings: Marther

Martina
Meaning: From the god Mars
Origin: Latin
Pronunciation: mar TEE nah
Description: Martina, a common girls' name of Latin origin, is the

female form of Martin. It is popular in English-, German-, Italian-, Romanian- and Spanish-speaking countries. The variation Martyna may come from Wales, where the male name is Martyn.
Alternative spellings: Martinah, Martyna

Marwa
Meaning: Flower
Origin: Arabic
Pronunciation: MAR wah
Description: Marwa derives from the Arabic name for a species of flower. It is also the name of a mountain in Saudi Arabia, Al-Marwa. The name is popular in the Middle East.
Alternative spellings: Marwah

Mary
Meaning: Sea dew
Origin: Hebrew
Pronunciation: MAIR ee
Description: Mary is a Middle English form of the Hebrew name Miriam. Mary was the name of the Mother of Christ, the Virgin Mary. As a result the name was very popular among early Christians. The name was popular until the 1960s, when it declined.
Alternative spellings: Mari, Marie

Maryama
Meaning: Sea dew
Origin: Hebrew
Pronunciation: MAH ree AH ma
Description: Maryama is an unusual spelling variant of the more common Mariama, a variant form of names such as Miriam and Marianna. All of the names are closely linked to the Hebrew name Mary,

meaning 'sea dew'.
Alternative spellings: Mariama, Mariamma, Maryam

Marzia
Meaning: Mars
Origin: Italian
Pronunciation: MAR tsya
Description: Marzia is the Italian form of the name Marcia, and the two share the meaning of 'Mars' or the Roman God of War. These names all come from the same root as the similar feminine name Marcella and the masculine name Marcus.

Masha
Meaning: Sea dew
Origin: Russian
Pronunciation: mah SHA
Description: Masha is the Russian form of the name Marie and as such, shares the same meaning of 'sea dew'. It is often used as a nickname for women named Marie or Maria.

Mason
See entry in 'Names for Baby Boys A–Z'

Matilda
Meaning: Mighty in battle
Origin: German
Pronunciation: muh TIL duh
Description: Matilda, the name of an early German queen, derives from the Old German words *'macht'* and *'hiltja'* meaning 'mighty' and 'battle' respectively. In recent times, the book by Roald Dahl and subsequent Hollywood film have kept this name in the spotlight.
Alternative spellings: Mathilda, Matildah, Matylda, Matilde

M

Maude
Meaning: Powerful battler
Origin: German
Pronunciation: maude
Description: Maude is an Old German name meaning 'powerful battler'. It is also seen as a variant of the name Matilda, so the two have very similar meanings.

Maureen
Meaning: Sea Dew
Origin: Irish
Pronunciation: more EEN
Description: Maureen is the Irish version of Mary and Miryam, and as such shares the same meaning of 'sea dew'. It is also the feminine version of Maurice.

Mavis
Meaning: Type of Bird
Origin: English
Pronunciation: MAY vis
Description: Mavis is actually a type of bird, more specifically the song thrush. It was used as a given name in Marie Corelli's 19th-century novel, *The Sorrows of Satan*.

May
Meaning: Month of May
Origin: English
Pronunciation: MAY
Description: A pet form of Margaret, Mary or Mabel, May also exists as an independent given name from the month of May. It is often chosen as a name for a girl born in May.
Alternative spellings: Mae, Mai

Maysa
Meaning: Graceful
Origin: Arabic
Pronunciation: MAY sah
Description: Although of Arabic origins, Maysa could also be a variant of the name Maisy. Maisy has become an extremely popular name recently and Maysa could be a nice alternative.
Alternative spellings: Maisa, Maysah

Meadow
Meaning: Meadow
Origin: English
Pronunciation: MED oh
Description: Although it has connotations of beauty and freedom, Meadow is a name that comes from the English word for a grassy field, and has no other meaning.
Alternative spellings: Medow

Medea
Meaning: Cunning
Origin: Greek
Pronunciation: meh DEE ah
Description: In Greek mythology, Medea was a sorceress who took revenge on her husband Jason of the Argonauts after being betrayed by him. She became a common antagonist of ancient playwrights.
Alternative spellings: Medeia, Media

Meera
Meaning: Prosperous
Origin: Sanskrit
Pronunciation: mee RAH
Description: Meera is an Indian name, meaning 'prosperous' in Sanskrit. Meera Bai was a popular Hindu mystical poet and her writings are well known in India. She was a 15th-century Indian princess whose poems

were devoted to the Indian god Krishna.

Meerab
Meaning: Unknown
Origin: Urdu
Pronunciation: MEE rab
Description: Meerab, an unusual name whose meaning is uncertain, seems likely to be of Urdu origin. It is often favoured by Muslim parents.
Alternative spellings: Merab

Megan
Meaning: Pearl; light's creation
Origin: Welsh
Pronunciation: MEG uhn
Description: Megan is a longer version of Meg, a pet name for Margaret. It is a very popular name in Britain, although Meghan is the more common spelling in America and Australia.
Alternative spellings: Meghan

Mehek
Meaning: Sweet smell
Origin: Arabic
Pronunciation: meh HEK
Description: Mehek is a variant of Mehak, a name of Arabic origins. It is quite rare in Britain but has more popularity in the Middle East.
Alternative spellings: Mehak

Mehreen
Meaning: Bright
Origin: Arabic
Pronunciation: mah REEN
Description: Mehreen is an Arabic girls' name often found in Pakistan.

Alternative spellings: Mehrene, Mehrine

Meisha
Meaning: Alive
Origin: Arabic
Pronunciation: MAY shah
Description: Meisha is an uncommon name of Arabic origin and a variant of Aisha, who was the third and favoured wife of the prophet Muhammad.
Alternative spellings: Mischa, Misha, Mysha

Melania
Meaning: Black; dark
Origin: Greek
Pronunciation: mee LAN ee ah
Description: Melania is actually a Greek word meaning 'black' or 'dark'. It was the name of two Roman saints who were known for their charity to the poor.

Melanie
Meaning: Dark-haired
Origin: Greek
Pronunciation: MELL ann ee
Description: Melanie derives from the Greek adjective *'melas'*, meaning 'black' or 'dark'. Melanie was the name of two 5th-century Roman saints, a grandmother and granddaughter. The name was introduced to England from France in the Middle Ages and became popular in the late 20th century.
Alternative spellings: Melaney, Melani, Melany

Melantho
Meaning: Dark flower
Origin: Greek

M

411

Pronunciation: mel AN tho
Description: In Greek mythology, Melantho appeared in Homer's epic poem *The Odyssey* as an unfaithful maid.
Alternative spellings: Melanthios, Melanthus

Melia

Meaning: Ash tree
Origin: Greek
Pronunciation: ME lee ya
Description: Melia is an uncommon girls' name of Greek origin and a variant of Amelia. The name means 'ash tree' in Greek and it is also the name of a nymph in Greek mythology.
Alternative spellings: Meliah, Melya

Melina

Meaning: Dark-haired
Origin: Greek
Pronunciation: meh LEE nah
Description: Melina is a name of ultimately Greek origin and may derive from *'meli'* (honey), *'melon'* (apple) or *'melas'* (dark). It is similar to the name Melanie, so could be seen as holding the same meaning of 'dark-haired'.
Alternative spellings: Meleena, Melena

Melinda

Meaning: No meaning
Origin: English
Pronunciation: meh LIN dah
Description: Melinda is thought to have been invented in the 18th century from the elements 'mel' and the suffix 'inda'. As such, it has no real meaning.

Melissa

Meaning: Honey bee
Origin: Greek
Pronunciation: meh LIS sa
Description: Melissa comes from the Greek word meaning 'honey bee'.
Alternative spellings: Melisa, Melisah

Melody

Meaning: A song
Origin: Greek
Pronunciation: MEL oh dee
Description: Melody comes from the Greek word *'melodia'*, meaning 'to sing'. According to the English dictionary, a melody is a pleasing arrangement of musical notes. Like Harmony, Melody has become a popular given name.
Alternative spellings: Melodey, Melodi, Melodie

Melrose

Meaning: Scottish town
Origin: Gaelic
Pronunciation: MEL roze
Description: Melrose is a name taken from the small Scottish town of the same name. It can be found as both a first name and a surname.
Alternative spellings: Mellrose, Melroze

Memphis

Meaning: Place in Tennessee
Origin: English
Pronunciation: mem FISS
Description: Memphis is a city in the American state of Tennessee. Like London and Paris, this name follows the trend of using place names for baby names.

Menna

Meaning: Unknown
Origin: Welsh
Pronunciation: MEH na
Description: The name Menna is found in several languages and therefore has an uncertain origin and meaning. It is a male ancient Egyptian name, as well as a modern Welsh girls' name.
Alternative spellings: Menah, Mennah

Mercedes

Meaning: Merciful
Origin: Spanish
Pronunciation: mer SAY dees
Description: The name Mercedes comes from a Spanish title for the Virgin Mary, 'our lady of the mercies', and has long been popular in that country. Its popularity may have been increased in the UK owing to the luxury car.
Alternative spellings: Merceydes, Mersaydes

Mercy

Meaning: Merciful
Origin: English
Pronunciation: MER see
Description: Mercy is from the English word for the virtue. It is used in the same way as Hope and both seem to be popular with Christian parents.
Alternative spellings: Mercey, Merci, Mercie

Meredith

Meaning: Great lord
Origin: Welsh
Pronunciation: ME re dith
Description: Meredith is the English form of the Old Welsh male name Maredudd. The name is well established in the US.
Alternative spellings: Meridith, Merredith

Merida

Meaning: One who has achieved a high honour
Origin: Latin
Pronunciation: mer ID ah
Description: Merida is a Latin name meaning 'one who has achieved a high honour'. It is the name of the main character from Disney's 2012 animated film, *Brave*.

Merryn

Meaning: Joyful
Origin: English
Pronunciation: MEH rin
Description: Merryn is a name of either Cornish or Old English origin, said to mean 'joyful'. St Merryn is the name of a village in Cornwall and the name may have originally been given to girls born here.
Alternative spellings: Merrin, Merin

Meryem

Meaning: Bitter
Origin: Turkish
Pronunciation: MERY am
Description: Meryem is the Turkish version of the Hebrew name Miriam, which in turn is a variation of the name Mary, meaning 'bitter'. Related names include Maryam and Maryann.
Alternative spellings: Mariam, Maryam

M

Meryl

Meaning: Bright; sea
Origin: Celtic
Pronunciation: mer RYL
Description: Meryl is the feminine version of the name Muriel. The name is composed of '*muir*' meaning 'sea,' and '*gheal*' meaning 'bright'. Meryl Streep is a famous American actress with this name.

Mia

Meaning: Sea dew
Origin: Danish
Pronunciation: MEE uh
Description: Mia is thought to be the Danish and Swedish form of Maria. The name enjoyed a sharp rise in popularity in the late 1990s and has since gained even more popularity. The name could have also come about as a pet form of names ending in 'mia', such as Hermia.
Alternative spellings: Mea, Miah

Miami

Meaning: Big water
Origin: Native American
Pronunciation: my AM ee
Description: Miami is a city in the south-eastern corner of Florida. The city was named for the nearby Miami River, derived from the Native American word *mayaimi* (meaning 'big water'), who were the people who lived around Lake Mayaimi.

Michaela

Meaning: Who is like God?
Origin: Hebrew
Pronunciation: me KAY lah
Description: Michaela is the feminine version of Michael, often shortened to Kayla. It is popular in English-, German- and Italian-speaking countries.
Alternative spellings: Makayla, Mikayla

Michalina

Meaning: Who is like God?
Origin: Hebrew
Pronunciation: me ka LEE nah
Description: Michalina is a variant of the masculine name Michael and it is found used mainly by Polish parents.
Alternative spellings: Michaelina, Michalena, Michalinah

Michelle

Meaning: Who is like God?
Origin: Hebrew
Pronunciation: MICH ell
Description: Michelle is the French feminine form of Michael, and soared in popularity during the 1970s and 80s. It is sometimes shortened to Shelley.
Alternative spellings: Michele, Mishelle

Mila

Meaning: Pleasant
Origin: Latin
Pronunciation: MEE lah
Description: Mila is used as a pet form for many Eastern European names, but is also a name in its own right, meaning 'pleasant'.
Alternative spellings: Melah, Milla

Milan

See entry in 'Names for Baby Boys A–Z'

Milana

Meaning: Favoured; from Milan
Origin: Slavic

Pronunciation: mee LAN ah
Description: Milana is a popular name in Slavic countries, and is an alternative spelling of the name Milena. It could also be an Italian name, meaning someone who comes from Milan.
See entry in 'Names for Baby Boys A–Z'

Mildred
Meaning: Gentle strength
Origin: English
Pronunciation: mill DRED
Description: Mildred is an Old English name composed of the elements of '*milde*' meaning 'gentle' and '*ðryð*' meaning 'strength'.

Miley
Meaning: Smiley
Origin: Hawaiian
Pronunciation: MY lee
Description: Miley is a phonetic spelling of the feminine Hawaiian name Maile. It has gained popularity owing to the teenage star Miley Cyrus and has taken on the meaning 'smiley'.
Alternative spellings: Mylee, Myley, Myli, Mylie

Millicent
Meaning: Hard-working
Origin: German
Pronunciation: MEE lee sent
Description: Millicent comes from an Old German word referring to having a strong work ethic. It was a popular name in France in the 12th century in the form Melisent, yet it has since returned to its original form. It is not a common name in Britain at the moment, although its pet form Millie is very popular.

Alternative spellings: Milicent, Milisent, Millisent

Millie
Meaning: Hard-working
Origin: German
Pronunciation: MILL lee
Description: Millie was originally used as the pet form of Millicent, but is now a first name in its own right.
Alternative spellings: Milli, Milly

Mimi
Meaning: Sea dew
Origin: Hebrew
Pronunciation: ME me
Description: Mimi is a pet form of the name Mary, a biblical name of Hebrew origin that means 'sea dew'.
Alternative spellings: Mimie, Mimy

Mina
Meaning: Love
Origin: German
Pronunciation: MEE nah
Description: It is thought that Mina first came about as a pet form of names ending in 'mina', such as Wilhelmina. Now as a name in its own right, it means 'love'. It could also be a variant of the Arabic Meena, meaning 'fish'.
Alternative spellings: Meena, Mena, Minah

Minahil
Meaning: Atmosphere of paradise
Origin: Urdu
Pronunciation: MIH na hil
Description: It is difficult to ascertain the precise origin and

M

meaning of Minahil, although a few sources claim it means 'atmosphere of paradise'.
Alternative spellings: Minahill

Minako
Meaning: Child of the beautiful Nara
Origin: Japanese
Pronunciation: Min A Ko
Description: Although Japanese, this name can be found right across Asia. The character *'mi'* means 'beautiful' and *'ko'* means 'child'.
Alternative spellings: Minakoh

Minami
Meaning: South
Origin: Japanese
Pronunciation: MEE nah mee
Description: Minami is most commonly found in Japan and only requires one Japanese character to be written, which means 'south'.
Alternative spellings: Miname, Minamie, Minamy

Mindy
Meaning: No meaning
Origin: English
Pronunciation: min DEE
Description: Mindy is a diminutive of the name Melinda. As Melinda is an 18th century invented name, neither names have any real meaning.

Minerva
Meaning: Intellect
Origin: Latin
Pronunciation: min ER vah
Description: Minerva is derived from the Latin word *'mens'* meaning 'intellect'. Minerva was the Roman goddess of wisdom and war. Minerva McGonagall is a character in the Harry Potter series.

Minnie
Meaning: Seeking protection
Origin: German
Pronunciation: MIH nee
Description: Minnie is a name that came about as the pet form of Wilma and Wilhelmina. Both of these names are feminine variants of the name William, meaning 'seeking protection'.
Alternative spellings: Minni, Minny

Mira
Meaning: Famed one; surprise
Origin: Latin
Pronunciation: MEER ah
Description: The name Mira is said to come from a Latin word used to express surprise. However, it is also used in Slavic languages to mean 'famed one'.
Alternative spellings: Mirah, Mirra

Mirabelle
Meaning: Wondrous
Origin: Latin
Pronunciation: mira BELLE
Description: Mirabelle is a Latin name meaning 'wondrous'. It stems from the Latin word *'mirabilis'*, giving the name its meaning.

Miracle
Meaning: Miracle
Origin: English
Pronunciation: MIH rih cul
Description: The name Miracle comes from the English word for an extraordinary event that surpasses all known human and natural powers. These virtues

names are often favoured by Christian parents.
Alternative spellings: Miracel, Miricle

Miranda
Meaning: Worthy of admiration
Origin: Latin
Pronunciation: mih RAN dah
Description: This name was supposedly invented by William Shakespeare for a character in his play *The Tempest*. He may have been inspired by the Latin name Mirabel, meaning 'admirable'.
Alternative spellings: Mirandah, Myranda

Miri
Meaning: Sea dew
Origin: Hebrew
Pronunciation: mi REE
Description: Miri is a diminutive of the name Miriam and both names are Hebrew in origin. The names mean 'sea dew'.

Miriam
Meaning: Sea dew
Origin: Hebrew
Pronunciation: MARE ee um
Description: This name was also spelt as Maryam and is an old version of the name Mary. It is thought to derive from the Hebrew *'harim'* meaning 'to raise'. It could also have the same meaning as Mary, which is 'sea dew'.
Alternative spellings: Miryam

Mischa
Meaning: Who is like God?
Origin: Hebrew
Pronunciation: ME sha

Description: Mischa derives from the masculine name Michael and so technically is a boys' name. However, due to its feminine sound the name has become popular as a girls' name.
Alternative spellings: Meisha, Misha, Mysha

Misty
Meaning: Thin fog
Origin: English
Pronunciation: MISS tee
Description: The name Misty derives from the English word 'mist' and may have started out as a nickname.
Alternative spellings: Misti, Mistie

Mitsuko
Meaning: Child of light
Origin: Japanese
Pronunciation: MEE tsoo koh
Description: This female name can be found throughout Asia, although it is most popular in Japan. It is written using two Japanese characters, *'mitsu'*, meaning 'light', and *'ko'*, meaning 'child'.
Alternative spellings: Mitsukoh

Miya
Meaning: The sacred house
Origin: Japanese
Pronunciation: mee YAH
Description: Miya could be an alternative spelling of the popular name Mia, although it is also a girls' name from Japan. It is said to mean 'temple' or 'sacred house'.

Miyuki
Meaning: Beautiful fortune
Origin: Japanese
Pronunciation: MEE yoo kee
Description: Miyuki is a Japanese

M

name of multiple meanings. It can be taken to mean 'beautiful fortune' or 'deep snow'. The pet form is Yuki.
Alternative spellings: Meyuki, Miyukie

Miyumi
Meaning: True bow; reasonable beauty
Origin: Japanese
Pronunciation: MEE yu mee
Description: Using traditional Japanese characters, Miyumi would mean 'true bow'. However, it can also be written using the character *'yu'*, meaning 'reason' and *'mi'*, meaning 'beauty'.
Alternative spellings: Meyumi, Miyumih

Moana
Meaning: Large body of water
Origin: Hawaiian
Pronunciation: mo ANNA
Description: Moana is a Hawaiian/Maori name meaning 'large body of water'. It was the name of the main character in the 2016 Disney animated film, *Moana*.

Molly
Meaning: Sea dew
Origin: English
Pronunciation: MOLL lee
Description: Molly first came about as a pet form of the name Mary and was coined in the 18th century. It is now a name in its own right.
Alternative spellings: Molli, Mollie

Momina
Meaning: Unknown
Origin: Arabic

Pronunciation: moh MEE nah
Description: There is not much in the way of documentation on the name Momina; however it is known that it is used in Persian and Urdu.
Alternative spellings: Mominah, Momyna

Mona
Meaning: Moon
Origin: English
Pronunciation: MOH na
Description: Mona, a unisex name though more usually feminine, is found in various forms in many languages and does not have a distinct origin. In Old English it means 'moon'.
Alternative spellings: Monah

Monica
Meaning: One with good advice
Origin: Latin
Pronunciation: MOH ni ka
Description: The name Monica is said to come from the Latin word *'monere'*, which refers to the giving of advice.
Alternative spellings: Monika

Monique
Meaning: One with good advice
Origin: Latin
Pronunciation: moh NEEK
Description: Monique is a variant of the Latin name Monica, meaning 'one with good advice'. The variant Monique is quite popular across Europe.
Alternative spellings: Moneke, Moneque, Monike

Monroe
Meaning: From the mouth of the

River Roe
Origin: Scottish
Pronunciation: mon ROW
Description: Monroe is a Scottish surname meaning 'from the mouth of the River Roe', the River Roe being a river in Ireland. This follows the contemporary trend of using last names as first names.

Montana

Meaning: State in the United States
Origin: English
Pronunciation: mon TAN uh
Description: Montana is the name of a state in the northwestern United States. Like London and Paris, this name follows the trend of using place names for baby names.

Morgan

Meaning: Great circle
Origin: Welsh
Pronunciation: MOR gun
Description: The name Morgan derives from the Old Welsh masculine name Morcant, which can mean 'bright' or 'great sea' or 'great circle'.
Alternative spellings: Morgann, Morganne

Morgana

Meaning: Sea; circle; bright
Origin: Welsh
Pronunciation: mor GAN uh
Description: Morgana is a Welsh name composed of the elements of '*môr*' meaning 'sea', '*cant*' meaning 'circle' or '*can*' meaning 'bright'.

Morwenna

Meaning: Maiden

Origin: Latin; Welsh
Pronunciation: mor WHEN nah; mor WEEN nah;
Description: Daughter of the Welsh King Brychan in the 12th century. Morwenna later became the patron saint of Morwenstow, a parish in Cornwall. Her name is thought to have derived from the Welsh word '*morwyn*' meaning 'maiden'.

Munira

Meaning: A wish
Origin: Arabic
Pronunciation: mu NEER ah
Description: Munira is a variant of the Arabic name Mouna, meaning 'a wish', and is popular in the Middle East.
Alternative spellings: Muneera, Munirah

Muskaan

Meaning: Smiling
Origin: Sanskrit
Pronunciation: mus KAHN
Description: Muskaan is a name often found used by Punjabi-speaking parents. It is said to come from a word meaning 'smiling'.
Alternative spellings: Muskan

Myla

Meaning: Mild and merciful
Origin: Latin
Pronunciation: MYA lah
Description: Myla is the feminine equivalent of the masculine name Miles, which is thought to derive from the Latin name Milo. It could also have come into usage as a shortened form of Michael.
Alternative spellings: Milah, Mylah

M

Myra

Meaning: Myrrh
Origin: Latin
Pronunciation: MY rah
Description: It is said that the name Myra was invented by the poet Fulke Greville and is based on the Latin noun *'myrrh'*. In Christian belief myrrh was given to Jesus upon his birth.
Alternative spellings: Myrah

Mysha

Meaning: Alive
Origin: Arabic
Pronunciation: ME sha
Description: As well as being a variant for the Arabic name Meisha, meaning 'alive', Mysha could also be considered a variant of the Hebrew name Mischa, meaning 'who is like God?'.
Alternative spellings: Meisha, Mischa, Misha

N

Nabila

Meaning: Noble
Origin: Arabic
Pronunciation: nah BEE lah
Description: Nabila is the feminine version of the name Nabil and shares its meaning. It is a popular name in the Middle East.
Alternative spellings: Nabeela, Nabilla

Nada

Meaning: Dew
Origin: Arabic
Pronunciation: nah DAH
Description: Nada is a feminine Arabic name meaning 'dew', as in the small water droplets that form on cool surfaces during the night. It is also the Spanish word for 'nothing'.

Nadia

Meaning: Hope
Origin: Russian
Pronunciation: NAR dee ah
Description: Nadia is the English form of the Russian name Nadya, short for Nadezhda, which means 'hope'.
Alternative spellings: Nadiah, Nadya

Nadine

Meaning: Hope
Origin: Russian
Pronunciation: NAY deen; nuh DEEN
Description: Nadine shares its roots with the name Nadia as they both derive from the Russian name Nadezhda.
Alternative spellings: Nadeene, Naydine

Nafisa

Meaning: Delicate and valuable
Origin: Arabic
Pronunciation: nah FEE sah
Description: Nafisa is uncommon in Britain but found throughout Arabic- and Swahili-speaking countries.
Alternative spellings: Nafeesa, Nafisah

Nahla

Meaning: To drink water
Origin: Arabic
Pronunciation: NAH lah
Description: Nahla is a name of Arabic origin; however, there are many similar names found in neighbouring languages such as Nala, which means 'gift' in Swahili.
Alternative spellings: Nala

Naila

Meaning: One who accomplishes
Origin: Arabic
Pronunciation: nah EEL ah
Description: In the history of the Islamic Empire, Naila was the name of the wife of Uthman, a caliph. The name is more popular with Muslim parents.
Alternative spellings: Nahlia, Naliah

Naima

Meaning: Content
Origin: Arabic
Pronunciation: nah EE mah
Description: Naima is an uncommon name in the UK but is more frequently found in Africa and America.
Alternative spellings: Naema, Naemah, Naimah

Naina

Meaning: Content
Origin: Arabic
Pronunciation: na AY na
Description: Naina is a variant of the name Naima, meaning 'content'.
Alternative spellings: Nainah, Nayana

Naira

Meaning: Shining; glittering
Origin: Indian
Pronunciation: NAI rah
Description: Naira is an Indian girls' name meaning 'shining' or 'glittering'.
Alternative spellings: Nairah

Naiya

Meaning: Vessel
Origin: Sanskrit
Pronunciation: NAY ah
Description: Naiya is of Sanskrit origin and probably means 'a vessel'. Names ending in 'ya' are becoming popular.
Alternative spellings: Naiyah, Naya

Najma

Meaning: Star
Origin: Arabic
Pronunciation: NAHJ mah
Description: Najma seems to be mostly found in the Middle East and in parts of Africa, and so is presumably of either Arabic or Swahili origin. The meaning of the name is also uncertain, but is generally accepted to mean 'star'.
Alternative spellings: Najmah

Nala

Meaning: Unknown
Origin: African
Pronunciation: nah LAH
Description: Nala is an African name that is commonly used throughout the Middle East, but the meaning is unknown. The name was made famous in the Disney film *The Lion King*, where she was Simba's wife.
Alternative spellings: Nalah

Nana

Meaning: Springtime
Origin: Hawaiian
Pronunciation: NAH na
Description: Nana comes from the springtime Hawaiian month of Nana. The name has spread somewhat in America; however it is not particularly popular in Britain because the title Nana is often used as an affectionate name for a grandmother.
Alternative spellings: Nanah, Nanna

Nana

Meaning: Various
Origin: Japanese; Greek; Ghanaian
Pronunciation: Na na
Description: Nana is a unisex name. In Japan and Korea it is a girls' name, as well as in Georgia where it is the fifth most popular girls' name. In Ghana, among the Akans, Nana is the title of a king or a queen, signifying royalty.
Alternative spellings: Naana, Nanah, Nanna

Nancy

Meaning: Favoured by God
Origin: Greek
Pronunciation: NAN see
Description: Nancy was originally a pet form of the Latin name Ann, but is now a name in its own right.
Alternative spellings: Nancey, Nanci, Nancie

Naomi

Meaning: Pleasantness
Origin: Hebrew
Pronunciation: nay OH mee
Description: Naomi means 'pleasantness' in Hebrew. In Christian belief Naomi was the mother-in-law of Ruth, an ancestor of Jesus.
Alternative spellings: Naomie, Naomy

Nat

Meaning: Birthday of Christ
Origin: Italian
Pronunciation: NAT
Description: Nat is a pet form of a number of names, such as Natalie, Natasha and Nathaniel. It is most often seen in a feminine context and is still rare as a given name in its own right.
Alternative spellings: Natt

Natalia

Meaning: Birthday of Christ
Origin: Italian
Pronunciation: na TAH lia; na TAR lia
Description: Natalia derives from the Italian word *'natale'*, meaning 'birthday' – especially that of Christ. It is therefore often given to children born around Christmas. St Natalia is regarded as a Christian saint.
Alternative spellings: Natalya

Natalie

Meaning: Birthday of Christ
Origin: Italian
Pronunciation: NAT a li
Description: Natalie is the French form of the Italian name Natalia. It appeared in the early 20th century, possibly as a result of the touring Ballets Russes, which was established in 1909.
Alternative spellings: Nataley, Natali, Nataly, Nathalie

Natasha

Meaning: Birthday of Christ
Origin: Russian
Pronunciation: na TA shuh
Description: Natasha is the Russian pet form of Natalia, but now exists as a well-adopted name worldwide.
Alternative spellings: Natacha, Natascha, Natassja

Nausicaa

Meaning: Excelling in ships
Origin: Greek
Pronunciation: NAW sik e a
Description: In Greek mythology, Nausicaa appeared in Homer's epic poem *Odyssey* as a young and beautiful princess who aids the shipwrecked Odysseus.
Alternative spellings: Nausica, Nausika

Nawal

Meaning: Gift
Origin: Arabic
Pronunciation: nah WAHL
Description: Nawal is an Arabic girls' name meaning 'gift'. Other names related to Nawal are Munal, Nawal, Nawl and Nawlaa.

Naya

Meaning: Resolve
Origin: Swahili
Pronunciation: nah YA
Description: Naya is an alternative spelling of the Swahili name Nia, meaning 'resolve'. It is one of the days of Kwanzaa, the African-American cultural holiday that is celebrated at the end of December and early January.

Neda

Meaning: Born on Sunday
Origin: Greek
Pronunciation: NEE dah
Description: In Greek mythology, Neda was a nymph who nurtured Zeus as a child. A river and a town were named after her.
Alternative spellings: Needa, Neyda

Neel

See entry in 'Names for Baby Boys A–Z'

Neha

Meaning: Raindrop
Origin: Sanskrit
Pronunciation: NEY ha
Description: The name Neha derives from the Sanskrit word *'nehal'*, meaning 'rain'. It is quite a popular name in India.
Alternative spellings: Nehah, Neyha

Nehir

Meaning: Unknown
Origin: Arabic
Pronunciation: neh HIR
Description: Nehir is an unusual name of uncertain origin and meaning. It is thought the name may be Turkish.
Alternative spellings: Nehire

Nela

Meaning: Horned
Origin: Latin
Pronunciation: NEE lah
Description: Nela originally came about as a pet form of Cornelia, meaning 'horned'. Although uncommon, it is now a name in its own right.
Alternative spellings: Neela, Nelah

N

Nell

Meaning: Ray of sunshine
Origin: Latin
Pronunciation: NELL
Description: The name Nell has roots in Old English, Latin, Greek and Arabic; however, its meaning is always associated with light. Nell was originally a shortened form for names such as Helen, Eleanor and Danielle.
Alternative spellings: Nel

Nella

Meaning: Bright one; light
Origin: English
Pronunciation: nehl AA
Description: The origins of Nella are very mixed; it and is often said to be the short form of several different names, including: Antonella, Cornelia and Fenella. However, in Old Greek, the word Nella means 'bright one' or 'light'.

Nellie

Meaning: Various
Origin: English
Pronunciation: NEL lee
Description: Nellie is a spelling variant of Nelly, the shortened form of Helen or Eleanor.
Alternative spellings: Nelli, Nelly

Nephele

Meaning: Cloudy
Origin: Greek
Pronunciation: NEH fel leh
Description: Nephele is an uncommon girls' name of Greek origin. In Greek mythology, Nephele was a goddess formed out of the clouds in the shape of the goddess Hera, by Zeus.

Alternative spellings: Nefele, Nephelee

Neriah

Meaning: Lamp of Yaweh
Origin: Hebrew
Pronunciation: ni RIE ya
Description: A unisex name meaning 'lamp of Yahweh' in Hebrew, Neriah was also the name of the father of Baruch in the Old Testament.

Nevaeh

Meaning: Heaven
Origin: English
Pronunciation: neh VAY ah
Description: Nevaeh is an alternative spelling of the popular modern name Neveah, which is 'heaven' spelt backwards. This is a relatively modern creation.

Nia

Meaning: Purpose
Origin: Gaelic
Pronunciation:
Description: Although this female name has mainly Gaelic origins it is also influenced by African-Swahili languages, in which it means 'purpose'. It is thought that Nia derives from the Welsh name Niamh, pronounced Neev, who was a goddess in Irish mythology and a queen in the land of eternal youth.

Niah

Meaning: Intended
Origin: Sanskrit
Pronunciation: NEE ah
Description: As well as being a spelling variant of the name Nia, Niah is also a name of Sanskrit

origins.
Alternative spellings: Nea, Nia, Nya, Nyah

Niamh
Meaning: Radiant
Origin: Gaelic
Pronunciation: NEEV
Description: Niamh is a popular name in Ireland. It first appears in Irish mythology where Niamh was the princess daughter of a sea god.
Alternative spellings: Neave, Neive, Neve

Nicol
See entry in 'Names for Baby Boys A–Z'

Nicola
Meaning: Victory of the people
Origin: Greek
Pronunciation: NIK olla
Description: Nicola is the Latinate feminine form of the masculine name Nicholas. The spelling Nikola can sometimes be used for boys.
Alternative spellings: Nickola, Nikola

Nicole
Meaning: Victory of the people
Origin: Greek
Pronunciation: NI cole
Description: Nicole is the French feminine form of Nicholas, meaning 'victory of the people'.
Alternative spellings: Nichole, Nikole

Nicolette
Meaning: Victory of the people
Origin: Greek
Pronunciation: NIC oll ETT
Description: Nicolette is a French

variation on the name Nicola, the feminine version of Nicholas.
Alternative spellings: Nicollette, Nikolette

Nicky
Meaning: Victory of the people
Origin: Greek
Pronunciation: NIK ee
Description: Nicky is a unisex name of Greek and English origin. It is a shortened variant of the Greek Nicholas.
Alternative spellings: Nickee, Nicki, Nickie

Nida
Meaning: Voice
Origin: Arabic
Pronunciation: nee DAH
Description: Nida is a feminine name of Arabic origins and because much documentation on the name is scarce in English translation it is difficult to give reliable information. It is used mainly by Muslim parents. The name is said to come from an Arabic word meaning 'voice'.

Nieve
Meaning: Snow
Origin: Spanish
Pronunciation: ne AY vay
Description: Nieve derives from the Spanish for 'snow' and is not common outside Spain. Names with a soft 'v' sound are, however, currently becoming more popular in Britain.
Alternative spellings: Niave, Niayva

Nihal
See entry in 'Names for Baby Boys A–Z'

N

Nika

Meaning: Good
Origin: Persian
Pronunciation: nee KAH
Description: Nika has Persian origins and the name means 'good'. However, it has other roots as well; in Greek, it means 'victory' and in Croatia and Slovenia it is the female variation of Nikola or Nikolaj.

Nikita

Meaning: Undefeated
Origin: Russian
Pronunciation: nee KEE ath
Description: In its original Russian form Nikita is a masculine name said to mean 'undefeated'. It has since been found in many languages used as a unisex or a feminine name.
Alternative spellings: Nichita, Nicita, Nikitah

Nikki

Meaning: Victory of the people
Origin: Greek
Pronunciation: NIK kee
Description: Nikki came about as a pet form of Nicola, but is now found as a given name in its own right.
Alternative spellings: Nicki, Nickie, Nicky, Nikkie, Nikky

Nikola

Meaning: People of victory
Origin: Greek
Pronunciation: nik O la
Description: There are many spelling variations of this female name including Nicola and Nickola and it is mainly used in English- and Italian-speaking countries. The name comes from the Greek '*nike*'

meaning 'victory' and 'loas' meaning 'people'. The name developed into this feminine form from the male form Nickolas and has been used in the English tongue since the 12th century.
Alternative spellings: Nicola

Nimra

Meaning: Cheetah
Origin: Arabic
Pronunciation: nim RAH
Description: Nimra is a name that is found used by Muslim parents, although its meaning is uncertain. It could derive from the word '*nimravidae*', meaning 'cheetah', or the Punjabi word '*nimrata*', meaning 'humility'.
Alternative spellings: Nimrah, Nymra

Nina

Meaning: Unknown
Origin: Russian
Pronunciation: NEE na
Description: The name Nina originated as the pet form of many Russian names ending in 'nina' such as Antonina and Tatynina. As such it does not have a specific meaning of its own.
Alternative spellings: Neena, Niina

Niobe

Meaning: Fern
Origin: Greek
Pronunciation: NEE o bee
Description: In Greek mythology, Niobe was a boastful queen of Thebes whose children were killed by Apollo as a reprimand for her arrogance.
Alternative spellings: Niobee, Niobi, Niobie, Nioby

Nisa

Meaning: Follower of Dionysus
Origin: Greek
Pronunciation: NEES ah
Description: Nisa is a pet form of the name Denisa, which derives from the Greek name Dennis, a follower of the Greek god Dionysus.
Alternative spellings: Neesa, Nisah

Nisha

Meaning: Night-time
Origin: Sanskrit
Pronunciation: NEE sha
Description: The name Nisha is often found in India and might be appropriate for a baby born during the night.
Alternative spellings: Neesha, Nichsa, Nishah

Niya

Meaning: Intended; caring
Origin: Arabic
Pronunciation: NEE ah
Description: In Arabic the name means 'intended', but in Ireland and Wales the name is thought to derive from Gaelic and could mean 'bright'. Niya could also be a pet form of the Arabic Anniyah, meaning 'caring'.
Alternative spellings: Neeya, Niyah

Noa

Meaning: Motion
Origin: Hebrew
Pronunciation: NOH ah
Description: Noa is an uncommon girls' name of Hebrew origin, meaning 'motion' and 'movement'. In the Old Testament, Noa was a daughter of Zelophehad.
Alternative spellings: Noah, Nua

Noel

See entry in 'Names for Baby Boys A–Z'

Noelle

Meaning: Christmas
Origin: English
Pronunciation: no EL
Description: Noelle is the feminine version of the name Noel. Noel comes from a French word meaning 'birthday' and is associated with the day of Christ's birth, Christmas Day. Noel is the original spelling but the variation Nowell can be found in Britain.
Alternative spellings: Nowell

Noemi

Meaning: Pleasant
Origin: Hebrew
Pronunciation: no EE mi
Description: Noemi is a variant of the Hebrew name Naomi, who was the mother-in-law of Ruth in the Bible.
Alternative spellings: Noemie, Noemy

Nola

Meaning: Charming; pale shoulders
Origin: German
Pronunciation: NOH la
Description: Nola could have come about as the pet form of several names. It could be short for the German name Winola, meaning 'charming', or derive from the Gaelic name Fionnuala, meaning 'pale shoulders'.
Alternative spellings: Nolah

Noor

Meaning: Light

N

Origin: Arabic
Pronunciation: NOOR
Description: This name is a variation of the Arabic name Nura, borne by the former queen of Jordan. Noor can most commonly be found in Malaysian-, Arabic- and Indian-speaking countries.
Alternative spellings: Nore, Nour, Nur, Nure

Nora

Meaning: Honour; pale shoulders
Origin: Latin
Pronunciation: NOR ra
Description: Nora is most probably a pet form of the Latin name Honora, meaning 'honour'. It is also thought of as a variant of the Irish name Fionnuala, meaning 'pale shoulders'.
Alternative spellings: Norah

Nova

Meaning: New
Origin: English
Pronunciation: no VAH
Description: Nova comes from the Latin word '*novus*,' meaning 'new'. It was first used as a name during the 19th century.

Nuala

Meaning: Fair-haired; pale shoulders
Origin: Gaelic
Pronunciation: NOO lah
Description: Nuala is a shortened form of the Gaelic name Fionnuala, which appears in Irish mythology and means 'pale shoulders'. For a baby, we can probably take Nuala to mean 'fair-haired'.
Alternative spellings: Nualah

Nuha

Meaning: Sun god
Origin: Arabic
Pronunciation: NOO hah
Description: Before the advent of Islam, northern tribes in Arabia worshipped three deities: Ruda, Nuha and Atarsamain. The goddess Nuha was associated with the sun.
Alternative spellings: Nuhah

Nusaybah

Meaning: Noble bloodline
Origin: Arabic
Pronunciation: noo SAY ba
Description: The name Nusaybah was originally given to a baby of a noble bloodline. Nusaybah Bint Ka'ab was a companion of Muhammad and the first woman to fight for the cause of Islam.
Alternative spellings: Nusayba, Nusaybaa

Nyah

Meaning: Lustrous
Origin: Gaelic
Pronunciation: nee AH
Description: Nyah is a spelling variation of the feminine name Nia, which can be traced to Gaelic origins where it is said to mean 'lustrous'. However it is also found used as a pet form of names ending in 'nia' such as Antonia, whereby its meaning would differ. The form Nyah was probably invented to give the name more credit as an independent name.

Nyla

Meaning: Champion
Origin: Gaelic
Pronunciation: NYE lah

Description: Nyla could be a feminine form of Nyles, deriving from the Irish name Neil, meaning 'champion'. The name could also be Hebrew or Arabic, come from the name of the river Nile.
Alternative spellings: Nilah, Nylah

Nylah
Meaning: Cloud
Origin: Gaelic
Pronunciation: nye LAH
Description: Nylah is a feminine name of uncertain origin and meaning. It seems it could come from Gaelic origins, where it is said its meaning is 'cloud'.

However some also trace it back to Egyptian origins, where it is thought to stem from the name of the River Nile, and is thought to be the feminine version of the masculine name Nile.

Nyx
Meaning: Night
Origin: Greek
Pronunciation: Nyks
Description: In Greek mythology, Nyx is the goddess of the night. She was found only in the shadows of the world and only ever seen in glimpses.
Alternative spellings: Naix, Niks, Nix

O

Ocean
Meaning: The ocean
Origin: English
Pronunciation: oh SHUN
Description: Ocean is a name that comes from the noun in the English language. It is found used for both boys and girls. It is an uncommon name but mostly used in English-speaking countries.

Octavia
Meaning: Eighth
Origin: Latin
Pronunciation: ok TAY vee uh
Description: Octavia is a Latin female name derived from the Roman family name Octavius.
Alternative spellings: Octayvia

Ola
Meaning: Descendant of an ancestor
Origin: Norse
Pronunciation: OH la
Description: Ola is a unisex variant of the Old Norse masculine name Olaf, meaning 'descendant of an ancestor'. It is most often found in Germany.
Alternative spellings: Olah, Olla

Olga
Meaning: Holy
Origin: Norse
Pronunciation: ol GAH
Description: Olga is a variant of the Old Norse feminine name Helga, which is mainly found in Russia. Saint Olga was a Russian

N
O

saint and many take the name after her. The name in its various forms has long been popular across Scandinavia. The Old Norse name is said to mean 'holy'.

Olive

Meaning: Olive
Origin: Latin
Pronunciation: OL iv
Description: Olive refers to the Mediterranean fruit and the olive branch is considered a symbol of peace.
Alternative spellings: Olife

Olivia

Meaning: Olive
Origin: Latin
Pronunciation: oh LIVY uh
Description: Olivia was first used by Shakespeare in his play *Twelfth Night*. Shakespeare may have taken it as a feminine form of Oliver or he may have derived it from the Latin for 'olive'.
Alternative spellings: Oliviah, Oliwia

Ollie

See entry in 'Names for Baby Boys A–Z'

Omari

See entry in 'Names for Baby Boys A–Z'

Ondine

Meaning: Little wave
Origin: Latin
Pronunciation: on DINE
Description: Ondine is a Latin name meaning 'little wave'. Ondines are mythical beings

associated with water and are found throughout classical literature.

Onyx

Meaning: Gemstone
Origin: Greek
Pronunciation: on ICKS
Description: Onyx is the name of a gemstone that is usually jet-black in colour. Like Opal and Ruby, this follows the trend of using gemstone names as given names.

Opal

Meaning: Precious stone
Origin: English
Pronunciation: opal
Description: Opal is taken from the precious stone of the same name. Like Ruby and Sapphire, these gemstone names are a popular trend for baby naming.

Ophelia

Meaning: Help; serpent
Origin: Greek
Pronunciation: o FEE lee a
Description: Ophelia, the name of the tragic female character in *Hamlet*, was made famous by Shakespeare. It is thought that the name either derives from the Greek *'ophelos'*, meaning 'help', or *'ophis'*, meaning 'serpent'.
Alternative spellings: Ofelia, Ofeliah, Opheliah

Oprah

Meaning: Fawn
Origin: Hebrew
Pronunciation: OH pruh

Description: Oprah is a spelling variant of the name Ophrah. It has been popularised by the success of US chat show hostess Oprah Winfrey.
Alternative spellings: Ophrah

Oreoluwa
Meaning: A gift from God
Origin: African
Pronunciation: oh REE oh LOO wa
Description: Oreoluwa originates from the Yoruba tribe in Nigeria and means 'a gift from God'. It is an uncommon name outside Africa.
Alternative spellings: Oreoluwah, Orioluwa

Oriana
Meaning: Golden sunrise
Origin: Greek
Pronunciation: or ree AN ah
Description: The exact origin of Oriana is uncertain. It could have derived from the Latin name Aurara, meaning 'sunrise' or 'dawn'. It could also have roots in Gaelic, where it would mean 'golden'.
Alternative spellings: Orianah, Oryana

Orla
Meaning: Golden princess
Origin: Gaelic
Pronunciation: OR lah
Description: Orla is a Gaelic name derived from the original Irish spelling Orlaith, meaning 'golden princess'. Orla and Orliath are popular in Ireland, with Orla also becoming popular elsewhere.
Alternative spellings: Orlagh, Orlah, Orlaith

Orlagh
Meaning: Precious princess
Origin: Gaelic
Pronunciation: or LAH
Description: Orlagh is a feminine name of Gaelic origin, and is said to mean 'precious princess'. Its original Irish spelling is Orlaith and although not often found in England, both the original and the modern form are popular in Ireland. This is one of the anglicised spellings of Órfhlaith, others being Órlaith and Órla.

Orleanna
Meaning: Golden
Origin: English
Pronunciation: or LEE anna
Description: Orleanna is an English name that is related to the Latin name Aurelius and French name Orlina, both of which mean 'golden' or have something to do with gold.

Ottilie
Meaning: Rich
Origin: German
Pronunciation: OTT eh lee
Description: The name Ottilie derives from the German masculine name Otto, which means 'rich'. Ottilie is mainly found in Germany.
Alternative spellings: Otili, Otilie, Otily, Ottili, Ottily

Ottoline
Meaning: Wealth
Origin: English
Pronunciation: otto LINE
Description: Ottoline is a diminutive of the name Ottilie, which in turn was the German version of the name Odilia, meaning 'wealth'.

O

P

Padme

Meaning: No meaning
Origin: English
Pronunciation: pad MA
Description: Padme is a modern, invented name and as such has no meaning. It was made for Padme Amidala, a character in the Star Wars franchise.

Paige

Meaning: Page
Origin: English
Pronunciation: PAYJ
Description: Paige was originally a surname given to those who served as pages to the lord. Paige then became a popular given name in the US during the 20th century and is usually found on girls.
Alternative spellings: Page, Payge

Paisley

Meaning: Persian pattern
Origin: Gaelic
Pronunciation: PAYZ lee
Description: Paisley is the name of a town in Scotland famous for its weaving. The name could have come about as a surname for those who lived there before it transferred to a girls' name.
Alternative spellings: Paislee, Paisleigh, Paislie, Payslee, Paysleigh, Paysley, Payslie

Paloma

Meaning: Dove
Origin: Latin
Pronunciation: Puh LOH muh
Description: Popular in other European countries, particularly in Spain and Italy, Paloma derives from the Latin word '*palumbus*' meaning a pigeon, or a dove.

Pamela

Meaning: Honey bread
Origin: English
Pronunciation: PAM eh la; pah MEH la
Description: This name was invented by the Elizabethan poet Sir Philip Sidney, who may have combined the Greek words '*pan*' and '*meli*'. At this time, the emphasis was on the second syllable.
Alternative spellings: Pamelah, Pamella

Pandora

Meaning: All gifts
Origin: Greek
Pronunciation: pan DAWR ya
Description: Pandora was a famous figure from Greek mythology. She was the first mortal woman and Zeus gave her a jar containing all the troubles and ills of mankind, telling her not to open it. She did, however, and unleashed the evil spirits into the world. The name is a combination of '*pan*' (all) and '*doron*' (gift).

Paris

Meaning: Paris
Origin: Greek
Pronunciation: PA riss
Description: Paris, the capital city of France, was a name often given

to boys in the Middle Ages. In Greek legend Paris carries Helen from Sparta to Troy, causing the Trojan War.
Alternative spellings: Pariss, Parys

Patience
Meaning: Endure suffering
Origin: Latin
Pronunciation: PAY shunce
Description: This name derives from the English word, which itself comes from the Latin *'pati'*, meaning 'to suffer'. Patience is a name often favoured by Christian parents.

Patricia
Meaning: Noble
Origin: Latin
Pronunciation: pa TRISH ah
Description: Patricia is the feminine version of the Gaelic name Patrick. Both names derive from the Latin *'patricius'*, a title given to a nobleman, so the name means 'noble'.
Alternative spellings: Patricjia, Patricya, Patrycia, Patrycja

Paula
Meaning: Modest
Origin: Latin
Pronunciation: PAW luh
Description: Paula is the Latin feminine form of Paul, meaning 'small' or 'modest', and is the name of various early saints.
Alternative spellings: Paulah, Paulla

Paulina
Meaning: Modest
Origin: Latin
Pronunciation: pall LEE nah
Description: Paulina is the Spanish feminine version of the

popular name Paul, from the Latin name Paulus meaning 'small' or 'modest'. Paulina is especially popular in Poland and Italy.
Alternative spellings: Paulinah, Paullina

Pauline
Meaning: Modest
Origin: Latin
Pronunciation: pall LEEN
Description: Pauline is the French feminine version of the popular name Paul, from the Latin name Paulus meaning 'small' or 'modest'.
Alternative spellings: None

Pavani
Meaning: Purifying
Origin: Sanskrit
Pronunciation: pah VAN ee
Description: Pavani is a Sanskrit girls' name meaning 'purifying'. It has connotations of holiness and purity.

Payton
See entry in 'Names for Baby Boys A–Z'

Peaches
Meaning: Fruit name
Origin: English
Pronunciation: peech ES
Description: Peaches is taken directly from the fruit name. It was made famous by the late British socialite, Peaches Geldof.

Pearl
Meaning: Light's creation
Origin: English
Pronunciation: PERL
Description: The name Pearl comes from the English word

P

for the valuable gemstone and the name carries connotations of beauty. Pearl is also the birthstone for June.

Alternative spellings: Pearle, Pearll

Peggy

Meaning: Pearl; light's creation
Origin: Latin
Pronunciation: PEG ee
Description: Peggy was originally a pet form of the name Margaret but is now often found as a name in its own right.
Alternative spellings: Peggi, Peggie

Penelope

Meaning: Weaver
Origin: Greek
Pronunciation: pen EL lo pe
Description: In Greek mythology Penelope was the wife of Odysseus, who waited for him to return home for 20 years. The name therefore has associations with faithfulness.
Alternative spellings: Penelopi, Penelopie, Penelopy

Penny

Meaning: Weaver
Origin: Greek
Pronunciation: PEN ee
Description: Penny is a pet form of the name Penelope and has become a name in its own right.
Alternative spellings: Penni, Pennie

Peony

Meaning: Flower name
Origin: English
Pronunciation: pee ON ee

Description: Peony comes from the pink flowers of the same name. Like Rose and Tulip, Peony is part of the trend of using flowers as given names.

Perdita

Meaning: Lost
Origin: Latin
Pronunciation: per DEE tah
Description: Perdita is the Latin word for 'lost'. This was the name of the heroine in Shakespeare's play, *The Winter's Tale*.

Perrie

Meaning: Pear tree
Origin: French
Pronunciation: pe RIE
Description: Perrie is a French name meaning 'pear tree'. Perrie is actually a unisex name, although there are more girls with this name than boys. It is also an alternative spelling of the French boys' name, Perry, which has the same meaning.
Alternative spellings: Perry

Perry

See entry in 'Names for Baby Boys A–Z'

Persephone

Meaning: To Destroy; murder
Origin: Greek
Pronunciation: per SEF e nee
Description: Persephone is the name of Demeter and Zeus' daughter in Greek mythology. She was famously abducted by Hades, god of the Underworld, and made to be his bride. She is allowed to return to the surface for part of the year, and her movements helped explain the changing of the seasons.

Petal

Meaning: Flower petal
Origin: English
Pronunciation: pet ALL
Description: Petal comes from the English vocabulary word of the same spelling, referring to the petals on a flower. It is also often used as a nickname as well as a given name.

Petra

Meaning: Rock
Origin: Greek
Pronunciation: PET ra
Description: Petra is the feminine form of Peter, meaning 'rock'. It is a fairly uncommon name in Britain.
Alternative spellings: Peitra, Pettra

Peyton

Meaning: Farm of Paege
Origin: English
Pronunciation: PAY ton
Description: The name Peyton is actually a unisex name and so can be used for both boys and girls. There is a different spelling variation, which is Payton, and the Farm of Paege was often referred to as peacock town. The name derives from two elements of '*pawa*' meaning 'peacock' and '*tun*' meaning 'town'.
Alternative spellings: Payton

Phaedra

Meaning: Bright
Origin: Greek
Pronunciation: fay DRAH
Description: Phaedra is derived from the Greek word '*phaidros*', meaning 'bright'. She was the daughter of King Minos and wife of Theseus in Greek mythology.

Pheobe

Meaning: One who glows
Origin: Greek
Pronunciation: FEE be
Description: Pheobe is a variant spelling of the name Phoebe, which is a feminine name of Greek origin and is said to mean 'one who glows'. It is also sometimes found as a pet form of the Greek name Euphemia, which means 'beautiful silence'. This name is extremely rare in Britain; however its variant Phoebe is currently a popular name for girls.
Alternative spellings: Phoebe

Phil

See entry in 'Names for Baby Boys A–Z'

Philippa

Meaning: Lover of horses
Origin: Greek
Pronunciation: FILL ih puh
Description: Philippa is the feminine form of Philip. It is often shortened to Pippa or Pip.
Alternative spellings: Philipa, Philipah, Phillipa, Phillippa

Phoebe

Meaning: Bright
Origin: Greek
Pronunciation: FEE bee
Description: Phoebe is the feminine version of Phoebus, from the Greek name for the god of light. Phoebe is also an irregular satellite of Saturn. The name has experienced a boost since its use in hit TV sitcom *Friends*.

P

Alternative spellings: Febe, Phebe, Phoebee, Phoebie, Phoeby

Phoenix
See entry in 'Names for Baby Boys A–Z'

Phyllis
Meaning: Green bough
Origin: Greek
Pronunciation: fill US
Description: Phyllis is a Greek name meaning 'green bough'. In Greek mythology, she is the daughter of a Thracian king and wife of Demophon.

Pia
Meaning: Devout
Origin: Latin
Pronunciation: PEE ah
Description: Pia is the feminine version of the Latin name Pius, which shares the same root as the word 'pious', meaning 'devout'.
Alternative spellings: Pea, Piah

Piper
Meaning: Pipe player
Origin: English
Pronunciation: PIPE er
Description: Piper, originally a surname for families whose father played the pipe, is now a unisex name.
Alternative spellings: Pypa, Pyper

Pippa
Meaning: Lover of horses
Origin: Greek
Pronunciation: PIP pah
Description: Pippa originally came about as a shortened female version of the name Philip. Now it is

seen as the short form of the name Philippa or a given name in its own right.
Alternative spellings: Pipa, Pippah

Pixie
Meaning: Mischievous fairy
Origin: English
Pronunciation: PIX ee
Description: Pixie comes from the word for the sprite-like creature. Its origin is uncertain since many fairy tales are shared between cultures. The name became more popular when Bob Geldof gave it to his daughter.
Alternative spellings: Pixey, Pixi, Pixy

Pocahontas
Meaning: Playful one
Origin: Native American
Pronunciation: poh CAH hon tas
Description: While Pocahontas was a real-life Native American figure, many most likely know her through Disney's 1995 film *Pocahontas*. She was the daughter of Chief Powhatan, of the Powhatan Indian tribe in Virginia. The name Pocahontas is most likely a childhood nickname that referred to her spirited nature, and also why it means 'playful one'.

Pola
Meaning: Poppy
Origin: Arabic
Pronunciation: POH la
Description: Pola is the pet form of the Arabic name Amapola, meaning 'poppy'. It is now seen as a name in its own right and has associations with beauty.

Alternative spellings: Polah, Polar

Polly
Meaning: Sea dew
Origin: Gaelic
Pronunciation: POL lee
Description: Polly actually derives from the name Molly, as in the Middle Ages it was commonplace to replace 'M' with 'P' to form a pet name.
Alternative spellings: Polley, Polli, Pollie

Pollyanna
Meaning: Optimistic
Origin: Hebrew
Pronunciation: POH lee AH na
Description: Pollyanna was originally a double-barrelled name. Owing to the use of the name in E.H. Porter's children's novel *Pollyanna*, the name is associated with optimism and bravery.
Alternative spellings: Poliana, Polianna, Polliana, Pollianna, Pollyana, Polyana, Polyanna

Pooja
Meaning: Prayer; worship
Origin: Indian
Pronunciation: poo JAH
Description: Pooja is a popular Indian girls' name meaning 'prayer' or 'worship'.

Poppy
Meaning: Poppy flower
Origin: English
Pronunciation: POP ee
Description: Poppy is the name of a flower and often given to girls born on Remembrance Sunday. Poppies are seen as symbols of remembrance owing to their link with World War I.
Alternative spellings: Poppey, Poppi, Poppie

Posey
Meaning: Flower bouquet
Origin: English
Pronunciation: poh ZEE
Description: Posey comes from the English vocabulary word of the same spelling, referring to a small, decorative flower bouquet usually tied with ribbon.

Precious
Meaning: Precious
Origin: English
Pronunciation: PREH shus
Description: Precious is a name that comes directly from the English word, which means 'of high value'. It is often used as a term of affection and is now a name in its own right.

Primrose
Meaning: Flower
Origin: English
Pronunciation: PRIM rose
Description: Primrose comes directly from the name of the flower. The name means 'first rose' because it is one of the first flowers to bloom in the spring.
Alternative spellings: Primroze, Prymrose, Prymroze

Princess
Meaning: Royalty
Origin: English
Pronunciation: PRIN sess
Description: This name was originally only used as a title for particular members of the royal

P

family; however in recent years it seems to have transferred into a popular forename.
Alternative spellings: Pryncess

Priscilla
Meaning: Long life
Origin: Latin
Pronunciation: pre SIL ah
Description: Priscilla is an elongated version of the Roman name Pricsa, which derives from the Latin word *'pricus'*, meaning 'old'. It is thought the name would have been given to wish long life on the bearer.
Alternative spellings: Priscila, Pryscilla

Prisha
Meaning: Gift
Origin: Arabic
Pronunciation: PREE sha
Description: Prisha is a unisex name often favoured by Hindu parents and is most commonly found in India.
Alternative spellings: Preesha, Prishah

Priya
Meaning: Beloved
Origin: Sanskrit
Pronunciation: PREE yah
Description: The translation of Priya is 'beloved'. In Hindu texts the name is often used to denote a romantic lover or a wife. Priya was a daughter of Daksha, the creator god.
Alternative spellings: Preeya, Priyah

Priyal
Meaning: Beloved
Origin: Indian

Pronunciation: pee YAL
Description: Priyal is an Indian girls' name meaning 'beloved'. The name is directly translated from the Sanskrit word.

Priyanka
Meaning: Symbol of love; beloved symbol
Origin: Sanskrit
Pronunciation: pre YANK ah
Description: Priyanka comes from the Sanskrit words *'priya'*, meaning 'beloved' and *'anka'*, meaning 'symbol'. We can take the name to mean either 'symbol of love' or 'beloved symbol'.
Alternative spellings: Preeyanka, Priyankah

Pru
Meaning: Good judgement
Origin: English
Pronunciation: proo
Description: Pru is the shortened version of the name Prudence, meaning 'good judgement'. Although it is a nickname, it can also be used as a given name.
Alternative spellings: Prue

Prudence
Meaning: Good judgement
Origin: English
Pronunciation: proo DENCE
Description: Prudence is an English name from the word of the same meaning. The name means 'good judgement,' and in England it was used during the Middle Ages and revived in the 17th century by the Puritans.

Purdy
Meaning: For God

Origin: French
Pronunciation: pure DEE
Description: Purdy is a French surname translated from the words 'pour Dieu,' meaning 'for God'. This follows the contemporary trend of using last names as first names.
Alternative spellings: Purdie

Purity

Meaning: Pure
Origin: English
Pronunciation: pure IT ee
Description: Purity comes from the English vocabulary word of the same name and means 'pure'. Like Charity and Grace, Purity is a virtue name.

Q

Queenie

Meaning: Queen
Origin: English
Pronunciation: KWEE nee
Description: The name Queenie derives from the English word 'queen' and comes from the Old English 'cwen', meaning 'woman'.

Queenie was also used as a pet name for Queen Victoria.
Alternative spellings: Queeney, Queeni, Queeny

Quinn

See entry in 'Names for Baby Boys A–Z'

R

Rabia

Meaning: Garden in flower
Origin: Arabic
Pronunciation: RAH bee ah
Description: Rabia, the name of an Islamic saint, is popular with Muslim parents. Rabia is also the name of a small town in Iraq.
Alternative spellings: Rabbia, Rabiya

Rachel

Meaning: Ewe
Origin: Hebrew

Pronunciation: RAY chul
Description: This biblical name means 'ewe' in Hebrew. Rachel was the wife of Jacob and mother of Joseph.
Alternative spellings: Rachael, Rachelle

Rachelle

Meaning: Ewe
Origin: Hebrew
Pronunciation: rash EL
Description: Rachelle is an elaboration upon Rachel with a French influence.

P
Q
R

439

Alternative spellings: Rachel, Rachael

Rae
Meaning: Ewe
Origin: Hebrew
Pronunciation: ray
Description: Rae is a pet form of the name Rachael which is originally a Hebrew name meaning 'ewe'. It could also be the feminine form of Ray, but this is less common.
Alternative spellings: Ray

Rahma
Meaning: Compassion
Origin: Swahili
Pronunciation: rah MAH
Description: Rahma is a name that has its origin in Africa, and most likely among Swahili-speaking people. It is a name that means 'compassion'.
Alternative spellings: Rahmah

Rain
Meaning: Rain fall
Origin: English
Pronunciation: rain
Description: Rain comes from the English vocabulary word of the same spelling referring to the type of weather.

Raina
Meaning: Queen
Origin: Slavic
Pronunciation: rain AH
Description: Raina is a Slavic name meaning 'queen' and likely has the same roots as the English vocabulary word 'reign'. Therefore, the name refers to a ruler or leader.
Alternative spellings: Rayna

Rainbow
Meaning: Rainbow
Origin: English
Pronunciation: RAYN bo
Description: The name Rainbow comes from the English word. It was popularised as a name during the 'flower power' movement of the 1960s.
Alternative spellings: Rainbo, Raynbow

Raisa
Meaning: Rose
Origin: Yiddish
Pronunciation: rai SAH
Description: Raisa is a Yiddish name meaning 'rose'. Another name that is similar to Raisa is Raisel, and is the male variation to the name.

Raja
Meaning: Optimism
Origin: Arabic
Pronunciation: rah-JAH
Description: Although the Arabic name Raja is considered unisex, the feminine and masculine forms are often pronounced differently. For boys the pronunciation is 'rah-juh'.
Alternative spellings: Raija, Raijah, Rajah

Ramla
Meaning: Seer
Origin: African
Pronunciation: RAM lah
Description: The name Ramla is found across several African languages and its exact origin is unclear. However, it generally translates to mean 'seer', which means a person who has the gift to see into the future.

Alternative spellings: Ramlah, Ramlla

Ramona
Meaning: Wise protector
Origin: Spanish
Pronunciation: rah mo NAH
Description: Ramona is the female version of the name Ramon and it means 'wise protector'. It became popular in English-speaking regions after the publication of Helen Hunt Jackson's novel, *Ramona*, in 1884.

Rana
Meaning: Mesmerising
Origin: Arabic
Pronunciation: RAH nah
Description: Rana is a unisex Arabic name; however it is more commonly found on girls due to the feminine 'a' sound.
Alternative spellings: Raina, Ranah, Rayna

Rania
Meaning: Singing queen
Origin: Sanskrit
Pronunciation: RAN yah
Description: Rania is a variant of the Sanskrit name Rani, meaning 'singing queen'. It has increased in popularity by association with Queen Rania of Jordan.
Alternative spellings: Raniah, Raniya

Rashida
Meaning: Righteous; wise
Origin: Arabic
Pronunciation: ra SHEE dah
Description: Rashida is an Arabic word that means 'righteous' or 'wise', and has connotations of someone who knows their way. Rashida Jones is a famous American actress with this name.

Raven
Meaning: A black bird
Origin: English
Pronunciation: ray VEN
Description: Raven comes from the black bird that shares the same name. Raven Symoné is a famous actress who has this name, and was the star of the Disney show, also called *That's So Raven*.

Rawan
Meaning: River that feeds
Origin: Arabic
Pronunciation: rah WAN
Description: Rawan derives from the Arabic verb *'rawi'*, meaning 'to feed with water'. A popular girls' name, it is also the name of a river that flows through heaven in Islamic belief.
Alternative spellings: Rawanne

Raya
Meaning: Friend to all
Origin: Arabic
Pronunciation: RAY ah
Description: The name Raya appears in many languages and is likely to have derived as a shortened form of a longer name such as Rayan. It is believed to be Arabic in origin.
Alternative spellings: Raiya, Rayah

Rayaan
Meaning: Young maid
Origin: English
Pronunciation: ray AN
Description: Rayaan is a variation

R

of the name Rayann, which in itself is an unusual name of uncertain origin and meaning. It is found used in several different languages. It sounds similar to a group of Welsh names including Rhianna, which are said to mean 'young maid'. Rihana is another similar name, this time from Arabic origins, and is said to refer to a kind of herb. Rayann could also have come about as a compound of the two names Ray and Ann.

Rayah
Meaning: Friend
Origin: Arabic
Pronunciation: RAY ah
Description: Rayah is an Arabic Muslim girls' name meaning 'friend,' and would be a good choice for parents looking for something with a sweet meaning.
Alternative spellings: Raya, Reaya

Rayan
See entry in 'Names for Baby Boys A–Z'

Rayann
Meaning: Great goddess
Origin: English
Pronunciation: ray AN; RAY an
Description: As well as being a spelling variant of the Sanskrit name Rayan, Rayann could derive from a group of Welsh names, including Rhianna, which mean 'great goddess'. It may also be a combination of the names Ray and Ann.
Alternative spellings: Raiyan, Rayan, Rayanne

Reba
Meaning: Binding

Origin: English
Pronunciation: ree BAH
Description: Reba was originally a shortened form of the name Rebecca and as such, shares the same meaning of 'binding'. However, it is not established as a given name in its own right. Reba McEntire is a famous American country singer and actress.
Alternative spellings: Reeba

Rebecca
Meaning: Binding
Origin: Hebrew
Pronunciation: REH beh cuh
Description: In the Bible, Rebecca was the wife of Isaac. It derives from a Hebrew word meaning to tie or constrict and its meaning is 'binding'.
Alternative spellings: Rebeca, Rebeka, Rebekah

Reem
Meaning: Little deer
Origin: Arabic
Pronunciation: REEM
Description: From the Arabic word for a 'little deer', Reem is popular across the Middle East and Africa.
Alternative spellings: Ream, Reeme

Reese
Meaning: Enthusiastic
Origin: Welsh
Pronunciation: REECE
Description: Reese is another anglicised version of the Welsh name Rhys. It is unisex and especially popular with girls in America.
Alternative spellings: Reece, Rhys

Reeva

Meaning: Shore, riverbank; the sacred Narmada River
Origin: French
Pronunciation: ree VAH
Description: Reeva has both French and Sanskrit roots, meaning 'shore' and 'riverbank' in the former, and 'the sacred Narmada River' in the latter.
Alternative spellings: Riva

Regan

Meaning: Royalty
Origin: Gaelic
Pronunciation: RAY gen; REE gan
Description: Regan is a unisex Gaelic name first featuring in Shakespeare's play *King Lear*. The name has associations with the word 'regal'.
Alternative spellings: Raegan, Reagan, Reagun, Reegan

Regina

Meaning: Queen
Origin: Latin
Pronunciation: reh GEEN ah
Description: Regina comes directly from the Latin word of the same spelling, meaning 'queen'. It is also the feminine version of the name Reginald.

Reiko

Meaning: Courteous child; thankful child
Origin: Japanese
Pronunciation: REH eh ko
Description: The name Reiko is traditionally written using the Japanese characters *'rei'*, meaning 'thanks' or 'salute', and *'ko'*, meaning 'child'. This gives the name

the meaning 'courteous child' or 'thankful child'.
Alternative spellings: Rehiko, Reikoh

Remi

Meaning: From Rheims
Origin: French
Pronunciation: REH me
Description: The name Remi derives from the French town Rheims and would have originally been given to those who lived in the town. There was also a French saint who bore the name Remi.
Alternative spellings: Remy

Remy

See entry in 'Names for Baby Boys A–Z'

Renee

Meaning: Reborn
Origin: French
Pronunciation: REH nay
Description: Like many French names, Renee is often spelt using an accent. The name comes from the Latin word *'renatus'*, meaning 'reborn'.
Alternative spellings: Renae, Rene, Rennee

Reya

Meaning: Singer
Origin: Sanskrit
Pronunciation: RAY ah
Description: Reya is a feminine Sanskrit Indian name that comes from the word 'riya,' meaning 'singer'. Other related names include Rea, Reeya, Rheeya, Ria and Riyah.
Alternative spellings: Rhia, Riya, Rhea

R

Rhia

Meaning: Flowing water
Origin: Greek
Pronunciation: ree AH
Description: Rhia is a variation of Rhea, a feminine name of Greek origin. The Greek meaning is said to refer to flowing water. The name is widely used in Welsh and probably comes from the same origin, as it is the name of a river that flows through Wales as well as being a popular girls' name. In Greek mythology Rhea was the name of the mother of the influential gods Zeus, Poseidon, Demeter and Hera. Like many Greek gods, Rhea is also found in Roman mythology.
Alternative spellings: Rhea, Reya, Riya

Rhian

Meaning: Great goddess
Origin: Welsh
Pronunciation: REE an
Description: Rhian is the shortened form of the Welsh name Rhiannon, meaning 'great goddess' or 'young maid'.
Alternative spellings: Reeanne, Rhiann, Rhianne

Rhianna

Meaning: Great goddess
Origin: Welsh
Pronunciation: ree AHN aah
Description: Rhianna is a combination of the Welsh name Rhiannon and the Irish name Riane.
Alternative spellings: Reeana, Reeanna, Rhiana, Rhiannah, Rianna, Rihana, Rihanna

Rhiannon

Meaning: Great goddess

Origin: Gaelic
Pronunciation: ree ANN on
Description: The name derives from the Welsh *'rigantona'*, meaning 'great queen'. In the *Mabinogion*, a collection of stories from Welsh mythology, Rhiannon was the horse goddess.
Alternative spellings: Reeannon, Reeanon, Rhianon, Riannon, Rianon

Ria

Meaning: Sea dew
Origin: Hebrew
Pronunciation: REE ah
Description: This name is a spelling variant of the Greek name Rhea. It can also be considered the shortened and more unusual form of the name Maria.
Alternative spellings: Rhea, Rhia, Rea, Reah, Riah

Ricky

See entry in 'Names for Baby Boys A–Z'

Rida

Meaning: Right
Origin: Sanskrit
Pronunciation: REE dah
Description: Rida is a pet form of the name Afrida, said to come from a Sanskrit word meaning 'right'. Rida is now a given name in its own right.
Alternative spellings: Reeda, Ridah

Rihanna

Meaning: Basil
Origin: Arabic
Pronunciation: ree AN nah

Description: Rihanna is a spelling variant of the Arabic name Rihana, meaning 'basil', as well as being a variant of the Welsh name Rhianna, meaning 'great goddess'. The name has become extremely popular recently, no doubt due to the fame of singer Rihanna.

Alternative spellings: Reeana, Reeanna, Rhiana, Rhiannah, Rianna, Rihana

Riley

See entry in 'Names for Baby Boys A–Z'

Rio

See entry in 'Names for Baby Boys A–Z'

Rita

Meaning: Virtuous; pearl
Origin: Sanskrit
Pronunciation: REE tah
Description: Rita is used by Hindu parents and comes from a Sanskrit name meaning 'virtuous'. However, it has also been found for centuries throughout Europe as a pet form of Margarita, meaning 'pearl'.

Alternative spellings: Reeta, Ritah

River

Meaning: River
Origin: English
Pronunciation: RIH vuh
Description: River is a fairly modern name, borne out of the so-called 'flower power' era in the 1960s. It is considered unisex.

Alternative spellings: Riva, Ryver

Rivka

Meaning: Young calf
Origin: Hebrew
Pronunciation: riv KAH
Description: Rivka is a variation of the name Rivkah, which is the traditional Hebrew form of Rebecca. The name itself means 'young calf'.

Alternative spellings: Rivkah

Roberta

Meaning: Bright fame
Origin: German
Pronunciation: roh BER tah
Description: The feminine form of Robert, meaning 'bright fame'. Roberta is most popular in continental Europe.

Alternative spellings: Roburta

Robin

See entry in 'Names for Baby Boys A–Z'

Robyn

Meaning: Bright fame
Origin: German
Pronunciation: ROB in
Description: A popular feminine spelling of the name Robin, especially common in the US. It shares the same meaning as Robin, meaning 'bright fame'.

Alternative spellings: Robin

Rochelle

Meaning: Rock
Origin: French
Pronunciation: roh SHELL
Description: The name Rochelle derives from the place name of La Rochelle in France. It comes from the French word *'roche'*, meaning 'rock', and would have been given

R

as a surname to those from La Rochelle.
Alternative spellings: Rochell, Roshelle

Roisin
Meaning: Little rose
Origin: Latin
Pronunciation: ro SHEEN
Description: This name can most commonly be found in Irish- and English-speaking communities. It comes from the Irish name Rois, meaning 'rose'.
Alternative spellings: Roisheen, Rosheen

Roksana
Meaning: Star
Origin: Persian
Pronunciation: rok SAH nah
Description: Roksana is the Polish variant of the name Roxanna. It ultimately derives from the Persian name Roshan, meaning 'star'. Although Roshan is unisex, Roksana is specifically feminine.
Alternative spellings: Roksanna, Roxana, Roxanna

Roma
Meaning: City of Rome
Origin: Latin
Pronunciation: ROH ma
Description: Roma is the Latin word for the city of Rome. It has transferred into a unisex given name.
Alternative spellings: Romah

Romana
Meaning: Citizen of Rome
Origin: Latin
Pronunciation: roh MA na
Description: Romana is the specifically feminine version of the

unisex name Roman, derived from the Latin word for citizens of Rome.
Alternative spellings: Romanah, Romona

Romilly
Meaning: Rosemary herb
Origin: Latin
Pronunciation: RO mil ee
Description: Romilly is believed to be an elaboration of the name Romy, itself a pet form of the name Rosemary, which is a herb. Romilly seems to be rising in popularity as a baby name.
Alternative spellings: Romilley, Romilli, Romillie

Romola
Meaning: From Rome
Origin: Latin
Pronunciation: rom OH lah
Description: Romola is the feminine version of Romulus, meaning 'from Rome'. It was the titular character of George Eliot's 1862 book. Romola Garai is a British actress with this name.

Romy
Meaning: Sea dew
Origin: Latin
Pronunciation: RO mee
Description: Romy is a pet form of the name Rosemary, which comes from the English noun for the herb.
Alternative spellings: Romey, Romi, Romie

Ronit
Meaning: Song
Origin: Hebrew
Pronunciation: ron IT
Description: Ronit is a Hebrew

name and the feminine version of the name Ron, meaning 'song'.

Ronni
Meaning: Bringer of victory
Origin: Greek
Pronunciation: ROH ni
Description: Ronni could be either a pet form of the Greek name Veronica, meaning 'bringer of victory', or a feminine version of Ronny, meaning 'open-minded'.
Alternative spellings: Ronnie, Ronny

Ronnie
Meaning: Open-minded
Origin: Norse
Pronunciation: RON ee
Description: Ronnie is a spelling variant of the feminine name Ronni or the masculine name Ronny. It is unisex.
Alternative spellings: Ronni, Ronny

Rory
See entry in 'Names for Baby Boys A–Z'

Rosa
Meaning: Rose
Origin: Latin
Pronunciation: ROH za
Description: Rosa is the Latin word for the flower and also the Italian version of the name. Rosa could also be the shortened form of the German name Rosalind, meaning 'gentle horse'.
Alternative spellings: Roza

Rosabelle
Meaning: Beautiful rose
Origin: Latin

Pronunciation: rosa BEL
Description: Rosabelle is a combination of two elements, '*rosa*' meaning 'rose' and '*belle*' meaning 'beautiful'.

Rosalie
Meaning: Rose
Origin: French
Pronunciation: roh ZAH lee
Description: Rosalie is a French variation on the Italian Rosalia. It has gained in popularity over recent years due to the character in the Twilight series of books with the same name.
Alternative spellings: Rosalia

Rosalind
Meaning: Gentle horse
Origin: German
Pronunciation: ROZ a lind
Description: The name Rosalind was originally popularised in England by Shakespeare in his play *As You Like It*.
Alternative spellings: Rosalynd, Rozalind, Rozalynd

Rosalyn
Meaning: Beautiful rose
Origin: Latin
Pronunciation: ROZ ah lin
Description: Rosalyn could be a variant of the German name Rosalind, meaning 'gentle horse', or a combination of the names 'Rose' and 'Lyn' to mean 'beautiful rose'.
Alternative spellings: Rosalin, Rosalynn, Rosalynne, Rozalin, Rozalyn

Rosamund
Meaning: Horse protection
Origin: German
Pronunciation: rosa MUND

R

Description: Rosamund is a German name composed of the elements of '*hros*', meaning 'horse', and '*mund*', meaning 'protection'. Rosamund Pike is a famous British actress with this name.

Rosanna

Meaning: Flower of grace
Origin: English
Pronunciation: roh ZAN ah
Description: Rosanna is a combination of the names Rose and Anna, and consequently it has the meaning 'flower of grace'. It has become increasingly popular in recent years as double-barrelled and combined names are sought.
Alternative spellings: Roseanna

Rosanne

Meaning: Rose
Origin: Latin
Pronunciation: ROZE an
Description: Rosanne, which is of Latin origin, was initially a compound name, combining Rose and Anne, but has since become a name in its own right.
Alternative spellings: Rosann, Roseann, Roseanne

Rosario

Meaning: Rosary
Origin: Spanish
Pronunciation: row SAR ee oh
Description: Rosario is a Spanish name that means 'rosary'. It is taken from the title for the Virgin Mary, Nuestra Señora del Rosario, meaning 'Our Lady of the Rosary.'

Rose

Meaning: Rose

Origin: English
Pronunciation: ROZE
Description: Rose is an elegant name for a girl, taken directly from the English name of the flower. It is considered a traditionally English name, taken from the phrase 'an English rose'.
Alternative spellings: Roze

Rosemary

Meaning: Rosemary herb; sea dew
Origin: Latin
Pronunciation: ROZE ma ree
Description: The name Rosemary was coined in the 19th century. Rosemary is a fragrant herb; however the girls' name was derived from the Latin words '*ros marinus*', meaning 'sea dew'. The name carries both of these meanings.
Alternative spellings: Rosemarey, Rosemari, Rosemarie, Rozemari, Rozemarie, Rozemary

Rosetta

Meaning: Rose
Origin: Italian
Pronunciation: roze ET tah
Description: Rosetta is the Italian version of the common name Rose, which refers to the flower of the same name.

Roshan

Meaning: Star
Origin: Persian
Pronunciation: roh SHAHN
Description: Roshan is a unisex name meaning 'star' in reference to fame and luminosity. The name is very popular in India. It is also a variant of the anglicised form Roxanne, which is specifically a feminine name.

Alternative spellings: Roshann, Roshanne

Roshni
Meaning: Light
Origin: Sanskrit
Pronunciation: rosh NI
Description: Roshni is a feminine name of Indian origins and because much documentation on the name is scarce in English translation it is difficult to give reliable information. The exact origin is uncertain and the name seems to be used by both Muslim and Hindu parents. It seems to be agreed that the name means 'light'.

Rosie
Meaning: Rose
Origin: English
Pronunciation: RO zee
Description: Rosie came about as a pet name for the English name Rose, taken from the name of the flower. Now it is seen as a name in its own right.
Alternative spellings: Rosi, Rosy, Rozi, Rozie, Rozy

Rosina
Meaning: Rose
Origin: Latin
Pronunciation: roh ZEE nah; roh SEE nah
Description: The name Rosina is an elaboration of the Latin name Rosa, meaning 'rose', and is most commonly found in Italy and Spain.
Alternative spellings: Rosinah, Rosyna, Rozina

Rosita
Meaning: Rose
Origin: Spanish
Pronunciation: roze EE tah
Description: Rosita is the Spanish version of the common name Rose, which refers to the flower of the same name.

Rowan
See entry in 'Names for Baby Boys A–Z'

Rowena
Meaning: Fame; bliss
Origin: German
Pronunciation: row EEN ah
Description: The meaning of Rowena is uncertain, but it is composed of the Germanic elements of '*hrod*' meaning 'fame' and '*wunn*' meaning 'bliss'. It was made famous by Sir Walter Scott's novel, *Ivanhoe*, which featured a character called Lady Rowena.

Roxanna
Meaning: Star
Origin: Persian
Pronunciation: rox AN ah
Description: Roxanna is a variant of Roxanne, which is itself an anglicised version of the Persian name Roshan.
Alternative spellings: Roksana, Roksanna, Roxana

Roxanne
Meaning: Star
Origin: Persian
Pronunciation: ROKS an
Description: Roxanne is an anglicised version of the Persian name Roshan. Its popularity may have been increased by the song 'Roxanne', a big hit in the 1980s.
Alternative spellings: Roksanne, Roxane, Roxann

R

Roxie

Meaning: Star
Origin: Persian
Pronunciation: ROK see
Description: Roxy is the pet form of Roxanne and from the Persian name Roshan, meaning 'star'. The name has associations with independence.
Alternative spellings: Roksi, Roksie, Roksy, Roxi, Roxy

Ruby

Meaning: Precious
Origin: English
Pronunciation: ROO bee
Description: The name Ruby comes from the precious red gemstone. Common in the late 19th and mid-20th century, the name is enjoying a partial revival in English-speaking regions. Ruby is also the birthstone for July.
Alternative spellings: Rubee, Rubey, Rubi, Rubie

Ruhi

Meaning: Spiritual
Origin: Indian
Pronunciation: rue HEE
Description: Ruhi has Indian origins and means 'spiritual'. The name also has Muslim and Hindu roots, and can also mean 'soul'. Similar names are Rahi, Raha and Rhea.
Alternative spellings: Ruhee

Rumaisa

Meaning: Unknown
Origin: Arabic
Pronunciation: roo MAY sa
Description: Rumaisa is an unusual name of uncertain meaning and origin. The name is likely to be Arabic and is used mainly by Muslim parents.
Alternative spellings: Rumaysa

Rumi

Meaning: Name of a poet
Origin: Persian
Pronunciation: ROO mi
Description: It is speculated that Rumi comes from the 13th-century Persian poet of the same name, Jalāl ad-Dīn Muhammad Rumi. In Japanese, the name Rumi also means 'beauty,' 'current,' 'flow', and 'water'. Beyoncé and Jay-Z named one of their newborn twins Rumi.
Alternative spellings: Roomi

Ruqayyah

Meaning: Delicate
Origin: Arabic
Pronunciation: ruh QUAI ah
Description: Ruqayyah is a name of Arabic origin, which means 'delicate'. This name is popular with Muslim parents and was the name of the second daughter of the prophet Muhammad.
Alternative spellings: Ruquaiah

Ruth

Meaning: Companion
Origin: Hebrew
Pronunciation: ROOTH
Description: The name Ruth is derived from the Hebrew meaning 'companion' or 'friend'. It also means 'compassion' in English.
Alternative spellings: Rooth, Ruthe

Ryan

See entry in 'Names for Baby Boys A–Z'

Rylee

Meaning: No meaning
Origin: Gaelic
Pronunciation: ry LEE
Description: The meaning of this name is unknown, although it can be traced back as an Irish surname. It has become a popular name in modern times, especially in America, for both girls and boys in its variously spelt forms. However, the version spelt Rylee is that usually given to a girl, along with Ryleigh.
Alternative spellings: Rilee, Riley

Ryleigh

Meaning: Courageous
Origin: English
Pronunciation: RI lee
Description: Ryleigh is a unisex name of Old English origin, meaning 'rye clearing' or 'courageous'. The name is a variant of the boys' name Ryley, and the girls' names Rylee and Rylie. Ryleigh is more commonly seen as a girls' name.
Alternative spellings: Reilley, Reilly, Rielly, Riley, Ryley

Ryoko

Meaning: Refreshing child
Origin: Japanese
Pronunciation: ree OH ko
Description: The name Ryoko originates from Japan and means 'refreshing or good child'.
Alternative spellings: Rioko

S

Saanvi

Meaning: One who follows
Origin: Sanskrit
Pronunciation: SAHN vee
Description: Saanvi is a name that comes from Sanskrit origins; the name means 'one who follows'. It is mainly used by Hindu families.
Alternative spellings: Saanvee

Sabah

Meaning: Dawn sunrise
Origin: Arabic
Pronunciation: sah BAH
Description: Sabah is a name of Arabic origin and it is said to come from an Arabic word for a 'dawn sunrise'. It is popular in Arab-speaking countries.
Alternative spellings: Saba

Sabiha

Meaning: Beautiful
Origin: Arabic
Pronunciation: sah BI ha
Description: Sabiha is a name that is quite popular in Africa. It is thought to be originally of Muslim origin, from the Arabic word meaning 'beautiful'. Its use has spread into Swahili.
Alternative spellings: Saabiha

Sabina

Meaning: Sabine

R
S

Origin: Latin
Pronunciation: sah BEE nah
Description: Sabina comes from Latin origin of the name Sabine, which is a region in Italy and the name of a saint.
Alternative spellings: Sabbina

Sabrina

Meaning: River Sabrina
Origin: Gaelic
Pronunciation: sah BREE nah
Description: Sabrina comes from the name of a legendary Celtic character whose name was lent to the River Severn.
Alternative spellings: Sabbrina, Sabreena

Sade

Meaning: Honoured one
Origin: African
Pronunciation: shah DAY
Description: Sade, a name of African origin, came about as a pet form of Folasade. This name means 'honoured'.
Alternative spellings: Saide

Sadia

Meaning: Honoured one
Origin: African
Pronunciation: sah DAY ah
Description: Sadia is a relatively rare name in Britain. The name is a variant of the name Sade and in Portuguese means 'healthy'.
Alternative spellings: Saddia, Sahdia

Sadie

Meaning: Princess
Origin: Hebrew
Pronunciation: SAY dee
Description: Sadie was originally a pet form of the name Sarah.
Alternative spellings: Saidie, Saydie

Safa

Meaning: Pure
Origin: Arabic
Pronunciation: SAH fah
Description: Safa is a name of Arabic origin and it means 'pure'. It is popular in Middle Eastern countries and is also a name given to a park in Dubai.
Alternative spellings: Safah

Safaa

Meaning: Large rock
Origin: Arabic
Pronunciation: suh FAH
Description: Safaa is a name that comes directly from the Quran. It is a hill in Mecca and is of importance during the Hajj proceedings every year.
Alternative spellings: Safa

Saffron

Meaning: Yellow
Origin: French
Pronunciation: SAF fron
Description: Saffron is an English name that is also the name of a rare and highly sought after yellow spice.
Alternative spellings: Saphron

Safiya

Meaning: Purity
Origin: Arabic
Pronunciation: sah FEE yah
Description: Safiya is a name said to mean 'purity' or 'sincere friend'. It is popular in Britain mainly among Muslim and African-American parents.

Alternative spellings: Safia, Safiyah, Safiyyah

Sage
Meaning: Herb
Origin: English
Pronunciation: sage
Description: Sage is a type of herb often used in cooking. Like Rosemary, it is part of the trend to use plants and flowers as baby names.

Sahana
Meaning: Melody
Origin: Sanskrit
Pronunciation: sah HA na
Description: Sahana is an Indian name and can mean 'melody' as it is the name of a raga, which is a melodic mode in Indian music.
Alternative spellings: Sahaana

Sahar
See entry in 'Names for Baby Boys A–Z'

Sahara
Meaning: Desert
Origin: African
Pronunciation: sah HAHR rah
Description: While the name Sahara is most commonly associated with the desert, it is also the feminine version of the masculine name Sahar and it is the Arabic name for 'desert'.
Alternative spellings: Sahaara

Sahra
Meaning: Desert
Origin: Arabic
Pronunciation: SAH ru
Description: Sahra is a variant of the name Sahara. This name is popular in the Middle East and Saharan regions.
Alternative spellings: Sahraa

Sakina
Meaning: Peace
Origin: Arabic
Pronunciation: sak KEE nah
Description: Sakina, which is Arabic in origin, comes from the word 'sakun', which means 'peace'. In the Quran, Sukaina is the name given to a spirit who brings peace to the prophet Muhammad.
Alternative spellings: Sakinah

Salina
Meaning: Moon
Origin: Greek
Pronunciation: sah LEE na
Description: Salina is a name of ultimately Greek origins. It is a variant form of the name Celina, which is derived from a Greek word referring to the moon. Salina is also a name of an island off the coast of Italy.
Alternative spellings: Salinah

Sally
Meaning: Princess
Origin: Hebrew
Pronunciation: SAL ee
Description: Sally, like Sadie, was originally a form of the name Sarah. Now the name stands alone.
Alternative spellings: Sallee, Salley, Sallie

Salma
Meaning: Whole
Origin: Arabic
Pronunciation: SAL mah
Description: This name is most

S

common in African, Arabic- and Swahili-speaking countries. It originates from the female name Salima.
Alternative spellings: Salmah

Salome
Meaning: Peace
Origin: Hebrew
Pronunciation: salom EH
Description: Salome is derived from the Hebrew word '*shalom*', meaning 'peace'. It was also the name of the daughter of Herodias and enemy of John the Baptist.

Sam
See entry in 'Names for Baby Boys A–Z'

Sama
Meaning: Sky
Origin: Arabic
Pronunciation: SAH ma
Description: Sama, from the Arabic for 'sky', is mainly used in the Middle East and popular with Muslim parents.
Alternative spellings: Samah

Samanta
Meaning: God listens
Origin: Hebrew
Pronunciation: sah MAN tah
Description: Samanta is a variant of the name Samantha, the feminine version of the masculine name Samuel. Samuel is a popular name of Hebrew origins and means 'God listens'. The version Samanta is most common in Italy, France and Germany.
Alternative spellings: Samannta

Samantha
Meaning: God listens
Origin: Hebrew
Pronunciation: sa MAN thah
Description: Samantha consists of a shortened form of Samuel, which means 'God listens', and the suffix 'antha', which means 'flower'.
Alternative spellings: Samanther, Sammantha

Samara
Meaning: Lively in conversation
Origin: Arabic
Pronunciation: sah MAYR ah
Description: Samara is a feminine variant of the masculine name Samir, which is Arabic in origin and is said to mean 'lively in conversation'.
Alternative spellings: Samarah

Sameeha
Meaning: Blessing from Allah
Origin: Arabic
Pronunciation: sah MEE hah
Description: Sameeha is an unusual name of Arabic origin and although its exact meaning and origin are uncertain, it may mean 'blessing from Allah'.
Alternative spellings: Sameehah

Sameera
Meaning: Lively in conversation
Origin: Arabic
Pronunciation: sah MEER ah
Description: Sameera is the feminine version of the masculine name Samir, which is of Arabic origins and is popular with Muslim parents. The name means 'lively in conversation'.
Alternative spellings: Samira, Samirah

Samia

Meaning: Lofty
Origin: Arabic
Pronunciation: sah MEE ah
Description: Samia is a name of Arabic origin and means 'lofty'. This name is mostly used in Pakistan.
Alternative spellings: Samiha, Samiya, Samiyah

Sammy

See entry in 'Names for Baby Boys A–Z'

Sana

Meaning: Dazzling; to shine
Origin: Arabic
Pronunciation: SAH nah
Description: Sana is a name of Arabic origin and means 'dazzling' or 'to shine'. It is found mainly in Arabic-speaking countries.
Alternative spellings: Sanaa, Sanah

Sanae

Meaning: Rice seedlings
Origin: Japanese
Pronunciation: sa NA eh
Description: This name is not often found outside Japanese-speaking countries. Although it uses the same Japanese characters required to write 'rice seedlings', the name may mean 'sand together' or 'seedling'.
Alternative spellings: Sahnae

Sanaya

Meaning: Noble
Origin: Arabic
Pronunciation: saan AH ya
Description: Sanaya is an Arabic name that means 'noble,' 'admirable' or 'praiseworthy'. Other related names include Sanayah Saniyya and Sonya.

Alternative spellings: Sanayah

Sandra

Meaning: Defender of man
Origin: Greek
Pronunciation: SAHN dra
Description: Sandra is a short form of Alessandra, the Italian form of Alexandra.
Alternative spellings: Sandraa

Sandy

Meaning: Defender of man
Origin: Greek
Pronunciation: SAN dee
Description: Sandy is a unisex name and pet form of either 'Alexander' or 'Alexandra'.
Alternative spellings: Sandie

Saniya

Meaning: Shining brilliance
Origin: Arabic
Pronunciation: sah NEE yah
Description: Saniya is a name of Arabic origin and it is said to come from the word *'sana'*, which means to shine. Saniya is a popular name with Muslim parents.
Alternative spellings: Saniyah

Sanjiana

Meaning: Gentle
Origin: Sanskrit
Pronunciation: san JAH nah
Description: Sanjiana is a name favoured by Hindu parents. Like many names with Sanskrit or Urdu origins, there is little translated documentation about its meaning. It may mean 'gentle'.
Alternative spellings: Sanjianah

Saoirse

Meaning: Freedom

S

Origin: Gaelic
Pronunciation: SEER sha
Description: Saoirse is a name of Irish origin and its meaning is said to be 'freedom'. It is the name of an Irish Republican newspaper and as such the name has patriotic connotations.

Sapphire
Meaning: Blue gemstone
Origin: English
Pronunciation: SA fire
Description: The name Sapphire comes from the name of the blue gemstone. This stone is also the birthstone for September.
Alternative spellings: Saphire

Sarah
Meaning: Princess
Origin: Hebrew
Pronunciation: SAIR uh
Description: Sarah, the biblical wife of Abraham and mother of Isaac, was originally named Sarai, which may mean 'contentious' in Hebrew. Her name changed to Sarah, which means 'princess'.
Alternative spellings: Saira, Sara, Saora

Sariah
Meaning: Princess
Origin: Hebrew
Pronunciation: sa RYE ah
Description: Sariah is a name of Hebrew origin from the same source as the name Sarah, and means 'princess'. The name is one of the original ancestors of the Mormon people in America.
Alternative spellings: Saryah

Sarina
Meaning: Princess
Origin: Hebrew
Pronunciation: sa REE nah
Description: Sarina is a modern variation of the name Sarah. Sarah is of Hebrew origin and means 'princess'.
Alternative spellings: Sarinah, Serena

Sasha
See entry in 'Names for Baby Boys A–Z'

Saskia
Meaning: Unknown
Origin: Dutch
Pronunciation: SASS kee uh
Description: Saskia is a name of Dutch origin. Its meaning is unknown but it does carry a phonetically pleasing sound.
Alternative spellings: Saskiah

Satin
Meaning: Satin
Origin: English
Pronunciation: SAT in
Description: Satin is a luxurious fabric and is now a name.

Savannah
Meaning: Treeless plain
Origin: Spanish
Pronunciation: sav AN nah
Description: Savannah is the name of two US cities in Georgia and South Carolina. They are linked to the local Savannah River, possibly derived from the word *'savanna'* meaning 'treeless plain'.
Alternative spellings: Savanna

Saya

Meaning: Quick arrow
Origin: Japanese
Pronunciation: say YAH
Description: Saya is a feminine name of Asian origins and because much documentation on the name is scarce in English translation, it is difficult to give reliable information. The name seems to come from a Japanese word and is said to mean 'quick arrow'.
Alternative spellings: Sayah

Scarlett

Meaning: Scarlet
Origin: French
Pronunciation: SCAR let
Description: Scarlett is a name of English origin and refers to a shade of red. Scarlett O'Hara is a character from the novel and film *Gone With The Wind*.
Alternative spellings: Scarlet, Scarlette

Seerat

Meaning: Inner beauty; fame; brightness
Origin: Indian
Pronunciation: see RAAT
Description: An Indian name meaning 'inner beauty,' 'fame' and 'brightness'. Seerat is a tradional girls' name used in the Hindu and Sikh religions. Some other related names are Sarat, Sarit and Soorat.

Sehar

Meaning: Early morning
Origin: Persian
Pronunciation: seh HAJ
Description: Sehar is an unusual name; it is thought to be of Persian origin and means 'early morning'.
Alternative spellings: Seher
See entry in 'Names for Baby Boys A–Z'

Selby

See entry in 'Names for Baby Boys A–Z'

Selena

Meaning: Goddess of the moon
Origin: Greek
Pronunciation: seh LEE na
Description: Selena is of Greek origin and means 'goddess of the moon'.
Alternative spellings: Celena, Selina

Selin

Meaning: Moon
Origin: Greek
Pronunciation: SEH lin
Description: Selin is an unusual name thought to come from the name Selina, meaning 'moon'.
Alternative spellings: Celin

Selma

Meaning: Beautiful
Origin: Gaelic
Pronunciation: SEL ma
Description: Selma is a name of Gaelic origin; it means 'beautiful'.
Alternative spellings: Selmah

Seraphina

Meaning: Burning ones
Origin: Hebrew
Pronunciation: SEH ra FEE na
Description: Seraphina is a Hebrew name, which means 'burning'. The Hebrew word that

S

it comes from is *'seraphim'*, which refers to an order of angels.
Alternative spellings: Serafina, Serrafina, Serraphina

Seren
Meaning: Star
Origin: Welsh
Pronunciation: SEH ren
Description: Seren is given to both males and females and means 'star', but is uncommon in the UK outside of Wales.
Alternative spellings: Sehren

Serena
Meaning: Calm; serene
Origin: Latin
Pronunciation: seh REE na
Description: Serena is a modern variation of the name Sarah. Serena comes from the Latin word *'serenus'*, meaning 'serene'.
Alternative spellings: Sarina

Serenity
Meaning: Peaceful
Origin: English
Pronunciation: seh REH nih tee
Description: Serenity is a name taken from the English word for 'calm'. Like Charity or Hope, it is a virtue name and is of English and French origin.
Alternative spellings: Serenitee, Sereniti, Serenitie

Setsuko
Meaning: Season child
Origin: Japanese
Pronunciation: SET su ko
Description: Setsuko is popular in Japanese-speaking countries. It means 'season child'.
Alternative spellings: Setsukoh

Shaan
Meaning: God is gracious
Origin: Welsh
Pronunciation: sha AN; SHARN
Description: Shaan (pronounced sha AN) is of feminine origin The name is of Punjabi origin that means 'respected one'. The name is a variant of the spelling 'Sian', which is of Celtic origin.
Alternative spellings: Sian

Shakira
Meaning: Thankful
Origin: Arabic
Pronunciation: sha KEER ah
Description: Shakira is a name of Arabic origin, which means 'thankful'.
Alternative spellings: Shakeera, Shakeira

Shalom
Meaning: Go in peace
Origin: Hebrew
Pronunciation: sha LOM
Description: Shalom is a name of Hebrew origin. The word can be used as a greeting and a farewell, and means 'go in peace'.

Shanae
Meaning: God is gracious
Origin: Gaelic
Pronunciation: sha NAY
Description: Shanae is a name of modern coinage that started in America. It is thought that the name is based on the Irish name Sinead.
Alternative spellings: Shanay, Shanea, Shannea, Shenae

Shania
Meaning: I am coming

Origin: American
Pronunciation: sha NEE yah
Description: Shania is an extremely popular American name. It is thought to be inspired by a Native American word from the Ojibwa language meaning 'I am coming'.
Alternative spellings: Shaniia, Shaniya

Shanice

Meaning: God is gracious
Origin: Hebrew
Pronunciation: sha NEECE
Description: Shanice is a modern name that was first used in America as a combination of the name Janice and the fashionable prefix 'sha'.
Alternative spellings: Shannice

Shannon

Meaning: Old river
Origin: Gaelic
Pronunciation: SHAN nun
Description: The increasingly popular name Shannon refers to the Irish river. The Gaelic for 'old river' is *'seanan'*.
Alternative spellings: Shanon

Sharon

Meaning: Forest
Origin: Hebrew
Pronunciation: SHA ron
Description: The name Sharon is a Hebrew name and refers to a fertile plain near the coast of Israel. The name is given to the rose of Sharon, a flowering plant of yellow and purple.
Alternative spellings: Sharron

Shaun

See entry in 'Names for Baby Boys A–Z'

Shauna

Meaning: God is gracious
Origin: Hebrew
Pronunciation: SHON ah; SHAW na
Description: Shauna is the name that comes from Sean, the Irish variant of the masculine name John.
Alternative spellings: Shawna

Shaye

Meaning: Admirable
Origin: Gaelic
Pronunciation: SHAY
Description: Shaye is a unisex name suitable for boys and girls. It is a variant of the Gaelic name Shea, which means 'admirable'.
Alternative spellings: Shae, Shai, Shay

Shayla

Meaning: Blind
Origin: Latin
Pronunciation: SHAY lah
Description: Shayla is a name that has developed in America as a variant of the Irish name Sheila. It is a relatively popular name in both America and Ireland and means 'from the fairy palace'.
Alternative spellings: Shaylah, Sheylah

Shayleigh

Meaning: Full of majesty in the woods
Origin: Gaelic
Pronunciation: shay LEE
Description: Shayleigh is a name of relatively modern coinage. It is a compound of the two names Shay and Leigh.

S

Alternative spellings: Shaelee, Shaeleigh, Shaylee

Shayna
Meaning: Beautiful
Origin: Hebrew
Pronunciation: SHAY nuh
Description: Shayna is a name taken from the Yiddish meaning 'beautiful'. It is a very unusual name in the UK.
Alternative spellings: Shaina, Shainah, Shaynah

Shayne
Meaning: God is gracious
Origin: Hebrew
Pronunciation: SHAY n
Description: This is the female variation of the common male name Shane, but can also be a variant of the name for boys. It has become popular only in recent years.
Alternative spellings: Chayne, Sheyn

Shea
Meaning: Descendant of the fortunate
Origin: English
Pronunciation: SHAY
Description: Shea is a unisex name originally used as an Irish surname. It means 'descendant of the fortunate' and may have become more common across the UK since the arrival of shea butter in many cosmetic stores.
Alternative spellings: Shae, Shay, Shey

Sheila
Meaning: Blind
Origin: Irish

Pronunciation: shee LAH
Description: Sheila is an Irish name, believed to be taken from the Irish Sile, which is a Gaelic form of Cecilia. As such, they all share the same meaning of 'blind'.

Shelby
Meaning: Area of willow trees
Origin: English
Pronunciation: SHEL bee
Description: Shelby would have originally been given to someone who lived in an 'area of willow trees'. It has since evolved into a first name.
Alternative spellings: Shelbee, Shelbie

Shelley
Meaning: Wood beside cliff
Origin: English
Pronunciation: SHEL lee
Description: Shelley is a transferred surname used by those in Essex, Suffolk and Yorkshire. It has become a name in its own right.
Alternative spellings: Shellie, Shelly

Sheri
Meaning: The plains
Origin: Greek
Pronunciation: SHER ee
Description: Sheri is a name of Hebrew origin now found in English-speaking countries. It means 'the plains'.
Alternative spellings: Sherie, Sherii, Sherry

Shifa
Meaning: Healer

Origin: Hebrew
Pronunciation: SHE fa
Description: It is uncertain whether the name Shifa is Arabic or Hebrew in origin as it is used by both Muslim and Jewish parents. The meaning is thought to be 'healer' or 'abundance'.
Alternative spellings: Sheefa

Shiloh

See entry in 'Names for Baby Boys A–Z'

Shion

Meaning: Sound of the water
Origin: Japanese
Pronunciation: SHEE on
Description: This feminine Japanese name is used throughout Asia. *'Shio'* means 'tide' or 'water', and *'ne'* means 'sound', so the name means 'sound of the water'. It is an uncommon name across the UK.
Alternative spellings: Shione

Shira

Meaning: Song
Origin: Hebrew
Pronunciation: SHEER ah
Description: Shira is thought to come from a Hebrew word meaning 'song'. The name is favoured by Jewish parents. It is a rare name in the UK.
Alternative spellings: Shirah, Shyra, Shyrah

Shirley

Meaning: Bright wood
Origin: English
Pronunciation: shir LEE
Description: Shirley is composed of the Old English elements of *'scīr'* meaning 'bright' and *'lēah'* meaning 'wood'. Shirley Temple was a famous American child star.

Shivani

Meaning: Mother of all
Origin: Sanskrit
Pronunciation: shih VAR nee
Description: Shivani, which means 'mother of all', is a name of Sanskrit origin. The name is mostly used by Hindu parents, as in Hindu belief it is the name of the wife of the god Shiva.
Alternative spellings: Shivanee, Shivarnee, Shivarni

Shona

Meaning: God is gracious
Origin: Hebrew
Pronunciation: SHO nah
Description: Shona is the Irish form of the name Joan, which is itself the feminine version of the masculine John.
Alternative spellings: Shonah

Shreya

Meaning: Fortunate one
Origin: Sanskrit
Pronunciation: SHREE yah
Description: Shreya, which means 'fortunate one', is an extremely popular name with Indian parents and is fairly popular in Britain.
Alternative spellings: Shreeya, Shriya

Shyanne

Meaning: Worthy
Origin: American
Pronunciation: shi AN
Description: The name Shyanne is thought to have originated as

S

a phonetic spelling of the name
Cheyenne, a Native American place
name. It became popular as a
boys' name; however, Shyanne is a
feminine name.
Alternative spellings: Shyenne

Shyla
Meaning: Goddess
Origin: Sanskrit
Pronunciation: SHY lah
Description: Shyla is a name of
Sanskrit origin that is particularly
popular among Hindu families. It
is one of the names of the Hindu
goddess Parvati.

Sia
See entry in 'Names for Baby Boys
A–Z'

Siân
Meaning: God has given
Origin: Welsh
Pronunciation: SHARN
Description: Siân is the Welsh
version of the name Jane, used
since the 1940s. The name means
'God has given'.
Alternative spellings: Shaan

Sianna
Meaning: God is gracious
Origin:
Pronunciation:
Description: Sianna is a Hebrew
name meaning 'God is gracious'. It
is also a variation on the English
name Seanna, and also the Welsh
name Siân. Sianna was also the
daughter of the Faerie Queen in
Marion Zimmer Bradley's *Lady of
Avalon*.
Alternative spellings: Siana,
Seanna

Sidney
See entry in 'Names for Baby Boys
A–Z'

Sidra
Meaning: Born from a star
Origin: Latin
Pronunciation: SID rah
Description: The name Sidra
comes from the Latin meaning
'born from a star'. It is also a place
name in Poland.
Alternative spellings: Sidrah,
Sydra, Sydrah

Sienna
Meaning: Brownish orange
Origin: Italian
Pronunciation: si EH nuh
Description: Sienna, a name of
Italian origin, is associated with
the city Siena.
Alternative spellings: Siena

Sierra
Meaning: Jagged mountains
Origin: Spanish
Pronunciation: see AIR uh
Description: Sierra is a feminine
Spanish name that literally means
'saw' and also refers to mountain
ranges.

Siham
Meaning: Arrow
Origin: Arabic
Pronunciation: see HAM
Description: The name Siham ap-
pears across the Middle East and
parts of Africa. The Arabic mean-
ing is 'arrow'.
Alternative spellings: Siiham

Simona
Meaning: Listen

Origin: Hebrew
Pronunciation: sih MOH nah
Description: Simona, a variant of Simone, is found in Eastern Europe.
Alternative spellings: Simonah

Simone

Meaning: Listen
Origin: Hebrew
Pronunciation: si MONE; see MOHN
Description: This is a feminine version of the masculine name Simon, which is of Hebrew origin and means 'hark'.
Alternative spellings: Semone

Simrah

Meaning: Heaven
Origin: Arabic
Pronunciation: SIM rah
Description: This name is used by Muslim parents and comes from an Arabic word meaning 'heaven'.
Alternative spellings: Simra

Simran

Meaning: Meditation
Origin: Sanskrit
Pronunciation: sim RAN
Description: Simran is a unisex name that is popular among Hindu communities. It means 'meditation,' and while it is more commonly given to girls the Sikh community often chooses it as a name for boys too.

Sinead

Meaning: God is gracious
Origin: Hebrew
Pronunciation: shan AID
Description: Sinead, a feminine Irish name, has its roots in Jane, which is itself the feminine version of John. The name means 'God is gracious'.
Alternative spellings: Shinead

Siobhan

Meaning: God is gracious
Origin: Gaelic
Pronunciation: shiv ORN
Description: Siobhan is the Gaelic version of the Hebrew name 'Joan'.
Alternative spellings: Sioban, Siobain, Siobhain

Siya

Meaning: Unknown
Origin: Arabic
Pronunciation: SEE ah
Description: Siya, a unisex name, appears to be of Arabic origin and is favoured by Muslim parents.
Alternative spellings: Siyah

Siyana

Meaning: Protection
Origin: Muslim
Pronunciation: see YAN ah
Description: Siyana is a feminine Muslim name meaning 'protection'. Related names include Siya, Siyah and Siyanna.
Alternative spellings: Siyanna

Skye

Meaning: Cloud
Origin: Norse
Pronunciation: SKY
Description: The name Skye comes from the Old Norse word for 'cloud'. It rose to prominence during the 1960s.
Alternative spellings: Sky

Skyla

Meaning: Fugitive

S

Origin: Dutch
Pronunciation: sky LA
Description: Although the name Skyla is thought to derive from the Dutch name Schuyler, it is most commonly found within England and America. The masculine version is spelt Skyler.
Alternative spellings: Skila, Skylar, Skyler

Skylah
Meaning: Scholar
Origin: Dutch
Pronunciation: SKY lah
Description: The name Skylah has Dutch origins and means 'scholar' in the langauage. It is also an alternative spelling of the more mainstream Skyler or Skyla, and could also be a variation of the name Kayla.
Alternative spellings: Skylar, Skyler

Sofia
Meaning: Wisdom
Origin: Greek
Pronunciation: so FEE uh
Description: Sofia is a variant of Sophia, the capital city of Bulgaria. The name is Greek and means 'wisdom'.
Alternative spellings: Sofiya, Sofiyah, Sophia

Sol
See entry in 'Names for Baby Boys A–Z'

Soleil
Meaning: Sun
Origin: French
Pronunciation: so LAY

Description: Translated directly from the French, Soleil means 'sun'. Note that the pronounciation of the name does not include the last 'L'.

Sommer
Meaning: Summer
Origin: Scandinavian
Pronunciation: SOH mer
Description: Sommer is a unisex name and a Scandinavian term for summer.
Alternative spellings: Summer

Sonia
Meaning: Wisdom
Origin: Greek
Pronunciation: SOHN yuh
Description: Sonia is a variant of the Greek name 'Sophia', meaning 'wisdom'.
Alternative spellings: Soniah, Sonya, Sonyah

Sophie
Meaning: Wisdom
Origin: Greek
Pronunciation: SO fee
Description: This popular name is of Greek origin and it means 'wisdom'.
Alternative spellings: Sofi, Sofie, Sofy, Sophi, Sophy

Soraya
Meaning: Princess
Origin: Persian
Pronunciation: sor RYE ah
Description: Soraya is a name of Persian origin and it means 'princess'. It is popular in the Middle East and in Spain.
Alternative spellings: Sorayaa, Sorayah

Stacey

Meaning: Fruitful
Origin: Greek
Pronunciation: STAY see
Description: Stacey is the feminine variant of the unisex name Stacy, derived from the Greek name Eustace.
Alternative spellings: Stacee, Stacy, Stayce

Star

Meaning: Bright
Origin: English
Pronunciation: STAR
Description: Star is a name that has associations with brightness and fame. The name is not common in Britain but it is used in other English-speaking countries.
Alternative spellings: Starr

Stefania

Meaning: Garland; crown
Origin: Greek
Pronunciation: ste fan NYAH
Description: Stefania is a Greek name meaning 'garland' or 'crown'. It is also the Greek version of the name Stephanie, which is a feminine variation of the male name Stephen. The Greek word for 'crown' is Stephanos.
Alternative spellings: Stephania

Stella

Meaning: Star
Origin: Latin
Pronunciation: STEH luh
Description: Stella is the Latin word for 'star'. In Catholic tradition, the Virgin Mary was given the title 'Stella Maris', meaning 'star of the sea'.
Alternative spellings: Stellah, Stellar

Steph

Meaning: Garland; crown
Origin: Greek
Pronunciation: STEFF
Description: Steph, a shortened version of Stephanie, is popular as a name in its own right across the English-speaking world.
Alternative spellings: Stef

Stephanie

Meaning: Garland; crown
Origin: Greek
Pronunciation: STEH fah nee
Description: Stephanie comes from the same derivative as Stephen and means 'garland' or 'crown'.
Alternative spellings: Stefanee, Stefanie, Stephanee

Storm

Meaning: Storm
Origin: English
Pronunciation: STORM
Description: Storm is a unisex name and means violent weather. It is a fairly unusual name.

Sue

Meaning: Lily
Origin: English
Pronunciation: SOO
Description: Sue is a short form of Susan, and, less commonly, of Susanna and Suzanne. The name means 'lily'.
Alternative spellings: Su

Suha

Meaning: Forgotten one
Origin: Arabic
Pronunciation: soo HA
Description: Suha is a name that comes from the Arabic word

S

for 'forgotten one' and also the Arabic for a star in the Great Bear constellation.
Alternative spellings: Suhar

Suhana
Meaning: Pleasing
Origin: Urdu
Pronunciation: soo HAH nah
Description: Suhana is a name of Urdu origin and can be found in Hindu, Sikh and Punjabi communities. Its Urdu meaning is said to be 'pleasing'.
Alternative spellings: Suehana, Suehanah, Suhanah

Sukhmani
Meaning: Bringing peace
Origin: Sanskrit
Pronunciation: sook MANI
Description: Sukhmani is an Indian name meaning 'bringing peace'. This name appears to be a more modern Indian girls' name and perhaps was not used as much throughout history.

Suki
Meaning: To love
Origin: Japanese
Pronunciation: SOO ki
Description: Suki is a name of Japanese origin; however, in Japan it is not used as a given name. It comes from a Japanese verb meaning 'to love'.
Alternative spellings: Sukii

Sumaiya
Meaning: Sacrifice
Origin: Arabic
Pronunciation: soo MAH ee YAH

Description: Sumaiya is a variant of the feminine name Sumayyah, which is of Arabic origin and was the name of the first martyr of Islam. This has given the name connotations of 'sacrifice'. It is a popular name with Muslim parents.
Alternative spellings: Sumayyah, Sumaya, Sumayah

Summa
Meaning: From Somma
Origin: Italian
Pronunciation: SOO mah
Description: Summa is a variant of the name Suma. The name may have come from Italy where it was the surname given to people from Somma.
Alternative spellings: Suma

Summer
Meaning: Summer
Origin: English
Pronunciation: SUM muh
Description: The name Summer comes from the English word for the season.
Alternative spellings: Sommer

Sunny
Meaning: Bright and cheerful
Origin: English
Pronunciation: SUH nee
Description: Sunny is a relatively modern name, taken from the adjective describing a person with a bright and cheerful disposition.
Alternative spellings: Sonni, Sonnie, Sonny, Sunni, Sunnie

Suraya
Meaning: Star constellation

Origin: Arabic
Pronunciation: su RAY ah
Description: Suraya is a variant of the name Soraya, which is found mostly in the Middle East. Both the names come originally from the Arabic name Thurayya. Thurayya is the Arabic name of the Seven Sisters constellation.
Alternative spellings: Suraaya

Suri
Meaning: Red
Origin: Persian
Pronunciation: SUR ee
Description: Made famous by Suri Cruise, daughter of Tom Cruise and Katie Holmes, the meaning of the name has been the subject of some debate. Tom and Katie originally stated that it was Hebrew and meant 'princess' but there is little evidence to support this.
Alternative spellings: Soori

Susan
Meaning: Lily
Origin: Hebrew
Pronunciation: SOO san
Description: Susan is a popular Hebrew name. Its original form was Susanna.
Alternative spellings: Susanne, Suzanne

Susanna
Meaning: Lily
Origin: Hebrew
Pronunciation: soo SAH na
Description: Susanna is the New Testament form of Shoshana, from the word meaning 'lily', which in modern Hebrew also means 'rose'. It carries connotations of purity and as the lily is a Christian symbol this name is popular with Christian parents.
Alternative spellings: Susannah, Suzanna, Suzannah

Suzie
Meaning: Lily; rose
Origin: Hebrew
Pronunciation: SOO zee
Description: Both Suzie and its variant Susie came about as pet forms of Susan or Susanna, which both mean 'lily' or 'rose'. The name is mostly found in Eastern Europe and the Netherlands.
Alternative spellings: Susie, Susy, Suzy

Sydney
Meaning: Wide meadow
Origin: English
Pronunciation: sid NEE
Description: Sydney, as well as being a major Australian city, is a unisex name meaning 'wide meadow'. It was introduced as a boys' name, but has now been overtaken by the female given name.
Alternative spellings: Sidney

Syeda
Meaning: Noble
Origin: Arabic
Pronunciation: SIGH yed ah
Description: Syeda is a name of Arabic origin, which is equivalent to the popular masculine Muslim name Syed. The meaning of the word is said to be 'noble'.
Alternative spellings: Sayyida

Sylvia
Meaning: Woodland woman

Origin: Latin
Pronunciation: SIL vee ah
Description: Sylvia is a name that comes from a Latin word meaning 'lives in the woods'. It was a popular name in Roman times because it was the name of the mother of Romulus and Remus, founders of Rome.
Alternative spellings: Silvia

Sylvie

Meaning: Woodland woman
Origin: Latin
Pronunciation: SIL vee
Description: Sylvie is a diminutive form of the name Sylvia. It is popular across the English-speaking world.
Alternative spellings: Silvie, Silvy, Sylvi

T

Tabitha

Meaning: Gazelle
Origin: Aramaic
Pronunciation: TA bi tha
Description: Tabitha is said to come from the word for a gazelle, which carries connotations of gracefulness. The name is found in the New Testament.
Alternative spellings: Tabbitha, Tabbytha, Tabytha

Tahani

Meaning: Best wishes
Origin: Arabic
Pronunciation: ta HAN ee
Description: Tahani is an Arabic name meaning 'best wishes' and is associated with congratulations or happy greetings.

Tahira

Meaning: Pure
Origin: Arabic
Pronunciation: tah HE rah
Description: Tahira is the feminine version of the Arabic masculine name Tahir. The name means 'pure' and

is often favoured by Muslim parents.
Alternative spellings: Taheera, Taheerah

Tahiya

Meaning: Security
Origin: Arabic
Pronunciation: tah HI ya
Description: Tahiya is an unusual name, which comes from around the Middle East and into Africa. It can be found in several languages around this area. Some speculate that the meaning of the name is 'security'.
Alternative spellings: Tahiyah

Tahlia

Meaning: Lamb
Origin: Hebrew
Pronunciation: TAL yah
Description: Tahlia can be seen as a variant of the Hebrew name Talya, which means 'lamb'; it is also the pet name of Natalie. Tahlia is a popular name with Jewish parents.
Alternative spellings: Tahliah, Talia, Taliah, Taliyah

Taiba

Meaning: Refrains from evil doings
Origin: Arabic
Pronunciation: tah IB ah
Description: Taiba, which is of Arabic origin, is the feminine form of the masculine Taib. This name is very rare in the UK, and would suit families looking for a unique baby name.
Alternative spellings: Taibah

Tala

Meaning: Christmas
Origin: Italian
Pronunciation: TAHL ah
Description: Tala is a pet form of Natalia, which comes from an Italian word meaning 'birthday', specifically that of Christ. It can be found in the Italian phrase *'buon natale'* meaning 'merry Christmas'.
Alternative spellings: Talah

Talia

Meaning: Dew of God
Origin: Hebrew
Pronunciation: tal EE ya
Description: This female name is mainly used in English and Hebrew-speaking countries and can also be spelt as Talya. The name derives from the Arabic word *'Tal'* meaning 'dew,' but is also thought to have roots in Old Greek.
Alternative spellings: Thalia, Taliah, Talya

Tallulah

Meaning: Leaping water
Origin: Gaelic
Pronunciation: TAHL oo lah
Description: Tallulah is an alternative spelling of the Gaelic name Tallula, which was a name borne by two Irish saints. It could also derive from the Native American Choctaws.
Alternative spellings: Tallula

Tamar

Meaning: Date
Origin: Hebrew
Pronunciation: tah MAR
Description: Especially popular in Israel, Tamar and its variant Tamara are names of Hebrew origin and are found in the Bible. They come from the Hebrew word for a palm tree.
Alternative spellings: Tahma, Tahmar, Tamah

Tamara

Meaning: Palm tree
Origin: Hebrew
Pronunciation: tah MAR ah
Description: The name Tamara has two separate roots. It can come from the Hebrew biblical name Tamar, which means 'palm tree'. It is also found in Indian languages originating from a Sanskrit word meaning 'spice'.
Alternative spellings: Tamarah

Tamia

Meaning: Spice
Origin: American
Pronunciation: tah ME ah
Description: Tamia is a relatively modern name that may be a compound of popular female names such as Tammy and Mia. It is very popular among African-American parents.
Alternative spellings: Tahmia, Tamea

T

Tamika
Meaning: Unknown
Origin: American
Pronunciation: tah MEE kah
Description: Tamika is a unisex name of uncertain meaning found across the English-speaking world.
Alternative spellings: Tameeka, Tamica

Tammy
Meaning: Twin
Origin: English
Pronunciation: tam EE
Description: Tammy is a nickname for names such as Tamsin and Thomasima, which in turn are the feminine version of the name Thomas. All of these names mean 'twin'.

Tamsin
Meaning: Twin
Origin: Aramaic
Pronunciation: TAM zin
Description: Tamsin is the feminine equivalent of the masculine name Thomas. It has become a very popular name in the UK over recent years.
Alternative spellings: Tamzin

Tanisha
Meaning: Born on Monday
Origin: African
Pronunciation: tan EE sha
Description: The origins of this name lie in the West African language Hausa, where it is the name for babies born on a Monday. Tani is the short form.
Alternative spellings: Taneesha, Taneisha, Tanishah

Tanvi
Meaning: Feminine one
Origin: Sanskrit
Pronunciation: tan vee
Description: Tanvi is a feminine name that comes from Sanskrit origins. The meaning of the name is said to be 'feminine one'. The name is mostly found used in India and Iran and is particularly popular with Hindu parents.
Alternative spellings: Tanvee

Tanya
Meaning: Roman name
Origin: Latin
Pronunciation: TARN yah
Description: Tanya is a very popular pet form of the name Tatiana.
Alternative spellings: Tania, Taniah, Tanyah

Tara
Meaning: Hill
Origin: Gaelic
Pronunciation: TAH ra
Description: Tara is a name that is common across all English-speaking countries and derives from a word that means 'hill'.
Alternative spellings: Tarah

Taran
See entry in 'Names for Baby Boys A–Z'

Taryn
Meaning: Unknown
Origin: Gaelic
Pronunciation: TAH rin
Description: Taryn is an unusual name of uncertain origin, and is found across many languages in various forms. It is now becoming popular across the UK.
Alternative spellings: Tarin, Tarynn

Tasha

Meaning: Birthday of Christ
Origin: Latin
Pronunciation: TASH ah
Description: Tasha began as a pet form of the name Natasha, but is now a name in its own right. It would originally have been given to girls born around Christmas time.
Alternative spellings: Tasher

Tasneem

Meaning: A spring in paradise
Origin: Arabic
Pronunciation: TAHS meen
Description: Tasneem is a variation of the Arabic name Tasnim, meaning 'a spring in paradise'.
Alternative spellings: Tasnim

Tatiana

Meaning: Unknown
Origin: Latin
Pronunciation: taht ee AHN ah
Description: Tatiana is a name of Latin origin said to come from the Roman family name Tatius. It is popular in continental Europe.
Alternative spellings: Tatianna, Tatyana

Taya

Meaning: Favourite
Origin: Russian
Pronunciation: TAY uh
Description: Taya is a pet form of the name Taisiya. It is very popular in Russia and means 'favourite'.
Alternative spellings: Tayah

Tayla

Meaning: Tailor
Origin: English
Pronunciation: TAY lah
Description: Tayla is a phonetically spelt variation of the name Taylor. Taylor is a unisex name that comes from an Old English surname, which denoted someone who was a tailor by trade. The variation Tayla is a specifically feminine name.
Alternative spellings: Taylah

Taylor

Meaning: Tailor
Origin: English
Pronunciation: TAY lor
Description: Taylor was originally a surname given to those with this occupation. Its popularity as a unisex name has risen in recent years.
Alternative spellings: Tailor, Tayla, Taylah, Tayler, Teyla, Teylah, Teylor

Teagan

Meaning: Beautiful thing
Origin: English
Pronunciation: tee GAN
Description: Teagan is a variation of Tegan, which is a feminine name of English origin and comes from a Cornish word for something pretty and ornamental. 'Teg' a Welsh and Cornish word meaning 'pretty'.
Alternative spellings: Teigan, Tegan

Tehya

Meaning: Precious
Origin: American
Pronunciation: TAY ah
Description: Tehya is a name of Native American origin and means 'precious'. It could also be a variant of the name Taya and is rare in the UK.
Alternative spellings: Taya, Thaya

471

Temperance

Meaning: Moderation
Origin: English
Pronunciation: temp ER rance
Description: Temperance comes from the English vocabulary word of the same spelling, meaning `moderation'. Like Chastity or Faith, this is a virtue name.

Teresa

Meaning: Summertime
Origin: Greek
Pronunciation: teh REES ah
Description: Teresa is a variant of Theresa. Mother Teresa was a Christian missionary who was awarded the Nobel Peace Prize.
Alternative spellings: Tereza, Theresa

Terese

Meaning: Summertime
Origin: Greek
Pronunciation: teh REES ah
Description: Terese is a variant of the name Theresa, which is Greek in origin.
Alternative spellings: Tereza, Theresa

Terry

See entry in 'Names for Baby Boys A–Z'

Tess

Meaning: Summertime
Origin: Greek
Pronunciation: TES
Description: While Tess is a shortened version of Teresa, it has become a very popular name in its own right.
Alternative spellings: Tes

Tessa

Meaning: Summertime
Origin: Greek
Pronunciation: TESS ah
Description: Tessa is a shortened version of the name Teresa, but it has become a popular name in its own right. Tessa Sanderson was a British Olympic javelin thrower.
Alternative spellings: Tessah, Tesza

Thalia

Meaning: Blooming
Origin: Greek
Pronunciation: TAHl ee ah
Description: Thalia is a feminine name of Greek origin and is said to mean 'blooming'. In Greek mythology, it was the name of one of the three graces along with her sisters, all daughters of Zeus. Thalia is an uncommon name in English-speaking countries and is mainly found used in Greece and its surrounding countries.
Alternative spellings: Talia, Taliah, Talya

Thandie

Meaning: Loving one
Origin: South African
Pronunciation: thaan DEE
Description: Thandie is a name from South Africa that means 'loving one'. Thandie Newton is a British actress with this name.

Thea

Meaning: Unknown; derived from Greek mythology
Origin: Greek
Pronunciation: THEE uh
Description: A shortened version of the given name Althea.

Alternative spellings: Thaea, Thaia

Theia
Meaning: Goddess
Origin: Greek
Pronunciation: the YA
Description: With origins from the Greek word meaning 'goddess,' this was the name of a Titan goddess of sight, glittering and glory. She was the wife of Hyperion and the mother of the sun god Helios, the moon goddess Selene and the dawn goddess Eos.

Thelma
Meaning: Will; volition
Origin: Greek
Pronunciation: thel MAH
Description: Thelma is a Greek name meaning 'will' and 'volition'. Thelma is one half of the famous female duo "Thelma and Louise" from the movie of the same name.

Theodora
Meaning: Gift of God
Origin: Greek
Pronunciation: thee ah DOR ah
Description: Theodora is the feminine version of the masculine Theodore. It means 'gift of God' and has become rare in the UK in recent years.
Alternative spellings: Theodorah

Thomasina
Meaning: Twin
Origin: English
Pronunciation: thoma SEE nah
Description: Thomasina is the feminine version of the name Thomas, and both names mean 'twin'.

Tia
Meaning: Aunt
Origin: English
Pronunciation: TEE uh
Description: Tia is a name that has recently become popular, but its origins are uncertain. It could come from the Spanish word for 'aunt', or derive from the Greek god of light Theia.
Alternative spellings: Tiah

Tiana
Meaning: Princess
Origin: Greek
Pronunciation: ti AH na
Description: This name is most popular in English-speaking countries such as the United States and Canada. It may have been a shortened version of Christiana or even Diana.
Alternative spellings: Tianna, Tiarna

Tiara
Meaning: Jewelled headdress
Origin: Latin
Pronunciation: tee ARH ah
Description: Tiara is a feminine name that comes from Latin origins. It comes from the Latin word for a 'jewelled headdress', which is still found today in the English language.

Tierney
Meaning: Lord
Origin: Gaelic
Pronunciation: TEER ney
Description: Tierney is a unisex

T

given name of Gaelic origin. It would originally have been a surname, O'Tiarnaigh.
Alternative spellings: Tearney, Teerney,

Tiffany
Meaning: Appearance of God
Origin: Greek
Pronunciation: tiff AN ee
Description: This girls' name derives from the word 'epiphany,' which was given to the appearance of Jesus to the three wise men. It is commonly associated with fashion brand Tiffany and Co.
Alternative spellings: Tiffani

Tigerlily
Meaning: Flower name
Origin: English
Pronunciation: tiger LILY
Description: Tigerlily comes from the bright orange flower of the same name. Like Rose and Tulip, Tigerlily is part of the trend of using flowers as given names.

Tilda
Meaning: Strength in battle
Origin: German
Pronunciation: till DAH
Description: Tilda is a shortened form of the name Matilda, which is a German name meaning 'strength in battle'. Tilda Swinton is a famous British actress with this name.

Tilly
Meaning: Mighty in battle
Origin: German
Pronunciation: TIL lee
Description: Tilly is the pet form of the name Matilda, but it has become popular as a name in its

own right.
Alternative spellings: Tillee, Tilley, Tilli, Tillie

Tina
Meaning: Follower of Christ
Origin: Latin
Pronunciation: TEE na
Description: Tina was originally the short form of any girls' name that ended in 'tina', although it is now also seen as a name in its own right.
Alternative spellings: Teena

Tisha
Meaning: Joy
Origin: American
Pronunciation: tish AH
Description: Tisha is an American name meaning 'joy'. It could also be seen as a shortened version of Letitia.

Tobey
See entry in 'Names for Baby Boys A–Z'

Tomoko
Meaning: Wise child
Origin: Japanese
Pronunciation: to MO ko
Description: This unusual name is most commonly found in Japan.
Alternative spellings: Tomokoh

Toni
Meaning: Protector
Origin: Latin
Pronunciation: TOE nee
Description: Toni is the feminine form of the male name Tony, and it could also be a shortened version of Antonia.

Alternative spellings: Toney,
Tonie

Tonia
Meaning: Protector
Origin: Latin
Pronunciation: TOE nee ah
Description: Tonia was originally
the short form of the name An-
tonia, but it is now a name in its
own right.
Alternative spellings: Toniah,
Tonya, Tonyah

Topaz
Meaning: Topaz
Origin: English
Pronunciation: TOE paz
Description: Topaz is a
gemstone and the birthstone
for those born in November. It
is a fairly uncommon name.
Alternative spellings: Topazz

Tori
Meaning: Victory
Origin: Latin
Pronunciation: TOR ee
Description: Tori is a name with
unisex roots in the United States. It
is usually a pet form of the name
Victoria, and it shares the same
meaning.
Alternative spellings: Toree, Tori,
Torie, Tory

Tracey
Meaning: French place name
Origin: French
Pronunciation: TRAY see
Description: A popular name in
the 60s and 70s. There are several
places in France named 'Tracy'
but 'Tracey' is the slightly more
popular spelling variation in the

UK.
Alternative spellings: Tracy

Trinity
Meaning: Three
Origin: Latin
Pronunciation: TRIN it ee
Description: Trinity is a popular
name with Christian parents owing
to its associations with the Holy
Trinity.
Alternative spellings: Trinitee,
Trinitey, Trinitie, Trinti

Trudie
Meaning: Spear strength
Origin: English
Pronunciation: troo DEE
Description: Trudie is a diminutive of the name Gertrude, which
is a German name composed
of the elements of '*ger*' meaning 'spear' and '*thrud*' meaning
'strength'. Trudie has also become
a name in its own right.
Alternative spellings: Trudy

Tulip
Meaning: Tulip flower
Origin: Turkish
Pronunciation: TOO lip
Description: Tulip comes from
the Turkish and Persian flower of
the same name. This name is part
of the popular flower name trend,
such as Rose and Violet.

Tulisa
Meaning: No meaning
Origin: English
Pronunciation: too LEE sah
Description: Tulisa is a name
that has only come to popularity
in recent years, owing to Tulisa
Contostavlos, who is a singer and

TV personality. It is a modern construction so it has no meaning.
Alternative spellings: Tulisah

Tulsi
Meaning: Basil
Origin: Indian
Pronunciation: tul SEE
Description: Tulsi is an Indian/Hindu girls' name meaning 'basil'.

Twiggy
Meaning: Name of supermodel
Origin: English
Pronunciation: twig EE
Description: Twiggy was made famous by the mod supermodel, Lesley Lawson. She changed her name to Twiggy based on her childhood nickname, Twigs.

Tyler
See entry in 'Names for Baby Boys A–Z'

Tyra
Meaning: Irish county
Origin: Gaelic
Pronunciation: TYE ra
Description: Tyra is the female equivalent of the masculine name Tyrone.
Alternative spellings: Tyrah

U

Ulrica
Meaning: Wolf power
Origin: Scandinavian
Pronunciation: ul REE kah
Description: Ulrica is derived from the German male name Ulric, and first gained popularity in Scandinavia.
Alternative spellings: Ulreka, Ulrika, Ullrika

Uma
Meaning: Tranquillity; splendour; fame; night
Origin: Sanskrit
Pronunciation: oo MAH
Description: Uma is a feminine Sanskrit name that has multiple meanings, including 'tranquillity', 'splendour', 'fame' and 'night'. It is also another name for the Hindu goddess Parvati. American actress Uma Thurman has this name.
Alternative spellings: Umma, Umah

Umaiza
Meaning: Beautiful and bright
Origin: Arabic
Pronunciation: oo MAY za
Description: Umaiza is a name that is found most often in Arabic countries, and is very popular among Muslim parents. It is rare in the UK and far more popular in the Middle East.
Alternative spellings: Umaizah

Umaymah
Meaning: Young mother

Origin: Arabic
Pronunciation: oo MAY mah
Description: Umaymah is a rare name of Arabic origins and a character in the Arabic book of folk tales *One Thousand and One Nights*.
Alternative spellings: Oomaymah

Una

Meaning: One
Origin: Latin
Pronunciation: OO nah
Description: Una comes from the Latin for the number one, and was traditionally given to the first-born child.
Alternative spellings: Unah

Ursula

Meaning: Girl bear cub
Origin: Scandinavian
Pronunciation: UR suh lah
Description: Ursula is a name found across Europe, although it is Scandinavian in origin. It is the name of a Christian saint and its popularity in Britain may stem from Shakespeare's play *Much Ado About Nothing*.
Alternative spellings: Ersula, Ursala

Urte

Meaning: God's gift
Origin: Slavic
Pronunciation: ur TEH
Description: Urte is a feminine name of uncertain origin and meaning. It is thought that the name may have come from Baltic origins, and may be a Baltic version of the feminine name Dorothy and as such shares the same meaning of 'God's gift'.

V

Valencia

Meaning: Brave
Origin: Spanish
Pronunciation: vall EN see ah
Description: Valencia is a Spanish name meaning 'brave'. It is also the name of a city in Spain.

Valentina

Meaning: Good health
Origin: Latin
Pronunciation: vah len TEE nah
Description: Valentina is the feminine version of the masculine name Valentine. It carries connotations of romance owing to Valentine's Day.
Alternative spellings: Valentena

Valeria

Meaning: Brave
Origin: Spanish
Pronunciation: vah leh REE yah
Description: Valeria is a Spanish name that is a variation of Valerius, which comes from the Latin word '*valere*', meaning 'to be strong' or 'brave'. The name Valeria was the name of a 2nd-century saint.

U
V

Valerie

Meaning: Healthy
Origin: Latin
Pronunciation: VAL er ee
Description: This French form of the name Valeria was originally masculine but is now almost exclusively female.
Alternative spellings: Valarie, Valary, Valery

Vanessa

Meaning: Star
Origin: English
Pronunciation: van ESS er
Description: The name Vanessa was invented by 18th-century poet Jonathan Swift. It has remained popular in English-speaking communities.
Alternative spellings: Vanesa

Venus

Meaning: Love
Origin: Latin
Pronunciation: veen US
Description: Venus, in Roman mythology, was the goddess of love. It is also the name of the second planet from the sun as well as Venus Williams, the tennis champion.

Vera

Meaning: Truth
Origin: Greek
Pronunciation: VEER ra
Description: Vera is a Russian name, but also has similarities to the Latin *'veritas'* meaning truth. Although the name peaked in the UK in the 1920s, it is associated with singer Vera Lynn and a *Coronation Street* character.
Alternative spellings: Veera, Viera

Verity

Meaning: Truth
Origin: Latin
Pronunciation: VEH ri tee
Description: Verity comes from the abstract noun meaning 'truth' and, although once popular, it is currently fairly rare in the UK.
Alternative spellings: Veritee, Veritey Veriti, Veritie

Verona

Meaning: Italian city
Origin: Italian
Pronunciation: ver OWN ah
Description: Verona is a city in northern Italy. It is famous for being the city in which Shakespeare's *Romeo and Juliet* is set.

Veronica

Meaning: Truth
Origin: Latin
Pronunciation: vuh RON ih ka
Description: Veronica is a name derived from Latin, which became popular due to the saint of the same name who is said to have wiped sweat from Jesus's face.
Alternative spellings: Veronika

Vesper

Meaning: Evening star
Origin: Latin
Pronunciation: VES per
Description: Vesper is a Latin name meaning 'evening star'. It is also the name of a popular scooter brand as well as a main character in the James Bond novel, *Casino Royale*.

Vicky

Meaning: Victory

Origin: Latin
Pronunciation: VIK ee
Description: Vicky is the short form of Victoria. This shorter version has become a popular name in its own right.
Alternative spellings: Vickie, Vikki

Victoria
Meaning: Victory
Origin: Latin
Pronunciation: vik TOR ee ah
Description: Victoria is the feminine form of Victor. It would have arrived in the UK from Germany and its most famous bearer was Queen Victoria, England's longest-reigning monarch.
Alternative spellings: Victoriah, Viktoria

Vida
Meaning: Life
Origin: Latin
Pronunciation: VEE da
Description: Vida is a name believed to derive from the Latin word that means 'life'.
Alternative spellings: Veda, Veeda

Vienna
Meaning: White; city of dreams
Origin: Latin
Pronunciation: vee EN ah
Description: Vienna is the name of the capital city of Austria. The name, which spread through Europe owing to the city's power, is now fairly rare.
Alternative spellings: Viena

Vilte
Meaning: Hope; people; nation

Origin: Lithuanian
Pronunciation: vil TE
Description: Vilte is a feminine Lithuanian name that is traced all the way back to the masculine name Viltautas. Both names have the Baltic elements of '*vil*' meaning hope and '*tauta*' meaning people or nation.

Viola
Meaning: Violet
Origin: Latin
Pronunciation: vee OH la
Description: Viola is one of the characters in Shakespeare's *Twelfth Night*. A shipwrecked orphan who has no one to protect her, Viola is a practical and resourceful character. Viola is a feminine name that is mainly found in Italy. It comes from the Latin word '*violet*', which is a shade of the colour purple. *Twelfth Night* introduced the name into England.

Violet
Meaning: Violet
Origin: Latin
Pronunciation: VI oh let
Description: Violet is the name of a flower and also one of the colours that make up a rainbow.
Alternative spellings: Violette

Virginia
Meaning: Virgin
Origin: Latin
Pronunciation: VER gin ee ah
Description: Virginia is a name that comes from the Latin word '*virgo*', meaning 'virgin'. It is also the name of a state in the United States of America.

Vivienne
Meaning: Alive

V

Origin: Latin
Pronunciation: VIV ee en
Description: Vivienne has gone out of fashion recently but it

is derived from the French for 'living'.
Alternative spellings: Vivian, Vivien Viviene

W

Wanda
Meaning: Wanderer
Origin: Polish
Pronunciation: WAN dah
Description: Wanda is a Polish name meaning 'wanderer,' and is probably derived from the name of the Wends tribe. It is a popular name in Poland due to the legend of Princess Wanda, who was queen of the Poles.

Wendy
Meaning: Friend
Origin: English
Pronunciation: WEN dee
Description: Wendy, the name coined by J.M. Barrie in the novel *Peter Pan*, comes from a childhood nickname he was given. The name peaked in the 1960s and has declined in recent years.
Alternative spellings: Wendee, Wendi Wendie

Whitney
Meaning: White island
Origin: English
Pronunciation: WIT nee
Description: Whitney is most commonly found in North America and means 'white island'.
Alternative spellings: Whitni, Whitnie, Whitny, Witnee

Willa
Meaning: Will, desire; helmet, protection
Origin: English
Pronunciation: will AH
Description: Willa is the feminine version of the name William, meaning 'will,' or 'desire,' and 'helmet,' or protection'. Willa can also be a short form of the name Wilhelmina, and is a popular modern name.
Alternative spellings: Willah

Willow
Meaning: Willow tree
Origin: English
Pronunciation: WIL low
Description: Willow trees are known for their grace and flexibility. It has been a popular name for many years.
Alternative spellings: Willo, Wilow

Winifred
Meaning: Fair; blessed
Origin: Welsh
Pronunciation: WIN ee fred
Description: An English variation on the Welsh name Gwenfrewi. Winifred was a 7th-century saint.
Alternative spellings: Wynifred, Wynyfred

Winnie

Meaning: Blessed with peace
Origin: Welsh
Pronunciation: win EE
Description: Winnie is the pet form of the name Winifred, but is now found used independently as a name in its own right. Winifred is an Anglicisation of the old Celtic Welsh name Gwenfrewi, which is said to mean 'blessed with peace'. Winifred is used as a name for both boys and girls, although nowadays Winnie is found mainly as a feminine name. An increase in popularity may be due to A.A. Milne's loveable bear, Winnie-the-Pooh.
Alternative spellings: Winny

Winona

Meaning: Firstborn daughter
Origin: Native American
Pronunciation: win OWN ah
Description: Winona is the English version of the Dakota word '*winúŋna*', meaning 'firstborn daughter'. Winona Ryder is a famous American actress with this name.

Winter

Meaning: Cold season
Origin: English
Pronunciation: WIN ter
Description: Winter comes from the English word of the same meaning, referring to the cold season during the year.
Alternative spellings: Wynter

Wren

Meaning: Small bird
Origin: English
Pronunciation: REN
Description: Wren, which is Old English in origin, is associated with the small bird and is an uncommon name.
Alternative spellings: Ren

X

Xanthe

Meaning: Yellow; bright
Origin: Greek
Pronunciation: ZAN thee
Description: Xanthe is an unusual name and was one of the Oceanids in Greek mythology as well as an Amazon.
Alternative spellings: Zanthe, Zanthi

Xena

Meaning: Stranger; foreigner
Origin: Greek
Pronunciation: zina
Description: Xena is a Greek name meaning 'stranger' or 'foreigner'. It was made popular by the television series, *Xena: Warrior Princess*.
Alternative spellings: Zena

Xenia

Meaning: Hospitality

W
X

Origin: Greek
Pronunciation: ZEE nee uh
Description: While this name is mainly used in Russia and Greece, it has spread in popularity. It is now more common across Europe, especially Spain.
Alternative spellings: Zenia

Y

Yana
Meaning: He answers
Origin: Slavic
Pronunciation: YAE nah
Description: Yana is a Slavic girls' name meaning 'He (God) answers'. The name is a variation of the similar name Jana, but has a different meaning.
Alternative spellings: Yanna, Yanah, Yannah

Yara
Meaning: Butterfly
Origin: Arabic
Pronunciation: YAH rah
Description: Yara means 'butterfly' and is popular across the Arabic world. As the name of a Brazilian goddess, it is also popular in South America.
Alternative spellings: Yahrah, Yarah

Yasmin
Meaning: Jasmine flower
Origin: Persian
Pronunciation: YAH smin
Description: Yasmin is a variant on

Xin
Meaning: Beautiful
Origin: Chinese
Pronunciation: SHIN
Description: Xin is a name of a Chinese dynasty that ran between AD 9–23. It was then passed down as a surname and first name throughout generations.

the name Jasmine. It has become very popular in the UK over recent years.
Alternative spellings: Yasmine, Yazmin

Yayoi
Meaning: Full life
Origin: Japanese
Pronunciation: yah YO ee
Description: While this name is uncommon in the UK it is popular across Asia and Japan. It is the name of one of the most important eras in Japanese history, the Yayoi Period.
Alternative spellings: Yahyoi, Yayoe

Yi
Meaning: Righteous
Origin: Chinese
Pronunciation: YE
Description: Yi is a name from Eastern Asia and associated with historical Chinese rulers.
Alternative spellings: Ye

Yoko
Meaning: Honoured child

Origin: Japanese
Pronunciation: yo KO
Description: Yoko is a variation on the Japanese name Youko and is popular across Japan and Asia.
Alternative spellings: Youko

Yolanda

Meaning: Violet
Origin: Greek
Pronunciation: yo LAN dah
Description: Yolanda comes from the Greek word '*iolanthe*' meaning 'violet', as in the purple flower. In many European countries, this name is spelt with a 'J'.

Yu

Meaning: Unknown
Origin: Chinese
Pronunciation: YOO
Description: Yu is unisex and its meanings depend on the 13 Chinese characters that make up the name.
Alternative spellings: Yoo

Yuka

Meaning: Fragrant
Origin: Japanese
Pronunciation: yoo KAH
Description: Yuka is a name found across Asia, but more commonly in Japan and Japanese-speaking communities. It means 'fragrant'.
Alternative spellings: Uka, Yooka

Yuki

Meaning: Snow; happiness
Origin: Japanese
Pronunciation: yoo KEE
Description: Depending on the kanji character used, Yuki can mean either 'snow' or 'happiness'.

Yumiko

Meaning: Helpful beautiful child
Origin: Japanese
Pronunciation: yu MI ko
Description: Yumiko is common across Asia, but is most popular among Japanese communities. Yumiko Abe is a Japanese professional wrestler.
Alternative spellings: Yumikoh

Yumna

Meaning: Lucky
Origin: Arabic
Pronunciation: YUHM na
Description: Yumna is an Arabic name that means 'lucky'. It has spread throughout the Middle East and into Africa, but is favoured mainly by Muslim parents.
Alternative spellings: Yummna

Yuriko

Meaning: Lily child
Origin: Japanese
Pronunciation: yur EE ko
Description: Yuriko is a common name across Asia and is most popular in Japan. It is said to mean 'lily child'.
Alternative spellings: Yureko

Yvette

Meaning: Yew
Origin: French
Pronunciation: ee VET
Description: Yvette is a common name in France. It means 'yew'.
Alternative spellings: Ivette

Yvie

Meaning: Full of life
Origin: Hebrew
Pronunciation: EE vee

Y

Description: Although Yvie could be seen as an alternative to Evie, it is also derived from the name Yvonne. It has grown in popularity in recent years.
Alternative spellings: Evee, Evie, Yvee

Z

Zadie
Meaning: Princess
Origin: English
Pronunciation: zay DEE
Description: Zadie is a variation of the name Sadie, which was originally a pet form of Sarah. All of these names mean 'princess'.

Zahara
Meaning: She will flourish
Origin: Arabic
Pronunciation: za HAR ah
Description: This name has become popular because of its similarity to Sahara. For Muslims, Zahara is the name of the prophet Muhammad's mother.
Alternative spellings: Zahaara

Zahra
Meaning: In flower
Origin: Arabic
Pronunciation: ZAH rah
Description: Zahra is a spelling variation of the feminine name Zara, which is of Arabic origin and is said to mean 'in flower,' as in to flourish. In Islamic belief it was the surname of the prophet Muhammad's mother, and is a popular name with Muslim parents, who use it in tribute to her.

Alternative spellings: Zahraa, Zarah, Zara

Zainab
Meaning: Fragrant
Origin: Arabic
Pronunciation: zay NAB
Description: Zainab is another way of spelling Zaynab, a feminine name of Arabic origin that is popular amongst Muslims. Its meaning is uncertain, although it is sometimes held to mean 'fragrant'. It is found in Islamic belief as the name for several members of the prophet Muhammad's family.
Alternative spellings: Zaynab

Zayna
Meaning: Beauty
Origin: Persian
Pronunciation: ZAY nah
Description: Zayna is a phonetic spelling of Zaina, the feminine equivalent of the masculine name, Zain, which is an Islamic name that means 'beauty' or 'handsome'. It does, however, also have a separate origin to this and can be traced to the Greek name, Xenia, which is said to mean 'stranger'.
Alternative spellings: Zaynah, Zaina

Zeenat

Meaning: Decoration
Origin: Sanskrit
Pronunciation: ZEE nat
Description: Zeenat is a name of Urdu origin that means 'decoration'. It is common among Hindu families.
Alternative spellings: Zinat

Zelda

Meaning: Dark battle
Origin: Germanic
Pronunciation: ZEHL dah
Description: This is a shortened version of Griselda, a German name meaning 'dark battle'. It can also be the feminine form of the Yiddish name Selig, meaning 'happy' or 'blessed'.

Zena

Meaning: Zeus's life
Origin: Greek
Pronunciation: ZEE na
Description: Said to derive from Zenobia, meaning 'Zeus's life', Zena is popular in English-speaking countries.
Alternative spellings: Xena

Zendaya

Meaning: Give thanks
Origin: African
Pronunciation: zen DAY ah
Description: Zendaya is an African name meaning 'give thanks'. Zendaya is also the name of a famous American actress and singer.

Zeynep

Meaning: Father's jewellery
Origin: Arabic
Pronunciation: ZEY nep
Description: Zeynep is a name of Arabic origin and is extremely popular in Turkey. It means 'father's jewellery' and is the name of one of the daughters of the prophet Muhammad.
Alternative spellings: Zeynip

Zhi

Meaning: Nature
Origin: Chinese
Pronunciation: JHEE
Description: Zhi is a unisex name of Chinese origin, common as both a given name and a surname.
Alternative spellings: Zhee, Zi

Zia

Meaning: Light; splendour
Origin: Arabic
Pronunciation: ZEE ah
Description: Zia, derived from the Arabic name Ziva, is usually given to girls. It is said to mean 'light', but also means 'aunt' in Italian.
Alternative spellings: Ziah

Ziva

Meaning: Light of God
Origin: Hebrew
Pronunciation: ZEE vah
Description: Ziva, derived from the Hebrew Ziv, means 'light of God'.
Alternative spellings: Zivah

Zoe

Meaning: Life
Origin: Greek
Pronunciation: ZO ee
Description: Zoe is a Greek name that was extremely popular during the classical period of Rome. It means 'life'.
Alternative spellings: Zoë, Zoé, Zoey, Zooey

Z

Zofia

Meaning: Wisdom
Origin: Greek
Pronunciation: zi FEE ah
Description: Zofia is a name that derives from the more common Greek name Sophia. It is common in Polish- and English-speaking communities.
Alternative spellings: Zophia

Zoha

Meaning: Morning light
Origin: Arabic
Pronunciation: ZOH ha
Description: Zoha is a name which is extremely popular among Muslim parents, and means 'morning light'.
Alternative spellings: Zohah

Zohra

Meaning: Flower blossom
Origin: Arabic
Pronunciation: ZOR ah
Description: Zohra means 'flower blossom'. There is a Hebrew city of the same name in the Bible.
Alternative spellings: Sora, Zora, Zorah

Zoya

Meaning: Life
Origin: Greek
Pronunciation: ZOI ya
Description: Zoya is derived from the Greek Zoe. It is extremely popular in Russia, where it is spelt Zoia. It means 'life and subsistence'.
Alternative spellings: Zoia

Zunaira

Meaning: Guiding light
Origin: Arabic
Pronunciation: zun AIR ah
Description: Zunaira is an Arabic feminine name meaning 'guiding light'. Zunairah al-Rumiya was a Muslim figure who was tortured until she became blind and her sight was restored by a miracle from Allah.
Alternative spellings: Zunairah

Zunairah

Meaning: A flower of paradise
Origin: Arabic
Pronunciation: zoo NAIR ah
Description: Zunairah is an unusual name of Arabic origin. It may mean 'flower of paradise'.
Alternative spellings: Zunaira

Zuri

Meaning: Good; beautiful
Origin: Swahili
Pronunciation: ZUR ee
Description: Zuri is a girls' name meaning 'good' and 'beautiful' in Swahili. It is often found in African-American communities to celebrate their heritage.

Zuzanna

Meaning: Lily
Origin: Slavic
Pronunciation: zoo ZAN ah
Description: Zuzanna is an alternative spelling of the name Susannah and it would have originated from the Slavic regions of Europe. It means 'lily,' referring to the flower, which is a popular Christian symbol.
Alternative spellings: Susanna, Susannah

Babynames.co.uk is the UK's favourite baby names website. If you want to extend your search online there couldn't be a better place to start. With a strong community of over 30,000 members providing help and advice, as well as entertainment, you can be sure that any question you have will be answered. Babynames.co.uk also offers a baby names generator for inspiration and quizzes to keep you entertained while you decide on your baby's name.